ARREST

*The Decision to Take a Suspect
into Custody*

ARREST

The Decision to Take a Suspect into Custody

BY

WAYNE R. LaFAVE

The Report of the American Bar Foundation's
Survey of the Administration of Criminal Justice
in the United States

* *

Frank J. Remington
Editor

LITTLE, BROWN AND COMPANY

1965

155415

Published simultaneously in Canada

PRINTED IN THE UNITED STATES OF AMERICA

THE AMERICAN BAR FOUNDATION, CHICAGO

DEDICATION

Dedicated to the late Justice Robert H. Jackson, first Chairman of the Project Advisory Committee on this study of the Administration of Criminal Justice — a great lawyer, a discerning judge, and indefatigable friend of the organized bar.

Any study of criminal justice administration should be permeated with the belief that dual objectives characterize any system of criminal justice that can be satisfactory to a just, free and orderly society. Such a system will aim promptly, firmly and impartially to detect, convict and punish the guilty and at the same time to avoid harassing the innocent or putting them in jeopardy. The dilemma is that no method for conviction of the wrongdoer has been devised that does not hold some danger to the bystander, while no system can fully safeguard the innocent without affording loopholes through which some guilty persons will escape. Achievement of proper balance between means to these two goals is the ultimate problem in criminal law administration.

> Robert H. Jackson
> Criminal Justice:
> The Vital Problem of the Future
> 39 A.B.A.J. 743 (1953)

PREFACE

This is the first of a series of several volumes to be published by the American Bar Foundation setting forth the analysis of field data obtained in the course of its Survey of the Administration of Criminal Justice. When the project was commenced in 1953 a comprehensive "Plan for the Survey" was prepared by the Project Director, Professor Arthur H. Sherry of the University of California.[1] In a foreword to this plan, Loyd Wright, then President of the American Bar Foundation, expressed his view of the important responsibility which lawyers have for the administration of criminal justice:

> We can no longer ignore our personal responsibility in this regard. We must adopt the same attitude in relation to the representation of those accused of crime as we have . . . in Lawyer Referral and in our participation in Legal Aid.
>
> Ours is a profession premised upon service. Material reward must no longer be an excuse for so many of our top flight members of the profession ignoring the basic need for all of our profession to contribute to the uplifting and establishment of a thoroughly responsible bar for the practice of Criminal Law.[2]

At the start of the survey the project had to its invaluable advantage a most imaginative leader, Justice Robert H. Jackson, the first Chairman of the Advisory Committee. He saw the need of the survey, and he brought to the project a wealth of experience at the bar, a broad understanding of criminal procedure, and a degree of stimulation that proved to be of immense value in the development of the research program. We regard it a great privilege to dedicate this volume to Justice Jackson, and we wish thereby to acknowledge his valued contribution.

Justice Jackson's varied personal experiences, as Supreme Court Justice, as Attorney General of the United States, and in other posts in the Federal Department of Justice, as defense lawyer in a relatively rural New York county, and as a member of the Roosevelt Commission to investigate New York State administration of justice, all left him convinced that we know too little about how

[1] Sherry, The Administration of Criminal Justice in the United States, Plan for a Survey (1955).
[2] Id. at iii.

the criminal justice system in this country actually works. He therefore proposed that there be careful and intensive on-the-scene examination of the policies and practices of agencies responsible for the administration of criminal justice.

A pilot study was undertaken in the states of Michigan, Wisconsin, and Kansas. Field studies started in February, 1956, and ended in June, 1957. A large amount of data was gathered and recorded in some 2000 "field reports," averaging about ten pages each and totaling over three million words. More than a thousand exhibits were assembled. In December, 1957, this material was summarized in a seven volume, mimeographed *Pilot Project Report.*

This preliminary report was circulated widely among persons interested in the study of criminal justice administration. It was hoped that the material would stimulate new interest in the study and teaching of criminal justice and that this interest would in turn strengthen the basis for assessing the contributions and limitations of the Bar Foundation data. This hope was largely fulfilled. Numerous papers have used the Bar Foundation data to good advantage,[3] and these articles have contributed to the further analysis of the data by the Bar Foundation staff. The seven-volume Pilot Project Report has been distributed by the Foundation on loan to persons doing research in the area of criminal justice administration. In response to an almost constant demand, the one

[3] For example: Abernathy, Police Discretion and Equal Protection, 14 S.C.L.Q. 472 (1962); Allen, Federalism and the Fourth Amendment: A Requiem for Wolf, in Kurland, The Supreme Court Review (1961); Barrett, Police Practices and the Law — From Arrest to Release or Charge, 50 Calif. L. Rev. 11 (1962); Goldstein, H., Full Enforcement vs. Police Discretion Not to Invoke the Criminal Process, May 22, 1963 (paper presented at the National Institute of Police and Community Relations, Michigan State University); Goldstein, H., Police Discretion: The Ideal Versus the Real, 23 Public Administration Rev. 140 (1963); Goldstein, J., Police Discretion Not to Invoke the Criminal Process: Low-Visibility Decisions in the Administration of Justice, 69 Yale L.J. 543 (1960); Kadish, Legal Norm and Discretion in the Police and Sentencing Processes, 75 Harv. L. Rev. 904 (1962); Kadish, The Advocate and the Expert — Counsel in the Peno-Correctional Process, 45 Minn. L. Rev. 803 (1961); LaFave, Detention for Investigation by the Police: An Analysis of Current Practices, 1962 Wash. U.L.Q. 331; LaFave, The Police and Nonenforcement of the Law — Part I, 1962 Wis. L. Rev. 104; LaFave, The Police and Nonenforcement of the Law — Part II, 1962 Wis. L. Rev. 179; Miller and Remington, Procedures Before Trial, 339 Annals 111 (1962); Newman, The Effect of Accommodations in Justice Administration on Criminal Statistics, 46 Sociology & Social Research 144 (1962); Ohlin and Remington, Sentencing Structure: Its Effect upon Systems for the Administration of Criminal Justice, 23 Law & Contemp. Prob. 495 (1958); Remington, Criminal Justice Research, 51 J. Crim. L., C. & P.S. 7 (1960); Remington, The Law Relating to "On the Street" Detention, Questioning and Frisking of Suspected Persons and Police Arrest Privileges in General, 51 J. Crim. L., C. & P.S. 386 (1960); Remington and Rosenblum, The Criminal Law and the Legislative Process, 1960 U. Ill. L.F. 481; Rotenberg, The Police Detention Practice of Encouragement, 49 Va. L. Rev. 871 (1963).

hundred original sets have been circulated among scholars in this country and in England, Japan, and New Zealand. The Pilot Project Report has also been used as a basis for three summer faculty seminars and a substantial number of seminars for law students. The consequence has been a constructive effect upon the teaching of criminal justice administration.

A major objective of the pilot project was to determine whether the methods of research which were used would produce factual knowledge of a kind that would make a meaningful contribution to a greater understanding and an ultimate solution of important criminal justice problems. We believe that this volume demonstrates that research of this kind does make a significant contribution in this respect.

The task of analysis has been complex and time-consuming. Such success as has been achieved was made possible by the efforts of many individuals and agencies. It is with profound appreciation that the American Bar Foundation acknowledges their splendid cooperation.

Except for some relatively minor expenses, the entire cost of the project has been met through a series of grants from the Ford Foundation, totaling $520,000. For its encouragement, patience, and generous support we gratefully acknowledge our special indebtedness to this organization.

Because it was necessary to establish proper liaison in the states studied, initial assistance was sought and obtained from several national societies, which passed formal resolutions calling for cooperation with and support of the survey. These included the International Association of Chiefs of Police, the Conference of Chief Justices, the National Association of Attorneys General, the American Correctional Association, and the National Association of District Attorneys. Other organizations, such as the American Sociological Society and the Council of State Governments, appointed committees to cooperate with and advise the staff of the survey. Many letters to state and local officials asking for cooperation were written in behalf of the study by these national groups.

In Kansas, Michigan, and Wisconsin, the American Bar Foundation received splendid cooperation. The governors formally announced the study and urged cooperation with it. The attorneys general cooperated by furnishing valuable advice and information. State bar associations, leading universities, research organizations, and professional societies in the three states also gave their unqualified support.

Cooperation and assistance at the local level was equally impressive. It was here that cooperation was most crucial to the success of the survey, for local agencies were the primary object of the study. These agencies were told that the objective of the research was to better understand important current issues and to learn of methods which exist at the local level for dealing with these issues. Assurance was given that the identity of individuals and agencies would, wherever possible, be kept confidential and that no statement of fact clearly identifying an agency would be made without affording that agency an opportunity to comment upon the accuracy of the statement. The Bar Foundation has made every effort to fulfill this commitment.

It is well known in the profession that contemporary conditions insistently demand thoughtful attention to the criminal processes as they are actually working in our system. The tremendous growth in population, the industrial development of the last forty years, the vast sociological changes that have accompanied increasing urbanization in the United States, all have served to create the conditions that spawn crime and especially organized crime in an ever increasing degree. Concurrently they create problems of enforcement of the criminal law that did not exist in an earlier and a less complicated period. These facts furnish the social setting for the survey.

At the same time, although crime has intensified in almost every aspect of contemporary society, the processes utilized for the apprehension and prosecution of criminals have remained substantially unchanged over the years. True, there have been a few encouraging developments. Progress has been made in some areas of criminal procedure, e.g., in the detection of crime, in the organization of prosecutors' offices, and in the principles and techniques of trial, sentencing, and parole. Yet these improvements have been geographically spotty and of widely varying effectiveness. These facts furnish the legal setting for the survey, and, coupled with the magnitude and complexity of crime today, they more than justify an intensive survey of the administration of criminal justice by the legal profession.

Grateful acknowledgement is made to those who participated in the phase of the project in which data were gathered. These persons include the members of the Special Advisory Committee, the consultants, and the field researchers, whose names are listed in the front of this volume.

Able members of several law faculties have from time to time given stimulating reactions to the material being written. An attempt to list those who have contributed most creates the risk that someone may be inadvertently omitted. For this we make apology in advance. Among those to whom we want to give thanks are Francis A. Allen of the University of Chicago, Edward L. Barrett, Jr., of the University of California, William Beaney of Princeton University, Fred Cohen of the University of Texas, Joseph Goldstein of Yale University, Sanford H. Kadish of the University of Michigan, Yale Kamisar of the University of Minnesota, Edward L. Kimball of the University of Wisconsin, Victor Rosenblum of Northwestern University, and Herbert Wechsler of Columbia University.

Finally, acknowledgment must by all means be made of the indefatigable services and the very great professional skill of Professors Wayne LaFave and Frank Remington, who have brought the present volume to its state of completion. Their understanding of the subject matter and their infinite patience in dealing with the enormous number of ramifications of the available field evidence, and their skill in presentation, are deserving of the highest commendation. Moreover, we must acknowledge our indebtedness to their respective institutions, the law schools of the University of Illinois and the University of Wisconsin, which have made their services available and have borne many of the incidental costs connected with the preparation of the manuscript.

The Bar Foundation Committee on Administration of Criminal Justice under the chairmanship of Mr. Harold A. Smith of Chicago has approved this study of arrest for publication as a Foundation research monograph. It is standard practice within the Foundation to submit each manuscript prior to publication to review and approval, either by a special Advisory Committee or by the standing Research Committee of the Foundation. In addition to formal approval, each member of these two committees is given an opportunity to make suggestions and recommendations to the author. This exchange of views and review of the research is an essential part of the research program of the Foundation. Nevertheless, neither the committee members nor the Foundation assumes responsibility for the positions taken by the author, nor do they necessarily agree with all of the statements in the text. These responsibilities are naturally assumed by the author himself.

Harold A. Smith
Chairman, Advisory Committee

E. Blythe Stason
Administrator

ACKNOWLEDGMENTS

Grateful acknowledgment is made for permission to quote from the following publications:

Harvard Law Review (copyright, Harvard Law Review Association).

The University of Chicago Law Review and Social Service Review (copyright, University of Chicago).

Giardini, The Parole Process; Houts, From Arrest to Release; Wilson, Police Planning (copyright, Charles C Thomas, Publisher).

Code of Criminal Procedure; Restatement of Torts; Model Penal Code (copyright, American Law Institute).

EDITOR'S FOREWORD

This volume focuses principally upon police policies and practices which relate to the arrest of persons suspected of criminal behavior. It is one of a series of volumes which will, in the aggregate, cover the major stages in criminal justice administration from the time a crime is committed until the offender is finally released from parole supervision. These other volumes deal with Detection of Crime, Prosecution, Adjudication, and Sentencing.[1]

The scope of the series is deliberately broad. We are convinced that there is a genuine need for a continuing research and teaching commitment to the over-all process of criminal justice administration and that it is important for the legal profession and for law teaching and law research to assume a greater responsibility for the total process of criminal justice administration than they have in the past.

Many of the major and most neglected current issues involve relationships between the various stages of the criminal justice process and between various agencies given responsibility for the detection of crime and the apprehension, prosecution, conviction, and correctional treatment of offenders. From the point of view of either the individual suspect or the community as a whole, the issue is not so much whether police are efficient, or whether the correctional process is effective, but whether the system of criminal justice administration in its entirety is sensible, fair, and consistent with the concepts of a democratic society.

A broad interest in the process of criminal justice administration is properly a responsibility of the legal profession. This is the process by which government applies its most severe sanctions against individuals who have engaged in socially deviant conduct. In our constitutional system, law has as a principal function the control of the use of official power. Whether one considers the work of police, lawyers, or correctional workers, the operations of criminal justice processes have such severe impact upon the lives of individuals suspected, charged, or convicted of crime as to make this an area of essential study.

A broad interest in the over-all process of criminal justice ad-

[1] Although references are made in this volume to the other volumes in the series, these are necessarily inexact, since this is the first volume to appear.

ministration is also responsive to the needs of practice. Increasingly the trial judge finds himself involved in what were in the past exclusively police or correctional issues. The exclusionary rule of evidence as a means of controlling police practice is perhaps the best known illustration. But the methods used by the trial judge and their effect upon actual police administration have not been well understood. Adequate understanding, if it is to be achieved, requires recognition of the fact that the lawyer has an important function, and thus an important professional responsibility, outside the traditional confines of the courtroom and the trial of contested cases.

The author has tried, in this volume, to describe the role of the police and the role of the law and lawyer in respect to the arrest decision. Their functions are more complex than they are generally assumed to be, even by police and lawyers themselves. Police in particular have not recognized that they have the difficult task of making those complex social decisions which must be made in the development and implementation of a proper law enforcement policy. Nor have judges and lawyers been sufficiently aware of the nature of the police function, which in many respects is more like that of an important administrative agency than it is like the job of the fireman with whom the policeman is often compared. There has been inadequate appreciation of the difficulty of the court's role in reviewing enforcement policies as a safeguard against arbitrariness. Police often seem more concerned with criticizing the courts than with developing law enforcement policies which will receive judicial approval and lawyers seem often to feel that understanding prior case law is an adequate substitute for understanding the day-to-day problems of the law enforcement agency which will be vitally affected by the judicial decision.

We try to stress those issues which are important and difficult for the well-staffed, competent, and honest police department, prosecutor's office, trial court, or correctional agency. Problems of inefficiency, incompetence, and dishonesty have been and will no doubt continue to be matters of concern to criminal justice administration. Certainly there is need for better personnel, better training, and better methods of preventing dishonest administration. But these are problems of local government which are not confined to police or to criminal justice administration. And even where they have been solved and criminal justice agencies are staffed with efficient, competent, and honest personnel, there remain some difficult and important issues. It is these issues which are stressed in this volume.

This is not the first survey of the administration of criminal justice in the United States, and it no doubt will not be the last. We have benefited from the contributions and what we think are the mistakes of the surveys of the 1920's and early 1930's. The ingenious use of the so-called mortality tables in the early surveys served to identify those stages in the criminal justice process where important decisions were being made as to whether to release a suspect or to subject him to prosecution, conviction, and sentencing. Where the early surveys assumed that a decision not to proceed further was an indication of inefficiency, incompetence, or corruption, we make no such assumption and try, instead, to understand the policy and practice at each of these critical stages. Where the early surveys seemed to assume that the ideal system was one in which all suspects are arrested, prosecuted, convicted, and sentenced, we assume that the ideal is one where intelligent and consistent decisions are made as to who, among even the clearly guilty, will be arrested, prosecuted, convicted, and sentenced. The aim is not, in other words, statistically measurable efficiency but rather a much more difficult to measure, intelligent, and responsible exercise of discretion. As a consequence, quantitative or statistical data are largely absent from this volume. Instead it contains what might fairly be called an episodic or critical incident view of criminal justice administration, with the recorded incidents being used to identify the stages at which important decisions are made, the alternative courses of action, the criteria which underlie the choices made, and the extent to which decisions are influenced or controlled by the legal order. This kind of concentration does not imply that quantitative, statistical measurement of criminal justice processes is impossible or unimportant. But it does reflect the judgment that elaborate measurement is a second step which has meaning only after there has been careful identification of the issues, practices, and policies which ought to be subjected to careful measurement.

In the analysis of current practice, we do not try to make value judgments about the practices described. The effort rather is to give an objective description even of policies and practices with which we may completely disagree. This is not to assert that value judgments are unimportant but merely that it is more important, in fact necessary, to first adequately identify the issues and the reasons for existing administrative policies and practices before attempting to evaluate them. In the past certain value positions have too often been assumed to be proper and have dictated the kind of data gathered, the purpose of the research being to support the value judgment rather than to produce a more adequate basis for dealing with the basic problem which is involved. This kind of advocacy by means of research has tended to distract attention from many important issues. It results in what may be viewed by some as an exposé and by others as a whitewash. It contributes ammunition for the advocate — which is important. But it seldom provides a basis for greater mutual understanding by courts of the complexity of the police task or by police of the difficulties which confront courts.

Stressing the total system of criminal justice administration has advantages, but there are also disadvantages which inhere in this approach. Since these result in significant limitations upon the value of this volume it is appropriate to give specific warning of them.

The effort to cover a broad range of issues prevents detailed concentration upon some significant aspects of important law enforcement policies and practices. As a consequence, we as yet know too little about many phases of criminal justice administration even though we have gained a great deal of knowledge about the over-all system and the interrelationships of the various stages of the process and the various agencies involved in the administration of criminal justice.

Although reference is frequently made to existing operations, we recognize that we know too little to assert categorically that all descriptions of current practice are entirely adequate. Certainly they accurately describe no more than what they purport to describe, namely, the practices observed in Kansas, Michigan, and Wisconsin. Statements or descriptions thus may not precisely reflect practices which exist in other states, although we have little doubt that many of the important practices found in the three states also exist in other places. The operational necessities of law enforcement tend to be the same even though the law of various jurisdictions may vary.

Despite the fact that most descriptive statements are in the present tense, they describe those practices which existed in Kansas, Michigan, and Wisconsin during the years 1956 and 1957 when the field research took place. For consistency and convenience we use the present tense, speaking as if the descriptive statements were made contemporaneously with the research. An effort has been made to take account of important developments which have occurred between the time of the field research and the time of the publication of this volume. Although the description is largely of practices which existed some years ago, this does not, in our view, limit the value of this volume. The basic objective of the research is to identify important issues confronting systems for criminal justice administration and to describe alternative practices for dealing with these issues. This is done on the assumption that understanding these issues and the experience of those who have been dealing with them is an important contribution to clarification and hopefully to long-range improvement. Neither major issues nor common practices in law enforcement change quickly, and even when change does occur it is important to know the pre-existing situation and why the change was made.

Throughout the analysis it will perhaps be apparent that situations are sometimes described without adequate indication of causal factors. For example, some police agencies, with dogged determination, seem to proceed against certain deviant behavior, such as prostitution and homosexuality, in spite of the fact that there may be little overt community support for such a program and, in fact, in spite of a great deal of hostility to the program on the part of at least some trial judges. It is not apparent why police do this, although some educated guesses can be made on the basis of the factual data contained in this volume. There is, however, need for more carefully focused research if we are to have greater confidence in our knowledge of factors which are important in explaining recurring police practices. This kind of additional knowledge is imperative if change is desired and if effective ways are to be devised to produce that change.

Because the emphasis of this research is upon important issues which confront criminal justice agencies and upon the policies and practices which these agencies have devised to deal with these issues, arrest is viewed as an important stage in the criminal justice process rather than as a significant, sometimes critical, episode in the life of the individual who is taken into custody. This does not mean that we are unconcerned with individual freedom. Quite the contrary. Knowing how criminal justice agencies act and why they act as they do is of obvious importance to those individuals who become involved. But our approach does result in another limitation of the data about which the reader should be warned. Adequate evaluation of current law enforcement policies and practices requires more knowledge than we now have about the impact of those policies and practices upon individuals and groups within the community who are affected by them.

The objective of this volume is a modest but important one. It is to identify and describe those aspects of arrest practice which seem to us most significant and to do so in a way which we think is most conducive to understanding and to improvement where improvement is needed and desired.

SUMMARY OF CONTENTS

T A B L E O F C O N T E N T S

CHAPTER 2

THE ISSUANCE OF THE WARRANT AFTER ARREST WITHOUT REVIEW BY THE PROSECUTOR

PART II

THE DECISION NOT TO INVOKE THE CRIMINAL PROCESS

CHAPTER 3

POLICE DISCRETION

CHAPTER 4

NONINVOCATION BECAUSE THE LEGISLATURE MAY NOT DESIRE ENFORCEMENT

C H A P T E R 5

C H A P T E R 6

C H A P T E R 7

CHAPTER 8

PART III

CHAPTER 9

CHAPTER 10

DELAY IN MAKING AN ARREST 208

PART IV

THE DECISION TO ARREST FOR PURPOSES OF PROSECUTION 227

CHAPTER 11

MISDEMEANOR ARREST: THE "IN-PRESENCE" REQUIREMENT 231

CHAPTER 12

FELONY ARREST: THE "REASONABLE CAUSE" REQUIREMENT 244

CHAPTER 13

FELONY ARREST: SOURCES OF INFORMATION 265

CHAPTER 14

CHAPTER 15

CHAPTER 16

C H A P T E R 1 7

C H A P T E R 1 8

C H A P T E R 1 9

C H A P T E R 2 0

PART V

THE DECISION TO ARREST FOR PURPOSES OTHER THAN PROSECUTION

CHAPTER 21

ARREST OF AN INTOXICATED PERSON FOR HIS OWN SAFETY

CHAPTER 22

ARREST TO CONTROL THE PROSTITUTE

CHAPTER 23

ARREST TO CONTROL THE TRANSVESTITE

ARREST

The Decision to Take a Suspect
into Custody

Arrest in Current Criminal Justice Administration

This volume deals with the decision to take custody of a person suspected of criminal behavior. This decision is obviously an important exercise of official power, from the point of view of both the individual involved and the system of criminal justice administration.[1] Arrest results in detention of the individual, usually a search of his person, sometimes the use of force, and often, with the possible exception of the chronic offender, damage to his reputation. In most cases, decisions to charge, to convict, and to sentence are made only with respect to those persons whom the police have first arrested. Thus, to a large extent, this decision determines those offenders against whom the official process is to be invoked.[2] Its importance necessitates concern with who makes the decision to arrest, how it is made, and particularly how it is controlled in order to insure its conformance with the basic objectives of consistency and fairness.

A. The Nature of the Arrest Decision

In this volume, the term "arrest" refers to the decision to take a suspect into custody. It is a critical decision in its own right, as it goes somewhat beyond the police investigative practice of "field interrogation," where a suspect is momentarily stopped for questioning, and as it is not limited to those situations in which a suspect is taken into custody for purposes of prosecution. Some confusion exists about the term "arrest" because it is often used in law to mean, in its narrowest sense, the taking of custody upon

---

[1] Jerome Hall has defined the objective of a sound arrest policy as the "maintenance of an equilibrium between official practices and political ideals, realized through effective legal remedies . . . ." Hall, The Law of Arrest in Relation to Contemporary Social Problems, 3 U. Chi. L. Rev. 345, 374 (1936).

[2] See Goldstein, Police Discretion Not to Invoke the Criminal Process: Low-Visibility Decisions in the Administration of Justice, 69 Yale L.J. 543 (1960).

sufficient and proper evidence for the purpose of prosecution or, in its broadest sense, any interference with a person which, if not privileged, would constitute false imprisonment.[3] Neither of these definitions adequately describes the subject matter of this volume. Arrest, as the term is used here, is a distinct operational step in the criminal justice process, involving all police decisions to interfere with the freedom of a person who is suspected of criminal conduct [4] to the extent of taking him to the police station for some purpose.

Arrest ordinarily occurs after a crime has been detected and before a decision is made to charge the suspect with the commission of the crime. However, the distinction between arrest and detection on the one hand and arrest and charging on the other is not always clear. In certain cases, for example, stopping and questioning, arresting, and charging are so telescoped that it is difficult to separate them. But it is nonetheless clear that the arrest decision has separate and distinct operational significance in the criminal justice process and thus merits separate and careful analysis.

1. *Arrest distinguished from detection.* A basic distinction employed in this volume is that between actually taking a suspect to the station and the preliminary investigative devices of stopping and questioning, frisking, and conducting an on-the-spot search. The former is called an arrest and is discussed in detail in this volume. Discussion of the latter devices, which are primarily investigative techniques, will be found in the volume on Detection of Crime. There are a number of reasons for maintaining this distinction. In the usual case, the degree of interference is substantially greater when the suspect is actually taken to the station. The stopping and questioning of a person on the street usually results in his detention for only a few minutes, after which the officer decides that the suspect should either be taken to the station or allowed to go his way. A frisk or search may take place during

---

[3] For a definition of "arrest" made for research purposes, see Note, 100 U. Pa. L. Rev. 1182, 1185-1188 (1952). It is there assumed that the term must be applied to any police interference with the freedom of locomotion in order to insure the right to a tort recovery against the officer who acts illegally.

[4] Arrests of such persons constitute the vast majority of all arrests made. But there are situations in which persons who are not suspected of criminal conduct are taken into official custody. In this sense there may be arrests of witnesses to crime, insane persons, and persons involved in civil litigation. These are not included in this analysis.

It should also be noted that a suspect may be either a person against whom there exists sufficient objective evidence of guilt for arrest, whether or not the officer believes him guilty, or a person arrested because the officer thinks it likely that he is guilty, even though the objective evidence of guilt may not be sufficient to support the arrest.

this brief detention. In contrast, the person who is taken to the station is ordinarily detained at least several hours.[5]

The police generally view the taking of a person to the station as entirely different from use of on-the-street investigative techniques. A person is taken to the station only in cases in which extended custody is required. This may be in cases where the person is to be held for prosecution, where a detailed investigation is to be carried out, or where the person is to be held in order to realize some deterrent, rehabilitative, or punitive function. On-the-street investigations are ordinarily employed in order to determine, in cases of uncertainty, which suspects should be taken to the station.

The person being dealt with also generally views the taking to the station as different from on-the-street investigation. For instance, if asked on a questionnaire whether he has ever been arrested, the person who was only questioned on the street, frisked, or searched would most likely answer no. The person who was taken to the station is more likely to answer yes, particularly if asked whether he has ever been "arrested or detained."

The consequences of being taken to the station are more serious from the point of view of the individual. For example, a person taken to the station is usually booked. This means that a record of arrest is made, often including fingerprinting and photographing. By contrast, a record is not ordinarily kept of on-the-street investigations. If a record is kept, it merely indicates that the suspect was observed at a certain time at a certain place.

The use of the term "arrest" to mean a decision to take a suspect into custody and to the station defines as well as possible the important operational step in the criminal justice process which exists between the detection and charging stages.

2. *Arrest distinguished from charging.* In many cases the first decision which is made in the process concerning a particular person is whether he should be arrested, that is, whether he should be taken to the station and detained. If the suspect is arrested, the next decision is whether to prosecute him for the crime of which he is suspected.

Although these two decisions have much in common, there are significant reasons for treating them separately. Such formal cri-

---

5 Of course, it must be admitted that this distinction does not always hold true. Sometimes persons taken to the station are released almost immediately, either because it is decided that further action will be taken but the person can be released on his own recognizance or because it is decided by a supervisory officer that no action should be taken. Sometimes persons stopped on the street are detained for a substantial period of time, particularly if the investigating officer is awaiting the arrival of witnesses in the area or a report from headquarters.

teria as are provided by law differ at the two stages or at least have long been assumed to be different. In some jurisdictions, the law requires more evidence to charge a suspect than is required to arrest him. As a consequence, in some situations an arrest may lawfully be made on the basis of evidence insufficient to justify charging the person arrested.

Another important distinction is that the prosecutor, with traditionally recognized discretion, may consider matters of policy unconnected with the guilt of the suspect in deciding not to charge him, while the police are assumed to be purely ministerial officers whose function is to arrest in all cases where the evidence of guilt is sufficient.

It is traditionally assumed that the arrest decision is made by the police while the decision to charge is made by the prosecutor, but this is not always the case. For purposes of this analysis, whether a particular decision is treated as an arrest or as charging depends less on who makes the decision than on its purpose and the circumstances under which it is made. For example, after an officer has made an arrest a supervisory officer will sometimes, even without booking, decide to release the suspect. Or the suspect may be released later by the detective assigned to the case. Such releases are directly related to the arrest decision whenever they are based on a review of the propriety of the arresting officer's action. This is the case when the releasing officer, after considering the information the arresting officer should have had and the factors he was supposed to consider, decides that the arrest was improper. In other situations the release is more appropriately related to a decision not to charge. This is so when the release is based upon the consideration of information ordinarily not in the hands of the arresting officer at the time of the arrest or upon factors or criteria which relate more to the probability or desirability of obtaining a conviction than to the decision to take the suspect into custody. In these cases, although the release may be made without the prosecutor being consulted, it is, in substance, a decision not to charge rather than a decision that the arrest was improper.

Similarly, not all decisions made by the prosecutor are charging decisions. While the prosecutor's approval of a request for an arrest warrant for a person in custody usually demonstrates his decision to charge, this is not necessarily true when he approves such a request for a person not yet in custody. When the matter is brought to the attention of the prosecutor before the suspect's arrest, either because a complainant has gone directly to the prosecutor or because the police desire to obtain a warrant before arrest, the prosecutor in approving the warrant request may be deciding to charge, or he may only be deciding that the circumstances are sufficient to justify an arrest of the suspect.

Treatment of arrest and charging as separate decisions is also justifiable on the grounds that the consequences of each are or can be quite different. Arrest is a step which may lead to further processing, but it may also be a terminal action. For the person involved, arrest and release is obviously a better alternative than arrest and charging, in terms of his freedom, reputation, and possible monetary loss.

B. Major Issues in Relation to Arrest

Observation of current criminal justice administration[6] indicates that there are at least five aspects of the arrest decision which ought to be of major concern to anyone interested in the exercise of governmental power in a democratic society: (1) To what extent should the decision to take a suspect into custody be made by a disinterested judicial officer? In practice this question relates to the function of the arrest warrant, a matter considered in Part I. (2) To what extent is it proper and desirable for police to exercise discretion not to arrest some persons who are guilty of criminal conduct? It is traditional to recognize the prosecutor's discretion, but insufficient attention has been given to police discretion, which is dealt with in Part II. (3) To what extent is it proper and desirable for the police not to avail themselves of an opportunity to take immediate custody of a person who is to be proceeded against? This issue is the subject of Part III. (4) How much evidence is needed to justify an arrest, and when is it proper to conduct an in-custody investigation to gain further evidence needed to charge and convict the suspect? Part IV deals with this question. (5) Are there situations in which it is proper to take a person suspected of crime into custody for purposes other than prosecution? This is considered in Part V.

Each of these issues, judicial participation in the arrest decision, police discretion, evidentiary requirements for arrest, the need for custody as an arrest criterion, and the use of arrest to achieve objectives other than prosecution and conviction, is important to an understanding of the arrest decision in current criminal justice administration. In addition, each of these issues is analogous to others which arise at other stages of the criminal justice process.

[6] All references to current practices in this volume are based upon observations in Kansas, Michigan, and Wisconsin by field research personnel of the American Bar Foundation conducted several years ago. It should not be assumed that the practices observed necessarily still prevail in those jurisdictions or that they prevail generally in all other states. See the Editor's Foreword for more on these limitations.

The five issues are briefly discussed in this introduction to give some indication of why they are selected for emphasis and also how they relate to other important criminal justice questions which will be dealt with in other volumes.

1. *The decision to seek and to issue an arrest warrant.* It is usually assumed that judicial participation in decision-making is desirable in a criminal justice system in order to insure a fair balance between the interests of society and of the individual. This balancing of interests is thought best served if there is a "disinterested determination" by a "neutral and detached" judicial officer.[7] At the detection stage it is important to know when a warrant, obtained from a magistrate, should be required in order to search. At the charging stage, the requirement of a postarrest warrant and a preliminary hearing involves judgment about the importance of judicial participation. At the conviction stage, the judge's role is more obvious, although the extent of his responsibility in plea of guilty cases is somewhat ambiguous. At the postconviction level there is current debate over the desirability of judicial participation in sentencing, parole, and revocation decisions.

At the arrest stage, it is often assumed that in the absence of any need for immediate action the normal and desirable method for determining whom to arrest is by the police presenting the facts to a magistrate, who is removed from the competitive task of detecting crime and bringing about the arrest of offenders. However, in current practice arrest warrants are seldom used,[8] and when they are used the participation of the judicial officer is usually a formality with little or no attention given by him to the question of whether an adequate basis exists for making an arrest. Major responsibility for the arrest decision when the warrant is used rests with the police and prosecutor. Usually nothing is done unless the police initiate the process.[9] It is important to know what the actual function of the arrest warrant is in current criminal justice administration and to learn, as far as possible, why there is so wide a gulf between the conception of the "judicial decision" and the practice of noninvolvement of a judicial officer.

2. *The decision not to invoke the criminal process.* The exercise of discretion is of major significance at every stage of the

---

[7] See the statement of Justice Jackson, writing for the Supreme Court, in Johnson v. United States, 333 U.S. 10, 14, 68 Sup. Ct. 367, 92 L. Ed. 436 (1948).

[8] However, warrants are commonly issued with respect to persons who were arrested without warrant and are already in custody when the police think that they should be prosecuted. In this case the warrant serves as a charging document, and in the ordinary case the prosecutor makes the decision with regard to issuance.

[9] However, complainants sometimes go directly to the prosecutor or a magistrate, in which case police approval is not a prerequisite.

criminal justice administration process. Before conviction, the exercise of the prosecutor's discretion has been traditionally recognized. Following conviction, discretion is expressly delegated to the judge in sentencing and to correctional authorities in determining treatment and release of offenders. Thus, at the charging and postconviction stages, discretion not only is commonly exercised but is also commonly recognized as being proper. At other stages, however, particularly at the time of the police decision as to arrest [10] and the judge's decision as to guilt or innocence, although discretion is often exercised it is seldom formally recognized as being proper.

It is helpful to look at the total criminal justice system as a series of interrelated discretionary choices, examining at each stage the extent to which discretion is and properly should be exercised, the criteria upon which the exercise of discretion is based, the nature and effectiveness of controls on it, and the effect of the exercise of discretion upon earlier and later stages of the process and upon the multiple objectives of the criminal justice system.

It is particularly important to be concerned about the exercise of discretion, most often by police, at the arrest stage. Many persons whose conduct apparently violates the criminal law are not arrested.[11] In some instances this may be explained by the fact that there really is no legislative purpose to enforcing some statutes which are obsolete or drafted in overly general or ambiguous

[10] "[I]t will be argued by many that the very nature of the police function denies the existence of such discretion. To this group of formalists, the police function consists of relating the provisions of the law to a fine measurement of the quantum of evidence. Out of this cold and somewhat mechanical calculation evolves an answer which provides the basis for subsequent police action. . . . The stereotype of a police officer as an individual having a purely ministerial function has been firmly planted in the minds of most Americans." Speech by Herman Goldstein, "Police Decisions and Police Discretion in the Criminal Law Process," Conference on Criminal Justice, University of Chicago Law School, January 7, 1960. See Fielding, Treatise on the Office of Constable, 290-291 (1761): "[A] Constable is to remember, that he is to apprehend Offenders and not to determine Offenses . . . ," cited in Hall, The Law of Arrest in Relation to Contemporary Social Problems, 3 U. Chi. L. Rev. 345, 355 n.48 (1936).

[11] The emphasis herein is upon decisions not to arrest for conduct which is or may be prohibited. While the same question could be raised concerning decisions to arrest, the former course seems most feasible. Failure by the police to enforce a legislative proscription typically merits explanation, but such an explanation may not be called for when there is enforcement. Thus it would seem superfluous to explain why the process is invoked by the arrest of a suspected armed robber. Failure to arrest for seriously dangerous conduct typically would be explainable on the basis of the unusual nature of a particular case (such as an armed robbery to recover money lost to a crooked gambler) or would be attributable to the gross inefficiency or corruption of officials. The highly unusual case is not of great concern to this analysis, nor is gross inefficiency or corruption. Major concern is with problems which cause recurring difficulty for the competent and honest official.

terms. In other instances the failure to make arrests results from the obvious fact that the resources available to law enforcement agencies make impossible the full enforcement of the existing substantive criminal law. A significant number of decisions not to arrest are unrelated to either legislative intent or resource allocation. Illustrative is the failure to arrest an informant as a reward for information. This type of decision may reflect an attitude shared by the prosecutor or judge, evinced by a previous refusal to prosecute, to convict, or to give a meaningful sentence, or it may sometimes indicate a judgment reached within the law enforcement agency itself.

Despite the obvious importance of discretion at the arrest stage, comparatively little attention has been given to it. Whether its importance is measured in terms of practice or of principle, it plainly deserves major consideration in this volume.

3. *The decision not to take immediate custody.* An issue which arises at some stages in the criminal justice process is whether it is necessary and desirable to take or to retain physical custody of the person. This is of obvious importance after conviction, when the judge must decide whether to imprison the offender or to place him on probation, and when correctional authorities must decide whether to release on parole and whether to revoke probation or parole. At the preconviction stages also the need for custody is and has traditionally been recognized as an important consideration. At least bail administration has been given a great deal of attention.

At the arrest stage a decision must be made as to whether to make an immediate arrest or to use an alternative such as the summons or notice to appear. In recent years there has been increased concern about whether it is necessary to take immediate custody of all persons against whom the criminal process is to be invoked. The Federal Rules of Criminal Procedure provide for the issuance of a summons in lieu of arrest,[12] and some state legislation has followed this lead.[13] However, the existence of this legislation has not resulted in the widespread use of the summons. To know why this is so requires an understanding of the functions which are served, in current practice, by taking a suspect into immediate custody rather than by utilizing some other alternative.

4. *The decision to arrest for purposes of prosecution.* At each stage in the criminal justice process the question arises as to whether there is enough evidence to carry the process further. It

---

[12] Fed. R. Crim. P. 4.

[13] E.g., Wis. Stat. §954.02 (1955). See ALI Code, Criminal Procedure §§12, 13, 14 (1930).

arises when a suspect is stopped and questioned and proceeds through arrest, charging, holding for trial, conviction, sentencing, release on parole, and revocation. At the point of conviction, it has long been recognized that the evidentiary requirement is "proof beyond a reasonable doubt." Conviction, of course, is the ultimate test of guilt. For this reason, and because of the necessity of interpreting the standard to lay juries, the requirement has been most frequently articulated. Less attention has been given to the requirements at other stages, particularly the postconviction and the charging stages.

At the arrest stage the requirement, in felony cases, has commonly been said to be "reasonable grounds to believe" or "probable cause," the two phrases being used interchangeably. The "probable cause" phrase has also been used to define the evidence needed to charge a suspect and to hold him for trial. As a consequence, it is sometimes assumed that the evidence required in each case is the same. Yet it is current practice for state and local law enforcement officers to arrest in situations where it is apparent that more evidence must be acquired in order to hold the suspect for trial.

The relationship between the evidentiary requirements for investigation, arrest, and charging has an important bearing on issues such as whether a suspect can be subjected to in-custody investigation when there are inadequate grounds for arrest and whether an in-custody investigation can be continued after sufficient grounds to charge become available.

5. *The decision to arrest for purposes other than prosecution.* Observation of current practice makes it apparent that a number of informal processes, or accommodations, are often used, sometimes routinely, at various stages of the criminal justice process. These accommodations often result from frustrations brought about by requirements of law which the administrators believe are excessively difficult to comply with or by an absence of adequate resources to invoke the entire criminal justice process. Thus suspected offenders are sometimes subjected to only a part of the full criminal process because it is thought that this achieves the objectives of the system, that the cost of invoking the full process would be excessive in view of the minimal additional achievements, or that use of the total process is not possible even if desirable because of limited personnel and facilities.

At the investigation stage, police may resort to the "tip-over" raid if convinced that it is not practicable to suppress organized vice by obtaining admissible evidence. In the "tip-over," gambling paraphernalia may be destroyed, the operation at least temporarily closed, and the professional gamblers kept "on the run." At the arrest stage, persons may be taken into custody without expectation of prosecution. Similarly, the prosecutor may resort to an alternative to charging, such as using his office to induce restitution in a bad check case. Administrative pressure may give rise at the conviction stage to a practice of reducing charges (in spite of sufficient evidence to convict on the higher charge) to elicit guilty pleas and avoid trials.

Many, no doubt a majority, of persons taken into custody are arrested for purposes of prosecution. This is clearly contemplated by the law. However, some are arrested for purposes other than prosecution. For example, it has long been a practice to arrest intoxicated persons and release them when they are sober. The purpose of the arrest is to provide for the well-being of the drunk; the purpose of his release is to avoid the cost of a judicial proceeding thought to accomplish nothing in the way of rehabilitation or prevention. Such use of the criminal process as a device for the administration of certain social services may be of doubtful propriety.[14] But, to the extent that arrest and temporary confinement are used to serve this objective in current administration, it is important to know when it is so used and with what apparent consequences. It is obvious, for example, that arrests in these cases will be on the basis of poverty and helplessness rather than moral character and social dangerousness.

Arrests are also made for purposes unrelated to prosecution in situations where subjecting the suspect to the total process would achieve only slightly more than is achieved by the arrest alone but would cost substantially more. Illustrative is the arrest of suspected prostitutes so that they can be subjectd to a brief period of detention, during which time a medical examination may be carried out. To invoke the total process it would be necessary to build an accosting case, an extremely difficult task and one which would require the expenditure of considerable enforcement resources. Furthermore, the result of conviction even if obtained would probably be the imposition of a small fine. In terms of time, effort, and cost, it may not seem worthwhile to proceed fully against the prostitute when there exists an alternative which is

[14] See Allen, The Borderland of the Criminal Law: Problems of "Socializing" Criminal Justice, 32 Soc. Service Rev. 107, 109 (1958), where the author concludes: "Whenever penal sanctions are employed to deal with problems of social service, two things are almost certain to happen and a third result may often occur. First, the social services will not be effectively rendered. Second, the diversion of personnel, resources and energy required in the effort will adversely affect the ability of a system of criminal justice to fulfill those functions that it can uniquely perform. Finally, the effort may sometimes result in the corruption and demoralization of the agencies of criminal justice."

simple to use and probably as effective in control and containment of the problem as conviction.

Police may arrest other types of offenders such as gamblers and confiscate their equipment without thought of prosecution. This practice may result from a continued lack of success in obtaining conviction of these persons. While there are a number of reasons why a prosecution may fail, the predominant one in gambling cases is that essential evidence is often excluded because of the manner in which it has been obtained by the police. Some police believe that evidence acquisition by means acceptable to the courts is not possible, so they subject the suspected offenders to only a part of the process. In this way they manage to impose a sanction without directly confronting the exclusionary rule.

The problems created by the arrest and release of a drunk for whom there are adequate grounds for arrest are obviously different from those created by the arrest of persons on insufficient evidence of guilt in order to achieve a punitive or deterrent objective. However, these two situations have seldom been differentiated in either law or practice. Careful study of each is necessary in order to understand the effect of leaving certain welfare services to the criminal process, of imposing only minor penalties upon conviction, and of attempting to control the actions of the administrators by blocking the full use of the process.

PART I

The Decision to Seek and to Issue an Arrest Warrant

The rule which permits arrest for felonies, as distinguished from misdemeanors, if there are reasonable grounds for believing a crime has been or is being committed . . . grew out of the need to protect the public safety by making prompt arrests. . . . Yet, apart from those cases where the crime is committed in the presence of the officer, arrests without warrants, like searches without warrants, are the exception, not the rule in our society.

JUSTICE DOUGLAS, dissenting
in *Draper v. United States,*
358 U.S. 307, 315-316 (1959)

It is frequently said that arrests should not be made, except in emergency situations, without the prior approval of an impartial judicial officer. In practice, however, it is routine to make arrests without warrant, and thus without the prior approval of a judicial officer, even though there is adequate opportunity to obtain a warrant.

The assumption that it is desirable to arrest with a warrant whenever it is feasible to do so undoubtedly rests upon the belief that a greater degree of protection against unwarranted police interference with an individual is afforded if arrest is delayed until an impartial evaluation of the evidence can be made. However, the requirement of judicial participation is not, in most situations, an explicit requirement of law. Felony arrests are lawful if made upon "reasonable grounds" and misdemeanor arrests are lawful if the offense is committed "in the presence" of the officer, without regard to whether it is feasible under the circumstances to obtain a warrant.

An obviously wide gulf separates the ideal stated above by Justice Douglas and the current practice in many jurisdictions. It is evident that judicial participation in the arrest decision is infrequent and that when it does occur it is largely perfunctory. Often a clerk signs the warrant or the judge may sign it himself but without reading it.

This situation probably results, at least in part, from a reluctance on the part of many judges to become too involved in what they may conceive to be the relatively ministerial task of issuing process. There is more interest, for example, in the trial of contested cases. In part it results also from a willingness by most judges to rely heavily upon the prosecutor, who usually gives careful attention to the advisability of arrest in those cases brought to his attention before arrest. Perhaps this is reinforced by an attitude, not expressed, that the decision to arrest is properly the responsibility of the police and prosecutor rather than the judge, who will, in any event, have an opportunity to review the decision at the preliminary hearing or, if one is waived, at the trial.

Analysis of the function of the arrest warrant is complicated by the fact that it serves two quite different purposes in current criminal justice administration. The warrant issued before arrest typically signifies a decision to arrest. It is this that Justice Douglas would presumably require, thus making arrest a judicial rather than a police decision. The warrant issued after arrest often, but not always, is a tangible indication of the prosecutor's decision to charge the suspect with a crime. The responsibility of the judicial officer in this situation is as uncertain as it is when the warrant is obtained prior to arrest. In addition, there is a significant number of cases in which the warrant is issued after arrest without the active involvement of either the prosecutor or a judicial officer. In these situations the police decision to arrest takes on added importance because it also constitutes the decision to charge the suspect with a crime.

The law relating to the issuance of an arrest warrant differs in the three states studied. In Kansas only the magistrate can issue a warrant, and he can do so without the concurrence of the prosecutor. In Wisconsin both the prosecutor and the magistrate can issue a warrant, and each can do so without the concurrence of the other. In Michigan only the magistrate can issue the warrant, but he can do so only if the prosecutor concurs. Thus an interesting basis for comparative analysis is afforded.

CHAPTER 1

Arrests with a Warrant

Although it is common current practice to make an arrest without a warrant, there are recurring situations in which warrants are obtained prior to arrest. It is the objective of this chapter to identify these situations and to explain, so far as possible, what function the arrest warrant serves when it is issued before arrest.

A. SITUATIONS IN WHICH EXISTING LAW REQUIRES A WARRANT BE ISSUED BEFORE ARREST

Generally, an arrest for a felony can be made without a warrant whenever adequate evidence exists to obtain a warrant. However, the grounds for arrest without a warrant for a misdemeanor are narrower than the grounds for obtaining a warrant. Thus, in misdemeanor cases there are situations in which the only way a lawful arrest can be made is by obtaining a warrant prior to arrest.

Under the early common law an offender could be arrested without warrant for a misdemeanor only if it constituted a breach of the peace committed in the presence of the person making the arrest.[1] This exception to the general requirement of a warrant for a misdemeanor arrest was apparently based upon the necessity of acting promptly to suppress a breach of the peace.[2] The prevailing rule today is a broader one which allows an officer to arrest for any misdemeanor committed in his presence. This is the rule in

[1] 9 Halsbury's Laws of England, Criminal Law and Procedure §117 (2d ed. 1933); 1 Anderson, Sheriffs, Coroners and Constables 166 (1941); A.L.I. Code of Criminal Procedure 231 (1931).

[2] Bohlen and Shulman, Arrest With and Without a Warrant, 75 U. Pa. L. Rev. 485, 488-491 (1927). The authors take the position that the subsequent change to allow arrest for all misdemeanors in the presence often resulted from a misreading of Carroll v. United States, 267 U.S. 132, 45 Sup. Ct. 280, 69 L. Ed. 543 (1925). Recognizing the old rule as too restrictive, they view the modern provision as unnecessarily broad, "like killing all the cattle in a state because a few are suspected of having foot-and-mouth disease." Bohlen and Shulman, *supra*, at 491.

Michigan by statute[3] and apparently in Kansas and Wisconsin as a matter of common law development.[4]

The "in-presence" norm for misdemeanor arrests without warrant is not strictly correlated to the necessity for immediate arrest in either its permissive or its prohibitive aspects. An arrest for an offense committed in the presence of an officer can lawfully be made even though there is adequate opportunity to obtain a warrant prior to arrest.[5] Conversely, an arrest for a misdemeanor committed outside the presence of the officer ordinarily cannot lawfully be made even if the probable cause needed for a warrant[6] is in the officer's hands and it appears that the failure to make an immediate arrest will result in further damage or in the successful flight of the suspect. An exception to the latter rule is to be found in Wisconsin, where a statute provides:

> An arrest by a peace officer without a warrant for a misdemeanor or for the violation of an ordinance is lawful whenever the officer has reasonable grounds to believe that the person to be arrested has committed a misdemeanor or has violated an ordinance and will not be apprehended unless immediately arrested or that personal or property damage may likely be done unless immediately arrested.[7]

3 Mich. Stat. Ann. §28.874 (1954).

4 State v. Merrifield, 180 Kan. 267, 303 P.2d 155 (1956); Hawkins v. Lutton, 95 Wis. 492, 70 N.W. 483 (1897). However, there is uncertainty in both of these states as to whether these are the controlling norms. See page 232.

5 Early cases can be found, such as Sarah Way's Case, 41 Mich. 299, 1 N.W. 1021 (1879), or Robinson v. Miner, 68 Mich. 549, 37 N.W. 21 (1888), which contain language strongly condemning misdemeanor arrest without warrant when not shown to be necessary for the protection of public security. However, these cases merely explain the rationale behind the earlier breach of the peace exception, and appear to have no validity today under the general "in-presence" rule.

6 The probable cause requirement is usually a matter of state constitutional law. Kan. Const., Bill of Rights §15; Mich. Const., art. II, §10; Wis. Const., art. I, §11. It now appears, however, that the states are bound by the Supreme Court's definition of probable cause as used in the Fourth Amendment. Aguilar v. Texas, 378 U.S. 108, 84 Sup. Ct. 1509, 12 L. Ed. 2d 723 (1964).

7 Wis. Stat. §954.03(1) (1955). This statute goes on to say that it is supplemental to the statutory powers of city police to arrest for in-presence violations. It is evident therefore, in regard to such officers, that neither of the two qualifications (possibility of escape or of damage) is necessary for in-presence violations. However, as to officers without statutory arrest power, it is not clear: (a) whether the common law in Wisconsin allows arrest for all misdemeanors committed in the presence or only for breaches of the peace, Comment, 1959 Wis. L. Rev. 489, 496-499; and (b) whether, if the former is the case, the above statute supersedes the common law power. Id. at 495 n.26.

The origin of this unique Wisconsin provision is uncertain. However, it is similar to §6(1)(b) of the Uniform Arrest Act, which permits a police officer to arrest without a warrant when "he has reasonable grounds to believe that the person to be arrested has committed a misdemeanor out of his presence, either within the state or without the state, if law enforcement officers of the state where the misdemeanor was committed so request, and will not be apprehended unless immediately ar-

In felony cases, police in Kansas, Michigan, and Wisconsin can arrest without a warrant whenever there is sufficient evidence to obtain a warrant. Notwithstanding considerable ambiguity as to the application of the governing norms to given fact situations,[8] it seems clear that the "probable cause" needed for a warrant is certain to meet the "reasonable grounds" or "reasonable cause to believe" test for felony arrest without warrant.[9] And there is no need to obtain a warrant merely because there is an opportunity to do so. Early cases in which this conclusion was reached [10] might be explained on the ground that at that time all felonies were capi-

---

rested." Such a statute does not exist in Kansas or Michigan and perhaps would violate the constitutions of these states. In In re Kellam, 55 Kan. 700, 41 Pac. 960 (1895), habeas corpus proceedings were begun challenging a misdemeanor arrest without warrant made upon the basis of information received from a reliable informant. Though the officer cited as his arrest authority a state statute of that era allowing arrest "upon reasonable suspicion that an offense has been committed," and a Topeka city ordinance allowing arrest of "all persons found under suspicious circumstances who cannot give a good account of themselves," the court held: "The powers of officers to make arrests have been extended to some extent by the statutes but it is generally held that officers cannot be constitutionally clothed with authority to arrest without warrant for minor offenses not committed in their presence or view." 55 Kan. at 702, 41 Pac. at 961.

Shortly thereafter, in State v. Dietz, 59 Kan. 576, 584, 53 Pac. 870, 873 (1898), the court refused to recognize any common law extension of the power to arrest without warrant, stating: "The rule in In re Kellam cannot be relaxed to permit arrests without warrant because the acts and language of an accused person are such as to induce the officer as a reasonable man to believe an offense has been or was about to be committed. The liberty of the citizen . . . cannot be thus made to depend upon the correctness of a sheriff's or constable's inductive conclusions."

Oddly enough, in a much more recent Kansas case, Hill v. Day, 168 Kan. 604, 610, 215 P.2d 219, 224 (1950), the court declared that "a properly qualified officer" could arrest "the perpetrator of a . . . breach of the peace without a warrant when he has reasonable grounds — and probable cause — for believing the person arrested is guilty." However, this case is probably explainable on other grounds. See page 414.

In Michigan the constitutional limitations in this respect are much less clearly defined. In early cases it was held that breach of the peace was the only constitutional exception, Robinson v. Miner, 68 Mich. 549, 37 N.W. 21 (1888); Sarah Way's Case, 41 Mich. 299, 1 N.W. 1021 (1879), and it was said "that no arrest can be lawfully made without warrant, except in the cases existing at common law before our Constitution was adopted," People v. Swift, 59 Mich. 529, 546-547, 26 N.W. 694, 698 (1886). However, in Burroughs v. Eastman, 101 Mich. 419, 59 N.W. 817 (1894), a city ordinance allowing arrest for all ordinance violations in the presence was upheld, which seems adequate support for the constitutionality of the present statute which allows arrest for all misdemeanors in the presence. Also, it strongly suggests that the warrant requirement for misdemeanors not in the presence is based merely on statute rather than on constitutional principles.

[8] A discussion of this will be found in the volume on Prosecution.

[9] Indeed, the fact that the exigencies of the situation are such that a prompt arrest is necessary is an important consideration in determining whether the "reasonable grounds" are present. See page 248. This would suggest that there may be instances in which an arrest without warrant might be proper, yet, if there were time to seek a warrant, the evidence might be insufficient for issuance.

[10] E.g., Davis v. Russell, 5 Bing. 354 (1829); Mure v. Kaye, 4 Taun. 34 (1811).

tal offenses, so that there was a serious risk of escape in all felony cases if arrest were delayed to seek a warrant.[11]   While most felonies are no longer capital offenses, there appear to be few exceptions to the no-need-for-warrant rule in this country today.[12]   Even the United States Supreme Court, in the course of reaching the since-repudiated conclusion that a search warrant must be obtained when there is time to do so, expressly declared that a felony arrest without warrant was valid notwithstanding the "more than adequate opportunity" to obtain an arrest warrant beforehand.[13]

Thus, despite law to the contrary in many foreign jurisdictions[14]

[11] Williams, Arrest for Felony at Common Law, 1954 Crim. L. Rev. (Eng.) 408, 419.

[12] A unique provision is found in the following Texas statute: "Where it is shown by satisfactory proof to a peace officer, upon the representation of a credible person, that a felony has been committed, and that the offender is about to escape, so that there is no time to procure a warrant, such peace officer may, without warrant, pursue and arrest the accused." Tex. Code Crim. Proc., art. 215. However, Texas statutes also allow an officer to arrest upon finding a person in a suspicious place under circumstances that reasonably show he has committed a felony or breach of the peace or is about to commit an offense, *provided* that the city or town has previously established rules authorizing such arrests. Tex. Code Crim. Proc., art. 214. See Potts, The Law of Arrest, 1 Baylor L. Rev. 397, 399-400 (1949).

[13] Trupiano v. United States, 334 U.S. 699, 68 Sup. Ct. 1229, 92 L. Ed. 1663 (1948), overruled by United States v. Rabinowitz, 339 U.S. 56, 70 Sup. Ct. 430, 94 L. Ed. 653 (1950).   In Trupiano, although agents had known for three weeks that a building was being used as a distillery, they made a nighttime raid without a warrant of arrest or search.   One of the defendants was arrested when the agents, looking through an open door, saw him engaged in distilling.   Curiously enough, the court upheld the failure to obtain an arrest warrant on the basis that there was an offense in the officers' presence, even though the presence of the officers on the farm was attributable to prior information in their hands sufficient to justify a warrant for the defendant's arrest: "Warrants of arrest are designed to meet the dangers of unlimited and unreasonable arrests of persons who are not at the moment committing any crime.   Those dangers, obviously, are not present where a felony plainly occurs before the eyes of an officer of the law at a place where he is lawfully present.   Common sense then dictates that an arrest in that situation is valid despite the failure to obtain a warrant of arrest." 334 U.S. at 705, 68 Sup. Ct. at 1233, 92 L. Ed. at 1669.

[14] A recent summary of the arrest law of the various countries states: "The requirement of a prior written order may be dispensed with in certain cases defined by law.   The most familiar group of such cases are embraced in the concept of *flagrante delicto*.   In some jurisdictions, the law authorizes arrest without warrant in such cases, subject, however, to additional requirements, such as, that the offense is serious, that the arrest is necessary in order to prevent flight or secure the evidence, or that the offender cannot be identified immediately.   In a few countries the power to arrest without a warrant is limited to *flagrante delicto* cases." Study of the Right of Everyone to Be Free from Arbitrary Arrest, Detention and Exile, Commission on Human Rights, U.N. Doc. E/CN.4/813, par. 110 (1961).

Similarly, another study notes that examination of the warrant requirements in many countries reflects "a belief that arrest is too serious a matter to entrust to the judgment of the police alone and that, except where circumstances require immediate action, some more disinterested observer should pass on the case before a deprivation of personal liberty occurs." Foote, Problems of the Protection of Human Rights in Criminal Law and Procedure (Santiago, Chile, May 19-30, 1958), U.N. Doc. TE 326/1 (40-2) LA, pp. 41-42.

Illustrative of the kind of provision to be found in some other countries is the

and criticism by some commentators,[15] the arrest warrant requirement is seldom keyed to necessity. In the three states observed, as
is generally true, there is no warrant requirement for felonies, and
the usual in-presence rule for misdemeanors only roughly corre-
sponds to the actual needs for immediate custody. Only in Wisconsin has express recognition been given to certain immediate
custody needs with regard to misdemeanors occurring out of the
officer's presence.

B. Noncompliance with the Misdemeanor Warrant Requirement

The misdemeanor warrant requirement causes police concern in
some situations, but does not in any way interfere with effective
law enforcement in others. It is apparent, for example, that the
prohibition against an arrest without a warrant causes no difficulty
in cases where the officer would use a notice to appear even if the
offense occurred in his presence. Thus, the local resident who has
an accident under circumstances indicating that he committed a
traffic offense will ordinarily not be arrested whether the offense
occurred in or out of the presence of the officer. In other situations officers actually benefit from the prohibition against an arrest
without a warrant. When an offense arises out of a domestic quarrel, there is often pressure on the police from the wife to arrest the
husband. Police experience is that the wife's enthusiasm for prosecuting the husband disappears by the next day, and therefore the
husband must be released, since there is no one willing to give
testimony against him.[16] For this reason, the police prefer not to
arrest, and they justify their failure to act to the wife by explaining
their lack of authority.

Norwegian requirement that arrest be made only upon a warrant, but that if waiting for a warrant entails danger, e.g., of escape or tampering with evidence, the
arrest may be made on the orders of a police official or, when even more pressing
circumstances make dangerous the procurement of such an order, by a policeman
without either warrant or order. Yet one observer has said of Norway: "Arrest by
warrant hardly exists." Bratholm, Arrest and Detention in Norway, 108 U. Pa. L.
Rev. 336, 339 (1960).

15 "No arrest should ever be made except on the authority of a warrant of arrest
if it is at all practicable to obtain one." Houts, From Arrest to Release 26 (1958).
"Arrest without warrant should be the exception rather than the rule: where there
is time and opportunity to procure a warrant, this should be done." Williams,
Arrest for Felony at Common Law, 1954 Crim. L. Rev. (Eng.) 408, 419.

16 The police are usually of the opinion that the criminal process need not be
invoked for minor offenses if the victim is not seriously interested in prosecution.
See page 114. But if the police deem prosecution desirable when the victim does
not, they may resort to the complaint-warrant process in order to commit the victim
to cooperation in the prosecution. See page 49.

Yet there are other situations in which arrests are made without warrant despite the fact that the offense has not occurred in the presence of the officer. Sometimes this is a matter of expediency, since it is easier to arrest first and then obtain the warrant. In other cases, the police make an immediate arrest because they believe it is necessary to prevent escape of the offender, to prevent the occurrence of further harm, or to prevent destruction or loss of important evidence.

1. *Reasons for noncompliance.*

a. *Immediate arrest because the offender may otherwise avoid apprehension.*

> *Illustration No. 1:* Traffic officers responded to an accident call and found that a car had left the roadway, resulting in some front-end damage to the car. The driver had been drinking and was quarrelsome, but clearly was not drunk. The officers, after questioning the driver, concluded that the accident had been brought about by a misdemeanor driving violation. Because the driver was not a resident of the state, and was presently on his way back to his home, he was placed under arrest.

One significant case where the police often ignore the warrant requirement is that in which it appears the offender might not later be found if a warrant were first sought. This is most likely to be so, as in the above illustration, when the offender is a non-resident of the area within the jurisdiction of the officer on the scene. City police often arrest violators with addresses outside the city (unless it clearly appears that they work in the city),[17] county officers arrest persons not residents of the county, and state patrolmen arrest only out-of-state offenders.

In other instances, knowledge that a misdemeanor has been committed outside his presence may lead the officer to believe that it is likely that the offender has also committed other, more serious offenses. In such a case the officer knows that the offender may have a strong inducement to flee because of the risk that the other offenses will be traced to him. Consequently, an immediate arrest may be made in this situation even though there is inadequate evidence to justify an arrest for the felony or felonies suspected.

Finally, later apprehension may appear improbable because the

---

[17] Because in Wisconsin arrest for a misdemeanor without warrant is allowed if there are reasonable grounds to believe that a misdemeanor has been committed and also that the person "will not be apprehended unless immediately arrested," Wis. Stat. §954.03(1) (1955), Milwaukee police arrest for misdemeanors not committed in their presence when the offender has an address outside the city.

violator has no regular address. Said a member of a "bum squad" in a Michigan city:

> Many times a citizen will come up to us and tell us he has been mooched. Even though we don't happen to see the guy in that particular offense, we will look for him and watch for a while. If he hooks a mooch on someone, we grab him. But if the description is a good one, we will take him in without waiting. Sometimes we charge him with mooching even if we didn't see him do it, and sign the complaint ourselves.

Often this problem is resolved by utilizing the broad reach of the vagrancy laws, which make arrest possible because the vagrancy offense occurs in the officer's presence. The more limited statute in Michigan means that this alternative is not available in that state.[18]

b. *Immediate arrest because the offender may otherwise cause further harm.*

Illustration No. 2: Officers were called to a domestic disturbance. Upon their arrival at the apartment in question, they found the husband and wife in a vigorous argument, although it was not loud enough to warrant a breach of the peace arrest. The wife, who had called the police, related to them what had happened. The officers concluded that a misdemeanor assault and battery had occurred. Also, the circumstances suggested that recurrence after the officers left the premises was not at all unlikely. Consequently, they decided to arrest the husband.

The domestic disturbance, whether or not it occurs in the officer's presence, usually does not lead to arrest. The police, knowing that the wife will later not desire prosecution, usually restore order and then leave without making an arrest. If the injured spouse is insistent, then the police may tell her to see the prosecutor the next day about obtaining a warrant.[19] However, there are situations, including some where the offense has occurred outside the presence of the officer, in which an immediate arrest appears desirable in order to prevent further harm. While Wisconsin police do have power to arrest in such a case,[20] officers in Kansas and

---

18 Vagrancy is included in the disorderly persons statute, as is begging. Mich. Stat. Ann. §28.364 (1938). However, the common law definition of vagrancy is read into the statute, and thus the Michigan court has said that it must appear that the person is idle *and* seeking to live on the charity of others. In re Jordan, 90 Mich. 3, 50 N.W. 1087 (1892). Thus observation of the begging may still be necessary in order for the offense to be considered as having occurred in the officer's presence.

19 See page 50.

20 The Wisconsin statute allows misdemeanor arrest without warrant if there are reasonable grounds to believe that a misdemeanor has been committed and also "that personal or property damage may likely be done unless [the suspect is] immediately arrested." Wis. Stat. §954.03(1) (1955). Thus Milwaukee police, if they are called

Michigan do not, and the arrests made in those states under these circumstances are without a basis in law.

c. *Immediate arrest as an aid in investigation.*

Illustration No. 3: Officers saw a group of youths leave a tavern and enter a vehicle. Because of darkness it was uncertain how many there were and whether they were under age. The officers approached the vehicle and asked the six occupants to identify themselves. They did so, and the officers learned that two of the girls were under age. The group of six, all local residents, were then taken to the sheriff's office, where each could be questioned separately. When each of the six gave the same story, the officers concluded that the two girls had not been furnished beer by the others nor had they entered the tavern. All the youths were promptly released.

Illustration No. 4: The police received a complaint of window-peeping in a residential neighborhood. A patrol car was sent to the area, and the patrolling officers observed a man running down an alley. They stopped the man and asked him to identify himself. The man explained that he was just out for a walk, and gave identification establishing his residence and employment in the community. The officers took the man to the home of the complainant, who was unable to make positive identification, but said the man's clothing resembled that of the Peeping Tom. At this, the man was taken to the station for questioning.

Both of these cases seem to involve adequate evidence to give the officer reasonable grounds to believe that a misdemeanor had been committed, though not in his presence,[21] and thus under the prevailing rule lawful arrest could not be made without a warrant. The police proceeded, however, as they would in a felony case, by taking the suspects into custody and conducting an inquiry at the station in order to determine if the suspected offenses were in fact committed or if the suspects were in fact guilty.

There is, as is pointed out elsewhere, considerable ambiguity in current law as to whether grounds for arrest must exist when a suspect is stopped and questioned on the street,[22] when he is taken

---

to a fight in a tavern and arrive after order has been restored, arrest if blood is seen (this is thought to be sufficient evidence that further harm might occur).

21 In Illustration No. 3, it could be argued that the officers, upon seeing some of the youths leave the tavern, had reasonable grounds to believe that an offense was presently occurring. However, it is not entirely clear that this satisfies the in-presence requirement. See page 238. In Illustration No. 4, the conduct would come within some vagrancy provisions. See page 354 for more on vagrancy statutes and their use.

22 E.g., People v. Esposito, 118 Misc. 867, 194 N.Y. Supp. 326 (Ct. Spec. Sess. 1922). See page 344 for more about on-the-street questioning. Detailed consideration of this problem will be found in the volume on Detection of Crime.

to the station for interrogation, or only when he is taken into custody for purposes of prosecution. Where a right to stop and question exists, although grounds for arrest are lacking, an on-the-street investigation is possible when the offense suspected is a misdemeanor not committed in the presence of the officer. This on-the-street investigation may at least serve to identify the suspect, making it possible to procure a warrant for his arrest.[23] However, in the absence of a showing that the suspect consented, courts have said that a taking to the station does require that grounds for arrest exist. Thus the in-presence requirement does limit this power of the police.

The two illustrative cases reflect the police view that interrogation is more likely to be successful if it is conducted at the station as soon as possible after the suspect knows he is the object of official attention.[24] In the case of the youths, there was an advantage in having an opportunity to question each of the six persons apart from the others before they had a chance to agree on a story. In the case of the suspected window peeper, there also was an advantage in interrogating him before he had an opportunity to fabricate a story concerning his presence in the neighborhood.

Illustration No. 5: Police officers came upon a vehicle in a ditch alongside the highway. The car was still warm, indicating that it had only recently been driven off the road. By police radio the officers learned the name and address of the owner. They went immediately to his home, which was nearby, and were admitted by him. He appeared to be in an intoxicated condition, and in response to questioning said that he had been driving when the car ran into the ditch. The officers thought it desirable to obtain a urine specimen, so they gave him the choice of being arrested or giving such a sample. At the subsequent trial for driving while intoxicated, the trial judge excluded the urine sample on the ground that the defendant could not be given such a choice, as no arrest could have been lawfully made.

---

23 Thus express recognition of a right to question as to identity might be considered a means of limiting police arrest authority granted under a statute such as Wis. Stat. §954.03(1) (1955).

24 Wigmore, in noting the frequency with which confessions are obtained promptly upon arrest, says that the "explanation seems to be that the long-continued nervous inhibition of all utterances, in fear of revealing clues to guilt, imposes a terrific strain, like that of a tightened steel spring; that the arrest shows the guilty person that this strain of repression is futile and is no longer needed; and that hence, in the sudden release of the inhibition, it is a genuine relief to be able to tell freely the whole story. After this sense of nervous relief has passed, the inclination to tell disappears; and most confessions are in fact made within a short time after arrest." 3 Wigmore, Evidence §851 n. 3 (3d ed. 1940). This futility is shown, perhaps to a lesser extent, when the offender knows that his conduct has come to official attention.

Although this incident was observed in Wisconsin, where a more liberal misdemeanor arrest rule prevails, the police were not empowered to make an immediate arrest. Driving while intoxicated is only a misdemeanor;[25] the offense did not occur in the officer's presence; and since the driver was already at his residence, it did not appear that he would escape apprehension or do further damage if not immediately arrested. Had it been possible to make an arrest, the obtaining of a urine sample after arrest would not have been an illegal search,[26] and would have been admissible if not obtained by methods which violate due process because they "shock the conscience." [27]

In current practice, it appears that arrests are made for misdemeanors not committed in the presence of the officer in order to make possible an in-custody investigation but not in an effort to use the arrest as a basis for conducting a search for physical evidence.[28] This may reflect the effect of the rule, which existed until recently, excluding physical evidence obtained as an incident to an unlawful arrest but allowing an admission or confession so obtained. A recent decision of the United States Supreme Court, holding the statement also inadmissible, may have abolished this distinction.[29]

Some supervisory police officers have expressed the opinion that the limitation on the right to make a misdemeanor arrest seriously interferes with the police ability to make an effective search for physical evidence. Typical is the statement of a captain in a Michigan department. He said, "If one of my officers should come upon a man at night who was carrying away hubcaps under circumstances suggesting he had shortly before stolen them off a parked car, I would certainly expect him to make an arrest." [30] Apparently the captain would risk rendering the evidence inadmissible in order to make an arrest which would allow investigation directed toward other evidence, perhaps of other offenses.[31]

[25] Wis. Stat. §346.63 (1957), then Wis. Stat. §85.13 (1955).

[26] State v. Kroenig, 274 Wis. 266, 79 N.W.2d 810 (1956).

[27] Rochin v. California, 342 U.S. 165, 72 Sup. Ct. 205, 96 L. Ed. 183 (1952).

[28] This statement might not be strictly accurate if a very restrictive view were taken of what constitutes an offense in the presence. On this problem, see page 236. Also, there may be some exceptions where it is known that the arrest is made for purposes other than prosecution, although often there is suspicion of a felony offense, a matter often overlooked. See page 480.

[29] Wong Sun v. United States, 371 U.S. 471, 83 Sup. Ct. 407, 9 L. Ed. 2d 441 (1963).

[30] Where the value of the property is under $50, the offense is only a misdemeanor. Mich. Stat. Ann. §28.588 (1954).

[31] Conviction might still follow, especially if the defendant decided to plead guilty or if the police were later able to put forward another explanation for the arrest, such as that the offender resembled a man wanted for a felony. On this practice, see page 296.

Or perhaps he would be satisfied to make an arrest in such a case, even if it diminished the chances of conviction, in exchange for an opportunity to determine if the suspect was in fact guilty, so that he could be watched in the future, and an opportunity to recover the stolen articles, so that they could be returned to the owner.

Although the necessity for a prompt search for physical evidence may be most important in felony situations, there are misdemeanor offenses where the obtaining of critical evidence is important and where delay, particularly if the suspect is aware of the suspicions of the officer or another person, may result in the loss of an opportunity to secure the evidence.[32] Petty thefts,[33] property damage,[34] carelessness in the use of weapons,[35] and the like may come to the attention of an officer shortly after the offense occurs and while the suspect might still have the fruits of the crime or the implements of its commission on his person.[36]

The extent of the problem depends in part upon the substantive law of the state. For example, in cases of suspected shoplifting an officer is likely to be called to the scene only after its supposed commission but while important evidence may still be in the possession of the suspect. Whether the officer can lawfully arrest may depend upon whether all larceny from a store is a felony, as in Michigan,[37] or whether theft of small items is only a misdemeanor, as in Wisconsin.[38] It also depends upon the extent to which the

[32] There is no evidence that legislative characterization of an offense as a misdemeanor or felony involves any real judgment as to the need to secure evidence. Indeed, in many cases the characterization appears to be fortuitous. For example, in the modern Wisconsin code the causing of death by a high degree of negligence in the use of a vehicle or weapon, Wis. Stat. §940.08 (1955), is a misdemeanor inasmuch as it is punishable by imprisonment only in the county jail, while the same conduct causing only bodily harm, Wis. Stat. §940.24 (1955), is a felony because the possible one year sentence in that case is not expressly limited to the county jail. See Wis. Stat. §§939.60, 959.044 (1955).

[33] E.g., Mich. Stat. Ann. §28.588 (1954) (under $50); Wis. Stat. §943.20 (1955) (under $100).

[34] E.g., Mich. Stat. Ann. §28.609(1) (1954) (under $50); Wis. Stat. §943.01 (1955) (under $1000).

[35] E.g., Wis. Stat. §§940.08, 941.20 (1955).

[36] Of course, sometimes if there are grounds for thinking that the suspect still has the evidence on his person, this may itself justify arrest on another charge. Thus reasonable grounds to believe that a person has shortly before committed a misdemeanor by use of a weapon might also be said to justify the belief that the instrument is still in his possession. However, if the possession of the concealed instrument also constitutes a misdemeanor, e.g., Wis. Stat. §941.23 (1955), there again arises the question of whether reasonable belief in present criminality constitutes a basis for arrest under the in-presence norm. See page 238. If the instrument is not concealed, there is no offense under the above statute; however, connecting the suspect with the offense may call for more careful examination of the weapon than is possible by mere observation.

[37] Mich. Stat. Ann. §28.588(1) (1954).

[38] Wis. Stat. §943.20 (1955) (under $100). In Wisconsin, the added arrest power

arrest law in the particular jurisdiction is broadened to allow for an arrest for a misdemeanor committed outside the presence of the officer generally[39] or for specific offenses where the problem is acute.[40]   But, in any event, the existence of the problem is attributable to the fact that, while arrest serves as the predominant means of making a lawful search, the law of arrest has developed without consideration of the kinds of cases in which immediate search would be necessary.

2. *Tactics employed when arrest is desired for a misdemeanor not in the presence.*   The police in Kansas and Michigan do not have the power, which Wisconsin officers do have, to arrest for a misdemeanor not committed in their presence.   However, certain tactics are frequently employed in order to minimize the chance of such an arrest being successfully challenged.

a. *Insuring the cooperation of the complainant in obtaining conviction so as to preclude a false arrest action.*

Illustration No. 6: An officer responded to a family dispute call.   Husband, wife, and children were all hysterical when the officer arrived at the scene.   It appeared that before his arrival a fight had taken place in which the husband blackened his wife's eye.   The officer found a neighbor who would care for the children and then took both husband and wife to headquarters.   The wife was pressured into immediately signing a complaint, and the officer stressed the importance of her appearing in court the next morning.   The husband was held in jail until the trial the following morning, at which time a conviction was obtained on the basis of the wife's testimony.

This tactic was observed occasionally in Kansas.   One officer explained that it was the policy of the police department to proceed in this way because otherwise the wife probably would not cooperate in the prosecution of her husband, making his conviction unlikely.   From the arresting officer's point of view, a conviction is important because it bars tort recovery against him for the

---

under §954.03(1) must also be kept in mind.   However, the suspected shoplifter might be known to be a local resident, and it is unclear whether the qualification that "personal or property damage may likely be done" includes the risk that the property already taken will not be recovered unless an immediate arrest is made.

[39] For example, in Illinois an officer may arrest when "he has reasonable grounds to believe that the person is committing or has committed an offense." Ill. Rev. Stat., chap. 38, §107-2 (1963).

[40] For example, by a recent revision, the arrest law in Louisiana has been changed so that, while a warrant is still generally required for misdemeanors out of an officer's presence, an officer can arrest a shoplifter on "reasonable grounds to believe," which are stated to include an allegation by a merchant. La. Stat. Ann., tit. 15, §84.5 (Supp. 1961).

illegal arrest.[41] For example, in *Hill v. Day*[42] the Kansas court said that probable cause, which constitutes an absolute defense in a false imprisonment action, is conclusively shown by a conviction even if reversed on appeal.

b. *Encouraging another offense and thus creating a basis for a lawful arrest.*

Illustration No. 7: Officers responded to a wife's complaint of an assault by her husband. The disturbance had subsided by the time they arrived at the home of the couple. The wife showed her bruises to the police, but the husband, who appeared to be intoxicated, had little to say. One of the officers suggested to the husband that because it was a warm night the matter could be discussed further outside the house. The husband followed the officer out to the sidewalk, where he was promptly arrested for public intoxication.

Officers in both Kansas and Michigan sometimes attempt to bring about an event which will provide another basis for arrest when the misdemeanor for which arrest is actually desired was not committed in their presence. The most common use of this tactic is, as in the illustration above, for purposes of protecting a wife and children from further abuse. By luring the husband outside and making the arrest for public drunkenness, the officers not only provide grounds for making an immediate arrest but also create a basis for prosecution and conviction without having to rely upon the uncertain later cooperation of the wife.[43]

c. *Persuading the suspect to remain voluntarily in custody while warrant is obtained.*

Illustration No. 8: An officer reporting to the scene of a traffic accident concluded that the accident was caused by a misdemeanor violation by one of the drivers, a nonresident. The officer told the offending driver that a complaint would have to be made against him for the violation, and that the driver should accompany him to the station while this was done. After a warrant was obtained a formal arrest was made, and the driver then posted bail.

Illustration No. 9: Officers were called to a family disturb-

---

[41] For detailed consideration of this kind of defense, see page 414.

[42] 168 Kan. 604, 215 P.2d 219 (1950).

[43] The same tactic is sometimes used for other purposes. Thus the police occasionally receive an anonymous call complaining of a disturbance or unusual activity at a private residence. The usual case is one in which a motorist or passer-by reports that a man is walking in front of his home partially clothed or is staggering as if drunk. If, in the case of the drunk, the offender is indoors when an officer arrives, the policeman may enter the building if he can do so without violence and induce the party responsible to step outside, at which point an arrest is made for being drunk in public.

ance, but when they arrived at the scene no offense was occurring. The wife indicated that she would sign a complaint against her husband for assault. One officer accompanied her to the station where a complaint and warrant were prepared. Meanwhile another officer remained at the scene with instructions to "use all lawful means" to induce the husband to remain until they returned with the warrant.

In Kansas officers were sometimes observed to retain control over the offender by his supposed consent until an arrest warrant could be obtained. Either the offender would accompany the policeman to the station while a warrant was obtained or an officer would stay with the violator while another officer obtained the warrant.[44] This procedure is proper only if the suspect consents to the detention, a fact which is often difficult to ascertain later if the action is challenged.[45]

d. *Justifying the arrest as a felony arrest.*

Police often fail to consider whether an arrest of a suspected misdemeanant can be justified on the basis that reasonable grounds exist for believing the suspect has committed a felony. This may be the case, for example, in a theft case where the amount stolen is uncertain, in a criminal damage case where the amount of damage is in doubt, or in an assault case where the amount of injury caused or intended may not be clear. Where the higher amount or value or the more serious injury will result in the offense being a felony, an officer may in fact have reasonable grounds to believe that the more serious offense has occurred.

Some officers did say that they would try, where it was thought necessary, to establish grounds for making such a felony arrest. Some also indicated that they would try to find some basis for connecting the suspect with an outstanding felony, even though he was not in fact suspected of that offense. For example, following the arrest for a misdemeanor, the officer might find a description of some wanted felon resembling the person arrested and then use it as the explanation for the arrest.

C. Nature of the Warrant-Issuance Process

The assertion is frequently made that police action in response to a warrant is the best course whenever it is a possible alternative. For example, Jerome Hall has said:

[44] Another alternative in such a case would be for the officer to have the wife make a citizen's arrest of the husband and then turn him over to the police. No such instance was observed.

[45] See page 351 on the difficulties of determining whether appearance at a police station in response to an officer's request is with or without consent.

There is certainly no police obligation to satisfy only the minimum legal requirements. They must conform to law but where there are several legal avenues, the police are free to take any of them. That a search is legal if it is reasonable, despite the fact that there was opportunity to obtain a search warrant, does not therefore require the police to omit search warrants in such cases. Instead, the duty of the police in our kind of society requires them to follow that legal course which conforms most to democratic values.[46]

Presumably the arrest warrant process is, like the search warrant process, more consistent with democratic values than is the arrest without a warrant. However, whether this is so under the current methods of issuing arrest warrants is not at all clear.

1. *The practice in Kansas.* In Kansas the law requires that an arrest warrant for a state offense be issued by a magistrate, that is, a judge of a district court, a justice of the peace, or a similar officer. No mention is made of concurrence or participation by the prosecutor.[47] However, in practice it is the prosecutor or his assistant who is actually consulted by the police officer or private person desiring to initiate a prosecution. The complainant appears at the county attorney's office, where the county attorney or his assistant listens to the facts and, if he decides a warrant should be issued, dictates a complaint (the carbon copy of which is the warrant) to his stenographer. The papers are prepared in his office and then sent to the office of the deputy clerk of court. There the deputy clerk swears the party who is to sign the complaint, the complaint is signed, and the deputy clerk then issues the warrant. A judicial officer does not enter the picture at any point.

If a city ordinance is involved there is some statutory basis for the clerk issuing the warrant.[48] The clerk of police court does issue such warrants during regular business hours but does not appear to exercise any independent judgment when the warrant is requested by the police. Police control is even more striking when a warrant is obtained after regular business hours, as then the city ordinance warrants are issued by a supervisory officer of the police department who has been designated as a clerk pro tem.[49] If the clerk or clerk pro tem does not desire to issue a

---

[46] Hall, Police and Law in a Democratic Society, 28 Ind. L.J. 135, 172 (1953).

[47] Kan. Gen. Stat. §62-602 (1949).

[48] The law provides for warrants to be issued by the police judge of the city. Kan. Gen. Stat. §§13-606, 14-806, 15-506 (1949), for first, second, and third class cities, respectively. But in first class cities the clerk of police court is authorized "to make out, sign and issue all processes of said court," which apparently includes the right to issue such warrants. Kan. Gen. Stat. §13-628o.

[49] Officers of the rank of field sergeant and up are deputized as clerks pro tem in Wichita. They exercise their powers whenever the clerk of court is not present. The field sergeants act only when higher ranking officers are not available. While

warrant demanded by an insistent complainant, the matter is referred to the city attorney.[50]

2. *The practice in Michigan.* In Michigan the law provides that an arrest warrant shall be issued by a magistrate, that is, a judge of a circuit court, a justice of the peace, or a similar officer. But these judicial officers cannot issue a warrant without the concurrence of the prosecuting attorney, except in certain specified minor cases.[51] Generally, the practice is for the prosecutor to approve the issuance of the warrant, and no meaningful review of his decision is made by the magistrate at the time of warrant issuance.

In Detroit an officer requesting a warrant takes a typed report of the case[52] to the prosecuting attorney's office and selects one of the five or six assistant prosecutors from whom to request warrant approval. The assistant looks at the case report and may also question the officer. If approval is granted, he signs the back of the report, which constitutes authorization for the officer to have one of the typists prepare a request for warrant form. He then goes to one of the two senior assistant prosecutors, who must review the case.[53] If the senior assistant prosecutor also approves, he will sign the request form, which is the authorization for the warrant clerk to prepare the complaint and warrant. The officer then takes these documents to the court, where the clerk takes them and either asks the officer to swear to the matter in the complaint or merely asks him if the information is correct and if the signature is his. The clerk or officer then passes the documents on to the judge, who signs the warrant without any independent inquiry.

The practice observed elsewhere in Michigan is generally in accord with that in Detroit. Sometimes the warrant request is made directly to the magistrate, who will then contact the prosecutor by telephone and describe the facts of the case to him. If the case

---

this allows for some control by supervisory police officers, it generally appears that the opinion of the investigating officer is relied upon.

50 The Wichita City Attorney indicated that most instances of referral to him resulted in denial of the warrant.

51 The exceptions are warrant requests by members of the state department of public safety concerning traffic offenses, Mich. Stat. Ann. §§28.860, 28.1195 (1938) (for offenses not cognizable by a justice of the peace and offenses cognizable by a justice of the peace, respectively), and warrant requests by conservation officers for violation of the fish and game laws, Mich. Stat. Ann. §13.1222 (1951).

52 The report includes a synopsis of the case against the person to be arrested and the suggested charge for the complaint and warrant.

53 This double check on the issuance of warrants was inaugurated in 1935 because officers were "shopping around" for assistant prosecutors who would approve their warrant requests. It has not entirely eliminated the difficulty, however, as the probability of the ultimate issuance of the warrant is greatly enhanced if approval is forthcoming from the assistant initially contacted.

is complex, the prosecutor might come to the courtroom or the person seeking the warrant might be sent to the prosecutor's office. The magistrate relies entirely upon the judgment of the prosecutor.

3. *The practice in Wisconsin.* Warrants for arrest may be issued in Wisconsin by a magistrate, that is, a judge of a court of record, a court commissioner, or a justice of the peace, and also by a district attorney.[54] There is no requirement that either the district attorney or the magistrate obtain the concurrence of the other party. Yet, as in Kansas and Michigan, the prevailing practice is for the matter to be brought first to the prosecutor, who makes the actual decision of whether an arrest should be made.

Thus in Milwaukee County a policeman or private complainant who desires an arrest warrant goes first to the office of the district attorney. Investigators in the office have the task of assigning these persons to one of the assistant district attorneys on duty. Assignment usually is to whoever is free, the exceptions being in cases of obscene literature, narcotics, or automobile financing, which are thought to require the attention of the assistant specializing in the particular type of case. If the assistant decides that a warrant should be issued, the police officer or complainant goes to the complaint stenographic pool in the office of the district attorney, where a stenographer prepares a complaint. The complaint is signed by the complainant, if present, and otherwise by the police officer. It must also be initialed by an assistant district attorney before a warrant can be obtained, although one of the investigators in the office may initial the complaint in minor cases. The complaint is then taken to the office of the clerk of criminal court,[55] where the warrant is prepared. The warrant is signed by the chief clerk or deputy clerk of the criminal court, notwithstanding the statutory requirement that the warrant be signed by a magistrate or district attorney.[56]

Similar practices were noted elsewhere in Wisconsin. In some areas the warrant is also prepared in the district attorney's office. There is some variation with respect to signing the warrant. In some counties it is signed by either the clerk or the judge, in some always by the judge, and in others ordinarily by the district attorney. But, regardless of who actually signed the warrant, nowhere did it appear that any discretion was exercised at this point. Rather, it was in all cases treated as a mere ministerial duty, with the real decision having been made in the office of the prosecutor.

54 Wis. Stat. §954.01 (1955).
55 He serves both the municipal and the district courts.
56 Wis. Stat. §954.02(5)(a) (1955).

4. *Significance of the practices.* The warrant-issuing process usually involves the request for a warrant by a police officer, the approval of the request by the prosecutor or his assistant, and finally the signing of the warrant by the judge or the clerk. In situations where no warrant is requested, the police obviously play a dominant role, since it is typically they who make the decision not to arrest or to arrest without a warrant. In situations where a warrant is requested, the prosecutor plays a dominant role. Although often influenced by the attitude of the police officer requesting the warrant, the prosecutor usually does give careful attention to the facts of the individual case and does in fact decide whether an arrest or prosecution is permissible and desirable. The participation of the judicial officer is less meaningful.

Where only the clerk is involved, as is true in many areas, the judge obviously plays no part. The clerk's role is limited to merely signing the warrant, perhaps after asking the officer if the information is correct or asking him to swear to the facts. The clerk knows what the answer will be in every case and signs the warrant without hesitation. In those locales where the judge signs the warrant himself, he will at most merely scan the documents. Often the warrant is signed without any examination of its contents.[57] The reason for the complete abdication of control was explained simply by one judge: "I have complete confidence in the police and prosecutor's office." No instance was observed in which a judge refused to issue an arrest warrant. This obviously occurs very rarely when a request is made by the police with the approval of the prosecutor.

The assumption that the decision to issue a warrant is properly a judicial decision is reflected by the fact that most states, like Kansas, have given the magistrate exclusive power to issue a warrant. Although somewhat different assumptions may underly the Michigan provision, requiring the concurrence of the magistrate and the prosecutor, and the Wisconsin law, giving each of these two officials the power independently, the practice in the three states is remarkably similar. In all three the prosecutor plays an important role, and the judicial officer a very insignificant role.

The practice is understandable when it is considered that in the vast majority of cases the warrant is issued only after an arrest has been made. In these cases the warrant usually manifests the decision to prosecute, an obviously important responsibility of the

[57] Thus in one observed instance an officer met a judge in the hallway just as he was leaving. They exchanged a brief greeting and the officer handed the judge a warrant. Without completely unfolding it and without reading it, the judge signed the document. The officer thanked the judge and departed.

prosecutor, and one which receives judicial review in serious cases at a preliminary hearing and in a sense in all cases because of the prerequisite of a trial to conviction. Because warrant issuance for purposes of arrest occurs relatively infrequently, separate procedures, different from those employed in the usual case, in which the warrant serves a charging function, have not developed.[58]

The fact that the arrest warrant serves multiple functions undoubtedly is responsible for much of the uncertainty on the issue of who ought to have warrant-issuing authority. This was noted by Alfred Bettman, commenting in the Wickersham Report on the inadequacies of earlier crime surveys, when he said that they failed to provide the basis for answering one basic question about the warrant process: "Should the clerk of a court be the official in whom this function is placed, and using clerical methods, or the prosecuting attorney using methods appropriate to his office, or the magistrate using methods of a judicial nature?"[59] How one ought to answer this question may depend upon the function being served by the warrant in a particular case. Thus, when the warrant serves a charging function, it might be thought preferable for the prosecutor to make the approval, as is required by a Michigan statute and allowed by a statute of Wisconsin. But when the warrant is being used to obtain custody of a suspect, the Kansas statute, which gives sole authority to the magistrate, might be considered more appropriate.

This latter position rests upon the assumption that a "disinterested observer should pass on the case before a deprivation of personal liberty occurs."[60] But the current practice of having the prosecutor rather than the magistrate pass on the desirability of arrest also affords some protection to the individual. Actually, in one sense the prosecutor may be better qualified to exercise control over police action than the magistrate would be, as the district attorney and his staff possess greater competence in weighing the evidence than do many minor judicial officers. But the prosecutor, while probably more objective than the police officer, is not a "disinterested observer." He shares with the police responsibility for an effective law enforcement program.

This is not to say, however, that in practice the prosecutor ap-

[58] This does not explain the Wisconsin and Michigan statutory provisions, however, as they are addressed to the warrant-before-arrest kind of case. The necessity of a warrant after a without-warrant arrest is not contemplated in these statutes, but rather is a creature of the courts. Discussion of this will be found in the volume on Prosecution.

[59] National Commission on Law Observance and Enforcement, Report No. 4, Prosecution 88 (1931).

[60] Foote, Problems of the Protection of Human Rights in Criminal Law and Procedure (Santiago, Chile, May 19-30, 1958), U.N. Doc. TE 326/1 (40-2) LA, pp. 41-42.

proves all police requests for warrants to arrest persons not already in custody. Warrants are sometimes refused because of an insufficiency of evidence. The prosecutor may find that "probable cause" is lacking or may refuse the warrant because there is not evidence sufficient for conviction and further evidence is not likely to be forthcoming. However, refusal is more likely to be based upon a decision by the prosecutor that the case does not call for prosecution, even assuming the guilt of the suspect. Thus the decision of whether a warrant for arrest should issue is more likely to involve the exercise of "the prosecutor's discretion," rather than a meticulous testing of the evidence against the "probable cause" norm. Therefore, perhaps the principal guarantee afforded by the warrant requirement in current practice is that it prevents the arrest of some minor offenders who the prosecutor feels ought not to be prosecuted.[61]

D. Function of the Warrant Issued Prior to Arrest

In most of the instances in which a warrant is obtained before arrest, the law requires a warrant for a lawful arrest.[62] In these cases, ordinarily involving only misdemeanors, the prosecutor's decision is usually whether or not the case deserves prosecution. This is the kind of decision that the prosecutor regularly makes in approving warrant requests for persons who have already been arrested.

Although the prevailing practice in the observed jurisdictions is to arrest without first acquiring a warrant,[63] there are recurring situations in which warrants are issued prior to arrest. In some situations, the prosecutor in approving the warrant has decided to subject the person to prosecution, but in other instances his approval of the warrant signifies merely that he is authorizing an arrest. In any case, the function served by the prearrest warrant is determined by the circumstances under which it is obtained, as discussed in the following sections.

1. *Complainant goes directly to prosecutor because no police action is necessary.*

Illustration No. 10: A number of thefts from boxcars wait-

---

[61] The police, while sometimes critical of the warrant requirement, on other occasions are thankful that they can refuse to arrest because a warrant is needed and thus avoid having to act in cases not likely to result in prosecution.

[62] However, it must be remembered that there are some instances in which the prearrest warrant requirement is not adhered to. See page 21.

[63] This has also been found to be the practice elsewhere. See, e.g., Note, 100 U. Pa. L. Rev. 1182, 1183 (1952).

ing on sidings for transfer to other trains had occurred. The railroad company assigned a private investigator to the area in order to stop the thefts, and he uncovered the perpetrator. The investigator assembled all his evidence and then went to the office of the local prosecutor to request that a warrant be issued.

Complaints about certain kinds of offenses are more likely to be presented to the prosecutor directly than to the police department. In many of these cases the complainant goes directly to the prosecutor because he knows that no further investigation is needed and that the real issue is whether the prosecutor is willing to prosecute or to use some alternative which will satisfy the complainant.

The best illustration is the check drawn against insufficient funds, where typically the complainant goes directly to the prosecutor. If such a complaint is made to the police, they will refer the complainant to the prosecutor. In part, the reluctance of the police to become involved results from the fact that there is no need for investigation in such cases since the identity of the person who wrote the check is already known.[64] In current practice, the major issue is whether the prosecutor will aid the complainant to regain his money by threatening the suspect with prosecution if payment is not made. Ordinarily a warrant is issued only after efforts at settlement have failed.[65]

Nonsupport cases are referred directly to the prosecutor. This practice no doubt also results partly from the fact that nonsupport cases do not require police investigation. The needed investigation is almost always done by a social welfare agency.[66] The nonsupport case differs somewhat from the insufficient funds check case in that it has already been through a negotiation process before it is referred to the prosecutor. Usually the social welfare agency will try to persuade the husband to make support payments and will refer the matter to the prosecutor only when efforts at settlement have failed. Thus, in the nonsupport case, a decision to prosecute has in effect been made by the social welfare worker and the prosecutor routinely concurs in that decision.

Some cases are brought directly to the prosecutor because the

[64] In Madison, however, there is referral to the police, but only to see if they have knowledge of any other bad checks by the suspect, and it does not appear that they are expected to arrest at this point.

[65] For example, in Milwaukee the prosecutor sends the offender a letter reading: "Sir: You are requested to be in this office to see the undersigned on [date]. Upon failure to comply with this request, a warrant will be issued." If the offender fails to appear after two such requests, or fails to make restitution after having appeared, a warrant is issued.

[66] The welfare agency conducts the investigation in the course of determining whether aid should and can be given. Often prosecution is a prerequisite of aid.

complainant has conducted the needed investigation himself. Thus private investigators employed by large department stores often go directly to the prosecutor and present the results of their investigation. These cases, like the bad check cases, may involve a process of negotiation to see if a settlement can be reached.

The reporting of other types of offenses directly to the prosecutor rather than to a police agency is more likely to occur in rural counties than in the urban centers.[67] This is in part due to the fact that the district attorney is known personally to a considerable number of citizens and frequently comes in contact with many of them informally. Also, citizens in smaller communities often doubt the capability of the local city or town police to cope with cases of any complexity. In these situations, the prosecutor may turn the matter over to the county sheriff for further investigation or may have a warrant issued if no prearrest investigation seems called for.

In cases where the complainant goes directly to the prosecutor, the prosecutor's decision that an arrest warrant should issue is ordinarily a charging decision. By approving the warrant the prosecutor is actually deciding to subject the offender to prosecution, having concluded that the evidence is sufficient and that no policy considerations make prosecution inappropriate. There are, of course, some exceptions. Issuance of the warrant at the complainant's request may sometimes merely evidence a judgment that probable cause exists and that an arrest should be made promptly, either because in-custody investigation is thought desirable or because of a risk that custody cannot be obtained if there is further delay. In these instances the decision as to prosecution is deferred. The cases in which the prosecutor does not decide to charge when he issues the warrant before arrest are much more apt to occur in the rural areas, where the prosecutor is presented with a broader range of cases directly from complainants.

2. *Police seek warrant to facilitate ultimate apprehension of a suspect who cannot presently be arrested.* In the usual case, the police do not seek a warrant prior to arrest because to do so would only delay the arrest without any advantage being achieved. However, if a delay in making the arrest is necessary or desirable for some other reason, then a warrant is more likely to be acquired before arrest.

a. *Whereabouts of the person to be arrested unknown.*

Illustration No. 11: A particular person was wanted in con-

---

[67] Thus while the Oakland County, Michigan, prosecutor said that felonious assault victims often contacted him directly, in Detroit these matters would be brought to the attention of the police.

nection with a recent murder. Officers sent to the man's residence did not find him, and he failed to appear there during a brief stakeout. Members of his family reported that they thought he had fled to a neighboring state. The police obtained an arrest warrant through the prosecutor's office.

In cases where the suspect has apparently fled the locality, so that his ultimate arrest is likely to be accomplished elsewhere in the state or in a neighboring state, there is an advantage to be gained from the issuance of a warrant of arrest. It serves a bookkeeping function. The warrant list provides a record of persons for whom that department and perhaps other departments as well will be continually watching.[68] Moreover, the fact that the warrant is issued may make certain the legality of the subsequent arrest without the necessity of communicating to other agencies or other officers all the facts which together constitute grounds to arrest. While arrests merely upon the request of another officer or department are sometimes subject to question,[69] statutes often make arrest upon notice that a warrant exists clearly legal.[70]

If the suspect is found in another state, the warrant becomes a practical necessity. The Uniform Criminal Extradition Act, adopted by a great majority of the states, provides in part:

> The arrest of a person may be lawfully made also by any peace officer . . . without a warrant upon reasonable information that the accused stands charged in the courts of a state with a crime punishable by death or imprisonment for a term exceeding one year . . .[71]

There has been little appellate litigation anywhere on the meaning of the quoted language. The requirement that the person be "charged" in the other state might be subject to various interpretations, but it apparently means that a warrant must have been issued.[72]

---

[68] The bookkeeping function of the warrant is emphasized by the practice of the Michigan State Police. Warrants are used there for defendants whose whereabouts are uncertain, and the operations office is responsible for the service of all warrants that cannot be served by a post within the district area. The lieutenant in charge explained: "All warrants are initially sent to the operations office for subsequent routing to districts and posts. If the post finds that the person named in the warrant has fled from the district in which the post is located, the post must send or return the warrant to the operations office, where it is re-routed to the area in which the fugitive is now believed to be located. When there are no leads as to the whereabouts of the person named in the warrant, the warrant is kept on file in the operations office."

[69] See page 285.

[70] Mich. Stat. Ann. §28.874(e) (1954); Wis. Stat. §954.03(2) (1955). See page 281.

[71] 9 U.L.A., Uniform Criminal Extradition Act §14.

[72] The word "charged" in the Uniform Act is apparently taken from the constitutional provision on extradition in U.S. Const., art. IV, §2, cl. 2. In respect to

Finally, the warrant may be needed in order to obtain the co-operation of federal authorities in apprehending the offender thought to have crossed state lines. Flight across state lines "to avoid prosecution" for a felony is a federal offense,[73] but has been interpreted on at least one occasion to require that there have been in the state "proceedings instituted by appropriate process." [74] It is the practice of the FBI to render assistance to the local police in cases of unlawful flight to avoid prosecution if the local district attorney has had a warrant issued and there is some evidence that the subject has fled the state.[75]

In cases where the issuance of the warrant serves some purpose connected with obtaining custody, such as insuring grounds for arrest by police elsewhere in the state, by officers in other states, or by federal officials, the prosecutor may approve the warrant for such purpose even though he is uncertain about prosecution. For example, the prosecutor may decide that it is necessary to have a murder suspect returned to the state so that he can be interrogated or viewed by witnesses, even though a decision as to whether to prosecute the suspect will be made only after this later investigation. In less serious cases careful consideration of the need for prosecution is likely to be a part of the warrant decision because of the expense of returning a suspect, especially from another state.

b. *Immediate arrest would reveal identity of informants or presence of undercover agents.*

Illustration No. 12: Agents of the state Beverage and Tax Division, Department of Taxation, charged with enforcement of liquor, gambling, and prostitution laws, had just entered a county to conduct an undercover investigation. Finding youths drinking in a bar, they did not make an arrest but followed the youths from the tavern, stopped them to insure they were under age, and obtained brief statements from them. A week later, after having uncovered a number of other violations in the county, the agents sought a warrant from the local prosecutor.

---

this, the Supreme Court has said: "Doubtless the word 'charged' was used in its broad signification to cover any proceeding which a State might see fit to adopt, by which a formal accusation was made against an alleged criminal." Pierce v. Creecy, 210 U.S. 387, 404, 28 Sup. Ct. 714, 719, 52 L. Ed. 1113, 1121 (1908).

[73] 18 U.S.C.A. §1073 (1950).

[74] United States v. Rappoport, 156 F. Supp. 159, 160 (N.D. Ill. 1957).

[75] The FBI advises the United States Attorney, and, if he so authorizes, the local United States Commissioner will issue a warrant, and the FBI will then issue a nationwide wanted notice. If the person is apprehended and returned to the local state, the charge of unlawful flight to avoid prosecution is dismissed, but if local prosecution fails there may be prosecution by the federal authorities. However, the federal authorities first determine whether it appears that the suspect knew he was wanted for the local offense and deliberately fled the local jurisdiction.

If the making of an immediate arrest will disclose the identity of an informant or the presence of an undercover officer, then a warrant may first be obtained. In the illustration above, an immediate arrest would have disclosed the agents' identity and the fact of their presence in the county. By delaying arrest, they were able to discover a number of other violations before their presence became generally known.

Similarly, an investigation utilizing the services of an informant will not necessarily culminate in arrest as soon as sufficient evidence is obtained. These informants are often used to purchase narcotics, and in such cases the police usually promise not to "burn" the informant by making an arrest immediately after the illegal sale. Rather, they wait until the seller has probably made a number of other sales, delaying the arrest for days and sometimes weeks. This minimizes the chance of the informant being identified.[76]

In these cases a warrant is usually obtained before an arrest is made, often for no reason except that the necessary delay gives the police more than adequate time to do so. They consult the prosecutor who, because of the kind of offense involved and the amount of evidence already in hand, usually makes a decision to prosecute when he approves the warrant. But the warrant may serve other functions in such cases. If the offense is a misdemeanor committed in the presence of the officer, a warrant is essential unless the arrest is made immediately. Even if not necessary, the warrant generally gives the arrest an air of legality sufficient in many cases to deter or overcome challenge of the arrest by defense counsel. In a case where the arrest is delayed, counsel for the defendant may argue that the delay shows that grounds for arrest were not present. The fact that the delay may be explained as necessary to obtain a warrant makes this argument less effective. From the police viewpoint inquiry into the grounds for arrest in an informant case is undesirable since it may require disclosure of the informant's identity. This is less likely when a warrant is used.

3. *Police seek warrant as an aid to investigation.* Arrest serves not only to obtain custody over the suspect in order to insure his appearance at subsequent proceedings, but also as a means of gath-

[76] By resort to the "supervised buy," successful prosecution is often possible without disclosure of the informant at the time of trial. The officers give the informant marked money, search him to insure that he has no narcotics on his person, and then watch from a distance the transaction between informant and seller. The informant returns to the officers immediately, and another search is conducted, this time disclosing narcotics and no money. Thus the officers can make a good case on the basis of their own testimony. While the accused is entitled to know the identity of the informer who participated in the offense, Annot., 76 A.L.R.2d 262, 313 (1961), this has been overcome in practice by charging the offender with possession rather than sale.

ering essential evidence. Arrest is the principal way in which searches are justified, and arrest also is the major device employed to obtain the presence of a suspect for questioning. If the police feel that the success of this investigation technique is enhanced by arrest with warrant, they may seek a warrant before arrest. Consequently, in such cases the prosecutor may approve the warrant without necessarily deciding that the suspect should be prosecuted.

a. *To insure legality of an incidental search.*

Illustration No. 13: Officers of the narcotics bureau had observed a number of "buys" from a particular narcotics seller. Desiring to build the best case possible against him, they thought it best to be able to acquire, by means which could not be challenged successfully, narcotics thought to be in the offender's apartment. The officers obtained an arrest warrant and then went to the apartment, placed the offender under arrest, and searched the apartment for narcotics.

This kind of situation occurs frequently in current practice. The usual police explanation is that the arrest warrant enlarges the right to search the premises on which the arrest was made. There seems, however, no basis in legislation or case law for this assumption.[77]

A more logical explanation is that the warrant makes it more certain that the evidence seized will be admissible. Defense counsel's argument of illegality is not likely to be as persuasive when directed toward an arrest with warrant. Also, by applying for a warrant before arrest, the police can better determine whether the arrest will later stand up in court.[78] If the prosecutor indicates that the grounds for arrest are doubtful, the officers may be able to obtain further evidence against the narcotics supplier. Application to the prosecutor for a warrant most often occurs in instances where the police have already expended considerable time in investigation and do not want to risk failure by a premature arrest.

Where insuring the validity of the search is a primary purpose, an arrest warrant rather than a search warrant is usually obtained.

[77] Treatment of this will be found in the volume on Detection of Crime. Indeed, it has been suggested that if an arrest warrant is used the limitation is even more evident "because the warrant specifies a particular crime, . . . [and thus] is to an extent self-limiting as to the area of search." Sobel, The Law of Search and Seizure, 1962 The Pleader 56, issued by Kings County (N.Y.) Criminal Bar Association. Of course, the same restriction would apply to arrest without warrant, except that there would be more freedom after the event to reconsider for which precise offense the arrest was being made.

[78] This is particularly true in Milwaukee, where one assistant prosecutor handles all warrant requests for narcotics cases. Because of this specialization, he has had a high degree of success in determining what searches will stand up in court.

The arrest warrant has most of the advantages of a search warrant and none of the disadvantages. Perhaps most important is that the evidence for a search warrant must relate to the items sought and their location,[79] while the evidence for an arrest warrant relates to the guilt of the person to be arrested. In the illustration given above, it may be doubtful whether the earlier observed "buys" afford probable cause to believe that the seller has a cache of narcotics in his apartment, but there certainly is sufficient evidence to arrest for the offense of selling. When the arrest is made for a sale of narcotics, the police routinely search the apartment, or other place where the arrest is made, for more narcotics. These searches are upheld, as the Kansas, Michigan, and Wisconsin courts have not insisted that the search be strictly limited to instrumentalities and fruits of the past offense for which the arrest is made.[80] And if the earlier purchase was made with marked money, the search incident to the arrest can be justified as a search for this money.

Another important reason for using an arrest warrant rather than a search warrant is that a search warrant in Kansas, Michigan, and Wisconsin can be issued only on direct information,[81] while an arrest warrant may be obtained by at least partial reliance on hearsay.[82] In a narcotics case a search warrant often could be obtained only if the police informant himself supplied the affidavit. The police, desiring not to disclose the identity of the informant, consequently prefer to use an arrest warrant.[83]

b. *To induce a statement by the arrestee.*

Illustration No. 14: Officers suspected a man of a recent burglary. Available circumstantial evidence made him an extremely likely suspect and was sufficient for arrest. It was the police view that conviction would be impossible without additional evidence and that no other evidence would become

[79] Discussion of this will be found in the volume on Detection of Crime.

[80] Treatment of this will be found in the volume on Detection of Crime.

[81] People v. Perrin, 223 Mich. 132, 193 N.W. 888 (1923); Glodowski v. State, 196 Wis. 265, 220 N.W. 227 (1928). It is assumed that the same result would be required in Kansas: "A search warrant may issue only on evidence which would be competent on trial." Wilson, Basic Rules of Arrest, Search, and Seizure, Univ. Kan. Govt. Res. Center Spec. Rep. 106, p. 23 (1961). However, there are no cases directly in point. Kansas did not have an exclusionary rule, and consequently had no problem in this regard.

[82] In Wisconsin, the statute declares "information and belief" to be adequate. Wis. Stat. §954.02(1) (1955). The law is less clear in the other two jurisdictions. In Michigan, compare People v. Lynch, 29 Mich. 274 (1874), with Currow v. Kessler, 110 Mich. 10, 67 N.W. 982 (1896). In Kansas, compare State v. Carey, 56 Kan. 84, 42 Pac. 371 (1895), with In re Kellam, 55 Kan. 700, 41 Pac. 948 (1895).

[83] Other search problems arising out of a desire to retain the confidentiality of informants will be found in the volume on Detection of Crime.

available unless a confession by the suspect were obtained. The police decided to obtain an arrest warrant prior to arrest in the hope that the arrestee's awareness of its existence would prompt a confession.

Modern interrogation techniques stress the importance of convincing the offender that nothing is to be gained by concealment of his crime. Officers are cautioned not to disclose the limitations of their case but instead to create the impression that they already have all the information necessary.[84] The objective is to create a "what's the use" attitude in the suspect, to convince him that resistance to questioning is futile. The suspect is also likely to be particularly susceptible to questioning immediately after arrest, as his apprehension actually brings about a feeling of relief after days or weeks of evading the police.[85]

Occasionally, because of the added impact which the warrant may have, the police will obtain a warrant when they intend to interrogate the suspect. The suspect may be impressed with the supposed weight of the case against him at his most vulnerable moment, immediately following arrest. An arrest with a warrant may have greater shock value by creating the impression that the arrest is not a spur-of-the-moment decision but rather a deliberate conclusion reached after the amassing of much evidence. The degree of success attained in this way is not known.

4. *Police seek warrant to minimize chances of individual or public objections regarding arrest or manner of arrest.* The police are often extremely sensitive to criticisms and objections voiced by individual citizens being proceeded against and by the public at large. As will be noted later, this police concern often influences enforcement policy.[86] When the police do feel that it is necessary to arrest a violator who might be very argumentative or that it is necessary to employ methods which might lead to criticism, they may obtain a warrant first in the hope of avoiding much of this conflict.

a. *To avoid an altercation with the offender.*

Illustration No. 15: A conservation agent came upon a man in a boat running a set line in violation of the law. The man apparently had been drinking and was quite belligerent. At first he refused to identify himself, and then he refused to accept a summons from the officer, saying he would not appear in court. The officer did not then arrest the violator,

---

[84] See, e.g., O'Hara, Fundamentals of Criminal Investigation 105 (1956).
[85] See 2 Wigmore, Evidence §851 n.3 (3d ed. 1940).
[86] See pages 127 and 146.

though he had authority to do so,[87] but rather left for the prosecuting attorney's office in order to obtain a warrant. He returned with the warrant shortly thereafter and placed the offender under arrest. The offender did not resist upon being shown the warrant.

An officer may obtain a warrant prior to arrest in cases where it appears that the person to be arrested is likely to be belligerent or argumentative, where the person is of some prominence in the community, or where the law involved is not generally understood or accepted by the public.

The existence of a warrant tends to minimize the possibility of trouble in making the arrest, since the officer can explain his actions to the offender by saying he is merely doing his duty in carrying out the command directed to him in the warrant. Even when, as in the above illustration, it is apparent that the warrant was issued at the officer's insistence, the warrant itself is a manifestation to the offender that others have concurred in the officer's decision.

b. *To justify resort to forcible entry.*

Illustration No. 16: Officers went to the home of a man they suspected of being implicated in some recent burglaries. Although the wanted man was observed through a window, he refused to answer the door. Some officers were left posted around the residence while another left to obtain an arrest warrant. When he returned with the warrant, force was used to gain entrance.

It is the policy of the Milwaukee department to obtain a warrant in the event that arrest will require breaking into a residence. A supervisory officer in the department said that such a precaution would be taken even if it required contacting an assistant district attorney and clerk of court on a weekend or holiday when their offices were not open for the regular transaction of business.

There is no indication that Wisconsin law requires a warrant before entry of a building, and it does not appear that the existence of the warrant gives the police any greater authority in this regard in situations where a right to arrest without warrant exists. Because of the way in which warrants are issued, there is no meaningful judicial review of the decision to use force to gain entrance to a residence, although the prosecutor may exercise some control in such cases. But, because police entry into private homes is undoubtedly one of the most sensitive of all law enforcement practices, the warrant serves the very important function of insulating the police from criticism by giving the appearance that they have

[87] Mich. Stat. Ann. §13.1226 (1951).

selected "that legal course which conforms most to democratic values." [88]

5. *Police seek warrant because they desire advice of prosecutor before arrest.* In other cases an arrest is made with a warrant because the police have thought it advisable to seek the advice of the prosecutor prior to the arrest. This may occur when the police are aware that the case involves a difficult legal question or a policy question best answered by the prosecutor, or where an arrest would be extremely harmful to the individual and consequently should be avoided unless prosecution is certain to follow. In these cases the prosecutor quite clearly makes a decision to prosecute when he approves the warrant.

a. *To resolve a difficult legal question.*

Illustration No. 17: A plainclothes officer purchased a number of magazines at a newsstand. Upon examining the magazines, he reached the conclusion that they contained obscene matter. However, rather than make an immediate arrest, the officer took the magazines to the prosecutor's office, where an assistant prosecutor examined them with great care, concluded they were obscene, and approved the issuance of a warrant for the arrest of the newsstand operator.

When the police are dealing with routine kinds of criminal conduct such as robbery, assault, burglary, and similar offenses, they usually have no difficulty determining whether an offense has been committed. However, there are cases which pose difficult questions as to whether a crime has occurred. This is frequently true where the suspected offense is negligent homicide, sale of obscene literature, embezzlement, violation of the blue-sky laws, or certain other "white collar" crimes. The questions of law may be most complex, even to the extent that in a large prosecutor's office certain assistants specialize in dealing with warrant applications for these offenses.

The hesitancy of the police to trust their own judgment in such cases is understandable. In fact, the law seems to assume that police should not make these kinds of decisions, since police are said to be responsible for damages resulting from any error of law in regard to an arrest without warrant. While police may make reasonable errors of fact without liability,[89] an error of law may result in liability no matter how reasonable the officer's interpretation.[90]

[88] See quotation from Hall, *supra* page 31.

[89] See Chapter 12.

[90] 1 Restatement of Torts §121, Comment *i* (1934). See page 86 for the substance of the Restatement view and further discussion.

b. *To resolve a policy question thought best determined by the prosecutor.*

> *Illustration No. 18:* A merchant presented to the police evidence indicating an insufficient funds check violation and demanded arrest and prosecution of the offender. The police refused to take any action whatsoever and instructed the complainant to take the matter up with the district attorney. He did so; the district attorney made some attempts at accomplishing restitution, and when these failed he authorized the issuance of a warrant for the offender's arrest.

It has long been recognized that in the performance of the duties of his office the prosecutor must make many policy decisions on whether to prosecute persons who, under a great variety of circumstances, have technically violated the criminal law.[91] The police also make these kinds of policy determinations day after day in deciding whether to arrest certain offenders,[92] although this practice has not received as much attention as has that of "prosecutor's discretion." In part, police discretion is exercised because it is impractical to delay such questions in all cases until the matter can be brought to the attention of the prosecutor.[93] This is not to suggest, however, that the police necessarily believe that the prosecutor's office would be the best repository of such discretion if practical considerations did not sometimes demand the contrary. There may be disagreement between the police and the prosecutor as to what circumstances justify noninvocation of the criminal process against a guilty person.[94] However, there are recurring situations in which the police do concede that the prosecutor is best equipped to make the policy decision involved.

Insufficient funds check cases are the best example. The general policy is to prosecute the writer of an insufficient funds check only if he refuses to make restitution or if this conduct occurs habitually. Although this policy is known to the police, they are willing to have the prosecutor handle these cases. The prosecutor is best equipped to conduct the process of negotiating for restitution and to do it in a way that does not subject enforcement officials to liability for improper use of the criminal process.[95]

91 Discussion of this will be found in the volume on Prosecution.

92 These decisions are the subject of Part II.

93 See page 72.

94 See page 75.

95 Bergeron v. Peyton, 106 Wis. 377, 82 N.W. 291 (1900). An officer took Bergeron to the bank where he had been overpaid on a check and when Bergeron refused to return the excess the officer took him to the magistrate. The jury found (and the Supreme Court upheld the finding) that the arrest was not "for the purpose of

c. *To avoid the harm of arrest unless prosecution is certain to follow.*

   Illustration No. 19: After a woman returned home in a disheveled condition and told her husband that she had been kidnapped and raped, he called the police. When later police investigation uncovered some discrepancies in the woman's story, she admitted to the investigating officer that she had concocted the story in order to cover up an affair with another man. Rather than make an arrest for a false felony report, the officer decided to consult with the prosecutor first, as arrest under these circumstances, even if prosecution did not follow, would have jeopardized the marriage.

As will be noted later,[96] sometimes the criminal process is not invoked against a person guilty of criminal conduct because it is felt that the resultant risk to society is less than the harm which would result to the defendant and his family if prosecution were undertaken. Unfortunately, perhaps, the facts of the particular case which indicate such a possible situation usually do not come to light until after an arrest has been made, so that what really occurs is a decision not to prosecute. In such a case the person is released from custody and steps are taken to insure that the arrest receives no notoriety.

One of the facts of the case which often indicates that excessive harm to the offender would result is that of his standing in the community as a respectable citizen. The very fact of arrest may do substantially more harm to him than it would to the usual criminal suspect. Thus, if the police officer involved is aware of the suspect's standing in the community, he may decide to consult with the prosecutor before arrest. Then, if the prosecutor decides not to prosecute because of a similar balancing of social risk and cost, the person will not have been unnecessarily harmed by an arrest. On the other hand, if the prosecutor does decide to proceed, he will probably authorize the issuance of a warrant before the arrest is made.

6. *Police seek warrant because they want to involve the victim or witness in the complaint-warrant process.* There are cases in which the police refuse to make an arrest until the victim or complaining witness has signed a complaint upon which a warrant is issued. This is done when the police believe that the victim or

---

taking him before the magistrate, but for the sole purpose of compelling and inducing him to repay . . . the $43 thus overpaid." 106 Wis. at 381, 82 N.W. at 293.
   [96] See page 137.

complaining witness will later change his mind and refuse to co-operate in the prosecution of the offender.

a. *To "commit" the person to cooperate in the prosecution.*

Illustration No. 20: The police investigated a burglary com-mitted in a barbershop. They finally learned that the prop-erty had been taken by a man who until recently had been employed in the shop as a barber. The owner of the shop, upon learning this, indicated his reluctance at pursuing prose-cution, especially if it would mean spending time in court which could otherwise be spent operating the shop. The po-lice, having devoted considerable time and effort to investiga-tion of the case, persuaded the owner of the shop that he should cooperate. Having done so, they immediately went to the prosecutor with the owner and had him sign a complaint. One of the officers commented that the owner was now "com-mitted" to cooperate in the prosecution.

In many cases involving minor offenses, police feel that prosecu-tion should be undertaken only if this is the desire of the victim. Consequently, if the victim manifests a reluctance to have the of-fender prosecuted, the police probably will not even make an ar-rest.[97] However, the police are not always willing to adopt the victim's attitude. If the offense is too serious, if the offender is a "bad actor" whom the police desire to have prosecuted because he is suspected of being implicated in other more serious offenses,[98] or if the police have already expended considerable energy in investi-gation of the case, they will take all steps possible to commit the victim to full cooperation in prosecution. In these cases, it is com-mon for the police to persuade the victim that prosecution is desir-able and then to rush him to the office of the prosecutor so that he will sign a complaint before changing his mind.[99]

The signing of a complaint undoubtedly has some psychological effect in causing the complainant to follow through with the case. Having affixed his name to a statement of the charges against the suspect, the complainant is in a position in which it is difficult for him to withdraw. In addition, some courts, as in Wichita, assess court costs against persons who sign complaints but fail to appear

97 See page 114.

98 See page 149.

99 Sometimes the victim is hurried into signing a complaint without any prior persuasion that prosecution is the proper course. In one instance observed, the officers hurried a merchant into signing a complaint though they knew that he only wanted his money back on a bad check. Said one detective, "I don't think he knew what he was signing when he signed the complaint. He probably thought it was some legal paper which would authorize him to squeeze money out of the guy."

to testify. In Detroit an assistant prosecutor described a different procedure:

> When a woman comes into our office and tells us that she wants to drop the complaint against the defendant, we usually give her a standard routine. We tell the woman that it will cost her $50 to drop the charge. I then take her down to Mr. G's secretary and inform her of the situation. Mr. G.'s secretary takes her through the red tape and finally tells the individual that it will cost only $15 considering the special circumstances of her case. . . . The idea is to try to discourage people from registering complaints which they subsequently will drop. . . . I have a standard line of patter which I give them, but the whole purpose of all this is to impress upon these individuals that once having initiated a criminal proceeding, it is not to their advantage to drop the charge, no matter what their husband, boyfriend, or both have told them.

b. *To ascertain the complainant's true desires concerning prosecution.*

Illustration No. 21: Officers were called to a disturbance at an apartment. The man and wife who were the participants in the disturbance were still arguing in loud voices when the police arrived. The wife said that she had called the police because her husband had just beaten her up. At this the fight broke out again, but the police quickly restored order. One officer advised the couple, "Either get a divorce or quit fighting. Whatever you decide to do is none of our business." The other officer made out a referral memorandum which the wife could use to obtain a battery warrant against her husband from the district attorney.

As indicated above, in many minor cases the police deem it inappropriate to invoke the criminal process unless the victim is seriously interested in having the offender prosecuted. The major difficulty in applying this criterion is that the victim is likely to demand prosecution when in the heat of the conflict but will have a change in attitude later. Because this is so, police often insist that the victim seek a warrant, knowing that the delay will give the victim time to reflect upon the matter.

If a misdemeanor has not occurred in the police presence, the officer can accurately state that he cannot lawfully make an arrest without a warrant. Police indicate that this limitation is beneficial in at least this respect. Even if police can lawfully arrest without warrant, they often refuse to do so when it appears likely that the victim will later change his mind. The referral memorandum, mentioned in the illustration above, is used in Milwaukee to show the prosecutor that the police on the scene thought an offense had occurred. However, a spouse is not able to obtain a warrant immediately on the basis of this memorandum. Under local policy no warrant will ordinarily be issued in a common drunk or assault case involving husband and wife until after a three-day "cooling-off" period has passed.

In some cases a victim may strongly assert a desire for prosecution only because he wants to employ the threat of prosecution for his own benefit. For example, a merchant often asserts a desire to prosecute in a shoplifting or a bad check case, but really only wants to pressure the offender into making restitution. Because the police are aware of this, they often tell the merchant that he must sign a complaint before any action will be taken. In such cases the police are primarily interested not in committing the victim to prosecution but in ascertaining whether he actually desires prosecution and is willing to cooperate in that prosecution.

E. Conclusion

Existing arrest law is in some respects most liberal, as arrest without warrant is often allowed notwithstanding the fact that there is more than adequate time to obtain a warrant. The only general warrant requirement is for misdemeanors not occurring in the presence of the arresting officer. However, the police view even this limitation as too restrictive in some cases, and consequently an immediate arrest will sometimes be made nonetheless if it is thought that the offender would otherwise avoid apprehension, cause further harm, or prevent the obtaining of critical evidence.

Although the three jurisdictions studied provide three interesting variations in the legal requirements regarding responsibility for warrant issuance, the practice in the three jurisdictions is substantially the same. The magistrates have largely abdicated their responsibilities, and the prosecutor decides when a warrant should be issued before arrest as well as after arrest, the latter decision manifesting a decision to charge. The principal protection afforded when the warrant is obtained in practice is that some offenders are spared the indignity of arrest because the prosecutor is not interested in prosecuting them.

The prevailing practice is for the police to arrest without first seeking a warrant. However, there are a number of recurring situations in which a warrant is issued before arrest. On some occasions, particularly when there is no need for police investigation, the complainant goes directly to the prosecutor. In such a case, the prosecutor will issue a warrant if he decides that official action should be taken. Typically, when he does so, the warrant manifests not only the decision to arrest but also the decision to subject the suspect to prosecution. This is also true when the police go to the prosecutor before arrest because they want his advice or want to commit the victim or witness to cooperation in prosecuting the offender. However, in other situations the prosecutor may well approve the warrant request without having decided to prosecute. This may be the case when the warrant is desired for a person who cannot presently be found, when it is needed to facilitate an investigation, or when it is desired to serve a public relations function.

CHAPTER 2

The Issuance of the Warrant After Arrest Without Review by the Prosecutor

To the extent that it is possible to generalize, the typical situation is one in which the police make an arrest without a warrant and then bring the suspect to the prosecutor with a request that he approve the issuance of a warrant. The decision to arrest is clearly made by the police. The decision as to whether to charge the suspect and the selection of the charge are the responsibility of the prosecutor. The prosecutor's charging decision is manifested by his approval or refusal of the issuance of the warrant.[1]

In all those instances in which the process operates in this manner, it is clear that the arrest decision does not constitute a selection of those to be prosecuted. Rather, it is by the process of arrest that, for the most part,[2] those persons are selected as to whom the charging decision is later made. This is equally true in some other cases where the process operates somewhat differently, such as those in which the determination as to prosecution is made by supervisory police officers or specialists in the police agency. In either event, the second decision is ordinarily not merely a review of the first; the inquiry is not as to whether the arrest was properly made. Rather, the charging decision is of a different quality than the arrest decision and involves factors and skills not ordinarily expected to be employed at the arrest decision level.[3]

There are two important situations in which only one decision

---

[1] A more detailed description of the charging process will be found in the volume on Prosecution.

[2] Of course, some cases come directly to the prosecutor without prior arrest. See page 36.

[3] The one basic difference is that the prosecutor usually applies a higher evidentiary standard at the time of charging than the police officer had to apply at the time of arrest. See page 320. Also the policy considerations are different, as will be seen by comparing those applied by the police, Part II, with those applied by the prosecutor, volume on Prosecution.

instead of two is involved. The first of these, discussed in the preceding chapter, is the case in which the arrest decision is merged with the charging decision. The prosecutor may approve a warrant prior to arrest which in effect may constitute both a decision to arrest and a decision to charge. The second situation is the case in which the charging decision is merged with the police decision to arrest. This occurs when the arrest is made without a warrant and the warrant is subsequently issued without any meaningful review.[4] In such a case the responsibility of the police is obviously greater than it is when they only decide to arrest and must then convince the prosecutor of the desirability of prosecution. This situation is dealt with in some detail in this chapter.

A. Situations in Which the Police Decision to Arrest Also Constitutes the Charging Decision

1. *In Kansas.* In Wichita, approximately ninety per cent of the city ordinances are re-enactments of comparable state statutes, usually concerning misdemeanors. Because these ordinances provide for a money fine or jail sentence, it is not uncommon for an officer to make an arrest with the objective of a prosecution under the ordinance rather than under the state statute. In such cases there is no separate charging decision either by the city attorney or by supervisory personnel within the police department.

The arresting officer usually acts as complainant in these cases. The law provides for warrants to be issued by the police judge of the city, but in first-class cities the clerk of police court is authorized "to make out, sign, and issue all processes of said court."[5] This apparently includes the right to issue warrants. This clerk issues warrants during the regular business day and, in doing so, he exercises no independent judgment, but performs a mere clerical function in response to the officer's request for a warrant.[6] Warrants can be issued outside regular working hours by certain supervisory members of the Wichita police department who have been deputized as clerks pro tem. This, of course, would make it possible to

---

4 Of course, it really is not necessary that an arrest be made for the two decisions to be merged. The police officer, at the time of the arrest decision, may conclude that the offender should be proceeded against but that custody of his person is not necessary to accomplish this result. Assuming no later review, this would be an instance of no arrest in which the decision to charge was made at the arrest decision level.

5 Kan. Gen. Stat. §§13-606, 14-806, 15-506 (1949), applicable to first, second, and third class cities, respectively.

6 Occasionally the clerk may spot a particularly difficult legal or policy question, and he is then likely to require the approval of the city attorney first.

have an independent charging decision within the department, but in practice the supervisory officers ordinarily rely completely upon the arresting officer. Members of the city attorney's staff usually do not even learn of these cases until they appear in police court to prosecute them the next morning.

2. *In Michigan.* Because Michigan law requires participation by the prosecutor in the warrant-issuance process, a separate and distinct charging decision is usually made by him. However, the statutes except cases where the warrant is for a traffic violation and is requested by a member of the state department of public safety[7] or is for violation of the fish and game laws and is requested by a conservation officer.[8] Sometimes even other exceptions are made in practice. Thus, in the early sessions branch of the Detroit Recorder's Court, the judge routinely issues, without the prior approval of the prosecutor, all of the warrants for lesser offenses triable by that court. These offenses include, for example, drunkenness, vagrancy, and disturbing the peace. However, the prosecutor's approval is required for accosting and soliciting cases, even though they are triable in early sessions court. Elsewhere in the state the practice in some counties is for the prosecutor not to be involved in warrant issuance with regard to any misdemeanors.

Thus, even in Michigan, where the statute apparently contemplates a decision being made by the prosecutor, he is sometimes bypassed in practice. Failure to obtain the prosecutor's concurrence has been held not to affect the court's jurisdiction, however.[9] Hence prosecutors and magistrates in each area are free to determine what kinds of cases require the prior approval of the prosecutor before a warrant is issued and prosecution is undertaken.

3. *In Wisconsin.* In Wisconsin some of the minor misdemeanors which would not reach the prosecutor's office elsewhere are routinely passed through the district attorney's hands. However, it appears questionable in many of these cases whether the prosecutor's approval of the warrant involves any real consideration of the case. There are some offenses which are rarely even brought to the attention of the prosecutor before trial and which seldom involve a review within the police agency itself. Included are minor traffic offenses and fish and game violations.

---

7 Mich. Stat. Ann. §§28.860, 28.1195 (1954).

8 Mich. Stat. Ann. §13.1222 (1951).

9 "While an omission to secure an order from the prosecuting attorney before issuing process in criminal cases might subject the magistrate to censure, and possibly, in some cases, to pecuniary injury and official embarrassment, it was never intended to deprive the court of jurisdiction in any case . . ." People v. Griswold, 64 Mich. 722, 723, 31 N.W. 809, 810 (1887).

B. The Reasons Why the Police Decision to Arrest Also Constitutes the Decision to Prosecute

Why is it that in some cases the arrest decision is allowed to be determinative on the charging issue as well? Although there is no obvious answer to this question, the following factors appear to be of major significance.

1. *The prosecutor is not involved in the trial.* In nearly all of the cases in which the arrest decision also serves as the charging decision, the prosecutor or his assistants are not actively involved in the prosecution of the case. Thus in Wisconsin the traffic and conservation cases are presented in court by the arresting officer and without prior review by the prosecutor or anyone else. Similarly, the minor misdemeanors heard in the first half of early sessions in Detroit are tried without the assistance of the prosecutor.

Cases that are obviously serious receive the prior attention of the prosecutor, in part at least because he needs an opportunity to prepare for trial. But in less serious cases the approval of the prosecutor is still obtained if a member of his office will be in charge of the prosecution, even though he will make no advance preparation. This suggests that prosecutors ordinarily want an opportunity to decide in advance on the desirability of prosecution if their office will have to devote time to the prosecution and appear in court. Of course, the correlation between the prosecutor's approval of and participation in the prosecution may merely indicate that the complexities which require a separate and distinct charging decision, discussed below, also necessitate participation of a prosecutor in the trial.

2. *The police have adequate knowledge of the substantive law.* Generally speaking, cases in which no separate charging decision is made involve offenses of which the elements are fully understood by the arresting officer. Because of this there is no need for review to insure that the officer has not misunderstood the law. This is particularly true where the officer is a specialist, such as the conservation agent as to fish and game violations and the state or county traffic officer as to lesser traffic violations.

3. *Evidence needed for prosecution is no greater than that needed for arrest.* In felony cases, the law in some jurisdictions requires more evidence of guilt for charging than for arrest.[10] In this situation, the fact that grounds for arrest exist does not mean that there is adequate evidence to prosecute. A prosecutor con-

10 See page 324.

cerned with the possibility of conviction in a contested case may apply a significantly higher evidentiary standard in deciding whether to prosecute than was applied by the police in deciding whether to arrest.

However, the rule in most states as to misdemeanors is that arrest without warrant is lawful only when the offense takes place in the officer's presence. Assuming such an arrest is properly made (a matter sometimes reviewed by police supervisory personnel), then there is no higher probability of guilt test which must be met before the suspect can be brought to trial. It is perhaps significant that there is greater participation by the prosecutor in misdemeanor cases in Wisconsin, where a misdemeanor arrest can sometimes be made on "reasonable grounds," [11] than there is in Kansas and Michigan, where the offense must occur in the presence of the officer. The exception in Wisconsin is in traffic and conservation violations, which do usually take place in the officer's presence.

Obviously this probability of guilt factor is not in itself determinative, for not all in-presence misdemeanor cases go directly to court without a decision by the prosecutor being made first.

4. *There are no policy factors which cannot be adequately considered at time of arrest.* It has long been assumed that the prosecutor, as an elected representative of the public, may consider matters of policy unconnected with the probability of guilt in deciding whether to prosecute.[12] Police, on the other hand, are often assumed to be ministerial officers whose only function is to assess the evidence and to arrest whenever sufficient evidence exists. Though current practice shows this distinction is not entirely meaningful,[13] it is still significant. As a general rule, cases not reviewed after arrest are those in which it is assumed either that no policy questions are present or that the policy questions can be adequately considered at the time of the initial contact between the police and offender. An example of the latter case would be minor traffic violations. The police are expected to exercise some discretion in deciding whether to proceed in a minor traffic case, and they generally think that their decisions in such cases should not be subject to reversal for policy reasons.

On the other hand, where the prosecutor is expected to eliminate some of the cases initiated by the police, a separate charging decision is likely. In Detroit none of the minor cases handled

---

11 Wis. Stat. §954.03(1) (1955), discussed in Chapter 2.

12 See, e.g., the series of articles by Baker and DeLong, 23-26 J. Crim. L., C. & P.S. (1933-1936).

13 The great range of situations in which the police exercise discretion by resort to policy considerations is considered in Part II.

during the first half of early sessions court are cleared through the prosecutor except those for accosting and soliciting. The court has asked the prosecutor to screen these cases because of what the judges view as improper actions by the police in building these cases.

Similarly, if there has been a loss of confidence in the police ability to make policy determinations in certain kinds of cases, special procedures may be adopted to insure review by the prosecutor. Thus, in one Wisconsin county, because of dissatisfaction with the county traffic officers' ability to select those traffic offenders who ought to be prosecuted, new procedures were put into effect requiring these officers to obtain the approval of the county prosecutor in all traffic cases.

5. *A requirement of a separate charging decision would be inconvenient.* In many cases it would be inconvenient for the offender, the officer, or the prosecutor if the process included a separate and distinct charging decision. In rural areas particularly, minor cases often are taken to the local justice of the peace as a matter of convenience to the offender and officer. When this is done, the prosecutor does not enter the picture. Even where the prosecutor is readily available, the volume of certain kinds of offenses may make it inconvenient for him to have to give approval for prosecution on each one. Thus, in a busy office of a large city like Detroit, the prosecutor gladly abdicates his authority to make the charging decision as to minor misdemeanors. Even in rural areas, the volume of certain minor offenses is likely to be sufficient to cause inconvenience to a part-time city attorney or district attorney.

C. Conclusion

While the arrest decision quite clearly sets the outer limits of law enforcement, it does not in the usual case set the actual limits of prosecution. The separate and distinct decision on whether to prosecute, ordinarily made by the prosecutor, serves both as a safeguard to insure that individuals are not prosecuted when adequate evidence is lacking or when sound policy reasons dictate to the contrary and also as a screen against the system becoming clogged with insignificant cases.

It is not clear that the special situations in which the warrant is routinely issued after arrest without review by the prosecutor reflect a considered policy that these cases can be adequately dealt with by the police at the time of arrest. However, generally the separate review by the prosecutor, or in some cases by specially designated, ranking police officers, has been dispensed with only in those situations where it does appear likely that the officer can resolve the evidentiary and policy questions involved. To the extent that this is so, the absence of a second decision prior to trial does not operate to the detriment of either the system or the individuals subjected to it. Rather, it frees offenders and officers from one time-consuming step, and at the same time leaves the prosecutor free to devote his limited resources to other cases more in need of the special skills of his office.

PART II

The Decision Not to Invoke
the Criminal Process

The police, in our legal tradition, are essentially ministerial officers. To them have been delegated relatively few grants of discretionary power which require interpretation of meaning before application. Thus a simple and logical hypothesis can be constructed: Police are ministerial officials charged with the enforcement of laws; success in police administration is directly related to completeness and perfection in the performance of this task.

> PARRATT, How Effective Is a
> Police Department? 199 *Annals*
> 153 (September, 1938)

I do not consider police officers to be robots who are prohibited from exercising discretion. Each of you — every day — is called upon to decide whether or not to search, to arrest, or to hold an individual. This is as it should be. If we took discretion out of the job of a police officer, we would reduce the task to one which could be performed by people of far less capability and much less pay.

> SUPERINTENDENT O. W. WILSON,
> Chicago Police Department,
> *Pax 501* (June 11, 1962)

Perhaps the most significant feature of current criminal justice administration is the great amount of discretion which is exercised by police. Decisions not to arrest because of the nature of the offense, the circumstances of its commission, or some other factor are made routinely. The use of judgment in deciding whether one apparently guilty of criminal conduct should be subjected to the criminal justice process is an obviously important exercise of governmental power. Arrest is the usual intake point for persons who are channeled into the criminal justice system. Therefore, the police to a large extent define the outer limits of law enforcement by the way in which they make this decision.

There is a common stereotype of police as ministerial officers whose only function is that of gathering evidence and making an arrest whenever sufficient evidence exists. This is illustrated by the assumption, frequently made, that police and firemen are similar since both are uniformed and are concerned with the safety of persons and property. Police themselves tend to reinforce this conception of their function by denying that they exercise discretion and by failing to specify the standards or criteria upon which they base their decisions.

A wide gulf thus separates theory and practice. Discretion is exercised by the police but this takes place largely without the knowledge of the general public, without the concerted efforts of police administrators to insure that it is exercised properly, and without adequate attention from legislatures and courts.

Whatever one may conclude about the necessity or desirability of the exercise of discretion by police, it is apparent that this is an issue deserving a great deal more attention than it has traditionally been given in the past.

CHAPTER 3

Police Discretion

Because the exercise of discretion involves decision-making not strictly governed by legal rules, but rather with a significant element of personal judgment,[1] it is sometimes said to be totally improper in criminal law enforcement, where the consequences of official action directly affect a citizen's freedom and property.[2]

No one would assert that law enforcement agencies have a right to exercise discretion beyond the outer boundaries of the law de-

[1] Roscoe Pound defines discretion as "an authority conferred by law to act in certain conditions or situations in accordance with an official's or an official agency's own considered judgment and conscience. It is an idea of morals, belonging to the twilight zone between law and morals." Pound, Discretion, Dispensation and Mitigation: The Problem of the Individual Special Case, 35 N.Y.U.L. Rev. 925, 926 (1960). Judge Breitel defines it as "the power to consider all circumstances and then determine whether any legal action is to be taken. And if so taken, of what kind and degree, and to what conclusion." Breitel, Controls in Criminal Law Enforcement, 27 U. Chi. L. Rev. 427 (1960). A typical dictionary definition of discretion is the "ability to make decisions which represent a responsible choice and for which an understanding of what is lawful, right, or wise may be presupposed." Webster, Third New International Dictionary 647 (1961).

Pound asserts that merely distinguishing technical and discretionary administration is "an unfortunate simplification. There are in truth four categories: (1) cases governed by and to be decided according to rule in the strict sense — according to the literal exactness of the strict law; (2) cases not within the first category but to be decided by reasoning from authoritative principles as starting points, using an authoritative technique guided by authoritative ideals; (3) cases calling for judicial discretion, i.e., discretion guided by the analogy of principles of law as starting points for reasoned determination; and (4) cases left to the personal discretion of judge or official or person authorized to act, without any organized grounds of or guides to decision. In the last case, however, the person to whose discretion the determination is left must act honestly in good faith without reckless indifference or from bad motives." Pound, supra, at 929-930.

[2] "Nobody disputes the fact that, in order to make efficient use of the means at its disposal, the government must exercise a great deal of discretion. But, to repeat, under the rule of law the private citizen and his property are not an object of administration by the government, not a means to be used for its purposes. It is only when the administration interferes with the private sphere of the citizen that the problem of discretion becomes relevant to us; and the principle of the rule of law, in effect, means that the administrative authorities should have no discretionary powers in this respect." Hayek, The Constitution of Liberty 213 (1960). See also Hayek, The Road to Serfdom 72 (1944).

fining criminal conduct, such as by arresting for conduct which the legislature has not declared to be a crime. The issue is rather whether discretion within these boundaries, exemplified by the common police decision not to arrest in some situations where criminal conduct has occurred, in proper. Some assert that the two situations are essentially the same and that both involve an abuse of power: "[T]he rule of law [means] . . . that the citizen should be free from arbitrary power. A discretion to withhold a punishment may result in just as much arbitrary power as discretion to use extra-legal punishment." [3]

Whatever their status in principle, it is clear that the two situations are dealt with differently in current practice. It is not common to arrest a person unless he is at least suspected of having engaged in criminal conduct. It is common for some persons not to be arrested even though it can easily be proved that they have engaged in criminal conduct.[4]

A. CURRENT ATTITUDES TOWARD POLICE DISCRETION

There has been a traditional failure to recognize the existence and importance of police discretion. This results, at least to some degree, from attitudes about (1) the mandate of the substantive criminal law; (2) the proper allocation of power between the legislative, judicial, and administrative agencies in American government; (3) the requirements of the rule of law or principle of legality; (4) the extent to which there is an actual necessity for discretion in the existing system; and (5) the extent to which any needed discretion can be exercised by the prosecutor.

1. *The mandate of the substantive law.* The substantive criminal law, insofar as it is addressed to the public, consists of a series of "thou shalt not's." Less clear is the extent to which it must be read as a mandate to law enforcement agencies to proceed against all conduct which is defined as criminal. While some view the substantive law as such a mandate,[5] other observers of the process

---

[3] Hargrove, Police Discretion, 25 Sol. 337 (1958), stating the views of Dicey.

[4] A considerable part of the formal law is devoted to protecting innocent persons from arrest, charging, or conviction. This will be seen in Chapters 11-13 and the volumes on Prosecution and Conviction. Another substantial segment of the law concerns improper police methods. Treatment of this subject will be found in the volume on Detection of Crime. Compare with the paucity of legislation and judicial opinion on invocation discretion, page 75.

[5] Goldstein, Police Discretion Not to Invoke the Criminal Process: Low-Visibility Decisions in the Administration of Justice, 69 Yale L.J. 543, 557 (1960). The Goldstein article is a thoughtful and detailed presentation of the view that discretion in the police agency not to invoke the process is highly undesirable.

have characterized it in different terms. Thurman Arnold has said that the criminal law should be looked upon by the law enforcers "not as something to be enforced because it governs society, but as an arsenal of weapons with which to incarcerate certain dangerous individuals who are bothering society." [6] Others have stated the duty of the law enforcement agency to be enforcement only when "in the public interest . . . , [considering] the effect . . . upon public morale and order and all other considerations affecting public policy";[7] enforcement "in such manner that the greatest degree of social protection will be secured";[8] enforcement only when it will secure "the real purpose of a police service, the prevention of crime";[9] or enforcement which will "winnow and sift from the offenders those who are the most guilty." [10] These attitudes reflect a view of the substantive criminal law as something less than a mandate for enforcement in all cases.[11]

2. *The proper allocation of power between legislature, court, and administrative agency.* It has been common in the criminal law field, particularly in recent decades, to assume that the legislature should play an almost exclusive role in deciding what conduct is criminal. The proper system is often said to be one in

[6] Arnold, The Symbols of Government 153 (1935). He says: "[T]he problem of the police and prosecutor is the suppression of the occasional dangerous individual. For this purpose the ideal that all laws should be enforced without a discretionary selection is impossible to carry out. It is like directing a general to attack the enemy on all fronts at once." Ibid.

[7] Devlin, The Criminal Prosecution in England 23-24 (1958).

[8] Smith, Police Systems in the United States 21 (1940). Smith goes on to say that by following this objective: "The degree of enforcement and the method of application will vary with each neighborhood and community. There are no set rules, nor even general guides to policy, in this regard. Each policeman must, in a sense, determine the standard which is to be set in the area for which he is responsible." Ibid.

[9] Dunning, Discretion in Prosecution, 1 Police J. 39, 47 (1928).

[10] Crownhart, Address to the Meeting of the District Attorneys' Convention, 16 Ops. Wis. Atty. Gen. xlix (1927). Justice Crownhart was of the view that there should be strict enforcement as to offenses mala in se, but that considerable discretion might be exercised with regard to those mala prohibita.

[11] But whether a court will consider the law on the books or the law as actually enforced as the true criminal law will depend upon the context within which this question arises. If a defendant attempts a defense based upon lack of enforcement of a particular provision of the criminal law, then the answer is: "The failure of the executive branch to enforce a law does not result in its modification or repeal. . . . The repeal of laws is as much a legislative function as their enactment." District of Columbia v. John R. Thompson Co., 346 U.S. 100, 113-114, 73 Sup. Ct. 1007, 1014, 97 L. Ed. 1480, 1492 (1953). But where the question was one of standing to challenge the constitutionality of a statute, the court indicated that the record of continued violation without prosecution "bespeaks more than prosecutorial paralysis. What was said in another context is relevant here. 'Deeply embedded traditional ways of carrying out state policy . . . are often tougher and truer law than the dead words of the written text.'" Poe v. Ullman, 367 U.S. 497, 502, 81 Sup. Ct. 1752, 1755, 6 L. Ed. 2d 989, 995 (1961).

which the legislature makes the policy decisions reflected in the enactment of criminal statutes, the court is limited to the resolution of ambiguities in these statutes, and the administrative agency merely executes the policy which has been legislatively prescribed. This position is consistent with the often stated rule that the legislature cannot constitutionally delegate the power to define criminal conduct.[12]

In other fields of law, particularly the field of governmental regulation of economic behavior, it is commonly recognized that administrative agencies do have major responsibility for important policy decisions.[13] In part this results from the fact that legislators sometimes avoid policy determinations, particularly those likely to have political repercussions greater than their importance warrants.[14] In part it also results from the obvious fact that there are limitations upon a legislature's ability to decide in advance all of the important policy issues which may arise. Roscoe Pound has observed:

> No lawmaker has been able to foresee more than the broad outlines of the clash of interests or more than the main lines of the courses of conduct to which the law even of his own time must be applied. Moreover, a legal system which seeks to cover everything by a special provision becomes cumbrous and unworkable.[15]

These factors are also applicable to the field of criminal law administration, and, therefore, the explanation for the different attitude toward criminal justice agencies and other governmental agencies must be found elsewhere.

Perhaps there is an assumption that the other agencies are more

---

[12] 1 Davis, Administrative Law §2.13 (1958); Dession, Criminal Law, Administration and Public Order 24 (1948); Schwenk, The Administrative Crime, Its Creation and Punishment by Administrative Agencies, 42 Mich. L. Rev. 51 (1943). Compare: "The law placed before an administrative official represents merely a statement of policy. Even if couched in mandatory language, it is still subject to administrative interpretation." Roucek, Social Control 87-88 (1947).

[13] "The executive and judicial branches of the government are and must be coordinate branches not only for carrying out policies determined by the legislative branch but also for determining basic policy." 1 Davis, supra, §2.05 (1958). The current legislative practice of sharing policy-making responsibilities with the executive and administrative agencies is a product of historic development. See Hurst, The Growth of American Law: The Law Makers, chaps. 2 and 3 (1950).

[14] Gross, The Legislative Struggle 106 (1953). For other references to studies of the limitations of the legislative process as a policy-making device, see Remington and Rosenblum, The Criminal Law and the Legislative Process, 1960 U. Ill. L.F. 481, 481-482 n.2.
  That there may be politically charged issues even in the drafting of substantive criminal law provisions seems clear. Consider, for example, the political wisdom of a legislator actively working toward repeal of the unenforced provisions on fornication and adultery.

[15] Pound, Criminal Justice in America 40-41 (1930).

competent to make important policy decisions than is the average police department. Perhaps the assumption is that discretion in the hands of a regulatory agency is proper when the sanction is noncriminal but improper when the sanction is criminal prosecution. The difficulty with this latter explanation is that economic regulatory agencies have been expressly delegated discretion to define as criminal any conduct falling within limits set in advance by the legislature,[16] provided that no conduct is subjected to a criminal penalty unless it has been defined as criminal by a precise, pre-existing, and published administrative regulation.[17] Similarly, where the legislature has itself defined the conduct which is criminal, there have been delegations to these agencies of power to declare exemptions to general statutory prohibitions or power to suspend the operation of a statute or regulation for a time, if a sufficiently definite legislative standard is provided.[18]

[16] The Supreme Court, in United States v. Grimaud, 220 U.S. 506, 522, 31 Sup. Ct. 480, 485, 55 L. Ed. 563, 570 (1911), upheld an express delegation of power to define criminal conduct because "A violation of . . . [the administrative provision] is made a crime, not by the Secretary, but by Congress. The statute, not the Secretary, fixes the penalty."

Some state courts have reached a similar conclusion, e.g., Commonwealth v. Diaz, 326 Mass. 525, 95 N.E.2d 666 (1950), upholding a statute authorizing the commissioner of airport management to "make such rules and regulations 'for the use, operation, and maintenance of state-owned airports as he may . . . deem reasonable and expedient'" on the ground that the statute laid down a sufficiently definite legislative mandate so that the commissioner "may constitutionally fill in the details."

Express delegations by statute to local municipalities to define criminal conduct are usually upheld. This fact was relied upon in Smallwood v. District of Columbia, 17 F.2d 210 (D.C. Cir. 1927), which upheld a statute authorizing the D.C. Director of Traffic "to make reasonable regulations with respect to brakes, horn, lights, mufflers, and other equipment, the speed and parking of vehicles, the registration of motor vehicles, the issuance and revocation of operators' permits, and such other regulations with respect to the control of traffic in the District, not in conflict with any law of the United States, as are deemed advisable . . ." Is it possible that "the same considerations that sustain a delegation of power to a local municipality are equally applicable to and should sustain to the same extent a delegation of power to a commission or other administrative body"? Foster, The Delegation of Legislative Power to Administrative Officers, 7 Ill. L. Rev. 397, 398 (1913).

Some other state courts have not upheld such delegation, e.g., Casey v. People, 139 Colo. 89, 336 P.2d 308 (1959), holding unconstitutional a statute, Colo. Rev. Stat. §66-2-7(4) (1953), which delegated to local boards of health the power to "adopt such rules and regulations not inconsistent with the public health laws of this state nor with the orders, rules and regulations of the state board of health . . ."

[17] See Gellhorn and Byse, Cases on Administrative Law 142 (4th ed. 1960).

[18] See cases cited id. at 119-124, and Note, 87 U. Pa. L. Rev. 201 (1938).

The suspending and dispensing power has sometimes been upheld even where there were no clear standards. For example, in State v. Davis, 178 Ark. 153, 10 S.W.2d 513 (1928), the court was concerned with a statute which, rather than directly relieving public officers and their bondsmen of liability for loss of funds put in banks which became insolvent, gave the governor authority to grant such relief in individual cases. The court upheld the delegation and indicated it would have done likewise had this power been given to a board, commission, or other such agency. Compare Montgomery v. State, 231 Ala. 1, 4, 163 So. 365, 368-369 (1935),

There has been no express legislative delegation of discretion to the police, although it is arguable that such a delegation would be constitutional because police are in a position comparable to other administrative agencies. Such a delegation might even be implied, particularly where the substantive criminal law is ambiguous. However, police have not claimed to have this kind of discretion; rather, they exercise a wide range of discretion without attempting to give explicit justification for the practice. As a consequence, police currently function differently from other administrative agencies. While even broadly defined criminal statutes are more precise in setting outer limits of discretion than are many statutes delegating authority to regulatory agencies, enforcement policies of these agencies are often explicit, whereas enforcement by the police is seldom preceded by an announcement indicating specifically what conduct the police intend to subject to enforcement. Also the common police practice of suspending the effective operation of certain penal statutes or of creating exemptions to them occurs without any standards having been prescribed in advance by the legislature.

3. *The rule of law or principle of legality.* Undoubtedly the exercise of discretion in the administration of the criminal law raises more difficult issues than the exercise of discretion in other areas because of the American commitment to the "rule of law" [19] or "principle of legality." [20]

These concepts are said to be inconsistent with the exercise of discretion in deciding not to arrest the person who has committed a crime.[21] Jerome Hall has stated this position:

> . . . there is an inevitable incompatibility between the principle of legality and complete exculpation even in marginal cases where very good motivation combines with a minimum of the proscribed harm. . . . If we agree that it is preferable to have a legal system with the attendant guarantees against official abuse, then we are bound to accept the limitations of any such system and recognize

---

where the court took the position that "the Legislature cannot authorize the suspension of a law by another agency, even in cases where it has the power to suspend the law."

[19] The term "rule of law" is rather nebulous, and may be used to mean (1) law and order, (2) fixed rules, (3) elimination of discretion, (4) due process or fairness, (5) natural law, (6) preference for judges, or (7) judicial review. See 1 Davis, Administrative Law §1.08 (1958).

[20] "The essence of this principle of legality is limitation on penalization by the State's officials, effected by the prescription and application of specific rules. That is the actual meaning of the principle of legality so far as the criminal law is concerned." Hall, General Principles of Criminal Law 28 (2d ed. 1960).

[21] See quotation from Hayek, *supra* page 63, note 2; and from Hargrove, *supra* page 64.

that mitigation, not exculpation, is the relevant recourse in meritorious cases.[22]

On the other hand, adherence to the principle of legality may require only that criminal sanctions not be imposed without fair notice that the conduct is susceptible to the sanction. Thus the boundaries of the criminal law must be drawn in advance of their application and with sufficient precision to allow compliance.[23] The exercise of discretion not to enforce the law would not depart from the principle of legality because there need be no advance notice of the boundaries of exculpation.[24]

There are obviously middle positions between the refusal to recognize any right to exercise of discretion and the recognition as proper of any discretion within the outer limits of conduct defined as criminal by the legislature. "Fair notice" may require advance notice not only of what conduct might be treated as criminal but also of what conduct is treated as criminal according to existing enforcement policy. It is certainly arguable that exculpation must be based upon differential factors which might properly have been considered by the legislature in drawing the line between criminal and noncriminal conduct.[25] Thus race or religion would clearly be an improper basis upon which to rest the decision not to enforce.

Whatever the proper position is, the concern and uncertainty about the "rule of law" or "principle of legality" has tended to prevent explicit recognition of police discretion and has, to that extent, contributed to the lack of an adequate understanding of the function of police discretion in current criminal justice administration.

4. *The need for discretion.* It is obvious that in practice some discretion must be employed somewhere in the existing criminal justice system. The exercise of discretion in interpreting the legislative mandate[26] is necessary because no legislature has suc-

22 Hall, General Principles of Criminal Law 55 (2d ed. 1960).

23 "In order that there be no doubt regarding the meaning of the principle, it has two important corollaries: penal statutes must be strictly construed, and they must not be given retroactive effect." Id. at 28.

24 Thus, in a criminal case, the defendant's complaint that other persons have not been proceeded against will usually be dismissed, e.g., People v. Flanders, 140 Cal. App. 2d 765, 296 P.2d 13 (Dist. Ct. App. 1956).

25 Such was the view taken in one case in which the defendant in a criminal prosecution raised equal protection arguments because other violators were not proceeded against. Taylor v. City of Pine Bluff, 226 Ark. 309, 289 S.W.2d 679 (1956).

26 Sometimes it is assumed that such exercise of discretion can be adequately controlled. "In acting under the rule of law the administrative agencies will often have to exercise discretion as the judge exercises discretion in interpreting the law. This, however, is a discretionary power which can and must be controlled by the possibility of a review of the substance of the decision by an independent court."

ceeded in formulating a substantive criminal code which clearly encompasses all conduct intended to be made criminal and which clearly excludes all other conduct. Poor draftsmanship and a failure to revise the criminal law to eliminate obsolete provisions[27] have contributed to existing ambiguities.[28] However, even where care has been taken, it has not been possible to draft substantive provisions which are entirely free from ambiguity. This is a result not only of limitations upon the effectiveness of language but also of the inability of a legislature to envisage all of the day-to-day law enforcement problems[29] which may arise.

Even more important is the fact that not enough financial resources are allocated to make possible enforcement of all the laws against all offenders.[30] The legislative body responsible for granting appropriations makes a general decision as to how much it is willing to pay for law enforcement, but usually provides no guidance as to how this sum is to be expended.[31] Allocation of resources to enforcement agencies is ordinarily decided by a municipal legislative body, while the criminal law is defined by the state legislature, which often leaves the administrator subject to

---

Hayek, The Constitution of Liberty 213 (1960). However, currently decisions not to invoke the process based upon interpretation of statutes are not likely to be reviewed by a court.

[27] Wechsler, The Challenge of a Model Penal Code, 65 Harv. L. Rev. 1097, 1101 (1952); Remington and Rosenblum, The Criminal Law and the Legislative Process, 1960 U. Ill. L.F. 481, 483-487.

[28] Wechsler, *supra*, at 1113.

[29] See quotation from Pound, *supra* p. 66.

[30] Although this lack of resources is generally recognized, there is no agreement on what would be a proper level of enforcement. See Goldstein, Police Discretion Not to Invoke the Criminal Process: Low-Visibility Decisions in the Administration of Justice, 69 Yale L.J. 543, 561 nn.31, 32 (1960).

[31] It has been suggested that the maximum sentence authorized for the various offenses might be some guide to enforcement priorities. Id. at 568. It might also be said that, to the extent that local legislative bodies actually prescribe in detail the structure of the law enforcement agencies (e.g., setting by ordinance the size of the police department vice bureau or narcotics squad), some guidance is being given. However, such restrictions on police organizations have been criticized:

"Policy is also established by budgetary appropriations; the budget represents the department work program. If the chief is to be held responsible for the accomplishment of the police purpose within this policy framework, he must have authority to organize and direct his resources to this end.

"Many communities unwisely restrict the authority of the chief to manage his force in the manner he considers most effective. Restrictions are frequently imposed on the chief in the management of his personnel and in the organization and direction of his force. . . .

"The practice of establishing the organization of the department by charter provision or even by ordinance places the force in a straitjacket. The progressive chief then finds himself powerless to modify the structure of the organization to meet changing conditions. No part of the organization structure should be established by law." Wilson, Police Planning 20 (2d ed. 1957).

conflicting legislative mandates. The same conflict occurs when the state legislature appropriates money to a state police unit, since the crime-defining and budget decisions are essentially unrelated even within the same unit of government. Because of the obvious dilemma created by limited resources and lack of established priorities for enforcement, the necessity of discretionary enforcement on this basis has received some recognition.[32] Yet there are no suggested principles to guide the exercise of such discretion.[33]

Finally, the exercise of discretion seems necessary in the current criminal justice system for reasons unrelated to either the interpretation of criminal statutes or the allocation of available enforcement resources. This is because of the special circumstances of the individual case, particularly the characteristics of the individual offender which "differentiate him from other offenders in personality, character, sociocultural background, the motivations of his crime, and his particular potentialities for reform or recidivism." [34] The infinite variety of individual circumstances complicates administration by mere application of rules.[35] Justice Charles D.

[32] See Pound, Criminal Justice in America 19-20, 62-63 (1930); Wilson, *supra*, at 20; Breitel, Controls in Criminal Law Enforcement, 27 U. Chi. L. Rev. 427, 431 (1960); Hall, Police and Law in a Democratic Society, 28 Ind. L.J. 135, 149-150 (1953). Even those generally opposed to recognition of discretion in the hands of law enforcers are apt to make an exception here, e.g., Hayek, The Constitution of Liberty 213 (1960); Goldstein, Police Discretion Not to Invoke the Criminal Process: Low-Visibility Decisions in the Administration of Justice, 69 Yale L.J. 543, 560-561 (1960).

[33] Police materials are usually devoted to *how* to make an arrest and *when* to arrest in terms of probability of guilt, with the allocation of resources problem completely ignored. An exception is California State Department of Education, California Police Officers' Training Bulletin No. 71, Police Supervisory Control 26-27 (1957): "Finally, note must be made of one insurmountable obstacle to supervisory control which confronts every chief of police: the fact that it is absolutely impossible to enforce all laws. One illustration will suffice.

"A study of traffic violations at Rose and Grove Streets, Berkeley, California, revealed that if conditions at other intersections were similar, three million violations of traffic regulations were occurring daily in Berkeley and that it would take more than fourteen thousand traffic officers to enforce the traffic laws in that city. With hundreds of thousands of federal, state and municipal laws to be enforced, it becomes obvious that considerable discretion must be exercised in the direction of the enforcement policy.

"It is at this point that the difficulty is met. The general enforcement policy of a police department is partly the result of traditional practices, partly the general orders of the chief modifying or amplifying these unwritten laws, and partly the character that the intelligent and honest official puts into his work."

[34] Glueck, Predictive Devices and the Individualization of Justice, 23 Law & Contemp. Prob. 461 (1958).

[35] "Although an important group of neo-analytical jurists still think of law as a body of rules attaching prescribed detailed sanctions to prescribed details of socially undesired conduct, it has become generally well perceived that the judicial process cannot be held solely to rules. . . . All legal experience shows that the power of

Breitel, who has had extensive administrative, legislative, and judicial experience, stresses this point:

> If every policeman, every prosecutor, every court, and every post-sentence agency performed his or its responsibility in strict accordance with rules of law, precisely and narrowly laid down, the criminal law would be ordered but intolerable.[36]

Individualized treatment of an offender, based upon the circumstances of the particular case, is well recognized at the sentencing stage, where discretion is provided.[37] These same circumstances may be apparent at the arrest stage and may seem to the police to dictate that the criminal process not be invoked against a particular offender. While sentence discretion is widely recognized, arrest discretion is not. This may reflect an assumption that, while individual circumstances may justify mitigation, the individualization of criminal justice should never go so far as to result in the complete exoneration of a particular offender.[38] The contrary view is that the individual circumstances sometimes make conviction and even arrest excessive,[39] so that proper administration requires the exercise of discretion at the early as well as at subsequent stages in the process.

5. *The extent to which necessary discretion can be exercised by the prosecutor.* It has been traditional to give explicit recognition to the propriety of discretion on the part of the prosecutor and either to deny or, more commonly, to ignore the issue of police discretion. To some extent this attitude is based upon an assump-

---

adjusting the operations of legal precepts to the exigencies of special circumstances is unavoidable if there is to be a complete system of justice according to law." Pound, Discretion, Dispensation and Mitigation: The Problem of the Individual Special Case, 35 N.Y.U.L. Rev. 925-926, 936-937 (1960).

36 Breitel, Controls in Criminal Law Enforcement, 27 U. Chi. L. Rev. 427 (1960).

37 See Glueck, Predictive Devices and the Individualization of Justice, 23 Law & Contemp. Prob. 461 (1958); Goldstein, Police Discretion Not to Invoke the Criminal Process: Low-Visibility Decisions in the Administration of Justice, 69 Yale L.J. 543, 549 n.12 (1960). Treatment of this will also be found in the volume on Sentencing.

38 See quotation from Hall *supra* pages 68-69.

39 Sometimes dispensation has been postponed until after conviction because of a view that the pardon is the only appropriate device to take care of such situations. Pound has criticized this: "We have been in the habit of covering up the actual process of dispensation in criminal cases where exceptional and formally unprovided for circumstances make application of a rule grossly unjust, by formal conviction and reservation of execution of the judgment for a formal pardon. . . . We have learned to look discretion in the face and not be shocked. Should we not also look dispensation in the face and not cover up what actually takes place by formal conviction and formal pardon, leaving one whom we hold innocent branded as a pardoned convict?" Pound, Discretion, Dispensation and Mitigation: The Problem of the Individual Special Case, 35 N.Y.U.L. Rev. 925, 936 (1960).

tion that the prosecutor is qualified to exercise discretion[40] while the average police agency is not.[41] This may result from the fact that the prosecutor has ordinarily been better educated than most police officers and, unlike most police, is directly responsible to the electorate.

The effect upon traditional attitudes of assumptions about the comparative competence of the prosecutor and the police is difficult to assess. Different educational requirements may be the result rather than the cause of the different attitudes about their respective responsibilities. There is, however, reason to believe that the assumption that the average municipal police agency lacks any special competence to make policy decisions is an important current factor. For example, the United States Supreme Court held it proper for the Federal Trade Commission to follow a policy of proceeding criminally against only major violators because there were insufficient resources to proceed against all violators.[42] This kind of judgment was said to be within the expertness of the enforcement agency, which is familiar with the economic problems being dealt with. Under similar circumstances, a Philadelphia court held an identical policy of the Philadelphia Police Commissioner to be improper.[43] The Philadelphia court gave no indication that it believed that the police commissioner was particularly qualified to decide how best to allocate the limited enforcement resources made available to him.

Although it is theoretically possible to have a system in which all discretion is exercised by the prosecutor, this would be difficult,

---

40 See the series of articles by Baker and DeLong, 23-26 J. Crim. L., C. & P.S. (1933-1936). Additional citations will be found in the volume on Prosecution.

Such discretion is properly exercised for precisely those reasons discussed earlier: interpretation of the legislative mandate, allocation of limited enforcement resources, and consideration of the special circumstances of the individual case. For a recent judicial opinion giving detailed recognition to this, see Pugach v. Klein, 193 F. Supp. 630 (S.D.N.Y. 1961).

41 Parratt, How Effective Is a Police Department?, 199 Annals 153 (Sept. 1938).

42 The Federal Trade Commission obtained a cease and desist order against one firm engaging in illegal pricing. The firm contended that the order should be suspended because certain of its competitors were engaged in the same practices but had not been proceeded against, with the result that this one firm suffered serious financial loss. The court held it would not disturb the FTC decision to put the order into operation immediately, saying: ". . . the commission alone is empowered to develop that enforcement policy best calculated to achieve the ends contemplated by Congress and to allocate its available funds and personnel in such a way as to execute its policy efficiently and economically." Moog Industries, Inc. v. FTC, 355 U.S. 411, 413, 78 Sup. Ct. 377, 379, 2 L. Ed. 2d 370, 373 (1958).

43 Bargain City U.S.A., Inc. v. Dilworth, 29 U.S.L. Week 2002 (Pa. C.P., June 10, 1960). Compare the statement in Gowan v. Smith, 157 Mich. 443, 473, 122 N.W. 286, 297 (1909), quoted in the text at page 81.

perhaps impossible, to implement in practice. There are a number of alternatives:

(a) The police could make no arrests until the matter had been reviewed by the prosecutor. Referrals often are made in doubtful cases,[44] but the feasibility of doing so is limited by the need to make an immediate arrest in some cases[45] and the fact that prior consultation in all cases would place a considerably greater strain on police resources than does the current practice.[46]

(b) The police could arrest all violators, leaving to the prosecutor the responsibility for exercising discretion when he decides whether to charge the suspect.[47] Carried to its extreme, this would require the police to construe all criminal statutes liberally, leaving it to the prosecutor to decide whether ambiguity ought to be resolved in favor of prosecution or release.[48] As a consequence, more persons would be arrested and later determined not to have violated the statute than is the case under current practice. The police would thus be liable for damages, at least in theory, because current tort law seems clearly to hold the officer liable for any mistake in the determination of the meaning of a criminal statute.[49] The imposition on the persons arrested would be great,[50] particu-

---

[44] For example, questions involving difficult interpretation are often referred to the prosecutor in obscene literature and negligent homicide cases. See Chapter 1.

[45] For the reasons why immediate arrest may be essential, see Chapter 9.

[46] Particularly in the numerous cases in which the officer and offender are face to face, it is far less time consuming to make an immediate arrest than to consult with a prosecutor or magistrate.

[47] Because police training materials rarely deal with the invocation discretion problem, few opinions have been expressed on this point. An exception is found in the Oakland, California, Police Academy materials, advising that "we should . . . remember that it's our job to turn in the evidence and it's the Prosecuting Attorney's job to determine when a complaint will be issued." See Goldstein, Police Discretion Not to Invoke the Criminal Process: Low-Visibility Decisions in the Administration of Justice, 69 Yale L.J. 543, 560 n.28 (1960).

[48] Jerome Hall has cautioned the police that, where the law is uncertain, "the law that must be enforced is the narrow, strict interpretation of the relevant statutes and decisions. . . . This does not oppose the standard that the police must enforce definite law impartially and regardless of their private opinion of its merits." Hall, Police and Law in a Democratic Society, 28 Ind. L.J. 133, 171 (1953). A less than broad interpretation is also implied by Goldstein, who notes that full enforcement by the police is not a realistic expectation due to ambiguities in the substantive law. Goldstein, *supra*, at 543, 560.

[49] See page 86.

[50] This is sometimes conceded by opponents of discretion by the police. Thus Goldstein, who is of the view that the "ultimate answer is that the police should not be delegated discretion not to invoke the criminal law," admits that full enforcement now would be improper because too many persons have come to rely upon nonenforcement. Goldstein, Police Discretion Not to Invoke the Criminal Process: Low-Visibility Decisions in the Administration of Justice, 69 Yale L.J. 543, 586, 588 (1960).

larly in cases where arrest in itself is damaging to reputation.[51] To the extent that such a practice would require more arrests to be made, it would necessitate the allocation of greater resources to law enforcement, an expense which municipalities would probably not be willing to incur for the purpose of eliminating police discretion.[52]

(c) Police could confine their decisions to policies made known in advance by the prosecutor and courts. The formulation of self-executing policies presents the same kind of difficulty as is presented by the effort to draft self-executing statutes. The range of individual variations is so great that it is difficult to deal with all of them in a brief verbal formulation. If the policy statements are elaborate, police training would need to be greatly improved to communicate effectively these statements to the individual officer. Most important, perhaps, is the fact that the prosecutor's policies may not adequately take account of limited police resources, particularly since the prosecutor, a county officer, is not directly concerned with the fiscal policies of the cities in the county, upon which most police departments in the area must rely for their support.

B. POLICE DISCRETION AND THE LAW

Police decisions not to enforce the law rarely become known to the public. Consequently, these decisions are seldom challenged either in the legislature[53] or in the trial or appellate courts.[54] Where there is challenge in court, the person making the challenge

51 See page 137.

52 It is not clear whether the police are, or should be, aware of the limited resource problems of the subsequent agencies in the criminal justice process and whether they exercise invocation discretion on this basis. Certainly the burden upon these agencies is lessened by the various kinds of decisions not to invoke which are made. However, no evidence has been found which indicates that the police follow a particular pattern of nonenforcement specifically to avoid a strain upon the resources of another agency. General observations about the police knowledge of and sympathies concerning these related agencies suggests that such action, if it demonstrates any concern at all, occurs only with regard to the burden upon the prosecutor's office.

53 Legislative action presupposes a number of persons sufficiently interested in obtaining legislative declaration of a given principle that they will work together toward that end. Interest groups objecting to police discretion have not taken form, and while the police might be expected to work toward an express legislative grant of discretion, they have been satisfied to exercise it without explicit authorization and in such a manner that it is not brought to general attention.

54 Of the cases observed, most involved nonenforcement which was clearly a result of corruption or neglect of duty, rather than an attempt to exercise discretion of the kind to be described herein. These opinions rarely refer to the problem of non-invocation in the absence of such circumstances.

is confronted with a very difficult burden of proof [55] and often by the lack of an available remedy.[56]

1. *Legislation on police discretion.* Almost every state has some legislation relevant to police discretion. However, there is a distinct lack of originality in the statutes defining the powers and duties of the police agencies. It is obvious that the question of police discretion has not received careful legislative attention. Most of the statutes have existed for many years, usually without the benefit of judicial interpretation. Therefore, while a good case can be made for the proposition that the state legislatures have generally denied the police authority to exercise discretion,[57] a review of all the applicable laws leaves the matter in some doubt.

The most convincing evidence that the police have been denied discretion is found in statutes which set forth the duties of various police agencies. Some impose a duty upon sheriffs[58] or city police[59] to arrest "all" violators of the criminal law. Others employ more limited terms, declaring it the officer's responsibility to arrest "all felons" [60] or "all persons committing an offense in his presence." [61] A lesser number state a duty to enforce "all" the crim-

---

[55] The problem of proof may be a considerable one. In People v. Winters, 171 Cal. App. 2d Supp. 876, 342 P.2d 538 (Sup. Ct. 1959), a trial judge's dismissal of a case on grounds of discriminatory enforcement of gambling laws against Negroes was reversed on the basis that such intentional and purposeful discrimination had to be proved, judicial notice not being sufficient. In Bargain City U.S.A., Inc. v. Dilworth, 29 U.S.L. Week 2002 (Pa. C.P., June 10, 1960), prosecution under the Sunday blue laws was enjoined because of a deliberate policy of selective enforcement, but the case is unusual in that the police commissioner, because of limitations in resources, had previously articulated a policy of enforcement directed only at large retail establishments.

It should be noted that the problem may be equally great when other decisions in the criminal justice process are challenged. In the recent case of Oyler v. Boles, 368 U.S. 448, 456, 82 Sup. Ct. 501, 506, 7 L. Ed. 2d 446, 452 (1962), the court observed that petitioner's proof that 904 men with similar records had not been prosecuted under the recidivist statute (as petitioner had been) was insufficient, as there was "no indication that these records of previous convictions . . . were available to the prosecutors."

[56] See page 157.

[57] See Goldstein, Police Discretion Not to Invoke the Criminal Process: Low-Visibility Decisions in the Administration of Justice, 69 Yale L.J. 543, 557 (1960).

[58] Ariz. Rev. Stat. Ann. §11-441 (1956); Ark. Stat. Ann. §12-1110 (1947); Cal. Govt. Code §26601 (1943); Hawaii Rev. Laws §31-5 (1955); Idaho Code §31-2202 (1961); N.D. Cent. Code §11-15-03 (1960); Utah Code Ann. §17-22-2 (1962); Wash. Rev. Code §36.28.010 (1961).

[59] Colo. Rev. Stat. §139-3-15 (1953); Hawaii Rev. Laws §150-10(b) (1955); Iowa Code Ann. §748.4 (1950); Mo. Ann. Stat. §74.203 (1952); Neb. Rev. Stat. §16-323 (1954); Utah Code Ann. §10-6-66 (1962); Wyo. Stat. §7-155 (1957).

[60] Minn. Stat. Ann. §387.03 (Supp. 1960); Mo. Ann. Stat. §57.100 (1959); N.M. Stat. Ann. §15-40-2 (1953).

[61] Ill. Rev. Stat., chap. 38, §655 (1961); Ind. Stat. Ann. §48-6107 (1950), §49-2802 (1951); Neb. Rev. Stat. §27-1706 (1956); Ohio Rev. Code Ann. §2935.03 (1954).

inal laws.[62] Seldom are the statutes phrased in permissive terms.[63]

Statutes frequently impose a duty of full enforcement in a particular, sensitive areas of the criminal law such as gambling,[64] prostitution,[65] narcotics,[66] or liquor[67] violations. While these provisions do seem to demonstrate a special legislative desire for full enforcement in these areas, it is questionable whether one can properly infer from them a recognition that discretion does exist in regard to crimes not specifically mentioned. In practice, police do tend to conform to specific commands for full enforcement while at the same time exercising considerable discretion in other enforcement areas.[68]

Over two-thirds of the states have passed general arrest statutes prescribing the circumstances under which police can make an arrest without warrant. A great majority are in permissive terms, usually indicating that the police "may" arrest upon a given quantum of evidence.[69] By comparison, only a few states have declared

[62] Alaska Comp. Laws Ann. §40-12-8 (Supp. 1958); Ark. Stat. Ann. §19-1705 (Supp. 1961); Colo. Rev. Stat. §139-75-5 (1953); Del. Code Ann., tit. 11, §8303 (1953); Hawaii Rev. Laws §150-9 (1955); Idaho Code §19-4804 (1948); Ky. Rev. Stat. Ann. §70.570 (1960); Mich. Stat. Ann. §5-1752 (1952); Mo. Ann. Stat. §85.060 (1952); Ohio Rev. Code Ann. §737.11 (1954); Va. Code §15-557 (Supp. 1960); W. Va. Code §509 (1961).

Sometimes the statutes take different forms, such as requiring the police to "suppress and prevent all disturbances and disorder," Mass. Ann. Laws, chap. 41, §98 (1961); or making it their duty "to report within 24 hours to the district attorney . . . every crime which shall come to his knowledge," La. Rev. Stat. §15:575 (1950). The latter provision is interesting in that it suggests that the police might properly refrain from arrest and, instead, refer the matter to the prosecutor for his invocation decision.

[63] The closest approach to express recognition of discretion in the police duty statutes is found in N.M. Stat. §39-1-1 (1953), which makes it a police duty "to investigate all violations of the criminal laws . . . which are called to the attention of any such officer or of which he is aware, and it is also declared the duty of every such officer to diligently file a complaint or information, if the circumstances are such as to indicate to a reasonable prudent person that such action should be taken . . ."

Statutes elsewhere are sometimes in permissive terms, such as those indicating that the police "shall have power to arrest," Kan. Gen. Stat. §§13-623, 13-625 (1949); that the police "may arrest," S.D. Code §45.1133 (1939); or that the police are "empowered . . . to make arrests," Pa. Stat. Ann., tit. 71, §252 (1942).

[64] E.g., Cal. Penal Code §335 (1960); Miss. Code Ann. §2478 (1942).

[65] E.g., N.D. Cent. Code §44-04-06 (1960).

[66] E.g., Ore. Rev. Stat. §475.120 (1959).

[67] E.g., Okla. Stat. Ann., tit. 37, §88 (1953); R.I. Gen. Laws §3-12-1 (1956).

[68] Thus, while the police in Michigan exercise considerable discretion, the Director of the Enforcement Division of the Michigan State Liquor Commission noted that local officers were resisting pressures for nonenforcement of the liquor laws because a duty of full enforcement is stated in the Liquor Control Act, Mich. Stat. Ann. §18.971 (1937).

[69] Ala. Code, tit. 15, §154 (1958); Alaska Comp. Laws Ann. §66-5-30 (1958); Ariz. Rev. Stat. Ann. §13-1403 (1956); Ark. Stat. Ann. §19-1706 (1947); Cal. Penal Code §836 (1960); Colo. Rev. Stat. §39-2-20 (Perm. Supp. 1960); D.C. Code §4-141 (1961); Fla. Stat. Ann. §530.15 (1960); Hawaii Rev. Laws §255-5 (1955); Idaho Code §19-603

that police "shall" arrest when such evidence exists.[70]   Occasionally courts have suggested that even the permissive language must be read as imposing a duty to arrest when the officer obtains the necessary evidence.[71]   A similar assertion has been made with regard to common law arrest powers.[72]

Statutes commonly make it a criminal offense for an officer to refuse or neglect to make an arrest pursuant to a warrant directed to him.[73]   This is understandable.   Once the prosecutor or magistrate has decided that an arrest should be made, the police officer has only the ministerial duty of executing the warrant.[74]   It may be of some significance that there are few comparable statutes dealing with the failure of an officer to arrest without warrant.[75]   A few western states make it a crime if an officer "willfully refuses to . . . arrest any person charged with a criminal offense," [76] but it is not clear whether "charged" means charged by the prosecutor, charged by a private complainant, or merely that sufficient evidence exists to make a legal arrest without warrant.[77]   In a few

---

(1961); Ill. Rev. Stat., chap. 38, §657 (1961); Ind. Stat. §9-1024 (1956); Iowa Code Ann. §755.4 (1950); La. Rev. Stat. §15:60 (1950); Mass. Ann. Laws, chap. 276, §28 (1956); Mich. Stat. Ann. §28.874 (1938); Minn. Stat. Ann. §629.34 (1947); Miss. Code Ann. §2470 (1956); Mont. Rev. Codes §94-6003 (1947); Nev. Rev. Stat. §171.235 (1957); N.Y. Code Crim. Proc. §177 (Supp. 1961); N.D. Cent. Code §29-06-15 (1960); Ohio Rev. Code Ann. §2935.04 (1954); Okla. Stat. Ann., tit. 22, §196 (1937); Ore. Rev. Stat. §133.310 (1959); R.I. Gen. Laws §12-7-4 (1956); S.C. Code §17-253 (1952); S.D. Code §45.1133 (Supp. 1960); Tenn. Code Ann. §40-803 (1955); Tex. Code Crim. Proc., art. 215 (1954); Utah Code Ann. §77-13-3 (1953); Va. Code §52-20 (1958); W. Va. Code §489 (1961); Wis. Stat. Ann. §954.03 (1961).

While the above statutes use the term "may," other statutes merely denote that "arrest is lawful whenever" certain evidence is available. Del. Code Ann., tit. 11, §1906 (1953); N.H. Rev. Stat. Ann. §594.10 (1955).

[70] Conn. Gen. Stat. Ann. §6-49 (1961); Me. Rev. Stat., chap. 147, §4 (1954); Neb. Rev. Stat. §29-401 (1956); N.C. Gen. Stat. §15-41 (Supp. 1959); Wyo. Stat. §7-155 (1957). Of these, only the Connecticut and North Carolina statutes refer to persons other than those "found" violating the law.

[71] Lees v. Colgan, 120 Cal. 262, 52 Pac. 502 (1898); Monson v. Boyd, 81 Idaho 575, 348 P.2d 93 (1959); Schultz v. United States Fidelity & Guaranty Co., 134 App. Div. 260, 118 N.Y.S. 977 (1909), aff'd, 201 N Y. 230, 94 N.E. 601 (1909).

[72] E.g., Hoch v. State, 199 Wis. 63, 225 N.W. 191 (1929).

[73] E.g., N.M. Stat. §40-31-09 (1953); N.D. Cent. Code §12-17-02 (1960).

[74] Consequently, it is generally agreed that the police officer can incur no liability if the warrant is fair on its face and he acts in accordance with it.

[75] Of course, it can hardly be contended that this conclusively establishes the existence of police discretion. It would be questionable policy, in an area such as this where the officer himself must weigh the evidence to determine if he can arrest, to leave the officer open to tort liability, if he erred in making an arrest, and to criminal liability, if he erred in the other direction. Yet criminal liability could be limited to those instances where the police officer, knowing he could lawfully arrest, failed to do so. See statutes cited in note 76.

[76] Cal. Penal Code §142 (1960); Colo. Rev. Stat. §40-7-34 (1953); Idaho Code §18-701 (1947); Nev. Rev. Stat. §281.280 (1959).

[77] In the only case found in which an appellate court interpreted this term in such a statute, it was observed that "it may be said that the words 'charged with

states it is an offense only if the officer should "neglect making any arrest for an offense . . . committed in his presence." [78] Similarly, only a few states expressly declare failure to make an arrest to be grounds for removal from office.[79]

The Wisconsin statutes suggest that there is a duty to arrest,[80] while equivalent provisions in Kansas[81] and Michigan[82] are in permissive terms. However, it seems likely that the choice of language was fortuitous.

2. *The courts and police discretion.* Generally, appellate courts have not recognized the propriety of police discretion. In part this is due to the fact that strong language denying the propriety of such discretion has been used in opinions in cases involving a clear abuse of authority. For example, in a Kansas case the court stated emphatically: "There is a discretion to be exercised, but that discretion is reposed in [the legislature and city council]. They have left no room for the exercise of discretion on the part of officials charged especially with the duty of seeing that the laws are enforced." [83] This use of unqualified language makes it difficult to reach a different result in situations where the exercise of discretion is more defensible.

Even within a single case a court may treat as identical a clearly improper decision not to arrest and a decision not to arrest for

criminal offense' limit the application of this statute to cases in which a formal charge has been made . . ." Monson v. Boyd, 81 Idaho 575, 348 P.2d 93 (1959).

78 D.C. Code §4-143 (1961); Tex. Penal Code, art. 382 (1952).

79 Okla. Stat. Ann., tit. 11, §577 (1959), removal for refusal to "make an arrest in the proper case"; W. Va. Code §509 (1961), for violation of the "duty to . . . arrest . . . any offender"; Wyo. Stat. §7-13 (1957), for failure to arrest for a violation in the officer's presence.

80 The statute on constables states as a duty: "To cause to be prosecuted all violations of law of which he has knowledge or information," Wis. Stat. §60.54(6) (1955), incorporated by reference in the city police and village marshal statutes, Wis. Stat. §§61.28, 62.09(13) (1955). City police and village marshals are further directed in these statutes to "arrest . . . every person found . . . violating any law of the state or ordinance" of the city or village. Conservation wardens shall ". . . cause proceedings to be instituted if the proofs at hand warrant it." Wis. Stat. §29.05(2) (1955). The statute on sheriffs and their aides is less clear, although it indicates that they ". . . shall keep and preserve the peace in their respective counties . . ." Wis. Stat. §59.24 (1955).

The arrest law itself has not been codified in Wisconsin, except that the general misdemeanor statute enlarging on the common law power exists. However, it speaks in terms of neither duty nor privilege, but merely says that an arrest under the stated circumstances is legal. Wis. Stat. §954.03(1) (1955).

81 Kan. Gen. Stat. §§13-623, 14-819 (1949), on police of first and second class cities. But see Kan. Gen. Stat. §19-813 (1949), on the county sheriff, drafted in language similar to the Wisconsin sheriff provision. See note 80 *supra.*

82 The general peace officer statute, Mich. Stat. Ann. §28.874 (1938), is permissive, as are many dealing with the duties of particular officers, e.g., Mich. Stat. Ann. §4.436 (1952), on state police, and Mich. Stat. Ann. §13.1226 (1951), on conservation officers.

83 State ex rel. Parker v. McKnaught, 152 Kan. 689, 107 P.2d 693 (1940).

which a sensible reason can be given. For example, the Wisconsin court recently reveiwed the conviction of a sheriff on counts which included allowing prostitution to continue in return for certain favors and failing to make an arrest in an assault case where the victim, who was the adult son of the offender, told the sheriff that he did not want to sign a complaint against his father.[84] A decision not to arrest in a case like the latter is certainly not unusual in current practice.[85] Yet the court held that the failure to arrest the father for assault justified conviction under a statute punishing a public official who "intentionally fails or refuses to perform a known mandatory, nondiscretionary, ministerial duty of his office." [86] The court, therefore, apparently assumed that the sheriff's decision in this situation was as improper as it was in the prostitution case.

Some other courts have nevertheless expressly recognized that some discretion, such as that involved in interpreting the meaning of a statute defining the crime, must be exercised by the police.[87] However, this right has been carefully limited, and where the legislative mandate is clear and unambiguous, it has been held that the police are not justified in concluding that the legislature did not contemplate enforcement against conduct clearly within the scope of the statute.[88] But there are cases suggesting that such an assumption by the police is justified if the legislation has remained unenforced for a substantial period of time.[89]

There has rarely been judicial recognition of the right of police

[84] State v. Lombardi, 8 Wis. 2d 421, 99 N.W.2d 829 (1959).

[85] See page 121.

[86] Wis. Stat. §946.12(1) (1955).

[87] Thus, an officer has "the duty . . . of interpreting the statutes he is called upon to enforce. He must act according to his best lights." State ex rel. Pacific American Fisheries v. Darwin, 81 Wash. 1, 13, 142 Pac. 441, 444 (1914). See also Jumonville v. Herbert, 170 So. 497 (La. App. 1936).

[88] Thus a city ordinance providing that no person shall sell liquor without first obtaining a license may not be interpreted to exclude wholesale liquor dealers on the basis that it was the legislative intent that it apply only to saloon keepers. Such an ordinance imposes on the police "an official duty . . . purely ministerial. No judicial discretion is anywhere involved." State ex rel. School District of Omaha v. Cummings, 17 Neb. 311, 313, 22 N.W. 545, 546 (1885). But see Rohrer v. Hasting Brewing Co., 83 Neb. 111, 119, 119 N.W. 27, 30 (1908), where the court, engaging in statutory interpretation under similar circumstances, relied on nonenforcement, stating: "After a careful and deliberate consideration of all of the legislative acts concerning said traffic and the conduct of the various officers whose duty it has been for the past 20 years to enforce those laws, we conclude that a corporation may be licensed to sell intoxicating liquors . . ." See also Lay v. Common Council of Hoboken, 75 N.J.L. 272, 67 Atl. 1024 (1907); People ex rel. Brown v. Kennedy, 102 Misc. 450, 169 N.Y.S. 1022 (Sup. Ct. 1918).

[89] Thus, in refusing to mandamus the police, one court observed that "the ordinance [in question] seems, whether for adequate or inadequate reasons, to have been a dead letter for a number of years." Carmody v. City of Elmira, 160 Misc. 916, 290 N.Y.S. 1021, 1023 (Sup. Ct. 1936).

not to enforce certain laws where available resources make full enforcement impossible. An exception is the Michigan case of *Gowan v. Smith*,[90] where the court declared that the police commissioner

> . . . is bound to use the discretion with which he is clothed. He is charged not alone with the execution of the liquor laws of the State within the city of Detroit, but he is likewise charged with the suppression of all crime and the conservation of the peace. To enable him to perform the duties imposed upon him by law, he is supplied with certain limited means. It is entirely obvious that he must exercise a sound discretion as to how those means shall be applied for the good of the community.[91]

Other courts have reached the opposite conclusion.[92]

Where discretion is recognized as proper, courts have not indicated what standards ought to control the exercise of such discretion. One court did suggest that police might appropriately divert resources away from those cases in which the possibility of conviction seems slight.[93] However, other courts have insisted that the police have a duty to arrest even when reasonably certain the prosecutor or judge will dismiss.[94] Some have held it improper to divert resources away from the enforcement of laws which do not enjoy public support.[95]

Certainly enforcement criteria must accord with constitutional guarantees such as the right to equal protection. However, the state cases on equal protection in law enforcement are not con-

[90] 157 Mich. 443, 122 N.W. 286 (1909).

[91] 157 Mich. at 470, 122 N.W. at 297. While opinions expressly recognizing police discretion in this fashion are most unusual, it might be said that a number of courts have accomplished approximately the same result by denying to the relator the extraordinary writ requested, on the grounds that such a remedy was not available to him. Compare State ex rel. Clark v. Police Board of Columbus, 10 Ohio Dec. 256, 19 Wkly. L. Bull. 341 (C.P. 1888), where mandamus was granted to compel enforcement of blue laws, with State ex rel. Clark v. Murphy, 30 Ohio C.C.R. 332 (Cir. Ct. 1888), also arising in Columbus, where the court refused, on procedural grounds, to grant the writ to compel enforcement of the same laws.

[92] After the Philadelphia Police Commissioner, because of lack of funds and personnel, adopted a policy of limiting enforcement of the blue laws to large retail establishments, the Philadelphia Court of Common Pleas enjoined prosecution of a complaining defendant. Bargain City U.S.A., Inc. v. Dilworth, 29 U.S.L. Week 2002 (Pa. C.P., June 10, 1960).

[93] "If it be true that petit jurors will not convict in such cases, it might well be doubted whether it would be best to summarily arrest the parties . . ." Graham v. Gaither, 140 Md. 330, 345, 117 Atl. 858, 863 (1922).

[94] Thus, "derelictions of other officials cannot excuse . . . failure to do what the law plainly required . . ." State ex rel. Thompson v. Reichman, 8 Tenn. 653, 680, 188 S.W. 225, 232 (1916) (claimed courts would not convict). See also Goodell v. Woodbury, 71 N.H. 378, 52 Atl. 855 (1902) (suggested prosecutor would not charge).

[95] Clark v. Police Board of Columbus, 10 Ohio Dec. 256, 19 Wkly. L. Bull. 341 (C.P. 1888).

sistent. Aside from those cases holding that the equal protection clause has no application to discriminatory penal enforcement,[96] the only agreement is that the prohibition is of purposeful and intentional discrimination.[97] It is probably accurate to conclude that the constitutional requirement is only that the enforcement agency refrain from using classifications impermissible to the legislature, such as race or religion, although some courts have stated other tests.[98] Wherever the line is ultimately drawn, the equal protection cases neither specifically affirm nor deny the propriety of police discretion. Rather they serve only to identify certain enforcement criteria as unconstitutional.

The exercise of discretion by the police, which seems inevitable in current criminal justice administration, continues unrecognized. In practice, policies to guide the individual officer in deciding whether to make an arrest are not formally developed within the police agency, and no sustained effort is made to subject existing practices to re-evaluation. This being so, the first step toward better understanding of the problem is identification and analysis of the criteria presently employed in practice. This is the objective of the next four chapters.

[96] See page 161.
[97] See Comment, 61 Colum. L. Rev. 1103, 1113 (1961).
[98] See page 162.

CHAPTER 4

Noninvocation Because the Legislature May Not Desire Enforcement

Because it is obviously important for criminal justice agencies to know what conduct constitutes a crime, those responsible for law enforcement often find it necessary to interpret the statutes defining such conduct. Although this process of administrative interpretation does involve the ordinary judicial techniques of construing statutes, it goes far beyond this to include other kinds of interpretation not traditionally engaged in by appellate courts.

This interpretation, which is unique to administrators of the law, is ordinarily directed toward statutes which are not ambiguous but which have in fact been drafted in overly broad language. In drafting such statutes, it may be that the legislatures are attempting to: (a) eliminate the possibility of loopholes, as is often the case with gambling statutes; (b) resolve certain enforcement problems, as is usually true in the case of vagrancy provisions; or (c) reflect the ideals rather than the immediate expectations of the community, as is the case with some legislation proscribing certain sexual conduct. An appellate court interpreting this kind of statute would be unlikely to hold that it does not mean what it says. Thus, for example, a statute prohibiting all gambling would not be interpreted by a court to allow social gambling. Yet an administrative agency, for purposes of enforcement policy, might not hesitate to conclude that the statute applies only to commercial gambling.

Some statutes drafted in unambiguous language were enacted so long ago that there may be real doubt as to whether they reflect the current attitude of the legislature. Although an appellate court would, nonetheless, be understandably reluctant to conclude that the statute is inapplicable because obsolete, an administrative agency might very well, and in appropriate cases perhaps should, make this kind of judgment.

Law enforcement agencies seldom articulate the reasons for the decisions that they do make. Because of this, analysis such as that which follows may give the impression that the process is much more orderly and consistent than it really is. The criteria identified in this analysis are helpful in understanding current practice. However, they do not reflect written policies of law enforcement agencies and, since the policies that do exist are seldom made explicit even within the enforcement agencies themselves, there is doubt as to how consistently the policies are carried out.[1]

A. AMBIGUITY IN STATUTORY LANGUAGE

Illustration No. 1: A police officer received a complaint that an itinerant salesman was selling obscene magazines. The officer examined the material objected to but was unable to determine whether such matter was covered by the rather ambiguous obscenity statute of the state. The officer refrained from making an arrest even though the salesman was about to leave the jurisdiction.

One objective of the law is to serve as a guide to behavior by defining criminal conduct with the greatest possible clarity and explicitness. This fair-warning objective is embodied in the principle of nullum crimen sine lege. Thus some criminal statutes are strictly construed, while others, impermissively vague, are sometimes invalidated. Interpretation is often based upon the literal meaning of the words rather than on evidence of legislative intention.[2] Despite this, limitations upon the effectiveness of even the most carefully selected language make it impossible to achieve a completely unambiguous definition of criminal conduct. This, together with the fact that many criminal statutes are not carefully drafted, sometimes makes it unclear whether certain conduct is within the legislative proscription.

The situation is further complicated by the fact that the legislature has deliberately delegated to the jury some of the responsibil-

---

[1] It should not be assumed that these policies have necessarily originated in the police department. While this often is the case, criteria regularly applied by other agencies in the process in making subsequent decisions sometimes influence police decisions on invocation, as noted in Chapter 3. In many instances it is not possible to determine whether the police, the prosecutor, or trial court is most responsible for the existence of the particular noninvocation policy.

[2] Indeed, there is rarely any evidence of legislative purpose available. Only the newer recodifications, which are few, typically contain supplemental legislative comments. Of the states studied, only Wisconsin has such a recodification, and it took effect during the course of observations in that state. See 5 Wis. Legis. Council, Judiciary Committee Report on the Criminal Code (1953).

On the general subject of the relationship between nullen crimen sine lege and interpretation of criminal statutes, see Hall, General Principles of Criminal Law 35-55 (2d ed. 1960).

ity for defining criminal conduct. This is true, for example, in the case of statutes which incorporate the concepts of negligence and obscenity. The definitions of these terms deliberately leave room for the jury to consider the particular standards of the community at the time the case arises. This makes even more difficult the task of the law enforcement agency, which must decide under a variety of circumstances whether conduct is criminal.

It is obviously important to determine how such criminal statutes should be interpreted by law enforcement personnel who must decide whether to arrest. There are at least two identifiable positions. On the one hand, some say that, while the canon of strict construction should be applied by courts, it should not be considered in deciding whether to arrest. Under this view, statutes would be much more broadly construed at the arrest level than at the conviction stage. This would be analogous to the situation in regard to evidence, where the requirements for arrest are less restrictive than those for conviction. Thus in both situations the criminal justice system would become more selective as the person is dealt with at successive stages in the process, and guilty persons would be less likely to benefit from erroneous interpretations by the police. Also, with the sole responsibility for this more precise interpretation being upon the courts, the decisions would be both more consistent and more visible.[3]

The contrary view is that criminal statutes ought to be strictly construed not only by the courts but also by the police.[4] Implicit in this view is an attitude that the fair-warning requirement makes it improper for persons who have engaged in conduct not clearly defined as criminal to be subjected to arrest and prosecution, even if conviction does not follow.[5]

In fact, a police officer often has alternatives other than arrest in a questionable situation. In most instances where a difficult question of statutory interpretation is presented, it is possible for him to consult the prosecutor. This is the normal practice, for ex-

---

[3] Judicial clarification cannot occur unless some uncertain cases reach the courts. Also, say the proponents of this view, "if a criminal law is . . . poorly defined . . . efforts by the police to achieve *full enforcement* should generate pressures for legislative action." Goldstein, Police Discretion Not to Invoke the Criminal Process: Low-Visibility Decisions in the Administration of Justice, 69 Yale L.J. 543, 586-587 (1960).

[4] Thus Hall cautions the police that where the law is uncertain, "the law that must be enforced is the narrow, strict interpretation of the relevant statutes and decisions." Hall, Police and Law in a Democratic Society, 28 Ind. L.J. 133, 171 (1953).

[5] Of course, conviction might follow: "Erroneous conclusions of this kind may not reach the appellate court because the legal representation available to a defendant in many criminal cases is not likely to engage in careful law research, and thus may not call into issue prevailing assumptions as to the meaning of the substantive criminal law where that law is not clearly expressed." Remington and Rosenblum, The Criminal Law and the Legislative Process, 1960 U. Ill. L.F. 481, 488.

ample, in negligence and obscenity cases.[6]   However, as in the case in the illustration, there are instances in which immediate action is needed.[7]   In these cases, to the extent that the law deals at all with police interpretation of criminal statutes, it seems to require police, for their own protection, to employ a very strict construction, particularly in doubtful cases.   If an officer is sued for false arrest, he cannot defend his action on the ground that his construction of the statute was a reasonable one.   As was held in a recent Michigan case, "An officer of justice is bound to know the law, and if he makes an arrest which the facts on which he proceeds would not justify, if true, he is a wrongdoer." [8]   The harshness of this rule is made clear in the Restatement of Torts:

> [N]o protection is given to a peace officer who, however reasonably, acts under a mistake of law other than a mistake as to the validity of a statute or ordinance.   Thus, an officer is not privileged to arrest another whom he reasonably suspects of having committed an act which the officer, through a mistake of law reasonable in one of his position, believes to be a common law felony.   So too, a peace officer is not privileged to arrest another whom he reasonably suspects of having committed an act which the officer, through a mistaken construction of a statute, believes to have been made a felony by such statute.   And this is so although the reasonable character of the officer's mistake is proved by the fact that at the time of the arrest the statute is generally understood to make such an act a felony and is not judicially construed to the contrary until after the arrest is made.[9]

Thus the law requires "certainty" in place of "reasonable cause" as to the relationship between the suspected conduct and the substantive law.[10]

---

[6] Thus, officers in the Detroit Censor Bureau were not in the habit of making arrests without first obtaining a determination from the prosecutor that the objectionable material was covered by the obscenity statute.   Similarly, complaints of questionable business practices were referred to the prosecutor's office in Detroit because of the difficult legal questions usually involved.   In Milwaukee it was also observed that those cases requiring careful statutory interpretation, e.g., negligent homicide, obscene literature, embezzlement, violations of the blue-sky laws, and other "white collar" crimes, were regularly brought to the attention of the prosecutor before arrest.

Someone other than the prosecutor may also be in a better position than the patrolman to interpret the statute.   Certain police officials, after considerable experience in a specialized agency such as one dealing exclusively with obscenity or business crimes, become very capable in this regard.

[7] See page 177.

[8] Donovan v. Guy, 347 Mich. 457, 80 N.W.2d 190 (1956).   Though this is the holding of the court, the facts of the case suggest that the court could have said that there was not even "reasonable cause" for so believing.

[9] 1 Restatement of Torts §121, Comment i (1934).

[10] As to whether the conduct in fact occurred and whether the suspect was the actor, only "reasonable cause" is required for felonies.   See Chapter 12.

Thus the police act at their peril. To the extent that this influences police conduct, it causes them not to arrest when in doubt as to the meaning of the criminal statute involved. Although knowledge of police practices in this regard is limited, it is unusual for either the prosecutor or the court to find that the police have arrested on an erroneous understanding of the statutes.[11] Perhaps one exception is the Detroit practice of making arrests for accosting and soliciting even though it is doubtful that the suspect has performed sufficient acts to constitute the offense,[12] but this particular situation is complicated by other factors which probably explain such action.[13]

B. Conduct Declared Criminal to Alleviate Administrative Problems

Illustration No. 2: A police officer came upon a "bum," a man wandering the streets clearly without any means of support. Though such conduct is explicitly proscribed by the vagrancy statute of the state, no arrest was made.

Elsewhere in this volume detailed consideration is given to the arrest and detention of persons suspected of engaging in criminal conduct. It is there noted that vagrancy or disorderly conduct statutes are sometimes used to justify detention and interrogation

---

While the police officer must make no mistakes in statutory interpretation, his understanding of constitutional law need not be as great. The arrest is valid, as to a statute later found to be unconstitutional, unless the statute is clearly, on its face, unconstitutional; e.g., Hill v. Taylor, 50 Mich. 549, 15 N.W. 899 (1883). This would appear to produce an anomalous situation, in which, if an officer arrests for conduct thought to be criminal, but the court declares the statute unconstitutional, he is protected, while, if the court should instead conclude that in order to find the statute constitutional it must construe it as not covering this conduct, the officer is liable.

11 However, sometimes cases are dismissed for policy reasons, but the reason given is that the conduct did not violate the statute. Such concealment of the actual reason is made necessary because the trial judge is not given the right to acquit the guilty. State v. Evjue, 254 Wis. 581, 37 N.W.2d 50 (1949).

12 The statute makes it a crime to "accost, solicit, or invite another in any public place, or in or from any building or vehicle, by word, gesture or any other means, to commit prostitution or to do any other lewd or immoral act." Mich. Stat. Ann. §28.703 (1938). Though the Michigan Supreme Court has not indicated exactly what acts are required, the trial courts frequently are very particular, but often for the reason stated in the preceding footnote.

13 There is a very active vice bureau in Detroit, but at least some of the Recorder's Court judges feel that the activities of this agency are too extensive. Actually, when the police are seriously interested in "making a case," they are often very careful to make sure that there has been an actual accosting, including a statement of the act to be performed and the price. But, where arrest is for purposes other than prosecution, these elements are not required. See Chapter 22.

of persons suspected of more serious crimes.[14]   While the Michigan vagrancy provision is relatively restrictive,[15] the Kansas statute covers those "found loitering without visible means of support." [16] The Wisconsin provision prior to the 1953 recodification included "persons having no visible occupation and unable to give a satisfactory account of themselves," [17] and now covers any "person found in or loitering near any structure, vehicle or private grounds who is there without the consent of the owner and is unable to account for his presence." [18]   In addition, city ordinances often include persons failing to account for their presence, persons associating with disreputable characters, and persons with bad reputations.[19]

These very broad and rather ambiguous statutory provisions cover a wide range of conduct.[20]   But, because it is believed that these statutes provide a necessary basis for the detention and investigation of suspects, no attempt is made to repeal them or to narrow their scope.[21]   Police assume that these statutes are intended primarily as aids to investigation.   Consequently, a person to whom they could be applied will normally not be arrested unless other

14 See page 354.

15 The statute, Mich. Stat. Ann. §28.364 (1938), on disorderly persons, applies to "any vagrant," but it is unclear whether persons who could not account for their presence were considered vagrants at common law.   For details, see page 356.

16 Kan. Gen. Stat. §21-2409 (1949).

17 Wis. Stat. §348.351 (1953).

18 Wis. Stat. §947.02 (1955).

19 These are set forth in detail at page 356.

20 This is not unusual.   On these statutes elsewhere, and the problems which they create, see Foote, Vagrancy-Type Law and Its Administration, 104 U. Pa. L. Rev. 603 (1956); Perkins, The Vagrancy Concept, 9 Hast. L.J. 237 (1958); Sherry, Vagrants, Rogues and Vagabonds — Old Concepts in Need of Revision, 48 Calif. L. Rev. 557 (1960); Comment, Who Is a Vagrant in California, 23 Calif. L. Rev 506 (1935); Ames, A Reply to "Who Is a Vagrant in California," Calif. L. Rev. 616 (1935); Note, Use of Vagrancy-Type Laws for Arrest and Detention of Suspicious Persons, 59 Yale L.J. 1351 (1950).

21 The recodification or other reconsideration of these provisions which does occur seems to reflect an awareness of these administrative problems, even if more clarity is achieved.   In addition to the change indicated above in the Wisconsin recodification, another section was proposed to cover "a person who loiters on the streets, whose actions give rise to suspicion of wrongdoing and who is unable to give a satisfactory account of himself." 5 Wis. Legis. Council, Judiciary Committee Report on the Criminal Code 210 (1953).   This proposal would seem to be an express recognition that the statute would be used to arrest and detain persons suspected of other criminal conduct.

When a proposed new California disorderly conduct statute was vetoed by the governor because, in repealing the prior broad and ambiguous provisions, it "unfortunately removed from police control certain dangerous conduct, regulation of which is necessary in the public interest," the draftsman then added a section to the proposal in order to cover one "who loiters or wanders upon the streets or from place to place without apparent reason or business and who refuses to identify himself and to account for his presence when requested by any peace officer so to do." Sherry, supra, at 569 n.67, 570-571.

factors make it desirable to conduct an in-custody investigation of him.[22]

C. CONDUCT DECLARED CRIMINAL TO INSURE AGAINST LOOPHOLES

Illustration No. 3: A police officer was led by a complainant to a private residence where, through a window, the occupants could be observed playing poker for money. The officer refused to take any action against the card players, although the state statute expressly covered all forms of gambling.

Undoubtedly a narrower definition of certain criminal conduct has been resisted not because of any disagreement as to what conduct ought to be subject to the criminal process, but rather because of fears that a more limited definition would create loopholes through which serious offenders could regularly escape. Thus enforcement of these statutes against the entire range of literally proscribed conduct would conflict with the real purpose of the legislature.

The gambling laws are the best illustration of this. In the jurisdictions studied, the gambling statutes are drawn in broad terms, covering all forms of gambling.[23] In this respect, they are in contrast to the optional provision in the Model Anti-Gambling Act, sponsored by the American Bar Association, which exempts from prosecution gambling which is "incidental to a bona fide social relationship, is participated in by natural persons only, and in which no person is participating, directly or indirectly, in professional gambling." [24] However, the risks inherent in this formulation were well recognized by the draftsmen:

> The Commission has also had great difficulty with this problem of finding a formula which would exclude the social or casual gambler from prosecution and punishment, yet which would not result in opening a large breach in the statute for the benefit of professional gamblers and their patrons. The Commission recognizes that it is unrealistic to promulgate a law literally aimed at making a criminal offense of the friendly election bet, the private, social card game among friends, etc. Nevertheless, it is imperative to confront the professional gambler with a statutory façade that is wholly devoid of loopholes.

22 See page 151.

23 Such broad coverage is the pattern in about half the states. 2 A.B.A., Commission on Organized Crime, Organized Crime and Law Enforcement 75 (1952). For the states studied, the applicable provisions are Kan. Gen. Stat. §21-924 (1949); Mich. Stat. Ann. §28.533 (1954); Wis. Stat. §945.02 (1955), formerly §348.092 (1953).

24 2 A.B.A., Commission on Organized Crime, Organized Crime and Law Enforcement 74 (1952).

It should be noted that the prosecuting attorneys who were asked for comment on prior drafts of the Model Act were also divided in their opinions as to the desirability of making an express exemption for the casual or social gambler. Many prosecutors were flatly opposed to any such exemption because it offered a loophole for the professional gambler.

Many state laws at the present time penalize all forms of gambling without exceptions for the social gambler. It is doubtful whether the latter has been unduly harassed under such laws.[25]

Observed practice conforms to the A.B.A. provision exempting social gambling, despite the broad language of these state statutes. There is no attempt to proceed against private dice and card games, so long as there is no house "cut" and no evidence of a syndicate operation.[26]

The police do experience some difficulty, however, in drawing a line between social gambling and professional gambling. Generally, gambling occurring in private homes is exempted from enforcement,[27] as was the case in the illustration, but the police must assure themselves that a professional game has not been moved into a private home in order to give the appearance of a social gathering. One tactic used by Detroit police when they are called to such a gathering is to take a number of the persons in the group aside and ask them to identify all other members of the group. This device, to some extent, allows the police to distinguish the gathering of a group of friends from the professional operations at which customers come and go at intervals and are not socially acquainted.

Gambling outside private homes is generally proceeded against unless it is clearly social in nature.[28] Professional gambling in so-

25 Id. at 75.

26 Generally, the fact that the operator of the game taking the cut is a church, veteran, or nationality group organization is not considered sufficient to characterize it as social in nature. This would seem to be in accord with the A.B.A. distinction. However, some leniency may be shown where the game is for a charitable purpose, though there may also well be other compelling reasons for enforcement in such a case. See page 147. While Wisconsin is most strict in this regard, the law is still occasionally not enforced against charitable groups, though unfavorable newspaper comment may follow in such cases. For example, the Milwaukee Journal of July 18, 1956, alleged that the sheriff of Grant County had been present at a Fourth of July picnic at which dice games and bingo were played, and asserted that the sheriff had said he was not sure it was up to him to enforce the anti-gambling laws. This is one instance of local law enforcement officials viewing gambling as the sole responsibility of the State Beverage and Cigarette Tax Division agents, though the statutes expressly state that this is not the case. Wis. Stat. §73.035 (1955).

27 Some states have attempted by statute to exempt such gambling, e.g., Mont. Rev. Codes §94-2403 (1947), excluding "all private homes."

28 Gambling tolerated in private homes may not be tolerated elsewhere, even though in private. Wichita detectives, in a hotel on another matter, overheard three men engaged in a crap game in a room, and arrested them although only ten cents

called private clubs is a subject of strict enforcement, although detection is difficult.[29]   Some uncertainty has been expressed, however, as to whether minor gambling in such places as pool halls ought to be looked upon as social or commercial.   It is not professional in the sense of any substantial income to the proprietor of the establishment.   He will collect a small sum from the players for the use of the table, but may receive no portion of the gambling money directly.   While this situation comes to the attention of the police fairly frequently during routine inspection of such licensed premises, arrest is not likely so long as the social aspects outweigh the professional aspects.   It is usually recognized that such activity is the equivalent of social gambling engaged in at home by persons higher in the community class structure.[30]

Illustration No. 4: A game warden came upon a hunter carrying a rifle in a closed hunting area.   Under the fish and game laws, the presence of a person with a gun in such an area in itself constitutes a violation.   However, it was decided not to arrest when the warden learned the hunter was not familiar with the country and apparently had made a mistake as to his location.

A legislative desire to eliminate loopholes is probably a major reason for the great mass of criminal statutes imposing liability without regard to criminal intent.[31]   Despite the broad language of such statutes, enforcement is characteristically limited to those

---

was involved and the men said it was just a "friendly little game."   Perhaps the fact that the conduct was not private enough, in that it could be overheard in the corridor, was a contributing factor.

29 For some of the consequences of this, see Chapter 24.

30 The Michigan police on one occasion arrested eight persons engaged in minor gambling in a pool hall, but the prosecutor promptly refused a warrant, on the basis that this type of activity was taking place in many homes in the area.   It was intimated that the police intended to make no more such arrests in the future.

In one enforcement study it was noted that the kind of gambling against which the process was not invoked was that sanctified by the tradition of the people in the area.   Esselstyn, Crime and Its Control in the Hinterland 201 (unpublished Ph.D. thesis, New York Univ. 1952).   Elsewhere it has been observed that this tendency may go so far as to result in nonenforcement against the numbers racket because this kind of gambling fits the prevailing pattern of behavior of the people involved. Whyte, Street Corner Society 135 (2d ed. 1955).   From the observations in the three jurisdictions studied, it did not appear that any such criterion was applied where there was a serious problem of professionalism.   Thus, while playing the numbers is part of the usual behavior pattern of some minority groups in Detroit, there is vigorous enforcement against this conduct, just as there is against horse race "books" and other gambling operations of a clearly professional nature.

31 Attempts to justify strict liability statutes on this ground have been severely criticized in that "the convenience of investigators and prosecutors is not, in any event, the prime consideration in determining what conduct is criminal."   See Hall, General Principles of Criminal Law 342-351 (2d ed. 1960); Hart, The Aims of the Criminal Law, 23 Law & Contemp. Prob. 401, 423 (1958).

instances where there is an indication of unlawful intent.[32]   Enforcement of these statutes is usually the responsibility of a specialized regulatory agency rather than of the police, and these enforcement agencies are often more willing to give explicit recognition to their discretionary policies in the utilization of the broadly worded statutes[33] than are the police.

> *Illustration No. 5:* A Negro informed a police officer that he had just been refused service in a nearby restaurant. The officer accompanied the complainant to the establishment, where the proprietor admitted the charge. The officer then advised the proprietor of the state civil rights law, which makes it a misdemeanor to refuse public accommodations on the basis of race, creed, or color. When the proprietor then agreed to serve the Negro, the officer took no further action.

Police will not invoke the criminal process in some circumstances unless the violator was actually aware that his conduct was prohibited by the criminal law. However, with some minor limitations,[34] the legislature does have the power to punish persons who have violated laws of which they are ignorant. Indeed, the doctrine of ignorantia juris neminem excusat makes this the rule unless a contrary legislative intention appears.[35] This doctrine is

[32] See Remington and Rosenblum, The Criminal Law and the Legislative Process, 1960 U. Ill. L.F. 481, 490 n.26, for an objection by one law enforcement officer to the requiring of intent to commit a burglary in the Wisconsin burglarious tools statute.

In Michigan there is a statute prohibiting the carrying of a concealed weapon and another prohibiting carrying a concealed weapon with intent to use the same unlawfully. While the penalties are the same, the prosecutor's office will prosecute only for the latter. It might be that this is a case of an enforcement policy narrower than possible under a broad statute. While the police do not completely concur in the attitude of the prosecutor's office, it may well be that there is no real disagreement in the limitation of enforcement to unlawful intent cases, but only lack of agreement as to what cases sufficiently suggest unlawful intent to warrant prosecution.

[33] Enforcement practices of these agencies were not observed. However, a study made of the administration of the Wisconsin Food and Drug Act concluded: "In actual effect then the principal functional significance of the liability without fault character of the food and drug sections is not to make possible wholesale convictions of inadvertent offenders untinted by subjective fault; it is rather to provide widened areas of administrative discretion within which the department of agriculture can administer and enforce the regulations with greater flexibility and effectiveness than would be possible if proof of subjective fault were necessary." Comment, 1956 Wis. L. Rev. 625, 655. The illustrative case in the text is found therein at 665.

[34] Lambert v. California, 355 U.S. 225, 78 Sup. Ct. 240, 2 L. Ed. 2d 228 (1957), held that ignorance of the law should have been recognized as a defense because the proscribed conduct (failure of a "convicted person" to register with the police in accordance with a Los Angeles ordinance) was an omission.

[35] The legislature can declare such intention: "If the legislature cannot, in good conscience, regard conduct which it wishes to forbid as wrongful in itself, then it has always the option of declaring the conduct to be criminal only when the actor knows of its criminality or recklessly disregards the possibility that it is criminal. For knowing or reckless disregard of legal obligation affords an independent basis of blameworthiness justifying the actor's condemnation as a criminal, even when his

often rationalized on the ground that effective administration of justice requires such a presumption[36] because it is difficult to prove knowledge of the law. Although in some situations ignorance of the law is due to the neglect of the individual defendant, in other cases failure to know the law is understandable and excusable, so that it is not surprising to find enforcement policy reflecting the opinion that the relevant statute ought to be applied only where it is fair to do so.[37] This policy rests upon the assumption that the legislature desired actual enforcement of the statute only against offenders who knew or should have known that the conduct was prohibited.[38]

Noninvocation because the offender did not know his conduct was criminal occurs more often with specialized enforcement agen-

conduct was not intrinsically antisocial. It is convenient to use the word 'wilful' to describe this mode of culpability, although the term is by no means regularly so limited in conventional usage." Hart, The Aims of the Criminal Law, 23 Law & Contemp. Prob. 401, 418 (1958).

[36] Thus Austin contended that the doctrine was required because it was impossible to determine the relevant issue. "Whether the party was *really* ignorant of the law, and was *so* ignorant of its provisions, could scarcely be determined by any evidence accessible to others." As to showing that the defendant was ignorant in not being aware, it would be "incumbent upon the tribunal to unravel his previous history, and to search his whole life for the elements of a just solution." 1 Austin, Lectures on Jurisprudence 498-499 (4th ed. 1879). "Without it justice could not be administered in our tribunals." 1 Bishop, Criminal Law 197 (9th ed. 1923). For an excellent discussion of the doctrine and its rationale see Hall, General Principles of Criminal Law 376-414 (2d ed. 1960).

[37] Pound has criticized the "covering up" of cases where persons ignorant of the law are excused by conviction and pardon (as in the classic case of Rex v. Bailey) or by employing unwarranted presumptions and fictions. Pound, Discretion, Dispensation and Mitigation: The Problem of the Individual Special Case, 35 N.Y.U.L. Rev. 925, 936 (1960). Thus he would allow exculpation for the express reason of lack of knowledge of the law, where appropriate, and perhaps he would approve of noninvocation on this score.

The Model Penal Code would recognize a limited defense here, allowing the defendant to show "by a preponderance of evidence" that he believed his conduct did not "legally constitute an offense" and that "the statute or other enactment defining the offense is not known to the actor and has not been published or otherwise reasonably made available to him prior to the conduct alleged." Model Penal Code §2.04(3) and (4) (Proposed Official Draft, 1962).

[38] But when might the legislature not intend enforcement where the actor is unaware of the relevant substantive provision? Ignorance of the law, it is said, should hardly be excused as to acts "immoral regardless of the actor's ignorance of their being legally forbidden (e.g., the felonies and principal misdemeanors)." Hall, General Principles of Criminal Law 403 (2d ed. 1960). This view might be considered "a demand that every responsible member of the community understand and respect the community's moral values." Hart, The Aims of the Criminal Law, 23 Law & Contemp. Prob. 401, 419 (1958). However, the theorists add that knowledge of the law should be essential to culpability "where normal conscience (moral attitudes) and understanding cannot be relied upon to avoid the forbidden conduct." Hall, *supra*, at 404. To some, the latter group includes those offenses "merely mala prohibita," while others would attempt a more subtle distinction. Compare Hart, *supra*, at 419, with Hall, *supra*, at 402-406.

cies than with a regular police department, as "it is a frequent practice in the exercise of [business regulations] for field investigators to lay the foundation for future successful prosecution by establishing knowledge of regulations." [39] But the police sometimes have occasion to do likewise, as in the above illustration involving the civil rights law. The applicable statute, the Michigan Civil Rights Law, does not stipulate that offenders be arrested only if they have refused to comply after notice of this law,[40] although the Detroit Police Manual does instruct the officer receiving such a complaint to go to the establishment and

> . . . advise the alleged violator of the substance of the Civil Rights or Equal Accommodations Law. He shall also advise both the complaintant and alleged violator of their responsibilities and rights, and shall urge the compliance with the law.[41]

However, the language in the manual goes on to make it appear that the process should be invoked whether there is compliance or not (which seems to make the purpose of the above procedure unclear). But the actual practice of the department is not to proceed when the proprietor agrees to comply.

Other cases of noninvocation because of the offender's unfamiliarity with the law may occur from time to time without any such formal policy, especially where the relevant criminal statute is new or not widely known.[42]

D. Conduct Declared Criminal in Order to Reflect the Ideals of the Community

Illustration No. 6: A local welfare director presented positive proof to the police that a local welfare recipient was engaging in an adulterous relationship. Notwithstanding a repetition of the complaint on another occasion, the police refrained from taking any action against the violator.

The criminal law may often be both a command to the general public and a mandate to those who enforce the law. However, some criminal statutes appear to be "state-declared ideals" rather than definitions of conduct which is to be routinely subjected to

---

[39] Hall, *supra,* at 350. Empirical data to support this conclusion have been gathered for one of the jurisdictions of this study. See Comment, 1956 Wis. L. Rev. 625.

[40] Mich. Stat. Ann. §§28.343, 28.344 (1938).

[41] Detroit Police Dept., Revised Police Manual, chap. 16, §24 (1955).

[42] Thus police in one city excused an instance of driving the wrong way on a newly designated one-way street. But this informal policy appeared to be restricted to drivers who (a) probably were not aware of the change and (b) had used the street before so as to have recollection of its being a two-way street (which apparently was thought to offset the fact that the one-way sign had not been observed).

penal sanction.[43]   It is said that certain lawmaking is intended to educate, to guide the individual conscience, but is not intended to be used to coerce compliance.[44]   The wisdom of using the criminal law for this purpose is frequently questioned, on the grounds that this educational objective cannot be realized and also that it compounds the difficulties of law enforcement.[45]   Yet it has been practically impossible to repeal these provisions.   As Thurman Arnold has written: "Most unenforced criminal laws survive in order to satisfy moral objections to established modes of conduct.   They are unenforced because we want to continue our conduct, and unrepealed because we want to preserve our morals." [46]

The observation that these laws are not enforced is not a new one.   It has been made repeatedly over the years,[47] although opinion differs as to whether the responsibility lies upon the legis-

---

[43] Pound, Criminal Justice in America 67 (1930).

[44] "The Puritan conceived of laws simply as guides to the individual conscience. The individual will was not to be coerced. . . . But as all men's consciences were not enlightened, laws were proper to set men to thinking, to declare to them what their fellows thought on this point and that, and to afford guides to those whose consciences did not speak with assurance. . . . [M]any still think of law after the Puritan fashion."   Pound, The Limits of Effective Legal Action, 3 A.B.A.J. 55, 69 (1917).
One might query whether legislation declaring it a crime to use artificial birth control devices, certainly an expression of the moral and religious views of a substantial segment of the community, known by the legislature to be completely unenforced but continued in effect notwithstanding numerous bills asking for repeal, is an illustration of just such a view of the law.   See Poe v. Ullman, 367 U.S. 497, 81 Sup. Ct. 1752, 6 L. Ed. 2d 989, *rehearing denied,* 368 U.S. 869, 82 Sup. Ct. 21, 7 L. Ed. 2d 69 (1961).

[45] "However impressive the state-declared ideal may be to the contemplative observer, the spectacle of statutory precepts with penal sanctions, which are not and perhaps are not intended to be put in force in practice, casts doubt upon the whole penal code and educates in disrespect for law more than the high pronouncement can educate for virtue."   Pound, Criminal Justice in America 67 (1930).   See also Pound, The Limits of Effective Legal Action, 3 A.B.A.J. 55 (1917); Taft, The Legislature and the Execution of the Laws, 12 Rep. Pa. Bar Assn. 239 (1906).   Compare: "Admitting that these moral qualities cannot be legislated into human beings by *fiat* of the State, does it necessarily follow that such legislation is futile and meddlesome? In other words, where legislation holds men to certain standards of conduct which have moral implications, must it be said that the purpose of such legislation is to instill into them the moral qualities on which such standards are based, and that since moral qualities cannot be created by law, the legislation is therefore bad? . . .   In other words, the aim of the law is not to accomplish the hopeless task of altering human character, but merely to insist on conformity of conduct to a standard deemed advisable for the protection of the other individuals who compose the community."   Dickinson, Legislation and the Effectiveness of Law, 37 Rep. Pa. Bar Assn. 337, 348-349 (1931).

[46] Arnold, The Symbols of Government 160 (1935).   See also Cohen, Positivism and Idealism in the Law, 27 Colum. L. Rev. 237, 246 (1927).

[47] See quotation from the seventeenth-century philosopher Spinoza in Cohen, id. at 246, for early recognition of this.   See also Arnold, *supra,* at 160; Pound, Criminal Justice in America 67 (1930).

lators for making laws without regard to the practicalities of enforcement[48] or upon the nonenforcing administrators.[49]

Some sexual conduct between adults, although engaged in by mutual consent and not seriously abnormal or homosexual, is made criminal. Although few of these violations actually come to the attention of the police, there is ample evidence of a pattern of nonenforcement in each of the three states studied. Of these states, only Wisconsin has a fornication statute prohibiting single isolated acts of intercourse between nonmarried adults,[50] but this conduct is no more a matter of official concern in Wisconsin than in the other two states.[51] Intercourse with the spouse of another is a criminal act in all three states,[52] though in Michigan an adultery prosecution may be brought only upon complaint of the husband or wife of one of the adulterers.[53] But arrest for adultery is very

[48] "Successfully to understand the science of practical lawmaking requires close observation of the nature, customs and traditions of the people to be affected by the laws, the degree of efficiency of the persons to be charged with their execution, the method by which such executives are to be selected, the difficulties with which those violating the laws may be brought to justice, and many other circumstances . . . The tendency of Legislatures in the enactment of such laws is to pass them and then rid themselves of the responsibilities for their enforcement by saying that the duty of enforcement rests on the executive and not on the legislative branch." Taft, The Legislature and the Execution of the Laws, 12 Rep. Pa. Bar Assn. 244-245 (1906).

[49] "If we thus come to the conclusion that in the last analysis the effectiveness of law depends not so much on the nature of the subject-matter dealt with as on the particular forces of support or opposition which from time to time make for or against the enforcement of the law, it seems impossible to say that legislation is futile merely for the reason that is deals with this or that subject-matter. . . . What we need rather is to say that legislation is useless if no honest and sincere attempt is made to enforce it; but when that is the case the blame belongs to the administrative departments charged with enforcing the law, and not to the Legislature which enacted it." Dickinson, Legislation and the Effectiveness of Law, 37 Rep. Pa. Bar Assn. 337, 355 (1931).

[50] Wis. Stat. §944.15 (1955). This recodification broadened the prior statute, Wis. Stat. §351.05 (1953), under which only a single woman could be guilty of fornication, while a man, married or single, could be guilty if he had intercourse with a single woman. State v. Roberts, 169 Wis. 570, 173 N.W. 310 (1919).

Twenty-eight states consider single, isolated acts of sexual intercourse as no crime at all. Bensing, A Comparative Study of American Sex Statutes, 42 J. Crim. L., C. & P.S. 57, 69 (1951).

[51] This is not to say, however, that no fornication arrests, prosecutions, or convictions occur. But, if they do, it is most likely for one of the reasons set forth in Chapter 7. See an example of this in Remington and Rosenblum, The Criminal Law and the Legislative Process, 1960 U. Ill. L.F. 481, 493-494.

[52] Kan. Gen. Stat. §21-908 (1949); Mich. Stat. Ann. §28.218 (1938); Wis. Stat. §944.16 (1955), formerly Wis. Stat. §351.01 (1953), except that under the old section an unmarried woman was not considered to be committing adultery if she had intercourse with a married man.

Thirteen states do not punish isolated acts of adultery. Bensing, A Comparative Study of American Sex Statutes, 42 J. Crim. L., C. & P.S. 57, 67 (1951).

[53] Mich. Stat. Ann. §28.220 (1938). It would not appear that complaint of the spouse is a prerequisite to arrest, however. The issue is one of whether a police officer, upon discovery of a couple engaged in adulterous conduct, may make an

unusual, even when the police receive a complaint from an offended spouse[54] or another official agency.[55]   Finally, all three states prohibit the continuous act of cohabitation by unmarried persons, and in Kansas and Michigan the conduct need not be open and notorious to be considered a crime.[56]   The police do not regularly proceed against this conduct in any of the three states except in cases of substantially notorious cohabitation, and even then usually only when the conduct is thought to deviate considerably from the moral standard of the group involved.[57]

E. Conduct Presently Defined as Criminal Only Because of Legislative Inaction

Illustration No. 7: A police officer came upon a merchant who was operating his business on Sunday. Such conduct was prohibited by a Sunday blue law, passed in 1860, covering all gainful employment. The officer knew that for years merchants had operated on Sundays without complaint and without enforcement of this law. No action was taken.

---

arrest and afterward determine the desires of the offended spouse as to prosecution. This happened in People v. Payment, 109 Mich. 553, 67 N.W. 689 (1896), but the court did not determine the validity of the arrest. Rather it was noted that since a proper complaint was later made the conviction in the case could not be attacked. Because "the complaint required by statute is not an element of the offense, but . . . a condition to its prosecution," People v. Isham, 109 Mich. 72, 75, 67 N.W. 819, 821 (1896), it would seem that such an arrest would be proper. Though such action seems unlikely in view of the usual decision not to invoke, it might be deemed necessary for one of the reasons set forth in Chapter 7.

54 For example, a policewoman in the Wayne County, Michigan, Sheriff's Department was heard to tell a telephone caller, "If you don't sign a delinquency complaint there's not much we can do for you." The policewoman explained that the caller had found his wife and his sixteen-year-old daughter together with two young men in an automobile behind the tavern he owned, all engaged in sexual intercourse. She said that the complainant had called once before and was told at that time that the only possible crime involved was contributing to the delinquency of a minor.

55 A local police chief in a rural Wisconsin county recalled that the district attorney had told the police during training sessions that the laws against fornication and adultery were not to be enforced. This chief later received an adultery complaint from the director of welfare concerning a local welfare recipient, but hesitated to take any action. When the director made a second complaint the chief invited him to accompany him to the district attorney. The district attorney, after hearing the complaint, said, "You two fellows forget about this. Anyone can do that in this county and we're not going to do anything about it."

56 The Michigan statute, §28.567, is directed toward unmarried persons who "lewdly and lasciviously associate and cohabit together." People v. Smith, 231 Mich. 221, 203 N.W. 869 (1925). The Kansas statute does not require open cohabitation, Kan. Gen. Stat. §21-908 (1949), whereas the Wisconsin provision does, Wis. Stat. §944.20 (1955), formerly Wis. Stat. §351.04 (1953).

57 Thus police regularly became aware of such cohabitation while investigating complaints in the Negro areas of Detroit, but no arrests were made.

It would be incorrect to assume that existing criminal statutes reflect the current attitude of the legislature. Hundreds of laws are added to the statute books each year, so that today's criminal law contains many provisions which were enacted because of "the mood that dominated a tribunal or a legislature at strategic moments in the past, a flurry of public excitement on some single matter, the imitative aspects of so much of our penal legislation." [58] Although many of these statutes are forgotten in time, few are repealed, and over a period of years a great mass of obsolete legislation accumulates.

Legislative failure to bring the criminal law up to date is common in the United States. Time and energy are devoted instead to issues thought to be of more current importance and to activities more responsive to public demands. Those few states which have accomplished recodification have done so only after very substantial periods of operation under admittedly obsolete statutes.[59] Even these states have not exercised all the obsolete provisions, as a majority of the statutes carrying penal sanctions are usually found outside the criminal code itself.

Police of the three states do not arrest for conduct which violates statutes thought to be obsolete. Although no attempt has been made to categorize those provisions which the police consider out of date, comparison of the range of conduct defined as criminal in the statutes with conduct actually proceeded against leaves no doubt that there are many existing laws which the police do not enforce. This police inaction is often based upon the supposition that the statute would be repealed if the issue were presented to the legislature. Thus, if the police are correct in their belief, there is here, as in the situations described previously, no difference in policy judgment between the legislature and the police.[60]

Statutes are still a part of the enforceable criminal law notwith-

[58] Wechsler, The Challenge of a Model Penal Code, 65 Harv. L. Rev. 1097, 1101 (1952).

[59] Thus the 1953 Wisconsin revision, which had among its objectives "simplifying the criminal law by removing obsolete material," was accomplished as to a body of laws which had not been thoroughly revised since their enactment in 1847. See 5 Wis. Legis. Council, Judiciary Committee Report on the Criminal Code ii (1953). Similarly, the 1961 Illinois revision was the first over-all revision of their criminal code since 1874, though in 1931 the Judicial Council had reported to the governor and assembly the acute need for revision because of outdated laws, and though the state bar had presented drafts to the assembly in 1935, 1937, and 1939. Illinois State & Chicago Bar Associations' Joint Committee to Revise the Illinois Criminal Code, Proposed Illinois Revised Criminal Code of 1961, pp. 3-4 (1960).

[60] Furthermore, the level of nonenforcement of the obsolete law does not appear to change significantly in relation to the amount of enforcement resources provided, so this situation cannot be classified with those in the following chapter.

standing their age.[61]   A legislative enactment does not become inoperative by nonuse or obsolescence, nor is it repealed by the failure of the administrators to enforce it.[62]   Such statutes can be
enforced and, in the opinion of some, should be enforced in order
to provoke the legislature to repeal them if they no longer represent the legislative intention.   Though addressed to judicial nonenforcement, the following quotation states this position:

> If the judiciary, influenced doubtless by the sincerest motives for
> the public welfare, did not tend to assume a quasi-legislative atti-
> tude in the interpretation and application of enactments of this
> character, the popular demand would necessitate the repeal of the
> laws in question. . . . Where the law, as declared, is jcdicially
> conformed to accord with the people's will, as conceived by the
> court, the generality of people remain in ignorance of their repre-
> sentatives' actual declarations.   There is a necessary fiction in the
> administration of justice that all men know the law.   The citizen
> who gains an actual knowledge of a law through its application to
> his own case and is dissatisfied therewith, may vote to compass its

[61] It is interesting to note that Justice Frankfurter, speaking for the majority in
the recent case of Poe v. Ullman, 367 U.S. 497, 81 Sup. Ct. 1752, 6 L. Ed. 2d 989,
(1961), held that some actual threat of enforcement is necessary to raise the issue
of the constitutionality of the criminal statute, presumably in the view that no one
is otherwise in sufficient jeopardy to give him standing to raise the issue. This may
mean either that someone actually must be prosecuted, a substantial imposition on
the individual, or that no issue is raised as to the constitutionality of an apparently
obsolete statute until the enforcement officials give adequate warning of their intention to enforce. The latter interpretation would seem to require administrative
notice of a purpose to take the statute out of its obsolete status prior to its use.

[62] District of Columbia v. John R. Thompson Co., 346 U.S. 100, 73 Sup. Ct. 1007,
97 L. Ed. 1480 (1953) (where it was no defense that the statute apparently had not
been enforced for 78 years); Jayhawk Construction Co. v. Topeka, 176 Kan. 517, 271
P.2d 769 (1954); Board of County Road Commissioners v. Michigan Public Service
Commission, 349 Mich. 663, 85 N.W.2d 134 (1957); 1 Sutherland, Statutory Construc
tion §2034 (3d ed. 1943).

"On the Continent there was some speculation during the middle ages as to
whether a law could become inoperative through long-continued desuetude. In
England, however, the idea of prescription and the acquisition or loss of rights
merely by the lapse of a particular length of time found little favour. . . . There
was consequently no room for any theory that statutes might become obsolete."
Plucknett, A Concise History of the Common Law 301 (2d ed. 1936).

A clear pattern of nonenforcement, however, may make it impossible for the statute's constitutionality to be challenged in court. Poe v. Ullman, 367 U.S. 497, 81
Sup. Ct. 1752, 6 L. Ed. 2d 989 (1961). Harlan, in dissent, said: "Indeed it appears
that whereas appellants would surely have been entitled to review were this a new
statute, . . . the State here is enabled to maintain at least some substantial measure
of compliance with this statute and still obviate any review in this Court, by the
device of purely discretionary prosecutorial inactivity." 367 U.S. at 537-538, 81 Sup.
Ct. at 1774, 6 L. Ed. 2d at 1016.

On the matter of obsolete statutes generally, see Bonfield, The Abrogation of
Penal Statutes by Nonenforcement, 49 Iowa L. Rev. 389 (1964).

repeal. Knowledge in this regard is power. There is no more certain manner in which this knowledge can be disseminated than by the literal application and enforcement of all statutes by the courts.[63]

Whether such strategy would be effective is not certain. Some, doubting that the legislature would thus be stimulated to action, declare that only by discretionary action in administration of the law can we be freed from the ideas of past generations.[64] Even if strict enforcement had the desired effect on the legislature, perhaps the harm to the persons who would be arrested could not be justified by the good which might be achieved in terms of law revision:

> . . . too many people have come to rely on the nonenforcement of too many "obsolete" laws to justify the embarrassment, discomfort, and misery which would follow implementation of *full enforcement* programs for every crime. *Full enforcement* is a program for the future, . . . when the states . . . enact new criminal codes clearing the books of obsolete offenses.[65]

One court has expressed the opinion that if law enforcement officers were to to proceed to enforce a statute which has long remained unenforced, and to which it has become a matter of custom not to comply, it would amount to "a decision legislative in character," which is therefore not correctly theirs to make.[66]   The

63 Mitchell, Legislative and Judicial Desiderata, 25 Rep. N.Y.S.B.A. 289, 300-301 (1902). See also Hayek, The Constitution of Liberty 155 (1960); Goldstein, Police Discretion Not to Invoke the Criminal Process: Low-Visibility Decisions in the Administration of Justice, 69 Yale L.J. 543, 586-587 (1960); Williams, Turning a Blind Eye, 1954 Crim. L. Rev. (Eng.) 271, 273.

64 Pound, Criminal Justice in America 42 (1930).

65 Goldstein, Police Discretion Not to Invoke the Criminal Process: Low-Visibility Decisions in the Administration of Justice, 69 Yale L.J. 543, 588 (1960).

66 In Thompson v. District of Columbia, 92 App. D.C. 34, 203 F.2d 579 (D.C. Cir. 1953), the court, although holding a criminal statute on refusal to serve a Negro unenforceable on other grounds, added: "But we think it appropriate to comment, in this connection, that the enactments having lain unenforced for 78 years, in the face of a custom of race disassociation in the District, the decision of the municipal authorities to enforce them now, by the prosecution of the instant case, was, in effect, a decision legislative in character. That is to say, it was a determination that the enactments reflect a social policy which is now correct, although it was not correct — else the enactments would have been enforced — heretofore. Such a decision were better left, we think, to the Congress." 92 App. D.C. at 48, 203 F.2d at 592.

Compare United States v. Morton Salt Co., 338 U.S. 632, 647-648, 70 Sup. Ct. 357, 366, 94 L. Ed. 401, 413 (1950), in which the Supreme Court observed: "The fact that powers have been unexercised well may call for close scrutiny as to whether they exist; but if granted, they are not lost by being allowed to lie dormant, any more than nonexistent powers can be prescripted by an unchallenged exercise."

Similarly, another court declared: "The Anglo-Saxon sheds statutes which grow obsolete and obnoxious the same as a snake sheds his skin. He has seldom bothered

rationale of this position would seem to be that legislative acquiescence in the long-continued practice of nonenforcement amounts
to a legislative decision that enforcement is no longer desired.[67]

to repeal them as every one acquainted with the history of laws very well knows.
No citizen any longer makes a complaint under them [or observes them], and thus
they become dead letter laws. It is not the business of the police to revive them.
They are not employed and paid by the citizens for any such purpose." People
ex rel. Poole v. Hesterburg, 43 Misc. 510, 513, 89 N.Y. Supp. 498, 500 (Sup. Ct. 1904).

[67] One must assume that this opinion applies only to cases in which the continued
practice of nonenforcement of a particular statute, and the legislative acquiescence
in this practice, are based on its supposed obsoleteness and not on considerations
of conservation of resources, expediency, or the greater urgency of other concerns.

CHAPTER 5

Noninvocation Because of Limited
Enforcement Resources

There are not sufficient resources available to the police for them to proceed against all the conduct which the legislature may actually desire subjected to enforcement. As a consequence, discretion must be exercised in deciding how to allocate the resources that do exist. As Thurman Arnold has said, to deny discretion at this point would be "like directing a general to attack the enemy on all fronts at once." [1] The police and other enforcement agencies are given the general responsibility for maintaining law and order under a body of criminal law defining the various kinds of conduct against which they may properly proceed. They are then furnished with enforcement resources less than adequate to accomplish the entire task. Consequently, discretionary enforcement occurs in an attempt to obtain the best results from these limited means. In this sense, the budgetary appropriation is an establishment of policy (the general level of enforcement for which the public is willing to pay) and an indirect delegation of power by the legislative to the administrative branch.[2]

Much of the criminal conduct coming to the attention of the police does not lead to arrest. Often a warning is given; this is the form of action least demanding on available enforcement resources.[3] Though warnings are generally issued on a haphazard

[1] Arnold, The Symbols of Government 153 (1935).

[2] See Wilson, Police Planning 20 (2d ed. 1957).

[3] In this analysis, warning is not considered a form of invocation of the process. Warning might be viewed as one kind of invocation, inasmuch as the offender learns that his violation has come to official attention and the warning, hopefully, serves to prevent future offenses. However, no established policy exists with regard to the issuance of a warning, except that some police manuals state that a warning may be given for "minor offenses." See note 8 *infra*. It is generally quite an arbitrary matter whether a decision not to invoke, as the phrase is used here, is accompanied by a warning. Thus any attempt to select for separate discussion decisions to invoke by warning would tend to give a distorted picture of current practice.

basis, they are regularly used in some situations where the conduct is thought not serious enough to justify an arrest.

Even more serious offenses do not necessarily lead to arrest, however. This may occur, for example, when the police view the conduct as conforming to the normal standards of the group involved; when the victim is not seriously interested in prosecution; or when the victim's plight, considering his own misconduct, is not thought worthy of official attention. Factors such as these influence the police in their adjustment of enforcement priorities.[4]

Before discussing the particular criteria employed, one general observation can be made. Although police decisions not to arrest do lessen the burden upon the prosecutor's office, the courts, the prisons, and the correctional agencies, there is no evidence to indicate that they are especially prompted by this consideration.[5] Rather, the practice of not arresting is generally adopted to conserve *police* resources, either those which would be used to arrest, book, and detain the suspect or those necessarily involved later in the process, such as for police testimony at the trial.

This is not to say that the predictable action at later stages of the process has no bearing on police allocation of enforcement resources. Police may not arrest if they believe that there is no likelihood of prosecution or conviction. Also, if the predictable punishment is thought to be either too strict or too lenient, arrest is less likely unless the police have means of influencing the nature of the penalty.[6] Finally, if the conduct is such that it is thought

---

[4] Of course, not all police attempts to allocate law enforcement resources take the form of decisions on whether or not to arrest a particular offender. Priorities of enforcement are largely set by the manner in which a particular police agency is organized. An examination of the distribution of manpower among specialized sub-agencies may be particularly revealing in this respect.

[5] Criticism of police lack of consideration for these other agencies was noted only once. A judge of Recorder's Court, Detroit, was critical of the police going into a bar to arrest a drunk, and said: "If the police did this in every bar in Detroit they would have time for nothing else, and if they did the jails would not hold all the drunks."

[6] Thus if the officer views the punishment as too severe, he may attempt to have a lesser offense charged. In Wisconsin, the officer can often significantly alter the possible punishment by channeling the case through the ordinance violation process rather than the state statute process. Since city ordinance violations in Wisconsin are not criminal, they involve no jail sentence, and the fines are correspondingly lower than those for violations of state statutes. Conversely, in more serious cases, particularly in those involving second offenders, the person may be charged under the state statutes because the officer thinks that time in jail will be beneficial.

The Michigan State Police indicated that they were able to influence the penalty by their choice of the justice of the peace to whom they sent the violator. Thus, if they felt the violation was not serious enough to warrant the usual penalty, they would send the violator to a lenient justice. Conversely, if they desired a more severe penalty, the offender would be sent to a justice who usually imposed such penalties.

that the criminal process cannot provide the appropriate punishment, deterrence, or rehabilitation, the police may again devote their resources to other cases.[7] Combinations of these factors will appear in the situations which follow.

A. TRIVIAL OFFENSES

Police manuals often advise the officer that warning rather than arrest is appropriate when only minor violations are concerned.[8] This has the effect of conserving enforcement resources for more serious conduct.

1. *Traffic violations.*

Illustration No. 1: A police officer saw a motorist make an illegal left turn. The officer stopped the driver, brought the violation to his attention, but did not make an arrest and did not write a ticket.

The use of a warning rather than making an arrest or issuing a ticket is common in cases involving minor traffic offenses. Indeed, the discretion which the officer has the power to exercise in such cases is so well known to the motoring public that an individual motorist is likely to protest if arrested or given a ticket.[9] The practical necessity for the warning alternative in traffic cases

---

[7] The police may consider the alternative methods available. The conduct may be best dealt with by a private agency of a civic, recreational, religious, educational, or welfare nature, or by a governmental agency not under the criminal justice system.

Where the conduct calls for penal treatment, it would appear that it could be effectively dealt with by the criminal administration process. However, the distinction between penal treatment and the administration of welfare services is often not clear, even in theory. See Allen, The Borderland of the Criminal Law: Problems of "Socializing" Criminal Justice, 32 Social Serv. Rev. 107 (1958). Even when welfare services are called for, law enforcement agencies may have to handle the situation because of a lack of appropriate public or private welfare facilities. Thus Allen notes that unmarried pregnant women were convicted when they were unable to pay for the necessary hospital expenses and the subsequent care of the child, so that the burden was shifted to the state. Id. at 109.

[8] Detroit and Milwaukee police are cautioned that "a polite warning" will suffice for "minor offenses" and that arrests should not be made in such cases unless the violations are "willful or repeated." Detroit Police Dept., Revised Police Manual, chap. 16, §34 (1955); Milwaukee Police Dept., Rules & Regulations, Rule 30, §31 (1950). Wichita police, in their "square deal code," are cautioned to "save unfortunate offenders from unnecessary humiliation, inconvenience and distress" and "never to arrest if a summons will suffice; never to summons if a warning would be better." Wichita Police Dept., Duty Manual i (undated). Similarly, Kansas City police are instructed, "Don't make trivial arrests when a warning will suffice." Kansas City Police Dept., Rules & Regulations, Reg. 121(2) (1956). Pontiac (Michigan) police are told to use warnings, but are then "enjoined against the indiscriminate use of this rule to the detriment of the peace and order of the city, and will be held accountable for undue leniency toward offenders." Pontiac Police Dept., Rules & Regulations §237 (undated).

[9] See page 156, note 18.

is widely acknowledged even by those who deny the propriety of police discretion for more serious offenses.[10] The volume of minor traffic cases is so great that it would be very costly to subject them all to the formal criminal process.[11]

Officers engaged in traffic enforcement in each of the three states studied indicated that the decision to issue a warning rather than a regular citation in a given case is left to the discretion of the individual patrolman. Specific guidance as to what kind of case deserves only a warning is rarely given, except for some written policy on the toleration levels on speeding.[12] The result is that warnings are sometimes given for illegal turns, rolling stops, and the like, but the process is invoked for the same conduct on other occasions, and it is not possible to observe any uniform enforcement pattern in this area. Invocation is the rule, however, if the violation results in a person actually being injured or put in a dangerous situation.[13] Of course, when a warning proves ineffective, then invocation of the process against the violator can be expected. But, unless warnings are made a matter of record, these repeated violations usually are not known.[14]

2. *Juvenile offenses.*

Illustration No. 2: Residents near a drive-in restaurant complained to the police that a disturbance of the peace was occurring in their neighborhood. A patrol car was dispatched to the scene, and the officers found a group of teenagers singing, shouting, and racing the engines of their cars, which

---

[10] For example, one writer, after asserting that the police should enforce *all* the law, adds: "Nor is it really relevant to point out that the police in this country do already exercise some degree of discrimination in the enforcement of the law. Many traffic offenders, for example, receive a word of advice on the spot instead of a summons. That speaks merely for the good sense of the police, and for our good fortune in being served by sensible officers. The point is that these are exceptions to the general rule, and are made under strictly controlled conditions, for a particular purpose; . . . ." Williams, Turning a Blind Eye, 1954 Crim. L. Rev. (Eng.) 272. His justification for the exception seems questionable, as it is not readily apparent that there is any greater control over noninvocation here than in other areas.

[11] In one study it was concluded that in Berkeley, California, three million traffic violations were occurring daily, and that full enforcement would require 14,000 traffic officers. Cal. State Dept. of Education, Cal. Peace Officers Training Publication No. 71, Police Supervisory Control 26 (1957).

[12] Thus the radar unit in one Wisconsin community was instructed that when operating in a 25 m.p.h. zone, speeds up to 32 m.p.h. were to be ignored, speeds from 32 to 38 m.p.h. were to be considered cases for warning cards, and drivers going above 38 m.p.h. were to receive regular traffic citations.

[13] Therefore, whereas a speeder on a lonely road might not be arrested, another person driving at the same place, and at the same speed, would be if the traffic were heavy.

[14] Probably the best system observed was in Eau Claire, Wisconsin. There, when a warning is issued, the driver signs a warning card, a copy of which is placed on file. Should a particular driver receive three warnings within a year, the process is invoked with respect to the third violation.

created a considerable disturbance. The officers administered severe warnings to the youths and then left.

Minor offenses by juveniles are not usually considered important enough to warrant expenditure of any substantial amount of police enforcement resources. The usual opinion is that such conduct, while proscribed by the penal statutes, is merely a consequence of the minor's immature judgment or youthful exuberance and poses no major threat to society if not proceeded against fully. Thus youthful offenders are often given a warning and sent on their way when the violation is not serious. This frequently occurs in small cities,[15] but in the larger metropolitan areas, such as Detroit and Milwaukee, the warning is more likely to come after arrest.[16] Even in large urban areas, however, it is still common for individual patrolmen to dispose of cases by some means other than arrest.[17]

The level of toleration of juvenile offenses cannot be stated with any great degree of certainty.[18]   However, the chance of arrest is

[15] Thus the chief of police in a small Michigan community indicated that petty juvenile offenses there are dealt with on an informal basis and without an arrest routinely being made. He said that this method of settling these kinds of cases "behind the kitchen stove" is particularly suited to a small town, but would probably not be possible in a larger city.

[16] In a smaller town the officer may know whether the youth is a first offender or a habitual troublemaker, or, in any event, whether he can be easily located later. But arrest is more usual in the larger city. The Detroit Police Manual instructs: "All violators under the age of twenty-one (21) years [who are guilty of purchasing, possessing, or transporting intoxicating beverages] shall be brought into the Precinct Station, and if it is determined that this is their first offense and there are no aggravated conditions involved, all such minors or juveniles may be released with a warning except juvenile girls [who will be transported home by the Women's Division]. . . . The provisions of this procedure may be applied to other types of cases involving juveniles and minors found in disorderly parties or other difficulties where liquor violations are not involved." Detroit Police Dept., Revised Police Manual, chap. 12, §74(a)(1), (b)(4) (1955). The Milwaukee regulations put the invocation question in the hands of supervisory officers, which suggests that arrest will be the first step. "Whenever a juvenile case is brought before any commanding officer, and in his judgment the offense involved is of a minor nature and the case can consistently be kept out of the Juvenile Court, such commanding officer may release the offender with a reprimand." Milwaukee Police Dept., Rules & Regulations, Rule 32, §9 (1950). In Wichita, juvenile officers are told to "dispose of all juvenile offenders in the way that will be to the best interest of the offender and to society in general." Wichita Police Dept., Duty Manual 61 (undated). Sometimes these juvenile officers do not enter the case until after the arrest, but it is not uncommon for a patrolman in Wichita to radio for a juvenile officer and to have him make the determination on the spot.

[17] See Carr, Delinquency Control 150 (1940), where it is said that in a city such as Detroit the police annually make from 10,000 to 14,000 nonofficial contacts in which youngsters may be reproved or admonished because of undesirable conduct. Of these, only one in three will be apprehended and placed in the detention home, and less than one in seven will be brought before juvenile court.

[18] Field research for this study did not focus upon crimes by juveniles as a special problem. Consequently, the factual data reported here are rather limited, having

great when force or violence has been used against an innocent victim outside the juvenile's social group. Nonviolent property crimes are not thought to warrant arrest unless the amount of damage involved is great or the technique employed is professional in nature.[19] The juvenile's past record is considered very important; it is for this reason that the decision whether to proceed against the juvenile must sometimes wait until after arrest, when it can be determined whether the youth has a record.[20]

The most obvious reason why the police do not feel that petty juvenile offenders need to be arrested is that the offenses are not serious enough to justify official concern. In many cases a warning appears to accomplish all that is necessary. In other cases, although the police consider the juvenile's conduct serious enough to merit punishment, no arrest is made because the officer feels that the juvenile court is too lenient.[21]

The fact that special treatment is given to the juvenile offender following arrest, during trial, and in sentencing and correction might be thought to bring nonenforcement in this area into question. Since these procedures are designed to rehabilitate, it might be argued that it is desirable to subject all youths who commit crimes to arrest and thus to rehabilitative treatment.[22] This consideration does sometimes prompt a police officer to make an arrest in circumstances which would not be thought to merit the expend-

---

been obtained merely incidentally to other inquiries. For a recent study on the appropriate degree of toleration of juvenile offenses, see Myren and Swanson, Police Work With Children (1962).

19 The limited observations are entirely consistent with the conclusions reached in another study, which focused on juvenile offenders. It was there noted that auto theft was considered a serious offense by the police and that burglary and robbery generally resulted in arrest unless they were very minor and restitution was made. Sexual relations between juveniles without coercion do not often result in arrest unless they are abnormal. Purse snatching is usually looked upon as a grave offense — an attack on the weaker sex — and restitution will rarely prevent arrest. Shoplifting and other larceny is not generally considered worthy of arrest if the victim will accept restitution (but see note 23 *infra*). The mode of commission of the offense may be significant. Carefully planned offenses, professional in nature, such as burglary with burglary tools, are viewed as much more serious than offenses committed on impulse. Use of force is an important factor, as is the fact that the offense was committed at night. Goldman, The Differential Selection of Juvenile Offenders for Court Appearance 148-156 (unpublished Ph.D. thesis, Dept. of Sociology, Univ. of Chicago, 1950).

20 While taking a juvenile offender to headquarters for a check on his record is considered an arrest, it may not be recorded as such if it is later decided that the youth will be released with a warning.

21 Such opinions were not infrequently voiced by the police, and were particularly vehement when the police had expended a considerable amount of their resources. For example, one Detroit officer said, "We may go around here for months trying to figure out who in hell is committing a bunch of petty crimes. We finally apprehend the guy and bring him before a judge. But, since he is a juvenile, he gets off easy."

22 This problem is considered at page 139.

iture of police resources were an adult involved.[23]   However, in many other cases, the police conclude either that the need for rehabilitative treatment is not great enough to justify the expenditure of their resources or that an arrest would have harmful consequences for the juvenile regardless of what the objectives of the juvenile process are in theory.

3. *Drunkenness.*

Illustration No. 3: A patrolman came upon a man staggering down the street. The man was clearly intoxicated but, while his gait was unsteady, he was able to walk without any great risk of falling. Upon questioning the man, the patrolman learned that he was on his way home and that he lived about a block away. No arrest was made.

Another offense which occurs frequently but is not subject to full enforcement is drunkenness. Even though the statutes in Kansas and Michigan[24] prohibit being intoxicated in public, a substantial number of persons observed in such condition are not arrested.[25] If the person is not a habitual drunk, it is unusual for him to be taken into custody unless he cannot care for his own safety[26] or is likely to cause harm to another. If the drunk is creating a nuisance, this will increase the probability of arrest, but if the disturbance can be stopped and there does not appear to be a significant likelihood of further trouble, an arrest still might not be made.[27] Drunks are often told at the time of arrest that they are being arrested for their own protection, and this fact may be

[23] Thus, although police do not usually arrest a shoplifter unless there is a prior assurance from the merchant that he desires prosecution (see page 115), some juvenile offenders are arrested for shoplifting without such assurance. This is because the officers know that the juvenile will be given special consideration later in the process, and they feel that this presents an opportunity for his guidance.

[24] Kan. Gen. Stat. §41-802 (1949). In Michigan a disorderly person is "any person who shall be drunk or intoxicated . . . in any public place." Mich. Stat. Ann. §28.364 (1938).

[25] Statutory language tending to reflect legislative recognition of such discretionary action is to be found only in Michigan. There the provision setting forth the duties of the chief of police of a city says: "He shall arrest upon view, and with or without process, any person found in the act of committing any offense against the laws of the state or the ordinances of the city amounting to a breach of the peace, and forthwith take such person before the proper magistrate or court for examination or trial, and *may* also without process *arrest and imprison persons found drunk in the streets.*" Mich. Stat. Ann. §5.1674 (1949) (emphasis supplied).

[26] The statutory definition of a drunken person in Wisconsin is "A person who is so intoxicated that he is unable to care for his own safety and is found in a public place in such condition." Wis. Stat. §947.03 (1955). This is not significantly different from the prior provision in Wis. Stat. §351.59 (1953).

[27] Thus, in Detroit, a drunk who had been arguing with patrons in a restaurant calmed down upon the arrival of the police and so was allowed to leave, whereas another highly intoxicated man who was found urinating on the sidewalk was arrested.

incorporated into the arrest report. An arrest is not usually made when the person evinces a willingness and ability to go home, and in this respect the proximity of the offender's home is a relevant factor.[28] In practice there is a lower level of tolerance for the "skid row" drunk, but this is because arrest is the only way in which to insure his safety.[29]

The intoxicated person who is most likely to cause harm to others is the one who is driving or who is likely to drive if not arrested. While arrest under these circumstances is more likely, the police sometimes utilize an alternative if one is available. Persons under the influence of alcohol who are seen entering cars may be allowed to take a cab home, and even those who have been stopped for erratic driving are sometimes permitted to park their car and resume their journey home by taxi.[30] One tactic which an officer may use when he finds a drunk sleeping in a car is to remove the keys from the ignition and either take them with him or hide them in the back seat of the car, or under the floor rug, thus insuring that the person will not drive until he is sufficiently sober to recover the keys.[31]

One situation which appears to provoke some disagreement between different agencies in the process, particularly in Michigan, is that concerning drunks found in taverns. The police apply the same test to these persons as that applied to those found drunk on the street. If the person appears to be unable to care for himself, and no responsible person is available to help him reach home safely,[32] an arrest is made. This practice is not approved by some judges,[33] who apparently feel that no arrest should be made unless

28 Milwaukee officers entered a tavern in which the bartender pointed to a man slumped over a drink and said that he had refused to pay for his drink. When the officers ordered the man to pay, he did so and then stumbled off the stool and weaved toward the door. The officers learned that he lived only four doors away at a hotel, so they told him to get to the hotel as fast as he could or he would be arrested.

29 This type of drunk creates the greatest problem in Detroit. A specialized "bum squad" patrols the skid row there, picking up the habituals and those who are "down and out."

30 Other drunks who are driving recklessly may not be so leniently treated, even though they are but a few blocks from home, if it is known by the officers that they have been apprehended for such conduct in the past.

31 A Dane County, Wisconsin, deputy upheld this practice by stating that in his opinion a person who is intoxicated but who does get off the road should be commended and not punished by being brought in as a drunk. He indicated that the "hidden key" trick was commonly used in the county.

32 While the police feel justified in telling bartenders or owners to see that the drunk gets home safely, they may doubt whether these persons are sufficiently reliable to be entrusted with the drunk's safety.

33 An officer in one Michigan community ignored persons whom he found to be "stone drunk" while checking a local bar. He said: "Why bother to arrest them? There is just no use to this type of enforcement. The case will get thrown out of court in the municipal court."

a risk of harm on the street or highway is directly shown by actions of the drunk.

The police practice in all three states is substantially the same, though only Wisconsin has a statute which defines intoxication as a crime only when the person thereby puts himself in a helpless condition. The case of the occasional drunk is not considered serious, and even arresting the habitual drunk does not accomplish much, since there is little the system can do for him. The officer's knowledge of postarrest alternatives may influence his decision. Thus in Kansas, where the only procdure following arrest is prosecution, fewer arrests are made than in Detroit, where many arrests are followed by release without prosecution.[34]

Although the practice of not arresting for minor offenses is not limited to the three kinds of cases described above, the policy factors usually involved are indicated by these examples.

B. Conduct Thought to Reflect the Standards of a Community Subgroup

Illustration No. 4: A report that a stabbing had taken place came in to the station of a precinct predominantly Negro in population. An officer reported to the address and learned that a Negro woman had seriously stabbed her husband with a pair of scissors. The husband commented that there had been a little argument and requested transportation to the hospital. The officer, who had served in the precinct for some time, had reported to such calls in the past and had received similar responses. Although the conduct constituted a felonious assault, no official action was taken.

Differential treatment of racial groups may take many forms in law enforcement. One possibility is that members of minority groups may be arrested or may have even more serious action taken against them when they have not in fact engaged in criminal conduct.[35] This quite obviously is improper. A second possibility is that laws which generally are not enforced may be enforced only when violated by members of certain minority groups. Such a

---

In a case observed in Recorder's Court, Detroit, the judge severely criticized the arresting officers for their actions in such a case. He said that although the defendant might have been drunk, he could not understand why the police were checking bars for drunks in the first place or why they had attempted to arrest the defendant when he was not "doing anything." See page 103, note 5.

[34] For the postarrest alternatives in Michigan and Wisconsin, which the police may think more appropriate, see Chapter 21.

[35] E.g., Thompson v. City of Louisville, 362 U.S. 199, 80 Sup. Ct. 624, 4 L. Ed. 2d 654 (1960).

practice is not so easy to evaluate, and it is harder for the individual defendant to establish, because it is almost impossible to present adequate proof of the discrimination.[36] A third possibility, and the one of concern here, is the failure to enforce certain laws which are enforced when members of certain minority groups are not involved. This obviously is not thought disadvantageous by the offender himself, but it may be of concern to the victim or to other members of the minority group.[37]

This kind of unequal enforcement of the law frequently occurs when Negroes are involved, particularly in large metropolitan areas such as Detroit. Such offenses as bigamy and open and notorious cohabitation are overlooked by law enforcement officials,[38] and arrests often are not made for carrying knives[39] or for robbery of other Negroes.[40] However, the practice is most strikingly illustrated by the repeated failure of the police to arrest Negroes for a felonious assault upon a spouse or acquaintance unless the victim actually insists upon prosecution.

This practice is most apparent in one predominantly Negro precinct in Detroit. The average officer, after spending several months in that precinct, becomes accustomed to the offenses

---

[36] In People v. Winters, 171 Cal. App. 2d Supp. 876, 342 P.2d 538 (Super. Ct. 1959), when a Negro trial judge dismissed a case on the basis of discriminatory enforcement of the gambling laws against Negroes, the court reversed his decision but without prejudice to the defendant's right to prove intentional or deliberate discriminatory enforcement. This would appear a formidable task, however.

While no instances of this kind of discriminatory law enforcement were observed, allegations to this effect were made. A Negro attorney objected to a police lieutenant in one Michigan community that while Negro gambling was proceeded against, a horse racing book for whites only two blocks from the police station was not. The lieutenant offered to make an arrest if the attorney would make a formal complaint, but the attorney declined the offer. These same charges were repeated in the Negro press shortly thereafter.

[37] "Equality of treatment implies also that there will be one standard of law enforcement in all areas within the community. Respectable members of a minority group do not appreciate the fact that minor criminals in their areas are sometimes treated like children, or are laughed at, when their violations are the type that run down the minority community, but do not seriously annoy the police or vocal complainants. It becomes particularly galling to them when, on the other hand, they feel that excessive police attention is given to other violations by their members. They sometimes allege the police make or fail to make arrests of their members to suit police convenience rather than the ends of justice." Brown, The Police and Community Conflict 19-20 (1962). This is a pamphlet distributed by the National Conference of Christians and Jews. It is prepared by a retired inspector of the New York City Police Department who had twenty-two years of service.

[38] These offenses came to official attention principally when aid to dependent children was sought or when a domestic dispute was being dealt with.

[39] A car occupied by ten Negro youths was stopped and switch-blade knives were found on each of them. The knives were taken, but no arrests were made.

[40] Only one such case was observed, and the facts are unusual because the offender recouped his losses at gunpoint from his co-gamblers but then returned the money before the police located him.

which he is regularly called upon to handle; he accepts the double standard and applies it without question.[41] He does not look upon a stabbing, for example, with the same degree of seriousness as would an officer in one of the other precincts. While settling differences with a knife cannot properly be called the established standard of behavior for Negroes, the officer repeatedly called to cases of this kind is apt to conclude that it is, particularly since his contacts with Negroes are usually confined to the law-breaking, and not the law-abiding, Negro. Thus what might appear to be an aggravated assault to an officer assigned elsewhere would, to the officer in this precinct, be looked upon merely as a family disturbance.

Usually the victim of such an assault does not wish to have the offender prosecuted. Even arrest is not usually desired; the police are called because they are able to provide the victim with ambulance service to the hospital. While the attitude of the victim is an important factor in the exercise of police discretion generally, the assault cases between Negroes are the only apparent situations in which the victim controls the arrest decision when the offense is a serious one. Although the reluctance of the victim to cooperate makes successful prosecution difficult and in many cases impossible, the willingness of the police to accept the decision of the victim indicates that they are not greatly concerned about the problem.

The Negro press sometimes accuses the police of discrimination solely on the grounds that more Negroes are being arrested than whites.[42] Nonenforcement in Negro assault cases has the effect of keeping down Negro arrest statistics and thus is sometimes thought to have the added benefit of deterring criticism. While there is no reason to believe that this is the only cause of the practice, the

[41] One exception was the officer who reflected that perhaps the department should begin signing complaints in these cases despite the protest of the victim. This officer appeared principally concerned with decreasing the number of calls to the police. This proposal would seem to approve the present lower standard of enforcement in Negro communities, since, if successful, it would result not in less crimes being committed, but in less crimes coming to police attention.

[42] Frequent criticism of the Negro press was heard. Similarly, one Philadelphia policeman is quoted in another study as saying: "I don't know what the answer is. I think the Negro press plays up the wrong angle. Sometimes they hurt things instead of helping. It's got so now that some white cops hate to arrest a Negro. They know if there's any trouble the press will play it up to look bad for the cop." Kephart, Racial Factors and Urban Law Enforcement 66 (1957). Similarly, a Negro patrolman, when asked if he was discouraged by the high Negro crime rate, replied: "No, I don't get discouraged. It's just being handled all wrong. The cops, the magistrates, the judges — everybody's afraid to crack down, especially with the Negro press yelling discrimination all the time." Id. at 119. Kephart reports that police of all ranks and both races were interviewed and all condemned local Negro newspapers. Id. at 147.

attitude of the Negro press is hardly conducive to the adoption of a nondiscriminatory policy.[43]

The fact that the practice of not arresting in Negro assault cases is more prevalent in Detroit than elsewhere[44] undoubtedly reflects the higher concentration of Negro population there.[45]   In such areas, there is apt to be more of a disparity between Negro crime and the resources which the police administrator has to deal with the problem.

The basic question is: To what extent, if at all, is it ever justifiable to take into account the customs, practices, and prevailing standard of conduct of an identifiable subcultural group in determining whether the process should be invoked against a member of that group? [46]   The problem was defined by a Negro assistant prosecutor in these terms:

[43] Chief Parker of Los Angeles, in one of a series of interviews on the American character published by the Center for the Study of Democratic Institutions, said: "One of the real problems has been the resentment of some minority groups because of the publication of the high amount of crime attributed to these groups. From the police standpoint, however, that incidence of crime is a fact. The social and economic conditions that contribute to this high rate of criminal activity is another matter. . . . In the last meeting with the commission on human rights I made it clear that I was disturbed about the consistently inflammatory criticism of the police in the press published by one of these minority groups. I challenged this group. . . . They accepted the challenge. A little later there was a most amazing editorial in the leading newspaper of this group. It stated, calmly and objectively, that their people must stop blaming the police for their own criminal activity. It admitted that there was a great deal of crime and it went on to say that a man who holds up another person with a gun must expect vigorous and prompt action by the police, regardless of whether he is a member of a minority group or not. It was a magnificent, thorough treatise on the subject and represents a real breakthrough in this matter. We had never seen such an editorial." Center for the Study of Democratic Institutions, The Police 15-16 (1962).

[44] In Milwaukee a definite attempt has been made to eliminate any prejudice against, and unfair treatment of, the Negro section of the community. Great care is taken in the selection of officers for duty in Negro areas. Police commanders said that, if a policeman was believed to be prejudiced against Negroes, he was assigned to an area where he was not likely to be called upon to deal with them; and cases of overt prejudice would be grounds for disciplinary action. The Negro in Milwaukee VII, The Milwaukee Journal, May 30, 1960, p. 22, col. 1-5. On more than one occasion observation was made of the courteous manner in which these officers treated Negroes.

It might be argued that the double standard can still prevail despite these highly successful attempts to combat the other manifestations of discrimination. The data from Milwaukee do not allow a conclusive judgment, as noninvocation against Negroes was observed only with regard to lesser assaults. But in some of the instances it appeared likely that an arrest would have resulted had the parties been white.

[45] Detroit had a population 16.2 per cent Negro in the 1950 census, while Milwaukee had only 3.4 per cent. See Kephart, Racial Factors and Urban Law Enforcement 135 (1957).

[46] The criminal law has rarely considered cultural differences, although the problem has arisen when a given set of laws has been imposed upon territories with a population unlike that of the lawmakers. See Howard, What Colour Is the "Reasonable Man"? 1961 Crim. L. Rev. (Eng.) 41; Marsack, Provocation in Trials for Murder, 1959 Crim. L. Rev. (Eng.) 697.

Negroes have been struggling for many years to secure their civil and legal rights through such organizations as the NAACP, but there has been too little emphasis placed upon the Negro's duty to assume responsibility for acts of violence and not to expect differential treatment. But it will take cooperation by the white people as well. There is too much of a tendency on the part of police officers, juries, and even judges to dismiss Negro crimes of violence with the saying, "It's only Negroes, and they've always been like that." Too many Negroes expect to escape lightly in crimes of this nature, and with some justification, as those in authority have actually condoned such offenses by taking them so lightly.

The obvious dilemma is that the Negro continues to be judged by a different standard because it is assumed that he has a greater tolerance for certain kinds of antisocial conduct, and existing differences in attitude are probably reinforced by the fact that different standards are applied by enforcement agencies.

C. Victim Does Not or Will Not Request Prosecution

Police nonenforcement is also the rule when the victim of a minor offense does not wish to expend his own time in the interests of successful prosecution. This occurs not only with minor property crimes, when the victim is concerned primarily with restitution, but also with many offenses arising out of family relationships or other associations, such as that between landlord and tenant or employer and employee.

The reluctance of the victim to prosecute makes conviction difficult or impossible and is at least some indication that the offense is not serious enough to justify the expenditure of time and effort of the police and prosecutor.[47] In those cases arising out of a

[47] The fact that the victim does not desire prosecution will be disregarded in some offenses where the damage is minor if the police consider the conduct serious. The following excerpt, from a newspaper report on enforcement against the hit-and-run offender, is particularly revealing. "Often his offense is minor, but affects the owner of the other car disproportionately. In a routine case handled in the traffic court last week, for example, the owner of a damaged parked car spent an entire morning 'doing nothing,' he said, 'but following the policeman around.'

"In this case, the other driver pleaded not guilty, said he did not think he had damaged the other car much, accepted a fine of $10 (with costs, it came to $24.50) and went home. The owner of the damaged car received assurances that his car would be fixed, collected a witness fee of $5.50 but lost $25 in wages because he had to appear in court instead of at his job.

"Some car owners, not wanting to be bothered with the lengthy processes of justice, refuse to sign complaints against hit-run drivers if they know their own damages will be taken care of.

"This attitude, needless to say, does not serve the cause of justice. Investigating officers, questioning a witness reluctant to give information about a hit-runner, ask:

private relationship, resolution of the difficulty without prosecution may appear to be a more desirable alternative. For these reasons, the police frequently decide to apply their resources to other offenses.

1. *Victim interested only in restitution.*

Illustration No. 5: A merchant called the police after having apprehended a shoplifter in his store. When the merchant was asked by the officer whether he was willing to appear in court to testify, he replied that he could not take time out from his work for this. The officer declined to arrest the shoplifter.

When small amounts of property have been taken without force or violence, the criminal process is not usually invoked unless the victim indicates that he is willing to cooperate in the prosecution of the case. In cases in which the police recover all or a substantial portion of the stolen property, it is likely that the victim will ask that the matter be dropped so that he need not take the time to appear in court. The police usually do not take further action in such cases.[48] Cases of larceny are frequently concluded in this way, as is an occasional burglary. If force or violence has been used in obtaining the property, however, the victim's desire is seldom determinative, although action might not be taken if the act was impulsive and the victim is an acquaintance of the offender.[49] In any of these cases, if the police have already expended considerable resources in investigating the offense, they are less likely to abide by the victim's wishes. In fact, in such a case steps will probably be taken to persuade the victim to commit himself to cooperate in the prosecution.[50]

'How would you feel if it had been your car — or your child — that was hit?' The witnesses usually come through." Milwaukee Journal, Dec. 10, 1959, pt. 1m, p. 4, col. 3.

[48] For example, in Wichita, a man found that his wallet, containing $750, was missing the morning after he had been on a drinking spree with two other men. He could not recall the events of the prior evening. The police suggested that his two companions of that evening take a lie detector test. One did so, but the other refused. The police continued to pressure the latter, who eventually reported that he had "found" $680 in his clothes. He agreed to turn this over to the victim. The police learned that the victim did not wish to prosecute, so no arrest was made.

[49] For example, when a man who had been participating in a gambling game retrieved his losses by taking $64 from the other players at gunpoint, the victims complained to the police and a warrant was obtained, apparently because the offender's whereabouts was then unknown. An attempt to serve the warrant was made a few days later, and the offender told the officers that when he had sobered up after this incident he had had feelings of remorse and had since returned the money and given the gun to a friend. The officers told him the incident could be closed if he would turn the gun in to the police, which he promised to do. No arrest was made.

[50] A Wichita barber reported a burglary from his shop. After considerable in-

Probably the most significant category of conduct in which recovery of the stolen property concludes the victim's interest in
prosecution is shoplifting. When shoplifters are caught, they are
usually apprehended in the act, which results in immediate recovery of the stolen goods. Merchants generally are unwilling to
prosecute, asserting that they cannot afford the time away from
the store to testify in court or that they do not want to risk a loss
of good will.[51] The police reaction is typified by the following
statement by an experienced officer to a "rookie":

> Now if that situation ever comes up with you, don't take the per-
> son to the station unless you can get somebody to agree to sign a
> complaint. When I first got on, I went to this store just like we
> did tonight. I took the shoplifter to the station, booked him
> through, and then one of the policewomen came up and asked me
> who the complainant was. Being green, I just looked at her and
> said, "I don't know." The policewoman informed me that the
> best thing to do was to turn the individual loose, and that it was a
> good thing we had not booked him in county jail.
>
> For a while this store manager would not sign complaints; all
> he wanted the police to do was to throw a little scare into the sus-
> pect and get him out of his hair. Now, however, since we have
> adopted the policy of not taking them unless he will sign a com-
> plaint, things have improved, and he only calls when he intends to
> sign a complaint.

Thus nonenforcement in this type of situation conserves police
resources in two ways: no further action need be taken in the particular case, and calls for police service from merchants are substantially diminished.[52]

---

vestigation, the missing items were found in local pawnshops by the police. The
pawn tickets bore the name of a recent employee of the barber. The barber indicated that he did not want to prosecute. This was probably because he had recovered the property and he would have had to spend time away from his shop as a witness. Nonetheless, the detectives pressured him into signing a complaint, and a
search for the offender was begun. Very likely the victim's attitude was not honored
here because the police had already expended considerable time in investigation of
the crime. The fact that the former employee had a long criminal record, including
two prior felony convictions, may also be significant.

[51] In a recent commentary on the increase of shoplifting and the means being
employed to combat it, the following appears with regard to shoplifting by youths.
"Reactions of parents are equally distressing: a few bring the child back to the store
to apologize, but most parents in this well-to-do community either (a) stop trading
at that particular store or (b) become highly indignant and overprotective, claiming
the manager doesn't know what he's talking about: 'Why, Junior goes around all
the time with $5 in his pocket!' " Wharton, Shoplifting — Newest Crime Wave,
Family Weekly, March 17, 1963, p. 8.

[52] For similar conclusions, see Goldman, The Differential Selection of Juvenile
Offenders for Court Appearance 161-166 (unpublished Ph.D. thesis No. T 914, Dept.
of Sociology, Univ. of Chicago, 1950).

Illustration No. 6: A merchant turned over a "no account" check to the police, requesting apprehension of the writer. The merchant was asked whether he was willing to appear in court when the offender was prosecuted, and he replied that he only wanted to collect the amount of the check. The police refused to take any action.

Usually, when a minor property crime is reported, the police ask whether the victim is willing to prosecute before deciding whether to arrest. While this issue may arise in a variety of situations,[53] it occurs most often in reports of bad checks by merchants.

It is important at the outset to distinguish between three kinds of bad checks. One is the check with a forged signature; the second is the no-account check, to which the writer has signed his own name but which is written on a bank where he has no account; and the third is the "NSF" check, to which the writer has signed his own name but for which his account has insufficient funds. Police view the forgery as the most serious and the no-account check as more serious than the check written without sufficient funds. The victim's reluctance to prosecute, therefore, is likely to be given the greatest weight in the insufficient funds situation.

In Michigan, the practice is to proceed against forgers regardless of the attitude of the victim, although forgery ordinarily requires the expenditure of police time and resources to identify the offender.[54] In some parts of Kansas, on the other hand, the police are hesitant to proceed with investigations unless the victim promises to cooperate in prosecution of the offender after he is found. The Milwaukee policy is to refer these check complaints to the documents examiner. After identification is made, the complainant is contacted, and, if he is willing to appear in court, a warrant is obtained and the case is assigned to detectives, who then arrest the suspect. The fact that in Milwaukee the investigation is made first suggests that the police will make an effort to prosecute regardless of the victim's desires if the case involves a serious forgery or a repeating offender.

[53] Thus when a woman called a Detroit precinct and reported that in the course of paying for her meal in a restaurant she had been cheated of some money, the lieutenant answering the call suggested she report to the station so that a complaint could be made out against the person who had cheated her. When the woman replied that she only wanted her money back, the lieutenant said: "Then, madam, you have the wrong department. Please call the Lonely Hearts Club of the Detroit Free Press."

[54] In Detroit, forged checks are handled by a specialized unit, the check detail of the general services bureau of the detective division. The Michigan State Police have a fraudulent check section of the special investigation squad, which maintains a statewide central record file on bogus checks passed in Michigan. A highly developed system is employed for determining, from examination of the check, whether it was written by a known forger.

The victim's attitude is most often decisive in the case of insufficient funds checks and is only slightly less so in the case of no-account checks. Many of these cases are not brought to the attention of the police. Instead, complainants go directly to the prosecutor's office, probably because it is widely known that the prosecutor sometimes aids in the collection of bad checks.[55] In cases which do come directly to the police, the victim is first asked whether he is willing to take the time to appear in court to testify, and if the answer is negative the police indicate that they will take no action in the case. Thus in Detroit a set of instructions for the use of precinct detectives in such cases asks: "Is the complainant willing to prosecute? (If the check is being reported merely as an aid to collection, the police department is not interested, and the check cannot be accepted as a complaint.)" Insuring that the complainant will prosecute may be more essential when considerable expense will be involved in preparing the case for prosecution. These instructions continue:

> It is well to caution the complainant that in the event that the check is drawn on an out-of-state bank account, unless the writer of the check admits that he has no account (or insufficient funds in that bank) it will be necessary for the county to bring in an officer from that bank to testify as to the status of the defendant's account (or lack of it). For that reason, the complainant may be required to post a cash bond guaranteeing prosecution in the case.

Customarily in Wisconsin, and to a somewhat lesser extent in the other two states, bad check complainants are referred by the police to the prosecutor's office, thus leaving the decision whether to invoke the process to the prosecutor.[56] There appear to be several reasons for this. First, there is usually no need for immediate police action, so that the decision whether to arrest can be made after such investigations as the prosecutor wishes to make. Second, except in forgery cases there is no particular need for police investigative skills, as the identity of the offender is known. Also, the typical bad check case is not of particular concern to the police because there is no connection with organized crime. Another important factor is that resort to the complaint-warrant process, which involves the prosecutor, tends to commit the complainant to further cooperation. Finally, the police view restitution as insufficient cause for expenditure of their resources,[57] and

---

[55] On complainants going directly to the prosecutor, see page 36.

[56] On police referral to the prosecutor generally, see page 47.

[57] The police policy of not aiding merchants seeking only restitution results in fewer complaints being made to the police. One inspector in the Detroit department, after reading some statistical sheets, said: "There was an 11% drop in com-

they are also concerned with the possibility of tort liability result-ing from an arrest to effect restitution.[58]

A decision not to invoke is clearly involved here, in the sense that the police are aware of an offense but take no affirmative ac-tion. This becomes more apparent when one considers the gen-eral facts already noted concerning the practice in the three states: (a) the initial inquiry of the police is always as to whether the complainant is willing to prosecute; (b) arrests, if any, are made only when the police are certain that the victim agrees to prosecution;[59] (c) referral to the prosecutor is not always made, since reluctant victims are sometimes told that nothing can be done for them; and (d) even when there is referral, the police do not try to de-termine whether the victim will cooperate, leaving the burden solely on the prosecutor.

2. *Victim in continuing relationship with offender.*

Illustration No. 7: An officer responding to a call learned that the complainant wanted his neighbor arrested for tearing down a part of his fence. The officer's investigation disclosed that this was merely the latest chapter in a continued neigh-borhood dispute between the complainant and offender. Al-though the property destruction was a criminal violation, the officer declined to take any official action.

A combination of factors may result in nonenforcement when the criminal conduct involves two persons who are in a continuing legitimate relationship with each other, such as neighbors, land-lord and tenant, or parties to a contract. Generally, the police feel that such disputes are principally private in nature and that so long as the conduct is not serious, enforcement resources need not be diverted to it.

---

plaints, department wide, from 1955 to 1956. This was due to greater selectivity in taking a case from a merchant who would indicate immediately his unwillingness to prosecute on an NSF check."

58 Bergeron v. Peyton, 106 Wis. 377, 82 N.W. 291 (1900). An officer took Bergeron to the bank where he had been overpaid on a check, and, when Bergeron refused to return the excess, the officer took him to the magistrate. Since the jury found the arrest was "for the sole purpose of compelling and inducing him to repay . . . the $43 thus overpaid . . . ," the court held the arrest illegal and the officer liable for damages, even though the officer had taken the offender directly to the magis-trate when he refused the opportunity to make restitution. But in a Kansas case, apparently in answer to an assertion that an arrest had been made to influence pay-ment of a debt, the court said that "if the arrest was lawful the motive for it was immaterial" but that the arrest must have been made "in good faith." Atchison, T. & S.F. Ry. v. Hinsdell, 76 Kan. 74, 90 Pac. 800 (1907).

59 In Detroit, the police also usually give the offender an opportunity to make restitution and thus avoid being arrested. There is some evidence that this is less usual in other parts of Michigan, where the offender may be arrested and brought before a justice of the peace, and only then given the opportunity to make resti-tution.

Obviously an arrest should not be made when the conduct is not criminal and would warrant only a civil action. The police are warned against acting in such cases[60] and in fact do refuse assistance.[61] However, they may not arrest even when the conduct is criminal if a civil remedy is available to the injured party. The availability of a civil remedy is thought adequate by the police, and their hesitation to act may be increased by a fear of giving an undue advantage to one of the parties. Also, the fact that the victim can resolve his difficulty by terminating his relationship with the offender is important. Thus a landlord was advised to evict his tenant when he wanted criminal action brought against a member of the tenant's household who caused malicious damage to the premises.[62] Similarly, an employer was told that he could handle the situation himself when a minor burglary was found to be an "inside job" perpetrated by an employee.

In such cases, the police are not likely to take any action unless the victim asserts a strong desire for prosecution. They may even discourage the complainant if they feel that he is motivated by spite and that prosecution would only strain a necessarily continuing relationship, such as that between neighbors. The continuing relationship also makes it more likely that the victim will change his mind about prosecution.

Often the police refer these matters to another agency. Putting the burden on the victim to see the prosecutor or magistrate con-

---

60 Detroit police are told: "Members of the Department shall render no assistance whatever in civil cases, or advise parties involved, except to prevent a breach of the peace or to quell a disturbance actually commenced." Detroit Police Dept., Revised Police Manual, chap. 10, §25 (1955). Similarly, in Wichita the police are instructed: "Officers shall not render assistance in civil cases, except to prevent an immediate breach of the peace or to quell a disturbance actually commenced." Wichita Police Dept., Duty Manual 11 (undated).

61 For example, a Detroit station lieutenant received a call from a man who said that his wife had left him and was now in a bar. The lieutenant told the complainant that no police action was warranted in this case and that the man should go to the bar himself and tell his wife to come home. "You want an officer to be a witness in a civil matter and we are not going to do it. I will give you help if it is a criminal matter and a criminal matter only. If she is leaving you that is a civil matter."

62 The Michigan state policeman responding to the call learned that the landlord's primary interest was in having his door replaced. The trooper advised: "That won't do very much good. He probably is smart enough to know that there is not much that can be done unless you swear out a complaint form. And then if you do that there is no telling what will happen after that. If the man does go to jail for thirty days, you still haven't got your door repaired, and in a sense you are still paying for it because you are supporting him while he is in jail. It may be that you will have to handle this case civilly. Frankly, I think the best thing for you to do would be to order these people to move and get rid of the problem that way."

serves police resources in two ways: first, no action is necessary unless the victim fails to "cool off" and continues his demand for prosecution;[63] and, second, future complaints of this kind to the police are likely to diminish. The police feel that other agencies should take care of restitution cases. The exception is Detroit, where a specialized agency within the police department itself will aid insistent complainants in obtaining restitution.[64]

3. *Victim a member of offender's family.*

> *Illustration No. 8:* A call was received at the precinct reporting a disturbance of the peace. The officer responding to the call found that the disturbance was due to a family squabble. Although the man was still hitting his wife when the officer arrived, the officer did not make an arrest but merely restored order and left.

The police are sometimes advised to avoid arrest in domestic disputes where possible. For example, the Detroit Police Manual provides:

> When a police officer is called to a disturbance in a private home having family difficulties, he should recognize the sanctity of the home and endeavor diplomatically to quell the disturbance and create peace without making an arrest.[65]
>
> In any case where an officer suspects that a disturbance may result in the injury of any person, it is advisable for the officer to take the person causing such disturbance into custody, at least temporarily, even though it may be against the wishes of the family involved.[66]

---

[63] The clerk of police court in Wauwatosa, Wisconsin, said that the police often refer complainants in neighborhood quarrels to the justice of the peace for the determination of whether a warrant should be issued. It does not appear that the police believe that this justice is any more qualified to make the determination. Rather, this referral, which usually entails a "cooling-off" period since the justice is available only on Mondays and Tuesdays, again tests the complainant's willingness to see the case through prosecution.

[64] This specialized agency is the prosecutor's bureau of the detective division. Within this bureau is the Misdemeanor Complaint Bureau, which handles neighborhood disputes and other quasi-civil cases. In 1956 this bureau investigated 5791 cases, of which 123 were found to be civil in nature, which may mean either purely civil or primarily civil. Also within the prosecutor's bureau is the felony detail, which handles embezzlement, larceny by conversion, false pretenses and other frauds, blue sky violations, and similar offenses. Unlike the average patrolman, felony detail personnel are not concerned with the motive of the complainant; if restitution appears to be the motive they work toward this result.

[65] Of course, if the offense is only a misdemeanor, arrest without warrant is not possible, except in Wisconsin, if it occurred prior to the officer's arrival. But the officers could obtain a warrant, and if immediate arrest were actually desired they might resort to a variety of devices to accomplish this. See page 28.

[66] Detroit Police Dept., Revised Police Manual, chap. 16, §22 (1955).

This is the policy generally followed in all three states.[67]   The police dislike becoming involved in family disputes,[68] and calls for service may be refused when it does not appear that arrest is essential to maintain order,[69] or when demands upon police services are particularly heavy.[70]

In any event, an officer is unlikely to make an arrest in cases of intrafamily disturbances involving minor offenses such as unaggravated assaults[71] if the offended spouse does not insist upon prosecution.[72]   Even if the victim-spouse asserts a desire to prosecute, the officers may still refrain from arresting if it appears likely that the victim will later change his or her mind.[73]   Because the police do not wish to expend resources on cases in which the victim will later refuse to cooperate in prosecution, steps are sometimes taken to make it difficult for the insistent victim to change his mind later. In Wichita, the victim-spouse may be taken to the station immedi-

[67] For example, when a Detroit officer reported to a family dispute in which a man had struck his wife, the officer told the man that he was acquainted with the man's employer and cautioned him that any further trouble might result in his losing his job.   When the husband promised not to resort to physical violence again the officer departed.

[68] Confirming this is the statement of a police official quoted in another study: "You know, if there is one thing these men hate more than anything else it is to go out on a call for a family quarrel.   You ought to see their faces when they hear that call come over the radio."   Westley, The Police: A Sociological Study of Law, Custom and Morality 115 (unpublished Ph.D. thesis No. 1197, Dept. of Sociology, Univ. of Chicago, 1951).

[69] For example, a woman called a Michigan State Police post to complain about domestic trouble.   The corporal on duty suggested that the woman spend the night elsewhere and then reprimanded the husband over the phone, but declined to send an officer out to make an arrest.   Both parties were informed that the state police have no right to take action in a problem such as this except to preserve the peace.

[70] Especially during the hours when police patrol cars are most busy, Detroit precinct dispatchers screen out those family disturbances in which there does not appear to be any threat of excessive violence.

[71] Occasionally officers also decide not to arrest in cases of intrafamily felonious assault, but this was rarely observed except where the parties were Negroes (see page 110) or persons the police referred to as "hillbillies."

[72] Undoubtedly the law could be drafted so as to require such demand by the spouse in this case, just as with adultery and intrafamily thefts. See Model Penal Code §§206.13(4), 207.1, Comment (10) (Tent. Draft No. 4, 1955)..   The adultery provision was subsequently deleted from the Code, and the theft provision was changed so that misappropriation of household and personal effects, or other property normally accessible to both spouses, is characterized as theft only if the parties have ceased living together. Model Penal Code §223.1(4) (Proposed Official Draft, 1962).

[73] A Detroit scout car was dispatched to a family dispute.   Questioning disclosed that each party was guilty of having assaulted the other.   Both asserted that they desired to have the other party prosecuted.   However, one officer recalled having been called to this household on a previous occasion and having made an arrest because the victim expressed a desire to prosecute.   But he also recalled that the victim had undergone a change of heart the following day, which resulted in the offender's release.   Therefore no arrest was made on this occasion.   Rather the husband was told to leave the house for the remainder of the night.

ately to sign a complaint before arrest,[74] or the victim may also be arrested in an attempt to insure appearance in court the following day. In Milwaukee the police determine the victim's true desires by giving him a referral memorandum which may later be used to obtain a warrant. The clerk of municipal court, who issues warrants in both ordinance and statute violation cases, will issue warrants under a charge of common drunk or assault upon complaint of the spouse only after a three-day "cooling-off" period.[75] In Detroit the police try to discourage prosecution by the victim-spouse, but they may refer the spouse to the Misdemeanor Complaint Bureau, which does undertake to mediate more serious family disputes. The full burden is on the victim, who must go to the Misdemeanor Complaint Bureau, and no arrest is made in cases where mediation is the goal.[76]

There are exceptions to this policy. Sometimes the circumstances are such that arrest becomes necessary regardless of the offended spouse's attitude. For example, if the police have had to respond to the same address on a number of occasions, an arrest will be made. Also, if the officer feels that the incident cannot be closed by a brief lecture, the offender will be taken into custody.[77] Finally, a threat of subsequent serious harm will prompt a decision to arrest even when the victim does not desire prosecution.[78]

D. Victim Involved in Misconduct

Illustration No. 9: A man entered a precinct station and complained that he had just been cheated of $20. Asked to explain, he said that he had given the money to a prostitute who had agreed to meet him at a certain time and place, but that she had failed to appear. The police, although familiar with this kind of racket, subjected the complainant to some ridicule, suggested that he had learned his lesson, and sent him on his way.

[74] Use of this method may also be prompted by an attempt to circumvent the in-presence arrest requirement. This matter is considered in detail in Chapter 1.

[75] Occasionally, in an aggravated case such as one in which it appears that the husband is likely to resume the conduct, an attempt may be made by the prosecutor to have the warrant issued immediately.

[76] For more on this, see page 197.

[77] Of course, the police are not always able to predict whether any further trouble is likely. In the situation described in note 73 *supra,* the husband later returned to the house and the dispute was resumed. This time the officers arrested without any inquiry concerning the victim's desire to prosecute.

[78] When Kansas City Police, in response to a call, found a woman cowering in a corner and were told by her that her mentally unbalanced son had threatened her with violence, they attempted to find the son so that he could be arrested, despite the fact that the mother did not want him jailed.

In some situations a crime is committed upon a person who is himself engaged in criminal conduct at the time. Indeed, the person's misconduct often increases the likelihood that he will become a victim of criminal action. Such is the case, for example, when a prostitute is mistreated as a direct result of her illegal activity,[79] or when both parties to a fight are at fault. Despite the fact that the criminal activity of the victim would not be a defense in a criminal prosecution of the other party, the police are reluctant to arrest in such cases.[80]

The most frequently observed situation of this kind is that in which a man has been tricked out of funds given to a prostitute or pimp. If the victim is insistent the police may attempt to shame him out of desiring police action, but if this is unsuccessful they may proceed to arrest the offender. Often the police will question the victim in an attempt to determine the extent of his own culpability. He will be asked how long he has lived in the vicinity, and an attempt will be made to learn whether he was sufficiently familiar with the area to know that he was exposing himself to this kind of offense by going there.

There is no established department policy to refuse to arrest under these circumstances, and informal policy has not developed to the point where all such cases are treated in the same way. An officer may detain the prostitute long enough to obtain a return of the victim's money; he may arrest and jail the prostitute; he may detain for a while both the prostitute and the man; or he may release the prostitute but detain the victim for a short time. Those officers who refuse to take action in these cases probably do so in part because they know that such a case cannot be successfully prosecuted. It is not likely that a warrant will be issued if the complainant does not have "clean hands," and judges are reluctant to convict in cases of this kind.[81]

---

[79] One case of this kind in which the police will take action is that in which a prostitute is beaten or otherwise mistreated by her pimp. The police strongly desire to prosecute panderers, and such a situation is about the only one in which they can hope to have the prostitute testify against her pimp.

[80] No similar police reaction is to be found regarding the multitude of offenses which involve what might be termed a "willing victim," such as prostitution, gambling, and the illegal sale of liquor or narcotics.

[81] For example, in one case the judge asked the complainant to explain what had happened. The complainant stated that he had given the defendant $15 upon the defendant's promise to obtain some girls, and that the defendant had disappeared with the money. The judge asked again, "And you gave him the money?" The complainant answered, "Yes." The judge said, "And you did this on Hastings Street?" Again the complainant nodded in the affirmative. The judge dismissed the case.

CHAPTER 6

Noninvocation for Reasons Unrelated to Legislative Intent or Resource Limitations

Arrests are deliberately not made for reasons other than those which relate to limitations upon available law enforcement resources or to the presumed desires of the legislature. Although these additional reasons are many and varied, there are four important recurring instances in which an arrest might not be made: (a) the conduct is of a kind which, according to police experience, is not dealt with in an appropriate or effective way by the criminal justice process; (b) the conduct is tolerated and perhaps even supported by the particular local community; (c) more is gained, from a law enforcement point of view, by giving the offender immunity than would be gained by arresting him; or (d) the circumstances of the case are such that the harm caused to the offender or the victim of the offense by an arrest outweighs the good which would be achieved thereby.

A. ARREST WOULD BE INAPPROPRIATE OR INEFFECTIVE

Illustration No. 1: A police patrol came upon a number of skid row bums in an intoxicated condition. The officers knew them all, having found them in this state on numerous other occasions. Although all of them were violating the statutes on public drunkenness and habitual drunkenness, no arrests were made. Another intoxicated derelict, found unconscious on the sidewalk, was arrested for his own safety, but was released the following morning.

Even with sufficient resources, the police would probably view the result of an arrest in certain situations to be so ineffective or so inappropriate that a decision not to arrest would still be justified.[1] They may consider arrest ineffective because (a) the judge will be too lenient; (b) there are no effective means in the system for dealing with the conduct; or (c) utilization of the criminal process will serve only private ends.

Communication between the police and other agencies in the process is generally very poor.[2] An officer's knowledge of how the prosecutor or judge will react to a given case is based on hearsay or his own limited observations. Even so, the police officer often has an idea of what the action of these agencies will be. If he predicts what he considers to be leniency so extreme that the criminal sanction is rendered ineffective, he may arrest and release the suspect without prosecution, a practice discussed elsewhere,[3] or he may not arrest at all.[4] This police dissatisfaction often results in a decision not to arrest some traffic violators, juvenile offenders,[5] and other offenders.

Many of those not now arrested in order to conserve resources would still probably not be arrested even if police resources were unlimited. The habitual drunk would not be arrested because the criminal process lacks the means to treat the alcoholic effectively. Assaults among Negroes probably would be dealt with as they are now because of the belief of officers in the ghetto areas that "they've always been that way and always will be." Similarly, the assumption that the criminal process is not an effective means of dealing with the domestic dispute would prevail even if more resources were available.

This is not to say, however, that the belief that the criminal process cannot effectively deal with certain conduct will always lead to a decision not to arrest. Although it is frequently said that the criminal law cannot effectively deal with drug addicts[6] or homosexuals,[7] they are the object of regular enforcement, undoubtedly reflecting a police and public attitude that their conduct is very undesirable.

---

[1] Because the current system is one in which enforcement resources are not adequate to allow full enforcement of the law, this section must remain somewhat speculative. To what extent the supposed inappropriateness or ineffectiveness of the criminal process would influence invocation decisions, even with adequate resources, is not entirely clear.

[2] See page 153.

[3] See Part V.

[4] Of course, he can sometimes take steps to influence the later results. See page 103, note 6.

[5] See page 107, note 21.

[6] See Joint Committee of A.B.A. and A.M.A., Narcotic Drugs, Drug Addiction: Crime or Disease? (1961) and many citations therein.

[7] See Comment, 70 Yale L.J. 623 (1961) and numerous citations therein.

In some situations the police may find the criminal process effective but inappropriate. This is particularly true when the victim only desires restitution, or if the dispute is primarily civil in nature. The police may also regard the criminal process as inappropriate if the victim has exposed himself to criminal activity by his own misconduct. Even if resources were unlimited, it is not likely that police would take official action in such cases.

B. Arrest Would Cause Loss of Public Respect and Support

Illustration No. 2: A police officer came upon open gambling in a local tavern. The community was known as a "wide-open" town, and much of the revenue in the city came from operation of gambling and entertainment houses. A considerable majority of the community appeared to favor the continuance of such conditions. No arrest was made.

It has long been recognized that public attitudes concerning which laws should or should not be enforced can have a significant effect upon law enforcement.[8] Most of the criteria already discussed are in accord with general public opinion. In many cases in which the public would find enforcement objectionable, such as those concerning social gambling, minor traffic violations, and the like, the police have already adopted a practice of nonenforcement because of doubts as to the legislative desire for enforcement and the belief that resources are more needed elsewhere.[9] Yet other instances of nonenforcement clearly result from public attitudes in certain localities. Although some of this pressure converges upon the prosecutor, it has been said that it is the individual policeman "who usually determines how far popular attitudes shall control." [10]

Law enforcement agencies are often made subject to popular control. Popular election of the sheriff is the general rule and has been in the United States since early times.[11] The appointment of a police administrator, such as the local chief, usually involves careful consideration of the responsiveness of the various candi-

[8] See, for example, Arnold, The Symbols of Government, chap. 7 (1935); Smith, Police Systems in the United States 5-7, 18-19, 285-286, 366-367 (1940).

[9] Indeed, these factors may be traced back to public opinion, as legislative desires and budget appropriations are likewise responsive to it.

[10] Smith, Police Systems in the United States 19-20 (1940).

[11] Id. at 84-85. Thus one study concludes: "In summary it would appear that as chief conservator of the peace of this county the social function of the sheriff is not to enforce the law but to keep that kind and degree of peace which the people want kept." Esselstyn, Crime and Its Control in the Hinterland 239 (unpublished Ph.D. thesis, New York Univ. 1952).

dates to local opinion.[12]   Eligibility may be limited to local residents, just as membership in the police department usually is, in order to insure a department more responsive to the community.[13] In fact, our whole scheme of police organization is largely based upon the concept of local autonomy.   Decentralization and fragmentation "are the most striking characteristics of American police patterns, since no other part of the world has carried local autonomy in police management to such extreme lengths." [14]

Necessary reliance upon public support may have some benefits; it may insure "reasonable" law enforcement and may provide protection from "unfair" enforcement methods.[15]   Yet it is obviously inconsistent with full enforcement of all criminal statutes.   It might be argued that this is also desirable, but, if local opinion were to prevail, the criminal law would have to be viewed not as a mandate for uniform enforcement throughout the state, but rather as a restriction on what conduct the localities could subject to serious sanctions.

It is apparent that complete, state-wide uniformity is not contemplated in the present system.   Local governments can, within limits, pass ordinances which impose minor sanctions on conduct not prohibited by the criminal law.   Usually they can likewise enact ordinances concerning conduct prohibited by the criminal law, thereby providing an alternative basis of action with a lesser penalty.   Also, localities have been given control over appropriations to the police department, which has the effect of rendering full enforcement of state laws totally impossible.

However, it is one thing to acknowledge that these powers have been granted to the local legislative body — city council, county board, and the like; it is another to assert that police administrators should directly attempt to ascertain the desires of the local citizenry and fashion their enforcement program accordingly.   This would result in a complete lack of uniformity throughout the state

[12] Thus open recruitment of a new chief of police is usually opposed. "More than any other position in the municipality, it seems as if the citizen wants to feel assured that the police chief understands the community and its feelings." Sherwood, Roles of City Manager and Police, Public Management 110, 112 (May 1959).

[13] See Smith, Police Systems in the United States 162, 246 (1940). He notes that if public opinion is to be interpreted by the police administrator to determine the extent and direction of popular control, then a local resident can probably do this better. But, he adds, popular control is not always the most vital issue.

[14] Id. at 342.

[15] Not all would agree that popular control produces police fairness. Some are of the opinion that the general public does not care how the police treat persons so long as they restrict their activities to those whom the public considers criminals. See Westley, The Police: A Sociological Study of Law, Custom and Morality 118 (unpublished Ph.D. thesis No. 1197, Dept. of Sociology, Univ. of Chicago, 1951).

and would give rise to numerous other problems.[16] But, if public cooperation is an essential ingredient of law enforcement, then complete aloofness on the part of the police agency would be equally undesirable. "In a democratic society, the corollary is the dependence of professional police upon the public with regard to detection, evidence, financial support, and in the last analysis, the police job itself." [17]

Variations in enforcement from place to place, attributable in part to differing public attitudes in different locales, were frequently observed. Most noticeable is the "wide-open" town, such as the one in Illustration No. 7, above, with a comparatively high tolerance of criminal conduct. Pressure against enforcement in such places may originate from various segments of the community. The chief in one such community indicated that the pressure against enforcing the liquor laws came not only from the tavern owners but also from those he termed the "blue bloods," who superficially support full enforcement but do not want enforcement to reach the point where the tavern operators are not able to pay rent to them. The problem becomes even more complex when public attitudes differ in various sections of the same community.[18]

16 For example, how would the desires of the majority of the local populace be determined? Would not enforcement, fashioned to comply with the public's wishes, tend to reflect the desires of a vocal and influential minority? Cannot more pressure usually be mobilized against enforcement of a particular kind than for enforcement? For example, in a Kansas city, after the police had received complaints that a number of youths were causing minor property damage and disturbing the peace because of their "drag-racing" and similar activities in a particular neighborhood, arrests were made of some of the offenders. Because of this action, however, the police received severe criticism from the parents of those arrested and also from the local newspapers. The police then stopped arresting "hot-rodders."

17 Hall, Police and Law in a Democratic Society, 28 Ind. L.J. 135, 143 (1953). Thus one leading police official flatly asserts: "The police cannot progress ahead of public sentiment." Wilson, Police Planning 48 (2d ed. 1957).

This dilemma is exemplified in the need of the individual officer to have the approval of the people on his beat. As Whyte concluded in his study of an Italian slum he called Cornerville: "There are prevalent in society two general conceptions of the duties of the police officer. Middle-class people feel that he should enforce the law without fear or favor. Cornerville people and many of the officers themselves believe that the policeman should have the confidence of the people in his area so that he can settle many difficulties in a personal manner without making arrests. These two conceptions are in a large measure contradictory. The policeman who takes a strictly legalistic view of his duties cuts himself off from the personal relations necessary to enable him to serve as a mediator of disputes in his area. The policeman who develops close ties with local people is unable to act against them with the vigor prescribed by the law." Whyte, Street Corner Society 136 (2d ed. 1955).

18 Whyte observes: "Under these circumstances the smoothest course for the officer is to conform to the social organization with which he is in direct contact and at the same time to try to give the impression to the outside world that he is en-

State or federal enforcement agencies are often unpopular in certain localities. To the extent that such agencies believe it necessary to maintain good local relations, they may be influenced toward a policy of less than full enforcement. As a result, they may merely report offenses to local officials for action,[19] or they may ignore some observed violations altogether.[20] However, because they are responsive to the state or nation as a whole and are to that extent immune to local pressure, such agencies are often better able than local police to deal with local crime, and vice in particular, especially when a sanction such as loss of liquor license is also administered by a state agency immune from local pressure.[21]

The reasons behind lack of public support for full enforcement vary. First, the average citizen does not really appreciate the need for enforcement in some areas. Thus, when the traffic laws and other safety regulations are violated, "there is serious menace to the general security in ways which the ordinary citizen, under the ordinary circumstances of his experience, does not perceive read-

---

forcing the law. He must play an elaborate role of make-believe, and, in so doing, he serves as a buffer between divergent social organizations with their conflicting standards of conduct." Id. at 138. See also notes 16 and 17 *supra;* Hall, Police and Law in a Democratic Society, 28 Ind. L.J. 135, 143 (1953); Wilson, Police Planning 48 (2d ed. 1957).

[19] Thus, although Michigan State Liquor Commission agents have power to arrest, they prefer to turn the matter over to the local police.

[20] Michigan state troopers passing through Detroit do not take any action against observed traffic violators unless the violation actually involves serious danger to life or property, which is a standard considerably lower than they otherwise apply. In Wisconsin it appears that city limits are considered out of bounds for county traffic officers, so that any attempts at enforcement within the municipalities are strongly resisted. In Madison, it was reported that a local judge had thrown out cases where county officers had arrested in the city, and consequently these officers now ignore most traffic violations while passing through the city.

The Michigan State Police are also cautious not to enter a local situation unless necessary. Particular care is taken by them to avoid local labor and racial disputes, in which they would be most likely to be viewed as interlopers. Care is also taken to insure that the state police are not being called in to be the "fall guy," by having to take action in unpopular cases which the local authorities wish to avoid. In a number of other states the state police are by law forbidden to act in a labor dispute. Wis. Legis. Ref. Lib., The Organization of the Traffic Law Enforcement Agencies in the United States, Research Bull. No. 107, p. 24 (1952).

[21] Enforcement of the liquor laws by local police officials tends to be something of a problem in each of the states. The Beverage and Cigarette Tax Division of the Wisconsin State Department of Taxation is also charged with the enforcement of these laws, but they do not appear to temper their level of enforcement by reacting to public attitudes. One reason for this might be that they are less subject to pressure. Moreover, since their enforcement is limited to gambling, liquor, and prostitution offenses, all of which are usually detected by undercover operations by the agents themselves, no great need for public cooperation is felt — at least not to the extent it would be felt by a state enforcement agency, such as a state police force, charged with general enforcement.

ily, and is not likely to appreciate until a gross instance or a whole-sale disaster shocks the conscience of the community into a spasm of activity." [22]   Second, many criminal statutes apply to the day-to-day conduct of many citizens, with the consequence that "the old easy division of the community into lawbreakers and law observers has thus been destroyed," and enforcement may therefore "prove irritating to the sensibilities of people who believe that they have a right to be let alone." [23]   Finally, public knowledge of a policy

[22] Pound, Criminal Justice in America 19 (1930).

[23] Smith, Police Systems in the United States 10, 18 (1940). A classic illustration of the lack of public support for full enforcement is the following article from the Chicago Daily News of Saturday, March 2, 1963. The article was written by John Justin Smith and entitled "Dear Supt. Wilson — Leave the Good People Alone."
"It was a very fine party . . . for a while. People laughed and had a good time.

"But, wait, let's start at the beginning.

"The party, called a Heart Social, was held last Sunday afternoon in the basement of the Central Park American Legion Post at 3356 W. 83rd St.

"Sponsors were the good women of the post auxiliary. Mrs. Bridget Musacco, head of the auxiliary, explained the purpose of the party thus:

" 'We needed money for our hospital program. We keep the boys in the West Side and Hines (Veterans Administration) hospitals supplied with stuff like socks, razor blades, combs, cigarets and whatnot.

" 'In the past we've raised money with things like bake sales, dances and rummage sales. Frankly, we didn't do so hot. Once we cleared about $6 and that's not enough.'

"SO SOMEBODY DREAMED up the Heart Social. It sounded like a sure-fire way to get more money and it was.

"The ladies of the auxiliary, Robin Hood fashion, ranged Archer Av. in their Brighton Park neighborhood, putting the sleeve on merchants for gifts . . . towels, dishes, pans, gift certificates for a dollar or two, costume jewelry.

"The good women augmented the list of gifts with homemade items, mostly baked goods.

"The idea proved to be a good money raiser. About 160 persons, mostly women, paid $1 each to attend the Heart Social.

"The party began at 3 P.M. and consisted of a game similar to, ahem, Bingo.

"AT ABOUT 5 P.M., the Heart Social came to a crashing halt.

"Let Mrs. Musacco tell you what happened:

" 'The post commander came down to the basement and told me three guys wanted to see me upstairs and I said, "What for . . . for heaven's sake?" And the commander said the cops were up there. The place was raided.'

"The three policemen were polite but firm. They said they had received a complaint that there was gambling in the place.

"They went downstairs and, as they say in Brighton Park and elsewhere, cased the joint. Mrs. Musacco said:

" 'They said they wouldn't arrest me because they couldn't see any money, but one of them told me: "You better close down before the dicks from downtown get here or they will pinch you." '

"Having done this brave thing, the policemen galloped away over the horizon.

"MEANWHILE, down in the basement, the patrons of the Heart Social got panicky, grabbed their hats and coats and fled the scene.

" 'We didn't even get a chance to serve coffee and cake to most of them,' Mrs. Musacco lamented.

"AN ANSWER FOR SUPT. WILSON.

"Many months ago, in a conversation with Police Supt. O. W. Wilson, the old professor parried a question by asking one:

of less than full enforcement in respect to certain criminal statutes results in an attitude by all violators of these statutes that they ought not to be arrested.   Thus the area of traffic enforcement, for example, is made most difficult because it is generally recognized that the police do engage in the practice of warning offending drivers,[24] while pressure from the public diminishes in other areas in which the police are commonly thought to have no discretion.[25]

C. Failure to Arrest Would Benefit the Law Enforcement System

Illustration No. 3: In a routine frisk of a group of persons found under suspicious circumstances, a small quantity of narcotics was found on one of them.   The officers recognized this

---

" 'Do you worry that Chicago will ever be too clean?'

"I laughed and never bothered to answer. I'll take the chance now.

"Yes, Prof. Wilson, I do think Chicago can be what is called 'too clean.' It is right now . . . in some respects.

"Most of the people of Chicago don't want you or your men to raid Heart Socials.

"They want you to go chase some crooks and leave the good people alone."

24 In Wichita the point has been reached where the police often avoid arresting for traffic offenses because of the loss of respect engendered by such action.   Assigning men to traffic work has become a personnel problem because the officers are subjected to considerable abuse and vituperation by the citizenry.   When a traffic offense is written up, the officer really has to "sell" the ticket, sometimes having to talk to the offender for as much as fifteen minutes.   In Milwaukee traffic violators sometimes complain to police supervisors about the fact that they were given a ticket instead of a mere warning.   Another study has also concluded that "for the policeman the traffic violator represents an unpleasant experience."   Westley, The Police: A Sociological Study of Law, Custom and Morality 109 (unpublished Ph.D. thesis No. 1197, Dept. of Sociology, Univ. of Chicago, 1951).

25 For example, the Director of the Enforcement Division of the Michigan State Liquor Commission noted that not infrequently local groups have attempted to exert pressure upon local law enforcement officers because of their strict enforcement of the Liquor Control Act.   He indicated that these local officials have been able to overcome this pressure successfully by emphasizing the fact that they have no discretion in this area.   To strengthen their position, they are able to assert that they are themselves subject to arrest and prosecution in the event that they do not proceed against a known violation of this act.   This is so because one section of the act makes it a misdemeanor for "sheriffs . . . and their deputies . . . , village marshals, constables, officers or members of the village or city police, and members of the department of state police" to "neglect or refuse to perform the duties imposed" by the act.   Mich. Stat. Ann. §18.971 (1937).   Although no officer has ever been proceeded against under this statute, the director was certain that it had been effective in terms of enabling local police to repel pressure for less than full enforcement.

Presumably an officer in Michigan could base his enforcement against any kind of conduct upon another statute which declares it to be a misdemeanor for an officer to neglect to perform a duty enjoined upon him by law.   Mich. Stat. Ann. §28.746 (1938).   This statute probably would not be so helpful, as (a) it does not itself declare full enforcement to be the officer's duty, and (b) assuming it does require full enforcement, knowledge that the law is not fully enforced as to all conduct would make it apparent that the statute is not the effective sanction the officer asserts it to be.

man as one who from time to time informed the police on narcotics peddlers. No arrest was made.

A decision not to arrest may be based upon the premise that it is desirable to trade an arrest for information which will contribute to the detection, arrest, and conviction of a more serious offender.[26] Preferred treatment for the informant may also occur at other stages in the process. He may be given a lighter sentence or may be placed on probation. Because of his willingness to give testimony in court, he may be granted formal or informal immunity by the prosecutor.[27]

The police make substantial use of informants in all three of the jurisdictions studied.[28] They are most often employed in the enforcement of law concerning narcotics but are also used to a lesser degree in cases concerning liquor, gambling, and similar offenses. They not only provide the police with information about persons with whom they associate, but they are also utilized in setting up purchases of illegal goods, in eliciting information from suspects, and in actually making purchases of narcotics. Officers, particularly those engaged in narcotics enforcement, strongly support the informant program. Great care is taken to protect the identity of the informant; often only one detective is aware of an informant's status.[29]

1. *Nature and extent of immunity from arrest.* Police inform-

---

[26] Noninvocation in order to benefit the law enforcement system may also occur if acting in a given case would expose police investigation with respect to other cases thought to be more important. Detroit plainclothesmen often overlook minor offenses for this reason.

Agents of the Beverage and Cigarette Tax Division, Wisconsin State Department of Taxation, who are charged with enforcement of the laws on liquor, gambling, and prostitution, usually operate on an undercover basis, moving from county to county in an irregular pattern. When agents pulled up near a tavern in a county they had just entered, one agent, with the aid of night field glasses, observed activity in the various cars parked outside. One car was observed in which the occupants, apparently minors, were drinking beer. All three investigators left the car and approached this vehicle from different directions. However, when the officers noted the Illinois license on the car it was decided that the arrest of six Illinois minors for drinking beer was not worth the risk of making their own presence known, as they were working on a number of prostitution cases in the county.

Compare the instances in Chapter 10, in which no immediate arrest is made on the same basis.

[27] See 2 A.B.A., Commission on Organized Crime, Organized Crime and Law Enforcement 157-186 (1953). The concern with proper controls over any such arrangement, whereby one person is not proceeded against because he aids in enforcement against others, is reflected therein. The model act set forth there provides for control over the prosecutor, with alternative provisions which require either prior approval of the attorney general or a court finding that immunity would not be "clearly contrary to the public interest."

[28] On use of informants elsewhere, see Deutsch, The Trouble with Cops 98 (2d ed. 1955); Kooken, Ethics in Police Service, 38 J. Crim. L. & C. 172, 174-175 (1947).

[29] Police are cautioned not to "burn" an informant by disclosing his identity. See Kenney, A Guide for Police Planning: Narcotics Operations 10-11 (1954).

ants sometimes assist in enforcement in return for money.[30]   More often, however, especially in narcotics cases, they are rewarded with immunity from arrest.   In all three states a user of narcotics is immune from arrest if he continually supplies information directed toward the apprehension of sellers of narcotics.   However, he is restricted to the use of narcotics; informants are warned that their status in no way gives them a "license to peddle."   An informant's immunity ends if he makes substantial and continued sales after a warning to refrain from doing so.[31]

Police knowledge that the informant is using narcotics is most apparent in cases in which the informant makes a "supervised buy," that is, a purchase of narcotics from a seller which is observed by the police.   In these cases, the narcotics detective expects that the informant will "shoot up a couple of caps" before turning the evidence over to him.[32]   This fact is known to the detective and is often included in the actual case report.   It is, however, rare for an informant to be furnished with narcotics by the police, although this is sometimes necessary when the informant has not been able to make a purchase recently.[33]

Other kinds of conduct may also be tolerated by the police in return for information.   A numbers writer may not be arrested because he has furnished the police with information on "blind pigs"

[30] The Milwaukee department budget of 1955 set aside $1500 as a secret service fund, used in part to buy information.   Elsewhere in the state, including Madison, funds often were not available for this purpose.

Personnel of the Detroit Narcotics Bureau said that they had ample funds for the payment of informants.   In Pontiac the police have a yearly fund of $1000 for this purpose, the usual price being $25 for information leading to arrest, and $25 more if conviction results.

The county board at first refused to provide informant funds for the Sedgwick County, Kansas, Sheriff's Department, but later granted such a fund when it was learned that many other departments had them.   The Wichita department has such funds, and the vice squad pays $25 for useful information.   In the first four and a half months of 1957 the squad paid $900 to informants, an increased amount due to additional activity in the liquor area after the State Alcoholic Beverage Control Board changed its policy and ceased using informants.

[31] Milwaukee officers were observed taking up a position near the apartment of a known user and pusher who had at one time been a minor informant of the narcotics squad, but was now rumored to be pushing heavily.   The narcotics squad officers reported that when they first obtained information that their ex-informant was so engaged, they went to see him and warned him to stop or suffer the consequences.   Since he did not stop, they had now decided to make a case against him.

[32] The following observed instance is typical.   The informer entered the house of the seller and came out in about seven minutes, at which time he returned to the officer's car.   The informant handed the officer ten red capsules of heroin wrapped in tinfoil, stating that he was keeping two for his trouble.

[33] A police supervisor in one Kansas city, noting that his informants had not been able to make any buys of late, said, "I know this is true because they have gotten sick on me a couple of times and I have had to go get them some Dilaudid.   In fact, only two days ago I saw them out on the street and they looked very sick indeed. I guess I will have to go get them some more Dilaudid."

(places where liquor is sold illegally), crap games, or prostitutes. A prostitute may be exempted from arrest and overnight detention[34] because she claims to be "copping for the Feds." A youth may be excused for a minor offense because he is a good source of information on juvenile crime in the area.[35] A traffic ticket may be overlooked if the offender has been a good source of information.[36]

The extent of immunity which informants enjoy is difficult to assess. It undoubtedly varies with the value of the informant. As a general rule, immunity will not be given for offenses as serious or more serious than those for which information is given. It also appears that informants are expected not to commit a crime against an unwilling victim who will report the offense to the police and expect action to follow. For this reason burglars or similar offenders are not granted immunity. It is such offenders as prostitutes, numbers writers, and drug addicts who are allowed to carry on their activities because they supply information. Even their immunity is likely to end, however, if the police receive a specific complaint as to their activity.[37]

The granting of arrest immunity to an informant in exchange for information is, for the most part, a decision made by the individual officer involved. Most of these decisions are made by

[34] This special arrest and overnight detention process is explained in full in Chapter 22.

[35] The sheriff in one Wisconsin county reprimanded a youth who had been involved in a barroom brawl, but then told him that the information he had given in the past had been appreciated and that this practice should continue. After the youth had left, the sheriff explained that this youngster had been a good source of information concerning the activities of young hoodlums in the area. He said that he frequently used this tactic, and in order to induce further cooperation he always had the offender who was being granted immunity write out a "confession" of the conduct in which he was involved.

[36] A supervisor of the Wichita Police Department stated that taxi drivers are often a great help to the vice and detective division, and that in exchange for their information they expect and receive assistance in having traffic citations dropped. He said that this matter is handled between the officer receiving the information and himself. Private persons also supply information in exchange for ticket fixing. A Wichita vice detective was observed receiving information on an auto accessory theft ring in exchange for a promise to fix a ticket obtained by the informant's wife. He said that this man was "of inestimable value as an informant," but he warned the man that he had fixed many tickets for him in the past, and that this was becoming more difficult. On another occasion he recalled that he had fixed about twenty-five tickets for this informant, and he stated that it was often difficult because the informant waited until a warrant had been issued before coming to him.

[37] Thus one Detroit addict, who was well known to detectives as an informant, was immediately arrested when he was reported for shoplifting, and the detectives told him that they were not interested in any "deals" regardless of how much new information he promised. In Pontiac a prostitute was granted immunity because she provided information from time to time. It is interesting to note, however, that when she was reported to the police as having robbed a customer, the police brought her in long enough to retrieve the money and then released her.

members of a narcotics or vice bureau, and there is little indication that the policy is given detailed consideration by anyone higher than the head of the bureau. There is no consultation with persons outside the police department.[38]

2. *Problems created by the informant policy.* The informant program not only creates administrative problems but also gives rise to a serious question of its compatibility with the over-all objectives of criminal justice administration. It is difficult for the individual officer to know who is and who is not an informant. Officers assigned to a particular unit may be aware of the informants serving that unit, but will usually have no knowledge of those serving other units, since considerable care is taken to conceal the identity of police informers. The problem is complicated by the fact that it is also customary to respect the status of informants serving other law enforcement agencies. Some informants are arrested because the officer is unaware of their informer status.[39] More serious is the fact that immunity is given to some persons who are not really informants, because the officer believes they are. It is not uncommon for the police, upon questioning persons on the street, to be told, "I'm working for the Bureau," or "I'm working for Sergeant Smith's crew." [40] The only way in which the patrolmen can be sure that these persons are in fact informants is by checking with the agency for which they claim to be working. Such a check is not usually made, however, unless the person claiming informer status has already been arrested and is in custody.[41]

---

[38] Consultation outside the police agency is unlikely, even when it is a matter of releasing a person already held. An assistant county attorney in Sedgwick County said that police officers, especially detectives, did not consult with his office when they made a deal of this sort, but that his office went along with any deal made. He felt that such cooperation was necessary in order to build up the confidence of the underworld in these detectives. Similar attitudes were expressed elsewhere.

It has been said that an informer program, when established by the police, "constitute[s] a usurpation of legislative function," but that such a program could properly be initiated by the prosecutor or court. Goldstein, Police Discretion Not to Invoke the Criminal Process: Low-Visibility Decisions in the Administration of Justice, 69 Yale L.J. 543, 568-569 (1960).

[39] Thus a federal informant was arrested by Detroit officers on the basis of information provided by a Detroit informant. After consultation with the federal narcotics agents the case was nol-prossed.

[40] For example, after Detroit officers stopped a vehicle in order to question the occupants, each person was searched separately. The driver of the car informed the officers that he was working for the narcotics bureau and was trying to get a buy off the other man in the car. The other man informed the officers that he too was an informant, but for the federal agency, and that he was associating with his companion in the hope of obtaining information on the sale of narcotics.

[41] For example, a Detroit narcotics user complained that his friend, a prostitute, had been arrested in violation of a promise that she would be immune from arrest as long as he continued as an informant. The lieutenant called the narcotics bureau and learned that no such arrangement had been made.

There is often a difference of opinion within a single department about the value of an informant program. Giving immunity to an informant may make one unit's job easier but it may complicate the task of another unit. Toleration of one class of offenders may seem justified to a specialized police unit but not to the department as a whole.[42] As a result, some units may complain that overly strict enforcement has dried up good sources of information, while other units feel that the information received does not justify immunity.[43]

Although the narcotics informant undoubtedly facilitates narcotics law enforcement in specific instances, his contribution to the deterrence of narcotics traffic generally has not been adequately assessed. There is no policy of continual re-evaluation to decide whether the benefits of the program outweigh its disadvantages.[44]

D. Arrest Would Cause Harm to the Offender or Victim Outweighing the Risk from Inaction

There are situations in which the police do not arrest because they believe that the risk involved in inaction is not so great as to justify the harm which would be caused to the suspect or others by

[42] Another study reports that for this reason detectives and officers granting immunity to informants try to conceal this tactic from others in the department. Westley, The Police: A Sociological Study of Law, Custom and Morality 69, 73 (unpublished Ph.D. thesis No. 1197, Dept. of Sociology, Univ. of Chicago, 1951).

[43] A supervisory officer of the Detroit Homicide Bureau objected, "All sources of information are dried up. In the past we used to be able to stop pimps and whores on the street and get something from them. Now they won't talk at all. We, as detectives, are not concerned with that aspect of police work. We feel it is much more important to catch murderers and stick-up men even if it means allowing a pimp or whore to operate another week or so before they get caught."

In response to this attitude, a high official in the department stated that in his view the source of information did not justify leaving these undesirable characters on the streets. Rather, he thought that these persons should have no immunity, and that the detectives should "have to get out and work instead of waiting for the telephone to ring."

[44] Not only do the police thus forfeit the opportunity to rehabilitate the person in terms of his addiction, but they are also taking a calculated risk that the addict will not indulge in more serious kinds of crime while he remains free. For example, one addict who was still free because he was a source of information was apprehended for shoplifting; but he and others could resort to yet more serious conduct in order to obtain the money needed to satisfy their addiction. If the informant program is desirable, this may suggest that furnishing informants with narcotics might be preferable to allowing the addict to remain free without access to the quantity of drugs he needs to satisfy his craving.

For one view on the questions of whether the program fulfills the retributive, restraining, and reformative functions of the state narcotics laws, and whether it implements the deterrent function of criminal law administration, see Goldstein, Police Discretion Not to Invoke the Criminal Process: Low-Visibility Decisions in the Administration of Justice, 69 Yale L.J. 543, 569-572 (1960).

the arrest itself. On one side of the balance is the risk of further criminal conduct and the loss of respect for criminal justice administration if an arrest is not made.[45] On the other side is the harm which might be caused to the person arrested because of his age, reputation, or other individual characteristics, and also the trauma which might be caused to the victim or his family by requiring degrading testimony in court.

> *Illustration No. 4:* A traffic officer stopped a car that had been going 15 m.p.h. over the speed limit. The driver was a youth, but he had a valid driver's license. Although the 15 m.p.h. excess was beyond the ordinary toleration limit for speeding violations, the officer only gave the youth a severe warning. The officer knew that the law required suspension of the license of a juvenile driver for any moving violation.

One kind of harm-risk balancing which usually results in no arrest being made arises from a disagreement between the police and the legislature on what the penalty should be for certain criminal violations. This may occur when the necessary punishment is thought to be excessive by the police, considering the circumstances of the particular case.[46] Thus, because Wisconsin law requires that the license of a juvenile driver be suspended or revoked for any moving violation,[47] traffic officers are likely merely to warn the youth unless the violation is really serious.[48] Similarly, high minimum sentences for traffic offenses have been opposed on the ground

---

[45] See page 147. Thus arrest, charging, conviction, and punishment may be deemed necessary notwithstanding the fact there does not appear to be any risk of further violation by the offender. See Mead, The Psychology of Punitive Justice, 23 Am. J. Sociology 577 (1918).

[46] It is interesting that a decision not to invoke also may be made in these areas because it is thought that the penalty will be too light. See page 125. This suggests that in these areas there is a considerable variation in penalties imposed by different judges and also considerable difference of opinion by police as to the appropriate punishment.

[47] Wis. Stat. §48.36 (1955).

[48] The following is a newspaper account of a talk on juvenile drivers by Deputy Inspector Dahl, in charge of police training in Milwaukee, given at the Public Affairs Forum. "He also recommended that 16 and 17 year old drivers 'pay fines and be handled like adults' in moving traffic violation cases. He said the teenagers should be under the point system as adults were.

"Now, 16 and 17 year olds have their licenses suspended for first offenses. Dahl said officers often did not like to arrest youngsters when it meant that their licenses would be suspended for a violation which would mean only the loss of points for adults. . . .

"Judge John J. Kenney of the children's court said juvenile offenders should be handled in his court, not just required to pay a fine in 'the cash register court.'

"He said that difficulties, such as problems between the juvenile and a parent, came to light in appearances in his court. He also said he thought the children's court judge should have discretion in the matter of license suspension.

"He noted that when a teen ager lost his driver's license, he sometimes lost a job for which he needed a car." Milwaukee Journal, April 13, 1960, pt. 2, p. 11, col. 3.

that they would induce traffic officers to overlook many violations.[49] The absence of discretion at the judicial level may result in discretion being assumed at an earlier and less visible point in the process.[50]

> *Illustration No. 5:* A police officer was called to a store where a youth had been caught stealing some minor items. The officer administered a severe warning and then allowed the youth to go on his way. No further action was contemplated, as the officer knew that the youth had not been in trouble before.

In evaluating the imposition upon the offender, consideration is given to the cumulative effect of the money fine, restrictions which may be imposed,[51] and the inconvenience involved in court appearance.[52] If one or more of these predictable consequences is viewed as excessive, considering the circumstances of the offense, the police may choose not to arrest rather than subject the offender to them.

Despite the fact that juvenile procedures are designed to minimize the harmful effects of arrest and detention and to maximize the rehabilitative effects of the correctional treatment that is given, arrest and prosecution are nevertheless likely to have harmful effects on a youth. Even when a youth is later released, arrest in itself is considered by some to cause excessive harm, and so to be avoided, especially if the offense is minor.[53]

---

[49] At the 1956 Wisconsin Traffic Court Conference in Madison, one county judge suggested that high minimum sentences for traffic offenses cause what he termed "court on the highway," with traffic officers often deciding not to invoke the full process.

[50] Of course, here again it is necessary to keep in mind the possibility of the police officer's being in a position to influence the later penalty. He may do this either by attempting to influence the charge selection or by determining which judge will hear the case. See page 103, note 6. Where the offense is more serious, the officer may view these possibilities as the only way in which to alleviate the situation, as invocation is necessary.

[51] Under the Wisconsin point system, a relatively minor violation, added to points for earlier violations, may result in the driver's losing his license.

[52] In Milwaukee, an ordinance was proposed which would allow drivers to stipulate to certain moving violations, including failure to yield the right of way, inattentive driving, and deviating in traffic. A local judge was reported as saying that the ordinance was "making the policeman a judge of the offense and the city attorney the prosecutor and the judge." The assistant city attorney who drew up the ordinance responded that "policemen and the city attorney must use their judgment in every case with or without the new ordinance." He said that "the new procedure would make it unnecessary for defendants to spend all day in court just to plead guilty on minor traffic violations." Milwaukee Journal, June 27, 1961, pt. 1, p. 21, col. 1.

[53] This is the assumption underlying one recent analysis of police responsibilities in this area. "Exercise of . . . [police discretion in juvenile delinquency cases] is necessary to effectuate individualized handling based on the principle that, in the usual case, the home is the best place for the rearing of a child." Myren and

Illustration No. 6: Officers responding to a call of a disturbance of the peace found the noise to be emanating from an apartment. After restoring order, they learned that the argument began when the husband appeared at his wife's apartment to attempt a reconciliation. Neighbors reported that the couple was currently seeking professional assistance from a marriage counselor. The police decided that arrest would only aggravate the situation, so they gave a warning and left.

In other cases an arrest may be thought undesirable because the victim and offender are in a continuing relationship which will be seriously disrupted if criminal proceedings are undertaken. This may be true in family disputes, in which case an arrest might make reconciliation impossible.[54] Similarly, an arrest for an offense resulting from a neighborhood quarrel may cause harm to the relationship which would exceed the benefit gained thereby.[55]

Illustration No. 7: A woman returned home from work in a disheveled condition and told her husband that she had been kidnapped and raped. The husband called the police, and they began an investigation. Upon questioning the woman the following day, the police discerned some discrepancies in her story, and she finally admitted that she and a man had engaged in lovemaking by mutual consent, and that she had fabricated the story in order to explain her absence to her husband. Since proceeding against the woman for a false felony report would have endangered her marriage, the police decided to take no action.[56]

The instances of harm-risk balancing which present the greatest difficulties are perhaps those based upon the unique circumstances of the individual case. The need for such individualized treat-

---

Swanson, Police Work with Children 28 (1962). For recommendations on how discretion should be exercised in certain recurring situations, see id. at 39-57.

[54] Indeed, even if agencies in the criminal process are going to play a part in mediation of the dispute, arrest is ordinarily avoided. See Chapter 9.

[55] What appears to be the attitude of the police in the states studied is reflected very well in the following excerpt from police training materials of another jurisdiction: "But promptness of action is not enough. Supervisors must also be concerned with the question of how the clearance or disposition was made. . . . Another policeman may dispose of a neighborhood quarrel report by arresting one of the parties concerned in the row, and through this act precipitate one of those never ending feuds which will be the cause of numerous calls for police assistance in the future." California State Dept. of Education, California Peace Officers Training Publication No. 71, Police Supervisory Control 8 (1957).

Other enforcement considerations may be operative in regard to continuing relationships, as seen at page 196.

[56] This incident was observed in Detroit. In 1955 and 1956, fifty-eight and sixty-three persons, respectively, were charged with filing a false felony report. Detroit Police Dept., 90th Stat. Ann. Rep. 40 (1955); 91st Stat. Ann. Rep. 40 (1956).

ment of cases is well recognized at the sentencing stage, when discretion is usually exercised to make it possible for the sentence to reflect the individual circumstances of the case.[57] While it is agreed that "the power of adjusting the operation of legal precepts to the exigencies of special circumstances is unavoidable if there is to be a complete system of justice according to law," [58] this may not be thought to necessitate discretion at the arrest stage.[59] The case for such discretion is stated by Justice Breitel:

> Discretion too must play its role very early — at the inception of a criminal matter. Criminal proceedings, by their very nature, are summary and often effected in immediate pursuit of the wrong and the wrongdoer. Mere arrest may destroy reputation, or cause the loss of a job, or visit grave injury upon a family. Hailing the arrestee promptly before a magistrate, though serving due process, may be no boon indeed, to the innocent or technical violator.[60]

A police decision not to arrest because of unique circumstances is most likely to occur in situations in which it is apparent that arrest itself, considering the nature of the offense, would greatly harm the suspect.[61] Thus a man with no police record, with a respectable position in the community, and with a wife and family, was not arrested for taking indecent liberties with a child because there was some doubt as to whether the offense had occurred, and future conduct of this nature appeared improbable.[62] A youth found involved in homosexual activities while intoxicated may not

[57] There is no agreement upon what the limits of individualizing should be, however. See Hall, General Principles of Criminal Law 56 (2d ed. 1960).

[58] Pound, Discretion, Dispensation and Mitigation: The Problem of the Individual Special Case, 35 N.Y.U.L. Rev. 925, 936-937 (1960).

[59] Thus Hall contends: "If we agree that it is preferable to have a legal system with the attendant guarantees against official abuse, then we are bound to accept the limitations of any such system and recognize that mitigation, not exculpation, is the relevant recourse in meritorious cases." Hall, General Principles of Criminal Law 55 (2d ed. 1960).

[60] Breitel, Controls in Criminal Law Enforcement, 27 U. Chi. L. Rev. 427, 431 (1960).

[61] Sometimes this harm is minimized by charging an offense with a less objectionable label. For example, a Detroit assistant prosecutor charged a young man with disorderly conduct rather than with contributing to the delinquency of a minor because of the connotation of the latter charge.

[62] The factors weighed were (a) the effect on the suspect (a recorded arrest for indecent liberties would be likely seriously to affect this man in his relationship with his family and the community); (b) the effect on the victim (the child would have to appear in court and testify as to what occurred); and (c) the risk from no action (the man was visibly shaken by what had transpired, and appeared to realize fully the damaging effect which official action would have on his life, so that recurrence seemed unlikely). This example is not from observation in the states studied but was related by New York Supreme Court Justice Charles D. Breitel in a talk entitled "The Controls in Criminal Law Enforcement," presented at the Conference on Criminal Justice, Univ. of Chicago Law School, Jan. 7, 1960.

be arrested.[63] A juvenile offender from a respectable family may not be arrested if the family reputation would thus be endangered, and if it appears likely that disciplinary action will be taken by his family.[64]

In the indecent liberties case referred to above, the fact that the young victim would have to appear in court and repeat the details of what transpired may also have prompted the decision not to arrest. Testifying in public in certain kinds of criminal cases is not only humiliating but may be a severely traumatic experience for the victim, especially for a child.[65] In other cases the decision not to arrest is made out of consideration for the victim because publicity concerning his involvement with the offender would be harmful to him.[66]

[63] Thus another study reports a "rookie" recollecting experiences from his training period with older officers. The rookie related a situation in which they came upon a parked car, and the more experienced officer "went up there, and pretty soon he called to me and there were a couple of fellows in the car with their pants open. I couldn't understand it. I kept looking around for where the woman could be. They were both pretty plastered. One was a young kid about 18 years old and the other was an older man. We decided with the kid so drunk that bringing him in would only ruin his reputation and we told him to go home. Otherwise we would have pinched them." Westley, The Police: A Sociological Study of Law, Custom and Morality 267 (unpublished Ph.D. thesis No. 1197, Dept. of Sociology, Univ. of Chicago, 1951).

[64] See Goldman, The Differential Selection of Juvenile Offenders for Court Appearance 167ff (unpublished Ph.D. thesis, Dept. of Sociology, Univ. of Chicago, 1950); Westley, *supra,* at 147.

[65] In another study it is reported that the police use on-the-spot force as an alternative to arrest in many cases involving sexual misconduct because they know the offender will be released in order to spare the victims from embarrassment. Westley, *supra,* at 118.

[66] For example, a woman notified the Milwaukee sheriff's office that she had received several anonymous telephone calls from a woman instructing her to meet with the caller at a given place. After trying unsuccessfully on several occasions to meet the caller, the woman obtained her name, which was passed on to the officers. The woman who had made the calls was interviewed, and she claimed that the calls were intended for the complainant's husband. At this point the police began to suspect an extortion plot. Consequently, the husband was privately interviewed, and he revealed that the woman was a known prostitute with whom he had had relations over a four-year period, and who for some time had been extorting money from him by threats to expose him. He was a prominent businessman in the community with four grown children, one of them a clergyman, and he stated that he did not want any publicity in connection with this matter, nor did he want his wife to learn of the situation. Therefore, the sergeant in the sheriff's office, who was handling the case, decided to proceed no further, and the matter was dismissed without arrest and without any attempt to bring it to the attention of the district attorney. It is likely that arrest of the woman would in itself have caused the harm it was hoped to avoid since the local newspapers would probably not have cooperated in keeping the matter secret.

Similarly, a sergeant of the Michigan State Police reported that a recurring situation is that in which they learn about some of the one-girl prostitution operations around the state. A man will report to the police that he woke up in a hotel room with his car gone, his money gone, the girl gone, and with a hangover. The police usually locate the car in the immediate area with little difficulty. However, no

Police officers often consult the prosecutor in cases in which individual circumstances create doubt as to whether an arrest ought to be made.[67] This may be because the police are uncertain of their right to make this kind of decision.

While a decision not to arrest is sometimes made because of the special circumstances of the individual case, this does not frequently happen, because the relevant circumstances are usually not known until after the arrest. The case in the illustration is unique because the woman was present for questioning as a supposed victim to a crime. In other cases these facts have become apparent only after arrest.[68] Thus, the most that can be done in the usual case is to "undo" the arrest by insuring it does not become known.[69]

---

attempt is made to apprehend and prosecute the girl, as the victim does not want his wife to learn of his indiscretion, and the police are willing to cooperate with him in this regard. Of course, another reason for noninvocation in this situation is that dealt with on page 122.

[67] Such consultation is also the usual procedure when these factors are considered after arrest, even when the officers feel strongly that the persons should not be held. However, sometimes the desk lieutenant makes such a determination.

[68] For example, a man was arrested when a woman complained that he had been exhibiting himself from an auto. After arrest, it was discovered that the man came from a wealthy family, could afford private psychiatric care, and was in fact undergoing such care. In another case, after an officer arrested a man who accosted him for purposes of performing a homosexual act, it was learned that the man had a fine medical practice in town, was supporting his parents, and was willing to consult a psychiatrist.

[69] For example, a patrolman arrested a transvestite walking down an alley and the driver of a car who had been following him and who admitted to the patrolman that the homosexual had offered to commit an act of sodomy. The lieutenant spoke briefly with the driver, and told him that he was letting him go only because he was a married man and that prosecution would lead to further complications. No record of the arrest was made, and the man was detained for only a short time.

Often when apparently respectable persons are arrested on charges of homosexuality, the officer will tell the arrestee that no notoriety will result from the arrest.

CHAPTER 7

Arrest in Cases in Which the Process Is Not Ordinarily Invoked

Preceding chapters have dealt with those generalized situations in which, for various reasons, it is decided that the offender should not be subjected to the criminal process. Nonenforcement in such situations is not, however, uniform. Exceptional circumstances sometimes exist which cause an arrest to be made despite the fact that the offense or conduct is of a type ordinarily not subjected to enforcement. The purpose of this chapter is to identify when and why this occurs.

A. ARREST TO AVOID A STRAIN UPON AVAILABLE RESOURCES

Illustration No. 1: Police reporting to the scene of a disturbance found a family squabble, involving a minor assault on a spouse. Although the usual procedure was merely to restore order and leave, the officers recalled that they had received repeated calls to this particular address in the past. Therefore the offender was arrested.

Arrests are sometimes made only because the police decide that such action must be taken to minimize the necessity of future police action. This supposed need to avoid future strain upon departmental resources may result in enforcement against persons who have required considerable attention in the past, as in the above illustration, or it may bring about a new policy of enforcement against a general class of conduct not previously subjected to arrest.

While domestic disputes are not ordinarily the object of enforcement, an arrest will often be made if the police have had to respond to the same address on a number of prior occasions, particularly if there are no other effective means of terminating the dispute. For example, in Detroit there is a Misdemeanor Complaint Bureau to which family disputes can be referred. At this bureau an effort is made by informal methods to mediate the dispute and to prevent its recurrence by putting one or both of the parties on a so-called peace bond. The patrolman faced with a family problem which he cannot effectively deal with on the spot is likely to refer the parties to this bureau rather than make an arrest.[1]

If the police believe that they are devoting an inordinate amount of their resources to certain kinds of conduct with regard to which nonenforcement has been the rule, there may be a general reversal of policy in the hope of either deterring such conduct or reducing the number of complaints. In one Michigan community the chief became disturbed over the great number of domestic disputes to which members of the department were being called. He issued a directive that in the future an arrest was to be made in all such cases, presumably because he felt that this would put an end to such calls for police service. The policy had been in effect only a week when it was reversed by the city attorney.[2]

The precise outcome of a continued policy of full enforcement in such cases is difficult to predict.[3] The policy was not continued long enough to determine whether it would have a significant impact on the incidence of such assaults in the community. More likely the effect would be to reduce the number of complaints when it became known that the spouse would be put in jail as a consequence of any complaint made. Such a consequence would

[1] This bureau is staffed by detectives who are very competent in handling family disputes because of their specialization in this kind of problem. At an informal hearing at which the husband and wife appear, the detectives may attempt to resolve the problem themselves or may decide to refer the case to a social agency or to another agency within the criminal justice system, or they may suggest that the parties consult an attorney. In this way the necessity for further police services is minimized. But, in any event, the couple is made aware of the fact that this bureau is the appropriate agency to handle such problems, so that in the future they will contact this bureau rather than the precinct station.

[2] This raises the interesting question of what the role of the city attorney should be in setting enforcement policy. While it was reported that the city attorney overruled the chief's policy of full enforcement against domestic disputes, it may be that he merely reminded the chief that his policy would require the police to act illegally in some instances. First, strict interpretation of the order might result in arrest when no offense had been committed. Second, compliance with the order would necessitate some arrests for misdemeanors not committed in the officer's presence.

[3] For a report of the decline in intrafamily assaults in Oakland, California, after a similar policy change from nonenforcement to enforcement, and a discussion of the inevitable question of whether the decline represents a decrease in actual or reported assaults, see Goldstein, Police Discretion Not to Invoke the Criminal Process: Low-Visibility Decisions in the Administration of Justice, 69 Yale L.J. 543, 577-580 (1960).

not necessarily be desirable, particularly if no other agency were ready to assume the task of mediating family disputes which had been handled by the police.[4]

B. Arrest to Maintain Respect for the Police

Illustration No. 2: A police patrol stopped a car that had been traveling at 39 m.p.h. in a 30 m.p.h. zone. They decided prior to leaving the squad car that they would only issue a warning. When the deputies approached, the driver said in a sarcastic tone, "What in hell have I done now?" Because of his belligerent attitude the driver was placed under arrest.

Just as an officer might decide not to arrest when to do so would result in loss of public support,[5] so he might arrest a person who ordinarily would not be arrested in order to maintain respect for the police or the law enforcement system as a whole.[6] A "spite arrest," where a person is taken into custody solely because he has incurred the disfavor of a particular officer, is certainly subject to criticism.[7] However, it is more difficult to judge an arrest of an offender who ordinarily would not be proceeded against, in a situation where a failure to make the arrest would result in loss of respect for the police.

Even if an offender's discourtesy is not intentional, it might be sufficiently abusive in the eyes of bystanders to cause the officer to make an arrest. For example, in one Michigan community a number of patrons were leaving a bar which was about to close. One of them was obviously in no condition to drive, so a plainclothes officer suggested that he take a taxi. The drunk did not realize that the officer was a policeman, and in front of the other patrons told him to "go to hell." The man was placed under arrest and taken to the station.[8]

---

[4] For a discussion of other, similar problems emanating from law enforcement agencies performing functions in the nature of social services, see Allen, The Borderland of the Criminal Law: Problems of "Socializing" Criminal Justice, 32 Social Serv. Rev. 107 (1958).

[5] See page 127.

[6] "The decision upon the part of the individual policeman as to what kind of action to take in a specific situation involves the interrelation of three variables: the enforcement of the law, the maintenance of respect for the police, and the apprehension of the felon." Westley, The Police: A Sociological Study of Law, Custom and Morality 197 (unpublished Ph.D. thesis No. 1197, Dept. of Sociology, Univ. of Chicago, 1951).

[7] In fact, such tactics, because they have no direct relation to policies and practices related to the ultimate objectives of the criminal justice system, are not considered herein.

[8] Similarly, another study reports that the drunk, usually treated with leniency, is arrested if he curses the officer in the presence of others. Westley, The Police:

Arrests of this kind occur most frequently in the case of drunks, traffic violators,[9] and juveniles.[10]   They occur less often in other minor offenses.[11]   A minor offender who lies about a past criminal record [12] may also be arrested.   If a complainant who has engaged in criminal conduct himself, such as patronizing a prostitute, becomes argumentative because he is dissatisfied with the police officer's action,[13] or creates difficulties for the officer by refusing to admit his own guilt,[14] he is likely to be arrested.

C. Arrest to Maintain Public Image of Full Enforcement

Illustration No. 3:   The police were aware of the operation of a private card game in which there was no house "cut." Since this operation therefore qualified as mere social gambling, no action was taken against the offenders.   However, the operators of the game made no attempt to conceal the operation, and it was soon apparent to the general public that the police must be aware of it.   Realizing this, the police arrested the gamblers.

A Sociological Study of Law, Custom and Morality 198 (unpublished Ph.D. thesis No. 1197, Dept. of Sociology, Univ. of Chicago, 1951).

9 For example, a local newspaper in Wisconsin reported an incident in which a village officer stopped a driver "for going 45 miles an hour in a 35 mile zone.   The officer claimed he only intended to warn her, but when she raised objections, he arrested her."   Milwaukee Journal, July 26, 1960, pt. 2, p. 1, col. 6.

Another study likewise noted that traffic violators who argued with the officer or claimed to know more about the law than he were arrested.   Westley, *supra,* at 153.

10 Another study concludes: "Almost all police officials agree that 'defiance on the part of a boy will lead to juvenile court quicker than anything else.'   Such damage to the dignity of the police will lead to court referral even in minor cases."   Goldman, The Differential Selection of Juvenile Offenders for Court Appearance 145 (unpublished Ph.D. thesis No. T 914, Dept. of Sociology, Univ. of Chicago, 1950).

11 The observed practice would appear to conform to Westley's conclusion: "The emphasis placed on the maintenance of respect for the police makes the attitude of the offender a major factor in the policeman's decision as to whether he will act against him except in the case of crimes on the felony level.   Thus there is a tendency to let the respectful offender off easily, but to give the works to the disrespectful offender."   Westley, The Police: A Sociological Study of Law, Custom and Morality 297 (unpublished Ph.D. thesis No. 1197, Dept. of Sociology, Univ. of Chicago, 1951).

12 For example, a Wichita officer stopped a drunken driver, who had almost hit the police car, just as he arrived at his home.   The officer stated that he had not intended to arrest the offender, and would not have done so had not a check with the dispatcher disclosed that the driver had lied about his past record.

13 Thus a drunken complainant who reported an attempted assault abused the police because no immediate arrest was made and was himself arrested.

14 A man who had engaged the services of a prostitute and then had become involved in a fight with her concerning the value of her services was locked up when he objected violently to the officer's statement that he too had violated the law.

This situation is similar to, but distinguishable from, the preceding illustration. The maintenance of the public image of full enforcement and thus respect for the law itself is sometimes thought to require that the law be enforced against conduct not usually considered a matter for official concern. The extremes to which such an attitude may be carried have been described by Thurman Arnold:

> It is important to keep in mind that we are concerned with Law Enforcement as a sort of creed, and not with the enforcement of any particular rule. When, by imperceptible gradations, emphasis is changed from the purpose or merits of a rule itself to the notion that the very prestige of government depends on enforcement as a kind of ceremonial, to be observed even toward obnoxious legislation — when the enforcement becomes directed, not to preserve public safety or convenience, but to justify a moral attitude toward law regardless of public convenience — then the common-sense idea with which we started has become the mystical ideal called Law Enforcement.[15]

Some social gambling cases illustrate this point. When police do arrest in cases of nonprofessional gambling, as in the above illustration, this is prompted by a desire to avoid the impression of nonenforcement.[16] Generally, however, it is possible to maintain a reasonably good image of full enforcement while following a policy of nonenforcement in regard to many offenses since most instances of a failure to arrest are less visible than those concerned with open gambling.[17] Sometimes, current public concern about a

[15] Arnold, The Symbols of Government 152 (1935). His Chapter 7 explores this matter in more detail and is an excellent statement.

[16] Thus the policy of the Michigan State Police racket squad was not to attempt to quash private dice and card games in which there was no house "cut" unless such games became public or flagrant. The Director of Public Safety in Pontiac moved to eliminate bingo games by fraternal, religious, and veterans' organizations when they began to be operated quite openly.

Because, in some cases observed, the most vocal groups in the community and the greatest concentration of pressure appeared to be for nonenforcement, it is evident that the real purpose behind the arrests was to promote this image of full enforcement, rather than to maintain public support.

[17] A review of earlier chapters will show that there is no likelihood of the public's becoming aware of the nonenforcement policy adopted in regard to the kinds of conduct discussed therein. See also page 153.

On other occasions, however, the police may go to considerable trouble to avoid the appearance of a policy of nonenforcement or unfair enforcement. For example, a United Press dispatch, Dec. 26, 1962, from Monroe, Wisconsin, reports that members of the county board there became embroiled with the local police because their cars were being ticketed for parking meter violations while parked around the courthouse square. The city police finally agreed that board members had a right to park free of charge around the square, inasmuch as it was county property. However, local officers charged with enforcement against meter violations were instructed to continue giving tickets in all cases, even if the car was known to belong

particular, widely-publicized incident also prompts a higher level of enforcement against certain conduct than otherwise would be undertaken.[18]

Basically the question is whether it is desirable for the public to be aware of a policy of less than full enforcement. Widespread recognition of the exercise of discretion by the police makes the appearance of impartiality more difficult to achieve. Public pressure on the police for nonenforcement in individual cases is greatest when it is known that the conduct is not usually subject to full enforcement.[19] Perhaps this is the implication of the assertion that "the worst evil of disregard for some laws is that it destroys respect for all law." [20]

D. ARREST TO PUNISH A PERSON SUSPECTED OF OTHER CRIMINAL ACTIVITY

Illustration No. 4: The police learned of a minor property theft. As the victim was not interested in prosecution, the police, in accord with their usual policy, decided not to arrest. However, when they learned that the offender was known to the police department as a "bad actor," and that the police had been unsuccessful in obtaining his conviction for other, more serious offenses, they arrested him.

If the police know or suspect a person to be responsible for a relatively serious offense, but cannot assemble sufficient admissible evidence to bring about his conviction, they may arrest him for an

---

to a county board member. Although tickets on board members' cars are later torn up at the police station, the police explained that the ticketing itself would continue "in order to carry out the intent of the law and not to give other violators an impression of favoritism."

18 For example, a twelve-year-old boy was arrested for taking liberties with a six-year-old girl. Examination showed that he had not raped or otherwise physically harmed the child. Although the boy came from a good home and the police authorities thought that the act was one of curiosity rather than evil intent, the boy was committed to the juvenile court. Such action was deemed necessary because of the disturbed state of the public resulting from the newspaper accounts of a brutal sex killing in a nearby community. Goldman, The Differential Selection of Juvenile Offenders for Court Appearance 144 (unpublished Ph.D. thesis No. T 914, Dept. of Sociology, Univ. of Chicago, 1950).

19 See page 127.

20 Arnold, The Symbols of Government 151 (1935). He quotes a statement made by President Hoover in connection with the report of the Wickersham Commission. See also Williams, Turning a Blind Eye, 1954 Crim. L. Rev. (Eng.) 271: "For the police to ignore breaches of a particular law, for whatever reason, is to offer a license to sections of the community to violate those laws at will. Further, it is to demand that the rest of the community ignore the breaches also. . . . If public servants such as the police are to choose which laws to enforce and which to ignore, then naturally the public will make such a choice too."

offense which can be proved even though that conduct would not ordinarily be proceeded against. So used, the large body of usually unenforced criminal laws becomes "an arsenal of weapons with which to incarcerate certain dangerous individuals who are bothering society." [21] Thurman Arnold has observed:

> . . . so far as the effect of the number of criminal laws on policemen or the prosecutor is concerned, they are more apt to be a help than a hindrance. Such persons are trying to apprehend individuals who at the time happen to be considered dangerous to society, and the wider the selection of laws which they have, the more chance there is of conviction.[22]

One Detroit police lieutenant said that he instructed his men that it is desirable to arrest, notwithstanding the fact that the conduct usually does not call for such action, whenever the offender is "a known criminal the police desire to get off the street." This practice was observed in all three states. The typical case is that of a bad check or a minor theft, in which the police make a strenuous effort to persuade the victim to cooperate in the prosecution because the offender is known to the police as a "bad actor." Ordinarily the offender would be allowed to make restitution and no official action would be taken.

Despite the efforts which are being made to eliminate certain statutes which seem to be only selectively enforced,[23] there remain, even in the newest, most carefully drafted criminal codes, many statutes which the individual police officer will continue to use at his own discretion as a basis for arresting offenders whom he suspects but cannot prove to be guilty of more serious offenses.[24] Although the use of such discretion increases the capacity of the police to take effective action against persons thought dangerous to society, the opportunity for improper use of discretion will continue to exist.[25]

---

21 Arnold, The Symbols of Government 153 (1935).

22 Id. at 160.

23 The Model Penal Code, in omitting some sexual offenses, presents the argument that they are used for purpose of discriminatory enforcement. See Model Penal Code 204-210 (Tent. Draft No. 4, 1955).

24 For example, it has already been noted that the laws on bad checks and theft, usually not invoked in certain circumstances, are so used. And the use of the income tax laws to deal with known gangsters is universally known. For a more detailed discussion of this problem, see Remington and Rosenblum, The Criminal Law and the Legislative Process, 1960 U. Ill. L.F. 481, 493-494.

25 See People v. Winters, 171 Cal. App. 2d Supp. 876, 342 P.2d 538 (Super. Ct. 1959); Hargrove, Police Discretion, 25 Sol. 337 (1958).

E. ARREST TO AID IN INVESTIGATION OF ANOTHER OFFENSE OR OFFENDER

Illustration No. 5: Narcotics officers were following a person suspected of carrying narcotics. The officers lacked grounds to arrest, however. Observing the suspect commit a minor traffic violation, one which ordinarily would only result in a warning, the officers placed the suspect under arrest and searched the car for narcotics.

Illustration No. 6: Officers saw a man leave an out-of-state car in the vicinity of a pawnshop with a jacket on his arm. The suspect, when questioned, said that he had no employment but had come to the city to find work. He could provide no identification, but explained this by saying that his wallet had recently been stolen. He was somewhat evasive in answering other questions. The police suspected him of burglary, but lacking evidence for this charge, they arrested him for vagrancy.

Illustration No. 7: Officers had reasonable grounds to believe that a particular man was responsible for a recent homicide. However, desiring an opportunity to conduct a prolonged in-custody investigation, they arrested him on a vagrancy charge. He was then convicted for vagrancy, and the murder investigation was continued while he served his sentence.

An arrest might be made for conduct not ordinarily subjected to the criminal process because the arrest facilitates the investigation of another, more serious offense. Arrest for the minor offense may aid in the investigation of the more serious offense because it provides a lawful basis for (a) taking custody; (b) conducting a search; or (c) if followed by a continuance or conviction, a longer in-custody investigation than would be possible if the arrest had been made for the serious offense.

Many courts have upheld without question the validity of searches made incidental to arrests for offenses not normally subject to arrest. Recently, however, the trend has been for courts to require that the search be in some way related to the minor offense for which the arrest is made[26] or be necessary for the protection of the arresting officer.[27] Thus an arrest for failing to stop

[26] E.g., Gilbert v. United States, 291 F.2d 586 (9th Cir. 1961); Taglavore v. United States, 291 F.2d 262 (9th Cir. 1961).

[27] See Note, 1959 Wis. L. Rev. 347. It is observed therein that few courts have analyzed such cases carefully, most of them being satisfied just to declare that a search incident to an arrest is valid. However, since that note was written some

at a stop sign does not justify a search of the trunk of the car. A detailed discussion of the host of problems accompanying the current practice of arresting for one offense in order to search for evidence of a more serious crime will be found elsewhere.[28]

Appellate courts have seldom had occasion to consider the legality of such arrests. No agreement is found in the few judicial opinions[29] or between the commentators who have considered the question.[30] The arrest and conviction, or the arrest and continuance, for a minor charge in order to provide time for an in-custody investigation of a more serious crime pose fundamentally the same kind of problem. These two situations are considered in greater detail later as a part of the broader discussion of arrest and detention for purposes of investigation.[31] They are mentioned here as notable examples of situations in which an arrest will be made for conduct ordinarily not subject to arrest.[32]

---

states have adopted the stricter approach, e.g., People v. Mayo, 19 Ill. 2d 136, 166 N.E.2d 440 (1960); People v. Watkins, 19 Ill. 2d 11, 166 N.E.2d 433 (1960); People v. Gonzales, 356 Mich. 247, 97 N.W.2d 16 (1959).

[28] In the volume on Detection of Crime.

[29] Compare People v. Craig, 152 Cal. 42, 91 Pac. 997 (1907), with Rex v. Dick [1947] 2 D.L.R. 213 (Ont. Ct. App.), quoted in Culombe v. Connecticut, 367 U.S. 568, 632 n.95 (1961).

[30] Compare Comment, 23 Calif. L. Rev. 506 (1935), with Williams, Requisites of a Valid Arrest, 1954 Crim. L. Rev. (Eng.) 6, 17.

[31] See pages 338, 354, and 371.

[32] Sometimes, from the nature of the offense for which the arrest is made and the surrounding circumstances, the police motives are quite obvious. For example, a suspect in a Milwaukee murder case was arrested and arraigned on a fornication charge, and his case was continued for two weeks. Milwaukee Journal, Feb. 10, 1960, pt. I, p. 12, col. 1.

Control of Police Discretion

Even those who acknowledge the need for police discretion in law enforcement recognize the hazards involved.[1] As Pound has observed, while all discretion is liable to abuse, the consequences of abuse are much more serious in the area of criminal justice.[2] Fear that effective controls over discretionary power cannot be provided may result in a failure to give the police needed power. It is important to know whether effective methods exist for challenging the propriety of such discretion as is exercised.

A. GENERAL AWARENESS OF DECISIONS NOT TO ARREST

A decision not to arrest in a specific case does not ordinarily come to the attention of members of the community. Even repeated decisions not to arrest for certain kinds of conduct may be unnoticed by the majority of people.[3] In most situations, the decision is known only to those who know of the crime and to the police officer who decides not to arrest. Frequently, the crime is of a kind which involves a willing victim[4] or a victim who concurs in the decision not to arrest,[5] or there may be no victim involved.[6] The offender obviously will not want to challenge the decision.

---

1 For example, Justice Breitel writes that ". . . discretion — even legally permissible discretion — involves great hazard. It makes easy the arbitrary, the discriminatory, and the oppressive. It produces inequality of treatment. It offers a fertile bed for corruption. It is conducive to the development of a police state — or, at least, a police-minded state." Breitel, Controls in Criminal Law Enforcement, 27 U. Chi. L. Rev. 427, 429 (1960).

2 Pound, Criminal Justice in America 75 (1930).

3 This is mainly because the police are more apt to invoke against a violation coming to the attention of the general public. See page 147.

4 E.g., gambling, prostitution, sale of narcotics.

5 This usually occurs in the case of domestic disputes, bad checks, minor property thefts, and the like. Sometimes the police will take steps to convince the victim of the desirability of not invoking the process. See the landlord incident reported at page 120.

6 E.g., minor traffic violations.

Consequently, the exercise of discretion is usually not known to any person who might be motivated to challenge it.

Usually the decision not to arrest is made by an individual police officer, and it is seldom brought to the attention of a supervisory officer in the department. The extent to which the decision becomes known may depend upon whether the officer is assigned to the case by the dispatcher or a supervisor in the department, is alerted by a private complainant, or personally observes the offense being committed.

Even when a complaint is made to the department and is referred to an individual officer for action, that officer's decision may never become known to the department. Whether it does may depend upon whether a record of this assignment is made by the dispatching officer and upon whether and in how much detail the officer files a report of his action. The practice varies considerably: some departments record all complaints on which an officer is dispatched;[7] some record them only on a selective basis;[8] and some make no record of these initial requests for action.[9] When there is a recording of the initial complaint on a regular basis, a report is usually also made by the officer dispatched in order to complete the record.[10] When the recording of dispatches is not routine, investigating officers are very loath to file any report unless an arrest was made. They feel that in such cases a report accomplishes no useful purpose.[11] Even when a report is routinely made on cases in which no arrest is made, the nature of the decision is often obscured by reporting those complaints which motivated the investigation as "unfounded." [12]

[7] This was the observed practice, for example, in the Madison and Wauwatosa, Wisconsin, Police Departments, the Sedgwick and Johnson County, Kansas, Sheriffs' Departments, and the Michigan State Police Department.

[8] This was the observed practice, for example, in the Milwaukee department and in the Eau Claire and Dane County, Wisconsin, sheriffs' offices.

[9] This practice was observed in many Detroit precincts. The great volume of complaints and requests for service received would make comprehensive reporting difficult, unless it were done by a recording device.

[10] Thus a Madison, Wisconsin, officer, responding to a complaint received from the radio dispatcher, indicated that he would have to follow up with an officer's report, as the dispatcher routinely makes a complaint report and assigns it a number. In the Sedgwick County, Kansas, sheriff's office, all dispatch calls are recorded on "dictabelts," so that the investigating officer must in all cases call in a report to the dispatcher, and this is likewise recorded.

[11] For example, after a cruiser car of a Michigan city department reported to a domestic dispute and learned that the victim, wounded by a knife, merely desired transportation to the hospital, the officers left without taking any action. No record was made of the incident and one of the officers remarked: "The chief wants us to write reports on all incidents we handle. Now, what the hell is the use of writing a report on that. Nobody wants to prosecute, they just wanted the police to give them a free ride to the hospital."

[12] Thus a Detroit detective interviewed a complainant who asserted that a woman

There is even less probability of a report being made when the officer observes the offense and decides not to make an arrest. In Milwaukee, for example, each patrolman makes out a daily report, which is supposed to include all complaints not resulting in an arrest or other major affirmative action.   However, officers exercise discretion to a considerable extent in determining what matters justify a criminal complaint report, as opposed to a mere entry in their daily report, and also with regard to what is to be reported at all.   Even when police regulations require a report "even though the results be negative," [13] and even when patrolmen are advised of the need for these reports for various reasons,[14] instances of nonarrest and the reasons therefor are not regularly reported.[15] When such reports are filed, however, review by supervisory officers is not usually made as a matter of course, but if such a review is made it is for the most part limited to insuring that the incident is closed.

This lack of written record or review continues in part because of police reluctance to acknowledge their use of discretion.[16]   Not

---

with whom he had frequently had intercourse had stolen some money from him. The detective decided no action should be taken, so he slapped the victim on the back and told him to go home to his wife and family. After the man had left, the detective drew a red line through the complaint report, explaining that in such a case the complaint is best classified as unfounded.

It is often uncertain how decisions not to invoke are reported when a complaint form has already been prepared. The Michigan State Police complaint form, Form UD-3, has a check list of alternatives printed on it as follows: "complaint unfounded," "complaint closed by arrest," "service rendered," and "other disposition." The complaint form used by the Wayne County, Michigan, Sheriff's Department lists: "unfounded," "cleared by arrest," "exceptionally cleared," and "inactive" as the choices. It was reported that "exceptionally cleared" was used there for the disposition in question.

[13] Wichita Police Dept., Duty Manual 71 (undated). One police administration text recommends reports of all violations except "city ordinance violations which are observed by the police (not reported to them) in which action consists only of a warning which is accepted without protest." Wilson, Police Planning 175 (2d ed. 1957). See also Wilson, Police Records (1942).

[14] Wichita patrolmen were made aware of the necessity of recording all incidents with which they dealt, the reason given being that such statistics were needed to justify requests for additional budgetary allocations.

This suggests that noninvocation practices and the budget affect each other. Noninvocation is in part due to the scarcity of enforcement resources, and the legislative body may provide less than necessary resources because it is not aware of the time spent on other than reported crime.

[15] On the incompleteness of police records elsewhere, see Goldstein, Police Discretion Not to Invoke the Criminal Process: Low-Visibility Decisions in the Administration of Justice, 69 Yale L.J. 543, 553 n.17 (1960).

[16] Official recognition by a police agency that the police may exercise discretion seldom occurs, and when it does it is usually prompted by a serious challenge to certain instances of nonenforcement. Following a recent John Doe investigation in Milwaukee, the head of the vice squad was charged with misconduct in office for alleged improper handling of tavern gambling device investigations, including failure

only does this support the image of the police as impartial enforcers of the law,[17] but it also makes the enforcement task easier to accomplish.[18]   Thus the regulations of the typical police department give the impression that strict adherence to the "letter of the law" is the ideal toward which all officers should strive.   Though suggestions that arrests need not be made in all cases are sometimes found,[19] the manuals usually call for full enforcement.   For example, the Milwaukee police are told that they

---

to arrest or report certain known violations. This officer's counsel was reported as saying: "It does seem entirely clear, however, that it has been the practice in the Milwaukee police department for many years to do precisely what Capt. Kuszewski is alleged to have done under these counts, that is, make a determination of whether arrests should be made for violations on a case by case basis. . . .

"Capt. Kuszewski's vice squad made about 7,500 arrests during the time alleged violations occurred. Only six nonarrest situations are involved in the charges. He has been making these determinations openly for 16 years, and he has never been told by anyone that it is not within his authority to do so." Milwaukee Journal, March 3, 1963, p. 1, col. 2.

The chief of police in Milwaukee, who asked for a legal opinion from the city attorney on whether the police could exercise discretion, was quoted as saying: "Use of good judgment is a primary function of a good policeman in every case involving possible violation of a city ordinance or state law.

"We must secure a legal opinion determining to what extent policemen may exercise judgment in possible law violations to safeguard the officers themselves from possible prosecutions. Police judgment in the enforcement of the law has been required since the first patrolman walked a beat anywhere in the world." Milwaukee Journal, March 4, 1963, p. 1, col. 6.

[17] See page 147 on the need to maintain this image.

[18] Because it is generally recognized that the police engage in the practice of warning offending drivers, pressures are increased to expand the area of nonenforcement. See page 132, note 24. Enforcement problems in generally recognized areas of nonenforcement can attain ridiculous proportions. In New York City, the habitual nonenforcement of the vehicle parking ordinances is well known. N.Y. Times, Nov. 14, 1958, p. 26, col. 2. Thus, when the police wanted the streets cleared during a visit by President DeGaulle, they covered the "No Parking" signs with paper signs reading "No Parking Today!" The streets were clear that day. Chicago Sun-Times, May 3, 1960, p. 25, col. 2.

[19] "Members of the police force shall instantly go to the scene of any unlawful disturbance occurring within their vicinity, and use their best efforts to restore peace and order by moderate means, if possible; but should such efforts fail, force must be used, if necessary, and the principals arrested." Milwaukee Police Dept., Rules & Regulations, Rule 29, §16 (1950); Madison Police Dept., General Rules and Regulations, Rule 13 (undated).

The foreword to the Detroit manual cautions officers that: ". . . no arbitrary rules can be established which will embrace all possible situations. In the general discharge of duty under our Laws and these Rules and Regulations, something must necessarily be left to the discretion and sound judgment of the individual. Nevertheless, all members are reminded that they may be required by vested authority to answer for abuse of authority or discretion." Detroit Police Dept., Revised Police Manual (1955).

Some manuals also specify instances when a warning is an appropriate alternative to arrest. See citations, page 104, note 8. For citations to other manuals with provisions suggesting that discretion might be exercised, see Goldstein, Police Discretion Not to Invoke the Criminal Process: Low-Visibility Decisions in the Administration of Justice, 69 Yale L.J. 543, 559 n.27 (1960).

... shall, at all times within the boundaries of the City, preserve the public peace, prevent crime, detect and arrest violators of the law, protect life and property and *enforce all the criminal laws* of the State of Wisconsin and the ordinances of the City . . .[20] [Emphasis supplied.]

B. METHODS OF CONTROLLING THE EXERCISE OF POLICE DISCRETION

Methods for review and control of police discretion have not generally proved effective, nor have they provided a basis for a legal determination of the proper use of discretion. However, since such methods do exist and are sometimes used, they deserve some attention at this point.

1. *Intradepartmental supervision and discipline.* The "real answer" to the problem of police discretion has been said to be the development of controls of an administrative nature, which would permit decisions to be carefully reviewed within the police department.[21] Effective control of this kind is generally absent in the current criminal justice system. The lack of regularized reporting and of review by superior officers has already been noted. Perhaps more significant is the fact that supervisory police officials

---

An unusually explicit direction by a police administrator to his personnel to utilize discretion in their daily tasks is that recently given by Superintendent O. W. Wilson of the Chicago Police Department: "Many members of the department are under the impression that it is my policy, and the department's policy, to insist that every traffic violator who is stopped must be issued a summons no matter what the circumstances. . . . *This is not true.*

". . . I have great confidence in your ability to exercise good judgment in traffic enforcement, and I will support any officer who exercises what appears to him to be proper judgment under a given set of circumstances.

"There will always be some errors in judgment on the part of any officer during a career with the department. This is to be expected. Occasionally, it may be necessary to investigate the exercise of discretion to establish the facts and to assure that the officer was not inspired by evil or malicious intent or that he was not acting for personal gain. It is only the officer who engages in these latter practices who needs fear an investigation. Members of the public will not complain of being politely warned about a traffic offense. They will complain of any improper actions on the part of officers which might be a source of embarrassment to all of us." Chicago Police Dept., PAX 501, June 11, 1962.

20 Milwaukee Police Dept., Rules & Regulations, Rule 29, §3 (1950). An identical provision is found in Madison Police Dept., General Rules and Regulations, Rule 2 (undated). Similarly, Eau Claire, Wisconsin, officers are cautioned to "enforce all laws in a fair and impartial manner." Eau Claire Police Dept., General Order No. 8 (1956). Detroit commanding officers are likewise made responsible for "the enforcement of all laws and ordinances within [their] command. . . ." Detroit Police Dept., Revised Police Manual, chap. 1, §9 (1955). For nation-wide citations to provisions of police manuals suggesting that the police duty is full enforcement, see Goldstein, *supra*, at 557-559 nn.26, 27.

21 Breitel, Controls in Criminal Law Enforcement, 27 U. Chi. L. Rev. 427, 435 (1960).

have not tried to articulate and disseminate criteria to be applied in deciding whether to arrest. Either because of fear that any such criteria would be challenged,[22] or for other reasons,[23] nonenforcement decisions continue to be made on an ad hoc basis. Patrolmen are thus left to make decisions on the basis of their own opinions, the observations of more experienced officers, and some informal, and often divergent, advice from precinct personnel who review those arrests which are made.

The typical police manual suggests that disciplinary action will follow a failure to arrest or to report any crime.[24] However, such disciplinary action is seldom taken. A decision not to arrest seldom comes to the attention of superior officers, and, if it does, there is no prescribed criterion for deciding whether it conforms to departmental policy. If disciplinary action is taken, it may be because the decision was clearly contrary to any reasonable policy and thus constituted a corrupt act or a serious error of judgment,

[22] A formalized nonenforcement program may very well be successfully challenged when an informal one would not. See page 76, note 55. It would be unfair to conclude, however, that the failure to define the criteria employed is unique in the police: "Again, reliance on the role of discretion has disinclined many agencies to make available for the use of interested parties any clear statements either of the exact practice and procedure of the agency or the criteria relied on by the agency in deciding cases. Discretion can be more freely exercised if procedural matters can be settled in accordance with the agency's convenience in each case. Similarly, discretion has a broader range if the agency has not committed itself to any stated bases or principles of decision comparable to common-law rules of decision, but has reserved the privilege of deciding each case on its 'merits,' permitting such departures from prior criteria of decision as may seem expedient in any particular case." Cooper, Administrative Agencies and the Courts 22-23 (1951).

However, articulation of the criteria would still give the police and indeed all administrative agencies the required flexibility. While restrictions akin to res judicata and stare decisis are sometimes imposed on administrative agencies, 2 Davis, Administrative Law, chaps. 17 and 18 (1958), the administrators are allowed to alter policies as need and experience dictate. As Judge Wyzanski has written, "The administrator is expected to treat experience not as a jailer but as a teacher." Shawmut Assn. v. SEC, 146 F.2d 791, 796-797 (1st Cir. 1945). See also FCC v. WOKO, Inc., 329 U.S. 223, 67 Sup. Ct. 213, 91 L. Ed. 204 (1946); Churchill Tabernacle v. FCC, 160 F.2d 244 (D.C. Cir. 1947); and Butler Oak Tavern v. Division of Alcoholic Beverage Control, 20 N.J. 373, 120 A.2d 24 (1956) for other judicial attitudes toward complaints that administrators had departed from prior policy to the detriment of a particular person.

[23] Such as that a formalized program would make the enforcement task more difficult in terms of relations with the public. See note 18 *supra*.

[24] The Detroit manual defines "neglect of duty" as "failure to report or take appropriate action in the case of any crime," and makes this and also failure to report a known violation punishable. Detroit Police Dept., Revised Police Manual, chap. 3, §49; chap. 10, §130 (1955). Similarly, "failure to take action respecting violations . . . coming to their attention or about which they have knowledge will be considered gross neglect of duty." Milwaukee Police Dept., Rules & Regulations, Rule 29, §19 (1950); Madison Police Dept., General Rules and Regulations, Rule 16 (undated). For citations to and comment on provisions found elsewhere, see Goldstein, Police Discretion Not to Invoke the Criminal Process: Low-Visibility Decisions in the Administration of Justice, 69 Yale L.J. 543, 592-593 (1960).

or because pressure upon the department requires some action to maintain the public image of full enforcement.[25] Action may not be taken even in these cases if it appears that the officer involved might refer the matter to a local council or commission and then to court, thereby possibly exposing department nonenforcement practices.

2. *Criminal action against the officer who fails to make an arrest.* Neglect of duty is generally regarded as a criminal offense,[26] and in some states there are statutes dealing with police inaction.[27] However, criminal prosecution is unlikely for the same reasons as those given to explain the infrequency of departmental discipline. Since decisions not to arrest do not usually become known, they rarely lead to conviction.   Only cases which involve clearly immoral conduct reach the courts,[28] and these cases, by their very nature, do not provide a standard by which to distinguish between the proper and improper exercise of discretion.[29]

[25] There is another possibility. Because many police regulations are couched in terms of full enforcement, a police supervisor might proceed against an officer for violation of such regulations, though the officer was acting in conformance with the informal nonenforcement policy of the department, if it is desired that the officer be disciplined for some other purpose. One writer has observed the close control which can be exercised by police supervisors because of the extensive and detailed regulations which govern subordinates' conduct. Westley, The Police: A Sociological Study of Law, Custom and Morality 93 (unpublished Ph.D. thesis No. 1197, Dept. of Sociology, Univ. of Chicago, 1951).

[26] Mich. Stat. Ann. §28.746 (1954); Wis. Stat. §946.12(1) (1955). On neglect of duty as a common law and statutory crime, see Goldstein, Police Discretion Not to Invoke the Criminal Process: Low-Visibility Decisions in the Administration of Justice, 69 Yale L.J. 543, 593 (1960); Note, 20 N.C.L. Rev. 110 (1941); Note, 4 U. Fla. L. Rev. 264 (1951).

[27] Sometimes a statute is enacted making failure to enforce a particular law an offense. For example, in Michigan it is a misdemeanor to neglect or refuse to enforce the Liquor Control Act, Mich. Stat. Ann. §18.971 (1937). On the possible effects of such a statute, see page 132, n.25.

Also in Michigan there is a statute which makes it a misdemeanor for an officer not to make an arrest under a warrant, Mich. Stat. Ann. §28.388 (1938), but no similar provision exists with respect to arrest without warrant. This in itself may suggest that a police officer's failure to carry out an arrest decision properly made by another is one thing, while his failure to make an affirmative arrest decision himself is another.

[28] See Goldstein, Police Discretion Not to Invoke the Criminal Process: Low-Visibility Decisions in the Administration of Justice, 69 Yale L.J. 543, 593 (1960).

[29] The presence of corruption and bad faith in these cases may result in the court's not giving adequate consideration to the propriety of other instances of noninvocation. Thus, in a recent Wisconsin case, these elements were present in some instances of the sheriff's failure to arrest, but the court also upheld conviction on the count that he had failed to make an arrest in an assault case in which the victim did not desire to sign a complaint against his assailant-father. State v. Lombardi, 8 Wis. 2d 421, 99 N.W.2d 829 (1959). Conviction was under Wis. Stat. §946.12(1) (1955), which declares a public officer guilty of a misdemeanor if he "intentionally fails or refuses to perform a known mandatory, nondiscretionary, ministerial duty of his office." This requires that the arrest decision be determined to be nondiscretionary and that it be shown that the officer was aware that he was under an absolute

3. *Quo warranto.* Quo warranto, which is a civil action to test a person's right to hold public office, is sometimes used to challenge police inaction.[30] Its use in this regard is limited, however, primarily because the writ is not available to all prospective petitioners. In some states the proceedings must be instituted by the prosecutor or a similar official, usually upon the report of a private person having a special interest in the matter.[31] Other states confine the action to persons who have an interest beyond that of taxpayer or citizen.[32] Another limitation found in a number of jurisdictions is that the only issue which can be raised by quo warranto is whether the respondent is a public official. Ouster for official misconduct is not possible.[33]

4. *Mandamus.* Mandamus, an action of a civil nature which generally can be maintained only when there is no other remedy,[34] is used to force a public official to perform a particular duty. In several ways, it is a better means for testing nonenforcement policies than many of the other remedies. First, although there is some authority to the contrary, a person interested only as a citizen or taxpayer may bring mandamus to challenge an instance or policy of nonenforcement.[35] Secondly, because the action can properly be used to challenge a failure to perform a ministerial act or an abuse of discretion, the question of the existence of discretion and of the propriety of its exercise is brought directly into issue.[36] Finally, because the objective of the action is not punishment of the officer, the courts tend to focus more carefully on these issues.[37]

---

duty in such circumstances. 5 Wis. Legis. Council, Judiciary Committee Report on the Criminal Code 174-175 (1953). There is no specific discussion in the opinion of this case as to why such an instance of nonenforcement should be considered improper.

30 See, for example, State ex rel. Parker v. McKnaught, 152 Kan. 689, 107 P.2d 693 (1940).

31 The prosecutor has considerable discretion in determining the advisability of instituting quo warranto proceedings, and his decision generally will not be disturbed. 17 McQuillin, Municipal Corporations §50.04 (3d ed. 1950). On the writ generally, see Chapter 50 of that treatise.

32 See Note, 57 W. Va. L. Rev. 120 (1955).

33 See 17 McQuillin, Municipal Corporations §50.07 (3d ed. 1950); Gellhorn and Byse, Administrative Law 398-399 (4th ed. 1960).

34 On mandamus generally, see 17 McQuillin, *supra*, chap. 51. For citations to other cases of mandamus actions against police officers, see Goldstein, Police Discretion Not to Invoke the Criminal Process: Low-Visibility Decisions in the Administration of Justice, 69 Yale L.J. 543, 593 (1960).

35 17 McQuillin, *supra*, §51.28.

36 Id. §§51.16 to 51.19.

37 For example, in a Michigan mandamus case the court recognized the need for police superiors to exercise discretion in order to apply limited enforcement means "for the good of the community." Gowan v. Smith, 157 Mich. 443, 122 N.W. 286 (1909).

There are limits to the extent to which judicial control over enforcement may be brought about through mandamus, however. All courts would undoubtedly refuse a writ in which the complaint is only a general allegation of nonenforcement of the laws.[38] Likewise, courts will not grant mandamus if they would be required to undertake the task of constant or recurring supervision over daily activities of the police.[39] Beyond this, the writ may still be granted or refused in the discretion of the court.[40] At least one court has taken the attitude that mandamus should not be used to compel enforcement, since the public can exercise control through the ballot box.[41]

5. *The constitutional right to equal protection.* It is familiar law that a defendant may not avoid conviction merely because other offenders have not been prosecuted.[42] This is not to say, however, that persons who are prosecuted may not complain that the process by which they were selected for enforcement violated the constitutional guarantee of equal protection of the laws. Such a challenge brings the criteria of invocation into direct question, and if the applied criterion is not consonant with this constitutional principle, the defendant may obtain dismissal of the action or have the pending prosecution enjoined.[43]

The extent to which the constitutional right to equal protection applies in cases in which police discretion was used is not clearly defined in appellate court decisions.[44] Some courts have said that

[38] E.g., People v. Dunne, 219 Ill. 346, 76 N.E. 570 (1906); State v. Brewer, 39 Wash. 65, 80 Pac. 1001 (1905). Thus suppressing instances of nonenforcement can minimize the chances of an action being brought against the officer concerned, as the petitioner must cite specific cases. The restriction appears sound if public administration is to be protected from harassment.

[39] See Gowan v. Smith, 157 Mich. 443, 122 N.W. 286 (1909); Walsh v. LaGuardia, 269 N.Y. 437, 199 N.E. 652 (1936); and numerous cases cited therein.

[40] 17 McQuillin, Municipal Corporations §51.08 (3d ed. 1950).

[41] "The Mayor and his appointee, the Police Commissioner, have their duties defined by law . . . , and if they fail in these duties remedies are afforded the public other than the appeal to the courts." Walsh v. LaGuardia, 269 N.Y. 437, 440, 199 N.E. 652, 653 (1936).

[42] E.g., People v. Flanders, 140 Cal. App. 2d 765, 296 P.2d 13 (Dist. Ct. App. 1956). For other citations, see Comment, 61 Colum. L. Rev. 1103, 1106 n.12 (1961); Note, 59 Yale L.J. 354 n.3 (1950). For those interested in a more detailed treatment of the equal protection problem, both of these student writings are highly recommended. The Comment is particularly helpful.

[43] For more on the exact nature of these two remedies, see Comment, *supra,* at 1131-1140.

[44] One study, in commenting on the cases recognizing the applicability of the equal protection doctrine in this area, observed that: ". . . these cases approach the issue in a superficial manner; making a facile assumption that *Yick Wo* [in which discriminatory enforcement was alleged and the equal protection clause was held by the court to be applicable] is controlling, they fail to consider thoroughly the conceptual and policy problems or to refute the objections to extending *Yick Wo* made in the cases rejecting its applicability. Thus, they furnish only limited aid in re-

a criminal has no "right to demand protection of the law in the commission of a crime." [45]   Other courts have taken a similar attitude, observing that failure to prosecute certain persons should not nullify valid penal laws and permit subsequent violators to go unpunished.[46] About half of the appellate courts which have considered the problem have concluded that the equal protection clause is not applicable to discriminatory penal enforcement.[47]

Those courts which do recognize the applicability of this clause are not in agreement as to the scope of the constitutional protection guaranteed thereby. Some courts require only that the criminal justice administrator refrain from making classifications impermissible to the legislature, such as those bearing unequally on persons similarly situated with respect to the subject matter of the law, and those which do not have some rational relation to the legislative purpose.[48] Those courts would hold that only classifications based upon "race, religion, color, or the like" violate the constitutional guarantee.[49] It has also been said that the defend-

---

solving the basic question of the existence and scope of the constitutional prohibition against discriminatory enforcement." Id. at 1109.

45 People v. Montgomery, 47 Cal. App. 2d 1, 14, 117 P.2d 437, 446 (Dist. Ct. App. 1941). Likewise, in People v. Flanders, 140 Cal. App. 2d 765, 769, 296 P.2d 13, 16 (Dist. Ct. App. 1956), in which the defendant attempted to show that he was arrested for gambling whereas advertized church bingo games continued undisturbed, the court said: "[T]he rule of the case of Yick Wo v. Hopkins . . . does not stand for the proposition that persons violating the law are to have equal protection from prosecution, but rather for the proposition that equal protection of the law will be extended to all persons in the pursuit of their lawful occupation regardless of their race." See also Society of Good Neighbors v. Mayor of Detroit, 324 Mich. 22, 36 N.W.2d 308 (1949), and cases cited in Comment, 61 Colum. L. Rev. 1103, 1107 n.13 (1961).

46 Sherman v. State, 234 Miss. 775, 108 So.2d 205 (1959). For other cases taking a similar approach, see Comment, *supra,* at 1107 n.15, and for a refutation of this argument, see id. at 1112.

47 The cases on both sides of this issue are collected in Comment, *supra,* at 1106 n.12.

48 For example, in Taylor v. City of Pine Bluff, 226 Ark. 309, 289 S.W.2d 679 (1956), the court upheld the enforcement of a comprehensive Sunday blue law against grocery stores only. "Against the assumption in *Taylor* that there is an administrative power of reasonable classification in law enforcement coextensive with the recognized legislative authority to make statutory classifications, it could be argued that the difference between legislative and administrative functions imports a distinction in the scope of permissible classification under the equal protection clause. This view finds support in the Supreme Court's early enunciation of the reasonable classification doctrine . . . , [but the later Supreme Court case of Kotch v. Board of River Port Pilot Commissioners, 330 U.S. 552, 67 Sup. Ct. 910, 91 L. Ed. 1093 (1947) would seem to support the Taylor rationale]." Comment, 61 Colum. L. Rev. 1103, 1117-1118 (1961).

49 State v. Jourdain, 225 La. 1030, 74 So.2d 203 (1954). See also People v. Oreck, 74 Cal. App. 2d 215, 168 P.2d 186 (Dist. Ct. App. 1946), in which a bookie alleged that other forms of gambling were not proceeded against. The court said, however, that the distinction, to allow dismissal, would have to be based upon race, religion, or political affiliation.

ant must show "that he alone is the only person who has been prosecuted under the statute." [50]   Other courts have held that the defendant must show not only that he was improperly selected but also that he would be in a better position if other persons were also subjected to prosecution.[51]   Thus it is evident that the equal protection clause does not constitute an adequate basis for a court to consider the propriety or impropriety of the exercise of police discretion.

Even in cases in which the equal protection clause would be applicable if the facts could be proved, the defendant is confronted with an extremely heavy burden of proof.   He must overcome a presumption that the police have acted in a regular and proper manner,[52] and establish that he was prosecuted because of intentional discrimination.[53]   The trial judge cannot take judicial notice of a policy of discriminatory enforcement even though such a policy may seem evident to him from the cases prosecuted in court.[54]   Except for the few instances in which police enforcement policies are a matter of record,[55] sufficient evidence can seldom be presented.[56]

In most of the equal protection in law enforcement cases reaching the appellate courts, the alleged distinction was based on: (1) personal attributes, such as race, religion, or political beliefs; (2) personal animosity toward the defendant; or (3) the nature of the violator's business, such as its size, type, or charitable character.   For alignment of the cases on this basis, see Comment, *supra*, at 1118 n.66.

The previously ambiguous Supreme Court position has been clarified somewhat by the most recent case of Oyler v. Boles, 368 U.S. 448, 82 Sup. Ct. 501, 7 L. Ed. 2d 446 (1962).   The court in this case held that conscious exercise of selectivity by state prosecuting authorities in the application of a West Virginia recidivist statute was not, in itself, a violation of equal protection of the laws since it was not founded upon unjustifiable standards such as race, religion, or other arbitrary classification.

[50] State v. Jourdain, 225 La. 1030, 74 So.2d 203 (1954).

[51] People v. Darcy, 59 Cal. App. 2d 342, 139 P.2d 118 (Dist. Ct. App. 1943).   This would be true, for example, where the Sunday blue laws are not equally enforced.

[52] "[I]n all cases it is presumed that official duty has been fully and regularly performed by the public authorities until there is judicial proof to the contrary."   People v. Winters, 171 Cal. App. 2d Supp. 876, 882, 342 P.2d 538, 543 (Super. Ct. 1959).

[53] "The unlawful administration by state officers of a state statute fair on its face, resulting in its unequal application to those who are entitled to be treated alike, is not a denial of equal protection unless there is shown to be present in it an element of intentional or purposeful discrimination."   Snowden v. Hughes, 321 U.S. 1, 8, 64 Sup. Ct. 397, 401, 88 L. Ed. 497, 503 (1944).

[54] People v. Winters, 171 Cal. App. 2d Supp. 876, 342 P.2d 538 (Super. Ct. 1959).

[55] The Philadelphia Police Commissioner announced his policy of proceeding against only "large retail establishments" in enforcement of the Sunday blue laws, and thus a particular merchant was successful in enjoining prosecution.   The Philadelphia Court of Common Pleas said: "The admitted discrimination in enforcement is a calculated result of a definite policy on the part of a public official and thus results in a denial to the plaintiff of the equal protection of the law to which he is entitled by virtue of the fourteenth amendment of the United States Constitution." 29 U.S.L. Week 2002 (Pa. C.P., June 10, 1960).   The Supreme Court refused to decide the issue since the police commissioner was no longer in office at the time of the

appeal. Bargain City U.S.A., Inc. v. Dilworth, 407 Pa. 129, 179 A.2d 439 (1962). The only other case found in which direct proof of the discriminatory practices was available is People v. Harris, 182 Cal. App. 2d Supp. 837, 5 Cal. Rptr. 852 (Super. Ct. 1960), in which police officers testified that the department policy was to investigate gambling when parked autos were grouped in a Negro neighborhood, but not in white areas.

"[A]bsence of such [direct] evidence in the preponderance of discriminatory enforcement cases suggests the difficulty of obtaining it; obviously, as a practical matter, enforcement officers are not likely to admit to practicing discrimination prohibited by the Constitution." Comment, 61 Colum. L. Rev. 1103, 1122 (1961).

[56] On the host of problems involved in attempting to establish the fact of discrimination by inferential proof, see id. at 1123-1131.

PART III

The Decision Whether to Take Immediate Custody

In England summons, rather than arrest, is used regularly for minor prosecutions, and this practice obtains in some States, although even in those States arrest is employed too indiscriminately. At common law all prosecutions began with arrest and this is the staple method of beginning petty prosecutions in the United States. The practice of summons in such cases should be introduced wherever it is not provided for, and its use should be extended everywhere. Indiscriminate exercise of the power of arrest is one of the most reprehensible features of American criminal justice.

> National Commission on Law
> Observance and Enforcement,
> Report No. 8, at 14 (1931)

The Department of Justice should review practices in the various districts relating to the use of the summons as a substitute for arrest. A national policy regarding the use of the summons should be expressed and communicated to all United States Attorneys. That policy should direct use of the summons in those cases in which an arrest is not required to protect the proper functioning of the criminal process.

> Report of the Attorney
> General's Committee on Poverty
> and the Administration of
> Criminal Justice, at vii (1963)

When the police decide to invoke the criminal process against a person suspected of criminal conduct, they normally do so by arrest, usually without a warrant. If the decision to arrest is followed by a decision to prosecute, the supect is usually kept in custody until he makes his initial appearance before the magistrate. At that time he is entitled to be released on bail if he can post the required bond.

A continuing criticism of criminal justice administration over the years has been that too many persons are arrested who would voluntarily appear in court if given an opportunity to do so. This has been part of a broader criticism that too many persons, particularly indigents, are taken and kept in custody prior to their conviction in cases where they could be left in the community without serious risk of their failing to appear in court.

The general question of the need for taking and retaining custody of a suspect prior to conviction is an important one. Like other important issues, it arises at various stages in the criminal justice process. Primary concern here is with the decision of whether to invoke the process by arrest or by an alternative such as a summons or an informal notice to appear. Because they are obviously related, subsequent decisions to release, whether by the police soon after arrest or by the magistrate when he sets bail, are also discussed.

Different considerations are operative in making the decision to take a suspect into custody by arrest, the decision to grant release promptly after arrest without requiring bail, and the magistrate's decision at the initial appearance to release on bail. From a defendant's point of view, it is obviously more desirable not to be taken into custody at all. If he is arrested, it is in his interest to be released with as little expense as possible at the earliest opportunity, so that he can return to his family, assist in the preparation of his defense, and do other things which are possible only when he is not confined. From the law enforcement point of view, the decisions concerning custody may involve significantly different considerations at the various stages of the process. The officer who must make a quick decision on the street may be in no position to evaluate the character of the offender and decide whether he is likely to appear voluntarily in court. For this reason alone, the decision made at the arrest stage regarding the need for custody may differ from that made at later stages. Also, arrest makes it possible to search and to interrogate the person arrested. The police may retain a man in custody in order to search or to conduct an in-custody interrogation when it would not otherwise be necessary to do so to insure appearance in court. The objective of the following chapter is to identify, so far as possible, the criteria which are used in current administration in deciding whether a person should be taken into custody and kept in custody when an opportunity for his release arises.

In some cases making an arrest and thus taking the suspect into custody is clearly a proper way in which to proceed, but there is a question as to the time at which the arrest ought to be made.

Delay of arrest in order to protect or advance some interest of the defendant or the prosecution has received careful attention from the law in some instances and none whatsoever in others. One basis for delay is that excessive force would be required to accomplish an immediate arrest. This issue has been the subject of continuing debate and has received fairly extensive legislative and judicial attention. By contrast, there has been relatively little concern with the question of whether it is proper to delay arrest in order to achieve what the police believe to be a greater law enforcement objective. These issues are the subject of Chapter 10.

CHAPTER 9

Use of Alternatives to Arrest

Considerable attention has long been given to the important decision of the magistrate at the time of initial appearance when he decides whether to require bail and, if so, in what amount. By comparison, almost no attention has been given to earlier need-for-custody decisions which take place at the time of or immediately following arrest. The reason for this is not clear. Perhaps the fact that the legality of a search and seizure or interrogation is often dependent upon the making of a prior arrest is in part responsible for the assumption that an arrest can properly be made even though there is no need to take the suspect into custody to insure his appearance in court. Or perhaps it is because the decision as to whether custody is necessary has traditionally been considered a matter for a judicial officer, who rarely becomes involved in the process as early as the arrest decision. Whatever the reason, neither courts nor legislatures have given sustained attention to this issue. In practice persons are often arrested and held until their court appearance without any prior consideration of whether the initial taking into custody is necessary.

A. Extent to Which Need for Custody Is Considered in Current Practice

1. *Alternatives to arrest.* The law which defines when a peace officer can make an arrest has developed with almost no concern with whether the taking of immediate custody is necessary. The "reasonable grounds to believe" standard for felony arrests does not take account of the need for custody at all, unless one assumes that all felonies are sufficiently serious to warrant taking the suspect into custody. This assumption is obviously untenable today when one considers the wide range of conduct defined as felonious in most states. Although the in-presence requirement for misdemeanors might be viewed as roughly correlative to the need for

custody,[1] it is only a limitation on the right to arrest without warrant and, in any event, an officer can lawfully arrest for a misdemeanor in his presence when the circumstances clearly indicate that there is no actual need for taking immediate custody.[2]

Of the three states, only Wisconsin has by legislation authorized the magistrate to issue a summons instead of an arrest warrant. The Wisconsin statute, which is similar to the provision in the Federal Rules of Criminal Procedure,[3] provides that the magistrate or district attorney "may" issue a summons rather than a warrant, but that the magistrate "shall" issue a warrant if the defendant fails to appear in response to the summons.[4] However, the summons is rarely used in practice in Wisconsin. Most arrests take place without warrant,[5] so that the magistrate or district attorney seldom has an opportunity to decide whether to use a summons rather than a warrant. When the arrest is delayed until process is issued, the magistrate usually relies upon the district attorney to ask for a summons and such a request is not often made. Consequently, the need for custody is a factor not ordinarily considered by the magistrate even in Wisconsin. Moreover, when a police officer has a warrant directing him to make an arrest, he will seldom allow the defendant an opportunity to appear voluntarily.[6]

---

1 See page 18.

2 The Michigan court, in Odinetz v. Budds, 315 Mich. 512, 24 N.W.2d 193 (1946), was critical of the arrest of a restaurant owner for the misdemeanor charge of operating his restaurant without a license, noting that a summons would clearly have been sufficient to bring this defendant, a resident of the locality for 20 years, into court. However, the court added that no liability could come from failure to use a summons instead of arrest.

The misdemeanor arrest law not only makes possible arrest where custody is not necessary, but also makes illegal some arrests where the circumstances are such as to indicate there is not time to obtain a warrant. See page 22.

3 Fed. R. Crim. P. 4(a) provides that "upon the request of the attorney for the government a summons instead of a warrant shall issue."

4 Wis. Stat. §954.02 (1955).

5 See page 36.

6 However, it was observed that members of the unit of the Milwaukee sheriff's office charged with the task of serving warrants do not always attempt to obtain immediate custody. Persons sought for failure to pay court-imposed fines are allowed to make payment to the officer and thus avoid arrest, or sometimes they will not be arrested upon a promise to make prompt payment. Not taking custody in these cases is understandable, as the threat of arrest is needed only to obtain payment.

Even in the case of other warrants, a card requesting the defendant to report to the sheriff's office is often left when the defendant named in a warrant is not at home. Thus in one instance the officer had a warrant issued for larceny by bailee. The defendant, who it was alleged had kept about $200 of company funds after termination of his employment, was not at home. The deputy told the defendant's wife none of the details, but merely said that he had a warrant for her husband's arrest. When the wife indicated that her husband would cooperate, the deputy left one of his cards requesting appearance at the sheriff's office. However, the cards are

None of the three states has general legislation authorizing the police themselves to issue a notice to appear rather than to make an arrest. The police ordinarily view arrest as the only way in which the process is invoked,[7] and they are seldom instructed to the contrary.[8] But police do sometimes refrain from making an arrest and instead give the defendant an opportunity to appear voluntarily if it appears that the person will not flee and that no good purpose would be served by taking him into custody.[9] This practice is usually limited to minor offenses of the kind committed by

---

apparently used only to simplify the warrant-serving process, as defendants who do appear are treated just as if they had been arrested.

[7] Practices in the United States are often compared with those in other countries in this regard: "There appears to be a surprising range in the extent to which the summons is employed. In the United States its use is negligible except in traffic cases. . . . On the other hand it is employed very widely in Canada and in some European countries. A British Royal Commission urged its extensive use, and the most recent British statistics indicate that this practice is followed even in serious cases; in 1955, for seven of the most serious offenses (homicide excluded), there were 6342 persons summoned compared with 14,408 arrests, and for lesser offenses the proportionate use of the summons was much higher." Foote, Problems of the Protection of Human Rights in Criminal Law and Procedure (Santiago, Chile, May 19-30, 1958), U.N. Doc. TE 326/1 (40-2) LA, p. 42. See also Study of the Right of Everyone to Be Free from Arbitrary Arrest, Detention and Exile, Commission on Human Rights, U.N. Doc. E/CN 4/813, pars. 196-197 (1961).

Sometimes, however, failure to use arrest alternatives in these other countries is criticized. Thus a close observer of the English practice has said that "the general police practice is not to obtain a warrant if there is the legal power to arrest without one; and it is also common for the police to arrest with the full intention of granting bail. At present there is no judicial authority for saying that an arrest, otherwise valid, is unlawful because unnecessary." Williams, Arrest for Felony at Common Law, 1954 Crim. L. Rev. (Eng.) 408, 419-420.

Similarly, it has been noted that while Norwegian arrest law expressly lists danger of escape as a special prerequisite to arrest, the practice often is to take custody without regard to whether the accused will evade punishment. Bratholm, Arrest and Detention in Norway, 108 U. Pa. L. Rev. 336 (1960).

[8] Of about fifty police manuals, rules and regulations, and training bulletins from a representative group of the major police agencies across the country, collected at the University of Wisconsin Law School, over forty fail to provide any guidance on when arrest alternatives might be employed. There is a caution in the Wichita duty manual, however, "never to arrest if a summons will suffice." Wichita Police Dept., Duty Manual, cover page (undated). And, at one Kansas training school, officers were instructed that with respect to offenses which do not constitute felonies or breaches of the peace "an arrest is 'unreasonable' if it would produce an undue hardship upon the person arrested." Sedgwick County School for Law Enforcement Officers, Arrests, Searches and Seizures, July 2, 1953, p. 4.

[9] Because use of alternatives to arrest is so unusual in most cases, invocation by means other than arrest sometimes raises the suspicion that the charge is unfounded. In a disorderly conduct prosecution arising out of the testimony of a policeman that he saw the defendants playing strip poker in a restaurant, defense counsel is reported as arguing that if the officer's testimony were correct "it is incredible that these people were only ordered to report to police headquarters instead of being arrested summarily." The presiding judge dismissed the charges. Milwaukee Journal, June 22, 1960, p. 4, col. 1.

the average citizen, such as traffic[10] or conservation violations by local residents.[11]   An offense arising out of the operation of a

10 By statute in Kansas, when a person arrested for a misdemeanor traffic violation is not given an immediate hearing, he is to receive upon demand a written notice to appear and then be released. However, he will be given an immediate hearing upon demand or if he should refuse to sign the notice. Kan. Gen. Stat. §§8-5,128, 8-5,129 (1949). In Wichita all except the more serious traffic violations are handled by the officer who stops the vehicle and gives the driver a ticket. The Uniform Traffic Ticket is employed. (On the form of this ticket and its adaptability to local requirements, see Economos, The Uniform Traffic Ticket and Complaint — A Judicial Function, 1958 Wis. L. Rev. 185.)

This is a vast improvement over earlier procedures there. The system once was that every time an officer made a traffic violation arrest he took the violator to the station, signed a complaint against him, booked him, and then obtained his release from jail, taking at least an hour for each arrest. The station lieutenant or a person of higher rank was authorized to release the person on his own recognizance, and this was usually done. This system caused disrupted public relations and inefficiency in the traffic enforcement program.

The Michigan statute provides that whenever a person is arrested without a warrant for a misdemeanor traffic violation (a few offenses excepted), the arresting officer is to give the offender a notice to appear in court. Failure to appear constitutes grounds for denial of renewal of the offender's driver's license. Mich. Stat. Ann. §§9.2427 to 9.2429 (1952). The police are instructed in the terms of the statute. Pontiac Police Dept., Training Manual, XIV.N. (March, 1954); Detroit Police Dept., Revised Police Manual, chap. 17, §45 (1955). However, the latter also indicates that an arrest could be made for leaving the scene of an accident. This goes beyond the statute for, while leaving an accident in which there has been an injury or death is a felony, and thereby excepted, leaving an accident in which there has been only property damage is a misdemeanor. Mich. Stat. Ann. §§9.2317, 9.2318 (1952).

This suggests another problem: the right of the police to detain persons involved in accidents for purposes of accident investigation. The Detroit police are told to detain all drivers involved in an accident, and witnesses, until Accident Prevention Bureau personnel arrive or until the patrolman at the scene has at least obtained advice from the bureau on the case, and the police are further instructed that "persons involved in fatal traffic accidents shall be detained at the Accident Prevention Bureau until instructed by the Prosecuting Attorney to release them." Detroit Police Dept., Revised Police Manual, chap. 13, §16 (1955). But the only duty imposed upon drivers by statute is that they are not to leave the scene of an accident until they have given their name, address, vehicle registration number, and the name and address of the vehicle owner to the other party, that they display their license to him, and that they render assistance to the injured. Mich. Stat. Ann. §9.2319 (1952). In Detroit, A.P.B. personnel review all the information collected and then decide whether a traffic offense has occurred. In the usual case they then mail a summons.

The police in Wisconsin, as in other states, often invoke the process for minor traffic violations by a traffic ticket or notice to appear, even though there is no specific statute authorizing this as there is in Michigan. A captain of one of the state traffic patrol districts sent out a bulletin stating: "physical arrest should only be made when the violator is unable to care for his own safety or the safety of others as in OAWI [operating automobile while intoxicated] cases, or when the arresting officer has reason to believe that the person arrested will flee the jurisdiction of the court." This would appear to be a fair statement of the general practice of all observed police agencies in Wisconsin with respect to traffic violations. It was noted that officers whose primary responsibility was traffic enforcement were more likely than other police to use a ticket when they occasionally handled minor nontraffic cases.

11 The Director of Law Enforcement for the Michigan Department of Conservation

permanent local business may also not lead to an arrest. For example, tavern owners are usually allowed to appear voluntarily to answer a charge of a liquor law violation.

2. *Release by the police following arrest.* None of the states studied has legislation of general applicability which authorizes the police to release, on their own recognizance, persons who have been arrested and who promise to appear in court at the designated time. However, all three states do have statutes authorizing police to release minor traffic offenders on bond.[12] Such releases

---

said that his officers used a notice to appear, in the following form, in 90 per cent of the cases.

You are hereby ordered to appear before Justice .... at ....
.... on .... to answer a complaint to be filed against you for violation of the Conservation Law. Property seized: ....

Officer's signature ....
Officer's station ....

[12] Both the Kansas and Michigan notice to appear statutes also provide for a taking of bail in some situations. In Michigan the statute reads: "When any person not a resident of this state shall be arrested without warrant . . . , the officer making such arrest shall upon demand of such arrested person forthwith take such person before a magistrate of the vicinity to answer to the complaint made against him. If no magistrate is available or such immediate trial cannot be had, the person so arrested may recognize to such officer for his appearance by leaving with him a sum of money not to exceed $25.00." Mich. Stat. Ann. §9.2428(e) (1952). Because the sections on notice to appear refer to all persons arrested, it seems that the statutes have not expressly made it possible to require the nonresident driver to post bond unless he asks for but cannot have an immediate trial. However, in practice the nonresident is treated differently, in that he is given the choice of immediate trial or posting bond.

The Kansas statute provides that, when a person is stopped by a member of the state highway patrol and no immediate hearing is given, "the arresting officer may require the person so arrested to give bond." The amount of bond for 18 offenses is listed in the statute, and the offender is to mail the set amount in the presence of the officer. Kan. Gen. Stat. §8-5,129 (Supp. 1955). Although the patrolmen are not obliged by the statute to demand bond, they usually do require it of nonresidents, even if this results in considerable delay to the offender. Thus the police will sometimes accompany the violator to a commercial establishment many miles away in an attempt to get a large bill changed or a check cashed. Or they may keep the violator's driver's license while he goes to attempt to change a bill or cash a check. In one instance the driver returned an hour and a half later, very much disturbed by the delay caused by the system. The nonresident offender who cannot post bond will be jailed, although an exception is often made for drivers who work in the state or near the borders of the state. These motorists are required to sign a promise to appear, and it was reported that about 50 per cent of them did appear.

In Wisconsin a statute provides for the acceptance of bail by the police in traffic cases only with respect to speeding violations; the sheriff or chief of police may take bail *at his office* in an amount not to exceed the maximum fine. Wis. Stat. §345.13(1), formerly 85.40(4)(a) (1955). While this statute may have been intended to eliminate the obvious hazards accompanying roadside bail-taking, the procedure prescribed obviously causes inconvenience to both the violator and the officer. In practice, the taking of bail has been extended to other traffic offenses. Of course, since localities may enact ordinances not inconsistent with the state vehicle code, Wis. Stat. §349.06, formerly 85.84 (1955), the action may be brought as an ordinance violation, in which case it would appear that bail is possible for any traffic violation. Wis. Stat. §345.15,

are frequently made in practice, but there is considerable hesitancy to release a traffic violator without any bail even if there is no doubt that he will appear for trial. This undoubtedly results from the lack of express authority to do so.[13] Similarly, officers in Kansas and Wisconsin do sometimes release ordinance violators and minor misdemeanants on bond,[14] but, for the same reason, release

---

formerly 85.84 (1955). In Milwaukee County, the judge of District Court No. 2, which is the traffic court, has established a bond schedule even for offenses other than speeding, and, because ordinance and state cases are generally handled alike, this applies to both.

Bail is often taken by officers other than those named in the statute. However, especially as applied to a large department like Milwaukee, the mention of the chief in the statute cannot mean that he must personally attend to the bail process. This authority has been formally delegated to commanders of the district stations, Milwaukee Police Dept., Rules & Regulations, Rule 7, §40 (1950), and they in turn allow all officers assigned to duty in the station to handle bail in traffic cases, with the desk sergeant in each station accountable.

Often the inconveniences involved in taking the violator to the station as required by statute are avoided. Various tactics are used. Thus when members of the Wauwatosa department are operating a radar unit, an extra squad is assigned for the purpose of transporting violators to the station to post bail. State traffic patrolmen and some county traffic officers will take offenders to the chief in the nearest town, though this officer has no official connection with their unit. (Actually, state troopers apparently have no alternative, as they are not named in the statute.) In Clark County, where a traffic arrest is usually based upon a county ordinance, offenders can post bail by mailing it to the county judge (the amount has been set by the county law enforcement committee). Similarly, the Milwaukee County sheriff's office radar detail often operates near a drugstore at which money orders are sold. When a nonresident driver is stopped, he is given the opportunity of purchasing a money order and then mailing it to the sheriff in the presence of one of the officers.

13 However, the Detroit manual provides: "Prisoners arrested for traffic violations, not on a warrant, capias, or other legal process may be released by the officer in charge without bond if, in his discretion, such release is advisable, provided that if such prisoner has been involved in an accident the officer in charge of the Accident Prevention Bureau shall approve such release. If the officer in charge of a Precinct, Bureau or Division does not wish to assume responsibility for a release of a prisoner without bond he shall require a cash bond to be posted in accordance with the current bond schedule published by the Traffic and Ordinance Branch of the Recorder's Court." Detroit Police Dept., Revised Police Manual, chap. 17, §50 (1955).

In all three states, release without bond is only likely when the driver has no money and he would otherwise have to remain in jail a considerable length of time before he could be taken to court.

14 Kansas police in first-class cities are authorized to set bond on ordinance violators arrested without warrant, Kan. Gen. Stat. §13-623 (1949), but in second-class cities only a person arrested without warrant at night for an ordinance violation is entitled to deposit a sum of money not less than the minimum fine for the offense charged. Kan. Gen. Stat. §14-807 (1949). Persons arrested on state offenses must be turned over to the sheriff, Kan. Gen. Stat. §13-623 (1949), and they then can be let to bail only by the judge or clerk of court where they are to appear, Kan. Gen. Stat. §62-1215 (1949). However, prompt release may ensue when, as in some Kansas counties, a member of the sheriff's department has been appointed a clerk for purposes of bail-setting.

In Wisconsin the police frequently release ordinance violators on bail up to the amount of the maximum fine. In Milwaukee a city ordinance allows the chief to admit ordinance violators to bail up to the amount of the maximum penalty, City

without bond is not common. The police in Detroit are instructed that they may release arrested persons without bond,[15] but they seldom do so, requiring instead a $300 bond.[16]

3. *Release by the prosecutor following arrest.* In Detroit minor offenders are not taken immediately to a local justice of the peace, as sometimes might occur in rural localities, but rather are held for the next regularly scheduled session of the Recorder's Court. Due to this fact and to the great volume of minor offenders taken into custody in that large metropolitan area, a unique agency called the Release Bureau has been established. This bureau is the responsibility of the prosecuting attorney's office and is staffed

---

of Milwaukee, Code of Ordinances, chap. 11, §139, and this duty has been delegated formally to district commanders, Milwaukee Police Dept., Rules & Regulations, Rule 7, §40 (1950), and further delegated to officers on duty in the station houses.

The police in Wisconsin likewise release misdemeanants on cash bail in an amount either set by the police in individual cases or previously established by a bail schedule. The Milwaukee department will not release misdemeanants on their own recognizance, but bail will be set by the district station commander up to $500. There is no bail schedule; the amount is within the discretion of the commander. Cash bail is accepted in Ashland County by the sheriff's office and local departments in accordance with a bail schedule established by the county judge for common misdemeanors. In Madison the police often release on bail persons brought in for being drunk and disorderly, for indecent exposure, and the like, the amount being set by the releasing officer.

[15] "The power of the officer in charge of releasing prisoners may be literally and intelligently exercised, and he will be held personally responsible for any abuse of such power. He shall have the discretionary power of releasing prisoners for appearance, except those arrested on a warrant, vice or gambling, or those held by the Prosecuting Attorney, taking into consideration the seriousness of the offense, previous record, number of dependents, person making the request, etc. Provided, that before releasing a prisoner who has been detained for the commission of a felony, the officer in charge shall obtain the sanction and approval of the investigating officers, and for a person involved in an accident, the approval of the officer in charge of the Accident Prevention Bureau. It is not necessary for the officer in charge to receive a request before releasing a prisoner if in his discretion he deems it safe and prudent to release such prisoner. However, before releasing any prisoner, the officer in charge shall obtain a clearance on fingerprints from the Identification Bureau." Detroit Police Dept., Revised Police Manual, chap. 16, §135 (1955).

[16] However, no attempt is made to insure that the person has sufficient property or money to support such a bond.

In other parts of the state, the state police expressed a belief that they could release persons on their own recognizance but could not require a bond. Such releases as were made were for minor misdemeanors when the arrest was without warrant. Since these observations were made, a statute has been enacted in Michigan regarding offenses cognizable by a justice of the peace or municipal judge: "If no magistrate is available or immediate trial cannot be had, the person so arrested may recognize to the direct supervisor of the arresting officer or department for his appearance by leaving with him a sum of money not to exceed $100.00. If, in the opinion of the arresting officer or department, the arrested person is under the influence of liquor or narcotic drug, is wanted by police authorities to answer to another charge, or it is otherwise unsafe to release him, the arrested person shall be held until he is in a proper condition to be released, or until the next session of court." Mich. Stat. Ann. §28.872(1) (Supp. 1961).

by at least one assistant prosecutor between the hours of 4:30 P.M. and 8:30 A.M. every day, and around the clock on weekends and holidays. These assistant prosecutors have been appointed deputy clerks of the Recorder's Court for purposes of releasing persons on bond. The bureau acts only with respect to persons arrested without warrant in misdemeanor cases, though occasionally arrangements are made through the bureau for release of a person held on a felony charge. When the assistant prosecutor in the bureau receives a request for release,[17] he contacts the officer in charge of the police agency (precinct or specialized bureau) holding the person and determines the facts of the case. The police attitude toward release is inquired into, and the assistant prosecutor usually concurs with the police if they object to release. Some release requests are refused because they are outside the bureau's authority in that they involve a felony or a warrant case.[18] Most are granted, however.[19]

4. *Release by the magistrate following arrest.* In all three states a release may be ordered by a magistrate. However, he ordinarily does not and perhaps legally cannot[20] set bail upon a person until

---

[17] Most requests for release made to the police are referred to this bureau. Also, many requests for release are made directly to the bureau by persons who know of its existence and purpose, usually local defense attorneys. The arrestee himself may call for release, as notices have been posted in jails advising persons of their right to request release. The printed placards, which are required to be prominently displayed in all precincts, have been revised to read:

ATTENTION:
PERSONS IN POLICE CUSTODY
YOU ARE ENTITLED TO USE THE
TELEPHONE
YOU ARE ENTITLED TO
CONSIDERATION FOR RELEASE
CONSULT THE OFFICER
ON DUTY

28 Detroit Lawyer 21 (1960).

[18] For example, in May, 1956, a total of 136 requests were received and 29 refused; in June, 1956, there were 211 requests and 26 refusals; in July, 1956, there were 180 requests and 21 refusals.

[19] When Release Bureau approval has been received, the police prepare an "application for release on bond" form, on which they indicate whether they concur in release, and a personal recognizance bond for the arrestee, on which the arrestee affirms that he is indebted to the state for the sum of $300 if he fails to appear in court. These papers are forwarded to the assistant prosecuting attorney for approval, though immediate release is allowed on the basis of the telephone approval.

[20] This would seem to be the limitation imposed by statutes allowing the setting of bail by "officers before whom persons charged with crime shall be brought." E.g., Mich. Stat. Ann. §28.888 (1954). In a libel action resulting from a Detroit newspaper's exposé of the practice of Recorder's Court judges of telephoning the police for release of suspects and sometimes appearing at the station to set bail, the Michigan Supreme Court approved the following language of the trial court: "A judicial officer can only exercise judicial power in a pending case. This power is not ubiquitous; it is a power of government which is conferred upon a person to exercise under definite restrictions and only in definite circumstances. A judge acts in a proceeding

that person is properly before him. This usually means at the initial appearance before the magistrate.

An offender may be brought before the court prior to his regularly scheduled appearance by resort to a writ of habeas corpus. Although habeas corpus is an appropriate means for having bail set,[21] in general practice it is not ordinarily resorted to for this purpose except in Detroit, where it is regularly used to obtain immediate release on bail.[22] If counsel has been retained, he will probably obtain the writ from one of the judges of Recorder's Court.[23] At the hearing on the writ, attended by the prisoner, his counsel, and a police officer, the judge determines if bail is to be set and, if so, what the amount should be.[24] As is generally true in Detroit when the question of release is before a judicial officer, a surety bond is required, though occasionally a person will be released on his own recognizance.[25]

---

which is brought before him, a proceeding instituted in the manner prescribed by law. . . . Only in that manner can a judicial officer take cognizance of a cause or a proceeding . . . and in the absence of any such cause pending, judicial power is inert; in other words, judicial power is exercised in a cause or proceeding." Sanders v. Evening News Assn., 313 Mich. 334, 341, 21 N.W.2d 152, 154 (1946). Prior Michigan cases have also held that judges cannot legally obtain the release of persons who have not been brought before them. In re Mead, 220 Mich. 480, 190 N.W. 235 (1922); Clute v. Iona Circuit Judge, 131 Mich. 203, 91 N.W. 159 (1902).

21 E.g., Mich. Stat. Ann. §27.2274 (1938): "If it appears that the party has been legally committed for any criminal offense, . . . the court or officer before whom such party shall be brought, shall proceed to let such party to bail, if the case be bailable, . . ."

22 Thus the Release Bureau was characterized in a report prepared by the prosecutor as a means for release "at hours when courts are not open for habeas corpus." Since the Release Bureau operates only when the Recorder's Court is not in session, a considerable number of writs are heard each year. In 1956, for example, the Recorder's Court handled a total of 5274 habeas corpus writs, compared with 6380 felony cases and 20,452 misdemeanor cases.

23 When an attorney learns that a client has been arrested he immediately fills out the writ and writ petition forms and contacts the clerk of Recorder's Court (who notifies the police), and then takes the forms to a judge for signature. The judges always sign them, as they are subject to $1000 damages to the party aggrieved if they refuse a writ legally applied for. Mich. Stat. Ann. §27.2260 (1938).

24 Bail may be refused if the police report that the person is being held incident to an ongoing investigation, but the judge will then continue the hearing, giving the police a set time within which they must charge or release the suspect. The implications of this practice are considered in detail in Chapters 14 and 15.

25 One reason that release on recognizance is not more prevalent is the fact that many of the best risks, for whom bail probably would not be required, have already been released by the police (or, in Detroit, by the Release Bureau).

B. Criteria Employed in Determining Need for Custody

The major concern in this chapter is with the issue of when it is appropriate to initiate the criminal process by arrest rather than by some less drastic method, such as a summons or notice to appear. The criteria identified and discussed in the material which follows are based upon observation of current practice at the stages of arrest, release by police, release by the prosecutor, and release by the magistrate. This composite treatment makes it possible to define the need-for-custody criteria more adequately and also furnishes a basis for a comparison of the need for custody at these various stages in the criminal justice process.

1. *The likelihood of appearance.* It is generally agreed that taking and retaining custody of a suspect is justified when this is the only way to insure that he will appear in court to answer charges against him. There is, however, debate over what circumstances make the risk of nonappearance great enough to justify immediate arrest, the setting of high bail, or the denial of bail entirely.

The federal courts[26] and most state courts[27] have held that the risk of nonappearance is the only valid basis for requiring bail or for setting a high bail before trial. This is also an important factor in the law of other countries.[28] Constitutional provisions

[26] Fed. R. Crim. P. 46(c): "If the defendant is admitted to bail, the amount thereof shall be such as in the judgment of the commissioner ·or court or judge or justice will insure the presence of the defendant, having regard to the nature and circumstance of the offense charged, the weight of the evidence against him, the financial ability of the defendant to give bail and the character of the defendant."

In Stack v. Boyle, 342 U.S. 1, 72 Sup. Ct. 1, 96 L. Ed. 3 (1951), the Supreme Court held as "excessive," under the Eighth Amendment, bail set at a figure higher than an amount reasonably calculated to assure the presence of the accused.

[27] Comment, 70 Yale L.J. 966 (1961); Note, 102 U. Pa. L. Rev. 1031, 1033 (1954); Annot., 72 A.L.R. 801 (1931). One might query whether Stack can be read through the due process clause of the Fourteenth Amendment so as to require that this be the sole criterion. The state cases have been interpreting similar language in their own constitutions. For the constitutional provisions, see Comment, *supra.*

Recently a federal court declared that the Eighth Amendment was applicable to the states through the Fourteenth Amendment, but added in dictum that a state could deny or postpone bail "beyond the purpose of assuring presence at trial" and "where this rationally appears to be necessary to prevent a threat or likelihood of interference with the processes of investigation or the orderliness of trial." Mastrian v. Hedman, 326 F.2d 708 (8th Cir. 1964). The Eighth Amendment declares that "[e]xcessive bail shall not be required," but does not expressly state in what cases there is a right to bail.

[28] See Study of the Right of Everyone to Be Free from Arbitrary Arrest, Detention and Exile, Commission on Human Rights, U.N. Doc. E/CN.4/813, pars. 89-91, 155, 164 (1961).

prohibiting excessive bail are common,[29] and statutes, such as those in Michigan and Kansas, often prescribe that bail is to be set at an amount sufficient to secure the defendant's appearance.[30]   Less effort has been made by the law to relate the right to arrest with the risk of nonappearance, although a Wisconsin statute does make the risk of nonappearance one of the only two proper bases for arresting a person upon reasonable grounds to believe that he has committed a misdemeanor.[31]   Of course, a misdemeanor arrest can be made with a warrant issued on probable cause without regard to risk of nonappearance.

In practice, whenever a decision is made to use the notice to appear, to release without bail, or to release on minimal bail, the risk of nonappearance is considered.   Even when the notice to appear is used without express statutory authority, the police are instructed to take this risk into account.   For example, state traffic officers in Wisconsin are instructed to arrest "when the arresting officer has reason to believe that the person arrested will flee the jurisdiction of the court."

The following are determining factors in the decision as to whether there is a real risk of nonappearance.

a. *Seriousness of the offense.*

> *Illustration No. 1:* A defendant charged with the sale of narcotics was brought before the magistrate.   Without inquiry into the defendant's background, the magistrate set bail at $10,000.   This amount is uniformly set for such an offense.   Sale of narcotics carries a minimum sentence of 20 years' imprisonment, although many defendants are allowed to plead guilty to the lesser offense of possession of narcotics, thus avoiding the high, mandatory minimum.

The seriousness of the offense is obviously an important consideration, and the possible penalty seems an appropriate indication

---

[29] In Kansas there is a right to bail except for capital offenses; the Michigan constitution gives a right to bail except for murder and treason when the proof is evident or the presumption great; and in Wisconsin a right to bail is granted except for capital offenses when the proof is evident or the presumption great.   In all three states there are constitutional provisions that bail not be excessive.   Kan. Const., Bill of Rights §9; Mich. Const. art. II, §§14, 15; Wis. Const. art. I, §§6, 8.

For the similar provisions elsewhere, see Comment, 70 Yale L.J. 966 (1961).

[30] The Michigan statute provides: "The amount of the recognizance shall be fixed with consideration of the seriousness of the offense charged, the previous criminal record of the defendant and the probability or improbability of his appearing at the trial of the cause."   Mich. Stat. Ann. §28.893 (1954).   While the statute appears to state three separate criteria, it would appear that the first two are merely factors which affect the third, the likelihood of appearance.

A host of Kansas statutes dealing with bail in a variety of situations all speak of bail which will secure the appearance of the person charged.   Kan. Gen. Stat. §§13-608, 13-611, 14-808, 14-815, 15-507, 15-515, 62-611, 62-619 (1949).

[31] Wis. Stat. §954.03(1) (1955).

of seriousness.[32] The offender who, at most, will receive a small fine is generally much more likely to appear than one who anticipates a severe prison sentence. For this reason the notice to appear is most often used in misdemeanor traffic violations and conservation offenses. The amount of bail required is also influenced by the seriousness of the offense. In Michigan, it is provided by statute that this is a factor which must enter into the bail decision.[33]

The question is sometimes raised as to whether too great an emphasis is placed upon this one factor. Defense counsel complain that high bail is set for persons accused of a serious offense even though other factors make it extremely unlikely that these persons will flee. Bail bondsmen are hesitant to give bond for a person accused of some serious offenses, such as bank robbery. This is due in part to the high risk of nonappearance and in part to a desire to cooperate with the police, who are likely to want to conduct a prolonged in-custody investigation in such cases.

b. *Nature of the offense.*

Illustration No. 2: A numbers writer was brought before the magistrate for the setting of bail. Without inquiry into any of the specific facts of this case, the magistrate immediately set an extremely low bail. "These people would not leave town if an atomic bomb were dropped on it," he remarked.

The nature of the offense, regardless of the penalty, may in itself disclose a great deal about the risk of nonappearance. The fact that the offense arises out of an ongoing established business enterprise, legal or illegal, may suggest the continued availability of the defendant. Thus, in Wisconsin, tavern owners who violate the liquor laws are ordinarily given a notice to appear rather than being arrested.[34] In Detroit the Release Bureau grants more releases to persons arrested for possession of numbers slips than for any other offense, and at habeas corpus hearings such persons are released on very low bail. It is known that these persons will continue in business and will regard prosecution as one of the costs of doing business.

Illustration No. 3: A woman just arrested for shoplifting was brought to the precinct station. After a records check, it

---

[32] Dicta in People v. McDonald, 233 Mich. 98, 206 N.W. 516 (1925), stated emphatically that as the penalty for a second offender was higher, so bail could be set higher for a second offender.

[33] See statute quoted in note 30 *supra.*

[34] In Michigan, the Supreme Court has taken note of the desirability of using a notice to appear in a similar situation. See Odinetz v. Budds, 315 Mich. 512, 24 N.W.2d 193 (1946), discussed in note 2 *supra* page 169.

was determined that she had not been apprehended for any offenses in the past. The station lieutenant authorized her release without bond upon her promise to appear in court.

Sometimes the nature of the offense suggests that its commission is attributable to a mental or emotional problem of an otherwise law-abiding citizen. For this reason, shoplifters without criminal records are often released without bond.[35] One Detroit judge commented that he usually sets low bail for sex perverts, as he considers their conduct to be attributable to a mental disturbance and he does not think it likely that they will flee jurisdiction once discovered.

c. *Residence of the individual*

Illustration No. 4: A traffic officer stopped a driver for a violation. The driver contended that he lived in a neighboring community but did not have his driver's license in his possession. When he could not produce any conclusive proof of his local residence, the officer placed him under arrest.

If the person is a local resident there may be no need to take or retain custody to insure his appearance. But if he lives outside the jurisdiction or has no fixed dwelling or known residence, the risk of nonappearance is greater.[36] Thus, a Michigan statute prescribing the use of a notice to appear for misdemeanor traffic violations has an exception for the offense of driving without a license, although it is further provided that the officer can nonetheless release the driver if he determines his identity and is assured that the offender can be readily located for subsequent apprehension in the event of his failure to appear.[37]

The notice to appear is ordinarily used only for persons who reside within the jurisdiction served by the particular officer. A county traffic officer is likely to arrest a violator who is not a resident of the county, while a state conservation warden will probably use the notice to appear for all state residents. Even in the case of residents, an arrest will be made if it is apparent that the person is about to abscond.[38]

---

35 In fact, it is the rule in Detroit that a shoplifter without a criminal record is under no circumstances to be detained overnight. In a year and a half under this rule, no released person has failed to appear.

36 This is made a determinative factor by law in some foreign jurisdictions with respect to the use of alternatives to arrest and to release without bail. See Study of the Right of Everyone to Be Free from Arbitrary Arrest, Detention and Exile, Commission on Human Rights, U.N. Doc. E/CN.4/813, pars. 91, 197, 198 (1961).

37 Mich. Stat. Ann. §§9.2427 to 9.2429 (1952).

38 The felony detail of the Prosecutor's Bureau in the detective division, Detroit Police Department, specializes in dealing with complaints of fraud arising out of business transactions. When a complaint is received, a "please come" letter is ordinarily sent to the suspect. See page 196. However, in one case the bureau received a number of complaints from women who asserted that a sewing machine salesman

For the most part police release after arrest only in the case of local residents.[39] This is also the practice of magistrates in habeas corpus hearings. Thus a Detroit judge denied bail altogether in one case, noting that the defendant was not a resident but had been merely passing through the city at the time of the offense.

d. *Character of the individual.*

Illustration No. 5: A defendant was brought before a magistrate on a burglary charge. The magistrate set bail at the usual amount for this offense. "He's been in more than he's been out," commented the police officer accompanying the defendant. At this, the magistrate raised the bail substantially.

The respected citizen is more likely to appear to answer charges against him than is the habitual offender, and therefore the decision as to custody is likely to include consideration of the character of the defendant. In Michigan the previous criminal record of the defendant is by statute a necessary consideration in setting bail,[40] and it is in fact a consideration in all three jurisdictions. One of the most frequent reasons given by the Detroit Release Bureau for refusing to release a suspect is his bad record. As is true in regard to the seriousness of the offense, however, it is not easy in this case to distinguish the desire to punish the offender from a conclusion that there is a high risk of nonappearance.

e. *Likelihood of conviction.*

Illustration No. 6: A Negro defendant was brought before the magistrate charged with felonious assault. The magistrate examined the case report and noted that the assault was on another Negro and that there were no other witnesses. He released the defendant on his own recognizance instead of requiring bail. "There'll probably be no conviction here," he noted. "In these cases the victim usually 'forgets' what happened."

Although the weight of the available evidence is a factor frequently mentioned in state constitutional provisions on bail in capital cases,[41] the sufficiency of the evidence is in practice generally not a consideration in decisions on arrest,[42] release, or bail-

---

had promised them $20 each for every new customer obtained, but that no payments had been made. When investigators learned that this salesman had recently moved all of the furniture from his office, they feared he was planning to leave town, so an arrest was made.

39 However, even local residents certain to appear may not be released without bail if the police doubt their authority for doing so. Thus in many Wisconsin communities local drunken drivers were released when sober only by posting bond.

40 See statute quoted in note 30 *supra.*

41 See the Wisconsin and Michigan provisions, cited note 29 *supra.* For similar provisions elsewhere, see Comment, 70 Yale L.J. 966 (1961).

42 Of course, probability of guilt may be an important factor in the determination

setting. However, the actual likelihood of conviction, often indicated by circumstances other than the adequacy of the evidence, is sometimes considered. The illustration above is an example of a case in which conviction is unlikely chiefly because of low enforcement priority.

Conviction may appear unlikely, notwithstanding the evidence in hand, because discretion will probably be exercised at the charging[43] or adjudication[44] level similar to that already noted with regard to arrest.[45] If the suspected offender is aware of the fact that he probably will not be convicted, he has less incentive to flee, and consequently there is a greater likelihood of his appearance. In any event, the mere fact that conviction is unlikely makes insuring appearance seem less important to those making decisions on arrest, release, and bail.

2. *The interest of the individual.*

a. *Hardship to individual or his family.*

> *Illustration No. 7:* A man was arrested for conspiracy to violate the gambling laws and was held in jail pending his appearance before a magistrate. The police received a call from the Release Bureau saying that, although the bureau did not ordinarily act in felony cases, there were some unusual circumstances in this case. There was a young baby at home, the person's wife was sick, and his home telephone had been confiscated at the time of the raid which resulted in his arrest. The police agreed to an immediate release.

The facts of an individual case may indicate that taking or retaining a person in custody will work an inordinate amount of harm upon him or his family. Thus the Detroit police are instructed to consider the number of dependents of the person in deciding whether to grant a release.[46] Sickness in the family is often recognized as a basis for release, because the family need is greater and flight is less likely under such circumstances.[47] Also, a person may be released if he has responsibilities in his daily work

---

of whether an arrest can be lawfully made. See Chapters 11-13. But once an officer determines that there is sufficient evidence available for arrest, he does not ordinarily then ask himself whether the strength of the evidence affects the need-for-custody issue.

[43] A discussion of noninvocation criteria will be found in the volume on Prosecution.

[44] Treatment of acquittal criteria will be found in the volume on Conviction.

[45] See Part II *supra.*

[46] Detroit Police Dept., Revised Police Manual, chap. 16, §135 (1955).

[47] A supervisory officer in one Michigan department said that in the last three years he had released only two persons without bail, and in both cases there was sickness in the family.

which cannot be performed by others.[48]   Even the desire to keep
a close relative from knowing about an offense may sometimes
prompt release.[49]

Some foreign jurisdictions have expressly made hardship, or
particular kinds of hardship, a basis for not arresting or for releasing a person already arrested.[50]   Since the special circumstances
are not usually known until after arrest, this factor is of more importance in the consideration of release than in the initial arrest.

   b. *Inability of individual to care for himself.*

   Illustration No. 8: A police officer made an arrest for public intoxication. The defendant was taken to the station, and,
   notwithstanding his demand for release and his ability to post
   bond, he was kept in custody until sober.

When the defendant is under the influence of alcohol, the police
in all three states view this as an adequate reason for arresting him
rather than giving him a notice to appear and also for refusing to
release him until he is sober. The Michigan statute prescribing
the use of the notice to appear in traffic cases makes an exception
in cases of drunken driving.[51] In Wisconsin, where the notice to
appear is used in practice even though there is no relevant statute,
a state traffic patrol bulletin states that an arrest should be made
only when the violator is unable to care for his own safety or the
safety of others, as in cases of operating an automobile while intoxicated. Only in unusual cases, where it is clear that there is
no further danger, will a ticket be given to the intoxicated driver.[52]
Similarly, persons arrested for public drunkenness or disorderly
conduct are not released until they are sober even if they have adequate funds to post bail.[53] In some cases, however, a drunk will

[48] Wisconsin conservation agents arrested a man for a serious game violation and
put him in jail. However, when it was learned that he had the responsibility of
operating a farm, he was allowed to leave the jail to attend to his work.

[49] Though they ordinarily do not attempt to obtain the release of prostitutes, the
Detroit Prosecutor's Bureau inquired into the possibility of release of a girl whose
mother was about to arrive in town for a visit.

[50] Study of the Right of Everyone to Be Free from Arbitrary Arrest, Detention and
Exile, Commission on Human Rights, U.N. Doc. E/CN.4/813, pars. 100, 162, 165
(1961).

[51] See statute quoted in note 30 *supra.*

[52] Wisconsin county traffic officers were summoned when a car was found in a
ditch. They checked the ownership of the car and went immediately to the home
of the owner, found him in an intoxicated condition, and learned from him that
he had just returned after driving the car into the ditch. He was left a ticket for
appearance in court.

[53] Statistics of the Detroit Release Bureau record many instances in which release
was denied because of the intoxication of the arrestee. However, the bureau did
grant release once the person was sober. In many Kansas communities the police
require drunks to remain in custody for a minimum of four hours as a matter of
policy.

be released to the custody of some sober, responsible party, such as his wife, close friend, or attorney.

In Wisconsin drunkenness is an offense only when the person is in public and unable to care for his own safety.[54] The draftsmen's comments state that "the police, as a matter of policy, should be permitted to take him [the helpless drunk] into custody, if for no other reason than that he needs protection."[55] However, continuation of custody on this basis is inconsistent with the notion that there is a right to prompt release on bail set only to insure appearance.[56] In *Schoette v. Drake*,[57] an officer arrested an intoxicated and boisterous offender at 5:00 P.M. but did not bring him before a magistrate until the following morning. The Wisconsin court held that the lower court erred in deciding as a matter of law that there had been no unreasonable delay, as the local court had been open immediately after arrest "for disposition of [the] case or for release on bail." There are cases to the contrary,[58] holding that the right to bail does not require the release of a person who cannot care for himself and who would commit another offense by being in public while still intoxicated.[59]

c. *Possibility of harm to individual by others.*

Illustration No. 9: A tavern owner, arrested by an officer

[54] The statutory definition of a drunken person is: "A person who is so intoxicated that he is unable to care for his own safety and is found in a public place in such condition." Wis. Stat. §947.03 (1955). This is not significantly different from the provision prior to recodification, Wis. Stat. §351.59 (1953).

[55] 5 Wis. Legis. Council, Judiciary Committee Report on the Criminal Code 45 (1953).

[56] Thus, in Markey v. Griffin, 109 Ill. App. 212 (1903), the court declared that an arrestee has an absolute right to bail regardless of his state of intoxication. Although the reported practice in Chicago is to deny bail to intoxicated persons except when release to a responsible relative or friend is possible, Note, 38 Chi.-Kent L. Rev. 22, 43 (1961), Markey is followed in some other parts of the state.

In one incident occurring in downstate Illinois, an intoxicated driver was arrested when found driving on the wrong side of a four-lane divided highway. He was able to obtain his release when a professional bondsman posted bond for him four hours later, but he subsequently killed himself and the occupants of another car when he again drove on the wrong side of the same highway. Although the police explained that they thought the man was sober at the time of his release, a local pathologist noted: "an individual who has 20 grams per cent blood-alcohol content has 10 to 12 ounces of alcohol in him. Alcohol is excreted at a rate of $\frac{2}{3}$ ounce per hour. If the individual is detained five hours, he would get rid of $\frac{2}{3}$ ounce times five, or about three to four ounces, when he would be released after five hours and would still have seven to eight ounces in him. A couple of beers would get him drunk again." Local law enforcement officials demanded legislation authorizing detention of intoxicated drivers for a minimum of six hours. Champaign-Urbana News-Gazette, March 14, 1963, p. 3, col. 6.

[57] 139 Wis. 18, 120 N.W. 393 (1909).

[58] Annot., Delay in taking before magistrate or denial of opportunity to give bail as supporting action for false imprisonment, 79 A.L.R. 13, 20-21 (1932).

[59] This view is also reflected in the recently enacted Michigan statute quoted in note 16 *supra* page 174.

for selling beer to a minor, was kept in custody over a week-end until he could be brought into court. In response to the district attorney's criticism that such offenders are not ordinarily arrested, the police noted that the youth to whom the liquor was sold had nearly died, and that as a result there was considerable public antagonism manifested toward the tavern owner.

In cases of crimes which cause a very emotional response by the victim, his friends or family, or the general public, the police may deem it necessary to take and retain the suspect in custody for his own protection. Thus it is the policy of the Detroit Release Bureau to deny release in a sex case involving an adult who has abused a child, on the basis that feelings are very intense in these cases and the family of the victim is likely to be aggressive toward the defendant.

While the safety of the accused is a factor which can be considered under the law of some foreign countries,[60] it is contrary to the common assumption in the United States that the likelihood of appearance is the sole criterion for setting bail. Certainly the safety of the accused is not a satisfactory basis for requiring a high bail, since the amount of bail required does not affect the danger to the accused. If properly considered, it would constitute a basis for denying release entirely. This issue has rarely been considered by appellate courts, although one court, while declaring that a higher bail could not be set because of a fear of mob violence, did intimate that at some time there might be a "danger so great" that the prisoner's "guaranty against excessive bail . . . should be withheld." [61]

This situation differs from the previous one in which the drunk is taken into custody because he has rendered himself unable to care for his own safety. The tavern keeper is taken into custody because of the threat of harm by others. To say that the suspect is responsible for this situation assumes his guilt. When there is readily available some means of preventing possible harm, perhaps by police protection, then the case for custody is not easy to support. The most difficult situation is that in which the police doubt their ability to keep order if the suspect is not taken and held in custody.

d. *Possibility of attempted suicide.*

Illustration No. 10: Officers arrested a man for homosexual

---

[60] Study of the Right of Everyone to Be Free from Arbitrary Arrest, Detention and Exile, Commission on Human Rights, U.N. Doc. E/CN.4/813, pars. 155, 165 (1961).

[61] State v. Richardson, 176 La. 750, 753, 146 So. 737 (1933). Thus the court rejected outright the proposal of the district judge to raise bond from $500 to $5000, saying that it "would not lessen the danger of mob violence," but to the suggestion to deny bail outright merely said that there was not sufficient indication of danger.

conduct. At the station it was determined that he was a local resident, unlikely to flee. The officer in charge said that under no circumstance were the police to grant a release to this man. He explained that a few years ago, after such a release had been made, the defendant, a schoolteacher, had committed suicide.

A person who has been arrested may be retained in custody pending his appearance in court if police feel that he will be a suicidal risk if released. This situation might occur, for example, when a prominent and respected person is arrested for homosexual activity. This criterion is apparently also utilized in practice in England [62] but is not formally recognized as proper in either England or the United States.

The risk of suicide is created by the arrest and pending public disclosure of the allegation of improper conduct.[63] The assumption is that the person is more depressed immediately following arrest than he is after the passage of some time and his appearance in court. In practice, both the police and the magistrate attempt to minimize the risk of suicide by impressing upon the homosexual that others are similarly afflicted and that he can be helped by psychiatric treatment.

3. *The obtaining of evidence.*

a. *Search incident to arrest.*

Illustration No. 11: Officers observed a numbers writer accepting bets from his customers. They recognized him as a local operator and a long-time resident of the precinct. They placed him under arrest, searched him to uncover the numbers slips in his possession, and then took him to the station.

Although a search may be made with a search warrant or, in a few limited situations, without either a warrant or an arrest, by far the commonest method of searching is incident to an arrest. An officer who has adequate grounds may arrest a suspect to make it possible to conduct a lawful search of his person.[64] Thus while

[62] Devlin, The Criminal Prosecution in England 93 (1958); Devlin, Criminal Courts and Procedure 53 (1960).

[63] Because possible public disclosure in the case of some offenses is thought to impose an undue burden upon certain defendants, the police sometimes decide against invoking the process at all. See page 137.

Even when an arrest is made in these cases the police often assure the defendant that all possible steps will be taken to avoid any publicity and that he probably will not be convicted if he agrees to seek private psychiatric help, which is usually the outcome.

For comparison of the sympathetic attitude of the police toward the respectable person who becomes involved in homosexual conduct with their attitude toward the troublesome transvestite, see Chapter 23.

[64] Arrest of a suspect in order to search, and taking a suspect into custody, are

the Detroit judge who released a numbers carrier on low bail may have been correct in his assumption that the average numbers carrier "would not leave town if an atomic bomb were dropped on it," the police do arrest persons suspected of such activity in order to obtain the evidence needed for prosecution and conviction. If the search fails to disclose any incriminating evidence, the suspect is usually released immediately, and in such a case most policemen would not consider that they had made an arrest. However, if incriminating evidence is found, then the suspect will be retained in custody, notwithstanding the high probability of his appearance in court, so that it will be readily apparent that the search was incident to arrest.[65]

> *Illustration No. 12:* Officers were following an automobile driven by a man suspected of being a narcotics pusher. Lacking evidence for arrest on this charge, they continued to follow the automobile until the driver committed a minor traffic violation. They stopped the car, arrested the driver, searched the car and found narcotics, and then took the driver to the station.

Reliance upon a traffic arrest as a basis for searching for evidence of a more serious crime is a common police practice, although an increasing number of state courts are finding the practice to be improper.[66] When official action is taken against a traffic offender, it is usually by means of a notice to appear rather than by arrest. However, because there is doubt about the validity of a search as an incident to a stopping and notice to appear,[67] an arrest is commonly made when a search is desired. Consequently, the suspect may be taken into custody under circumstances in which the risk of nonappearance would not be great.

A Michigan statute requires the use of a notice to appear "when-

---

both technically arrests, but they are sufficiently different to warrant being given separate analysis. In this volume we are concerned mainly with the decision to take into custody. Detailed consideration of the decision to arrest for purposes of search will be found in the volume on Detection of Crime.

[65] This decision is re-enforced by the common police attitude in numbers cases that the detention is appropriate as a sanction, since the money fine imposed in court can be regarded as a part of the cost of doing business.

[66] While a number of courts have upheld such searches by resort to the axiom that "a search incident to a legal arrest is lawful," more and more courts have recently adopted the opinion that the search can be justified only if its purpose is to obtain evidence of the offense for which the arrest was made or if it is made to protect the arresting officer and prevent escape. See Note, 1959 Wis. L. Rev. 347. Detailed exploration of all the ramifications of this problem will be found in the volume on Detection of Crime.

[67] Even when a right to arrest exists, it would not appear that the mere giving of a citation would justify a search. Id. at 352 n.33.

ever a person is arrested without a warrant for any violation of the motor vehicle code punishable as a misdemeanor." [68]   Perhaps this legislative characterization of the stopping while a ticket is written as an arrest is an attempt to avoid the necessity of taking a suspect into custody but to maintain the opportunity of search incident to the traffic arrest.   In any event, the assumption of the police operating under this statute is that they can search even though only a notice to appear can be given.

b. *In-custody investigation.*

Illustration No. 13: A suspect was arrested for a recent armed robbery on the statement of a reliable underworld informant.   When the suspect appeared before a judge on a writ of habeas corpus, the police informed the magistrate that they wished to have the robbery victims view the suspect so that it could be decided whether he should be charged or released.   For this reason, the magistrate remanded the suspect to police custody without bail.

Arrests are frequently made upon evidence which does not conclusively establish grounds for prosecution.   The person is taken into custody because it is thought that by conducting an in-custody investigation further evidence will be found which will either clear the suspect or provide an adequate basis for prosecution.   The in-custody investigation ordinarily involves questioning of the suspect.   But it may also include asking the suspect to do something, as in the case of the suspected drunken driver who is put through a series of coordination tests or the robbery suspect who is placed in an identification line-up.[69]

The need for in-custody investigation is a factor of major importance.   Police never use an alternative to arrest, such as a notice to appear, when there is a desire to conduct an in-custody investigation, nor do they release a suspect without bail before the investigation is completed.   The Detroit Release Bureau usually will not grant release if the police wish to conduct a further investigation.   Similarly, when the officer at a habeas corpus hearing makes a good case for the need for further in-custody investigation, bail is likely to be denied or a prohibitively high bail set.

Some foreign countries have made need for investigation a proper criterion for making an arrest or refusing to release the suspect after arrest.[70]   Whether this criterion is ever accepted in the

[68] Mich. Stat. Ann. §9.2427 (1952).

[69] For a detailed description of the various in-custody investigation methods used, see page 308.

[70] Study of the Right of Everyone to Be Free from Arbitrary Arrest, Detention and Exile, Commission on Human Rights, U.N. Doc. E/CN.4/813, pars. 155, 197 (1961).

United States and, if so, under what circumstances, is a most complex question. It is a part of the larger issue concerning the legitimacy of in-custody investigation, dealt with in later chapters in this volume.[71]

c. *Avoiding disclosure of continuing investigation.*

Illustration No. 14: A numbers carrier was arrested, and the evidence found on his person was turned over to detectives conducting a continuing investigation of the numbers syndicate. The arrestee was kept in custody while this evidence was analyzed and while the other conspirators whose identity was thereby disclosed were arrested.

Persons are sometimes retained in custody in order to prevent their alerting other suspects of the fact that a police investigation is being directed toward them. This is most likely to be true if the investigation concerns a number of conspirators, although unusual circumstances occasionally call for custody to be retained in order to avoid such a warning being given to a person who is not an accomplice of the person arrested.[72]

While retention of custody to avoid the warning of other suspects occurs with some frequency, it does not create a serious problem. Custody is usually needed only for the short period of time it takes to arrest the other suspects. Thus at most it may result in a brief delay in release.[73]

d. *Safeguarding evidence or witnesses.*

Illustration No. 15: A man was arrested after social workers interviewing his stepdaughter heard her allege that he had engaged in sexual intercourse with her. The magistrate set extremely high bail on this defendant, remarking that he wanted to insure that he was not released and in a position to induce his stepdaughter to change her story.

The possibility that the offender will tamper with important evidence or with a prosecution witness is another reason for taking or retaining custody in current practice. Threat of harm to witnesses is often more likely when an intrafamily offense has occurred. For this reason, arrests are made, releases denied, or a high bail set in cases in which a man has assaulted his wife or attacked his daughter, and in some situations when he is being prosecuted for nonsupport. A defendant who has been released may

71 See Chapters 14-17.

72 For example, the Release Bureau in Detroit was arranging the release of a well-known local gambler. However, the police indicated that somehow, while he was in custody, he learned of police plans for a raid on a numbers operation that evening. They feared that if released, he would divulge police plans, so the bureau authorized continued detention until the raid had been completed.

73 On the resulting delay of the appearance before a magistrate, see page 376.

be rearrested if it later appears that a witness[74] or a police informant[75] is in danger of harm from him.

In foreign countries it is common to provide by law that danger
of destruction of evidence or of harm to a witness justifies arrest
and denial of release.[76] This is in contrast to American bail law,
which usually recognizes the likelihood of appearance as the only
proper concern.[77] In support of the American view, it is said:

> Beside the fact that such a policy is implicit in the presumption
> of innocence, the soundness of our theory will be apparent to any-
> one who contemplates the almost insuperable difficulty of trying
> to contact witnesses and prepare and finance a defense from the
> enforced idleness of a prison cell.[78]

In contrast, the more strict English bail provisions are supported
in this statement:

> The public interest is weighed as well as that of the individual sus-
> pect, and — in the present writer's view — properly so. The "pre-
> sumption of innocence," in Britain at all events, is a rule of evi-
> dence to secure fair trial, and implies that the guilt of an accused
> must be proved at his trial beyond all reasonable doubt. It does

---

[74] In one Detroit case, the Release Bureau had granted a release, after which the complainant notified the police that the defendant had threatened him with bodily harm. The Release Bureau ordered that the suspect be rearrested.

[75] In Wichita a gang of hoodlums was arrested upon information provided by an informant. Upon gaining release on bail, they severely assaulted the man they suspected of having informed on them. On this occasion they attacked the wrong man.

Sometimes protection of witnesses is achieved by detention of the witness. For example, in pandering cases pending in Detroit the prostitute who is to testify is often willing to remain in custody as a police witness in order to insure that her former pimp will not do her any harm.

[76] Study of the Right of Everyone to Be Free from Arbitrary Arrest, Detention and Exile, Commission on Human Rights, U.N. Doc. E/CN.4/813, pars. 92-93, 156, 161, 164, 189 (1961). Where arrest is limited by legislation to situations in which custody is necessary, this danger is likely to be listed as one of those which establishes the necessity of taking custody. For specific provisions in Norway and Japan, respectively, see Bratholm, Arrest and Detention in Norway, 108 U. Pa. L. Rev. 336, 337 (1960); Dando and Tamiya, Conditional Release of an Accused in Japan, 108 U. Pa. L. Rev. 323, 324 (1960).

Where the granting of bail is discretionary, this kind of danger may be declared a proper basis for absolute denial of release. For specific provisions in England, France, Scotland, and Japan, respectively, see Devlin, The Criminal Prosecution in England 91 (1958) (declaring it is the "next most important consideration" to likelihood of appearance on the bail question); Vouin, Provisional Release in French Penal Law, 109 U. Pa. L. Rev. 355, 359 (1960); Smith, Bail Before Trial: Reflections of a Scottish Lawyer, 108 U. Pa. L. Rev. 305, 318 (1960); Dando and Tamiya, supra, at 325-326.

[77] Foote, Foreword: Comment on the New York Bail Study, 106 U. Pa. L. Rev. 685, 685-686 (1958). Compare the view taken as to the American constitutional requirements in the Mastrian case, note 27 supra.

[78] Ibid.

not mean that those who discharge executive or administrative functions prior to trial should be bound to act as though the suspect had behaved, and would pending trial behave, as a law-abiding citizen. This would be to contradict the experience of mankind over the ages. . . . Further, tampering with evidence and intimidation of witnesses does happen, and the duty to ensure fair trial and vindication of justice is not concerned with the interests of the accused alone.[79]

One alternative which is sometimes used, either because of the inability to have a high bail set or because of the ability of the defendant to meet the high bail which was set, is that of arrest of the witness. Thus, it is not uncommon in Detroit, in a case such as that in Illustration 15, for the daughter who is assumed to be the victim to be kept in jail for her own safety and to insure that she will testify free of threats from her father. Whether, under current bail law, a release is required of a suspect at the cost of the incarceration of an alleged victim has not been specifically litigated.

Although there are other alternative methods of safeguarding evidence and witnesses, there may be doubt as to their effectiveness. One court, on an appeal from a habeas corpus order denying bail, held irrelevant the prosecution's allegation that the defendant was likely to intimidate witnesses, as "detention without bail is not a substitute for a peace bond, or a method of crime prevention." [80] Peace bonds are generally available "if there is reason to fear" commission of an offense,[81] and penal sanctions exist for such conduct as bribery of witnesses,[82] subornation of perjury,[83] and inducement to commit perjury.[84] But some courts do not seem to consider these alternatives sufficient to prevent the threatened harm.[85] In a recent federal case in which a key witness received telephone threats, bail was denied during the trial notwithstanding

[79] Smith, Bail Before Trial: Reflections of a Scottish Lawyer, 108 U. Pa. L. Rev. 305, 309 (1960).

[80] Ford v. Dilley, 174 Iowa 243, 249, 156 N.W. 513, 516 (1916).

[81] Kan. Gen. Stat. §62-203 (1949); Mich. Stat. Ann. §28.1157 (1954); Wis. Stat. §962.06 (1955). The proceedings are begun upon a complaint that a "person has threatened to commit a crime." Kan. Gen. Stat. §62-202 (1949); Mich. Stat. Ann. §28.1155 (1954); Wis. Stat. §962.02 (1955).

[82] Kan. Gen. Stat. §21-708 (1949); Wis. Stat. §946.61 (1955).

[83] Kan. Gen. Stat. §21-703 (1949); Mich. Stat. Ann. §28.666 (1954).

[84] Kan. Gen. Stat. §21-705 (1949); Mich. Stat. Ann. §28.667 (1954). Also, committing any act tending to obstruct the due course of justice, such as intimidating a witness, was a misdemeanor at common law. Ruhland v. Cole, 143 Wis. 367, 127 N.W. 959 (1910).

[85] The peace bond may not be available unless the defendant has already "threatened" the interference, note 81 *supra,* and the threat of forfeiture of the bond or of added criminal sanctions may prove little deterrence to one presently facing prosecution for another offense.

the defendant's assertion that this witness was receiving round-the-clock police protection.[86] Justice Douglas, as circuit justice, denied bail pending an appeal for the same reason in this case, as there was a likelihood of a new trial.[87]

Thus the individual's interest in freedom and the public interest in the unobstructed administration of justice are at conflict. The difficult issue is whether, considering the alternative means available for preventing and punishing such interference, the risk is great enough to justify keeping in custody a person whom there is sufficient evidence to arrest but whose guilt or innocence has not as yet been established.

e. *Rewarding assistance in investigation.*

Illustration No. 16: Officers brought a woman before the magistrate on a charge of obtaining money by false pretenses. The magistrate set bail at $3000. A detective then spoke to the judge, informing him that the defendant had been extremely cooperative in identifying and leading the police to her accomplice. After further discussion, the magistrate said he would release the defendant on $500 bail on account. It was apparent that she was being released on her own recognizance.

Freedom pending trial may be used as a reward for cooperating with the police, as in the above illustration, or as an inducement to cooperation.[88] Thus in Detroit a narcotics pusher or user who has agreed to make further contacts for the police may be released on low bond or on his own recognizance.

The practice of releasing the cooperative suspect obviously does not raise a difficult question in regard to the individual's right to bail, provided there is no evidence that the uncooperative suspect is denied bail as punishment for his refusal to cooperate. Nor, in the view of the police, is the community interest sacrificed. They feel that the benefit resulting from the information received outweighs the possible risk that the suspect will not appear in court

---

[86] Carbo v. United States, 288 F.2d 686 (9th Cir. 1961). The decision has been criticized because (1) it recognizes a lesser right to bail during trial, while Fed. R. Crim. P. 46(a) speaks of a right to bail "before conviction," and (2) "the existence of criminal sanctions against those who obstruct justice . . . by threatening witnesses" is sufficient means for dealing with the threat. Note, 110 U. Pa. L. Rev. 118 (1961).

[87] Carbo v. United States, 369 U.S. 868, 82 Sup. Ct. 662, 667, 8 L. Ed. 2d 274 (1962).

It is not suggested that this case per se establishes the appropriateness of detention without bail *before* trial on the same basis. A balancing of the public and individual interests involved may show a preponderant need for freedom at that point. See quotation in text at note 78 *supra.*

[88] See page 132 on noninvocation on this basis.

and the fact that the cooperative suspect knows his sentence will be light minimizes the risk of his nonappearance.

4. *The prevention of future criminal conduct.*

> *Illustration No. 17:* A man arrested for burglary was brought before the magistrate for the setting of bail. The magistrate set a very high bail, explaining that he was concerned that persons arrested for such offenses might commit others while on bail pending trial in order to pay for their defense.

The risk that the suspect will commit further crimes if not arrested or if released has significant influence upon arrest and release decisions. A few statutes recognize the risk of future crimes as a proper basis for an immediate arrest. For example, the Michigan notice to appear provision for misdemeanor traffic violations makes an exception as to drunken driving and reckless driving, although as to the latter the officer may use the notice to appear if doing so will not create a danger to the public.[89] Even without such a provision, the police are often instructed not to use the notice to appear if it appears that further offenses might result.[90]

This risk of additional criminal conduct is also considered in the bail-setting decision. Judges often set extremely high bail if the suspect, by virtue of the nature of the offense, appears to be a habitual offender or a professional criminal. High bond is required for narcotics sellers, armed robbers, burglars, and similar offenders.[91] The police believe the risk of repetition of such offenses to be high and voice severe criticism of what they view as low bail when they apprehend a burglar or narcotics peddler only to find that he is currently on bail for another such offense.[92]

As with the threat of interference with witnesses, the risk of

[89] Mich. Stat. Ann. §§9.2427 to 9.2429 (1952).

[90] At one Kansas police school the officers were cautioned not to resort to arrest as the means of invocation in all cases, but were told that the possibility of "further harm by the offender" should be considered. Sedgwick County School for Law Enforcement Officers, Arrests, Searches and Seizures, July 2, 1953, p. 4.

[91] This was borne out by empirical studies in New York City and Philadelphia. Comment, 106 U. Pa. L. Rev. 693, 705 (1958); Note, 102 U. Pa. L. Rev. 1031, 1039 (1954).

[92] This is not an infrequent occurrence. An extreme example was reported by Herman Goldstein, Executive Assistant to the Superintendent, Chicago Police Department, at a panel discussion, "Use of Bail for Preventive Detention," at the National Conference on Bail and Criminal Justice, Washington, D.C., May 27-29, 1964.

"Massari was released from the Illinois State Penitentiary upon completion of a three-year term for burglary and armed robbery in 1961. On July 8, 1963, Massari was apprehended in the act of committing a burglary. He was indicted and released on bail totaling $7500. On August 24, 1963, while free on bail, the subject was apprehended in the commission of a second burglary and was found to have in his possession the proceeds of still another burglary committed earlier in the day. He was indicted on two counts of burglary and released on $4500 bail. The subject was again arrested on November 18, 1963, when he was found to be in the possession of a

further criminal conduct is a criterion which has received express approval in the law of many foreign countries, although generally not in the United States. In countries in which the power to arrest is limited to situations in which immediate arrest is necessary, it is commonly provided that arrest is proper if there is a risk that the suspect will commit further criminal acts or if there is a history of recidivism.[93] In many countries, threat of future criminality is also considered a proper basis for denying bail.[94]

The conflicting values are obvious: the desire to prevent future crimes and the desire to provide for freedom of the suspect prior to the adjudication of guilt.[95] It is said that "it is not the function of bail to prevent the commission of crimes between indictment and trial";[96] that "if it is feared that the defendants will commit further crimes if released on bail, the remedy is not preventive detention but a prompt trial";[97] and that "imprisonment to protect society from predicted but unconsummated offenses is . . . fraught with danger of excesses and injustice." [98]

Despite the difficulty of predicting future behavior,[99] experience

---

loaded firearm and burglary tools. On January 16, 1964, he was arrested in the act of committing a burglary and found to have the proceeds of two other burglaries in his possession. He was indicted the following day and released on $15,000 bail, only to be again arrested on the same afternoon while committing still another burglary for which he was indicted and bail set at $5000. Subsequently, he was arrested on February 8, 1964, with release on bail set at $10,000; again on February 21, 1964, with release on bail of $5000; and again on March 5, 1964, when bail was set at $5000.

"On April 24, 1964, when Massari went to trial he had been arrested nine times in the period from July 8, 1963, to March 5, 1964, indicted on ten counts and was free on $48,500 in bail. He entered a guilty plea to the ten indictments and was sentenced to from five to fifteen years in the penitentiary on each count — the sentences to run concurrently."

[93] Study of the Right of Everyone to Be Free from Arbitrary Arrest, Detention and Exile, Commission on Human Rights, U.N. Doc. E/CN.4/813, pars. 94-96 (1961). However, the Federal Republic of Germany has eliminated this as a reason on the ground that it is incompatible with the nature and purpose of pretrial detention. Id. at par. 99. For discussion of a specific provision limiting arrest to cases showing a need for custody, such as "when there is special reason to believe that [the accused] will repeat the criminal offense or complete a criminal offense which he has tried to commit or threatened to committ," see Bratholm, Arrest and Detention in Norway, 108 U. Pa. L. Rev. 336, 337-338 (1960).

[94] See U.N. Doc. E/CN.4/813 (referred to in note 93 *supra*) pars. 155, 164, 189 (1961). In England, this risk is the "next most important consideration" to likelihood of appearance. Devlin, The Criminal Prosecution in England 91 (1958). For more on denial of bail for this reason in England, France, and Japan, respectively, see Devlin, Criminal Courts and Procedure 54 (1960); Vouin, Provisional Release in French Penal Law, 108 U. Pa. L. Rev. 355, 359 (1960); Dando and Tamiya, Conditional Release of an Accused in Japan, 108 U. Pa. L. Rev. 323, 325-326 (1960).

[95] The excerpts in the text at notes 78 and 79 *supra*, it will be noted, apply equally well to the present problem.

[96] United States v. Foster, 79 F. Supp. 422, 423 (S.D. N.Y. 1948).

[97] Note, 102 U. Pa. L. Rev. 1031, 1077 (1954).

[98] Williamson v. United States, 184 F.2d 280, 282 (2d Cir. 1950).

[99] "Unfortunately there are apparently no statistics on either side of the Atlantic

seems to show that there is a high probability of the commission of new offenses in certain cases, such as those concerning narcotics offenders or burglars with a considerable record of past offenses.[100] The peace bond,[101] as an alternative to continued custody, is probably not available to deal with this risk when evidenced only by past offenses,[102] and, in any event, is of doubtful effectiveness. Where discretion may be used to refuse bail because of a risk of repeated criminal conduct, judges do deny bail on this ground,[103] and the risk of further criminal conduct is generally a matter of concern to judges.[104] Yet the law generally assumes that the risk of future crime does not justify the refusal of bail prior to the determination of guilt.

5. *The special objectives of the pending proceedings.*

a. *Objectives interfered with by custody.*

Notwithstanding the general tendency to invoke the process by arrest whether custody is actually needed or not, there is a significant number of cases in which the police do not arrest because to do so would directly conflict with another law enforcement objective. If an arrest is made, such considerations may be reflected at the time of the bail decision.

---

relevant to a determination of the likelihood that bailed defendants will commit a crime while on bail. In the absence of any reliable information we are left with the distasteful task of making value judgments which critically affect human liberty on no sounder premise than sheer speculation." Foote, Introduction: The Comparative Study of Conditional Release, 108 U. Pa. L. Rev. 290, 296 (1960).

[100] Perhaps the fact that the suspect has been convicted for past offenses of the kind being charged overcomes to some extent the criticism that such detention presupposes guilt. Some countries who deny bail through fear of future criminality do seem to assume the guilt of the offense charged. Foote, Foreword: Comment on the New York Bail Study, 106 U. Pa. L. Rev. 685 n.4 (1958).

[101] Williamson v. United States, 184 F.2d 280, 282 n.7 (2d Cir. 1950).

[102] See note 81 *supra.*

[103] Bail on appeal in the federal criminal justice system is not infrequently denied on this basis. "The pattern of his career to date indicates that whenever released he will soon be selling heroin again . . ." United States v. Wilson, 257 F.2d 796, 797 (2d Cir. 1958). "Bail should not be granted where the offense of which the defendant has been convicted is an atrocious one, and there is danger that if he is given his freedom he will commit another of like character." Estabrook v. Otis, 18 F.2d 689, 690 (8th Cir. 1927). Rule 33(f) of the Rules of the Circuit Court of Appeals for the District of Columbia makes the safety of the community a factor to be considered in deciding whether to allow release on bail pending appeal. For discussion of some recent cases, see Note, 9 DePaul L. Rev. 295 (1960).

However, likelihood of repetition may be "too restrictive a standard" under some circumstances, such as with crimes of a political nature and with appeals in which the constitutionality of the statute is at issue. Carbo v. United States, 369 U.S. 868, 82 Sup. Ct. 662, 667, 8 L. Ed. 2d 274 (1962).

[104] In People v. Benmore, 298 Mich. 701, 707, 299 N.W. 773, 775 (1941), the court quotes the suggestion of the trial judge that release of "a seasoned and dangerous professional criminal" is undesirable because it "gives him a fine encouragement to perpetrate additional crimes to repay the indebtedness he owes to those who aided him."

Illustration No. 18: Upon complaint of a woman, the prosecutor decided to commence a nonsupport prosecution against her husband. Instead of ordering his arrest, the prosecutor attempted to obtain the presence of the husband at the preliminary consultations by sending him a letter requesting appearance on "an important matter."

In a nonsupport situation, requiring bail diverts money which should be used for support, and keeping the offender in custody prevents him from earning needed funds. For this reason, nonsupport actions are routinely commenced in Detroit by a telephone call or a letter requesting the husband to appear. In Milwaukee an arrest is commonly made, but judges are likely to release the husband without bail.

Illustration No. 19: Police officers arrested a youth for a minor property theft. Rather than keep the boy in custody until he could be brought before a judicial officer the following morning, the police took him home and turned him over to his parents upon their promise to appear with the youth when notified.

Unless the offense is a serious one, steps are usually taken to avoid having to retain custody of a juvenile, as custody may not be consistent with the purposes of juvenile court.[105] Commonly, the youth is arrested [106] but is promptly released to the custody of his parents upon their promise to appear with the youth in juvenile court[107] or for consultation with the juvenile officer.[108]

Illustration No. 20: Detectives received a number of complaints concerning alleged fraudulent business practices. In order to get all the facts from each of the parties, they scheduled a "hearing" for the following week. Although the evidence was sufficient to merit arrest, a "please come" letter was

[105] Most juvenile court laws contain statements to the effect that juvenile court actions are not criminal in nature. Typical is N.P.P.A., Standard Juvenile Court Act §25 (6th ed. 1959).

[106] However, in many jurisdictions this taking into custody is not actually considered an arrest, which creates a number of problems concerning the rights and responsibilities of the police. Myren and Swanson, Police Work with Children 35-37 (1962).

[107] "A commanding officer may release an arrested juvenile when circumstances warrant, upon promise of the parent, guardian, or custodian to be responsible for the appearance of such juvenile in the Juvenile Court." Milwaukee Police Dept., Rules & Regulations, Rule 32, §8 (1950). For example, a youth was brought in for driving without a license. After a juvenile report had been prepared, the youth was taken home and released to the custody of his mother, who was given a referral memorandum instructing her to appear in juvenile court with her son, which she promised to do.

[108] In some communities the police use what is termed a "juvenile bond," which is merely a written agreement between the child's parents and the police that the child will appear at a given time to consult with the juvenile officers.

sent to the businessman. Arrest, the detectives felt, would not be conducive to settlement by restitution.

Arrest is unlikely when the objective is restitution or other settlement. This is illustrated by the procedure of the Prosecutor's Bureau in Detroit, which is actually a section of the detective division of the police department. The Prosecutor's Bureau consists of the Misdemeanor Complaint Bureau, which handles neighborhood and family disputes, and the felony detail, which deals with embezzlement, larceny by conversion, false pretenses and other frauds, blue-sky violations, and other such offenses.[109] If these cases come to the attention of other divisions of the police department, they are usually referred to this bureau, and seldom is an arrest made at the time of referral.[110] Complainants who are aware of the function of this bureau may contact it directly. Whether the offense is reported by the complainant or another law enforcement unit, the suspect usually is not arrested but is contacted and asked to appear voluntarily.

Both the Misdemeanor Complaint Bureau and the felony detail seek to avoid criminal prosecution. Because the offenses within their jurisdiction usually arise out of private transactions and are of such a nature that they would also be a basis for a civil action, it is thought best to settle the matter by resort to mediation where possible. An informal hearing is held, presided over by a detective or assistant prosecutor and attended by the complainant and the suspect, at which an amicable solution is sought. When the hearing involves a family dispute which has erupted into the commission of an assault and the threat of more violence, the bureau's mediator takes on the role of a marriage counselor. When a neighborhood squabble or supposed fraudulent commercial transaction is involved, an attempt is made to clarify for all parties the applicable law, since an erroneous view of their legal position may have contributed to the dispute, and an attempt is also made to obtain voluntary restitution when appropriate. Only when such a private settlement cannot be reached is a criminal prosecution undertaken.

Because the objective is mediation, arrest is not resorted to unless absolutely necessary,[111] because an arrest of one party on the

109 Detroit Police Dept., Revised Police Manual, chap. 4, §25 (1955).

110 One exception is the domestic dispute which is thought to be appropriate for referral (probably to avoid recurrence, see page 144), and in which it appears necessary to make an immediate arrest because of a threat of further harm to the victim.

111 Even if the offender fails to appear for the "hearing," another letter is usually sent unless it clearly appears that prosecution rather than mediation is called for. In one case a girl and her mother appeared at a scheduled hearing, but the other party, a boy who had been summoned by letter, did not appear. The girl reported that the youth, a former boy friend who had assaulted her, had said that he would

complaint of the other would seriously reduce the likelihood of a private settlement.[112] Rather, a so-called hearing is scheduled for about a week later,[113] and a letter is sent to the supposed offender asking him to appear concerning an "important matter." The letter is effective in the great majority of cases.

b. *Objectives attained by custody.*

Illustration No. 21: A woman was arrested on a charge of prostitution. Her request for release was denied, and she was kept in custody until the following morning, when she was transported to the city health department for purposes of physical examination. She was further detained for several more hours until a negative venereal disease test report was received.

The criminal administration process performs many welfare services, particularly when alternative resources for dealing with social problems are lacking.[114] For example, prostitutes arrested by the police are detained pending trial to make possible a medical examination and treatment, if necessary. In Wichita, prostitutes are booked under "hold for welfare and health department." This booking prevents release on bail. In Detroit prostitutes can be released only by an authorized representative of the department

---

ignore the letter. The assistant prosecutor in the office was displeased by this, but, after learning that the boy did not have a police record, he set a time for another hearing and said he would send another letter.

Likewise, an arrest may be avoided even if it would aid in the obtaining of significant evidence. The Better Business Bureau sent to the felony detail a number of complainants who alleged that they had been swindled by a freezer salesman. It appeared that the salesman had obtained their signature to a different contract by incorporating it in the freezer contract. The usual invitation was sent to the salesman, but he replied that he was too busy to attend the "hearing." Rather than order arrest, the assistant prosecutor said that he would attempt to see the salesman in the hope of determining the content of the alleged different contract.

However, if there is some risk that the offender will abscond, an arrest may be made. See note 38 *supra* page 180.

112 Among other factors which also prompt the use of alternatives to arrest are the facts that: (1) those offenses reported to the Misdemeanor Complaint Bureau usually come to the attention of the police only some time after they have occurred, so that a warrant would be needed in order to make a valid arrest; (2) an arrest for purposes of mediation and, perhaps, restitution rather than prosecution is of questionable legality, Bergeron v. Peyton, 106 Wis. 377, 82 N.W. 291 (1900); and (3) it is often difficult to determine whether the alleged conduct in many of the supposed business fraud cases constitutes a crime according to the law. In this last instance, an arresting officer might be liable should he arrest on an erroneous view of the substantive law. See page 86.

113 This time factor is significant, as it gives disputants the opportunity to settle their differences privately before the hearing, as often happens. But if arrest has been made necessary, see note 110 *supra*, then the hearing is held immediately.

114 See Allen, The Borderland of the Criminal Law: Problems of "Socializing" Criminal Justice, 32 Social Serv. Rev. 107 (1958).

of health. The Release Bureau[115] and judges hearing habeas corpus petitions[116] refuse to grant release without the approval of the department of health.

Whether the taking and retention of custody to achieve medical objectives is proper depends largely upon the circumstances and the existing legislation. Current practice in relation to prostitutes is discussed in more detail later.[117] If custody is essential to the achievement of proper medical objectives, an arrest and refusal to release on bail may be justified, even though the suspect would voluntarily appear in court.[118]

6. *The desired effect upon the individual or the public.*

a. *Impressing the individual with the seriousness of his conduct.*

Illustration No. 22: Police officers stopped two teenage drivers for drag-racing. Although both of the drivers were local residents and certainly could be expected to appear in court, the officers arrested them. "We've got to convince them that this is a serious matter," said one of the officers.

[115] One assistant prosecutor working in the Release Bureau said after having received a telephone call: "Now, that was a prostitute. She was calling from the eighth floor — women's detention quarters — and states that her mother is coming in from Hot Springs, Arkansas, today and she was unfortunate enough to be picked up last night. The custom here in the city of handling prostitutes is on the basis of a state law which allows segregation of prostitutes until they have been examined to find out whether they are active or not. Whenever a prostitute is picked up and placed in custody at police headquarters, she does not go to court and cannot be dismissed until she has been examined. Today is a holiday — the physician and nurse will not be in today, so these girls will have to remain in police custody until tomorrow morning when they will be here. . . . I will call the vice squad and find out why they have her in custody, what the nature of the charge is against her and whether or not she is eligible for release — although I know she will not be." A number of denials recorded by the Release Bureau are "hold for the Department of Health." Requests for release of prostitutes are unusual, however, as it is known that they will not be granted. In May, 1956, of the 29 refusals, 10 were on this basis; in June it was 5 out of 26; in July, 3 out of 21.

[116] The following incident is typical: A prostitute was brought before the bench with her attorney, and the investigating officer moved that the matter be adjourned. The defense attorney stated that he would go along with the adjournment provided the prisoner be allowed to be free from confinement on a bond. The court announced to the attorney that this was out of the question since he never released people charged with this offense unless he had a written approval from the department of health, certifying that the prisoner was free of venereal disease. The prisoner was taken back to the "bull pen," and orders were made for another hearing on the matter Monday morning.

[117] Another significant practice is the arrest of suspected prostitutes without the intention of prosecuting. In such cases the detention is often used for medical examination. This practice is discussed in detail in Chapter 22. The health statutes supposedly authorizing such detention are also considered at that point.

[118] Of course, if the girl is likely to appear in court, it might be thought that the inquiries needed to support the health examination might be made then. This would probably receive opposition, however, on the ground that the infected persons would not be discovered promptly.

Although a notice to appear might be adequate to insure appearance in court in such cases, it is sometimes felt that this procedure may not adequately impress the offender with the seriousness of his violation. In some jurisdictions the more serious traffic offenses automatically constitute grounds for arrest even though voluntary appearance would be almost certain. Thus in Wichita it is established policy to arrest for drunken driving (other reasons for this are explained earlier), or for reckless driving, driving with a revoked license, driving with an open bottle of liquor, or for speeding violations of 20 m.p.h. or more over the posted limit.

It is interesting to note that in Norway, where arrest is limited by statute to situations in which custody is required,[119] the current practice is apparently to violate the statute whenever a "shock effect" is desired.[120]

b. *Imposing a penalty where judicial leniency is anticipated.*

Illustration No. 23: Traffic officers stopped a vehicle traveling 20 m.p.h. over the speed limit. The officers, on the basis of their experience, viewed this as a major offense, one which could result in a serious accident, but they were aware that the local judiciary regularly imposed very small fines for speeding. Instead of writing a ticket, the officers immediately placed the speeding driver under arrest and took him to jail pending his appearance at the next regularly scheduled holding of court.

Whether because of a failure of communication[121] or because of differing assumptions about the seriousness of certain conduct, police sometimes consider judicial sentences grossly inadequate.[122] This may provoke a variety of responses by police. One, discussed earlier,[123] is that the police may no longer arrest such offenders because they feel it is a waste of their time. Another reaction, discussed in considerable detail later,[124] involves the use of arrest without any thought of prosecution. A third possibility is for police to continue to arrest and prosecute offenders with the hope that a meaningful penalty will be imposed.

[119] The needs for custody which are recognized by law and which allow arrest (assuming sufficient probability of guilt) are: (a) danger of escape; (b) danger of collusion; and (c) danger of repetition. Bratholm, Arrest and Detention in Norway, 108 U. Pa. L. Rev. 336, 337-338 (1960).

[120] Id. at 345-346.

[121] See page 126 for the details on the communication that does exist.

[122] The police are also concerned about those cases in which the victim or witnesses later conveniently "forget" what happened, making conviction impossible. They also criticize the agencies involved later in the process, because no action is ordinarily taken against those persons who, after giving an account of the crime, fail to testify later.

[123] See page 125.

[124] See Chapters 22-24.

Where the practice is to arrest and prosecute, the police consider that the likelihood of an inadequate sanction warrants the additional penalty of immediate arrest and detention until the offender is regularly brought before the magistrate for trial or setting of bail. This desire to use pretrial custody as a penalty apparently does not usually influence the bail decision itself, although such a result has been observed in some places.[125]

   c. *Maintaining respect for the police.*

    Illustration No. 24: A traffic officer stopped a driver because of a minor traffic violation for the purpose of giving him a ticket. The driver became extremely argumentative and abusive, so the officer decided to place him under arrest for the traffic violation.

As noted in an earlier chapter, it may be thought necessary to proceed against conduct ordinarily not subjected to the process in order to maintain respect for the police.[126] Thus a traffic offender whom the officer intended merely to reprimand may be given a ticket that necessitates a court appearance for his violation if the officer finds him argumentative. Similarly, as in the above illustration, the officer may, for the same reason, make an arrest rather than issue a ticket. If in this case the suspect at the time of arrest or subsequently fights with the police, the police commonly will not approve his release without bail.[127]

   d. *Satisfying the public that justice will be done.*

    Illustration No. 25: Considerable publicity was given by the press to the fact that a local tavern owner frequently served minors. An undercover officer was sent to the tavern and, upon observing the owner serve a youth, made an arrest notwithstanding the fact that voluntary appearance seemed likely.

The necessity, in the police view, of maintaining a proper public image of the processes of law enforcement has been noted earlier. One consequence observed was that criminal conduct not ordinarily subjected to the criminal process may be proceeded against because inaction in the given case would damage the public image of full enforcement.[128] Similarly, when the public realizes that

---

[125] An empirical study conducted in New York City reports the setting of high bail on those juvenile offenders likely to be acquitted or to receive a suspended sentence. Comment, 106 U. Pa. L. Rev. 693, 705 (1958).

[126] See page 146.

[127] In New York, where the pretrial right to bail has not been made a matter of right to the extent it has in most states, Comment, 106 U. Pa. L. Rev. 693, 697-699 (1958), bail has been denied altogether for instances of attacks on policemen. N.Y. Times, Nov. 27, 1961, p. 31, col. 8 ("Rare Rule Invoked to Deny Bail for 7 in Police Assault").

[128] See page 147.

the police must be aware of a violation, an arrest may be made notwithstanding the likelihood of voluntary appearance in order to represent to the public that justice is being done.[129] In such a situation, the arrest becomes a kind of ceremony whereby the retributive desires of the public are temporarily satisfied.

While custody criteria have generally been developed in some detail in foreign law, there has seldom been approval of taking or continuation of custody in order to impress the public that punitive action will be taken against the perpetrator.[130] It is again interesting to note that in one country in which arrests are lawful only when one of the legislatively declared needs for custody is present, it is said that the police sometimes exceed their powers in order to satisfy public retributive desires.[131]

C. The Need for Custody Prior to Trial

The question of whether a suspect should be taken into custody or, if already in custody, whether he should be released, arises at each stage in the criminal justice process. It is first involved when a decision is made as to whether to make an immediate arrest. If an arrest is made, the question of release from custody arises in the police station during the period prior to the initial appearance of the suspect before the magistrate. At the appearance before the magistrate the bail question is traditionally decided.

By viewing this series of custody decisions in relation to each other it is possible to construct a sort of "custody profile" of the criminal justice system. The most striking characteristic of the profile, reflected in both law and practice, is the almost complete lack of concern over whether custody is necessary at the arrest and police detention stages in contrast with the great concern about the need for custody at the initial appearance.

1. *Custody and the arrest decision.* Only about a third of the states have enacted statutes authorizing the use of a summons in-

---

129 This was observed in Wisconsin in cases of sale of liquor to minors.

130 However, the Belgian law makes the fear that the presence of the accused might cause a scandal among the people of the community a consideration. Study of the Right of Everyone to Be Free from Arbitrary Arrest, Detention and Exile, Commission on Human Rights, U.N. Doc. E/CN.4/813, par. 98 (1961).

131 "Retributive attitudes are especially to be expected in the case of serious crimes, the more so when the individual police official or judge considers mores of major societal value to have been offended, or when he is persuaded that a failure to confine may well give the public the impression that justice is lax. In actual fact, remand in these cases will often be a concession to the retributive desires of the public and of the individual official who requests or orders it." Bratholm, Arrest and Detention in Norway, 108 U. Pa. L. Rev. 336, 346 (1960).

stead of a warrant of arrest.[132] To the extent that the general practice conforms to that in the three jurisdictions studied, in that most arrests are made without warrant, such statutes can have only

[132] See A.L.I. Code, Criminal Procedure (1931).

"Section 12. *When summons shall be issued.*

(1) Where the complaint is for the commission of an offense which the magistrate is empowered to try summarily he shall issue a summons instead of a warrant of arrest, unless he has reasonable ground to believe that the person against whom the complaint was made will not appear upon a summons, in which case he shall issue a warrant of arrest.

(2) Where the complaint is for a misdemeanor, which the magistrate is not empowered to try summarily, he shall issue a summons instead of a warrant of arrest, if he has reasonable ground to believe that the person against whom the complaint was made will appear upon a summons.

(3) The summons shall set forth substantially the nature of the offense, and shall command the person against whom the complaint was made to appear before the magistrate issuing the summons at a time and place stated therein.

Section 13. *How summons served.* The summons may be served in the same manner as the summons in a civil action.

Section 14. *Effect of not answering summons.* If the person summoned fails, without good cause, to appear as commanded by the summons, he shall be considered in contempt of court, and may be punished by a fine of not more than twenty dollars. Upon such failure to appear the magistrate shall issue a warrant of arrest. If after issuing a summons the magistrate becomes satisfied that the person summoned will not appear as commanded by the summons he may at once issue a warrant of arrest."

Such provisions were found in the following jurisdictions: Alaska Comp. Laws Ann. §§66-5-2, 66-5-3 (1949) (upon request of attorney for government); Ariz. Crim. Rule 11; Ark. Stat. Ann. §43-102 (1947) (nonfelonies); Del. Super. Ct. Rule 4; Fla. Stat. §901.09 (1959); Hawaii Rev. Laws §257-3 (1955) (magistrate may issue a summons if the offense is not serious or subject to severe penalty and there is little threat of evasion); Ill. Rev. Stat. chap. 38, §107-111 (1963); Ind. Stat. Ann. §9-1001(b) (1956) (only for a misdemeanor if there is "reasonable ground to believe that the person will appear in response to a summons"); Iowa Code Ann. §754.3 (1946); Ky. Rev. Stat. §26.330(2) (1960) (applicable to second-class cities); Md. Code Ann. art. 52 §§23, 24 (Supp. 1962); Mass. Ann. Laws chap. 276, §§24-26 (1956) (in cases "punishable by fine only, or by imprisonment for not more than one year, with or without a fine"); Mo. Supreme Ct. Rule 21.05; N.H. Rev. Stat. Ann. §§592-A:14, 592-A:15 (Supp. 1961) (where municipal court has final jurisdiction); N.Y. Code Crim. P. Ann. §150 (Supp. 1962) (if magistrate is satisfied that a crime was committed which is within the exclusive jurisdiction of a court of special session or which is one of 41 enumerated in N.Y. Code Crim, P. §56, and also that person is a citizen of the state and a resident of the town or city where the information was received); N.C. Gen. Stat. Ann. §15-20 (Supp. 1961) (for misdemeanors where there is reason to believe summoned party will appear); Pages Ohio Rev. Code Ann. §§2935.10, 2935.11 (Supp. 1962) (for nonfelonies); Purdon's Pa. Stat. Ann. tit. 19, §§12.1 to 12.7 (Supp. 1962) (applicable to first-class cities, and only to offenses punishable by fine and/or not more than 2 years' imprisonment, or either larceny or fraudulent conversion where amount in question is $200 or less; offender must be a resident of the city, and magistrate *must* issue summons unless an affidavit is filed showing reasonable cause to believe that the person will flee); Utah Code Ann. §§77-12-12 to 77-12-23 (1953) (for nonindictable misdemeanors; a summons is to be issued unless it appears that the defendant will not appear); Wis. Stat. Ann. §954.02 (Supp. 1962).

Some of the provisions make failure to appear in response to a summons punishable by a contempt fine: Iowa ($20); Mass. ($20); N.H. ($20); N.Y. ($25); N.C. ($25); Ohio ($20); Pa. ($100); Utah ($20).

limited effect. Statutes giving the officer the right to issue a summons on the street instead of making an arrest without a warrant are rare.[133]

Some other states have provisions for issuance of a summons by a magistrate, but they apply to limited situations, such as ordinance violations only, e.g., Col. Rev. Stat. §139-86-2 (1953); only offenses with a penalty not exceeding $20, e.g., Va. Code §19.1-164 (1950); only juvenile court proceedings, e.g., N.D. Cent. Code Ann. §27-16-14 (1960); only traffic violations, e.g., N.D. Cent. Code Ann. §29-10-31 (1960); or only corporate defendants, e.g., N.D. Cent. Code Ann. §29-05-28 (1960).

[133] See Warner, Uniform Arrest Act, 28 U. Va. L. Rev. 315, 343-347 (1942):

"Section 9. *Summons Instead of Arrest.*

"(1) In any case in which it is lawful for a peace officer to arrest without a warrant a person for a misdemeanor, he may, but need not, give him a written summons in substantially the following form:

"[Insert form appropriate for your state]

"(2) If the person fails to appear in answer to the summons, or if there is reasonable cause to believe that he will not appear, a warrant for his arrest may issue. Willful failure to appear in answer to the summons may be punished by a fine of not over one hundred dollars or imprisonment for not over thirty days."

The only such provisions found are: Cal. Penal Code §§853.1 to 853.8 (Supp. 1962); Del. Code Ann. tit. 11, §1909 (1953); Ill. Rev. Stat. chap. 38, §107-112 (1963); N.H. Rev. Stat. Ann. §594.14 (1955); R.I. Gen. Laws Ann. §12-7-11 (1956).

The language of the Uniform Arrest Act contemplates use of the police-issued summons only in cases in which the officer could make an arrest. Similarly, a Michigan statute provides that a traffic ticket is to issue "whenever a person is arrested without a warrant." Mich. Stat. Ann. §9.2427 (1959). Similar statutory language has caused confusion elsewhere. In a book prepared primarily for police, it is noted that there is confusion as to the legal status of a summons, much of which is traceable to §728 of the Uniform Traffic Code, which provides that "whenever a person is arrested without a warrant for any violation of this act punishable as a misdemeanor . . . , the arresting officer shall prepare in duplicate a written notice to appear . . ." Houts, From Arrest to Release 44 (1958). The Michigan police interpret the provision as a prohibition against the issuance of a citation unless a misdemeanor is committed in their presence. For example, when officers of the state police came upon a rear-end collision, they filled out accident reports but issued no citations. They later observed that they could not have done so since the violation had not occurred in their presence. In other cases concerning the use of the notice to appear, arrest was usually possible. The exceptions are most likely to be cases in which the offender is asked to appear elsewhere than at an actual trial of the case. For example, in Detroit, a policeman called to a domestic disturbance may order the disputants to report to the Misdemeanor Complaint Bureau, an agency which attempts to mediate such disputes in order to prevent the necessity of prosecution.

There may be other reasons for the use of the quoted language. It may be thought necessary to protect the officer from tort liability for the mere act of stopping and giving a ticket. This assumption that any interference with individual freedom of movement must be denominated an arrest in order to guard against liability has caused difficulties in other contexts as well. See page 344. Another possibility is that the occurrence is designated as an arrest and release in order to validate searches conducted at the time of the stopping. See Note, 1959 Wis. L. Rev. 347, 352 n.33; Donigan and Fisher, Issuance of Traffic Citation Not an Arrest, Traffic Digest and Review, May, 1956. The issues raised by this in terms of articulating a no-arrest rule are considered elsewhere in this chapter. Perhaps the purpose is to establish a basis for punitive consequences accompanying a failure to appear. The Michigan statute, *supra* note 10 page 171, makes failure to appear grounds for denial of renewal of the offender's driver's license. And the U.A.A.

The summons and notice to appear have not become routine police methods in crimes other than traffic violations partly because legislation authorizing such alternatives is seldom to be found. But, even if legislation were passed, there are reasons in practice to continue to make arrests even in situations where it appears that the suspect will appear voluntarily in court. An immediate arrest may make it possible to conduct a search, an in-custody interrogation, or an in-custody health inspection. An immediate arrest may also minimize the risk of future crimes by the suspect pending his appearance in court.

2. *Release by the police after arrest.* Legislation authorizing police to release a suspect, after his arrest, upon his promise to appear in court at the designated time is not common.[134] There are

---

provision, 28 U. Va. L. Rev. 315, 343-347 (1942), provides a fine for willful failure to appear.

Subsequent to the observations in Michigan, the Attorney General advised that the notice to appear device could be used in the absence of grounds for arrest without warrant. He noted the quoted language, but then observed that the giving of a summons is not itself an arrest, and thus can be used when the officer comes upon a misdemeanor violation after its occurrence. However, because such a situation is not within the statutory provisions on notice to appear, the withholding of the driver's license for failure to appear would not be possible. Ops. Mich. Atty. Gen., May 27, 1957, No. 2872.

If the only consequence of nonappearance is the likelihood of issuance of a warrant, then the fact that no arrest could originally have been made without a warrant does not appear to be of significance. A contrary view might be based on the notion that the notice to appear is likely to be thought mandatory by the offender, so that his appearance is in fact brought about without prior adequate review of the grounds for prosecution. This assumes that some meaningful review takes place at the time of warrant issuance. This is not necessarily so, especially with regard to minor offenses thought to be within the capabilities of the arresting officer. See page 54. Perhaps the requirement is to insure some basis for the issuance of the warrant which will follow nonappearance.

Indeed, if some review does take place at the warrant-issuance stage, this review could still be conducted when the warrant is requested after the giving of a summons by the officer. Whether there is an arrest or not, issuance of a warrant is likely, as that document often serves as the basis of the charge in minor cases. If the reviewing authority overrules the officer, then the person summoned can be notified that he need not appear.

134 Some foreign countries provide police with this authority. See Study of the Right of Everyone to Be Free from Arbitrary Arrest, Detention and Exile, Commission on Human Rights, U.N. Doc. E/CN.4/813, par. 198 (1961). In the United States, such provisions were found only in Cal. Penal Code §849 (Supp. 1962); Del. Code Ann. tit. 11, §1910 (1953); R.I. Gen. Laws Ann. §12-7-12 (1956). See Warner Uniform Arrest Act, 28 U. Va. L. Rev. 315, 343-347 (1942).

"Section 10. *Release of Persons Arrested.*

(1) Any officer in charge of a police department or any officer delegated by him may release, instead of taking before a magistrate, any person who has been arrested without a warrant by an officer of his department whenever: . . .

(B) The person was arrested for a misdemeanor and has signed an agreement to appear in court at a time designated, if the officer is satisfied that the person is a resident of the state and will appear in court at the time designated."

These statutes should be distinguished from those which authorize the police to

a number of instances in which the police might grant a release if they were certain of their authority to do so. Often additional information is elicited after arrest which makes it clear that there is no substantial risk of the accused absconding. In other cases release would be possible because custody was originally taken for the purpose of accomplishing an objective already achieved by the time the suspect reaches the station, such as search of the person.

3. *Prompt appearance before a magistrate.* How soon a suspect must be taken before a magistrate depends in part upon whether making possible his early release is thought to warrant imposing upon the police the obligation of seeking out a magistrate outside of regular court hours. There is currently disagreement over this.[135] Whether the police may legitimately delay taking the accused before a magistrate when one is available or whether a magistrate may properly refuse to release on bail a person brought before him on a writ of habeas corpus involves consideration of the reasons for arrest and for detention. Some arrests are made because of a desire to conduct a lawful search or because of concern about the future availability of the suspect. These alone do not require a delay in the appearance before the magistrate. However, other arrests may be made in anticipation of detention continuing for a period of time. The arrest of the drunk is the most obvious example. Undoubtedly the most difficulty is created by arrests made in anticipation of a period of in-custody investigation by the police prior to the initial appearance before the magistrate. Its complexities will be explored later.[136]

4. *The setting of bail.* The only criterion generally recognized by law for determining the propriety and amount of bail is the

---

release on bail under some circumstances, e.g., Conn. Gen. Stat. Ann. §54-64 (Supp. 1961); Mo. Stat. Ann. §84.650 (1949).

[135] In Michigan it appears that the fact that the magistrate is not sitting because of a holiday or for other reasons is not in itself an excuse for delay, and it has been strongly suggested that the magistrate must be sought out during off-duty hours. Linnen v. Banfield, 114 Mich. 93, 72 N.W. 1 (1897); Malcolmson v. Scott, 56 Mich. 459, 23 N.W. 166 (1885). But in Wisconsin and Kansas it has been recognized that it is not the duty of the police to seek out a magistrate when one is not regularly sitting. Kiefer v. State, 258 Wis. 47, 44 N.W.2d 537 (1950); Torson v. Baehni, 134 Kan. 188, 5 P.2d 813 (1931). This issue is of considerable importance in federal criminal procedure, as statements obtained during illegal detention cannot be admitted into evidence. However, the federal courts are not in agreement here. Compare Watson v. United States, 249 F.2d 106 (D.C. Cir. 1957), and Carter v. United States, 252 F.2d 608 (D.C. Cir. 1957), assuming that the police must seek a magistrate during off-duty hours, with Trilling v. United States, 260 F.2d 677 (D.C. Cir. 1958), Porter v. United States, 258 F.2d 685 (D.C. Cir. 1958), and Lockley v. United States, 270 F.2d 915 (D.C. Cir. 1959), declaring that this is unnecessary.

[136] See Chapters 14-17.

likelihood that the suspect will appear voluntarily in court.[137]   This high regard for freedom from custody which is manifested when the case reaches the magistrate is in sharp contrast with the absence of such concern in law at the arrest and police detention stages. Factors such as risk of further criminal conduct, intimidation of the victim or witnesses, and the like, which are clearly relevant in practice and, so far as one can tell, in law at the arrest and police detention stages, are not recognized as proper in regard to the magistrate's decision as to bail.   Although some concern has been voiced about this,[138] the opportunity for change is extremely limited because of constitutional provisions on bail found in most states.[139]   At the same time, however, the substantially uncontrolled discretion of magistrates in setting the amount of bail makes possible the continuation of the current practice of denying release for reasons other than those recognized by the formal law. These reasons are seldom made explicit in current administration.[140]

[137] Such is the federal requirement, Fed. R. Crim. P. 46(c), and the states are generally in accord. Comment, 70 Yale L.J. 966 (1961).

[138] "It is incomprehensible to me, although I know and understand its history, that the bail system, as it stands, is still tolerated in the United States and not repudiated . . . We are compelled to release people before trial, who constitute an immediate danger to the community and who are free to collude and to obscure the truth in regard to evidence to be presented at the trial, just on the grounds of their posting bail." Frym, Administration of Criminal Justice in the United States and Europe, in A.B.A., Section of Criminal Law, 1962 Proceedings 110, 111. A return to the common law practice of using discretion in granting or refusing bail has been suggested, either in all cases or in certain kinds of cases. See Orfield, Criminal Procedure from Arrest to Appeal 110 (1947); Note, 41 Yale L.J. 293, 294 (1931); Note, 44 Ky. L.J. 447 (1956); A.L.I. Code, Criminal Procedure §70 (1931) (which would make bail discretionary as to recidivists).

[139] The provisions are collected in Comment, 70 Yale L.J. 966, 977 (1961).

[140] It will be noted that in this chapter the bail process is examined solely for purposes of understanding the need for custody problem. It should not be assumed, however, that there are not other problems of a most serious nature attendant to the bail process. However, for the most part these other problems either involve a corrupt system (the kind of problem excluded from the present study) or require a more detailed and extended observation of the bail process than was attempted by American Bar Foundation field research personnel.

For other empirical studies of the bail process, see Beeley, The Bail System in Chicago (1927); Comment, 106 U. Pa. L. Rev. 693 (1958); Note, 102 U. Pa. L. Rev. 1031 (1954).

For a description of an ongoing study, see Ares and Sturz, Bail and the Indigent Accused, 8 Crime and Delin. 12 (1962); Ares, Rankin, and Sturz, The Manhattan Bail Project: An Interim Report on the Use of Pre-Trial Parole, 38 N.Y.U.L. Rev. 67 (1963).

Recently, the host of problems relating to bail, and particularly those involving indigent defendants, have received considerable attention. A National Conference on Bail and Criminal Justice, under the co-sponsorship of the United States Department of Justice and the Vera Foundation, was held in Washington D.C., on May 27-29, 1964. For an excellent survey of existing bail problems, see the working paper prepared for that conference, Freed and Wald, Bail in the United States; 1964 (1964).

CHAPTER 10

Delay in Making an Arrest

In a case where the police have decided to arrest the suspect, the arrest is usually made as soon as possible. There are, however, some situations in which the police do not make an immediate arrest because it would cause undue harm to the offender or would interfere with some law enforcement objective. The legal system has long given careful attention to the first of these two situations, that concerning harm to the individual. An immediate arrest which would necessitate the use of excessive force is not proper. However, the appropriate limit upon the privilege to use force has been a matter of debate for many years. The arguments have been presented in extenso elsewhere,[1] and they will not be restated here. The discussion which follows on this situation is based upon limited data, because instances of use of force were not frequently observed.

The question of whether it is proper to delay an arrest to achieve some law enforcement objective of higher priority to the police has seldom been discussed and has not received careful attention from legislatures or courts. Because even temporary immunity from arrest can afford an offender an opportunity to commit other crimes, it is important to know when and why such decisions are made.

A. DELAY TO AVOID USE OF EXCESSIVE FORCE AGAINST THE OFFENDER

1. *Uncertainty regarding the governing legal norms.* Of the important decisions a police officer is called upon to make, perhaps none carry consequences so serious as the decision to employ force

---

[1] Model Penal Code §3.07, Comments (Tent. Draft No. 8, 1958); Moreland, The Use of Force in Effecting or Resisting Arrest, 33 Neb. L. Rev. 408 (1954); Pearson, The Right to Kill in Making Arrests, 28 Mich. L. Rev. 957 (1930); Perkins, The Law of Arrest, 25 Iowa L. Rev. 201, 272 (1940); Waite, Some Inadequacies in the Law of Arrest, 29 Mich. L. Rev. 448, 463-468 (1931); Note, 34 N.C.L. Rev. 122 (1955).

against a suspect in order to make an arrest. Because this is so, it is particularly important that the police have a clear understanding of their privilege in this regard. In Kansas, Michigan, and Wisconsin, however, police seem uncertain of the nature and extent of their authority to use force in making an arrest. This is partly due to lack of explicit guidance from the law itself. One Kansas statute declares a killing to be justifiable homicide only "when necessarily committed in attempting, by lawful ways and means, to apprehend any person for a felony committed," [2] whereas another statute suggests that the police have the right to kill in making an arrest for any offense.[3] While there are no Kansas cases directly in point, a few cases do indicate approval of this broader basis for using deadly force.[4] The Michigan statutes are silent on the use of force, and the few Michigan cases do not reveal any established policy in this respect.[5] In Wisconsin there is no specific statute dealing with the use of force, although the criminal code provides a privilege "when the actor's conduct is a reasonable accomplishment of a lawful arrest." [6] The few Wisconsin cases adhere to the common law view that only reasonable force is to be used, with deadly force limited to felony arrests.[7]

Police manuals and instructional materials in these three states tend to be ambiguous on the use of force in making arrests. Some police manuals make no mention of the problem at all.[8] One

2 Kan. Gen. Stat. §21-404 (1949).

3 "If after notice of the intention to arrest the defendant he either flee or forcibly resist, the officer may use all necessary means to effect the arrest." Kan. Gen. Stat. §62-1204 (1949).

4 The Kansas court, in State v. Dietz, 59 Kan. 576, 53 Pac. 870 (1898), noted that there were two opposing views on whether an officer could kill a fleeing misdemeanant, but that neither reached the issue inasmuch as both contemplated a lawful arrest, which was lacking in that case. Dicta in Harvey v. City of Bonner Springs, 102 Kan. 9, 22, 169 Pac. 563, 569 (1917), concerning use of force by police, states: "So long as they act with proper motives in seeking to arrest a person charged with an offense, the law protects them and those summoned to assist, even though, acting hastily or upon mistaken judgment, they unnecessarily take the life of the person charged."

5 On one occasion the court noted that force is proper when used to prevent escape, but that it is not necessary that the arrestee actually attempt escape or be of notoriously bad character to justify limited force such as the use of handcuffs. Firestone v. Rice, 71 Mich. 377, 38 N.W. 885 (1883). In determining whether the use of force was proper, the court will inquire into the circumstances, particularly the number of police present and the number of other persons present subject to the call of the police. Brown v. Wyman, 224 Mich. 360, 195 N.W. 52 (1923).

6 Wis. Stat. §939.45(4) (1955). See 5 Wis. Legis. Council, Judiciary Committee Report on the Criminal Code 39 (1953).

7 Krueger v. State, 171 Wis. 566, 177 N.W. 917 (1920); Goscinski v. Carlson, 157 Wis. 551, 147 N.W. 1018 (1914).

8 E.g., Madison Police Dept., General Rules and Regulations (undated); Eau Claire Police Dept., General Order No. 8, adopting police rules and regulations (1956).

common provision instructs officers (a) that no more force than necessary can be used, (b) that no amount of force is too great to overcome dangerous resistance, (c) that no force can be used when there is no fear of escape, and (d) that "the officer is charged with the duty . . . to compel submission." [9] Not only does this provision leave many questions unanswered, but it also implies that maximum force might be utilized against any offender. The Milwaukee regulations are unique in cautioning officers not to use a firearm except to defend life or prevent escape of a felon, and then only when all other methods have proved ineffectual.[10]

Police materials frequently fail to draw the common law distinction between felony and misdemeanor arrests.[11] This is most often true in Kansas, where there is some statutory basis for the view that deadly force can be used in making any arrest where lesser force is not sufficient,[12] although some police material in this state does draw the felony-misdemeanor distinction, advising that deadly force cannot be used in misdemeanor arrests.[13]

Even when the law is explicit, the legal norms governing police behavior are seldom communicated to the officer on the beat. This

[9] "In making an arrest an officer must be careful not to submit his prisoner to any greater severity or indignity than is necessary to effect the arrest and bring the prisoner safely to the police station. The State requires the officer to do his duty at all hazards, but in the performance of this duty it requires him to be as gentle and considerate as circumstances will permit. No amount of force is too great in making an arrest if it is necessary to overcome an obstinate and dangerous resistance; no measure of severity is justified where there is no reason to fear an escape. The officer must remember that he is responsible for his prisoner and required to do what is necessary to secure him. The officer must use his own discretion, and if he does his duty in a wise and careful manner he will be justified. While the officer is required to be as gentle and considerate in making an arrest as the circumstances will permit, he must always remember that he is the representative of the law, to whose lawful demands all must submit. The officer is charged with the duty and armed with the power to compel submission." Detroit Police Dept., Revised Police Manual, chap. 16, §28 (1955). Almost identical are Milwaukee Police Dept., Rules & Regulations, Rule 30, §30 (1950); and Pontiac Police Dept., Rules & Regulations §227 (1941).

[10] Milwaukee Police Dept., Rules & Regulations, Rule 30, §32 (1950).

[11] E.g., Michigan Assn. of Chiefs of Police, Michigan Police Law Manual §71 (1954).

[12] The Wichita manual merely states that "Officers shall use no more force than necessary in making arrests." Wichita Police Dept., Duty Manual 12 (undated). A manual produced for Kansas officers quotes the statute (Kansas Gen. Stat. §62-1204 [1949] *supra* note 3) and then goes on to say that what is necessary is within the discretion of the officer and that this discretion is "not subject to review by a court or jury unless wantonly or maliciously abused." Univ. of Kansas Governmental Research Center, Special Report No. 47, Arrest-Search-Seizure, Legal Problems of Peace Officers 7 (1954).

[13] Univ. of Kansas Governmental Research Center, Special Report No. 84, Eleventh Peace Officers Training School, A Report 41 (1957); Sedgwick County School for Law Enforcement Officers, Arrests, Searches and Seizures 5 (July 2, 1953); Somers, Not How to Shoot, But When: A Kansas Peace Officers Manual of Arrest 25-26 (1939).

is largely because police manuals, regulations, and training materials usually deal in generalities. Also, these materials are likely to be copied from manuals of other jurisdictions and so do not deal adequately with the law of the particular state.[14] Consequently, the average police officer is less influenced by his knowledge of the legal standards than by his observations of how more experienced officers react in such situations.[15] However, since the decision whether to use force does not arise frequently, particularly in smaller communities, an officer rarely has the opportunity to make such observations.

Without sufficient guidance from experience or administrative regulations and with the law being largely ambiguous in this regard, many officers are uncertain about their authority to employ force in making an arrest. Consequently, when an officer has to make a decision, he may be overly timid and fail to accomplish the arrest, with the result that the public faith is weakened. On the other hand, he may use excessive force when the occasion does not require it.

2. *Norms observed in current practice.* The courts of all states would undoubtedly agree that only that force reasonably believed necessary to accomplish the arrest should be employed to arrest a suspect. There is no consensus, however, on the matter of when it is better to allow the suspect to escape than to employ deadly force. While the common law view, that deadly force can be employed only in making a felony arrest, still prevails in most states,[16] some jurisdictions also state that the officer must not use force if he only suspects that a felony has occurred or if a felony is only threatened. He must have proof that the felony has actually been committed and that the fleeing person is in fact a felon.[17] Another

---

14 The University of Wisconsin Law School collection of about 50 police manuals, rules and regulations, and training bulletins from a representative group of the major police agencies across the United States reveals a high degree of similarity among most of these materials. Provisions on arrest, use of force, use of summons, and other matters of considerable importance in day-to-day police work are often identical, although the law on these subjects tends to vary somewhat between jurisdictions. Thus it seems that these materials are often prepared without a prior careful examination of the law actually governing the police to whom the manuals are addressed.

15 "Family quarrels, irate storekeepers, impudent teenagers, taunting drunks, ingratiating storekeepers, all pose situations in which the police school offers little help. . . . Thus he [the rookie] watches how his partner acts and the next time anything happens he does the same thing. From his partner he is receiving a constant stream of explicit and implicit definitions of behavior, . . . and from these explanations and assertions the recruit gets his actions defined." Westley, The Police: A Sociological Study of Law, Custom and Morality 254 (unpublished Ph.D. thesis No. 1197, Dept. of Sociology, Univ. of Chicago, 1951).

16 Model Penal Code §3.07, Comment 3 (Tent. Draft No. 8, 1958).

17 Ibid.; Perkins, Criminal Law 875 (1957).

variation limits the use of deadly force to cases of so-called dangerous felonies.[18] This is further refined in the Model Penal Code
proposal to limit the use of deadly force to felony cases in which
the officer believes that "there is a substantial risk that the person
to be arrested will cause death or serious bodily harm if his apprehension is delayed." [19] At the other extreme, some jurisdictions
approve the use of deadly force when necessary to accomplish an
arrest for either a felony or a misdemeanor.[20] Some evaluations
of these alternatives are possible on the basis of the few situations
in which the use of force was observed.

a. *Mistake as to amount of force needed.*

Illustration No. 1: Officers in a patrol car saw a man
slumped over the steering wheel of a car stopped in the middle of the street. The officers thought the man was intoxicated. When they approached the car and opened the door
the man lunged toward them. The police thought the man
was resisting arrest and used the force they thought necessary
to subdue him. After the man had been taken to the station
it was learned that his violent movements were due to an
epileptic seizure.

An officer's judgment of the amount of force necessary may
prove erroneous, and this may put the use of force into question
for two reasons. One is that a misinterpretation of the circumstances may render the arrest itself unlawful, and thus there would
be no right to use force at all. The felony arrest norm, "reasonable grounds to believe," leaves some room for error,[21] but the
courts have not always agreed that the "in-presence" norm for misdemeanor arrests allows room for even an understandable mistake
of fact.[22] The other reason is that, even when the police have the
right to arrest, they may wrongly predict the amount of resistance
the offender will offer and use force considered excessive.

The case in the above illustration shows that the need for force
may appear quite differently when a decision is made on the spot
rather than after the urgency of the situation is past. Because of
this, it is generally recognized that the right to use force depends
upon what the officer reasonably believed at the time to be necessary.[23] Yet in criminal trials arresting officers are sometimes

18 Ibid. The American Law Institute first adopted this view, Restatement of
Torts §131 (1934), but later changed its position in order to be in accord with the
prevailing common law view. Restatement of the Law, 1948 Supplement 628 (1949).
19 Model Penal Code §3.07 (Proposed Official Draft, 1962).
20 Model Penal Code §3.07, Comment 1 (Tent. Draft No. 8, 1958).
21 See, generally, Chapter 12.
22 See page 236.
23 Restatement of Torts §132 (1934); Model Penal Code §3.07 (Proposed Official
Draft, 1962).

reprimanded by the court for the use of force which only in retrospect might be viewed as unnecessary.[24]

b. *Deadly force toward misdemeanants.*

> *Illustration No. 2:* An officer on foot signaled a speeding driver to stop. The driver ignored the officer, who drew his revolver and fired five shots at the speeding car.

It was noted earlier that some provisions are found in the statutes and police materials which authorize the police to employ deadly force in order to arrest a fleeing misdemeanant. Because of this or because they are unaware of any rule to the contrary, officers occasionally use firearms in attempting to arrest a misdemeanant.

Courts have generally held that it is "better to allow one guilty only of a misdemeanor to escape altogether than to take his life." [25] In cases similar to the one above, officers have been found guilty of murder for shooting the driver[26] and guilty of manslaughter when death followed a disabling of the vehicle by gunfire.[27] Even under statutes apparently recognizing the use of any force necessary to make an arrest, deadly force has not been permitted against minor misdemeanants.[28]

> *Illustration No. 3:* A traffic officer saw a car speed through an intersection against the light. The car barely missed a pedestrian crossing the street. The officer stepped into the street to signal the driver to stop, but he drove on, almost hitting the officer. The officer drew his revolver and fired at the car.

The common law misdemeanor-felony distinction regarding the use of deadly force has been subjected to much criticism. The principal objection is that many felonies do not endanger life, so that force which might result in death should not be authorized in order to bring about arrests for such felonies. It can also be argued, however, that some misdemeanors involve such risks, and that consequently deadly force should be allowed in such cases. Some police officers say that they would feel justified in using

24 Thus the judge in one case criticized the officers' use of handcuffs to strike a violent drunk who had been resisting arrest, noting that the drunk had been injured but the officers had not.

The threat of such a reprimand may result in those officers who used the force not appearing at the time of the defendant's trial. In one observed case in which the defendant alleged excessive force was used, his accusation was directed not to the officer present to testify but to his partner. In another such case the judge remarked, "It's always the one that does the damage that stays away."

25 Reneau v. State, 70 Tenn. 720, 721 (1879).

26 Hill v. Commonwealth, 239 Ky. 646, 40 S.W.2d 261 (1931).

27 People v. Klein, 305 Ill. 141, 137 N.E. 145 (1922).

28 E.g., Johnson v. State, 173 Tenn. 134, 114 S.W.2d 819 (1938).

deadly force if the misdemeanor were a dangerous one. As an illustration they often mention cases such as that described above.

Uncertainty as to whether it is ever desirable to allow deadly force to be used in misdemeanor cases is also reflected in legal literature. The Restatement of Torts by caveat expresses no opinion on the extent to which force should be used in making an arrest for a misdemeanor involving danger of death or serious bodily harm.[29] The comments to the Model Penal Code note that many misdemeanors do endanger life and that "the felony-misdemeanor distinction is inherently incapable of separating out those persons of such dangerousness that the perils arising from failure to accomplish immediate apprehension justify resort to extreme force to accomplish it."[30]

It might be said, of course, that the legislative characterization of certain conduct, such as reckless driving, as a mere misdemeanor is a determination that the conduct is not so dangerous that deadly force is justified against it. However, police officers faced with the necessity of making a quick decision on the use of force sometimes employ only the criterion of danger without first considering whether the conduct is a misdemeanor or a felony. This is particularly likely when the continuing conduct of the offender presents some immediate threat of harm. But, even though there is this risk, it may not be considered serious enough for the officer to be said to be acting for the defense of third persons[31] or for the prevention of a dangerous felony.[32]

[29] Restatement of Torts §131, second caveat (1934). This caveat was retained in the later change to this section. Restatement of the Law, 1948 Supplement 628 (1949).

[30] Model Penal Code §3.07, Comment 3 (Tent. Draft No. 8, 1958). However, the Code does not privilege the use of deadly force in any misdemeanor cases.

[31] It can be argued, of course, that continued reckless driving constitutes a negligent threat of death or serious bodily harm to others, namely, other pedestrians and drivers. The Restatement recognizes a privilege of self-defense when the actor reasonably believes the threat is to himself and "that his death or serious bodily harm can safely be prevented only by the immediate use" of deadly force. Restatement of Torts §66 (1934). Defense of third persons rests upon the same basis, id. §76, Comment a.

[32] Deadly force, in the Restatement view, is privileged where "the actor reasonably believes that the commission or consummation of the felony cannot otherwise be prevented and the felony for the prevention of which the actor is intervening is of a type threatening death or serious bodily harm or involving the breaking and entry of a dwelling place." Restatement of Torts §143 (Supp. 1948). While the officer may successfully assert the privilege by reporting that he observed a person whose conduct suggested that he intended to commit a dangerous felony, he might experience some difficulty if he says that the observed conduct, such as reckless driving, led him to believe that an unintended dangerous felony was about to be committed (e.g., homicide by reckless conduct, Wis. Stat. §940.06 [1955]; manslaughter, Kan. Gen. Stat. §21-420 (1949), Mich. Stat. Ann. §28.553 [1954]).

c. *Deadly force toward all felons.*

Illustration No. 4: Police officers were summoned to a neighborhood where a door-to-door magazine salesman had been so persistent in attempting to sell his wares that he had committed a criminal assault in the process. When the officers arrived on the scene, they found a group of local residents pursuing the salesman. One of the officers fired a few shots in the direction of the salesman. He observed later that he felt such action was justified because the salesman was trying to escape from the custody of these residents, which was a felony.

The prevailing rule that deadly force can be used in making an arrest for any felony is often criticized on the ground that the felony category is not a reliable indication of the dangerousness of the offense or the offender. Thus, in Kansas, where the incident described above occurred, the crime of escape is a felony even if the offense for which the arrest was made is only a misdemeanor.[33] On this basis, officers in that state are instructed that any force necessary to prevent the escape of an arrested person may be used, including deadly force if all else fails.[34]

Illustration No. 5: Officers were pursuing a car thief. The squad car was unable to gain on the stolen car without traveling at an unsafe speed. The thief, in attempting to avoid arrest, was creating a considerable risk of harm to others. The officers, knowing that the thief was a minor, decided to refrain from use of firearms in order to avoid unfavorable publicity about the department should the youth be killed by their fire.

Even in jurisdictions where officers are privileged to employ deadly force against all felons, additional restraints are often imposed as a matter of practice. While instances that even suggest the need for deadly force do not occur frequently, the most conspicuous of all police decisions are made in those cases in which such force is actually used. Detailed reporting within the department is required;[35] the incident will probably receive substantial press coverage; and consequently the coroner or prosecutor may

33 Kan. Gen. Stat. §21-735 (1949).

34 Univ. of Kansas Governmental Research Center, Special Report No. 84, Eleventh Peace Officers Training School, A Report 41 (1957).

35 E.g., in Wichita, whenever force is used to effect an arrest, "the incident shall be reported in detail, including the amount of force used." Wichita Police Dept., Duty Manual 12 (undated). In Detroit the officer involved is to notify his superior immediately, and to follow this with a written report. His superior is to investigate the matter immediately and send a report of his findings to the superintendent. Detroit Police Dept., Revised Police Manual, chap. 16, §29 (1955).

feel compelled to conduct a detailed investigation. For this reason, even if the police generally are uncertain of the limits on their authority to use force, they are apt to limit their use of deadly force to those instances where they believe such action would receive public approval. Because, in the public view, the police department justifies its existence by the apprehension of the dangerous, professional criminal,[36] the tendency is to limit the use of deadly force to such persons. When dealing with a youthful violator or an adult who has engaged in felonious conduct but does not seem likely to take human life or cause bodily harm, there is considerable hesitation to employ deadly force. This reluctance is not so much the result of a belief that the law so limits the use of force as of a desire to maintain public approval of the police agency.

d. *Uncertainty as to whether the offense is a felony and the offender a felon.*

Illustration No. 6: Officers riding in a patrol car observed a moving vehicle with only one taillight. They stopped the car, and one of the officers approached the driver to give him a warning citation. As the officer reached the door of the car, the driver jumped out past him, holding something that gleamed like a knife. "You won't get me, I'm the holdup man," the man shouted as he fled. The officer, after firing shots into the air, fired at the fleeing man and killed him.

In some states, perhaps because of concern over a rule which allows the use of deadly force in all felony cases, the courts or legislatures have imposed a rule of absolute liability upon officers employing deadly force. If the felony has not in fact been committed or, in some instances, if the person apprehended is not in fact the felon, then the privilege does not apply.[37] Even in states without such a strict view, the police are sometimes advised in similar terms.[38]

36 "As we have pointed out, the apprehension of felons is one area where the police can create a favorable public impression, and therefore one from which they derive considerable gratification. . . . Each man obtains prestige and a greater chance for promotion by the publicity which attends the apprehension of the felon. The force as a whole is justified as an existing body. What public judgment of the police does occur is seldom in regard to the extensive time and activity they devote to their mundane service activities . . . but rather in terms of how they behave in more dramatic and newsworthy areas, of which the apprehension of the felon is the outstanding." Westley, The Police: A Sociological Study of Law, Custom and Morality 125-126 (unpublished Ph.D. thesis No. 1197, Dept. of Sociology, Univ. of Chicago, 1951).

37 Moreland, The Use of Force in Effecting or Resisting Arrest, 33 Neb. L. Rev. 408, 409-412 (1954); Note, 38 Ky. L.J. 618 (1950).

38 A Kansas manual says that "there is no justification in killing on suspicion of felony unless a felony actually has been committed." Univ. of Kansas Governmental Research Center, Special Report No. 47, Arrest-Search-Seizure: Legal Problems of Peace Officers 8 (1954). Kansas City officers are told that they may discharge their

Regardless of legal limitations, the police do use force, including deadly force, if there are grounds to believe that the person has committed a felony and to believe that the use of force is necessary. Indeed, the situations are few in which officers called upon to arrest are actually certain both that a felony was committed and that the person being arrested committed it.

B. DELAY TO AVOID FORCIBLE ENTRY

In Kansas it is provided by statute that an officer, in order to make an arrest, "may break open any outer or inner door or window of a dwelling house or other building . . . if after notice of his office and purpose, he be refused admittance." [39] A similar statute is to be found in Michigan, although it covers only cases of arrest with warrant or felony arrests without warrant.[40] Wisconsin has no such statute.

Illustration No. 7: Officers went to the home of a man for whom they held an assault warrant. They heard a radio playing within. They knocked on the door repeatedly, but no one answered. The officers then heard someone within changing the station on the radio. After knocking again, the officer in charge said that they would have to give up, as it was contrary to department policy to break into a home without specific knowledge that the person wanted is within.

Illustration No. 8: Officers went to the home of a man whom they suspected of being involved in some recent burglaries. Although the wanted man was seen through a window, he refused to answer the door. Rather than break down the door immediately, some officers stood around the residence while another left to obtain an arrest warrant. When he returned with the warrant, force was used to gain entrance.

Except where the arrest was for purposes other than prosecution,[41] few instances were observed in which officers had to decide

---

revolvers "to effect the arrest of a known felon." Kansas City Police Dept., Rules & Regulations 36-37 (1956). Michigan officers are warned that "no one can be justified in threatening or taking life in attempting to arrest on suspicion only." Michigan Assn. of Chiefs of Police, Michigan Police Law Manual §71 (1954).

[39] Kan. Gen. Stat. §62-1819 (1949).

[40] Mich. Stat. Ann. §28.880 (1954).

[41] Arrests for purposes other than prosecution are discussed in Part V. One example of forceful entry in this type of arrest occurred when a group of known prostitutes, having been located by the police, ran inside a building and locked heavy metal doors as the police approached. The lieutenant in charge of the "whore squad" suggested that the officers make use of the "master key," and handed them a sledge hammer. Similarly, officers raiding a gambling operation would often break in unannounced and arrest the participants without intention of prosecution.

whether to use force against premises to accomplish an arrest. As the above two illustrations, both observed in Milwaukee, suggest, the police view forceful entry of a home as a sensitive area of law enforcement. Police often do not use force in situations in which it would be lawful to do so.[42] Thus, while in cases of felony or arrest with warrant the Michigan statute allows forceful entry into buildings "in which the person to be arrested is or is reasonably believed to be," the Detroit police are instructed that such action is to be limited "to cases involving serious crimes and situations in which the officer knows that the person whom he is about to arrest is in the building, unless otherwise ordered by a superior officer."[43] While Wisconsin lacks a statute in point, the Milwaukee police regulations seem to imply that the officer should use force only when he has actual knowledge that the person to be arrested is within the building, and even then only "in extreme cases, or when an immediate arrest is necessary."[44]

Because of the general regard for sanctity of the home in the United States, such hesitancy by the police is understandable. Certainly there are many cases in which the situation does not warrant a forceful entry. Yet it is not clear that an absolute denial of a privilege to entry by force in misdemeanor cases would be the wisest limitation;[45] again the question is whether the felony-misdemeanor dichotomy always determines the needs of the individual case. To require that a warrant be obtained before force is used in a misdemeanor case might immunize the police against criticism, but it is doubtful that this would be an effective control over the use of force in cases where force ought not be used, because the routine practice of magistrates is to issue arrest warrants upon request without an independent determination of whether the facts justify the arrest.[46] There is no reason to believe that the magistrate's concern would be greater in practice in regard to whether force is proper in entering premises to arrest a misdemeanant.

[42] In the jurisdictions studied, the previously mentioned statutes constitute the only law on use of force. A few cases have upheld the right of police entry, but force was apparently not necessary in any of these instances. People v. Woodward, 220 Mich. 511, 190 N.W. 721 (1922); Hawkins v. Lutton, 95 Wis. 492, 70 N.W. 483 (1897) (both cases recognized the right of the police to enter for arrest for a breach of the peace heard from outside); Edwards v. State, 190 Wis. 229, 208 N.W. 876 (1926) (upholding the right to enter through an open door to arrest persons reasonably believed to be committing a felony within).

[43] Detroit Police Dept., Revised Police Manual, chap. 16, §31 (1955).

[44] Milwaukee Police Dept., Rules & Regulations, Rule 30, §21 (1950).

[45] The right to resort to forceful entry in misdemeanor cases appears rather uncertain throughout the United States. Annot., 76 A.L.R.2d 1432, 1443-1444 (1961).

[46] See page 30.

Illustration No. 9: An informant had just bought narcotics at a certain residence. Officers decided to arrest the seller. They rang the doorbell, but no one answered. Before attempting a forceful entry, they announced that they were police officers. They then broke through the door and found that the man within had just flushed what apparently was his narcotics supply down the toilet.

Illustration No. 10: Officers, outside an apartment door, could hear a card game underway within in which money was obviously changing hands. One officer knocked at the door, and as soon as the door was opened a little the officers used force to break the door chain and gain immediate entrance. Because they had broken in without announcement, the cards and money were still on the table.

Both the statutes and the police regulations on forceful entry emphasize the necessity of the police identifying themselves before employing force.[47] To do so affords added protection to the police, since it minimizes the possibility that the householder will employ force to repel what he might otherwise believe is an unlawful entry. However, giving notice may impair the opportunity of obtaining physical evidence as an incident to the arrest in a case where such evidence is necessary to obtain conviction. In current practice police do use force in such situations without previously notifying the person in the building.[48]

[47] See Kan. Gen. Stat. §62-1819 (1949) and Mich. Stat. Ann. §28.880 (1954); Detroit Police Dept., Revised Police Manual, chap. 16, §31 (1955); Milwaukee Police Dept., Rules & Regulations, Rule 30, §21 (1950).

[48] In Ker v. California, 374 U.S. 23, 83 Sup. Ct. 1623, 10 L. Ed. 2d 726 (1963), the Court held that the states could, consistent with the requirements of the Fourth and Fourteenth Amendments, allow entry without notice to prevent destruction of evidence. The majority, however, did so only after concluding that the prior "furtive conduct" of the defendant gave the police a basis for thinking destruction of evidence might be attempted. The dissenting justices were of the view that unannounced entry should be permitted only upon a showing that the persons within were actually aware of the officers' presence and purpose. Detailed discussion of this problem will be found in the volume on Detection of Crime.

Although entry without notice in other situations was not observed, some appellate courts have recognized additional exceptions to the notice requirement, such as: (1) where it reasonably appears that the occupants are already aware of the officer's objective, United States v. Frierson, 299 F.2d 763 (7th Cir. 1962); (2) where it reasonably appears that prompt action is required for the protection of a person within, People v. Woodward, 220 Mich. 511, 190 N.W. 721 (1922); (3) where it reasonably appears that unannounced entry is required for the protection of the arresting officer, People v. Hammond, 54 Cal. 2d 846, 357 P.2d 289 (1960); (4) where it reasonably appears that by unannounced entry actual commission of the offense can be observed, People v. Ramsey, 157 Cal. App. 2d 178, 320 P.2d 592 (1958); and (5) where it reasonably appears that by unannounced entry escape of the person to be arrested can be prevented, People v. Maddox, 46 Cal. 2d 301, 294 P.2d 6 (1956).

C. DELAY RELATING TO ANOTHER LAW
ENFORCEMENT OBJECTIVE

A person known to have committed a crime is sometimes not arrested at all if in this way another law enforcement objective can be realized.[49] Perhaps the most obvious example of this is the decision not to arrest an offender who is supplying the police with information concerning other, more serious offenses. Such decisions can clearly have significant consequences for the criminal justice system and for society.

Less significant perhaps, but still of importance, is the decision not to take advantage of a present opportunity to arrest an offender if such an arrest would interfere with another law enforcement objective. In this way, a known offender is allowed to remain free for a period of time, which may create a risk of further criminal conduct and which sometimes results in the offender not being amenable to arrest later. Thus it is important to identify those situations in which this temporary immunity from arrest is granted in current practice.

1. *Concealment of the identity of an informant.*

Illustration No. 11: Narcotics agents set up an "outside buy" whereby they might directly observe a narcotics sale to their informant. Immediately before the scheduled meeting between the informant and narcotics pusher, the officers searched the informant. They then gave him marked money and watched the exchange of money and narcotics from a distance. When the informant returned, the officers searched him again and found a packet of narcotics but no money. They did not immediately arrest the seller of the narcotics, although he was still in the area. Rather, the arrest was delayed for about 10 days.

Police are generally cautioned to avoid disclosing the identity of informants. For example, the Detroit police manual states:

Members shall not divulge to anyone, except to other members of the Department to whom it may be necessary in connection with police work, the name of any person giving information. Information presented to this Department in connection with crimes must be carefully guarded. The source of any information shall not be given publicity.[50]

Even the appellate courts sometimes caution against the disclosure of sources of information, noting that it would greatly impair the

49 See page 132.
50 Detroit Police Dept., Revised Police Manual, chap. 10, §32 (1955).

administration of justice by deterring persons from giving information to law enforcement agencies.[51]

Delay of arrest to avoid disclosure of the informant's identity most frequently occurs in narcotics cases. Narcotics informants are given guarantees by law enforcement officers, both federal and local, that they will not arrest the peddler immediately after the informant has made a purchase. Even if the informant has merely served as a contact man for a direct purchase by an undercover officer, the arrest will nonetheless often be delayed to minimize the possibility that those in the narcotics syndicate can learn the informant's identity. The police usually wait until the peddler has made a least three to five more sales, and may delay the arrest for as long as two weeks. Often a warrant is obtained for the arrest upon the strength of the earlier sale.

Such attempts at secrecy would be futile if the informant later had to appear at the trial of the narcotics peddler. Few informants ever have to appear in court; in fact, many peddlers are never charged with the sale of narcotics, but are given the opportunity to plead guilty to the lesser charge of possession. The desire to protect the informant may also be one factor prompting the prosecutor to agree to the lesser charge in these cases. Even if there is an actual trial for sale of narcotics, appearance by the informant is seldom made necessary. If, as in the above illustration, the transaction was an "outside buy" or a "supervised buy," the officers can testify to the entire transaction themselves. The question of whether the defense would have a right to call the informant as a witness did not arise in any observed case.[52] The defense was apparently willing to forego the opportunity of examining the informant, thinking that he would probably improve the prosecution's case. A right to be told the identity of an informant in such a case does exist in federal court.[53]

Most narcotics cases were observed in Michigan, where the prosecutor is required to list the names of all witnesses on the informa-

[51] The general rule is that the prosecution is privileged to withhold from the accused the identity of an informer. People v. Asta, 337 Mich. 590, 60 N.W.2d 472 (1953); People v. Laird, 102 Mich. 135, 60 N.W. 457 (1894). See the many cases taking this position cited in Annot., 76 A.L.R.2d 262, 271-275 (1961).

[52] No cases on this precise point are to be found in the three jurisdictions studied. The cases elsewhere present differing views, and are collected in Annot., id. at 262.

[53] In Roviaro v. United States, 353 U.S. 53, 77 Sup. Ct. 623, 1 L. Ed. 2d 639 (1957), the court held that the identity of the informant should have been disclosed in that narcotics case. The informant "had helped to set up the criminal occurrence and had played a prominent part in it. His testimony might have disclosed an entrapment. He might have thrown doubt upon petitioner's identity or on the identity of the package. He was the only witness who might have testified to petitioner's possible lack of knowledge of the contents of the package . . ." 353 U.S. at 64, 77 Sup. Ct. at 629, 1 L. Ed. 2d at 647.

tion.[54] However, the statute has been interpreted as referring to only res gestae witnesses,[55] meaning those persons who can testify to all parts of the transaction involving the crime charged.[56] It is not necessary to list a res gestae witness whose testimony would be merely cumulative to that given by others.[57] Whether this exception applies to the informant in a case where the sale was observed by officers is not entirely clear.[58]

If the charge is possession of narcotics found on the peddler at the time of arrest, the possibility of concealing the identity of the informant is increased. The original buy by the informant provides the grounds for the arrest. However, it would seem that the observation of the initial transaction would, under certain circumstances, afford officers reasonable grounds to believe the suspected seller possessed narcotics at the time of a later arrest. In establishing the adequacy of the grounds for arrest, the testimony of the informant would probably not be required.[59]

The immunity from immediate arrest does mean that the peddler can continue to sell during that period. The likelihood is that the sales will be to the pusher's "regular customers" rather than to persons who become new addicts, although this is not a certainty. Also, there is little chance that the seller will not later be found, because he will probably continue his business in the same area and with the same customers.

2. *Concealment of another investigation.*

Illustration No. 12: Officers in the conspiracy squad of the vice bureau observed a numbers runner making his rounds, collecting policy slips with bets for the day and paying off the winners for the day before. The officers' observations were sufficient to support an arrest and subsequent prosecution for possession of gambling equipment. However, the officers did not make an arrest but continued the surveillance of this runner and his associates for over a month, until a number of arrests could be made for conspiracy.

It was noted earlier that narcotics users may be granted immunity from arrest because they voluntarily furnish informa-

54 Mich. Stat. Ann. §28.980 (1954).

55 People v. Kayne, 268 Mich. 186, 255 N.W. 788 (1934).

56 People v. Bartlett, 312 Mich. 648, 20 N.W.2d 758 (1945).

57 People v. Swetland, 77 Mich. 53, 43 N.W. 779 (1889).

58 As suggested in Roviaro v. United States, 353 U.S. 53, 77 Sup. Ct. 623, 1 L. Ed. 2d 639 (1957), the informant's testimony is not necessarily "merely cumulative."

59 See People v. McMurray, 171 Cal. App. 2d 178, 340 P.2d 335 (1959), holding that "where the arrest is valid apart from the information received from the informer, the latter's identity need not be revealed." On the necessity to disclose the identity of an informer to show probable cause for arrest, see cases cited in Annot., 76 A.L.R.2d 262, 327-345 (1961).

tion concerning their supplier. Their supplier, in turn, may be granted temporary immunity from arrest because he is unwittingly leading the police to persons in the upper echelons of narcotics distribution. Similar tactics are employed with respect to all forms of criminality that involve an elaborate organization if the police either do not know the leaders or do not have sufficient evidence of their connection with the activity to support a conspiracy prosecution.

The decision to delay arrest in order to continue surveillance is most frequent in the case of the numbers carrier. In Detroit, a special agency, called the conspiracy squad, is charged with the responsibility of making conspiracy cases against those in the higher echelons of the syndicate. For such purposes, continued surveillance is necessary for a matter of weeks and often months. Many persons who could be arrested for carrying numbers, and many who could be arrested for conspiracy, are merely watched while a pattern of contacts with others is established. Only when it has been possible to fill in the gaps in the "organizational chart" of the syndicate is an arrest made simultaneously of all those involved.[60] By this method, the police can prosecute a great many persons involved in the policy racket and can obtain convictions for conspiracy. The resulting prison sentences are much more effective than the minor penalties imposed for the offense of possession of gambling materials.

Illustration No. 13: State tax agents, charged with the duty of uncovering instances of violation of the prostitution, gambling, and liquor laws across the state, move from county to county in their undercover work. Agents who had just arrived in a particular county entered a tavern and found a number of minors drinking on the premises. The agents left the tavern immediately without making any arrests. When a group of minors left the tavern, the agents followed the car until it stopped, then identified themselves and obtained statements from the minors. The officers did not return to the tavern but began checking for violations in other premises. Only when their stay in the county was nearly completed did they obtain a warrant and arrest the tavernkeeper who had served the minors.

Officers working under cover may not make an immediate arrest because they do not want to disclose their identity until they have

[60] An exception, however, is the situation in which an arrest is made to facilitate this investigation. The arrest is sometimes made to appear to be a means of harassing the numbers carrier, as discussed in Chapter 24, when it is actually intended to provide the police with some important piece of evidence, such as the code numbers on the numbers slips, which help to identify other persons in the conspiracy.

completed other investigations. Although this may occur in a variety of situations, the case in the above illustration is the kind in which continued secrecy is most essential. The success of these officers is based upon the fact that they are not known in the locality. An arrest shortly after the agents' entry into the area would result in other violators being "tipped off" and gambling and prostitution operations and after-hours liquor sales being suspended. Therefore, the agents attempt to gather evidence on as many violations as possible before revealing the reason for their presence by making arrests.

3. *Preventing dispersal of criminal activity.*

Illustration No. 14: An undercover officer entered a tavern known to be patronized by prostitutes. He was accosted by a prostitute but made no arrest at that time. He made arrangements for the girl to meet him off the premises at a later time, and the arrest was made at the subsequent meeting.

Certain establishments, usually taverns, are well known to the police as places frequented by prostitutes or homosexuals. Enforcement is easier if these offenders are localized rather than dispersed throughout the community.

The Detroit police are told:

> No licensee, his agent, or employee, shall permit his licensed premises to be frequented by or to become the meeting place, hangout, or rendezvous for known prostitutes, homosexuals, vagrants, or those who are known to engage in the use, sale or distribution of narcotics or in any other illegal occupation or business; provided, that no licensee shall be disciplined hereunder until he has been warned by the Commission or the law enforcing agency having jurisdiction thereof, and has failed for a period of not more than five days to comply with the requirements of this section.[61]

When arrests of such persons are made within licensed premises, a report of this fact must be made to the liquor control commission. Such action will result in pressure by the commission upon the tavern owner to bar these persons from the premises. Continued violations will result in withdrawal of the license and closing of the tavern.

The vice officers do not want either of these things to happen. Therefore, upon making an accosting and soliciting case against either a prostitute or a homosexual, the practice is to refrain from making an immediate arrest on licensed premises. The offender is arrested later off the premises, even though this may invalidate the arrest because of the requirement that misdemeanor arrests

[61] Detroit Police Dept., Revised Police Manual, chap. 12, §47 (1955).

without warrant be made at the time of the offense and not later.[62] The vice officers support this procedure on the ground that immediate arrest would have the ultimate result of making policing of these kinds of offenders more difficult.

The chances of further criminality or avoidance of arrest by the prostitute or homosexual are slight, since the arrest is usually made shortly after discovery, when the offender is observed leaving the premises. Whether it is proper for police to exercise discretion of this kind to avoid a license revocation is an aspect of the larger issue of the extent and propriety of police discretion discussed elsewhere in this volume.

[62] "To authorize an arrest without a warrant, the offense must be committed in the presence of the officer, and the arrest must be made immediately." People v. Johnson, 86 Mich. 175, 48 N.W. 870 (1891) (dicta on latter point). While Michigan arrest law has been codified and does not expressly state any such time limit, it has elsewhere been decided that this common law restriction should be read into the statutes. Jackson v. Superior Court, 98 Cal. App. 2d 183, 219 P.2d 879 (1950). The rationale underlying this requirement is uncertain. The reason often given is that, since a period of time is allowed to elapse, there is evidently no need for immediate arrest and therefore a warrant should first be obtained. Ibid. See also cases cited therein. However, the criterion of need for immediate custody was a limitation for misdemeanor arrests when the common law allowed arrest only for presently occurring breaches of the peace; it can hardly be said to apply to officers who can arrest for any misdemeanor occurring in their presence.

As to the instances of delay described in the text, it could be said that the delay is a reasonable way of accomplishing the arrest. See Annot., 58 A.L.R.2d 1056 (1958). Or it might be said that the accosting is a continuing course of conduct which is still taking place when the prostitute or homosexual leaves the bar with the officer. However, the failure to make an arrest at the time of the initial accosting may be used by the defense as evidence that an offense did not take place. See Larson v. Feeney, 196 Mich. 1, 162 N.W. 275 (1917).

PART IV

The Decision to Arrest for Purposes of Prosecution

Presumably, whomever the police arrest they must arrest on "probable cause." It is not the function of the police to arrest, as it were, at large and to use an interrogating process at police headquarters in order to determine whom they should charge before a committing magistrate on "probable cause."

JUSTICE FRANKFURTER
in *Mallory v. United States*
354 U.S. 449, 456 (1957)

A vital factor to bear in mind is that as these steps progress the burden of the law enforcement agency increases. What may constitute probable cause for arrest does not necessarily constitute probable cause for a charge . . . Hence at each stage, and especially at the early stage, when little is known that is sure, police must not be compelled prematurely to make the hard choices, such as arraigning or releasing, on incomplete information. If they are forced to make a decision to seek a charge on incomplete information, they may irreparably injure an innocent person; if they must decide prematurely to release, they may be releasing a guilty one.

JUDGE BURGER
in *Goldsmith v. United States*
277 F.2d 335, 345 (D.C. Cir. 1960)

In current practice, some persons are arrested on evidence clearly sufficient for charging them with a crime and holding them for trial. These arrests meet the standard assumed to be proper by Justice Frankfurter. However, many arrests, a majority of those for certain offenses, are made on evidence which the police believe to be adequate to justify a lawful arrest but insufficient for charging. In these cases further investigation, usually by interrogation, is needed before the prosecutor will charge the suspect.

These are presumably the situations which Judge Burger referred to when he said that probable cause for arrest is not necessarily the equivalent of probable cause for charging. The fact that such a practice does exist and that there is conflicting judicial opinion on its validity raises one of the most vital questions in current criminal justice administration: whether the system ought to be so structured as to make it proper to take custody of a suspect under circumstances in which further investigation must take place before a decision can be made to charge or to release the suspect.

The debate on this issue takes different forms. Sometimes, as illustrated by the declarations of Justice Frankfurter and Judge Burger, the question is put in terms of how much evidence should be required to support certain basic decisions in criminal justice administration. Thus it may be asked what evidence is necessary for arrest and how this relates to the evidentiary requirement for charging. If the two evidentiary standards are different, this may suggest the need for investigation in the interval between the two decisions. More often, however, the debate focuses upon the supposed benefits and detriments of in-custody investigation without express regard to similarities or differences in the requirements for arrest and charging.

These two approaches, while involving somewhat different considerations, are clearly related. Thus a court might conclude that more evidence is needed for charging than for arrest but that certain investigation methods, such as in-custody interrogation, are too dangerous for the individual to be permitted.

The degree of risk in a system which allows in-custody investigation between arrest and charging depends upon a number of factors. For example, one's reactions regarding the propriety of such investigation may be vitally affected by whether the permitted techniques are limited to the use of lineups, fingerprinting, records-checking, and the like, or are extended to include interrogation of the suspect under circumstances where there is a possibility of coercion. Evaluation of risk may also include such considerations as whether the suspect is afforded an opportunity to consult with counsel and whether the detention and investigation occur in an atmosphere of isolation and secrecy. Similarly, it is important to know whether the judiciary plays a part here, by allowing detention to be continued only after a showing of sufficient evidence for taking custody and a necessity for detention to gather additional evidence, by telling the suspect of his rights before the investigation is conducted, or by actually conducting the necessary interrogation.

Weighing the need for in-custody investigation also involves a number of factors, such as the extent to which such investigations are successful in solving outstanding offenses when other detection techniques have been exhausted. One's reaction will also depend in part upon one's attitude toward the right to conduct a prearrest interrogation, as the greater the right to stop and question, the less pressure there will be to conduct in-custody interrogation. Therefore, the practice of "field interrogation" [1] must also be considered here.

To approach the problem as one of sufficiency of evidence, in the manner of Justice Frankfurter and Judge Burger, requires careful consideration of the grounds upon which an officer can properly arrest. One's impressions of what is necessary and proper at one stage of the process may be greatly affected by considerations of what is and what ought to be allowed at other stages. Therefore, the requirements for arrest must be looked at in relation to both the decision to stop and question before arrest and the decision to charge a suspect following his arrest. The latter comparison is most difficult because the formal law requirements for charging, as reflected by the evidentiary requirements for post-arrest warrants and bindover at the preliminary examination, are not readily identifiable and because in practice prosecutors usually demand greater evidence for charging than the minimum required by law.

It is important also to consider the means used for gaining custody for purposes of investigation when the suspect cannot be lawfully arrested for the offense suspected. In current practice the police may arrest for another lesser offense, take custody based upon the parolee or probationer status of the suspect, or induce the suspect to accompany them to the station "voluntarily." The circumstances, if any, under which these practices are legitimate have not been clearly identified.

Arrest for purposes of prosecution is an important decision apart from the issue of in-custody investigation. Even if the arrested person is taken immediately before a magistrate, the mere fact of arrest may carry with it consequences harmful to him. His freedom of movement is interrupted, his reputation may be damaged, and he is usually searched.

The evidentiary requirements for this important decision have received a great deal of attention from legislatures and courts. Even so, considerable ambiguity remains today in the law of arrest. Because false arrest cases seldom reach the appellate court, the primary occasion for courts to consider the propriety of an

---

[1] Detailed treatment of this practice will be found in the volume on Detection of Crime.

arrest is in cases in which the defendant seeks to suppress physical evidence obtained as an incident to the arrest. Consequently, the problem is dealt with only in those cases where physical evidence is of central importance. Thus, because informants are often used in narcotics cases, where the narcotic drug itself is usually essential evidence, there are numerous appellate cases deciding whether a lawful arrest can be made on the basis of information from an informant. In comparison, there are few cases which decide whether a description by a witness or victim which fits more than one person is an adequate basis for arrest, because the essential evidence is oral testimony rather than physical evidence. The recent Supreme Court case of *Wong Sun v. United States*,[2] holding that the admissibility of the defendant's statement obtained subsequent to arrest may be affected by the legality of the arrest, will increase the range of factual situations which are brought to the attention of appellate courts.

[2] 371 U.S. 471, 83 Sup. Ct. 407, 9 L. Ed. 2d 441 (1963).

Misdemeanor Arrest: The "In-Presence" Requirement

In current practice it is common for police to make misdemeanor arrests without warrant when the facts and circumstances immediately observable indicate that a person at hand has committed a misdemeanor. These arrests are usually made upon the supposed authority of the police to arrest for the commission of any misdemeanor occurring in their presence. But whether all such arrests are actually within the existing legal norms is not always clear. There are two reasons for this. First, it is sometimes unclear to what extent the in-presence standard actually applies in a particular jurisdiction. While the early common law view with respect to misdemeanors was that arrest without warrant was proper only for breaches of the peace occurring in the presence of the arresting officer,[1] the trend in more recent years, through either legislation or judicial declaration, has been to expand this power to allow arrest without warrant for all misdemeanors occurring in the presence.[2] But, where the law of arrest is a matter of common law development, the scarcity of and ambiguity in the decided misdemeanor cases at the appellate level often leave the nature of the arrest privilege unclear. Second, the few decided cases, even if they establish an in-presence standard for all misdemeanors, often do not make clear exactly how certain the officer must be that a misdemeanor has in fact been committed by the person suspected. The in-presence requirement is a far more definite standard than the reasonable cause requirement for felony

[1] 9 Halsbury's Laws of England, Criminal Law and Procedure §117 (2d ed. 1933); 1 Anderson, Sheriffs, Coroners and Constables 166 (1941); A.L.I. Code of Criminal Procedure 231 (1931).

[2] One article suggests that many of the courts that have themselves changed this rule have done so because of an erroneous reading of the case of Carroll v. United States, 267 U.S. 132, 45 Sup. Ct. 280, 69 L. Ed. 543 (1925). Bohlen and Shulman, Arrest With and Without a Warrant, 75 U. Pa. L. Rev. 485-504 (1927). See also, Restatement of Torts, Comments at 40-45 (Tent. Draft No. 3, 1927).

arrests, but there remains some uncertainty as to its exact meaning.

The ambiguity as to whether in presence is the test and, if so, what it actually means is a significant problem in current criminal justice administration. It is of course important to know precisely what the limits are on the power of the police to arrest without warrant and detain for a time before bail is set for minor offenses. Also, how the misdemeanor arrest standard is construed vitally affects the power of officers to conduct lawful searches, because it is a frequent practice to search as an incident to a misdemeanor arrest. Finally, how the arrest power is defined in misdemeanor cases has a bearing on the question of whether in-custody investigation following arrest is proper. If the requirement is that the officer must be certain from direct observation that the individual has committed a misdemeanor, then there is no need for in-custody investigation to obtain added proof of that offense.

A. Ambiguity as to the Applicability of the In-Presence Requirement

The law in the three jurisdictions studied reflects how the common law development of misdemeanor arrest law may make it uncertain whether or not the police can arrest for all misdemeanors in their presence and whether they have even greater authority. In Michigan the legislature has provided that any peace officer may without warrant arrest a person "for the commission of any . . . misdemeanor committed in his presence." [3] While this can probably be said to be the arrest power applicable in Kansas and Wisconsin, the situation in these states is far from clear.

The earliest relevant Kansas case involved an arrest for a breach of the peace long after its commission, but the court said cryptically that "it must be presumed that the defendant . . . made the arrest on sufficient information. In such a case he would not at common law be liable." [4] However, a later case stated that any supposed power of an officer to make an arrest on reasonable grounds to believe that a misdemeanor had been committed was contrary to the Kansas constitution. [5] The Kansas court did not

---

3 Mich. Stat. Ann. §28.874(a) (1954). Although the authority was limited to breaches of the peace in the presence prior to the enactment of this statute, Robison v. Miner, 68 Mich. 549, 37 N.W. 21 (1888), the present expansion does not seem open to challenge on constitutional grounds. Burroughs v. Eastman, 101 Mich. 419, 59 N.W. 817 (1894).

4 Prell v. McDonald, 7 Kan. *426, *446 (1871). This was a false arrest action, and the court may have confused the conditions justifying arrest with the conditions sufficient for defense in such an action.

5 State v. Dietz, 59 Kan. 576, 53 Pac. 870 (1898).

again consider the issue until over fifty years later. In *Hill v. Day*,[6] a false arrest action, the court said, in response to the plaintiff's contention that probable cause is not always a defense:

> A properly qualified officer of the law has authority to arrest either a felon or the perpetrator of a misdemeanor involving a breach of the peace without a warrant when he has reasonable grounds — and probable cause — for believing the person arrested is guilty.[7]

In the most recent case, the Kansas court noted that the arrest was on an in-presence basis, and (apparently oblivious of the existing ambiguity) went on to say:

> The law is well settled in this state that in order for an officer to make a valid arrest without a warrant on the charge that the person arrested has committed a misdemeanor, the offense must have taken place in the officer's view and presence.[8]

Because of the court's failure on each occasion to recognize and refer to its prior, apparently contrary decisions and to distinguish its present holding, it is impossible to reconcile these four cases. The only possible explanation is that probable cause is sufficient if the arrest is later challenged by a false arrest action (if not for all misdemeanors, at least for breaches of the peace), but that the in-presence requirement remains when the question of arrest power arises in the context of an action involving use of force by the officer or resistance by the arrestee.[9]

[6] 168 Kan. 604, 215 P.2d 219 (1950). This was a false arrest case brought to the court on demurrer. The complaint stated that the plaintiff was arrested by the defendant, a city policeman, without warrant and that he was subsequently convicted in police court of disorderly conduct, but that on appeal to the district court the city dismissed the case. The court noted that conviction is a conclusive determination that probable cause existed, and then went on to say that it is well settled that probable cause is a sufficient defense in a false arrest action, citing Torson v. Baehni, 134 Kan. 188, 5 P.2d 813 (1931). The plaintiff objected that Torson was a felony case, but the court declared this irrelevant.

[7] Hill v. Day, 168 Kan. 604, 610, 215 P.2d 219, 224 (1950). The holding of this case is not clear. It seems unlikely that the case is speaking strictly in terms of what constitutes a defense in a tort action, as opposed to what norm is to control arrest, in the light of the quoted paragraph. Also, the uncertainty of the court's position is increased when at this point it speaks of breaches of the peace, while elsewhere the reference is always to misdemeanors generally. Finally, the relevance of all prior discussion in the case is brought into question when the court suggests in closing that the plaintiff here had waived all right to object to the validity of the arrest inasmuch as he had posted bond following arrest (a point which itself appears open to serious question and which is considered in relation to other supposed defenses in a false arrest action in Chapter 20).

[8] State v. Merrifield, 180 Kan. 267, 270, 303 P.2d 155, 158 (1956). No mention was made of the Hill case.

[9] No policeman, prosecutor, or judge was ever heard to comment on the ambiguous state of the law. First Assistant Attorney General Paul Wilson cautioned officers at the Kansas Peace Officers' Training School not to rely upon Hill v. Day.

The law remains unclear in a somewhat different respect in Wisconsin. Here there is ambiguity as to whether officers can arrest for all misdemeanors in their presence or only for breaches of the peace occurring in their presence. The former view is taken by the Attorney General,[10] but two of the cases cited in support are explainable on other grounds,[11] and the third does not make it clear whether the common law power was being extended to all in-presence violations or merely to vagrancy.[12] Dicta supporting the broader rule can be found in some Wisconsin cases,[13] while others adhere to the breach of the peace limitation.[14] This ambiguity need be of no concern to those officers who by statute have been given power to arrest for any misdemeanor committed in their presence — city, town, and village policemen and village marshals.[15] However, other officers, such as sheriffs, undersheriffs,

---

The general opinion of the police is that misdemeanor arrests should be made on an in-presence basis; arrests made otherwise are cases of the police responding to what they believe to be the exigencies of the situation. See Chapter 1.

[10] 45 Ops. Wis. Atty. Gen. 289, 290 (1956).

[11] One, a false arrest action in which a village constable arrested the plaintiff for failure to explain satisfactorily the absence of license plates on his vehicle, is explainable on the basis of a statute specifically empowering an officer to arrest anyone violating the statute requiring registration of motor vehicles. Bursack v. Davis, 199 Wis. 115, 225 N.W. 738 (1929). The statute was Wis. Stat. §85.04(1) (1927).

The second case, involving arrest of a driver without a license, is explainable on the basis of the statutory power of the city policeman to arrest persons found violating the law and also the equivalent at that time of §954.03(1) (1955), which would allow arrest of the driver because he could not prove his identity. State ex rel. Tessler v. Kubiak, 257 Wis. 159, 42 N.W.2d 496 (1950). The statutes were Wis. Stat. §§62.09(13) and 361.44 (1947), respectively.

[12] Gray v. State, 243 Wis. 57, 9 N.W.2d 68 (1943). Vagrants were arrested by a deputy sheriff, and the court assumed the arrest to be valid without explaining the basis for its conclusion. It may be that the common law power of arrest without warrant was merely being extended to vagrancy. 4 Wharton, Criminal Law and Procedure §1606 (Anderson ed. 1957) takes note of such extensions of the common law in other states.

[13] Mantei v. State, 210 Wis. 1, 245 N.W. 683 (1932) (offense was a felony); Edwards v. State, 190 Wis. 229, 208 N.W. 876 (1926) (sufficient statutory power); Hawkins v. Lutton, 95 Wis. 492, 70 N.W. 483 (1897) (offense was a breach of the peace).

[14] Two are clearly dicta, in that the issue at hand in those cases was whether there could be an arrest for offenses not occurring in the presence, Gunderson v. Struebing, 125 Wis. 173, 104 N.W. 149 (1905); Stittgen v. Rundle, 99 Wis. 78, 74 N.W. 536 (1898). A third case, Allen v. State, 183 Wis. 323, 197 N.W. 808 (1924), is very ambiguous. A city police officer arrested a man who admitted he was carrying liquor. The court suppressed the evidence because the arrest was illegal, but it is far from clear whether this was done because of the court's view that such an admission does not constitute an in-presence violation or because there was no breach of the peace. Statements to both effects appear in the opinion. The court further confuses the issue by not conceding that §62.09(13) of the statutes (giving city police the power to arrest for violation of the laws of the state) in any way changes the common law rule that a misdemeanor arrest can be made only for a breach of the peace committed in the presence.

[15] Town policemen have the powers of village policemen, Wis. Stat. §60.29(7) and

deputies, and village and town constables, do not have this added power.

As was noted earlier, the significant difference in the Wisconsin misdemeanor arrest law, as compared with that found in the other states studied, is that a statute provides:

> An arrest by a peace officer without a warrant for a misdemeanor or for the violation of an ordinance is lawful whenever the officer has reasonable grounds to believe that the person to be arrested has committed a misdemeanor or has violated an ordinance and will not be apprehended unless immediately arrested or that personal or property damage may likely be done unless immediately arrested.[16]

The problems raised by this statute are treated in other chapters.[17] This statute makes the ambiguity which exists in Wisconsin in regard to the meaning of the in-presence requirement less significant. It is only the officer who has not been given statutory power to arrest for any offense and who cannot establish one of the needs for immediate arrest in the above statute who is in jeopardy because of the ambiguity in Wisconsin.

The common law development in both Kansas and Wisconsin leaves the authority of the police uncertain. The police are generally unaware of the ambiguity, however, and tend to assume in both states that they have power to arrest for all misdemeanors committed in their presence.

---

(21) (1955), who have the powers of village marshals, Wis. Stat. §61.32(2) (1955). Village marshals' powers are granted in Wis. Stat. §61.28 (1955), and those of city police in Wis. Stat. §62.09(13) (1955).

16 Wis. Stat. §954.03(1) (1955). This statute expressly states that it is not intended to limit the powers granted by §62.09(13) (1955), which allows city police to arrest without warrant persons "found" violating the law. It is interesting to note that the statute does not expressly state that it was likewise not intended to limit the statutory powers of town policemen, village policemen, and village marshals to so arrest. But even more significant is the fact that the statute fails to indicate whether it is intended to replace the existing common law power of arrest. Since courts do not consider the common law as replaced unless the legislative purpose to effect such change is clearly expressed in the statute, Wisconsin Bridge and Iron Co. v. Ramsay, 233 Wis. 467, 474, 290 N.W. 199, 202 (1940), it would appear that §954.03(1) (1955) leaves the common law intact.

17 First, since an arrest may be made under circumstances where a warrant would be required in the other states, this matter has been considered in Chapter 1. Also, the conditions attached to the use of the "reasonable grounds" statute are discussed in Chapter 9 in relation to the need for immediate custody. Of course, this same statute also requires consideration of what the "reasonable grounds" test means and whether it allows brief detention to obtain evidence sufficient for charging. These problems are comparable to those frequently faced in the felony area, discussed in Chapters 12, 13, and 15.

B. Evidence Needed for an In-Presence Arrest

In practice the usual misdemeanor arrest takes place when the officer sees a person commit an act constituting a misdemeanor. This clearly conforms to the in-presence requirement.[18] However, police are sometimes faced with situations where the privilege to arrest is unclear because of ambiguity as to: (1) whether sight is the only sense the officer can employ in determining if an offense has occurred, (2) whether the senses must reveal the occurrence itself or if indirect evidence is sufficient, (3) whether the officer must be certain that the misdemeanor has been committed, and (4) whether the officer must be certain as to the identity of the offender.

1. *Senses which can be employed.*

Illustration No. 1: Police officers in an apartment building on other business heard noise emanating from an apartment. They could hear cards being dealt and money changing hands, and they overheard conversation which made it perfectly clear that a card game was being played for money. One of the officers knocked on the door, but when it was opened the money had been removed and the scene was one of a friendly card game. The officers arrested four of the occupants of the apartment who were seated around the card table.

While presence is usually thought of as the state of being in view,[19] it is often asserted that an offense is considered as taking place within the presence of an officer when any of his senses afford him knowledge that it is being committed.[20] The police, at least in Detroit and Milwaukee, are instructed in the broader view.[21]

A problem is most likely to occur in practice when a misdemeanor is detected by hearing rather than sight,[22] as in the above

---

[18] Because of the clarity of the norm, it is usually possible to determine when the police have decided to act without compliance. Usually, this means a failure to obtain a warrant when the offense was not actually committed in the presence. This is discussed in Chapter 1.

[19] Webster, New International Dictionary 1955 (2d ed. 1955); Black, Law Dictionary 1346 (4th ed. 1951).

[20] 4 Wharton, Criminal Law and Procedure §1599 (Anderson ed. 1957); 1 Restatement of Torts §119, Comment m (1934); Perkins, The Law of Arrest, 25 Iowa L. Rev. 201, 231-232 (1940).

[21] Milwaukee police are instructed that misdemeanor arrests may be made when "the officer knows from his own knowledge, from his own senses, that such misdemeanor was committed and cannot rely upon the statement of others that the person whom he arrests committed the misdemeanor." Milwaukee Police Dept., Rules & Regulations, Rule 30, §23 (1950). An almost identical provision may be found in Detroit Police Dept., Revised Police Manual, chap. 16, §16 (1955); Pontiac Police Dept., Rules & Regulations §219 (1941).

[22] The other senses are rarely important on the misdemeanor level. However odors

illustration.   Forceful entry without a prior request for permission to enter would make possible direct observation of the offense, but this would be unlawful.[23]   In misdemeanor cases,[24] officers currently make what they consider to be in-presence arrests when they hear an offense being committed.

The law gives little guidance in any of the three states as to whether such arrests are proper.   The Kansas court has not considered the question.   A Michigan case upheld an arrest made after officers in the street heard noise from within a house which amounted to a breach of the peace.   But the rationale was not that there had been an offense in the officers' presence, but rather that knowledge that a breach of the peace is occurring in a house gives officers a right to enter, at which time an arrest can be made for an offense then occurring in the presence of the officer.[25]   Similarly, the Wisconsin court upheld an arrest for keeping a disorderly house based upon what the officers heard before entry, but the court emphasized that this offense took place in the officers' presence while they were outside because it involved keeping a house in which people disturbed the repose of the neighborhood; that is, the fact that the disturbance was heard in the area made it an offense.[26]   Thus, in none of the three states have the police received express guidance from courts as to what to do in cases such as that in the above illustration.[27]

---

may be a factor in finding reasonable grounds to suspect a felony. See cases collected in Annot., 3 L. Ed. 2d 1736, 1740 nn.7-9 (1958).

[23] See Chapter 10 on forceful entry.

[24] Gambling is a misdemeanor in Wisconsin, Wis. Stat. §945.02 (1955), and Michigan, Mich. Stat. Ann. §§28.533 and 28.541 (1954), while in Kansas it depends upon whether the betting is at a gambling place — a place "to which persons are accustomed to resort for the purpose of gambling," Kan. Gen. Stat. §21-915 (1949) — in which case it is a felony. Kan. Gen. Stat. §21-923 (1949).   Otherwise it is a misdemeanor, Kan. Gen. Stat. §21-924 (1949).

Even the operator of such a "gambling place" is only guilty of a misdemeanor in Michigan, Mich. Stat. Ann. §28.535 (1954), while in the other two states studied a felony conviction might result. Wis. Stat. §945.03 (1955); Kan. Gen. Stat. §21-915 (1949).

[25] People v. Woodward, 220 Mich. 511, 190 N.W. 721 (1922). This rationale, of course, would not apply to the case of gambling heard outside, but not observed after entry.

[26] Hawkins v. Lutton, 95 Wis. 492, 70 N.W. 483 (1897).

[27] Apparently the Restatement would allow arrest in the case described. Though the Restatement restricts arrest to breaches of the peace in the presence, it says: "If the actor, by the use of any of his senses, perceives that an act is being done, and forthwith investigates and finds that the act constitutes a breach of the peace, he is privileged to arrest . . ." 1 Restatement of Torts §119, Comment m (1934). The following hypothetical case is given as an illustration: "A, while passing B's house, hears a woman's scream. He rushes into the house and discovers that the woman was screaming because B *was* beating her. A is privileged to arrest B." [Emphasis supplied.]   Arrest in this case would seem more questionable than in the gambling case set forth. In the latter, the actual gambling was heard, while in the case in the

It is likely that an appellate court would decide that an offense which is "heard" is committed in the presence of the officer if the issue were squarely presented. This would seem consistent with the rationale of the in-presence norm, which apparently is that an arrest is justified because the officer does not have to rely upon information from others (minimizing the chance of error) and because he is on the scene where an arrest can be made promptly and therefore should not be required to delay the arrest in order to obtain a warrant.

2. *Direct or indirect knowledge that an offense is being committed.*

> *Illustration No. 2:* A state traffic patrolman operating a radar speed timer on the highway determined by radar that an approaching car was exceeding the speed limit, although he could not actually see it at the time. When the car reached the point at which the officer was stationed, he stopped it and arrested the driver. The driver later initiated a false arrest suit against the officer, claiming that the offense had not taken place in his presence.[28]

There is uncertainty as to whether an officer can arrest only if he directly observes the offense or whether observation of circumstances indicating the offense is being committed will suffice. While this situation does not occur frequently, the above illustration shows the kind of difficulty which can arise because of doubt as to which requirement applies.

A literal reading of some police materials supports the broader view. Detroit police are told that an officer may arrest when "he receives knowledge of the commission of the offense through any of his senses."[29] Milwaukee officers are instructed that arrest is possible where "the officer knows from his own knowledge . . . that such misdemeanor was committed."[30] The Pontiac officer learns that arrest is proper if the offense is "made known to him

---

Restatement illustration what was heard did not itself establish that an offense had occurred.

[28] A member of the Michigan Attorney General's office was designated to defend the trooper. The outcome of the case is not known.

The Wisconsin Attorney General might consider such an arrest legal in that state in view of 42 Ops. Wis. Atty. Gen. 93 (1953), which says that Wis. Stat. §83.016 (1955) authorizes an officer to arrest on the basis of a radio report received from another officer who has observed speeding on a radar speed meter. In fact this statute allows arrest in such a case only if the violation occurred in the presence of the informing officer. The factual situation was one in which the officer using the device was in a position to see the speeding car, but there was no evidence to prove whether the officer became aware of the offense by actually seeing it committed or by means of the meter.

[29] Detroit Police Dept., Revised Police Manual, chap. 16, §11a (1955).

[30] Milwaukee Police Dept., Rules & Regulations, Rule 30, §23 (1950).

at the time by the use of any of his senses." [31]   While this language stresses observation giving indirect knowledge of the offense presently occurring, as opposed to direct observation of the actual offense, the Michigan statute requires that there be a "misdemeanor committed in his presence," and the courts of Kansas and Wisconsin have used similar language.   If the only policy is to prevent arrest without warrant when the officer must rely upon information from others,[32] then it is consistent to construe the in-presence language as encompassing the kind of case described above.

The only relevant judicial language found in the three states is in the Wisconsin case of *Edwards v. State*.[33]   Police were posted to watch the defendant's apartment, since it was believed to be a disorderly place.   They saw the defendant, a woman, engage in conversation with a man on the sidewalk, after which both parties went up the stairs to the apartment.   The police saw both parties enter the defendant's bedroom, after which she pulled down the window shade.   At this, the police entered the apartment and arrested both for the crime of sodomy.   The court upheld the entry of the officers and the arrest on the ground that an offense had been committed in the officers' presence.   The court said:

> A crime is committed in the presence of the officer when the facts and circumstances occurring within his observation, in connection with what, under the circumstances, may be considered as common knowledge, give him probable cause to believe, or reasonable ground to suspect, that such is the case.   It is not necessary, therefore, that the officer should be an eye or an ear witness of every fact and circumstance involved in the charge, or necessary to the commission of the crime.[34]

The case is somewhat weakened, however, in that the court does not make explicit whether the offense reasonably believed at the time of entry was a felony, for which reasonable grounds would be sufficient, or a misdemeanor.[35]

[31] City of Pontiac, Division of Police, Training Manual §VII.D.3 (1954).

[32] Some cases suggest that this is the policy, e.g., People v. Johnson, 86 Mich. 175, 48 N.W. 870 (1891).

[33] 190 Wis. 229, 208 N.W. 876 (1926).

[34] 190 Wis. at 231, 208 N.W. at 876, quoting Ex parte Morrill, 35 Fed. 261, 267 (9th Cir. 1888).

[35] The court notes at one point that "evidently" the apartment was suspected of being a disorderly place and, if this was the case, keeping such a place was a felony. Wis. Stat. §351.35 (1925).   The offense actually found, sodomy, was also a felony, §351.40, but it is unclear whether the officers thought this was the offense being engaged in or whether prostitution, a misdemeanor, §351.19, was the offense suspected.   The court notes only that the facts "were very convincing that a crime was either being committed . . . or about to be committed."   The case was later cited by the court as one in which there were reasonable grounds to believe a felony was

Illustration No. 3: An officer observed a youth who appeared to be trying to conceal something on his person. The officer asked what he had in his coat pocket. The youth answered that it was a pistol. The policeman placed the youth under arrest.

Even if the broader view of in presence discussed above is correct (which is unclear because of the ambiguity in *Edwards* and the lack of authority in the other states), it is not clear whether there are limitations upon the methods by which knowledge of the facts and circumstances can be obtained. In another Wisconsin case the police contended that a misdemeanor arrest was justified by the admissions of the defendant. The court said that an admission "was not the nature or kind of evidence" to allow arrest; rather there must be "evidence that comes to the officer through his sense of sight or other natural senses." [36]

3. *Certainty as to the misdemeanor.*

Illustration No. 4: Alcoholic Beverage Control Board agents were watching the actions of state residents at liquor stores located just beyond the state line in order to detect misdemeanor violations of the statutes prohibiting bringing into the state more than two quarts of liquor. They observed a person carry a cardboard whiskey case out of a store as if it were full, place it in the trunk of his car, and then drive across the state line. The agents placed this man under arrest and took him and his car to headquarters. There they opened the box and found that it was empty.

Illustration No. 5: An officer patrolling a beat on New Year's Eve noticed a car stopped in the middle of the street. Walking over to the car, the officer saw the driver slumped over the steering wheel. When the officer opened the car door the driver lunged toward him. The officer subdued the man and placed him under arrest for drunkenness. At the station it was determined that the arrestee was not intoxicated but had suffered an epileptic seizure.[37]

---

taking place, Mantei v. State, 210 Wis. 1, 245 N.W. 683 (1932), leaving the significance of the language quoted in the text above in doubt.

[36] Allen v. State, 183 Wis. 323, 197 N.W. 808 (1924). The Kansas court in State v. Dietz, 59 Kan. 576, 53 Pac. 870 (1898), indicated that it was not determining "whether a direct or open confession of guilt of a charge of misdemeanor made to the officer would justify an arrest by him."

[37] This resulted in a false arrest action which was ultimately settled out of court through the efforts of the Wichita Chief of Police. Because the case also involved questions of excessive force, and because it could be questioned whether reasonable belief was even present, the settlement can hardly be interpreted as reflecting a police view that misdemeanor arrest is illegal when it is subsequently learned that no offense was in fact committed.

Even when an officer arrests for what appears to be an offense actually happening before his eyes, it may later be established that no offense was being committed.

Some courts have held that an officer is liable in damages if no misdemeanor was in fact committed, even though he reasonably believed that the offense was occurring in his presence.[38] The officer thus acts at his peril. This is quite obviously not a workable standard to guide the conduct of officers who can only be expected to act upon the basis of what reasonably appears to be true at the time the decision is made.

In one Wisconsin case a man was arrested for driving an unregistered auto, although he had told the officer before arrest that he had made application for registration. After noting that application would be sufficient under the relevant statute, the court said:

> If, however, the defendant [officer], under the situation as presented to him, had reasonable grounds to disbelieve the statement that the conditions of the statute as to registration had been complied with by plaintiff, then he might still be justified in the eye of the law in making the arrest although, as a matter of fact, the plaintiff may not have committed the offense; for the police officer charged with the duties and responsibilities that such officers are is not required to justify his action in making an arrest by a subsequent showing that as a matter of fact the offense was committed. It is sufficient if he has reasonable ground for believing that the offense has been committed by the person whom he then arrests.[39]

The police in Michigan and Kansas, however, cannot be certain that they have the right to arrest in such circumstances. Frequent statements allowing arrest only for "misdemeanors *committed* in the presence" seem to deny such a right,[40] but it appears likely that the Michigan and Kansas courts would hold, in a proper case, that

[38] The cases are collected in Stone, Arrest Without a Warrant, 1939 Wis. L. Rev. 385, 387. The early commentators simply stated that there must actually be a misdemeanor committed but did not elaborate, which undoubtedly contributed to the confusion in this area. See Warner, Modern Trends in the American Law of Arrest, 21 Can. B. Rev. 192-214, 200 n.16 (1943).

[39] Bursack v. Davis, 199 Wis. 115, 121, 225 N.W. 738, 741 (1929).

[40] A different verbal formulation might prevent the ambiguity. For example, §6 of the Uniform Arrest Act would allow an officer to arrest without warrant for a misdemeanor whenever "he has reasonable ground to believe that the person to be arrested had committed a misdemeanor in his presence." See Warner, The Uniform Arrest Act, 28 Va. L. Rev. 315 (1942).

The Restatement, though limiting arrest power to breaches of the peace, uses a "reasonably suspects" formulation. 1 Restatement of Torts §121(c) (1934). Thus, "A . . . sees B and C fighting. Reasonably believing it to be a mutual combat, A arrests both B and C. In fact B was acting in self-defense. . . . [I]f A were a peace officer, the arrest would be privileged . . . ." 1 Restatement of Torts §119, Illustration 4 (1934).

a reasonable belief that a misdemeanor is committed in the officer's presence is sufficient.[41]

4. *Certainty as to the offender.*

Illustration No. 6: An officer on patrol at five o'clock in the morning saw a shot being fired from a parked automobile. When he reached the car he found two persons in it, and was unable to determine which of them had fired the shot. He therefore arrested both, but in order to protect himself from possible liability he brought another charge against both suspects.[42]

Illustration No. 7: Officers riding in a patrol car saw a bundle of papers being thrown from the vehicle immediately in front of them. Stopping to examine the papers, they discovered them to be numbers slips. They then overtook the car, and when none of the four occupants of the car would admit that he had possessed the slips, the officers arrested all four.[43]

In cases such as those in the illustrations it is not clear whether the police can lawfully arrest any or all of the persons in the small group known to contain the offender. One treatise has indicated that an offense occurs in the presence when it is "so near that [the

---

[41] The Michigan court has asserted that the standard is "whether or not [the officer] had probable cause to believe the plaintiff to be guilty of committing a misdemeanor at the time of the arrest." Doak v. Springstead, 284 Mich. 459, 461, 279 N.W. 898, 899 (1938). However, the case becomes questionable when it is asserted therein that probable cause at the time is established by a later conviction. This problem is considered in Chapter 20.

State v. Dietz, 59 Kan. 576, 53 Pac. 870 (1898), said that the constitution did not allow misdemeanor arrests without warrant "because the acts and language of an accused person are such as to induce the officer as a reasonable man to believe an offense has been or was about to be committed," but said nothing of when the belief is that an offense is being committed.

[42] The Kansas officer had both charged in police court on two counts; discharging a firearm and unlawful assembly. In the course of the trial it was determined which person had actually fired the weapon, and he was found guilty on both counts, while his companion was found guilty of unlawful assembly.

Whether the ordinance on unlawful assembly would cover the situation is unclear, but it seems unlikely. Clearly it would not if it is patterned after the state law, which requires three or more persons assembled with intent to do an unlawful act with force and violence against the person or property of another. Kan. Gen. Stat. §21-1001 (1949).

[43] All were charged with possession, but in court one of the four admitted that the slips were his. This man was therefore convicted and the others acquitted.

It may be that a felony arrest would be possible in this situation. While possession of policy slips is a misdemeanor in Michigan, where this offense occurred, Mich. Stat. Ann. §28.538 (1954), conspiracy to engage in gambling is a felony. The crime of conspiracy is not included in the Michigan code, but it is a common law offense, and by §28.773 an indictable common law offense is a felony. It has been held that this includes conspiracy. People v. Smith, 296 Mich. 176, 295 N.W. 605 (1941).

officer] cannot be mistaken as to the offender," [44] and the police are often instructed that such a limitation exists.[45] While neither Kansas nor Wisconsin law deals with this problem, the Michigan cases hold that the officer cannot lawfully make an arrest unless he can identify with certainty the offender.[46]

The wisdom of disallowing an arrest on this basis depends upon whether it is desirable to require the officer to obtain an arrest warrant. This issue is discussed in Chapter 1. When the officer can identify a small group within which the offender is known to be, and there is no other evidence as to the identity of the offender, it might be questioned whether the officer should be required to recite his observations to a magistrate before being entitled to make an arrest.[47] Also, when a bystander purports to know the precise identity of the offender, it might be asked whether the need for apprehension is so great that this bystander's veracity cannot first be tested by a magistrate.[48] However, such testing does not occur in current practice; if an immediate arrest is not made it is most likely that what the bystander told the officer will merely be reported to the magistrate who will decide whether to issue the warrant on the identical information available to the officer.

[44] 4 Wharton, Criminal Law and Procedure §1599 (Anderson ed. 1957). See also 1 Restatement of Torts §119, Comment m (1934), where it is said that in presence "means that the actor by the use of his senses knows that the other is committing the act . . ."

[45] Michigan police are instructed that an officer cannot make a misdemeanor arrest unless he "knows of his own knowledge, from his senses, and not from the statements of others that the party whom he arrests committed the act," Detroit Police Dept., Revised Police Manual, chap. 16, §16 (1955); Pontiac Police Dept., Rules & Regulations §219 (1941). For a similar provision in Milwaukee, see note 21 *supra*.

[46] Thus, in People v. Johnson, 86 Mich. 175, 48 N.W. 870 (1891), presence was found to be lacking where an officer heard boisterous shouting down the street but was unable to learn the identity of the offender without asking bystanders. In the earlier case of People v. Bartz, 53 Mich. 493, 19 N.W. 161 (1884), it was held that a discharge of a pistol on a dark night immediately across the street from the officer was in his presence. While language of the court indicated that it was sufficient if the officer was where he could have observed the offender, had it been light, the holding appears to be based on the fact that it was light enough for the officer to distinguish the form of the offender when the offense occurred and keep this form in sight until an arrest was made.

[47] The issue here is not unlike that of whether the "reasonable cause" norm for a felony arrest allows arrest of an entire group in which the offender is known to be. See page 259.

[48] It could be argued that the Johnson case, 86 Mich. 175, 48 N.W. 870 (1891), is not controlling on the kind of cases presented by the illustrations in the text, since there inquiry was made of bystanders.

CHAPTER 12

Felony Arrest: The "Reasonable Cause" Requirement

In Wisconsin and Kansas the felony arrest power has been left to common law development. In accord with the usual common law view found throughout the United States,[1] arrest without warrant is proper if the officer "has reasonable grounds to believe that a felony has been committed and that [the person to be arrested] participated in such felony." [2] Case law further defining this test, while available in Wisconsin, is largely lacking in Kansas. Prior to *Mapp v. Ohio*[3] Kansas did not have the exclusionary rule, and consequently its appellate court was seldom confronted with the necessity of deciding whether an arrest under given circumstances was proper. As has already been noted, false arrest actions seldom reach the appellate courts, and those that do are usually less satisfactory as an occasion for an explicit statement of the arrest norms[4] than are cases challenging the validity of a search made as an incident to an arrest.

---

[1] 4 Wharton, Criminal Law and Procedure §1596 (Anderson ed. 1957); A.L.I. Code of Criminal Procedure §21 (1931).

[2] Peloquin v. Hibner, 231 Wis. 77, 84, 285 N.W. 380, 384 (1939). The Wisconsin court on other occasions has expressed or quoted other verbal formulations undoubtedly intended to convey the same meaning. Some of these are: (1) "probable cause to believe or to suspect that [the arrestee] had participated in the commission" of a felony, Scaffido v. State, 215 Wis. 389, 392, 254 N.W. 651, 652 (1934); (2) "when the arresting officer has reasonable, probable cause to believe the person arrested has committed" a felony, State v. Phillips, 262 Wis. 303, 307, 55 N.W.2d 384, 386 (1952); (3) "a peace officer may arrest . . . one whom he has reasonable or probable grounds to suspect of having committed a felony," ibid., citing 6 C.J.S. Arrest §6 (1937); (4) an officer "may arrest any person whom he, upon reasonable ground, believes has committed a felony," ibid. citing 4 Am. Jur. Arrest §25 (1936).

The Kansas court held in Smith v. Hern, 102 Kan. 373, 375, 170 Pac. 990, 991 (1918): "An officer may arrest without a warrant where he has reasonable grounds to believe that a felony has been committed by the person arrested." This is the only Kansas holding on this point. Dictum in a prior case, Garnier v. Squires, 62 Kan. 321, 62 Pac. 1005 (1900), suggested this was the test, thereby clarifying a statement in an earlier case that an officer could arrest upon reasonable suspicion "in cases of felony actually committed." In re Kellam, 55 Kan. 700, 41 Pac. 960 (1895).

[3] 367 U.S. 643, 81 Sup. Ct. 1684, 6 L. Ed. 2d 1081 (1961).

[4] See page 412. On a similar statutory difficulty, see following footnote.

In Michigan, a statute provides that an officer may arrest a person without a warrant "when he has reasonable cause to believe that a felony has been committed and reasonable cause to believe that such person has committed it." [5] Notwithstanding the slightly different language, no deviation from the common law appears to be intended.[6] Many Michigan appellate cases add clarification to the statutory language.

Reasonable cause, then, is the requirement for a lawful felony arrest in each of the three states studied. It is important because it states not only the evidentiary standard for taking custody of a person, resulting in his loss of freedom and perhaps reputation, but also the standard governing the many searches which are conducted as an incident to an arrest. Despite its importance, however, the standard is not easy to define in terms which give explicit guidance to police under the wide variety of fact situations which arise. The question of what constitutes reasonable cause has been characterized as:

. . . one of those unclassified problems that is not a question of fact, in the sense that it is not an objectively appreciable proposition, and is not a question of law, in the sense that there are no standards or guides for its determination.[7]

It is not readily apparent whether the ambiguity in the meaning of reasonable cause results from the inevitable difficulty of giving specific content to a generalized requirement, from the existence of judicial procedures which afford appellate courts an occasion to consider some issues but not others, or from a deliberate attempt to leave lower courts and police sufficient flexibility to make appropriate decisions in the wide variety of factual situations which occur.

The objective of this and the following chapter is to show what content appellate courts have given the reasonable cause standard and also to describe the ways in which police have applied the

[5] Mich. Stat. Ann. §28.874(d) (1954). Some of the other sections of this statute apply to the felony arrest question but do not give any power beyond that quoted in the text. For example, subsection (a) allows arrest for felonies in the presence; subsection (c) for felonies in fact committed where the officer has reasonable cause to believe the person committed it; and subsections (e) and (f) refer to particular kinds of information which furnish reasonable cause, which will be dealt with later. Subsection (b) states that the officer may arrest "when such person has committed a felony although not in the presence of the officer." This is certainly broader than the power quoted in the text. However, since it says nothing about the nature of the evidence as it appears to the officer, but rather refers to the actual guilt of the arrestee, it seems appropriate to consider this not as an added power of arrest but as a possible source of defense in a false arrest action. As such, it is dealt with on page 414.

[6] Because no meaningful distinction is ordinarily made between "reasonable cause" and "reasonable grounds," the terms will be used interchangeably herein.

[7] Waite, Some Inadequacies in the Law of Arrest, 29 Mich. L. Rev. 448, 453 (1930).

standard in practice. An understanding of these issues is essential
to a determination of how much guidance the police have been
given and to an evaluation of the assertion that "what may constitute probable cause for arrest does not necessarily constitute
probable cause for a charge." [8]

The present chapter is concerned with some basic inquiries
about the meaning and application of the reasonable cause norm.
Chapter 13 considers this requirement in terms of the various
sources of information regularly utilized by the police in deciding
whether to make a felony arrest.

A. Fixed or Variable Test

One important question is whether the reasonable cause test
always requires the same amount of evidence or whether the
amount of evidence required varies, depending upon certain other
circumstances, such as the seriousness of the suspected offense.

Illustration No. 1: A county sheriff received an anonymous
call advising that a recent murder could be solved by questioning a certain person. The sheriff decided to arrest the
named person, though such a call would not, in itself, have
led to arrest in a less serious case.

If the seriousness of the offense committed is a consideration,
it might be said, for example, that a suspected murderer can be
arrested upon a lesser probability of guilt than a suspected gambler. The rationale of such a position is that a greater interference
with individual liberty is warranted if the crime is of a very serious
nature. Though addressing himself to the legality of a search,
Justice Jackson suggested this possibility when he said:

If we assume, for example, that a child is kidnapped and the officers throw a roadblock about the neighborhood and search every
outgoing car, it would be a drastic and undiscriminating use of
the search. The officers might be unable to show probable cause
for searching any particular car. However, I should candidly
strive hard to sustain such an action, executed fairly and in good
faith, because it might be reasonable to subject travelers to that
indignity if it was the only way to save a threatened life and detect a vicious crime. But I should not strain to sustain such a
roadblock and universal search to salvage a few bottles of bourbon
and catch a bootlegger.[9]

[8] Goldsmith v. United States, 277 F.2d 335, 345 (D.C. Cir. 1960).

[9] Brinegar v. United States, 338 U.S. 160, 183, 69 Sup. Ct. 1302, 1314, 93 L. Ed.
1879, 1894 (1949) (dissenting opinion).

Justice Jackson expressed a similar view in his concurring opinion in McDonald v.
United States, 335 U.S. 451, 459, 69 Sup. Ct. 191, 195, 93 L. Ed. 153, 160 (1948), where
he said: "whether there is reasonable necessity for a search [of premises] without

It is difficult to assess the police practice in this regard, but observation strongly suggests that the practice is to arrest upon less evidence when a serious offense is involved. However, this does not necessarily mean the police believe the standard to be flexible; there may be other reasons for their action.[10]

No court in any of the three states has expressly said that the nature of the crime affects the requirement of reasonable cause. While the Restatement of Torts lists this as a relevant factor,[11] express recognition by commentators[12] or courts[13] is most unusual. Nonetheless, it seems that the seriousness of the suspected offense does in fact influence courts' decisions. For example, the Michigan court has upheld an arrest for kidnapping made on the basis of an officer's observation of a car circling the block with the occupants "apparently closely watching all onlookers," [14] but has declared invalid an arrest for bootlegging made because the occu-

---

waiting to obtain a warrant certainly depends somewhat upon the gravity of the offense thought to be in progress." He observed that the offense in that case was only a gambling violation, which does not "involve . . . violence or threats of it," and further noted that most of the cases in which the Supreme Court held searches unlawful involved police action against acts malum prohibitum.

10 Police decisions to arrest on lesser evidence in serious cases may often be prompted by community pressure for action. For example, a Wichita officer indicated that public opinion was very strong regarding a group of robberies in which the responsible parties entered private homes and bound up the householders and took their valuables. He said "the heat was on" the department to make an arrest.

11 "The nature of the crime committed or feared, the chance of the escape of the one suspected, the harm to others to be anticipated if he escapes and the harm to him if he is arrested, are important factors to be considered in determining whether the actor's suspicion is sufficiently reasonable to confer upon him the privilege to make the arrest." 1 Restatement of Torts §119, Comment j (1934).

12 An exception is the following comment by Professor Caleb Foote: "If the police were reliably informed that a given crime was committed by a man fitting a certain description, and they could determine that there were in the vicinity 50 men answering that description, any one of these 50 would be the object of justified suspicion to the extent that it was much more probable than the average that he was guilty. Yet as the chances of guilt as to any one of these individuals would still be only one in 50, it would hardly seem proper to arrest all of them, in the hope that a process of interrogation at police headquarters would isolate the guilty person. In determining whether such drastic action would ever be reasonable, one would probably weigh the seriousness of the crime; a kidnapping where the life of the victim was at stake might be considered to warrant such greater invasion of personal liberty than would be the case in a routine burglary." Foote, Problems of the Protection of Human Rights in Criminal Law and Procedure (Santiago, Chile, May 19-30, 1958), U.N. Doc. TE 326/1 (40-2) LA, p. 36.

13 An exception is the following from United States v. Kancso, 252 F.2d 220 (2d Cir. 1958): "The word 'reasonable' is not to be construed in abstract or in a vacuum unrelated to field to which it applies . . . standards for arrest which might be reasonable for apprehension of bank robbers might not be reasonable for arrest of narcotics peddlers."

14 People v. Minchella, 268 Mich. 123, 255 N.W. 735 (1934), cert. denied, 293 U.S. 619, 294 U.S. 717 (1934), motion for writ denied, 297 U.S. 692 (1935). It remains questionable whether the court should have considered the serious nature of the offense here, however, as it is not clear that the arresting officer was aware of the kidnapping before the arrest.

pants of a car traveling very slowly looked back at the motorcycle officer who passed them.[15]   However, the extent to which the seriousness of the offense is a factor is left unarticulated.

Illustration No. 2: The police received a call from a woman in a hysterical condition.   She claimed that someone had tried to run her down with an automobile and had further threatened to kill her.   She was uncertain as to the identity of the person, and because of her hysteria was unclear on many of the details.   However, because of the imminent danger if the allegations were true, the police promptly arrested the suspect without further investigation into the charges.

A second factor which might affect the requirement of reasonable cause is the exigency of the situation, regarding either the risk of escape or the risk of further harm if an immediate arrest is not made.   It appears that the police do arrest on less evidence when immediate arrest appears desirable, such as when the suspect is leaving the jurisdiction, or when the suspect is thought to be carrying vital evidence.

Careful consideration of this factor by the courts and commentators is also lacking.[16]   However, the Michigan Supreme Court has indicated that in some cases such urgency will justify arrest on what would otherwise be insufficient evidence.   In one case the court said, in connection with a hypothetical case of a bank robber who could be expected to make a quick escape:

> If the officer must delay to ascertain that the information received comes from a responsible person, in many cases the opportunity to arrest will have passed.   That officers do make arrests on such information, and that they are complimented on their promptness in doing so, is a matter of common knowledge.[17]

The court has noted that "delay in arrest may endanger the public by permitting a felon to remain at large" or "may also permit his escape," [18] and further that there may be need for action without checking the story of the accuser (which might otherwise be necessary[19]), where further harm might be caused to the supposed victim if there were delay.[20]

Thus, in Michigan at least, the court has given explicit attention to the possible escape of the suspect, threat of harm to the public,

---

15 People v. Roach, 237 Mich. 215, 211 N.W. 742 (1927).

16 However, it is also listed as a significant factor by the Restatement.   See note 11 *supra.*

17 People v. Ward, 226 Mich. 45, 51, 196 N.W. 971, 972 (1924).

18 Leisure v. Hicks, 336 Mich. 148, 153, 57 N.W.2d 473, 476 (1953).

19 See pages 268 and 274.

20 Hammitt v. Straley, 338 Mich. 587, 61 N.W.2d 641 (1953).

and possible further harm to the victim.   Whether a court would give similar attention to the fact that the suspect might presently be carrying critical evidence is not clear.   The fact that evidence such as narcotics, illegal liquor, or policy slips might be destroyed if arrest is delayed in one sense presents an emergency situation. But recognition of this as a variable suggests that an arrest may be made upon less evidence where the real desire is to search, an unlikely position for a court to take.[21]   It is interesting to note, however, that in the Michigan case where the court used the hypothetical bank robber to illustrate a need for immediate arrest, the actual case involved a person suspected of carrying liquor.   His identity was known and there was no likelihood of escape or damage, but immediate arrest allowed the police to obtain the evidence of the offense.[22]

Illustration No. 3: A patrolman came upon a man walking in a residential neighborhood late at night. The community in question was experiencing a particularly serious wave of nighttime offenses. Although the man could identify himself, he did not live in that neighborhood, and his explanation for being there was equivocal. The officer placed him under arrest.

The requirement of "reasonable cause" has often been characterized by the courts as a balance between the needs of effective law enforcement and the interest of individual freedom.[23] It might therefore be concluded that a lesser quantity of evidence is needed to meet the reasonable cause test in an area where law enforcement agencies have a substantial and serious crime problem with which to deal.[24] As one leading police official has expressed it:

Now all people want complete security and complete liberty. This is impossible today. . . . [W]e are confronted with the question of how much must we sacrifice in liberty to assure a measure of security that is acceptable to a majority of people.

This, you see, is not a legal question. It is not a police question. It is a philosophical question that must be solved by statesmen. The scales of justice should be kept in balance with the security of

21 But see Ker v. California, 368 U.S. 974, 82 Sup. Ct. 480, 7 L. Ed. 2d 437 (1963). More detailed consideration of arrest when the dominant desire is to conduct a search will be found in the volume on Detection of Crime.

22 People v. Ward, 226 Mich. 45, 196 N.W. 971 (1924).

23 E.g., "The rule of probable cause is a practical, nontechnical conception affording the best compromise that has been found for accommodating these often opposing interests." Brinegar v. United States, 338 U.S. 160, 176, 69 Sup. Ct. 1302, 1314, 93 L. Ed. 1879, 1894 (1949).

24 We are now concerned with the general crime problem of a given community. The fact that a particular kind of crime is frequently committed in a specific locality may also be one item of evidence to be considered in finding reasonable cause.

the people on one pan and the liberties of the people on the other.

If you are living in a community where security is quite complete, where there is little criminality, then you can reduce the restrictions on liberty. But if you are in a society where security is in jeopardy . . . I think it is fair to say that the scales are out of adjustment, and that security is so low that our statesmen should give the police some greater authority, some greater privilege of arrest in order to restore balance.[25]

Whether such local conditions are relevant to the meaning of reasonable cause in a particular case is not clear. Courts in the three states have not expressly recognized such a factor.[26] But, in practice, arrests are more frequently made on a lesser amount of evidence in urban areas having a substantial crime problem.

B. Information to Be Considered

Illustration No. 4: A police officer noted that a transient staying at a local hotel strongly resembled a photograph of a man wanted by another department. The officer did not arrest immediately, but conducted further investigation at the hotel. The suspect had not registered in the name of the wanted man but had listed his home as being that of the wanted man. The hotel clerk also related some suspicious actions by the suspect, so the officer made an arrest. It was later learned that the suspect was not the man wanted and that he was innocent of any wrongdoing.

In determining whether an officer had reasonable grounds for arrest, the information to be considered is that information available to him at the time of arrest. Thus, what is to be considered is "knowledge of facts and circumstances" and not "the actual state of the case in point of fact, as it may turn out upon legal investigation." [27] For this reason, the later determined innocence or guilt of the arrested person does not decide the legality of the arrest.[28]

However, if an officer makes an arrest without first attempting

25 Statement by Police Supt. O. W. Wilson of Chicago, in Robert C. Nelson, A Police Chief Speaks, The Christian Science Monitor, May 16, 1960, Second Section, p. [9].

26 However, somewhat analogous is the recognition that in-custody investigation may gain added justification because of the unique problems of a large city. Bailey v. Loomis, 228 Mich. 338, 200 N.W. 148 (1934).

27 Odinetz v. Budds, 315 Mich. 512, 24 N.W.2d 193 (1946); State v. Cox, 258 Wis. 162, 167, 45 N.W.2d 100, 103 (1950).

28 This, however, should be contrasted with the possible defense in a false arrest action of actual guilt of the arrestee. See page 413. The possible existence of this defense should not be confused with the requirements of the "reasonable cause" norm.

to verify his information, his action may be considered improper. The Michigan court requires:

> [W]here there is an opportunity for inquiry and investigation, inquiry and investigation should be made. . . . An officer is not warranted in relying upon circumstances deemed by him suspicious, when the means are at hand of either verifying or dissipating those suspicions without risk, and he neglects to avail himself of those means.[29]

This, of course, does not imply that all investigation must be completed prior to arrest. The term "without risk" is critical. Seeking additional information against which to apply the "reasonable cause" norm would not seem necessary when in doing so "the opportunity to arrest will have passed," [30] or when there is threat of harm to the officer or others.

> *Illustration No. 5:* An informant disclosed to an officer that he had been told by an associate that a certain person was responsible for a recent holdup. Upon investigation, it was learned that the suspect had been convicted of such an offense in the past. The person was arrested.

In the trial of a criminal case, not all of the information available to the officer is necessarily admissible to prove the guilt of the accused. The hearsay rule, or other rules of evidence, may bar admission. But it is clear that it is not necessary for the officer to apply these evidentiary rules to the information he has in determining whether "reasonable cause" exists. Thus the officer may consider such things as the character of the suspect,[31] his past record,[32] and hearsay concerning the commission of the offense.[33] The United States Supreme Court, which has also upheld arrests where hearsay[34] and a prior police record [35] were considered, has said:

---

[29] Filer v. Smith, 96 Mich. 347, 354-355, 55 N.W. 999, 1002 (1893).

[30] Hammitt v. Straley, 338 Mich. 587, 594, 61 N.W.2d 641, 644 (1953).

[31] People v. Ward, 226 Mich. 45, 196 N.W. 971 (1924).

[32] Smith v. Hern, 102 Kan. 373, 170 Pac. 990 (1918).

[33] People v. Asta, 337 Mich. 590, 60 N.W.2d 472 (1953). In this case the court held that hearsay evidence was admissible at the preliminary examination for the purpose of showing that the officers were justified in making an arrest but not for the purpose of proving probable cause.

State v. Cox, 258 Wis. 162, 176, 45 N.W.2d 100, 107 (1950); Scaffido v. State, 215 Wis. 389, 254 N.W. 651 (1934). The dissenting judge in Cox said: "It does not seem to me to be logical to contend that an arrest can be justified if it is based only upon what an officer may have heard from others."

[34] Draper v. United States, 358 U.S. 307, 79 Sup. Ct. 329, 3 L. Ed. 2d 327 (1959). Justice Douglas, in his dissent, takes the position that hearsay might have been used if the informant had told the officer the basis for his suspicion.

[35] Brinegar v. United States, 338 U.S. 160, 183, 69 Sup. Ct. 1302, 1314, 93 L. Ed. 1879, 1894 (1949). Justice Jackson, in his dissent, takes the position that inadmissible evidence cannot alone establish probable cause.

For a variety of reasons relating not only to probative value and trustworthiness, but also to possible prejudicial effect upon a trial jury and the absence of opportunity for cross-examination, the generally accepted rules of evidence throw many exclusionary protections about one who is charged with and standing trial for crime. Much evidence of real and substantial probative value goes out on considerations irrelevant to its probative weight but relevant to possible misunderstanding or misuse by the jury. . . .

In dealing with probable cause, however, as the very name implies, we deal with probabilities. These are not technical; they are the factual and practical considerations of everyday life on which reasonable and prudent men, not legal technicians, act. The standard of proof is accordingly correlative to what must be proved.[36]

A similar issue may arise in connection with information which would be excluded at trial because it was illegally obtained. It is clear that the courts will not accept any circular reasoning whereby a search would be validated as incident to an arrest, the validity of which in turn depends upon what was found in the search.[37] But it is not clear what position a court might take if the question of the validity of this arrest should arise in another context. Consider this hypothetical case. An officer suspects a person of a recent armed robbery but lacks evidence to meet the "reasonable cause" test. He questions the suspect on the street, at which time he deems it advisable to conduct a frisk for his own protection. Because the frisk uncovers a distinctive weapon matching that used in the robbery, an arrest is made. If this information along with the prior suspicions would be sufficient to meet the "reasonable cause" test, but a frisk in that state is considered an illegal search,[38] is the officer justified in making an arrest? Can the arrestee recover for false arrest? If a full search

[36] 338 U.S. at 173, 175, 69 Sup. Ct. at 1309, 1310, 93 L. Ed. at 1889, 1890.

[37] "Had the officers made a legal arrest they would have been justified in their search of the defendant. Or had the officers made a legal search of the defendant they would have been justified in making an arrest upon finding defendant violating the law. But the officers did neither. . . . So, assuming that the arrest was made before the search, the arrest was illegal and the search following was illegal; or, assuming the search was made before the arrest, the search was illegal and the arrest based thereon without a warrant was illegal." Allen v. State, 183 Wis. 323, 333, 197 N.W. 808, 312 (1924). *Accord:* People v. Stewart, 232 Mich. 670, 206 N.W. 337 (1925). Kansas did not then have an exclusionary rule.

It is likewise clear that evidence cannot be considered legitimately obtained if knowledge of its existence resulted from the illegal search. Silverthorne Lumber Co. v. United States, 251 U.S. 385, 40 Sup. Ct. 182, 64 L. Ed. 319 (1920). This situation is likewise not contemplated in the hypothetical case following in the text.

[38] E.g., People v. DiDanna, 124 Misc. 872, 210 N.Y. Supp. 135 (Ct. Spec. Sess. 1925); People v. Esposito, 118 Misc. 867, 194 N.Y. Supp. 326 (Ct. Spec. Sess. 1922).

after arrest disclosed the property stolen, would this be admissible evidence?

This problem has not been dealt with by the courts in the jurisdictions studied and apparently has received little attention elsewhere.[39] While observations in the three states reveal that such situations do occur, the precise issue is not likely to reach a court. If a false arrest action were brought in such a situation, the usual defense would focus upon questions other than whether an officer should make an arrest in such circumstances.[40] Either the officer will allege that the arrest took place prior to the frisk or the court will assume that the frisk itself indicated that the arrest had already been made.[41]

While illegally obtained evidence may not be used to convict, it does not necessarily follow that it may not be used in determining who should be arrested. In the hypothetical case above, the victim may now identify the suspect and other evidence may be gathered which would result in conviction without direct use of the illegally seized weapon. But arrest might still be considered improper if the policy behind the exclusionary rule is to deprive the police of any benefit from the illegality. This is particularly so if the question becomes one of the admissibility of the stolen property found in the postarrest search. Though this issue is far from settled, the courts have hesitated to admit evidence to which the police were directed through prior illegal action unless the connection is "so attenuated as to dissipate the taint." [42] To a degree,

[39] But see second paragraph of note 37 *supra*.

[40] This is because the actual guilt of the arrestee is likely to be a defense. See page 413.

[41] Under different circumstances this defense would not be possible. The initial illegal search might be of the suspect's house in his absence, and the information thus obtained might lead to arrest, at which time evidence is found on his person.

See Somers v. United States, 138 F.2d 790 (2d Cir. 1943), where the search of the house did not supply the grounds for defendant's arrest, but only gave evidence of the fact that he would soon appear. The court held the evidence obtained during the subsequent search of the defendant's car, upon his arrival, was admissible only upon a showing that the officers would, in any case, have waited for the defendant's arrival.

[42] The quoted test is from Nardone v. United States, 308 U.S. 338, 341, 60 Sup. Ct. 266, 268, 84 L. Ed. 307, 312 (1939), where the prior illegality was interception of telephone messages. The same test has been applied where an illegal search directed officers elsewhere, Gregory v. United States, 231 F.2d 258 (D.C. Cir. 1956). For consideration of this general problem, see Maguire, Evidence of Guilt §5.07 (1959). See also Johnson v. United States, 333 U.S. 10, 68 Sup. Ct. 367, 92 L. Ed. 436 (1948), where it was held that a search of a hotel room was illegal because it was incident to an arrest which in turn was illegal because the officers had improperly gained entrance.

A similar problem may occur when the illegal search results in admissions by the suspect. For a definitive treatment of this problem, see Kamisar, Illegal Searches or Seizures and Contemporaneous Incriminating Statements: A Dialogue on a Neglected Area of Criminal Procedure, 1961 U. Ill. L.F. 78.

the propriety of the arrest may depend largely upon the court's view as to the propriety of admitting the evidence.[43]

C. SUBJECTIVE OR OBJECTIVE TEST

Illustration No. 6: An officer investigating a murder found that the assembled evidence made it highly probable that a particular person had committed the offense. The suspect was a long-time personal friend of the officer, and consequently the officer could not bring himself to believe that the suspect would commit such a crime. He nonetheless placed his friend under arrest.

The question arises whether an officer must believe the suspect committed the felony, or whether it is sufficient that adequate grounds exist for such a belief. Appellate courts have not infrequently said that the officer must believe in the guilt of the suspect.[44] Yet the Michigan statute, identical to those found in many states, suggests an objective test — "reasonable cause to believe." [45] The common law power has also been stated as an objective test.[46]

Some arrests may occur where reasonable grounds exist but the officer does not actually believe the suspect to be guilty.[47] Under-

---

[43] In this connection courts often erroneously assume that the right to arrest must necessarily carry with it a right to search. For one consequence of such an assumption, see Note, 1959 Wis. L. Rev. 347.

[44] E.g., "The rule is pretty well settled that if an officer believes, and has good reason to believe, that one has committed a felony . . . he has probable cause." People v. Licavoli, 245 Mich. 202, 203, 222 N.W. 102 (1928). "But no one, whether private person or officer, has any right to make an arrest without warrant in the absence of actual belief, based on actual facts creating probable cause of guilt." People v. Burt, 51 Mich. 199, 202, 16 N.W. 378, 379 (1883). In State v. Phillips, 262 Wis. 303, 55 N.W.2d 384 (1952), the court, after earlier indicating that the test was whether reasonable men would believe, then quoted language to the effect that the officer could arrest when "he, upon reasonable grounds, believes," and went on to decide that the arrest in question was valid because "the detective's belief" was supported by the evidence.

[45] Mich. Stat. Ann. §28.874(d) (1954). Also, one recent Michigan case, quoting from prior opinions, emphasized that the statutory test was whether there were "circumstances sufficiently strong in themselves to warrant a cautious man in believing," or whether there were "facts which would induce any fair-minded man of average intelligence and judgment to believe." Hammitt v. Straley, 338 Mich. 587, 594, 595, 61 N.W.2d 641, 644, 645 (1953).

[46] "An officer may arrest . . . without a warrant where [he] has reasonable grounds to believe . . . ." Smith v. Hern, 102 Kan. 373, 170 Pac. 990 (1918). The Wisconsin court said the test was whether there were "circumstances sufficiently strong in themselves to warrant a cautious man in believing the accused guilty." State v. Cox, 258 Wis. 162, 45 N.W.2d 100 (1950).

[47] Thus, "it may happen that the officer arrests because there is evidence on which a reasonable man would think it proper to arrest, though actually he himself does not believe that the suspect committed the crime — for example, because he knows that the suspect is a man of excellent character and cannot bring himself to believe

such circumstances, it has been said that "the duty of the officer is to proceed on the facts as they would appear to a reasonable man; he ought not to be required to pledge his personal opinion." [48] The general failure of the courts to consider the objective-subjective distinction has not caused serious difficulty.   Usually it is assumed that the officer did believe, and the court's attention is focused upon whether his belief was reasonable under the objective test.[49]   The question is not what the state of mind of the arresting officer was, but instead whether a reasonable man would have grounds to believe the arrested person guilty.   Likewise, it is important that officers recognize that the information must be sufficient to induce a state of belief in a reasonable man and that actual belief on their part is not necessarily sufficient.

D. EXPERIENCE OF THE OFFICER

Illustration No. 7: An officer with considerable experience on the narcotics squad smelled an odor coming from a particular apartment.   Because of his experience, he was able to identify the odor as being that of burning opium.   He entered the apartment and placed the occupant under arrest.

In tort law the special skills of the person are taken into account in determining whether his action was reasonable,[50] and it would seem that this should also be true in the case of arrest by a police officer.   The Michigan court has found reasonable cause to exist only after noting that the officer was possessed of skills and experience not held by the average person,[51] and the Wisconsin court has

---

the evidence against him."   Williams, Arrest for Felony at Common Law, 1954 Crim. L. Rev. (Eng.) 408, 417.

[48] Id. at 418.

[49] Perhaps the objective-subjective distinction has further significance, however. The Restatement takes the position that "it is not necessary that the actor shall believe that the other is guilty of the felony," and concludes that if belief of the actor were required only one suspect could be arrested.   1 Restatement of Torts §119, Comment j (1934).   See page 259.

[50] 2 Harper and James, Torts 919 (1956).   However, it should be noted that the reference to the skills of the particular arresting officer are likely to validate an arrest which would otherwise be invalid.   In the torts area, reference to these superior skills usually results in liability which would otherwise not result.

Considering the special skills of the officer also has an analogy in evidence law. An officer, because of his special skills, may be allowed to estimate what has occurred on the basis of physical facts observed after the occurrence.   White v. Zutell, 263 F.2d 613 (2d. Cir. 1959).

[51] In People v. Bommarito, 309 Mich. 139, 142, 14 N.W.2d 812, 813 (1944), the court carefully noted that the officer observed equipment "which he knew, from his experience as a police officer, was used in the policy, numbers, and mutuel business." In People v. Bartoletta, 248 Mich. 499, 500, 501, 227 N.W. 763 (1929), the court made special reference to the testimony of the arresting officers: "During my four years

made a similar observation.[52]   Consideration of special skill may also be a limiting factor.   An experienced officer may be held to have arrested illegally because a man with his skill should have concluded that grounds for arrest were lacking.[53]

E. Extent of Belief as to Felony

A police officer may not be absolutely certain that a felony has been committed either because of uncertainty as to whether certain known conduct constitutes a felony or because the information at hand does not clearly establish that conduct known to be felonious has occurred.   As discussed earlier,[54] in the former case the officer is left no margin of error; he must be certain of the meaning of the relevant substantive law.   However, it is no

---

as an officer, I have seen many burlap sacks, perhaps 1,000 or more, similar to the burlap sacks in this case and found that they contained beer. . . .   I had seen quite a number of similar burlap bags before that night and on previous experience had found that similar bags contained Canadian beer or ale."

Strong dissents in some other cases have berated the majority for failure to take into account the officers' training and experience, suggesting that these factors are not always considered.   People v. Stein, 265 Mich. 610, 251 N.W. 788 (1933); People v. Roache, 237 Mich. 215, 211 N.W. 742 (1927).   However, both of these cases involved situations of suspicious actions on the part of the defendants, suggesting that special skills and experience may not be accepted by the court as a basis for breaching the gap between generally suspicious conduct and conduct suggesting a particular felony.

52 Thus a search warrant was valid where based upon a report of the smell of mash by an officer who was experienced in enforcing the law against illicit liquor and therefore recognized this smell.   State v. Brockman, 231 Wis. 634, 285 N.W. 380 (1939).   In a similar case, State v. Harris, 256 Wis. 93, 100-101, 39 N.W.2d 912, 916 (1949), the court said: ". . . but the idea that a trained, experienced police officer may not state his conclusions from what he saw, heard, and smelled, the facts being stated, is certainly a novel one.   There would be little merit in securing able, trained men to guard the public peace if they could not conclude from what they saw, heard, and smelled, that the law was being violated."

53 This is similar to the notion in tort law that a reasonable man must be considered to possess the skills of the actor and also the skills which competent persons in the actor's line of activity possess.   2 Harper and James, Torts 917, 919 (1956).

In Jewell v. Hempleman, 210 Wis. 265, 268, 270, 246 N.W. 441, 442, 443 (1933), it appeared that a jury imposed liability for failure to use special skills possessed.   A conservation warden made an arrest for possession of part of a deer carcass during closed season.   The warden "testified that he had had a rather extended experience as a conservation warden, had seen lots of venison and deer bones, and was familiar with and knew the difference in texture, color, size of bones, etc., between venison and beef [which the meat turned out to be]; that after looking at the meat in the milkhouse and without cutting it up or particularly examining it he had considered it venison."   The appellate court concluded that "the jury might well have concluded that [the warden's] examination of the meat was, to say the least, cursory and careless, that his conclusion was a hasty one, and that as an experienced warden he did not act prudently."

54 See page 86.

longer required that the police be absolutely certain about what conduct the suspect actually engaged in.[55]

Police often are certain that a felony has been committed because they directly observe the offense, or the results of the offense, and they are uncertain only as to the identity of the offender. But frequently situations do arise in which it is difficult to know whether a felony has been committed at all. Usually these are cases in which the officer observes actions of a suspicious nature. He may, because of the suspicious actions of a person, conclude either that the suspect has probably committed or is committing some felony, or that the suspect has committed a particular kind of felony (perhaps not yet reported to the police).

> *Illustration No. 8:* In a residential neighborhood officers in a patrol car observed a car approaching very slowly. When the car passed the patrol car the occupants looked back, apparently to see if they were being observed by the police. The patrol car then turned around and passed the other vehicle, at which point one of the occupants was observed thrusting something under the seat. The police stopped the car and placed the occupants under arrest.

Actions which are only generally suspicious and which do not suggest a particular type of felony are apparently insufficient to justify arrest. The Michigan court has considered this question on more than one occasion, holding such conduct as looking back at a passing police car,[56] refusing to submit to search,[57] or hiding something under a car seat[58] insufficient for arrest. Yet it is clear that arrests are often made upon information which gives no greater indication of a specific offense than do these actions. If the result is in fact the apprehension of a person responsible for a serious offense, there seems to be a tendency to hold the arrest valid.[59]

---

55 In earlier times, no distinction between the arrest powers of a citizen and officer was recognized in this regard. Even today a citizen may arrest only for a felony in fact committed, and it was not made clear that a lesser standard applied to peace officers until 1827. For an excellent review of this development in the law, see Hall, Legal and Social Aspects of Arrest Without a Warrant, 49 Harv. L. Rev. 566 (1936).

56 People v. Roache, 237 Mich. 215, 211 N.W. 742 (1927).

57 People v. Lansing Municipal Judge, 327 Mich. 410, 42 N.W.2d 120 (1950).

58 People v. Stein, 265 Mich. 610, 251 N.W. 788 (1933).

59 For example, the Michigan court held legal an arrest made solely on the basis that an officer had observed a car continually circling the block with the occupants "apparently closely watching all onlookers." People v. Minchella, 268 Mich. 123, 129, 225 N.W. 735, 737 (1934), *cert. denied*, 293 U.S. 619, 294 U.S. 717 (1934), *motion for writ denied*, 297 U.S. 692 (1935). The court did not indicate what felony this conduct reasonably suggested; the actual crime later discovered was a kidnapping of which the arresting officer was not aware at the time.

Illustration No. 9: A patrolman observed a man walking slowly down a lonely street at night looking in the windows of parked cars. A number of unsolved thefts of and from cars had recently occurred. The officer placed the man under arrest so that he could be investigated concerning these offenses.

The police not infrequently observe conduct which leads them to suspect a certain type of felony, although the suspect is not linked with any specific offense. Thus persons prowling in a residential neighborhood late at night may be arrested as burglary suspects and persons looking into parked cars may be arrested as suspected car thieves. No case in any of the three states suggests that it is necessary to link the suspect with some specific past offense. Often the suspicious actions justify the conclusion that an offense is presently occurring, so that no such problem arises.[60]

The Wisconsin court has said that the suspect's actions must be "inconsistent with any innocent pursuit." [61] This is a strict test, and there may well be other factors which, if present, will justify arrest on a less clear indication. One qualification recognized by implication by the Wisconsin court is that if the suspect or his associates have been identified as previously having engaged in criminal conduct, then the fact that the present suspicious actions are not "inconsistent with any innocent pursuit" does not prevent arrest if these actions are also not inconsistent with the renewed pursuit of the criminal conduct.[62] However, the case law on this point is inconclusive in all three states.

[60] Thus, in People v. Schaub, 279 Mich. 457, 460, 464, 272 N.W. 867, 869, 870 (1937), an equally divided court upheld the arrest of two men, although it was made solely on the basis that the men had parked their car late at night in a residential section in which they admitted they did not live, and had been observed hiding something as they saw the police approach. The opinion for affirmance said: "I think the acts of the defendants, after they knew the officers were interested in the car, afforded reasonable belief by the officers that the occupants were either illegally armed or were attempting to conceal criminal goods. This would justify the officers in making a prompt arrest . . ." One opinion for reversal objected that the officer made the arrest on "mere and indefinite suspicion, not directed to any offense."

[61] State v. Leadbetter, 210 Wis. 327, 333, 246 N.W. 443, 445 (1933). The question in this case was whether a conservation warden had the right to make a search under a statute allowing such action upon "reason to believe." Such a test would explain another case, in which an arrest was held improper because knowledge that the defendant was holding a stag party at his home with admission by ticket was said not to allow a conclusion that there would be lewd dancing. Mantei v. State, 210 Wis. 1, 245 N.W. 683 (1932).

[62] For example, in State v. Cox, 258 Wis. 162, 45 N.W.2d 100 (1950), the dissent observed that Cox was arrested solely on the grounds that the officer had seen him driving an auto in which there were trousers in an unfinished state along with a considerable amount of other clothing, which was clearly not inconsistent with an innocent pursuit. However, the majority held the arrest legal, taking careful note that Cox had been seen, immediately preceding the arrest, in the company of two persons who had engaged in shoplifting a few years earlier.

F. EXTENT OF BELIEF THAT THE SUSPECT IS THE OFFENDER

Mere suspicion of a person does not justify arrest.[63] Therefore the fact that the information at hand makes one person a more likely suspect than any other known suspect is not necessarily sufficient for arrest. However, it is not necessary that the information be such as to justify belief beyond a reasonable doubt, which is the requirement for conviction.[64] The Wisconsin court has said that the information must be such that "reasonable men would conclude that in all probability" the suspect is the perpetrator.[65] However, the degree of probability required cannot be stated categorically.

Illustration No. 10: A reliable informant reported to the narcotics bureau of a police department that a Mexican presently staying at a particular hotel in the city had a large quantity of marijuana with him. Detectives were dispatched to the hotel, and from examination of the hotel register and interrogation of the clerk they learned that there were two Mexicans presently staying there. Only one was present at the time, and he was arrested, although there was no evidence making him a more likely suspect than the other Mexican.

Illustration No. 11: A householder called the police to report that a burglar had just been observed leaving his residence. The witness stated that the burglar was a Negro, but could give only a general description. Police went to the scene and arrested four Negroes found in the area who fitted this description.

The necessary amount of information connecting a suspect with a crime is of critical importance in cases in which the police know of a number of suspects who fit a general description given by a victim or informant. The basic question is when, if ever, it is permissible to arrest a group of suspects, or one suspect from a group of suspects, when it reasonably appears that the actual offender is within the group. The use of the "dragnet" arrest, which is clearly illegal, is a more indiscriminate practice than the one be-

---

[63] "Facts which warrant nothing but a suspicion are not sufficient," State v. Johnson, 210 Wis. 334, 336, 246 N.W. 446 (1933). "[T]here must be at the time in the possession of the officer information which goes beyond suspicion," State v. Cox, 258 Wis. 162, 166-167, 45 N.W.2d 100, 103 (1950). See also People v. Miller, 245 Mich. 115, 222 N.W. 151 (1928).

[64] This is consistent with the rule that an arrest on reasonable grounds to believe need not be justified by a later conviction. See, for example, Bursack v. Davis, 199 Wis. 115, 225 N.W. 738 (1929).

[65] State v. Phillips, 262 Wis. 303, 307, 55 N.W.2d 384, 386 (1952).

ing discussed here. The following situations, reported elsewhere, aid in understanding the dilemma of the police in this kind of case:

(1) "A sees B and C bending over a dead man D. B and C each accuse the other of murdering D. A is not sure that either B or C did the killing, but he has a reasonable suspicion that either B or C killed D." The Restatement of Torts adds: "A is privileged to arrest either or both." [66]

(2) X has been the victim of an armed robbery. He reports the matter to the police, who ask him to review photographs in their files of all persons who have used a similar modus operandi in the past. X, after study of the police files, cannot make up his mind between the photographs of Y and Z. The police pick up both Y and Z for inclusion in a lineup before X.[67]

(3) A patrolman fired at two burglars, but they escaped on foot. The only description he could give over the police radio was that both were young and both wore blue sweaters. A cordon was thrown around the area, and three cars joined in the search. The police arrested seven young men in blue sweaters within four blocks of the incident. At the station the patrolman picked out the two burglars, and the other five were released.[68]

(4) A rape occurred in the basement of an apartment house. The rapist was masked, and the victim could only report that the offender was a Negro of a certain build. Living in a basement apartment there were the Negro janitor, his wife, two grown sons, a younger son, and his half brother. The two grown sons and the half brother all fitted the general description. It did not appear likely that any other persons could obtain access to the basement. The three suspects were arrested.[69]

Arrests of several suspects for a crime committed by only one person are not infrequent occurrences in current criminal justice administration,[70] but the appellate courts of the jurisdictions

---

[66] 1 Restatement of Torts §119, Illustration 2 (1934).

[67] This is substantially the hypothetical case presented by Glanville Williams in his article, Questioning by the Police: Some Practical Considerations, 1960 Crim. L. Rev. (Eng.) 325, 334. He points out: "An arrest supposes that a charge is made and that the accused will be brought before a magistrate as the first step in legal proceedings. But it would be improper to bring a man before a magistrate merely with the evidence that either he or someone else committed the crime. The machinery of arrest is inappropriate until suspicion has been focused on a single person."

[68] This instance was observed by Sam Bass Warner while riding as an observer with police squads. See Warner, Investigating the Law of Arrest, 26 A.B.A.J. 151, 155 (1940).

[69] This was the fact situation in Mallory v. United States, 354 U.S. 449, 77 Sup. Ct. 1356, 1 L. Ed. 2d 1479 (1957).

[70] Multiple arrests in a variety of circumstances are frequently reported by the press, as they are most apt to occur with regard to a single serious offense or a series of offenses of public concern. For instance:

studied have not had occasion to rule on their validity. There appears to be a scarcity of authority on this point in the United States as a whole, although the *Mallory* case may be interpreted as prohibiting such arrests by federal officers.[71] *Mallory* aside, commentators who assert that the police are acting illegally when they arrest more than one suspect[72] and those taking the contrary position[73] rarely cite case authority.

In Milwaukee, a community was aroused by a wave of assaults upon women on the streets late at night. All of the victims identified their assailant as being a Negro between twenty and thirty years of age. In each case the woman had been dragged into a car. These offenses occurred between April of 1956 and January of 1957. In January approximately 140 Negroes were arrested by the police for inclusion in lineups to be viewed by the victims. Milwaukee Journal, Sept. 1, 1959, pt. 1, p. 1, col. 4.

The victim of a brutal attack in Milwaukee told the police, just before her death, that her assailant had been a "big white man" who said he "worked around bridges." Having only this description, and unaided by any physical evidence, the police arrested eight men for questioning. Milwaukee Journal, April 26, 1960, pt. 1, p. 1, col. 2.

71 The court in Mallory said: "Nor is there an escape from the constraint laid upon the police by that Rule [requiring appearance before a commissioner 'without unnecessary delay'] in that two other suspects were involved for the same crime. Presumably, whomever the police arrest they must arrest on 'probable cause.' It is not the function of the police to arrest, as it were, at large and to use an interrogating process at police headquarters in order to determine whom they should charge before a committing magistrate on 'probable cause.'" Mallory v. United States, 354 U.S. 449, 456, 77 Sup. Ct. 1356, 1360, 1 L. Ed. 2d 1479, 1484 (1957).

The facts of Mallory are reported in the text at note 69. One professor says of the case: "Remember that in the Mallory case the police suspicions extended also to the defendant's two nephews, and they were arrested and detained four hours without the slightest shadow of justification." Letter from J. D. O'Reilly, Boston College Law School, in Hearings on Confessions and Police Detention before the Subcommittee on Constitutional Rights of the Senate Committee on the Judiciary, 85th Cong., 2d Sess. 481 (1958). Thus the Mallory case is said to require evidence sufficient to charge one and only one person prior to arrest. Statement of National Bar Assn., id. at 179. Similarly, the president of the Washington Bar Assn. took the position that the "probable cause" arrest norm on the federal level prohibits arrest of more than one person for a crime committed by a single person. Hearings on H.R. 11477, S. 2970, S. 3325, and S. 3355 before Subcommittee of the Senate Committee on the Judiciary, 85th Cong., 2d Sess. 110-113 (1958).

72 Professor Waite, commenting on the famous Degnan murder case in Chicago, where two janitors were held for questioning, says: "As the news accounts make rather clear that no one supposed the two janitors had cooperated, but that if one was guilty the other was not, it would be extremely difficult to justify *both* arrests on this ground of reasonable belief in the arrestee's guilt." Waite, The Law of Arrest, 24 Texas L. Rev. 279, 297 (1949).

As to the English view, Glanville Williams, in reporting the case of seven suspects arrested, says that arrest is inappropriate until suspicion has been focused on a single person. This, he adds, seems to show "the need for some power of detention for evidentiary purposes on reasonable suspicion, distinct from the power of arrest." Williams, Questioning by the Police: Some Practical Considerations, 1960 Crim. L. Rev. (Eng.) 325, 334.

73 Concerning Mallory it has been said: "In that case there were three suspects. There was reasonable ground to arrest every one of them. After an interrogation of each of the three, two were cleared within a few hours and the third was held."

If the requirement of law is that the person arrested be more probably guilty than any other suspect, then more than one person obviously cannot properly be arrested. But, if the test is whether a reasonable man could believe the person guilty, an arrest of more than one person may be proper if there is a sufficient evidentiary link between the offense and each of the suspects.[74] The latter view probably would be accepted by most state courts, at least in some circumstances.

Other factors may be important in determining the validity of multiple arrests in a given situation. The degree of certainty that the actual offender is within the group would seem relevant, along with the size of the group.[75] The seriousness of the offense may affect the result.[76] Also of importance is the need for immediate action, as where two persons of unknown identity are running from the scene of a crime. The available means of postarrest selection may also be a deciding factor. For example, the arrest of three suspects to enable a witness to view them in a lineup may be less objectionable than the arrest of the same number for interrogation.[77] This is one interpretation of the restrictions imposed by the *Mallory* case on federal officers.[78]

Statement of the Honorable Alexander Holtzoff, U.S. district judge for the District of Columbia, in Hearings on Confessions and Police Detention before the Subcommittee on Constitutional Rights of the Senate Committee on the Judiciary, 85th Cong., 2d Sess. 4-5 (1958). Compare this with the situations presented in note 70 *supra*.

Perkins writes that reasonable cause requires only "grounds sufficient to induce a reasonably prudent man to believe the arrestee guilty of the crime for which the arrest is made or to cause him to believe there is likelihood of such guilt. The latter qualification is sufficient to permit an officer to arrest two persons, for example, if he has reason to believe a felony has been committed by one or the other." Perkins, The Law of Arrest, 25 Iowa L. Rev. 201, 238 (1940). In support he cites the Restatement of Torts.

[74] Thus the Restatement observes that the actor need not actually believe, because if that were the requirement, then "neither of two men could be lawfully arrested for a crime . . . although it is clear at the time of the arrest that one of them is guilty." 1 Restatement of Torts §119, Comment j (1934).

[75] Arrest of a large group would appear to make it very questionable whether there is an adequate connecting link between the crime and any one of the arrestees. In Bailey v. Loomis, 228 Mich. 338, 200 N.W. 148 (1924), the Michigan court held that the arrest of other suspects was admissible evidence in a false arrest suit. The court's theory was that such evidence was relevant to show that the defendant-officer had committed the act alleged, where the arrest was part of a pre-existing plan to bring in a number of persons for questioning. No mention was made of this evidence bearing upon the question of whether the officer had complied with the "reasonable cause" norm.

[76] See note 12 *supra* page 247.

[77] That is, the reasonableness of the detention may vary depending upon the nature and extent of the invasion of individual freedom involved. For a similar view as to other police actions, see Barrett, Personal Rights, Property Rights, and the Fourth Amendment, 1960 Sup. Ct. Rev. 46, 63-64.

[78] See detailed discussion on page 384, n.24, and page 434.

Would the problem differ if there were separate arrests of suspects matching the offender's description by two officers, each unaware of the other's action? It would seem difficult to label this a violation of the "reasonable cause" standard, since, if this were so, it would be impossible to insure compliance with the norm unless only one officer were given authority to make an arrest with respect to a given outstanding crime. Because there is no greater invasion of individual liberty when both arrests are made by a single officer than when the arrests are made by different officers, it might be argued that the former practice is also proper. Or it might be said that both instance are undesirable invasions of individual liberties, but that arrests by different officers must be allowed because organizational factors do not permit for any alternative.

G. Problems in Theory and in Practice

Despite the relative frequency of reported cases dealing with the evidentiary requirements for arrest, a great deal of ambiguity remains in regard to some prevalent and important police arrest practices. Police regularly require less evidence when certain factors, such as the seriousness of the offense, the exigencies of the situation, or the local crime problem, seem to so dictate. But there is only limited judicial attention to whether arrest on less evidence may be justified by the risk of escape or harm to another, or to the relevance of the seriousness of the offense or the existence of a serious local crime problem. Also, while it is not uncommon for the police to arrest more than one suspect when it is apparent that only one offender is involved, courts have not said when, if ever, such action is lawful. Courts, particularly in Michigan, have said that arrests based solely on the furtive actions of persons in the presence of the police are not proper. Yet this remains a common police practice. It is fair to say that one of the major issues in current criminal justice administration concerns what police must observe in order to make a proper arrest or to stop and question a person under generally suspicious circumstances. This issue is considered in more detail later.[79]

Uncertainty relating to the evidentiary requirements for arrest in comparison with those for charging makes more difficult an adequate analysis of the role of in-custody interrogation under current criminal justice systems sanctioned by law. This issue is discussed in detail in a subsequent chapter.[80] To the extent that

[79] See pages 295 and 344.
[80] See page 324.

arrest of more than one suspect, arrest upon hearsay, or arrest on little evidence when there is a need for immediate action is proper, it would appear that arrests can be made on less evidence than that required for charging. If this is an accurate appraisal of existing systems, one must then confront the problem of how enforcement officers may properly acquire the additional evidence necessary to decide whether to charge a person already in custody.

CHAPTER 13

Felony Arrest: Sources of Information

Police, in making felony arrests, rely upon information derived from a number of different sources. Among these are physical evidence, a victim or witness to an offense, an informant, the past record of the suspect, the police agency itself or another enforcement agency, direct observation of suspicious circumstances, or a combination of these sources.

Legislatures have seldom attempted to deal explicitly with certain kinds and sources of information and have not therefore provided guidance as to when such information is sufficient to justify an arrest. Most existing arrest law has developed from criminal cases in which defendants have attempted to suppress critical physical evidence obtained incident to arrest. Thus courts have had many opportunities to deal with questions concerning those sources which usually lead to the discovery of such evidence, such as informants in narcotics cases, but little, if any, occasion to deal with others. Hence the reliability of an informant has received considerable attention, while little is to be found regarding the veracity of a person claiming to be the victim of an offense.

The objectives of this chapter, as of the previous chapter, are to determine how much specific guidance the police have been afforded concerning recurring kinds of cases, to discover the areas of conflict between the existing legal norms and current practice, and to provide a basis for comparing the evidentiary requirements for arresting and charging a suspect.

A. Arrest on the Basis of Information from an Informant

Illustration No. 1: The police were told by an informant that a particular worker in an automobile plant would bring marijuana into the plant on a given date in an automobile of a particular description and license number. This informant had provided tips on previous occasions, and his information had been found reliable. Officers set up a stakeout and arrested the suspect when he appeared at the time predicted in the described vehicle.

Illustration No. 2: The police received a call from an informant known to them as a reliable source of information. He stated that on a given day a car of a particular description and license number would be driven into the city by one of either of two routes, and would be carrying illegal liquor. The two roads were watched on the given day and when the described vehicle appeared it was stopped and the driver was placed under arrest.

Illustration No. 3: The police received a telephone call from a man who refused to identify himself. He said that a man of a given description could be found on a certain street carrying a large black suitcase which contained narcotics. Officers were dispatched to the scene and arrested a man fitting the description.

Police frequently receive information from informers that a crime has been committed, is being committed, or will be committed at a particular place or by a particular person. Paid informants are often employed, particularly in narcotics enforcement, and to a lesser degree with respect to liquor and gambling offenses.[1] In addition, the police sometimes receive information from anonymous sources, either by telephone or by letter, usually concerning vice offenses.

There are two situations involving informants which are not dealt with in detail in this chapter. In some cases, especially where the reliability of the informant is in doubt, the information received is used not as a basis for arrest but only as a basis for further investigation of a person or place. If an arrest is later made, it is upon the basis of information developed during the investigation.[2] The reliability of the evidence in such a situation depends upon the adequacy of the investigation. In other cases the informant is an undercover agent and the arrest is based upon police observation of a transaction between the informant and another person.[3]

---

[1] See page 133.

[2] For example, in Detroit a mentally retarded informant told the police of the existence of a "blind pig," but the officers decided to arrest only if the investigation (knocking on the door and asking for a drink) confirmed the information. Treatment of this situation will be found in the volume on Detection of Crime.

[3] For example, narcotics officers often have their informant arrange for a "buy." The informant is thoroughly searched to make certain he does not possess narcotics, is given marked bills, and then is observed meeting the suspect. The arrest is based on the fact that the informant is searched again after the meeting and found to possess narcotics. This elaborate procedure is resorted to not because the police demand a high probability of guilt in these cases, but rather because in this manner

In this case the reliability of the evidence depends upon the accuracy of the police observations.

Primary attention in this chapter is given to cases in which police, after receiving information from an informant (usually concerning a continuing course of conduct or conduct to occur in the future), make an arrest on the basis of this information alone or in conjunction with other circumstantial evidence which alone would not have resulted in arrest. In this situation, the adequacy of the evidence depends on the completeness of the information received and on the important factor of the reliability of the informant.

1. *Completeness of the information.* Assuming the reliability of the informant, the police must consider whether the information is sufficiently complete to provide reasonable cause to believe that a felony has been, is being, or will be committed by a particular person. In a Michigan informant case the court said that the officer could not have made an arrest had the information been "in the nature of a mere rumor," as opposed to "when he is informed in positive terms that a crime has been committed by an individual, naming him." [4]

Information provided by informants is usually adequate in this respect because the informant usually makes a flat statement that a named person has committed or will commit a crime. Most often the informant gives information about a crime which will be committed in the future, as in the illustrations above. The assertion that a certain event will happen is usually made without any reasons being given as to why the informant thinks it will happen.[5] If the offender cannot be named, the informant is usually able to give a good description. Only occasionally is the information not specific enough for the police to focus upon one suspect. For example, one informant merely stated that a Mexi-

---

they are allowed to present the case in court without bringing in or disclosing the identity of their informant. Disclosure of the identity of the informant is not usually required where the probable cause for the search may be established independently. See Annot., Accused's Right to, and Prosecution's Privilege Against, Disclosure of Identity of Informer, 76 A.L.R.2d 262 (1961). While an accused is entitled to disclosure of the identity of an informer who participated in the offense, id. at 313, the usual practice is to charge with possession rather than sale, which apparently obviates this difficulty.

4 People v. Ward, 226 Mich. 45, 52, 196 N.W. 971, 972 (1924).

5 If the informant identifies the person and indicates he is or will be engaged in certain criminal conduct, the information is complete enough if reliability is otherwise established. That disclosure of the underlying facts or basis for the informant's assertions relates to the matter of reliability rather than to completeness of the information is supported by Draper v. United States, 358 U.S. 307, 79 Sup. Ct. 312, 3 L. Ed. 2d 298 (1959), where the court upheld an arrest based upon the word of an informer, although he did not disclose his grounds, only when they found the informer's reliability to be established by police confirmation of some predicted events.

can man, staying at a certain hotel, possessed marijuana, without further identifying the suspect.[6]

A lack of complete and specific information is most likely in cases involving anonymous letters and telephone calls, as they usually consist of reports of rumors or general reputation rather than a direct assertion that a crime has been or will be committed. This may in part explain the reluctance of the police to act in these cases, although the anonymity of the informant also casts doubt on his reliability.   But where an anonymous letter does give detailed information the police do not hesitate to make an arrest.

In the relatively infrequent case where the informant names the perpetrator of a past reported crime, more information is usually required by the police than when the informant tells them that a crime will be committed.   Because it is unusual for the informer to have been an actual witness to the offense,[7] the police usually ask these informants to give some indication of the basis for their suspicion.   However, the police may arrest upon less than a direct accusation without any further explanation when a serious crime is involved.[8]

The appellate courts of the jurisdictions studied have not indicated how indirect the informer's knowledge may be and still meet the reasonable cause test.[9]

2. *Reliability of the informant.*   By far the more serious problem with regard to the use of informants is that of determining when they can be considered sufficiently reliable to justify arrest of the person named.   Except for the public-spirited citizen, persons who furnish police with information are generally not the most reliable members of the community and are often engaged in some criminal activity themselves.[10]   In addition to the great number of narcotics users acting as informants, police receive in-

---

6 See Illustration No. 10 at page 259.

7 However, it was observed, particularly in Milwaukee, that narcotics addicts upon arrest may give information on other users, based on their personal knowledge.

8 See Illustration No. 1 at page 246.

9 People v. Ward, 226 Mich. 45, 196 N.W. 971 (1924), says "mere rumor" is not enough, but there is no indication there or elsewhere as to how far removed the informant may be, that is, how many persons the story may have passed through. The nature of the problem is illustrated by a recent federal case. The informant told the police that he had been told by a friend that the friend's brother and another had committed a certain robbery. The police, without first checking with the informant's friend, arrested the suspects, since they fitted the very general description of the offenders. Goldsmith v. United States, 277 F.2d 335 (D.C. Cir. 1960). The court upheld the arrest. However, one writer, citing cases from other jurisdictions, has asserted that when an informant gives information on a past crime, the officer must inquire whether his information is firsthand, and can arrest only if the answer is affirmative. See Note, 32 Ind. L. Rev. 332, 338-341 (1957).

10 See page 132 on the criminal activity of informants and the immunity they are given.

formation from such sources as mentally retarded persons and pimps acting with the ulterior motive of getting their competition off the streets. The police are also accustomed to getting a great deal of information, mostly false, from persons who have been arrested and who hope, by giving information, to obtain favorable treatment. Paid informants have also proved unreliable, since they sometimes fabricate stories in order to receive compensation. Nevertheless, since informers are a very important source of knowledge, the police must attempt in each case to ascertain whether the informer is sufficiently reliable to justify use of the information that he supplies.

While there is no law on this question in Kansas or Wisconsin, the Michigan court approved a jury instruction some years ago which stated:

> . . . if the officer arrested the respondent solely upon the information which he received over the telephone, the arrest was not lawful, for the reason that an officer has not the right to arrest a person without a warrant and upon information which is given anonymously, without the discloser [sic] of the informant and the source of his information. The officer cannot base a reasonable belief upon information which is secured in that way.[11]

Most problems of reliability concern anonymous letter writers and callers or paid or preferentially treated informants. But, while the language quoted in the Michigan jury instruction refers to the anonymous informant, it might also be said to apply to the known informant, since mere knowledge of a person's name adds little in the way of reliability. In any event, the police tend to view in the same way the informant whose identity is unknown and the informant whose identity they desire to keep anonymous to others.[12] This is presumably because in neither case will the identity of the informant be disclosed in court, and therefore the arrest will appear to have been made upon the basis of an anonymous

11 People v. Guertins, 224 Mich. 8, 10, 194 N.W. 561, 562 (1923).

12 In a 1960 Michigan case, which is excluded from the statement of the formal law under which the police were operating when they were observed, the court specifically applied the Guertins doctrine to the situation of the informer known to the police but not disclosed in court. People v. Zeigler, 358 Mich. 355, 100 N.W.2d 456 (1960). However, the court, erroneously it seems, failed to take note of other facts which are usually accepted as sufficient verification of the informant's reliability. In doing so, the court seemingly indicated that failure to disclose the informant would itself jeopardize the validity of the arrest. The court did not take note of People v. Asta, 337 Mich. 590, 60 N.W.2d 472 (1953), in which it was said that officers could justify arrest without disclosing the identity of the informant, but that this hearsay could not be admitted at the preliminary. A dissent in Zeigler objected to the finding of lack of reasonable cause because the informant's identity was not disclosed, but agreed that mere knowledge of an informant's name would not itself establish reliability.

tip unless there are other circumstances which tend to corroborate the informant's story.

The Michigan jury instruction indicates that the police must be told the source of the informant's information. But in practice, particularly where the informant is predicting future criminal conduct, the police usually act upon an accusation without knowledge of the source or exact nature of the informer's information. Arrests under this practice have been criticized as being based upon accusation rather than upon facts which are known by the officer and which justify a reasonable belief in the guilt of the person arrested.[13] But the Michigan court has indicated that an arrest may be valid even though the source of the information is unknown, if there are other factors which establish the reliability of the information. Some of the important, recurring factors are separately considered.

a. *Observation of predicted events.* The most frequently noted and apparently the most important factor in considering the propriety of an arrest based on information from an informant is the confirmation by direct police observation of some of the information given. Thus, where an informant states that a suspect will be at a certain place at an approximate time, it is of considerable significance that the officer later observes the suspect at the time and place given.[14] The more detailed the information given by the informant, that is, the more individual facts which can be verified by the officer's observation, the better the case.[15]

[13] In the recent federal case of Draper v. United States, 358 U.S. 307, 79 Sup. Ct. 329, 3 L. Ed. 2d 327 (1958), the court upheld an arrest upon an informant's accusation without requiring that the information in support be passed on to the officer, but other evidence of the informant's reliability was required. Justice Douglas, in dissent, agreed that hearsay information might be used as a basis for arrest, but took the position that the arrest was invalid because the officers, with their own information, could not have obtained a warrant. "They could swear only to the fact that the informer had made the accusation. They could swear to no evidence that lay in their own knowledge. They could present, on information and belief, no facts which the informer disclosed." 358 U.S. at 324, 79 Sup. Ct. at 339, 3 L. Ed. 2d at 339.

The view of the majority in Draper may have lost some of its vitality in the recent case of Aguilar v. Texas, 378 U.S. 108, 84 Sup. Ct. 1509, 12 L. Ed. 2d 723 (1964). There the court said that the probable cause needed for a search warrant may be based upon hearsay and need not reflect direct personal knowledge of the affiant, but the magistrate must be informed of some of the underlying circumstances on which the informant based his conclusions and of some of the underlying circumstances from which the officer concluded that the informant was reliable.

[14] People v. Mohl, 252 Mich. 469, 233 N.W. 383 (1930); People v. Brenner, 243 Mich. 688, 220 N.W. 714 (1928); People v. Ward, 226 Mich. 45, 196 N.W. 971 (1924). This factor was completely ignored in the recent Zeigler case, however. See note 12 *supra.*

[15] State ex rel. Pros. Atty. v. Martin, 314 Mich. 317, 22 N.W.2d 380 (1946).

Because of the kinds of offenses for which informers are most frequently utilized, such confirmation is often possible. The sale of narcotics or illegal liquor or the writing of numbers usually requires the offender to be at a particular place at an approximate time. Thus it is often possible for the informant to predict this event correctly, and for the officer to verify it by direct observation.

The idea that confirmation of predicted events establishes the reliability of an informant has been criticized.[16] Events may occur according to the informant's prediction without an offense actually taking place. For example, in Illustration No. 1 above, confirmation of the informant's assertion that the suspect will drive his own car to his place of employment on a given date does not directly substantiate the further assertion that the suspect will be carrying narcotics into the plant. Sometimes, notwithstanding corroboration of the noncriminal action predicted, the person arrested is later found innocent.[17]

Even if some suspects are later found to be innocent, it does not necessarily follow that arrest on the basis of an informant's statement plus confirmation of the predicted noncriminal events is contrary to the reasonable cause requirement. Reasonable cause can exist without the suspect being in fact guilty. It is arguable that allowing arrest on the basis of information from an informant, when collateral facts are confirmed, is a proper balancing of the values of individual freedom and effective law enforcement.[18]

b. *Failure of suspect to exculpate self.* A second factor which the Michigan court has recognized as contributing to the informant's reliability is the failure of the suspect to explain what he is doing or to submit to a search. The court has taken note of one suspect's failure to give a reasonable account of himself,[19] another's

---

16 Thus, in Draper v. United States, 358 U.S. 307, 79 Sup. Ct. 329, 3 L. Ed. 2d 327 (1958), Justice Douglas in dissent took the position that the confirmation of the appearance of the defendant at the time predicted, dressed as predicted, and carrying a zipper bag as predicted, made no difference, as these facts were "not evidence of any crime."

17 In Illustration No. 1 arrest and search disclosed the person was not carrying narcotics, though narcotics were later found at his residence. Similarly, search of the suitcase in Illustration No. 3 disclosed no marijuana.

18 In view of the definition of arrest given in the Introduction, as a decision to interfere with a person's freedom to the extent of taking him to the police station for some purpose, it might be thought that the preceding discussion has more relevance to the decision to investigate. It is true that an informant's information plus confirmation of the noncriminal events predicted often results in a mere decision to investigate, that is, a decision to search the person and see if he should be arrested. However, arrests are sometimes made even though the search discloses no presently occurring offense.

19 People v. Wallace, 245 Mich. 310, 222 N.W. 698 (1929).

refusal to state his business,[20] and another's refusal to open his suitcase.[21]

The degree to which this kind of situation occurs in practice is not clear. In other situations a refusal to cooperate in an investigation is one factor which contributes to a decision to arrest,[22] and this probably is also the case when the investigation is commenced because of an informant's tip. Although no such instance was observed,[23] it seems likely that such situations do arise in practice, because an informant's tip will often lead to an investigation requiring the cooperation of the suspect.[24]

Whether an informant's information plus the refusal of the suspect to cooperate in the investigation can logically be said to afford adequate basis for arrest touches upon considerations dealt with elsewhere.[25] Whether a refusal or an inability to explain may properly be considered a factor requires a judgment as to the propriety of the questioning. Giving consideration to a refusal to submit to search is more questionable. The suspect in many cases would be left with the unpleasant choice of either submitting to a search or being arrested because of his refusal to cooperate and then searched as an incident to the arrest.

c. *Prior reliability of the informant.* A third factor contributing to the reliability of information is the proved reliability of the informant on previous occasions.[26] Prior reliability is of importance in practice because of the frequent use of professional, or at least habitual, informants. Persons who, in the past, were paid for information which proved reliable are likely to continue to be reliable. This is particularly true where the informant receives a greater payment for information which leads to conviction. Persons who receive immunity from prosecution in exchange for accurate information are also likely to continue to be reliable, since the giving of false information would probably terminate their immunity status. However, the mere fact that a person has given reliable information on a previous occasion does not insure his

---

[20] State ex rel. Pros. Atty. v. Martin, 314 Mich. 317, 22 N.W.2d 380 (1946).

[21] People v. Ward, 226 Mich. 45, 196 N.W. 971 (1924).

[22] See page 295.

[23] However, in one Michigan case in which the suspect readily submitted to a search, the officer said that an arrest would have been made had there been a refusal of the search request.

[24] When Milwaukee police obtain information from an arrested narcotics addict as to other users, they send an officer to the home of the person named for interrogation. At this time a discreet examination is made of their arms, and if the relevant physical signs are present an arrest is made. Search follows arrest, but the person is brought in regardless of what is found.

[25] Discussion of this will be found in the volume on Detection of Crime and at page 295.

[26] People v. Brenner, 243 Mich. 688, 220 N.W. 714 (1928).

reliability.[27] Information from informers whose past tips have frequently proved inaccurate is likely to be ignored.[28]

d. *Opportunity to judge the informer.* The Michigan court has also stressed the opportunity for the officer to judge the reliability of the informant. A distinction is drawn between an informant who supplies information by telephone or letter and one who reports it directly to the officer. In one case it was observed that "the information which the officer received did not come to him indirectly. The men came to him. He saw them, talked to them, and had opportunity to judge of their dependability." [29] Of course, it might be possible to judge the reliability of a telephone informant by asking him who he is and what led him to believe that the person named has committed or is committing a felony.[30]

It is not clear to what extent personal contact is an important factor in practice. Regularly used informants usually do have personal contact with the officer, and thus there is a greater opportunity to ascertain their reliability. However, police also act upon information received over the telephone. Since telephone conversations afford police at least limited means of checking the reliability of the information by asking questions even when the informant insists upon keeping his identity secret, they are more willing to act on the basis of this kind of anonymous tip than on one received by letter.

e. *Prior suspicion of person informed against.* A fifth factor considered in practice is the prior suspicion of the named person by the police. If police have suspected that the person is engaging in the kind of conduct alleged by the informant, they then have some corroboration of the informant's story.[31] Because of the nature of the offenses in which informants are usually used, there is often some knowledge by police of the possible involvement of the particular suspect. The informer's tip may itself result in the

---

27 One Wichita detective said of his best informant: "He gives me good information occasionally, but he is pretty cagey and tries to sell me bad information. My job then is to try to figure out which information is good and which isn't."

28 In Wichita, taxicab drivers will occasionally alert the police to an unusual circumstance that they have observed. But these drivers have "cried wolf" so often, said one police official, that the police have become discouraged and often ignore requests to investigate suspicious circumstances. For example, on one occasion a taxi driver notified the police that he had picked up a young man in a wealthy residential area, carrying a large laundry bag that rattled as though it contained hardware, and had taken him to Union Station. The police ignored the call and the man boarded the train. It later developed that many houses in that area had been looted.

29 People v. Wallace, 245 Mich. 310, 313, 222 N.W. 698, 699 (1929).

30 This was emphasized in the dissent in People v. Ward, 226 Mich. 45, 196 N.W. 971 (1924).

31 Ibid.

police checking for other information casting suspicion on the individual.[32]

Any one of these five factors alone may be insufficient to convert an informant's statement into reasonable grounds for an arrest. Most of the observed arrests based upon information from an informant involved more than one factor, although some were based only on observation of the noncriminal events predicted by the informant. This factor is mentioned most frequently in the appellate cases, but in none of the cases did it or any of the other factors above suffice alone for a lawful arrest.[33] The most common combination observed involved informants of proved reliability plus verification of the predicted noncriminal events. This has been held sufficient for reasonable cause.[34] Other combinations would seem equally supportable.

B. Arrest on the Basis of Information from a Victim or Witness

The making of an arrest upon the basis of information supplied by an alleged victim or witness to an offense raises essentially the same issues as the informant situation. Again, proper analysis requires separate consideration of the reliability of the information and its completeness and specificity.

1. Reliability of the information.

Illustration No. 4: The police were called to a burglary at a gasoline station. The owner and his wife said that they had observed the entry from the window of their home across the street. When the owner left his house to investigate, the three culprits were alerted and fled. The wife said she recognized one of them as a youth who lived nearby, although she had observed him only from across the street and it was a

---

[32] For example, the Eau Claire (Wisconsin) police were told by an anonymous caller that a particular woman had frequently engaged in shoplifting. Before taking action, the police conducted an investigation and found that the woman was on parole. Upon inquiry her parole officer indicated he had heard rumors to the same effect. The woman was arrested.

[33] Five Michigan cases were found in which some of these factors contributed together with an informant's tip to a finding of "reasonable cause." In State ex rel. Pros. Atty. v. Martin, 314 Mich. 317, 22 N.W.2d 380 (1946), factors (a) and (b); People v. Mohl, 252 Mich. 469, 233 N.W. 383 (1930), factors (a) and (b); People v. Wallace, 245 Mich. 310, 222 N.W. 698 (1929), factors (b) and (d); People v. Brenner, 243 Mich. 688, 220 N.W. 714 (1928), factors (a) and (c); and People v. Ward, 226 Mich. 45, 196 N.W. 971 (1924), factors (a), (b), and (e).

[34] This combination was approved in the Brenner case, 243 Mich. 688, 220 N.W. 714 (1928), and has also been held to be sufficient for arrest by the United States Supreme Court in Draper v. United States, 358 U.S. 307, 79 Sup. Ct. 329, 3 L. Ed. 2d 327 (1958).

dark night. The boy was arrested, but it later developed that he was not responsible.

In contrast to the informant, who usually gives information about an offense currently being committed or which is to be committed, the victim or witness generally reports an offense which has already been committed. In determining whether the information is sufficiently reliable to justify arrest the police must decide to what extent they can rely upon the victim's or witness' use of language, his perception, his memory, and his sincerity.[35]

There is always a possibility that words do not convey to the listener what the speaker intends. Because of this, police usually try to exact from the witness or victim the most precise statement possible of what has occurred.[36] As to perception, police questioning is usually designed to test whether the person had an opportunity to observe the occurrence in question. The question of memory does not appear to be a serious problem, as usually, especially with respect to serious crimes, police appear on the scene and conduct their questioning without delay. Memory is more of a problem in those routine matters which are not immediately reported to the police or which, once reported, are inquired into by detectives at a later date.[37]

Arrests are rarely challenged because of alleged defects in the use of language, perception, or memory. It seems sufficient if police exercise reasonable care to insure that they do not arrest solely upon the word of a supposed witness or victim who in fact did not observe, cannot remember, or cannot adequately relate what occurred. The police usually do take these precautions.

Illustration No. 5: The police were informed by a woman that she had listened in on a telephone conversation between her daughter and a teenage girl friend in which the friend asserted that she had engaged in sexual intercourse with her stepfather. The police did not arrest on this information, but asked the girl to come to police headquarters. She did so and repeated the accusation to the police. The police still declined to arrest, but instead sent the girl to the police physician for a physical examination. The doctor was unable to establish conclusively that the girl had been involved in sex-

[35] The situation is not unlike that in which a trier of fact hears a witness testify. See the helpful discussion in Morgan, Maguire, and Weinstein, Cases and Materials on Evidence 167-170 (4th ed. 1957).

[36] The police may not take the time to be so precise, however, if it appears likely that the offender will escape from the area.

[37] The ability to remember details drops off sharply in the first few hours and days after the event, and only slightly thereafter. See Brown, Legal Psychology 88-89 (1926); Burtt, Legal Psychology 54-55 (1931).

ual relations.   Finally, after a lie detector test indicated that the girl was telling the truth, an arrest was made.[38]

Illustration No. 6: A woman complained to the police that her former handyman had stolen some jacks from under her house trailer.   The officer recalled that on a previous occasion the woman had complained about this man stealing gas, but that the case had been nolle prossed for lack of evidence.   The officer felt that the woman was fabricating these stories because she held a grudge against the man.   He refused to make an arrest.

The problem of determining the sincerity of the victim or witness to a crime is analogous to that of checking the reliability of an informant.   However, the appellate courts of the states studied have never specifically indicated that any confirmation is necessary when a complaint is received from an alleged victim or witness.[39] But the general trend of common law development has been away from the position that an officer is absolutely privileged to arrest upon a charge of any private individual and toward a more strict rule requiring the officer to concern himself about the veracity of the accuser.[40]

Because witnesses or victims usually furnish information about offenses already committed, police cannot verify the information

[38] However, after the stepfather steadfastly denied the offense, the girl was interrogated for some time by the police, and she then admitted that the entire story was untrue.

[39] But the Michigan court, at least, has carefully noted when such steps were taken.   The opinions are cited later.

[40] The early case of Samuel v. Payne, 1 Doug. 359 (K.B. 1780), apparently gives carte blanche to an official to whom a charge is made, as the holding there was that a charge by a private person is sufficient justification to the constable and that "it would be most mischievous that the officer should be bound first to try, and at his peril exercise his judgment on the truth [reasonableness] of the charge."   For a careful analysis of the development of the law from this principle to the more strict one, see Hall, Legal and Social Aspects of Arrest Without a Warrant, 49 Harv. L. Rev. 566 (1936).   This development is also traced in Williams, Arrest for Felony at Common Law, 1954 Crim. L. Rev. 408.

Sometimes a return to the old view is suggested.   Thus, in Ploscowe, A Modern Law of Arrest, 39 Minn. L. Rev. 473 (1955), it is said: "We believe that the law should specify that probable cause exists in certain stereotyped situations in which police normally act in making arrests. . . .   Among such situations in which the police may be deemed to have acted on the basis of probable cause are . . . complaints by private individuals that a specific person has committed a crime; . . ." Id. at 475-476.   Compare Texas Code Crim. Proc., art. 215: "Where it is shown by satisfactory proof to a peace officer, upon the representation of a credible person, that a felony has been committed, and that the offender is about to escape, so that there is no time to procure a warrant, such peace officer may, without warrant, pursue and arrest the accused."

This interesting provision goes beyond the common law requirement in that not only must the officer be concerned with the credibility of the accuser, but in the absence of the need for immediate arrest the accuser is "tested" by first having to sign a complaint.

by attempting to observe the commission of the offense, as they can, for example, when they receive a tip that a narcotic sale is to take place. Nor can the information usually be verified by the proved reliability of prior information given by a witness or victim, since there will have been no prior dealings, except in the rare case of the persistent, unreliable complainant. However, police can and do check to see if the reported offense has occurred and thus corroborate, to that extent, the information received. They accept, without hesitation, the description or identification of offenders when they have by direct observation confirmed that there has been a breaking and entering, felonious assault, murder, or similar offense.[41]

In the absence of this type of confirmation, direct contact with the witness is an aid in checking veracity.[42] In most of the instances observed, either the victim or the witness reported directly to a precinct station or the police went to the crime scene and received the information there.[43]

If there is in fact a duty on the part of the police to check the reliability of statements received from victims and witnesses, it probably exists in those circumstances in which it appears that, because of some prior relationship between the witness or victim and the accused, there exists a motive for a false accusation. One recurring kind of case in which the police are particularly cautious because of the possibility of false accusation is that of intrafamily illicit sexual relations. Thus, in a Michigan case where a woman alleged that her estranged husband had had illicit relations with her daughter, the court noted that the officer made a very careful check prior to arrest.[44] In those cases observed where the police knew or became aware of such a prior relationship, they were hesitant to act without further investigation.[45]

41 It is interesting to note that the only Michigan appellate cases on arrest based on information from victims or witnesses involved crimes which were not subject to this ready confirmation: an attempt to run over the victim with a car in Hammitt v. Straley, 338 Mich. 587, 61 N.W.2d 641 (1953); illicit relations in Leisure v. Hicks, 336 Mich. 148, 57 N.W.2d 473 (1953); and a liquor sale in People v. Bressler, 223 Mich. 597, 194 N.W. 559 (1923).

42 See People v. Bressler, *supra.* In Hammitt v. Straley, 338 Mich. 587, 61 N.W.2d 641, the court observed that, although the victim reported the offense over the telephone, the officer then went to her home and obtained the details by direct interview. In Leisure v. Hicks, *supra,* at 154-155, 57 N.W.2d at 476, the victim was a young person, and the court noted that "the written statement of the minor child upon which defendant primarily based his belief . . . was clear and convincing and substantially unshaken by cross-examination."

43 In Milwaukee, if there is some doubt as to the veracity of the victim or witness, he may be asked to come to police headquarters and give a written statement.

44 Leisure v. Hicks, 336 Mich. 148, 57 N.W.2d 473 (1953).

45 However, in some cases, such attempts at verification before arrest are not made. For example, when a woman consulted the district attorney in Chippewa County,

In other cases the police may be aware of an existing grudge between accuser and accused and for this reason may refuse to arrest upon the accusation alone.[46] Sometimes a motive for the accusation becomes evident only after an arrest has been made.[47] In such a case, the validity of the arrest ought not to be in doubt unless the story was told to the police in such a way as to reasonably suggest its falsity. The story of the witness or victim is more likely to be accepted as true if there has been prior police suspicion of the accused [48] or if the police check and find that the accused has a record of engaging in conduct similar to that alleged.[49]

2. Completeness of the information.

Illustration No. 7: Two patrolmen were approached by a woman who said that her seven-year-old daughter claimed two boys had stolen her purse while she was on her way to the movies. The officers asked the daughter to describe the boys, and she told them that one boy wore a black jacket with orange seams, blue jeans, and sneakers, while the other wore a tan coat. The patrolmen went to a nearby theater, where the cashier told them the boy in the black jacket might be a youth who had just entered. The officers entered the theater, found the boy, and asked him and his two companions to come out into the lobby. The child did not recognize any of the boys and noted that none of them wore a black jacket. One of the officers noticed that one boy had on a reversible jacket and had him reverse it. On the reverse side it was black with red seams. The child still insisted that these were not the boys. Nevertheless, the officers decided to arrest.[50]

Whether the information received is sufficiently complete and specific to justify the arrest of a particular person is often an important problem when the information comes from a victim or witness who does not know the name of the person who committed the crime. Under these circumstances the police are likely to re-

---

Wisconsin, relative to a divorce action and disclosed her suspicions of an incestuous relationship between her husband and daughter, the district attorney directed the sheriff to arrest the husband immediately. The husband was then given a lie detector test.

[46] The situation under discussion should be distinguished from those similar situations in which, although a private grudge is thought to exist, there is no doubt that the offense complained of was committed. No arrest may be made in these cases because the police view the matter as a strictly personal affair. See page 119.

[47] For example, after the Detroit police arrested two suspects for investigation for kidnapping and rape, they learned that the supposed victim's story was untrue, and that the woman had told it to her husband to cover her own misconduct.

[48] People v. Bressler, 223 Mich. 597, 194 N.W. 559 (1923).

[49] Hammitt v. Straley, 338 Mich. 587, 61 N.W.2d 641 (1953).

[50] One of the boys later admitted he was involved, and the purse was recovered.

ceive only a general description of the offender's physical features, clothing, and mannerisms.

How complete must the description be to justify an arrest? On this issue the law is ambiguous,[51] perhaps because precise definition is not possible.[52] The less precise the description of the suspect, the more important it is that there be other circumstances present before an arrest is made. One circumstance, of obvious importance, is the presence of the suspect in the area shortly after the crime was committed. The seriousness of the crime and the need for immediate action are factors which result in an arrest upon a less precise description than would otherwise be required.[53]

The practice is to hold a lineup soon after arrest at which the witness or victim has an opportunity to identify the offender. Police are usually careful to assemble a group of persons who fit the description of the suspect and therefore look alike so that the identification, if one is made, will be meaningful. Courts have not considered whether the requirements for arrest are somewhat less rigid in such a case because the means for clearly ascertaining the suspect's possible innocence are readily available, requiring only brief detention of the innocent.[54]

C. Arrest on the Basis of Analysis of Physical Evidence

Illustration No. 8: The proprietor of a shoe store thought that a $100 bill handed to him by a woman customer "looked funny." Upon learning that she had just cashed another such bill at a clothing store down the street, the proprietor called the police. The officer reporting to the store examined the bill, noted it had a waxy texture, and found it was possible to rub off a part of Franklin's face by rubbing the bill against the wall. Despite the woman's protestations that the bill was genuine, the officer placed her under arrest.

Little is to be found in the law as to when physical evidence is sufficient to justify an arrest upon reasonable cause to believe that

[51] See page 259.

[52] The reports of the American Bar Foundation field researchers tend to highlight this problem, as they often refer to the arrest of persons who "resemble" the person described, suggesting that stating degrees of resemblance is in itself difficult.

[53] For example, when witnesses to a robbery-kidnapping said that they thought they saw the responsible parties in a nearby drive-in restaurant, arrests were made immediately, but it was later proved that these persons were not the offenders.

[54] An even briefer detention occurs when the suspect is taken back to the crime scene to be identified by the complainant, but this is prohibited in Detroit. Detroit Police Dept., Revised Police Manual, chap. 16, §56 (1955). Apparently the objective is to minimize the chances of erroneous identification.

a felony has been committed and that a particular person committed it. One Michigan case held that footprints leading to a building, in which arson was committed, from the home of one who might have a motive for the crime constituted reasonable cause.[55] In another case adequate grounds were found to exist for the arrest of a burglary suspect (later found not to be the offender) where tracks at the scene of the crime indicated that the car used had well-treaded front tires and worn rear tires, and the suspect's tires fitted this description. Also, the suspect was seen by the police a few blocks from the crime scene shortly after its commission early in the morning.[56] In both cases, there was a factor other than the physical evidence which directed attention to the suspect. In the second case the court suggested that the necessity of immediate action is a factor of importance and that an arrest to confirm the inference from the physical evidence is proper.[57]

Doubts as to the adequacy of the grounds for an arrest arise less frequently in cases involving physical evidence than in cases involving verbal identification of the suspect. However, as the illustration clearly demonstrates, an issue of the adequacy of the physical evidence may arise, not only with respect to whether it sufficiently identifies a particular suspect but also as to whether it sufficiently indicates that a felony has been committed. It is not clear whether the officer in the illustrative case had adequate grounds for a felony arrest. He apparently concluded that the possibility that he had discovered a large counterfeiting operation warranted detaining the woman until a more expert analysis of the bill was possible. The Secret Service agent who later examined the bill declared it genuine, noting that the face on any bill can be rubbed off and that the waxlike texture of the bill might have resulted from someone having spilled wax on it. While the officer could hardly be expected to possess the special skills of the federal agent, his method of investigation might have been inadequate under the circumstances.

[55] People v. Losinger, 331 Mich. 490, 50 N.W.2d 137 (1951).

[56] People v. Overton, 293 Mich. 44, 50, 291 N.W. 216, 218 (1940). The dissent asserted that "the slightest examination would have disclosed that the car used in the robbery was not the car used by respondent."

[57] Indeed, the dissent in the preceding footnote seems more properly directed to the fact that the police, after arrest, did not immediately make a check between the tires and the tracks, rather than go to the suspect's house for the purpose of search.

D. Arrest on the Basis of Information from Within the Department or from Another Criminal Justice Agency

The concern here is not with all instances in which the arresting officer has received his information from an official source. If the officer has, through departmental channels, been told of the information provided by an informant, victim, or witness, or by analysis of physical evidence, then the problems are not unlike those already discussed. The present concern is with those instances when an officer may be placed in a dilemma because of the nature of the evidence made available to him through department channels. Among the kinds of information on which the officer may act are: (1) that a warrant exists in the state for a person's arrest, (2) that a person is wanted in another state, and (3) that a certain person is to be picked up.

1. *That a warrant exists in the state for a person's arrest.*

Illustration No. 9: A patrolman observed a man who resembled a description given in a recent departmental bulletin of a suspect wanted on an outstanding warrant. Consulting the bulletin, the officer confirmed the resemblance and noted the wanted man's name. When the suspect admitted that was his name, the officer placed him under arrest.

A Michigan statute provides that an officer may arrest without warrant "when he has received positive information by written, telegraphic, teletypic, telephonic, radio, or other authoritative source that another officer holds a warrant for such arrest." [58] Similarly, in Wisconsin "an arrest may lawfully be made by a peace officer when advised by any other peace officer in the state that a warrant has been issued for the individual." [59] No similar statute exists in Kansas, so that the power of the police in that state in such situations depends upon how the courts there interpret the general common law arrest requirements. What probably is required in all three states is information that a warrant does exist from what appears to be some member of a criminal justice agency[60] who could reasonably be expected to be aware of that fact.

In current practice arrests made upon this basis involve a minimum of discretion by the arresting officer. Most officers do not

[58] Mich. Stat. Ann. §28.874(e) (1954).

[59] Wis. Stat. §954.03(2) (1955).

[60] Though the Wisconsin statute refers only to "peace officer," it is likely that the common law would support an arrest by an officer if so advised by some other "authoritative source," to use the words of the Michigan statute.

hesitate to arrest upon being told by teletype or departmental bulletin or a direct call on the police radio that a warrant exists.[61] This practice clearly accords with statutory authority.

Police in Detroit also learn of the existence of a warrant by a "sight slip," used principally in nonsupport and minor assault and battery cases. In these cases, when a warrant is issued for a defendant not in custody, the complainant (most likely the spouse of the defendant) is usually given a slip prepared and signed by a warrant clerk which states that a warrant has been signed for the apprehension of the person named. When the defendant later appears, the complainant may have him arrested by showing the sight slip to an officer.[62] Precautions have been taken to insure that an officer can determine whether a sight slip is genuine.[63]

Notwithstanding the general willingness of the police to arrest when told a warrant exists and the apparent basis for such a practice under the Michigan and Wisconsin statutes, some officers have expressed doubts as to whether it is proper to arrest when the information has been received from another officer who has no direct knowledge that a warrant exists.[64]

Illustration No. 10: County officers were told that city police held a warrant for grand theft on a man named Takula,

[61] Sometimes the dispatcher gives this information on a request from a patrolman who has stopped a suspicious person, learned his name, and called in to discover whether he has any outstanding warrants.

[62] In one such case two officers brought a man before the station lieutenant and informed him that the man's wife had pointed him out to them on the street as being wanted on a nonsupport warrant. She had displayed a slip of paper to the officers which indicated that a warrant had been issued for him. When the lieutenant inquired if the officers knew that a warrant had been issued, the officers indicated that they had no specific knowledge, but were acting on the information provided by the wife. Notwithstanding the lieutenant's questioning here, the practice of arresting on these "sight slips" has been formalized by the Detroit department. Detroit Police Dept., Revised Police Manual, chap. 15, §36 (1955).

[63] All sight slips are made out by one police officer who is in the warrant clerk's office. He signs all these forms with a very distinctive signature. He has performed this job for twenty-six years, and there is no doubt that most police officers would recognize his signature.

[64] One Michigan state patrolman, after receiving a radio call to pick up a man for whom another post had a warrant, said, "Now, that's the kind of arrest I hate to make. Here we get a call from our corporal telling us that the Romeo post has a warrant for this man's arrest. Actually, Corporal B. doesn't know any more than I know that they actually have the warrant, and yet they want me to go up there and arrest the man without a warrant. As for myself, if I were Corporal B., I certainly would have told the Romeo post to bring the warrant and then we would have served it."

Of course, the real problem is whether the police are always entitled to assume that the information regarding the warrant is correct. Error can occur because the information is not current. For example, in one case the police arrested a man on whom they knew an abandonment warrant had been issued. However, prior to arrest the warrant had been withdrawn. Milwaukee Journal, Jan. 5, 1959, pt. 2, p. 2, col. 1.

age 51, brown eyes, 5′ 3″, and of medium build, supposedly living at a given address. At that address the county deputies found a man about 50 years of age, blue eyes, 5′ 8″, and of wiry build, who claimed that his name was Maloney. They advised headquarters of this discrepancy, but were told to make an arrest. The arrestee was viewed by city detectives, who decided the wrong man had been apprehended.

It is necessary to insure that the person arrested is the person named in the warrant. In the "sight slip" cases the police are satisfied to accept the word of the complainant who possesses the slip, especially when the suspect does not make any assertions to the contrary. In other cases, where officers are sent out to pick up a named person, there may be uncertainty, because the person, in order to escape arrest, may not identify himself correctly. The problems here are not unlike those of uncertain identity discussed earlier. Whether such an arrest is viewed as being made without warrant on the basis of information that a warrant exists, or whether it is viewed as being made upon a warrant not in the hands of the arresting officer, the officer can arrest upon a reasonable belief that he has the person named in the warrant.[65] However, there is some questionable authority to the contrary as to arrest with warrant.[66]

2. *That a person is wanted in another state.*

Illustration No. 11: A call was received in a police department from an out-of-state department requesting that a particular person be arrested. The calling officer indicated that their department held a murder warrant for the man. On this information, the man was located and placed under arrest.

The Uniform Criminal Extradition Act, enacted in each of the three states studied, provides:

The arrest of a person may be lawfully made also by any peace officer . . . without a warrant upon reasonable information that

[65] The former is the case in Michigan, where the statute says that an officer may arrest "without a warrant" on the basis of positive information that another officer holds a warrant. Mich. Stat. Ann. §28.872 (1954). The latter is apparently the case under the Wisconsin provision, Wis. Stat. §954.03(2) (1955). This margin for error is obviously a part of the "reasonable cause" norm for an arrest without a warrant.

[66] In cases of arrests with warrant, the weight of authority is that the officer is excused for a mistake in identity if he has used reasonable diligence. Filer v. Smith, 96 Mich. 347, 55 N.W. 999 (1893); Wallner v. Fid. & Dep. Co., 253 Wis. 66, 33 N.W.2d 215 (1948). See cases collected in Annot., 127 A.L.R. 1057 (1939); Annot., 10 A.L.R.2d 750 (1948). However, some cases, cited in the annotations, ibid., take the view that the officer arresting with warrant must get the right person, unless the mistake is induced by the arrestee. This is also the view of Restatement of Torts §125 (1934).

the accused stands charged in the courts of a state with a crime punishable by death or imprisonment for a term exceeding one year . . .[67]

Though the Uniform Act has been adopted in most states, there has been little appellate litigation on the meaning of the quoted language.[68] The requirement that the person be "charged" in the other state might be subject to various interpretations, but it apparently means that a warrant must have been issued.[69] Doubts about the reasonableness of the information are to be resolved in favor of the arresting officer.[70]

The police do make arrests upon being informed that a person is wanted on a warrant in another state. Whether they have "reasonable information" may depend in part on the means of communication used. The Milwaukee police are more strict than other departments; they will not act upon a telephone request but require a wire from the authorities in the requesting state assuring them that a warrant is on file. In such a case the statute clearly appears to be complied with.

Illustration No. 12: Police in city A learned that officials in neighboring city B, just across the state border, wanted to question a man presently in city A about a murder. An officer was dispatched to find the suspect, and when he found him he "asked" him to come to the police station so that "the chief can talk to you." When the suspect arrived at the station, officials in city B were notified, and they came over to interrogate the suspect. On the basis of this interrogation, they decided that they wanted the suspect held for further investigation. At this, the police chief of city A told the suspect that he was not under arrest and that he could leave if he wanted to, but that it would be advisable to accompany the out-of-

---

[67] Kan. Gen. Stat. §62-740 (1949); Mich. Stat. Ann. §28.1285(13) (1954); Wis. Stat. §964.14 (1955).

[68] 9 U.L.A., Uniform Criminal Extradition Act §14 (1957).

[69] Michigan cases prior to this statute took the position that a prosecution must have been commenced or a warrant issued. Kratzer v. Matthews, 233 Mich. 452, 206 N.W. 982 (1926); Malcolmson v. Scott, 56 Mich. 459, 23 N.W. 166 (1885). The word "charged" in the uniform act is apparently taken from the constitutional provision on extradition in U.S. Const., art. IV, §2, cl. 2. The United States Supreme Court has said of this provision, "doubtless the word 'charged' was used in its broad signification to cover any proceeding which a State might see fit to adopt, by which a formal accusation was made against an alleged criminal." Pierce v. Creecy, 210 U.S. 387, 404, 28 Sup. Ct. 714, 719, 52 L. Ed. 1113, 1121 (1908).

[70] Johnson v. Reddy, 163 Ohio St. 347, 126 N.E.2d 911 (1955). The Michigan cases in the prior footnote emphasized the distinction between receiving information from one known to be a police officer in another state and from a person whose capacity is not known.

state officers back to city *B* in order to clear up the matter. The suspect left with the out-of-state police.

As this illustration shows, custody in border cities may appear to be voluntary both as to the initial appearance at the station for questioning and as to the return to the investigating state. However, it seems likely that in many of these instances the suspect goes to the station and back to the other state because he is convinced that he has no other choice.[71]

This procedure is quite significant. It is analogous in some respects to the prevailing practice with regard to in-state offenses by which arrests are made upon a probability of guilt less than that required by law for charging, or at least less than prosecuting attorneys require in practice for charging. Thus persons are arrested so that interrogation or other in-custody investigation can be conducted with a view to deciding whether there is sufficient evidence to charge them with the offense. Notwithstanding the lack of express authorization by law,[72] practices have been developed for out-of-state offenses so that persons suspected of crimes in neighboring states can be taken into custody in order to determine whether there is sufficient evidence to prosecute them.

3. *That a certain person is to be picked up.*

Illustration No. 13: An officer on patrol was instructed over the police radio to proceed to a certain hospital and "pick up a Mr. John Walker there at the hospital and bring him to the station." The officer went to the hospital and apprehended Walker, who had a bad cut on his head and who professed ignorance of the circumstances which resulted in his being in the hospital.

Often an officer is directed to arrest a particular person without being given the reason or basis for the arrest. Although this practice was not observed in Wisconsin,[73] it was frequently noted in the

71 On "voluntary" custody generally, see page 351.

72 Though there is no case authority in this regard in the states studied, it has been held elsewhere that independent of statute an arrest may be made "by showing that prima facie a felony or other crime has been committed by the prisoner in another state, or that he stands charged therewith." 4 Wharton, Criminal Law and Procedure §1661 (Anderson ed. 1957). See cases cited therein. The exact meaning of the language quoted above is unclear. Compare the Uniform Arrest Act §6, which allows a peace officer to arrest upon reasonable grounds to believe that the person has committed a felony, "whether committed within or without the state."

73 In cases observed there, the officer was told who was wanted, the nature of the offense suspected, and upon what basis the named person was suspected. For example, at an assembly of Milwaukee detectives at roll call it was announced that a particular person was to be picked up for the West Milwaukee police because they wanted him for armed robbery, and that they had apprehended the two associates of the suspect and had obtained his name from them.

other states.   The only objection voiced by officers was that, because they were not told whether a felony or misdemeanor was involved, they did not know how much force they might employ.[74]

In Kansas and Wisconsin the validity of an arrest on mere notice that a certain person is to be picked up depends upon whether the officer has reasonable cause to believe the person to be guilty of a felony.   In Michigan an amendment to the general arrest statute allows a policeman to arrest without warrant

> when he has received such positive information broadcast from any recognized police or other governmental radio station, or teletype, as may afford him reasonable cause to believe that a felony has been committed and reasonable cause to believe that such person has committed it.[75]

It does not appear that this language gives any power of arrest not provided for by the general "reasonable cause" provision.[76]

The validity of an arrest made under the direction of a person in authority is not clear.   It might be said that the arresting officer has "information . . . as may afford him reasonable cause" because he is entitled to presume that the arrest would not be ordered unless the person giving the order was aware of facts providing grounds for the arrest.   However, the Michigan court has held invalid an arrest by a police officer based upon instructions from the prosecuting attorney,[77] and it has been suggested that the same is true with respect to a police superior.[78]

It seems likely that the arrest is valid if the officer ordering the arrest does in fact possess information which meets the reasonable cause requirement.   Though the Michigan statutory language refers to the information in the hands of the arresting officer, it does not appear inconsistent with the statutory purpose to allow the superior's knowledge to be imputed to the arresting officer,[79]

---

[74] A Johnson County, Kansas, patrolman voiced his disapproval of dispatching an officer without describing the offense.   A call had just been received from the dispatcher to "pick up and hold for leaving the scene of an accident" the driver of a specific car.   The officer noted that no information had been given on the extent of damage or whether there was personal injury, which would change the incident from a misdemeanor to a felony.   He expressed concern not about the arrest powers, but about the different norms for the use of force.

[75] Mich. Stat. Ann. §28.874(f) (1954).

[76] It was noted at the time of the amendment that there were numerous decisions from other states upholding such arrests, and no Michigan decisions to the contrary. Waite, Enactments of the 1935 Legislature Concerning Crime, 14 Mich. S.B.J. 399-408 (1935).

[77] Linnen v. Banfield, 114 Mich. 93, 72 N.W. 1 (1897).

[78] People v. Bressler, 223 Mich. 597, 602, 194 N.W. 559, 561 (concurring opinion) (1923).

[79] This was the view taken in United States v. Bianco, 189 F.2d 716 (3d Cir. 1951). An F.B.I. agent who made an arrest upon the request of another agent had to jus-

nor is such a result contrary to Michigan case law.[80] Such a view is no less respectful of the value of individual freedom, because an arrest can be justified only if information constituting reasonable cause has been assembled.[81] And, at the same time, it would not be necessary to hamper law enforcement by requiring transmittal of all the information to the officer making the arrest.

The rules governing this situation have not been clearly indicated by the law. Despite this ambiguity, however, it is clear that in current practice officers have little choice but to arrest when ordered to do so by their superiors.

E. Arrest on the Basis of a Person's Past Police Record

It is appropriate to consider a person's police record in conjunction with other information in deciding whether there are grounds for arrest.[82] The difficult question is whether arrest can ever be proper when the primary basis for suspicion is the prior record of the suspect.

A person's past record does not in itself constitute reasonable grounds to believe that a felony has been committed and that the person has committed it. For example, a record of many past illegal liquor sales does not alone indicate that the person is presently engaging in the same conduct.[83] Arrests for purposes of prosecution are seldom made in practice on this evidence alone, although past record does frequently result in a decision to investigate,[84] which may ultimately lead to an arrest. Arrests for pur-

tify his action as being within a statute allowing arrest when the arresting officer has reasonable grounds to believe. The court said: "The agent who relies on the summary assertions of his coagent can acquire therefrom no greater authority than could have been exercised by the coagent had he been in the arresting agent's position." 189 F.2d at 719.

[80] In Linnen v. Banfield, 114 Mich. 93, 72 N.W. 1 (1897), the prosecuting attorney had no more information than the arresting officer; and in People v. Bressler, 223 Mich. 597, 602, 194 N.W. 559, 561 (1923), the concurring judge's assertion that "power to arrest without a warrant is not vested in police officers, high or low, but arises, if at all, upon reliable information creating a reasonable belief," seems addressed to the need for reasonable grounds by which arrest could be ordered.

There are no Wisconsin or Kansas cases on this question.

[81] In Schneider v. Shepherd, 192 Mich. 82, 158 N.W. 182 (1916), the lower court dismissed a false arrest action against the police but not against the prosecutor who directed the police to make the arrest. In Linnen v. Banfield, *supra,* however, the court held that the fact that the prosecutor directed the arrest did not excuse the arresting officer, but the case is distinguishable because the officer knew the prosecutor had only that information which he had given him. See Annot., 3 A.L.R. 647 (1919).

[82] E.g., Hammitt v. Straley, 338 Mich. 587, 61 N.W.2d 641 (1953).

[83] Odinetz v. Budds, 315 Mich. 512, 24 N.W.2d 193 (1946).

[84] Thus known narcotics users are often searched for narcotics and parolees are

poses other than prosecution, however, are often made on the basis of past record. This matter is considered elsewhere.[85]

> *Illustration No. 14:* Detectives investigating a safecracking took particular note of the means used to open the safe, as disclosed by the physical evidence at the scene. The officers studied the modus operandi file which had been prepared on past solved and unsolved safecrackings. Finding a similarity between the methods used in the case being investigated and those employed in the past by four different offenders currently living in the community, they decided to have the four men arrested.

When there is adequate evidence that a specific crime has been committed but insufficient evidence to identify the offender, persons with a record for the same offense or similar offenses may be arrested. These arrests are most likely to be made if the offense is an extremely serious one. For example, complete records are usually kept of persons with a record of sexual offenses,[86] and a considerable number of these persons may be apprehended when a serious sexual offense occurs.

Although there is no lawful basis for the so-called dragnet arrest, it does not necessarily follow that all arrests made primarily on the basis of the person's past record are unlawful. The law in the three states does not afford any specific guidance on this issue. Presumably, if the suspect's record discloses a close similarity in modus operandi to the offense being investigated, it is more likely that the past record does constitute reasonable cause.

> *Illustration No. 15:* A deputy sheriff, after investigating a burglary in a rural area, found an abandoned vehicle alongside a nearby country road. Checking the registration of the car, he learned that it belonged to a man presently on parole from a burglary conviction. On this basis, the deputy arrested the parolee for questioning concerning the offense.

An arrest is likely if a person with a police record is known to have been in the area of the offense at the approximate time of its commission. This situation occurs most frequently in Milwaukee because of the use there of field interrogation reports, in which a record is made of persons found by patrolmen under suspicious circumstances.

---

frequently searched for weapons. Discussion of this will be found in the volume on Detection of Crime.

85 See Part V.

86 Michigan law, for example, requires that the police submit a report of all persons against whom a warrant has been issued in sex-motivated cases. Mich. Stat. Ann. §4.467(1) (1952).

F. Arrest on the Basis of Direct Observation

When a patrolman observes suspicious actions, he is often prompted to investigate the suspect by such means as questioning, frisking, or searching.[87] The discussion here is limited to those direct observations (often including the results of such on-the-spot investigation) which lead to an actual arrest. Because of the large percentage of police officers engaged in patrol work,[88] these arrests occur with considerable frequency.

For purposes of analysis, two situations are discussed separately: (1) observations relating to a particular offense or kind of offense and (2) observations not relating to a particular kind of offense.

1. *Observations relating to a particular offense or kind of offense.* When officers in the course of patrol duty observe the actual commission of a felony, there is no question of adequate grounds for arrest and in such cases officers do not hesitate to make an arrest.

The very presence of an officer will often prompt a person who is or has been engaged in criminal conduct to take steps to avoid detection. Patrolmen are commonly instructed to be alert to actions suggesting an attempt at concealment. However, the extent to which furtive movements may constitute reasonable cause to arrest for a felony is not clear. The Michigan court has held that any fumbling in one's pockets or movements toward one's pockets or other possible hiding place would justify arrest, provided it is clear that the person is aware of the policeman's presence.[89]

[87] Treatment of these techniques will be found in the volume on Detection of Crime.

[88] For example, of a total of approximately 4500 noncivilian employees of the Detroit Police Department, about 2700 are assigned to routine patrol. Of these, approximately 500 are engaged in foot patrol, and most of the rest are assigned in pairs to scout cars used in routine patrol. The chances of offenses being directly observed have been further increased by the creation of a 250-man special patrol force, assignable on a saturation basis to selected precincts, in an attempt to reduce street crimes.

In Milwaukee, the bulk of the department's manpower is assigned to the six precincts for patrol duty. These officers man approximately 50 motor patrol beats and 140 foot beats on a twenty-four hour basis.

In Wichita the patrol division of the police department is responsible for general police patrol and for the transportation, booking, and taking custody of prisoners in the city jail. The division is headed by a captain, and consists of 3 lieutenants, 10 sergeants, 98 patrolmen, and 6 matrons.

[89] People v. Lewis, 269 Mich. 382, 257 N.W. 843 (1934); People v. Licavoli, 245 Mich. 202, 222 N.W. 102 (1928). The court has stated that it will not presume, in the absence of some credible evidence on the point, that the person was aware he was being watched by the police. People v. Stein, 265 Mich. 610, 251 N.W. 788 (1933).

It is important to distinguish the decision to investigate from the decision to arrest. Suspicious movements may prompt the patrolman to investigate. The investigation may in turn establish a sufficient probability of guilt for an arrest,[90] in which case the only question is the propriety of the investigative methods employed.[91] But there are situations in which the investigation does not clearly implicate the suspect. This may occur when the person refuses or is unable to explain what he is doing, or when the investigation reveals items the possession of which is not in itself criminal.

> *Illustration No. 16:* An officer noticed a man walking slowly down an alley looking into parked cars. The officer approached the man to question him. The suspect asserted that he had been living in the city for only six months. Asked for identification, the suspect produced a driver's license issued over a year earlier showing a local address. The patrolman placed the man under arrest for investigation of recent car thefts.

Often suspicion will develop into what the officer concludes is reasonable cause for arrest because of the action of the suspect when he becomes aware of police surveillance. It was noted in previous discussion that information from an informant plus the suspect's failure to account for his movements, his refusal to submit to a search, or his attempt to avoid police questioning may justify an arrest.[92] Similarly, suspicion aroused by direct observation plus one of these factors may constitute reasonable cause. The practice is to make an arrest under such circumstances.[93]

> *Illustration No. 17:* Officers were called late at night to a residential neighborhood by a householder who complained that someone had attempted to break into his home. They found a man running within a block of the complainant's home and stopped him to ask his reason for being out at that hour. The man refused to tell the police anything and would

[90] For example, officers in Detroit saw a man throw a shiny object over a fence as they approached. They picked up the object and found that it contained heroin capsules.

[91] Discussion of this will be found in the volume on Detection of Crime.

[92] See pages 271-272 for cases.

[93] The questioning of persons found on the streets under circumstances which suggest that they have committed a particular offense is not uncommon. Though the practice was observed everywhere, the police in Milwaukee are expressly instructed to conduct such questioning and to record this information on a "field interrogation report." Milwaukee Police Training School, Field Interrogation (1954). In the period from September 1, 1955, to December 3, 1955, a total of 8400 field interrogation reports were submitted.

not produce any identification.   The officers placed him under arrest.

The Wisconsin court has made it clear that refusal to answer does not itself furnish reasonable grounds for arrest,[94] but courts in the three jurisdictions have not decided whether such a refusal may be weighed together with other suspicious circumstances. Occasionally a court will assert that "no adverse inference may be drawn" from a refusal to answer,[95] but the majority view is that it is appropriate to consider the refusal along with other evidence.[96] One writer has stated the rationale of the latter view as follows:

> It may be said to be the constitutional right of a man to refuse to answer incriminating questions, so that his refusal to answer is not a circumstance of suspicion.   But this would appear to be too legalistic a view, for innocent people do in fact help the police in their inquiries, and the silence of the accused is even a circumstance to which the judge may draw the jury's attention.   After all, the policeman is not trying the guilt of the accused, but is only making an administrative decision whether to arrest.[97]

Whether the constitutional guarantee against self-incrimination actually has any application here is debatable,[98] but even if it does

[94] State v. Gibbs, 252 Wis. 227, 31 N.W.2d 143 (1948).

[95] Poulas v. United States, 95 F.2d 412, 413 (9th Cir. 1938).
Some courts apparently support the police right to stop and question on the supposition that refusal to answer cannot in any way adversely affect the suspect.   For example, in United States v. Bonanno, 180 F. Supp. 71, 86 n.21 (S.D.N.Y. 1960), the court said: "It must be borne in mind that the defendants in this case had a constitutional right to remain silent when questioned by police or other investigatory agents or bodies, but they chose not to do so.   Had they chosen such a course, they would have suffered no penalty."   See also the dicta in Brooks v. United States, 159 A.2d 876 (D.C. 1960); Green v. United States, 259 F.2d 180 (D.C. Cir. 1958).

[96] Dickerson v. United States, 120 A.2d 588 (D.C. 1956); People v. Simon, 45 Cal.2d 645, 290 P.2d 531 (1955); People v. Romero, 156 Cal. App. 2d 48, 318 P.2d 835 (1957); Gisske v. Sanders, 9 Cal. App. 13, 98 Pac. 43 (1908); Baines v. Brady, 122 Cal. App. Supp. 957, 265 P.2d 194 (1953); Harrer v. Montgomery Ward, 124 Mont. 295, 221 P.2d 428 (1950).
Of course, a completely innocent person may refuse to reply to police questioning, especially if he views the questioning as an invasion of his rights.   Thus the son of Supreme Court Justice William O. Douglas spent a night in jail for his refusal to respond to police questioning concerning the reason for his being about.   The incident occurred in Beverly Hills, California, where, so it was reported, the police view evening pedestrians as "suspicious or eccentric."   Chicago Tribune, Nov. 24, 1962, pt. 1, p. 12.

[97] Williams, Arrest for Felony at Common Law, 1954 Crim. L. Rev. (Eng.) 408, 413.

[98] "[T]he privilege covers only statements made in court under process as a witness; . . ."   8 Wigmore, Evidence §2266 (3d ed. 1940).   "Wigmore, differentiating from privilege against self-incrimination the rule excluding involuntary confessions, makes the obviously inaccurate assertion that 'the privilege covers only statements made in court under process as a witness . . .' [although he elsewhere correctly remarks] that a proffered confession 'may be inadmissible on both grounds,' namely

apply, it does not necessarily follow that refusal to answer cannot be a factor in finding reasonable cause.[99]   In the few observed instances in which a suspect refused to answer, an arrest was made.[100]

>   *Illustration No. 18:* Police officers stopped the driver of a car to warn him about a minor traffic violation.   Having done so, they noticed a length of chain lying on the front seat of the car.   Asked for an explanation, the driver said that it was used to pull the car if it stalled.   One of the officers observed that the chain was neither long nor strong enough to be used for this purpose.   The driver then said he used it to free the car when it became lodged in the mud by wrapping it around a tire for added traction.   The police observed that the chain was not even long enough to be used for this purpose.   The man was arrested.

>   *Illustration No. 19:* An officer in the pawn shop district of a large city noticed a shabbily dressed man approaching a shop with a suit coat over his arm.   The officer stopped to talk with the man and noticed that all the labels had been removed from the coat.   Asked for an explanation, the suspect said that he always removed the labels from his suits so that no one would know where he purchased his clothes.   Not satisfied with this answer, the officer made an arrest.

A person may be found in possession of items which are not per se illegal, but which suggest a past felonious act by the suspect.   It is difficult to state generally what the practice is in such situations. It does appear that arrests are made when a person is found in possession of property which may have been obtained from or used in an offense and the officer believes that this can be determined by an interrogation of the suspect by detectives, a checking of the files on stolen property, a lineup, or other investigative method.   Often, as in the illustrations, the arrest will be based not only on the possession of the suspicious items but also on the suspect's failure to explain adequately where he got them.   Sometimes the suspicious

---

(1) its involuntary nature and (2) violation of privilege against self-incrimination." Maguire, Evidence of Guilt 15 n.2 (1959).

99 However, if the suspect asserts the privilege against self-incrimination in such a case, a different conclusion may be required.   "The express claim of the privilege would explain the failure to deny the accusation thus destroying the inference which would otherwise be raised."   Remington, Police Investigation and the Privilege Against Self-Incrimination, 26 Wis. B. Bull. 7, 64 (Dec. 1953).

100 Some courts elsewhere have upheld arrest upon failure to answer where the suspect is found at an unusual hour in an area with a high burglary rate.   People v. Romero, 156 Cal. App. 2d 48, 318 P.2d 835 (1957); Gisske v. Sanders, 9 Cal. App. 13, 98 Pac. 43 (1908).

items are discovered by what clearly is an illegal search,[101] which was not the case in the illustrations, but the suspect usually will be arrested anyway.[102]

Other factors, such as the fact that the suspect is found in an area in which the suspected felonious conduct frequently occurs, make an arrest likely.[103]

> *Illustration No. 20:* An officer observed two men walking in a residential area at night. He recognized one of them as a man with a record of past offenses. He stopped to question the men and frisked them. The shakedown disclosed a pistol in the possession of the man known to have a record. Notwithstanding the protestations of the other man that he was unaware his companion was carrying a gun, both were arrested.

Police may observe a person in the company of another whom they know or suspect is engaging in felonious conduct. If there are adequate grounds to arrest the suspect, it is usual practice to also arrest his companions if the group is not large and is traveling together on foot or in a car. Such is the case, for example, when the principal suspect is arrested for carrying a concealed weapon. Possession of the weapon makes the entire group suspect of being confederates in the commission of crime. The entire group is taken into custody for interrogation and a lineup.[104]   Similarly,

---

101 Discussion of this will be found in the volume on Detection of Crime. For example, the Milwaukee police are instructed to make a "short shake-down" where there is doubt about a person. Milwaukee Police Training School, Field Interrogation 3 (1954).

102 Thus a Detroit officer arrested a person who had a distinctive ring of considerable value in his possession, though the man alleged that he had recently found it in the area; a man in the company of a suspected prostitute was taken into custody for investigation of a breaking and entering because he was without a permanent job but had $150 in small bills on his person; and a man with a toy gun resembling a .45 caliber automatic was arrested on suspicion that he was responsible for a holdup.

103 For example, Milwaukee officers drove past a service station and noticed an automobile parked in the driveway of the station, though it was closed for the night. The officers recalled that there had been a recent wave of service station burglaries in this area. They stopped to investigate, and when the occupant of the car could not account for his presence there he was placed under arrest.

Of course, if a crime has just been reported in the area, the chances of arrest are even greater. See Illustration No. 17. Milwaukee police are instructed to arrest suspicious persons whenever they are found near a crime scene.

104 Occasionally even though an investigation produces no incriminating evidence against the companion, he is still recommended for charging along with the possessor of the gun. One such case was observed in Detroit; the assistant prosecutor refused a warrant on the companion, asserting that the police had no business to arrest him, as the gun was not on his person and he alleged that he knew nothing about it.

the associates of persons involved in narcotics violations are usually taken into custody,[105] apparently because of a belief that users and sellers of narcotics generally associate with others similarly inclined.[106] Though there is no case law in the three jurisdictions relating to these practices, such arrests seem questionable when the companion is not necessarily aware of the possession of contraband by another member of the group.[107]

> *Illustration No. 21:* Two youths grabbed a number of jackets in a clothing store and ran out to a nearby car, in which they made their escape. The incident was witnessed by a number of persons, all of whom said that only two youths were involved. The license number of the car was reported. Some days later officers saw this car with three occupants being driven in the city and stopped it. The stolen goods were not in the car, but all three occupants were placed under arrest.[108]

Persons may also be arrested if they are in the company of another suspected of a past offense. The Wisconsin court has upheld such an arrest, but only after noting that there was additional evidence suggesting the companion was aware of and possibly involved in the prior offense.[109] Without such additional evidence, it seems doubtful that probable cause exists.

---

105 This is most apparent in Detroit. The 1956 statistical report of the Detroit Police Department Narcotics Bureau listed 2646 arrests, of which 1241 were listed as investigated and discharged. This group was said to comprise persons on whom "there was insufficient evidence for a court case" and includes nonusers who were arrested in most instances as associates of users and peddlers.

106 These cases of arrest of associates who are thought to be involved should be distinguished from arrest of a group because it is not known which one is involved, as discussed on page 242. In the case in which numbers slips were thrown from a moving vehicle, arrest of the four occupants might be explained on either basis — that the one offender was known to be in the small group and this justified arrest of the group, or that the fact that one member of the group threw the slips out of the car constituted reasonable cause to believe that all four were involved in the numbers syndicate.

107 "The argument that one who 'accompanies a criminal to a crime rendezvous' cannot be assumed to be a bystander, forceful enough in some circumstances, is farfetched when the meeting is not secretive or in a suspicious hide-out but in broad daylight, in plain sight of passers-by, in a public street of a large city, and where the alleged substantive crime is one which does not necessarily involve any act visibly criminal. . . . Presumptions of guilt are not lightly to be indulged from mere meetings." United States v. Di Re, 332 U.S. 581, 593, 68 Sup. Ct. 222, 228, 92 L. Ed. 210, 219, 220 (1948).

108 Though witnesses to the offense had observed only two persons, all three, while en route to the station, admitted they were involved and all three were prosecuted.

109 State v. Cox, 258 Wis. 162, 45 N.W.2d 100 (1950). There, an officer saw in a car driven by Cox two men who were believed to be guilty of shoplifting clothes fourteen months earlier. Shortly thereafter the officer saw the same car parked, looked in a window of the car, and observed a considerable amount of clothing, including a pair of trousers with pinked edges. When Cox returned to the car alone, he was arrested and the car was searched. The court upheld the arrest, since the

2. *Observations not relating to a particular kind of offense.* As already noted, it is not entirely clear whether the officer must have reasonable cause to believe that the suspect has committed a specific felony or whether it is enough that he have reasonable cause to believe that the suspect has engaged in felonious conduct of a particular type but not a specific crime.[110] In current practice arrests are made on the latter basis.[111] Arrests are also made upon general suspicion, not directed at any specific kind of conduct,[112] a situation in which it is even more doubtful that reasonable cause exists.

Illustration No. 22: Officers on patrol late at night saw a pedestrian turn to watch their car as it turned a corner. The driver circled the block, and the officers again found themselves the subject of close scrutiny by the pedestrian. They stopped to question the man, who asserted that he did not have to answer their questions. The officers placed him under arrest.

It is not uncommon for persons on the street late at night to be arrested when they are questioned by an officer concerning their presence and do not give a satisfactory explanation. The police are directed to question such persons and to make an arrest if the suspect fails to give a satisfactory account.[113] Such arrests are made

---

events were such "as to afford ground for inference that a concert of effort existed between the defendant Cox and the other two men." 258 Wis. at 171, 45 N.W.2d at 105. The dissent was of the view that the presence of clothing in the car and the association with persons suspected of committing an offense over a year earlier could hardly induce a reasonable belief that Cox was acting unlawfully. 258 Wis. at 173, 45 N.W.2d at 105.

It has been said that this case "represents a high-water mark beyond which the court is not likely to go." Comment, 1959 Wis. L. Rev. 489, 494.

110 See page 258.

111 For example, the person arrested because he was looking into parked cars, Illustration No. 16, was not arrested for a particular car theft, but because he was suspected of having engaged in some car theft, perhaps one or more of those outstanding in the police records.

112 Situations which the Michigan court has said do not in themselves suggest a particular offense include refusal to submit to a search, People v. Lansing Municipal Judge, 327 Mich. 410, 42 N.W.2d 120 (1950), and looking back at a passing policeman, People v. Roache, 237 Mich. 215, 211 N.W. 742 (1927).

113 Both the Detroit and Pontiac police manuals inform the policeman that he may question persons "whom he may have reason to suspect of unlawful design," but do not indicate when arrest may follow. Detroit Police Dept., Revised Police Manual, chap. 16, §25 (1955); Pontiac Police Dept., Rules & Regulations §230 (1941).

The Milwaukee police are cautioned to stop and question persons of suspicious nature, and private citizens frequently notify the police by telephone or police call box (open to use by private citizens) of persons acting suspiciously. Milwaukee officers are instructed that they "may arrest persons who are prowling around at night and are unable or refuse to give a satisfactory explanation of their conduct or who have in their possession dangerous weapons or other instruments ordinarily used in the commission of crime." Milwaukee Police Dept., Rules & Regulations, Rule 30, §25 (1950). The practice is further clarified by the following extracts from training

on the assumption that the suspect's refusal or failure to properly explain his presence suggests that he was out for the purpose of committing some felonious act.   Custody also enables the police to determine if the suspect is guilty of a past offense in the area.

Because these arrests are of doubtful legality, police sometimes make it appear that the person is arrested for a known offense. One common practice is to select an offense, for purposes of booking, which occurs with frequency in the area.[114]   Another technique used in all three states is to justify the arrest on the basis that the arrested person fits the description of a wanted person.   Thus a captain in a Kansas county sheriff's department indicated that investigating persons without a specific offense in mind was not a problem

> because there always is an outstanding burglary or robbery or something in the county for which the person can be investigated provided his description fits some description of a wanted person. . . .   By the same token, if the police department or sheriff's department wants to pick a man up and talk to him for a period of time, it is no difficult matter to find some sort of a "want" on the state teletype that will fit the man's description.   For example, if Topeka sends out a want from the Kansas highway patrol for a white male adult, 30 to 40 years old, 5′ 10″, medium build, a ruddy complexion, etc., that is a general enough description to fit practically anyone you want to bring in and talk to.

material: "The definition of a suspicious person, as used in police parlance, is one who is discovered under extraordinary or suspicious circumstances, or whose appearance is sufficiently unusual to raise a doubt in an officer's mind as to who he is and whether his motive for being where he is, is justified.   In short, a 'suspicious person' is one who, because of the peculiarity of his conduct, differs from the other persons an officer customarily meets during his tour of duty." . . . "The following is the proper procedure to be followed in questioning so-called suspicious persons: An officer not in uniform should always identify himself to the person he intends to interview.   He may then proceed with the questioning, first obtaining the suspect's name and address.   Satisfactory proof of identity should be required.   If the subject is a transient, the length of time he has been in the city should be ascertained.   He should be questioned regarding his activities and his reason for being in that particular vicinity.   If the suspect is vague and contradictory in his answers and if he is unable to give a satisfactory account of himself, he should be taken to the station and detained pending further investigation."   Milwaukee Police Training School, Interviews 5-6 (July, 1951).

114 Two arrests of persons found on the street in Detroit under suspicious circumstances were noted to be classified as "for mugging" in one case and "for strong-arming" in another because these offenses were prevalent in the area.   A member of another Michigan department stated: "We will usually try to talk the suspect into giving us his name and identifying himself.   If he could not do so, or was not willing to do so, we could put him in jail for seventy-two hours on investigation.   We make every attempt to invite people to cooperate with us, but if they cannot account for themselves we are not restricted from taking certain steps to satisfy ourselves as to who they are.   Of course we have to book them for investigation of a specific offense such as robbery, or burglary, or something."

This procedure is used in both Detroit and Milwaukee and is facilitated because each patrolman carries a notebook containing bulletins describing wanted persons. An instructor at a training session said: "It is a poor policeman who cannot find a description to fit the suspect, as you officers have at least thirty days of daily bulletins in your notebooks." Though this practice is not described in the manuals of these departments, it is apparently condoned by supervisory officers.

As already noted, it is not entirely clear whether the officer must have reasonable cause to believe that the suspect is responsible for a specific outstanding and unsolved felony or whether it is enough that he have reasonable cause to believe that the suspect has committed a particular kind of felony (e.g., burglary). In fact, offenders are identified by this method. The alternative, an adequate field interrogation giving weight to the suspect's answer or refusal to answer, has an uncertain status in most states. As a consequence, police attempt to fit the situation into a category expressly approved as adequate for arrest.[115]

The basic question is whether the police ought to have the right to arrest a person found under suspicious circumstances who fails to answer their questions adequately. In some jurisdictions the law appears to provide an affirmative answer in substantive statutes which make failure to give a proper account under certain circumstances a misdemeanor such as vagrancy or disorderly conduct. The misdemeanor arrest because of a general suspicion of a felony is considered in greater detail in a subsequent chapter.[116]

G. Adequacy of the Information in General

Assessing the adequacy of the information upon which arrests are made in current practice is made difficult by uncertainty as to what courts and legislatures would require if they were to deal specifically with the important issues which arise in practice. The likelihood that a court will deal with an issue depends upon procedural considerations. Information from informants in narcotics

---

[115] The courts may sometimes appreciate the police viewpoint and declare valid an arrest upon general suspicion, especially if it results in the apprehension of a person responsible for a serious offense. For example, the Michigan court held legal an arrest made upon the sole basis that an officer had observed a car continually circling the block with the occupants "apparently closely watching all onlookers." People v. Minchella, 268 Mich. 123, 255 N.W. 735 (1934), cert. denied, 293 U.S. 619, 294 U.S. 717 (1934), motion for writ denied, 297 U.S. 692 (1935). The court did not indicate what felony this conduct reasonably suggested; the actual crime later found to be involved was a kidnapping of which the arresting officer was apparently not aware.

[116] See page 354.

cases often results in arrest and incidental search. Using the narcotics in evidence is ordinarily essential if a conviction is to be obtained, and consequently the validity of the search and therefore the arrest is likely to be challenged. Thus there are frequent trial and appellate opinions which discuss the adequacy of information received from an informant under varying circumstances.

In contrast, other issues are not litigated because they do not ordinarily result in a search and, therefore, there is not the same reason for the defendant to raise the issue of the validity of the arrest. Little judicial attention has been given to arrests based on a general description of a witness or victim, an unsupported request from an official agency to "pick up" a designated person, a suspect's record of past misconduct, or observation of generally suspicious activity on the part of a suspect.

Despite the prevalent uncertainty as to precisely how much evidence of guilt is required to make an arrest under varying circumstances, there is no doubt that some of the current practices fail to meet even minimum requirements. To a degree this may be caused by a general failure to clarify proper methods of dealing with the particular problem. For example, the practice of justifying an arrest by finding a description on a wanted poster which could apply to the suspect would perhaps not be necessary if it were clearly proper to base an arrest on the suspect's failure to give a satisfactory answer together with other evidence of guilt. Current uncertainty about the propriety of field interrogation methods undoubtedly contributes to some extent to the use of such methods.

It would be difficult to find support for the practice of rounding up a large number of suspects because of their past record in an effort to solve a serious crime. Some explanation, although not justification, for the practice undoubtedly lies in the public approval of this kind of police action when the community is aroused by a particularly serious crime.

The roundup, like the informal extradition of a person from an adjoining state, reflects the desire to use in-custody investigation methods, especially interrogation, to try to solve a crime. In some situations information which may be adequate to justify an arrest is clearly insufficient, as a practical matter, to justify charging a suspect with a crime without further investigation. This is true, for example, of cases involving preliminary identification by a witness or victim, and cases of police observation of suspicious activities adequate to constitute probable cause. The general problem of in-custody investigation is dealt with in detail in later chapters.

In other situations, there may be doubt about whether the information was adequate to justify an arrest but no doubt of the adequacy of the information to charge the person with a crime after his arrest. This is true, for example, of the arrest of a narcotics suspect on the basis of information furnished by an informant. If the search, which inevitably accompanies the arrest, produces the narcotics, there is clearly an adequate basis for charging at least possession of narcotics.

Adequate understanding of the arrest decision, and certainly of the criminal justice process in general, requires understanding of the comparative requirements of amounts and kinds of information at the successive stages in the process. At the risk of emphasizing the obvious, it should be stated that the difference between the amount of information required to stop and interrogate a person on the street and that required for arrest will have an important influence on arrest practices; the amount of information needed to charge in comparison with that required for arrest will have an important influence on both arrest and in-custody investigation practices.

CHAPTER 14

Detention by Police for Purposes
of Investigation

One of the chronic and difficult problems of criminal justice administration is whether police ought to be entitled to conduct in-custody investigation, particularly interrogation, of a suspect, and, if so, under what circumstances and subject to what controls. In part, the debate focuses on when the police should be able to take a suspect into custody. This involves consideration not only of the meaning of the arrest standards but also of whether brief custody on the street or at the station ought to be allowed when adequate grounds for arrest are lacking. Such detentions are authorized by the Uniform Arrest Act, adopted in three states, but there is no agreement on either the desirability or the constitutionality of such an enactment.[1]

Even more controversy surrounds the related question of whether, after a proper arrest, the police may delay taking the next procedural steps in order to obtain additional evidence. The focal point of this aspect of the dispute has been *Mallory v. United States*,[2] in which the Supreme Court said that Rule 5(a)[3] permits "a procedure that allows arresting officers little more leeway than

---

[1] See Wilson, Police Arrest Privileges in a Free Society: A Plea for Modernization, 51 J. Crim. L., C. & P.S. 395 (1960); Foote, The Fourth Amendment: Obstacle or Necessity in the Law of Arrest? 51 J. Crim. L., C. & P.S. 402 (1960).

[2] 354 U.S. 449, 453, 77 Sup. Ct. 1356, 1359, 1 L. Ed. 2d 1479, 1482 (1957). See Confessions and Police Detention, Hearings Before the Subcommittee on Constitutional Rights of the Committee on the Judiciary, United States Senate, 85th Cong., 2d Sess., pursuant to S. Res. 234, Mar. 7 and 11, 1958; Admission of Evidence (Mallory Rule), Hearings Before a Subcommittee of the Committee on the Judiciary, United States Senate, 85th Cong., 2d Sess., on H.R. 11477, S. 2970, S. 3325, and S. 3355, July 17 and 30, 1958; Mallory and Durham Rules, Investigative Arrests and Amendments to Criminal Statutes of District of Columbia, Hearings Before the Committee on the District of Columbia, United States Senate, 88th Cong., 1st Sess., on H.R. 7525 and S. 486, Oct. 10, 15, 16, 17, 22, 23, 24, and Nov. 5, 6, 7, 1963.

The court first applied this type of sanction in McNabb v. United States, 318 U.S. 332, 63 Sup. Ct. 608, 87 L. Ed. 819 (1942).

[3] The reference is to Fed. R. Crim. P. 5(a), which requires federal officers to take arrestees before a commissioner "without unnecessary delay."

the interval between arrest and the ordinary administrative steps required to bring a suspect before the nearest available magistrate." [4] *Mallory* is not binding on the states,[5] and the law in many states is not in accord.[6] Some states have a statutory time limit on police detention, while others impose a "without unnecessary delay" or similar requirement,[7] which may or may not be interpreted by the courts of the particular state to allow delay for investigation.[8] States without such statutes are in similar disagreement.[9]

Analysis of the law of the several states indicates not only that different results have been reached but also that the problem has not received careful attention. Most state statutes are merely copied from another jurisdiction, and the great majority of the appellate cases deal only superficially with the basic issues which are involved. Understanding of these issues is facilitated by a brief description of current police practice.

A. POLICE IN-CUSTODY INVESTIGATION PROCEDURES

Suspects are sometimes briefly detained by the police for purposes of investigation without being taken to police headquarters. This practice, referred to by the police as "field interrogation," involves stopping and questioning and sometimes frisking persons who are found under suspicious circumstances. The questioning may lead to the arrest of the suspect, the filing of a report on the

---

4 Mallory v. United States, 354 U.S. 449, 453, 77 Sup. Ct. 1356, 1359, 1 L. Ed. 2d 1479, 1482 (1957).

5 Gallegos v. Nebraska, 342 U.S. 55, 72 Sup. Ct. 141, 96 L. Ed. 86 (1951).

6 The contrary is often assumed, e.g., "there is no law, statute, or judicial decision anywhere in the nation that designates a charge of 'investigation' or which permits prosecution officials to hold an accused in custody for 72 hours, before the official may make a personal determination to either charge the accused with a crime, or release him." 1 Varon, Searches, Seizures and Immunities vii (1961).

7 The statutes are collected and categorized in LaFave, Detention for Investigation by the Police: An Analysis of Current Practices, 1962 Wash. U.L.Q. 331, 332-333.

8 States with statutes employing identical language have placed different interpretations upon them. For example, the phrase "without unnecessary delay" has been interpreted most strictly in New York, People v. Kelly, 8 App. Div. 2d 478, 188 N.Y.S.2d 663 (1959); People v. Trinchillo, 2 App. Div. 2d 146, 153 N.Y.S.2d 685 (1956); Bass v. State, 196 Misc. 177, 92 N.Y.S.2d 42 (Ct. Cl. 1949), and the contention that delay was needed for purpose of investigation has been said to be "no excuse under the statutes." People v. Snyder, 297 N.Y. 81, 92, 74 N.E.2d 657, 662 (1947). But, in interpreting the same words, other courts have approved detentions where "the officers in good faith were energetically endeavoring to discover the true facts," Mooradian v. Davis, 302 Mich. 484, 489, 5 N.W.2d 435, 437 (1942), or where "the crime committed has not been fully solved," People v. Kelly, 404 Ill. 281, 289, 89 N.E.2d 27, 29 (1949).

9 Compare State v. Beebe, 13 Kan. 589 (1874), with Peloquin v. Hibner, 231 Wis. 77, 285 N.W. 380 (1939).

suspicious activities, or complete exoneration of the suspect. Suspects are also sometimes taken to the station for investigation under circumstances which the police do not view as constituting an arrest. One practice is to "invite" the suspect to headquarters; another is to take the suspect in without recording the detention as an arrest. In either case the suspect is detained only a few hours unless a formal arrest is ultimately made.

Most of the formal arrests which are followed by in-custody investigation are made in the early hours of the morning, especially in the larger cities. After the suspect is brought to the local district or precinct station by the arresting officer, the supervisory officer on duty will often conduct a preliminary and limited interrogation of the suspect. Usually this questioning is merely for the purpose of deciding whether the suspect should be released, held for a warrant (meaning the police feel that no further investigation is called for), or held for investigation.

Persons held for investigation in Kansas are frequently booked for "vagrancy and investigation," which is related to a procedure later used to justify detention, to be discussed shortly. In Milwaukee, a person held for investigation is usually booked on "suspicion of" a particular offense rather than "on the nose," a practice supported by regulations there.[10] An identical practice prevails in Detroit,[11] and again authority for it can be found in their police manual.[12] The investigation booking in both cities is merely a bookkeeping function, in that it distinguishes those cases which are to be handled by the detectives, and does not of itself show that the arrest was illegal.[13]

[10] While it was indicated that this booking procedure is not condoned by the department at the present time and reflects an older practice, the current regulations instruct: "Arrested persons brought to any station by any member of the police force shall be booked on the specific charge on which they are arrested. If an arrest is made on suspicion, the prisoner shall be booked in the Register of Arrests on Suspicion until the proper charge is determined, and then booked in the Register of Arrests accordingly, using as the date and time of arrest on such charge the same date and time as appear for the arrest on suspicion." Milwaukee Police Dept., Rules & Regulations, Rule 33, §2 (1950).

[11] The police sometimes commented that there was no statutory authority for this kind of booking. One police official also made this observation, but he thought the practice must have been informally endorsed by the local courts in order for it to have continued for many years.

[12] The distinction between when the booking will be for "investigation of" as opposed to "on the nose" is apparently the same as the distinction between what is termed in the police manual a preliminary arrest and regular arrest. A regular arrest includes only those cases in which the officer directly views the offense, in which the arrest was by virtue of a warrant or capias, or where the arrest is for violation of probation or for other authorities. Detroit Police Dept., Revised Police Manual, chap. 16, §98 (1955).

[13] It is sometimes assumed that all "investigation of" bookings are illegal: "Prior to the Mallory decision in the District of Columbia a very large percentage of all

In a great many cases no investigation is needed and appearance before the magistrate occurs on the day of arrest or the next morning.[14] Those held for investigation are processed to the detective bureau for interrogation or other checking. Thus the availability of detectives is a significant factor in the length of time a particular suspect is held, and this is dependent on the working hours of the detectives. For example, in Detroit the bulk of the detective force goes on duty at 8:00 A.M. Though cases involving a suspect in custody take precedence over others,[15] each detective team has a number of cases assigned to it, often more than can be disposed of in one day.[16] Most judges in Recorder's Court will not handle initial appearances after 11:00 A.M. and this means that the detectives must have satisfied themselves that there is sufficient evidence for a warrant and must be at the prosecutor's office not later than 10:00 A.M. so that the complaint and warrant can be prepared and approved. Thus, unless the investigation can be

---

arrests were arrests made on the so-called charge of investigation. Since there is no such crime and no such charge known to the law, naturally all of these arrests for investigation were illegal arrests." Statement of National Bar Association in Confessions and Police Detention, Hearings before the Subcommittee on Constitutional Rights of the Committee on the Judiciary, United States Senate, 85th Cong., 2d Sess., pursuant to S. Res. 234, Mar. 7 and 11, 1958, p. 180.

In Staples v. United States, 320 F.2d 817 (5th Cir. 1963), the court excluded evidence found incident to an arrest acknowledged to have been made on information which "may have been sufficient to support a reasonable belief," the basis of exclusion being the subsequent booking of the defendant for "investigation of passing counterfeit notes." See also United States v. Killough, 193 F. Supp. 905, 910 (D.D.C. 1961), where the court in dictum suggests that a "suspicion" booking in itself makes the custody illegal.

Similarly, it is assumed that "investigation of" bookings are useful in tabulating the number of illegal arrests. E.g., Foote, Safeguards in the Law of Arrest, 52 Nw. U.L. Rev. 16, 26 (1958). As to the Detroit practice, a Detroit Bar Committee reported: "The measures taken by the Department during the past year have been constructive and have undoubtedly reduced the number of illegal arrests. Statistics submitted to us show that 'investigation' arrests were reduced from 15,465 during the first six months of 1958 to 11,686 during the first six months of 1959 (a reduction of 3,767 [sic] or 24.4%)." 28 Detroit Lawyer 21 (1960).

14 Thus, in Milwaukee, most cases result in the arrestee being brought before the magistrate on the day following arrest. In Detroit, the clerk of Recorder's Court indicated that in the majority of cases the warrant is issued the day of arrest, with appearance following as soon as a judge is available. Wichita police said that in the usual case a warrant was obtained as soon as the county attorney could be located.

15 "Commanding officers will immediately assign personnel to investigate any person detained on a Preliminary Charge Investigation Arrest Ticket in order that a proper disposition of such person can be made without any improper delay." Detroit Police Dept., Revised Police Manual, chap. 16, §57 (1955).

16 Often the detectives must interrupt their investigation in a particular case in order to appear in court on another matter, and sometimes the detectives return at night without pay in an attempt to handle the backlog of assigned cases. Once a particular team has undertaken the investigation of a particular suspect, the case usually is not assigned to another team even if this team goes off duty, unless it h progressed to the point where the next step is to obtain the warrant.

completed in two hours, the suspect who is to be charged will probably be held over to the following day.[17]

Investigation of persons in custody usually involves questioning but may also include holding a lineup,[18] checking records on recent offenses, or checking physical evidence. Some of these investigative devices take considerable time, and additional time is required when the suspected offense is of a kind investigated by a specialized bureau in the department. If the suspect is still at the precinct, he must be transported to headquarters and then back to the precinct. This transfer to specialized bureaus occurs most frequently for robbery, breaking and entering, car theft, and narcotics offenses.[19]

Interrogation is the principal investigative device, though relatively little use is made of specialized and skilled interrogation techniques. In Detroit questioning begins with the officer obtaining basic information for completion of an "interrogation form," where the questions concern the suspect's prior record and the like. The interrogation then moves on to other matters which are suggested by the arresting officer's report or by the property found in the possession of the suspect. If the detective suspects that the person is not telling the truth, he may threaten to "throw the book at him," or threaten to test him on the polygraph or a similar device.[20] Use of the polygraph as a "psychological pry-bar" (as expressed by the polygraph examiner) is common in Wichita. In Milwaukee statements either are written out in longhand by the

17 If more detectives were on hand at night, many of the suspects could be charged or released by the next morning. At the urging of the Detroit Bar Association such a change has recently been instituted. The duty schedule of detectives at precincts has been altered to provide for a team of two available daily between the hours of 12:00 midnight and 3:00 A.M. See 28 Detroit Lawyer 21 (1960). See also Detroit News, Sept. 4, 1959, sec. B, p. 9, col. 5; Detroit Free Press, Sept. 4, 1959, p. 3.

18 In Milwaukee all such suspects are usually included in a special lineup for all detectives the first thing every morning.

19 For example, the Detroit department has the following special bureaus: Arson, Auto Recovery, Robbery and Breaking and Entering, Narcotics, Homicide, Special Investigation (extortion, abduction, impersonating an officer, counterfeiting, threats, bombings, racketeering, labor troubles), General Service (bad checks, larceny, confidence men, shoplifting and pickpocketing), Missing Persons, and Prosecutor's Bureau (misdemeanors such as family cases, assault and battery, and felonies such as embezzlement, fraud, etc.). Detroit Police Dept., Revised Police Manual, chap. 4 (1955).

20 One of the Detroit precinct stations maintains an instrument which is intended to resemble a polygraph to those unacquainted with such a unit. It actually is an instrument formerly used by a doctor, but it has nothing inside it. On the outside are dials and gauges with such labels as "timer," "power pilot," "timer pilot," "D.C. volts," "D.C. amps." Several cords emanate from the machine.

In another precinct, similar use was made of a "truth serum." A detective kept a large veterinarian's hypodermic syringe, complete with needle, and filled with blue-tinted water, in his desk. He merely places this object on his desk and makes some offhand reference to truth serum during his questioning.

arrested person or are taken in shorthand by a stenographer, in which case the question and answer method is used.[21] In practically all of the interrogations observed, more than one officer participated and sometimes as many as a dozen were involved. No excessively long interrogations were observed. There were a significant number of interrogations in which members of the press were present.

In most cases the investigation is concluded by the time the prosecutor's office becomes involved. If the police are uncertain as to the need for any further investigation they will sometimes confer with the prosecutor without taking the suspect to his office. Occasionally a statement may be taken by the prosecutor, but it is primarily intended as a review of the evidence and verification of the facts provided by the police.

In-custody interrogation is also employed in rural areas, but here the need for such investigation is not so great as in urban centers. The police in urban areas often justify in-custody investigation by referring to the unique problems of a large city, particularly the mobility of the population and the greater number of professional criminals,[22] a point which has received some judicial recognition.[23] Personnel of rural law enforcement agencies are

[21] The Milwaukee police are under instructions to secure a statement from the arrestee as soon as possible after arrest. Milwaukee Police Dept., Rules & Regulations, Rule 30, §42 (1950). They are periodically reminded of this duty, and failure to secure a statement before the arrestee reaches the district attorney's office may result in a reprimand from that office. Thus the usual practice is for a brief interrogation to be held upon the arrestee's arrival at the district station and at the detective bureau, with more detailed questioning by assigned detectives. The actual taking of a statement usually occurs at this later step.

[22] One Detroit official said: "The size of the city and the problem of transportation and communication are, of course, very great. If a person is detained for interrogation in an outlying precinct in the city of Detroit, he may be twenty miles from police headquarters. [This is apparently a reference to those cases in which the investigation must be conducted by members of specialized departments located at headquarters.] . . . And those of us that are in law enforcement understand that when the police are confronted with the ways of persons who know how to get around, they are at a disadvantage. . . . I'm well aware of the fact that in a large and complicated community there are certain practices that are developed by police and law enforcement officers that seem to be necessary." An assistant prosecutor in Detroit attributed the number of arrests for investigation to the "tremendous bulk of the population" in the city of Detroit. He said: "Arrests have to be made immediately even though there is an insufficient amount of evidence to warrant a prosecution, else when the information is gathered the defendant cannot be found. Sometimes the arrests are not warranted, but in most cases they are. It is my opinion, and the opinion of the judges, that a few people will be arrested that should not be, but the overall advantage of letting the police officers arrest and then gather the facts very definitely tips the scales in favor of justice."

[23] Bailey v. Loomis, 228 Mich. 338, 200 N.W. 148 (1934).

It has been asserted that the Mallory requirement of immediate appearance is particularly harsh upon the District of Columbia police, and that separate consideration should be given to the kinds of criminality with which this force must deal, as

less likely to be aware of the legal limitations on detention[24] and often are not adept at conducting investigations. A local municipal force may depend upon the sheriff to aid in a serious case and the sheriff in turn usually relies upon the district attorney when the case calls for obtaining a statement from the suspect.

When the police have made a formal arrest but feel that further investigation is needed, the practice is to detain the suspect for up to seventy-two hours.[25] At the end of this period the police ordinarily either release the suspect or have him charged and brought before a magistrate for his initial appearance,[26] at which time bail is set. Because this appearance marks the point at which police may lose custody of the suspect, they usually assume that it is necessary to complete their investigation by this time. In many localities even the suspect who cannot make bail will be insulated from the police to some extent by being remanded to other authorities.[27]

---

contrasted to the kinds handled by the other federal police agencies. See the colloquies between Sen. Carroll and witnesses Oliver Gasch (U.S. Attorney for D.C.), Robert Murray (Chief, Metropolitan Police Dept., D.C.), and Irving Ferman (Director, D.C. Chapter A.C.L.U.), in Admission of Evidence (Mallory Rule), Hearings before a Subcommittee of the Committee of the Judiciary, United States Senate, 85th Cong., 2d Sess., on H.R. 11477, S. 2970, S. 3325, and S. 3355, July 17 and 30, 1958.

[24] It is not always clear, however, whether this results in greater deviation from the legal norms or merely less of a pretense of compliance. For example, in a rural area a booking may merely read "Questioning" if that is the purpose of the arrest.

[25] In Detroit one of the Recorder's Court judges estimated the average time at two days and a prominent defense attorney estimated it at three days. A small sampling of cases selected at random averaged out to 3.4 days. In Milwaukee, though the police feel it would not be desirable to have a statute allowing detention for a specific length of time, they generally consider the "reasonable time" allowed them to be about seventy-two hours.

[26] This stage of the process is sometimes referred to as an arraignment, though use of this term tends to confuse this and another, later step. For example, see Exhibit 31 in Confessions and Police Detention, Hearings before the Subcommittee on Constitutional Rights of the Committee on the Judiciary, United States Senate, 85th Cong., 2d Sess., pursuant to S. Res. 234, Mar. 7 and 11, 1958, where the state statutes concerning arraignment on the information are collected, though the hearings were conducted to study the problem of arraignment on the warrant. Arraignment on the information comes substantially later and is the point at which the defendant is called upon to plead.

This first appearance is also sometimes called a preliminary hearing, but this also causes confusion. See Goldsmith v. United States, 277 F.2d 335, 338 n.2a (D.C. Cir. 1960), where the court indicates that "the hearing called for by Rule 5 is *not* an 'arraignment' but a preliminary examination of the arrested person." However, the court failed to note that the rule also makes it clear that this first appearance, with which the court was actually concerned, is not the preliminary. Fed. R. Crim. P. 5 merely calls it an "appearance before the commissioner," at which time the commissioner, inter alia, is to "inform the defendant . . . of his right to have a preliminary examination," which is to be held "within a reasonable time." Unlike the initial appearance, the preliminary involves the taking of testimony to determine whether there is probable cause to hold for trial.

[27] For example, the suspect may be placed in the county jail rather than back in

As noted earlier, the opportunities for release prior to initial appearance before the magistrate are few.[28] Even if some special procedures have been established for release, they are generally not made available to those whom the police want to retain in custody for further investigation.[29] The suspect may challenge his detention by way of writ of habeas corpus. Even when this procedure is used, particularly in Detroit, and to a lesser extent elsewhere in Michigan and in Wisconsin, judges at habeas corpus hearings will continue the hearing for twenty-four or forty-eight hours and return the suspect to police custody when the police make some showing that they are presently engaged in an in-custody investigation.

Special steps are sometimes taken by the police to insure that they will be able to complete an in-custody investigation without successful challenge. Such measures may be employed because it is doubtful whether there are adequate grounds for arrest for the offense suspected; because of uncertainty about the validity of any in-custody investigation (which is the case in Kansas); or because the police desire a period of time for investigation longer than that ordinarily allowed by the courts. One technique is to arrest for a minor offense, often vagrancy. Either the suspect is convicted

---

the local police station lockup. See page 402. Moreover, it is questionable whether a person who remains in custody because he cannot make bail should be subjected to any kind of investigation other than that which would be possible were he free on bail. Recently a federal court enjoined Philadelphia police from placing in a lineup a man held in jail on a rape charge for want of bail, explaining that such treatment would constitute a deprivation of equal protection of the laws in view of the fact that those out on bail were not subject to such treatment. Butler v. Crumlish, 229 F. Supp. 565 (E.D. Pa. 1964).

28 See page 172.

29 Detroit might be thought to present the greatest opportunity for release because of the unique arrangement whereby under certain circumstances arrestees, by appeal to the Release Bureau, described in Chapter 9, can be freed without appearing before a magistrate. However, the Release Bureau actually has little effect upon the detention of persons for investigation, as it has no authority to release persons who are being held for investigation of a felony. Because the great majority of investigations concern felonies, the Release Bureau usually does not become involved in the case at all. As to investigation of misdemeanors, where the Release Bureau does have power to order release, it appears that the bureau personnel will usually cooperate with the investigating officers.

Even if the Release Bureau insists upon release (and this is far more likely where the detention is being used as a sanction — see Part V — than for purposes of investigation), the police find it possible to delay the release while the investigation is continued. Department regulations require that no person be released until his fingerprints have been checked out. Detroit Police Dept., Revised Police Manual, chap. 16, §135 (1955). Even under normal circumstances, this is not done until the prints are picked up by the police mail system and routinely checked in the identification bureau. But, if the police feel that still more time for investigation will be needed, they will arrange with the identification bureau to delay clearance of the prints.

of vagrancy or the case is continued for a time. In either event the police will have about ten days to complete their investigation. A similar device, used when the suspect is a probationer or parolee, is to employ a "hold" booking, signifying that he is being held for the probation-parole authorities because his suspicious conduct may constitute possible grounds for revocation. This may or may not be with the concurrence of the probation and parole officials. The probation or parole "hold" is assumed to justify a detention for about ten days.

In those cases in which the investigation is made on the street or at the station prior to arrest, the objective of the officer is to decide whether to make an arrest. In the more frequent case in which an in-custody investigation is made after an arrest, the objective is to obtain additional information sufficient to meet the requirements for the next step in the process, charging the suspect with a crime. The charging decision is ordinarily made by a member of the prosecutor's staff and involves a judgment as to whether there is sufficient evidence to justify prosecution and whether the case is one which ought to be prosecuted under the policy of the prosecutor. In current practice the charging decision is made prior to the first regular appearance of the defendant before a judicial officer and is manifested by the prosecutor's approval of an arrest warrant.

In some cases the police conduct an in-custody investigation even though there is evidence already at hand sufficient to satisfy the prosecutor. Sometimes the objective is to gather more evidence to increase the probability of conviction. In other instances the investigation is directed toward discovering the identity of other offenders or of clearing up other outstanding offenses.

B. KINDS OF INVESTIGATION

Understanding the basic problems of in-custody investigation necessitates consideration of the kinds of cases in which such investigation is commonly used in criminal justice administration.[30] More specifically, it is important to know what kind of investigation

---

30 Two other empirical studies which have focused upon arrests in which in-custody investigation was contemplated disclose cases generally fitting into the pattern described below. See Barrett, Police Practices and the Law — From Arrest to Release or Charge, 50 Calif. L. Rev. 11, 47-50 (1962); Report and Recommendations of the District of Columbia Commissioners' Committee on Police Arrests for Investigation, Appendixes C and D (1962). On the latter, see Murray, Memorandum on Report and Recommendations of the Commissioners' Committee on Police Arrests for Investigation (1962), reprinted in 108 Cong. Rec. 19756 (daily ed. Sept. 26, 1962), for the response of the Chief of Police, and Kamisar, Book Review, 76 Harv. L. Rev. 1502 (1963), for a critique of the two documents.

is utilized in attempting to obtain further evidence and what the relationship is between the techniques used and the continuance of custody.

1. *Detention to check records or physical evidence.*

> *Illustration No. 1:* An officer saw a man walking in a residential neighborhood and noticed that he appeared to be attempting to conceal himself from view from the police car. The officer stopped the car, approached the man, and asked him for identification. He then had the suspect accompany him to the police car while he called headquarters. Within minutes he learned that the suspect had a burglary record and that he was wanted for questioning concerning a recent burglary. The officer placed the suspect under arrest.

> *Illustration No. 2:* An officer on patrol in a slum area noted a shabbily dressed man wearing what appeared to be a very expensive ring. Asked about the ring, the suspect said that he had recently found it. The officer arrested the man. The arrest was made at 12:50 Sunday morning, and no detectives would be available to conduct the investigation until Monday morning. On Monday, after a detective learned from the pawnshop detail that there was no record of such a ring being stolen, the suspect was released.

The time involved in a simple record check made to determine whether the suspect is wanted or has a record for engaging in conduct of the kind suspected varies depending upon what records must be examined. A check of the records of the department making the arrest can often be accomplished in a matter of minutes. Therefore such a check is sometimes made without even taking the suspect to the station; instead the officer receives the necessary record check via police radio or call box. Even if the suspect is taken to the station, the record check can usually be accomplished in a short time. Any extended delay, as in the second illustration, is attributable to the absence of the person familiar with the records when the suspect is brought in.[31]

> *Illustration No. 3:* Officers responding to a windowpeeping complaint arrested a man found running about two blocks from the house of the complainant. The complainant could not make positive identification but noted that the suspect's clothing was similar to that of the person he had seen peeping into a neighbor's house. The suspect was taken to the station, after which the records of that department were checked. The man was found not to have a record, so calls were put

---

[31] Presumably, with detectives now on duty during these early hours, see page 304 *supra,* note 17, such an extended detention would not occur.

out to the county sheriffs of that and neighboring counties. Shortly thereafter it was learned that the suspect had a record of peeping in a neighboring county.

Checks with nearby departments can usually be made promptly. This is particularly true with regard to different police agencies within a large metropolitan area. Checking with a more distant department takes considerably more time, often a matter of days, and a routine check with the Federal Bureau of Investigation may take up to ten days.[32] An apparent basis for such an extended detention may be provided by either charging the suspect with a minor offense or by placing a "hold" on him for probation or parole authorities.

Illustration No. 4: An officer arrested a woman who had been passing $100 bills, because he believed the money to be counterfeit. The arrest was made at 6:00 P.M. At 9:00 P.M. a secret service agent arrived at the precinct and declared the bill genuine, but it was then thought, since the woman had been cashing these bills one after another, that the money might be "hot." The serial numbers were checked against the F.B.I. list of ransom and stolen money, but the check was negative. The woman was released early the following morning.

Illustration No. 5: The police learned that a prime suspect in a recent safe burglary case was wearing a pair of shoes which it was thought were those worn by the burglar. The offender had left a clear heel impression on a piece of paper lying near the safe. The suspect was arrested on a warrant obtained for an outstanding parking violation, and the shoes were sent on to the state crime laboratory for comparison with the print, which took a number of days.[33]

Often the analysis of physical evidence takes longer than a record check. This is particularly likely when the physical evidence is sent to a specialized agency for analysis. Because the continued detention of the suspect is not essential to the analysis, he

[32] A number of departments indicated that the check might take this long. F.B.I. headquarters, however, indicated that they handle all searches of fingerprints within forty-eight hours. Often, if a request is made, the fingerprint checks will be made within one hour. However, several days may elapse, depending upon the method utilized by the contributing police department in sending in the fingerprints to be searched. The F.B.I. sends all returns to departments west of the Mississippi River by airmail in an effort to render as rapid a service as possible. Letter from F.B.I. Inspector H. Lynn Edwards to American Bar Foundation, Sept. 9, 1963.

[33] A parking violation case is usually immediately closed by the offender paying the fine involved. It is not known whether the suspect in this case was held until the report from the crime laboratory was received or was released shoeless on payment of the fine.

is sometimes released when the analysis is likely to take some time and the police are confident that he can later be located. Thus, when suspected addicts are arrested because of what appear to be fresh needle marks on their arms, a urine sample may be obtained and sent to the crime laboratory for analysis. This takes a matter of days, so the suspect is usually released and then rearrested if the test shows the use of narcotics.

Although continued detention is not essential for the analysis of physical evidence, police take and frequently retain custody of a suspect to achieve one or more of the following four objectives:

(1) To obtain the physical evidence. In current practice most searches are made without warrant and incident to a lawful arrest. Thus to achieve a lawful search requires that an arrest be made by taking the suspect into custody. Although subsequent release by the police is possible, it is commonly assumed by police that release casts doubt upon the legality of the arrest.[34]

(2) To prevent the destruction of the physical evidence. Immediate possession of the evidence is not always necessary for subsequent checking. In the case in Illustration No. 2 the officer could have merely recorded a description of the ring worn by the suspect and in the case in Illustration No. 4 the officer could have simply recorded the serial number of the bill (assuming that it was merely thought to be "hot" money). However, if a record check disclosed that the ring or the money was stolen, the police could not expect the evidence to be available when they subsequently arrested the offender. The prior notice to the suspect that he is being investigated would be sufficient inducement for him to dispose of the evidence.

(3) To insure that the suspect will be available. Because the suspect knows he is the subject of investigation, he might flee while police are examining the physical evidence if he is in fact guilty.[35] The risk of unavailability is greater in metropolitan areas and in serious offenses.

(4) To prevent the suspect from warning his co-conspirators. In the illustration involving suspected counterfeiting, the officer may have believed that he had discovered a large-scale operation involving a number of persons. The woman claimed to have gotten the money from her boyfriend and, if released, she would undoubtedly have informed him of the police suspicion. Retention of custody preserved an opportunity to apprehend all those involved if the bill was counterfeit or had been stolen.

[34] There is some basis for their apprehension. See page 404.

[35] See Chapter 9, particularly the discussion of Wis. Stat. §954.03, which makes risk of unavailability a prerequisite to a lawful misdemeanor arrest under the statute.

The four grounds described above show that there may be reasons in practice for taking and retaining custody even when investigation itself does not require the presence of the suspect, although it does not necessarily follow that arrest and continued detention of the suspect is legally justified under the circumstances described.

2. *Detention to hold a lineup or to observe the suspect.*

Illustration No. 6: An officer observed a person who resembled a man wanted for a recent robbery. After verifying the resemblance by checking the teletype description in his notebook, the officer approached the suspect and asked him for identification. The suspect could produce no identification, so the officer placed him under arrest. About fifteen hours later the police were able to assemble the victim and witnesses to the offense in question to view a lineup.

In another significant group of cases the in-custody investigation consists of a lineup at which the suspect and others of the same general appearance are viewed by the victim or witnesses to the offense being investigated. In these cases it is usually apparent to the police at the time of arrest that they will need more evidence to obtain a warrant. Often these arrests are based upon a general description by a witness or victim, which may be sufficiently definite to cause the police to make an arrest but not to persuade a prosecutor to charge the suspect without a lineup identification.[36] This is obviously true when more than one suspect matching the victim's or witness' description has been arrested.[37] It is even more obvious when the suspect arrested is not connected with a specific outstanding offense at the time of arrest, as, for example, when a disreputable person is found carrying a considerable sum of money in small bills or a realistic toy gun. Such a suspect is put in a special lineup to be viewed by the victims of recent hold-ups.[38]

The time needed for a lineup is usually less than that required

[36] For the problem presented by these general descriptions and the arrest norms, see page 278.

[37] See page 259.

[38] Of course, the police may not make an arrest if an alternative means of making the identification is readily available. For example, in one Kansas case a large number of grease guns were stolen from a warehouse, and the circumstances suggested an inside job. Later a local lumber dealer notified the police that a person had approached him and offered to sell him a number of grease guns at an extremely low price. He was able to furnish only a general description, but the owner of the warehouse indicated that he had an employee who might fit the description. This man was not arrested; instead, the police arranged for the warehouse owner to have a Polaroid picture taken of his entire crew on the pretense that it would be used for advertising, and this picture was then shown to the lumber dealer for purposes of identification.

for an in-custody interrogation but longer than that needed for a record check or analysis of physical evidence. It is rarely possible to hold a lineup immediately after arrest. Taking the suspect back to the scene of the crime for identification is often prohibited by department rule.[39] Other delays, such as that necessary to assemble a group of persons who look somewhat like the suspect, are obviously for the benefit of the suspect. Apart from this, it takes time to locate the witness or victim and to make arrangements for him to come to the station to view the lineup.[40] In current practice lineups are often held on the same day as the arrest and never later than the following day.[41]

Illustration No. 7: Officers observed a car being driven in an erratic fashion. They signaled to the driver to pull over to the curb and, after a brief conversation with him, decided that he was intoxicated. They placed him under arrest and took him to the police station. At the station the man was given a series of coordination tests and also a drunkometer test by a doctor, both of which confirmed the suspicion of intoxication.

In-custody investigation sometimes consists of a closer and more prolonged observation of the suspect than is practical without arrest. An obvious case is that of the suspected drunken driver, who is given a coordination, drunkometer, or similar test and observed closely. This kind of additional evidence is often required by prosecutors before they charge the suspect. Detention in such a case is probably not subject to challenge, assuming a lawful arrest initially, because the fact of intoxication means that the person need not be released on bail or taken immediately to court.[42] A suspected narcotic addict with fresh scars on his arms may be arrested and placed in confinement overnight to enable the police to watch for withdrawal symptoms.

3. *Detention to interrogate the suspect.* The greatest number of arrests for purposes of investigation are made with the objective of questioning the suspect. The questioning may be conducted by

[39] See, for example, Detroit Police Dept., Revised Police Manual, chap. 16, §56 (1955).

[40] Requiring the victim or witness to come to the station repeatedly at unreasonable hours might in itself be detrimental to effective law enforcement, as it would discourage public assistance in detection of offenders.

[41] In one Detroit case a man who fitted a teletype description of a wanted man was arrested at 11:55 P.M. At 10:05 the next morning a writ was received on the man, and a hearing was held at 11:00 A.M. The investigating officer explained to the judge that he desired to hold a lineup later in the day, so the judge granted a twenty-four hour continuance.

[42] But see Schoette v. Drake, 139 Wis. 18, 120 N.W. 393 (1909), in which the court held that it was improper not to take a man arrested for drunkenness to the magistrate for purposes of bail or trial. See page 184.

precinct detectives, usually the morning after arrest, or the suspect may be transferred to a specialized bureau, which usually results in at least a twenty-four hour detention.

The kinds of cases in which persons are most frequently detained for interrogation are identified below, not for purposes of either justifying or condemning the practice, but rather to indicate when police feel that in-custody interrogation is necessary in current practice.

a. *Person suspected of criminal conduct, but not of a particular unsolved offense.*

> *Illustration No. 8:* Officers on patrol at night observed a man walking slowly down the street looking into parked cars. They stopped him and questioned him. He gave an equivocal explanation for his actions and admitted having a criminal record. There had recently been a number of thefts from automobiles reported in the community. The suspect was arrested, and the next morning detectives questioned him in detail about each of the outstanding thefts.

When police observe a person acting in a way which suggests that he has engaged in a particular kind of criminal conduct, and they feel that questioning him may connect him with one or more unsolved crimes of the kind suspected, they may take him into custody. A known narcotics pusher may be brought in by the narcotics bureau when he is found with a considerable sum of money in his possession; a man carrying a realistic toy gun or an unemployed man found carrying a large amount of money in small bills may be detained for questioning at the holdup bureau. A person traveling in the company of one carrying a gun or narcotics may also be held for interrogation.

In none of these cases is it possible to charge the suspect on the basis of the evidence known to the police at the time of the arrest. Interrogation is essential if the suspect is to be prosecuted. These arrests are most likely to occur when there are a large number of unsolved offenses of a particular kind, such as breaking and entering, and where there are no witnesses and little or no physical evidence. These circumstances are more likely to be present in a larger city, and this type of arrest and in-custody interrogation is more common in these areas.

b. *Person suspected of a particular offense, the commission of which is uncertain.*

> *Illustration No. 9:* Officers noted the occupants of an automobile with an out-of-state license plate acting in a suspicious manner and apparently trying to avoid the police patrol car. They stopped the car and questioned the occupants, none of

whom could establish ownership of the car. The three men were placed under arrest and taken to police headquarters, where they were kept apart until they could be questioned in more detail by detectives. When each of the three gave substantially the same account of the circumstances they were released.

Illustration No. 10: A man complained to the police that he and his friend had been shot at by the friend's wife. Officers were sent out to see the woman, and she denied having used a gun. Even though her husband also asserted that no weapon had been involved, she was arrested for further questioning. The police felt that while the complainant might have fabricated the story because the woman had been critical of her husband associating with him, the husband and wife might also be lying because they did not want the police to discover a weapon used in some other offense.

Sometimes the police may be certain that they have the right person if a crime has actually been committed. As in the illustrations, this uncertainty as to whether a crime has been committed may be a result of initial police investigation or of conflicting stories by supposed witnesses.

In the two illustrations, it is easier to explain the detention for questioning of the transients suspected of car theft than it is the detention of the local residents who could be questioned at their home. However, the police feel that cases involving disparity in the stories given or involving a group of suspects call for arrest and prompt questioning to insure against the suspect or suspects having an opportunity to fabricate a plausible explanation for the suspicious conduct.

c. *Person suspected of a particular unsolved offense.*

Illustration No. 11: The police had been investigating the robbery-murder of a recluse for some months. An anonymous telephone caller told the police that the gun used and found by the police on the premises had been the property of a certain individual who was presently on parole. The man was arrested and questioned. He claimed that the gun had been stolen from him some months before the murder. No other evidence linking him with the crime was found. He was held for parole violation while he was intermittently questioned over a period of ten days.

In most of the cases in which suspects are held for interrogation the objective of the questioning is to determine whether the suspect is guilty of a particular unsolved offense. Usually one or more persons have been identified as suspects and interrogation is thought the best, or only, way to clear up the matter. This is especially true in the following four situations:

(1) A serious crime of a sensational nature has been committed, and no clues have been uncovered. For example, after the gang-type slaying of a local hoodlum, two of his associates were brought in for questioning, and a number of known sex deviates were detained for interrogation after a sensational rape-murder case.

(2) It is doubtful that the victim can make positive identification, and interrogation is necessary to obtain an admission of guilt. When a six-year-old boy was molested, a driver whose truck had, for no apparent reason, been parked in the area at the time of the offense was arrested and promptly admitted the offense. In a case where a complainant was unable to state definitely whether all three persons who had joined him when he was intoxicated were responsible for the theft of his car, all three were brought in so that their stories could be compared.

(3) It has been possible to link the suspect with other persons known to have been involved in the offense or with evidence such as the stolen goods or the weapons used, but the proof of his connection is insufficient. For example, persons traveling with a numbers carrier were taken in because it was thought that they might be part of the gambling conspiracy, and a man who pawned a stolen suit was arrested so that he could be questioned about the theft of the suit.

(4) It is learned that a person who has engaged in criminal conduct in the past was in the area where the crime being investigated occurred. This is particularly likely to result in an in-custody interrogation when there are no witnesses to the offense and physical evidence is lacking. For example, when a review of field interrogation reports disclosed that a known burglar was in the neighborhood where a burglary was later reported, he was brought in for questioning.

Detention for a considerable period of time is more likely when the arrest is for interrogation than when other investigation methods are used. While many suspects are freed after a brief interrogation, some are detained substantially longer than they would be if a lineup, a check of records, or an analysis of physical evidence were involved.[43]

---

[43] This does not mean that lengthy, continuous interrogations are held. Rather, questioning usually involves a small part of the time, the balance of the time being taken by the detectives for other duties or for checking out the suspect's story.

C. THE BASIC ISSUES

The detention practices in Kansas, Michigan, and Wisconsin raise a number of significant questions which merit detailed consideration.

(1) When, if ever, is it desirable to allow a taking and continuance of custody of a person who cannot be immediately charged with a crime? This is certainly the most significant issue. In current practice custody is often taken of suspects who, because of the added requirements for charging either as a matter of law or as a matter of practice, will not be either charged or released without further in-custody investigation, often interrogation. If it is not the function of the police to arrest and interrogate in order to determine who should be charged, then delay after arrest for purposes of investigation is difficult to support. If there are occasions when custody may be taken, on evidence sufficient to support an arrest, but a prosecutor would rightly refuse to charge without additional evidence, then it seems obviously proper to allow some in-custody investigation.

(2) When, if ever, is it desirable to allow a taking and continuance of custody of a person who cannot be arrested for the crime suspected? The Uniform Arrest Act, adopted in only three states, apparently would authorize a brief detention on the street and at the station on evidence insufficient to support an arrest. Although the act has not been adopted in Kansas, Michigan, or Wisconsin, police in those states do engage in on-the-street questioning of suspicious persons and sometimes take the suspect to the station for a brief period of investigation. These actions are not regarded or recorded as arrests, and adequate grounds for arrest are usually lacking. Alternative methods are to "request" a suspect to come to the station, to base detention upon an alleged violation of a condition of probation or parole, or to arrest for a known minor offense when evidence is insufficient to arrest for the crime with which the police are concerned.

(3) When, if ever, is it proper to continue to keep a suspect in custody without bringing him before a magistrate when the police already have sufficient evidence to persuade the prosecutor to charge the suspect? In current practice, police may engage in further in-custody investigation even though they already have sufficient evidence to charge the suspect and to show probable cause at the preliminary examination. This may be done to acquire more evidence in order to make conviction of the offender more certain if the case goes to trial. In other instances the police

have reason to believe that the suspect can provide information concerning another offense or another offender and desire to continue the investigation for this reason.

(4) What are the proper standards of in-custody investigation and what methods of control are necessary to insure adherence to these standards? The most common method of in-custody investigation is interrogation. The basic issue is to what extent, if at all, in-custody interrogation during the period between arrest and appearance before the magistrate is a proper police investigation practice. Consideration of controls on police practice raises here, as elsewhere, the question of what the alternatives are and particularly whether release of the defendant through exclusion of evidence or outright acquittal is a necessary and proper sanction for courts to employ.

Such ultimate value questions cannot be resolved through empirical research alone. But asking these questions does provide a useful frame of reference for describing current practice, and knowledge about current practice and current law is certainly essential to adequate consideration of these issues. Chapters 15 through 20 are devoted to a detailed consideration of these issues, with emphasis upon observed practices.

CHAPTER 15

Custody of a Person Who Cannot Be Charged

In a recent federal case two men were arrested because they were suspected of being the two masked gunmen responsible for an armed robbery.[1] The arrests were made because an informant reported that the brother of one of the suspects had told him that the two were responsible and the suspects fitted the general description given by the victims of the robbery. The suspects were not taken immediately before a magistrate but were detained by the police and questioned. The court approved the practice, saying, in dicta:

> Though the statements . . . afforded grounds for *arrest,* the officers must necessarily have had some doubts about whether the two suspects should be formally charged with the crime in the face of the vigorous denials of the suspects. . . . The quantum of evidence necessary to sustain an arrest is not, in all circumstances, the same quantum necessary to make out probable cause for charging a person with the crime. . . . We must not forget that interrogation is not an evil *per se* but an absolute necessity and that it often leads to releases, not charges. . . . Since the hearsay evidence . . . was undoubtedly sufficient probable cause for arrest, . . . the inquiry was not needed to bolster defendants' arrest; but it could be conducted to determine whether the suspects should be arraigned or released.[2]

[1] Goldsmith v. United States, 277 F.2d 335 (D.C. Cir. 1960).
[2] 277 F.2d at 342-344. A similar approach was taken by Justice Jackson in Watts v. Indiana, 338 U.S. 49, 58, 69 Sup. Ct. 1347, 1357, 93 L. Ed. 1801, 1808 (1949): "In each case police were confronted with one or more brutal murders which the authorities were under the highest duty to solve. Each of these murders was unwitnessed, and the only positive knowledge on which a solution could be based was possessed by the killer. In each there was reasonable ground to *suspect* an individual but not enough legal evidence to *charge* him with guilt. In each the police attempted to meet the situation by taking the suspect into custody and interrogating him. . . . [N]o one suggests that any course held promise of solution of these murders other than to take the suspect into custody for questioning. The alternative was to

In Kansas, Michigan, and Wisconsin it is common for the police to make an arrest in similar circumstances. In such cases, even when there are clearly adequate grounds for arrest, the police usually detain the suspect in order to obtain additional information for use in deciding whether to charge him with a crime. This in-custody investigation during the period following a lawful arrest and before the initial appearance before the magistrate is the subject of this chapter.

A. The Charging Decision

To understand fully why police sometimes detain a suspect before bringing him before a magistrate, in order to seek additional information for use in making the decision to charge, it is necessary to consider the place of the charging decision itself in the criminal justice process. The charging decision is usually made by the prosecutor or an assistant in his office, although in some cases it is the responsibility of a highly specialized and trained member of the police department. By whomever it is made, the decision involves a judgment of whether the suspect should be subjected to a trial. A decision to charge reflects a belief that there is sufficient evidence of guilt to warrant expending further resources of the criminal process for the purpose of obtaining a conviction[3] and, in so doing, to subject the suspect to the economic and social costs inevitably incident to defending oneself in a criminal prosecution.

In the states studied, the decision to charge is manifested in the usual case by the prosecutor's approval of a police request for a warrant.[4] The arrest warrant issued after a person is already in custody serves the primary function of a charging document.[5] Though the law in the three states varies as to who has authority to issue an arrest warrant,[6] it is clear that the only real decision

close the books on the crime and forget it, with the suspect at large. This is a grave choice for a society in which two-thirds of the murders already are closed out as insoluble."

[3] This does not mean, however, that it is always assumed that a full-scale trial will be necessary or that any substantial expenditure of the prosecutor's resources will be required. Most cases are followed by a plea of guilty. Discussion of this will be found in the volume on Adjudication.

[4] On the limited use of the warrant for arrest purposes, see Chapter 1.

[5] There is some evidence that the postarrest warrant is also viewed by the courts as a document of custody justification. Discussion of this will be found in the volume on Prosecution.

[6] In Kansas, the statutes provide that only a magistrate, after examining on oath the complainant and any witnesses produced before him, shall reduce the complaint to writing and issue a warrant. Kan. Gen. Stat. §62-602 (1949). In Michigan, also, a warrant may be issued only by a magistrate, but in this state it may issue (with some

in practice is that of the prosecutor or his representative.[7] The magistrate's role is a formality.

It is not possible to state categorically how much evidence is necessary before a prosecutor is justified in charging a suspect with a crime. This is because the law does not expressly provide a distinct probability of guilt standard for the charging decision. Though it is clear that an arrest warrant is to issue only upon "probable cause,"[8] this phrase has been dealt with by courts only in cases where the warrant has been challenged as a basis for arrest rather than as a basis for the decision to charge. Thus judicial interpretations of the evidentiary requirements have related to the arrest rather than the subsequent charging decision.[9]

The preliminary examination is a check upon the charging decision, since the magistrate can hold the defendant for trial only if he finds that an offense was committed and that there is probable cause to believe the defendant committed it.[10] This "probable cause" requirement, which must be satisfied at the preliminary,[11] may be the standard to which the prosecutor should conform when he decides whether to charge the suspect. However, neither cases nor statutes expressly require this. As a practical matter the fact that some time passes before the preliminary is held [12] means that the prosecutor does not need, at the time of charging, all the evidence which will be required later at the preliminary. It is clear

---

minor exceptions) only with the prior written approval of the prosecuting attorney. Thus concurrence of prosecutor and magistrate is required. Mich. Stat. Ann. §28.860 (1954). A different situation is found in Wisconsin, where a warrant may be issued by either the district attorney or the magistrate without the approval of the other. Wis. Stat. §§954.01, 954.02 (1955).

7 A detailed description of this process will be found in the volume on Prosecution.

8 Kan. Const., Bill of Rights §15; Mich. Const., art. II, §10; Wis. Const., art. I, §11.

9 In the few appellate cases which do consider the requirements for an arrest warrant, the issue is the validity of an arrest and subsequent search rather than whether there were adequate grounds to charge the suspect. Consequently, courts have not given careful attention to the use of the warrant as a charging document and have not specifically determined whether the evidence required to justify the issuance of a warrant after arrest should be greater than that required when the warrant is issued as a basis for taking custody in the first instance.

10 Kan. Gen. Stat. §62-620 (1949); Mich. Stat. Ann. §28.931 (1954); Wis. Stat. §954.13(1) (1955).

11 It should be noted at this point that the "probable cause" needed at the preliminary examination is not necessarily the same as the "probable cause" required for issuance of an arrest warrant, although the terms are the same.

12 In Kansas the preliminary is usually scheduled for about two weeks after the first appearance before the magistrate, although there is no specific statutory time limit. In Michigan the statutes require the preliminary be held within ten days of the initial appearance, Mich. Stat. Ann. §28.922 (1954), and they are usually scheduled for within a week. In Wisconsin, the statutes require the preliminary be held within ten days unless the defendant consents to a longer period. Wis. Stat. §954.05 (1955).

that he is not required to have more evidence for charging than he will need to present to obtain a "bindover" at the preliminary examination.

Most defendants waive the preliminary examination.[13] Therefore, the prosecutor does not usually have to be concerned about his ability to present sufficient evidence at the preliminary. But, as a practical matter, when he approves a warrant for a suspect in custody, he must be concerned about whether he will have admissible evidence of sufficient weight that, absent any presently unknown exculpatory evidence presented by the defendant, a conviction can probably be obtained.[14]

The fact that the prosecutor usually makes the decision to charge at the time of the issuance of a postarrest warrant is apparently a matter of custom rather than an explicit requirement of law. The decision to charge is not necessarily wedded to the warrant-issuance step, as is demonstrated in those occasional cases in which warrants are issued prior to arrest without a commitment to charge.[15] Because the preliminary examination is typically not held for a week or more after the issuance of the warrant, the charging decision could be postponed, although this would obviously cause some administrative inconvenience, particularly for the magistrate who must fit the preliminary into his calendar. The initial appearance before the magistrate, which does ordinarily follow the issuance of the postarrest warrant, does not involve a review by the magistrate of the grounds for the warrant and there is thus no requirement that the prosecutor demonstrate that there are sufficient grounds to charge the suspect.[16]

[13] The law in all three states contemplates that the defendant be allowed to waive preliminary examination. Kan. Gen. Stat. §62-805 (1949); Mich. Stat. Ann. §28.982 (1954); Wis. Stat. §§954.34, 955.18 (1955). Discussion of the waiver practice and its effects will be found in the volume on Prosecution.

[14] The following statement, although made by a California prosecutor, is typical of the position taken by prosecutors in the jurisdictions studied. "In this connection, I wish to advise that it is not the policy of this office to continue with the prosecution of any case, regardless of the offense charged, when in the opinion of the deputy charged with the responsibility for such prosecution the defendant is not guilty of such charge, or where we do not have available sufficient evidence to prove guilt beyond a reasonable doubt. We will not be a party to convicting an innocent person; nor will we make a farce of a trial, harass a defendant, or impose upon the time of the court, by continuing with the prosecution of a case when we know in advance that the evidence available to us is insufficient to sustain a conviction." Barrett, Police Practices and the Law — From Arrest to Release or Charge, 50 Calif. L. Rev. 11, 30-31 n.83 (1962).

[15] This may occur, for example, when it is desired to obtain prior testing of the evidence so as to minimize the chances of a search being invalidated or when the whereabouts of the suspect is unknown and the warrant is needed to allow arrest elsewhere. See Chapter 1.

[16] In Mallory the Supreme Court was concerned with prompt appearance "so that the issue of probable cause may be promptly determined." Mallory v. United States,

The charging decision has become associated with the issuance of the postarrest warrant for practical reasons. Although the prosecution is not required to establish probable cause at the initial appearance before the magistrate, the fact that a defendant is customarily released on bail [17] at that time makes it important for the prosecutor to decide that he has probable cause before bail is set.[18] The release of the defendant on bail usually means that the prosecutor will not be able to conduct any further in-custody investigation and thus he is not likely to develop further evidence between the initial appearance and the preliminary examination. There is also concern about the propriety of demanding bail or requiring continued custody of those unable to post bail when the prosecutor is as yet uncertain as to whether there is a sufficient basis for prosecution. And, as previously mentioned, magistrates would be understandably reluctant to schedule preliminary examinations until the prosecutor has decided that the suspect is to be prosecuted. For these reasons then, it is understandable that the decision as to charging is made at the time the postarrest warrant is issued.[19]

---

354 U.S. 449, 454, 77 Sup. Ct. 1356, 1359, 1 L. Ed. 2d 1479, 1483 (1957). The court was apparently referring to the fact that the federal rules require that a complaint be filed with the commissioner and that the commissioner determine the question of probable cause when issuing warrants upon complaints. Fed. R. Crim. P. 3, 4, 5.

[17] In Michigan the general bail statute provides for the setting of bail by "officers before whom persons charged with crime shall be brought. . . ." Mich. Stat. Ann. §28.888 (1954). In Kansas the statutes merely indicate that, where arrest is not pursuant to a warrant on which the bail is stipulated, the judge or clerk of court where the defendant is to appear may take and approve bail. Kan. Gen. Stat. §62-1715 (1949). The Wisconsin statutes recognize a right to bail set by the magistrate pending the preliminary examination. Wis. Stat. §954.05 (1955).

[18] Of course, many defendants cannot make bail, and in some cases this is apparent in advance. But the same procedure is followed in these cases, and there is no affirmative evidence that prosecutors delay the charging decision or make it on a lower standard of evidence because of the continued availability of the defendant for further in-custody investigation.

In the case of persons who cannot make bail, it does not appear that the initial appearance substantially affects the ability of the police to continue the investigation. Upon remand the suspect may be placed in the county jail rather than back in the local police station lockup, which may impair to some extent the opportunity of the investigating officers to interrogate or hold a lineup. See page 402. Also, the suspect may be less amenable to questioning if the magistrate warns him that he need not answer questions or that his answers may be used against him in court. However, such a caution is seldom, if ever, administered. Of the three states studied, only Michigan has a statute which clearly contemplates that the defendant be informed of his rights by the magistrate, and this statute does not enumerate these rights. Mich. Stat. Ann. §28.885 (1954). The practice in all three states is for the magistrate to inform the defendant of his right to a preliminary examination, of the nature of the charge against him, and of his right to later appointment of counsel if he is indigent.

[19] The police, in each of the three states studied, find it possible to detain after arrest for purposes of obtaining information sufficient for charging, and it is not

B. Recognition in Law of In-Custody Investigation Following Arrest

The common practice of arresting a suspect and then conducting an in-custody investigation to decide whether to charge has received some limited recognition in Michigan and Wisconsin but not in Kansas. There are two ways of assessing the attitude of courts and legislatures toward the issue of the propriety of in-custody investigation: by comparing the kind and amount of evidence required by law to arrest with that required by law to charge, and by considering appellate decisions in which specific in-custody investigations were challenged.

1. *Comparison of the evidentiary requirements for arrest and charging.* If more evidence is legally required to charge a suspect with a crime than is required to arrest him, then it obviously follows that the additional evidence must be acquired through postarrest investigation. But it does not necessarily follow that in-custody investigation, particularly in-custody interrogation, is authorized, although as a practical matter most postarrest investigation does take place while the suspect is in custody and does involve interrogation.

A comparison of the legal requirements for arrest and for charging is difficult for a number of reasons. First, neither courts nor legislatures have been explicit as to how much evidence is required for the decision to charge, with the result that there is no firm basis for comparison with the more often considered arrest standard.[20] Secondly, there has been no determination of the

---

possible to state whether the charging decision would take a different form if the police did not have this opportunity. Thus it is not clear whether the prosecutor would continue to make the charging decision at this point, either not applying the present high standard or applying it and charging fewer suspects, or whether he would delay his decision in the hope that more evidence could be uncovered following initial appearance, either without the custody of the suspect or with custody when the suspect could not make bail. It is also uncertain whether, if the charging decision were delayed, there would be pressure upon magistrates to set higher bail at the initial appearance to allow further custody while evidence for use in making the charging decision was sought.

[20] The postarrest warrant standard and the preliminary hearing standard are both stated as "probable cause," but there does not appear to be any justification for assuming that they are necessarily identical to the felony arrest standard, which is also sometimes stated in these terms. Some of the courts in the jurisdictions studied have on occasion implied this, however. See cases in note 32 *infra*. For a case from another jurisdiction equating these standards, see People v. Ingle, 53 Cal. 2d 407, 412-413, 348 P.2d 577, 580, 2 Cal. Rptr. 14, 17 (1960), discussed in Barrett, Police Practices and the Law — From Arrest to Release or Charge, 50 Calif. L. Rev. 11, 29 (1962). The Ingle court said that the test for the arresting officer to employ is "whether the person should stand trial," and then the court cited as authority on

legality of many types of arrests which are made on the basis of evidence insufficient to justify charging the suspect. This is true, for example, of arrests made on the basis of a description given by the victim of the crime. Despite these uncertainties it is possible to make a realistic, if not certain, comparison between the requirements for arrest and those for charging. The two decisions appear to require different amounts of evidence because they are made by persons of different educational and professional status, according to different rules of evidence, and under different circumstances.

The United States Supreme Court said with regard to the requirements for arrest: "In dealing with probable cause, however, as the very name implies, we deal with probabilities. These are not technical; they are the factual and practical considerations of everyday life on which reasonable and prudent men, not legal technicians, act." [21] A standard of conduct cannot be precisely defined without consideration of the persons to whom it is directed. Most arrest decisions are made by policemen; most charging decisions by prosecutors. Telling a police officer that he may arrest when there are "reasonable grounds to believe" the suspect is guilty may be different from telling a prosecutor that he may charge when there is "probable cause" to believe the suspect is guilty. The prosecutor, who is a "legal technician," may decide that the evidence is inadequate even though the arrest by the police officer on the same evidence was proper.

What this means in many cases is that the kind of evidence required by the prosecutor is different from that required by the police officer before arrest. While it is not clear what evidence is properly considered in deciding to charge, it is apparent that the prosecutor is concerned with evidence which will be usable at the preliminary examination, if one is held, and at the trial itself. At trial "[m]uch evidence of real and substantial probative value goes out on considerations irrelevant to its probative weight but relevant to possible misunderstanding or misuse by the jury." [22] And, in Michigan at least, hearsay cannot be considered in de-

what constitutes probable cause for arrest a leading case on probable cause necessary to justify a magistrate in holding the defendant.

[21] Brinegar v. United States, 338 U.S. 160, 175, 69 Sup. Ct. 1302, 1310, 93 L. Ed. 1879, 1890 (1949). Similarly, the Michigan court has said that whether there are grounds for arrest "depends in every case upon the peculiar circumstances confronting the arresting officer. . . . He makes his determination, and we review it, not as a legal scholar determines the existence of consideration in support of a promise, but as a man of reasonable prudence and caution would determine whether the person arrested has committed a felony." People v. Harper, 365 Mich. 494, 501, 113 N.W.2d 808, 811 (1962).

[22] Brinegar v. United States, *supra*, at 173, 69 Sup. Ct. at 1309, 93 L. Ed. at 1889.

termining whether there is probable cause at the preliminary.[23] Thus, the prosecutor at the time of the charging decision must be concerned with the rules of evidence.

In contrast, police, in deciding whether to make an arrest, may properly consider evidence other than that which is admissible at trial.[24]   Courts in Kansas, Michigan, and Wisconsin have had occasion to make it clear that an officer may take into account the character of the suspect,[25] his past record,[26] and hearsay concerning the commission of the offense.[27]

The arrest and charging standards may also vary because of the different circumstances under which the decisions are made.   Because a police officer must frequently make the arrest decision on the spur of the moment, he may decide to arrest on less evidence, and with less effort to weigh the information on hand, than if there were time for deliberation.   This is particularly true when a serious offense is involved.   Delay in arresting the suspected murderer of a child may expose the community to a continuing danger, while delay in the case of a suspected numbers carrier would create a minor risk.[28]   Often immediate action is necessary because the suspect will otherwise escape.   Courts have held that risk of escape, danger to the community, or risk of further harm to the victim may justify an arrest on the basis of evidence which would otherwise be insufficient.[29]

In contrast, the prosecutor makes the charging decision in his own office, faced with no emergency, and with time for reflection. Therefore, evidence sufficient to support an arrest in an emergency situation may not justify charging.   For example, while it may be proper for the police to arrest three persons who are leaving the

[23] People v. Asta, 337 Mich. 590, 60 N.W.2d 472 (1953).   Since the evidence at the preliminary is heard only by the judge, the reason for exclusion stated in Brinegar (text at footnote 22) could hardly apply.   Rather, the rationale seems to be that since the issue is whether there is enough evidence to justify subjecting the defendant to trial, it involves some consideration of the likelihood of conviction, in which case the evidence must be considered in terms of its admissibility at the trial.   See the excellent discussion of this point in Note, 1963 Wash. U.L.Q. 102.

[24] See page 251.

[25] People v. Ward, 226 Mich. 45, 196 N.W. 971 (1924).

[26] Smith v. Hern, 102 Kan. 373, 170 Pac. 990 (1918).

[27] People v. Asta, 337 Mich. 590, 60 N.W.2d 472 (1953).   In this case the court held that hearsay evidence was admissible at the preliminary examination for the purpose of showing that the officers were justified in making an arrest, but not for the purpose of proving probable cause at the preliminary.

State v. Cox, 258 Wis. 162, 176, 45 N.W.2d 100, 103 (1950); Scaffido v. State, 215 Wis. 389, 254 N.W. 651 (1934).   The dissenting judge in Cox said, "It does not seem to me to be logical to contend that an arrest can be justified if it is based only upon what an officer may have heard from others."

[28] See page 246.

[29] See page 248.

scene of a crime and fit the general description given by the victim, it does not follow that the prosecutor may charge all three, or any one of the three, without more evidence than was available at the time of arrest.

Thus, although there is a lack of express judicial recognition of a difference between the arrest and charging standards, it seems that police may sometimes properly arrest a person whom the prosecutor may properly refuse to charge. This is especially true when significant events occur after the arrest. For example, if two armed robbery suspects, arrested because of their resemblance to the description of the responsible parties and their being identified as such by a police informant, should vigorously deny any implication in the crime, it would seem unreasonable for the prosecutor to charge them without at least first requiring the accuser to confront them and repeat the accusation.[30] Denial following an arrest may justify a refusal to charge even though the evidence at the time of the arrest was also sufficient for charging purposes.[31]

2. *Judicial reactions to challenged detentions for obtaining evidence for charging.* Some courts have expressly upheld police detention of a suspect following a lawful arrest where police were seeking further evidence before deciding to charge or to release the suspect. Despite some earlier language to the contrary,[32] both the

[30] These facts are from Goldsmith v. United States, 277 F.2d 335, 337 (D.C. Cir. 1960), where the court said, "if a suspect, arrested or not, denies knowledge of a crime, the police are entitled, if indeed not obliged, to confront him with those who have implicated him."

[31] Even the Mallory court seems to grant this, saying: "Circumstances may justify a brief delay between arrest and arraignment, as for instance, where the story volunteered by the accused is susceptible of quick verification through third parties." Mallory v. United States, 354 U.S. 449, 455, 77 Sup. Ct. 1356, 1360, 1 L. Ed. 2d 1479, 1483 (1957).

[32] In Bailey v. Loomis, 228 Mich. 338, 200 N.W. 148 (1924), the police were investigating the case of a woman charged with the murder of her daughter's illegitimate baby. They had received information suggesting that Bailey, the cousin of the woman's husband, had been connected with the disposition of the body. He was arrested at 9:00 A.M. and was held until the questioning was completed, some time after 3:00 P.M. He later commenced a false arrest action. Judgment for the plaintiff was affirmed by an equally divided court, but in the opinion for reversal is found the following language: "If the defendants caused the arrest and detention of the plaintiff, the evidence is undisputed that they did so for the sole purpose of interviewing him in regard to his connection with the crime or his knowledge of it. . . . There was no intention to have him brought before a magistrate or to prosecute him. In fact the purpose of the interview was to determine if there was probable cause for public prosecution. . . . This is not a case such as police officers of large cities are sometimes called upon to investigate, where there is an urgent and immediate necessity for bringing in parties suspected of a felony." 228 Mich. at 345-347, 200 N.W. at 150.

This language is directed precisely at the not uncommon practice of questioning persons to determine if they should be charged. However, a careful reading of the Bailey case indicates that the quoted language was prompted by evidence that the

Michigan and Wisconsin courts have adopted this view and thus present an interesting contrast to the position taken by the United States Supreme Court in the *Mallory* case. Michigan has recognized the practice of detention following a lawful arrest notwithstanding a statutory requirement that officers take arrested persons before a magistrate "without unnecessary delay." [33] And the Wisconsin court has construed a requirement that the arrested person be brought before a magistrate "without unreasonable delay" as being consistent with delay reasonably necessary for an adequate investigation prior to the decision as to whether to charge.[34]

The Michigan case of *Mooradian v. Davis*[35] is an excellent example of a situation in which the prosecutor might properly want more evidence before charging the arrested person. After a fire of apparently incendiary character, all of the evidence seemed to point toward the man who was purchasing the building on a land contract: he was in default of payments; foreclosure was threatened; because of a previous fire he had received insurance payments which

---

police did not have sufficient grounds for the arrest of Bailey and that they followed the practice of bringing in a number of suspects for questioning. It is not clear what is meant by the court's distinction between the case at hand and those sometimes handled by police in large cities, but the court may have been referring to the apparent availability of Bailey for questioning without being arrested.

The earliest Wisconsin case on this question is Geldon v. Finnegan, 213 Wis. 539, 252 N.W. 369 (1934), in which a thirty-six-hour detention of an arson suspect by a deputy fire marshal was held illegal. The court held that because the detention was based upon a nonexistent power of the fire marshal to detain for investigation, it was illegal even if some lawful basis was available. Although the court also said that "it was not until the investigating officer had satisfied himself that in his opinion there was evidence sufficient to charge the plaintiff with arson that he was authorized to make an arrest," 213 Wis. at 547, 252 N.W. at 372, this result was compelled by a statute so limiting the arrest authority of the state fire marshal.

[33] Mich. Stat. Ann. §§28.872, 28.885 (1954).

[34] Peloquin v. Hibner, 231 Wis. 77, 285 N.W. 380 (1939); Schoette v. Drake, 139 Wis. 18, 120 N.W. 393 (1909).

In a recent federal case involving a false arrest action against Wisconsin officers, the court took note of this judicially declared "without unreasonable delay" requirement, saying that it appeared to be "no different from that followed in courts generally, both State and Federal," and added that it is "analogous to that contained in Rule 5(a) of the Federal Rules of Criminal Procedure." Czap v. Marshall, 315 F.2d 766, 770 (7th Cir. 1963). The court gave no attention to the conflict between the statements in the Wisconsin cases that there may be delay for purposes of gaining additional evidence for charging and the notion expressed in Mallory and other federal cases that a person should not be arrested unless he can be charged. It is interesting to note that the court found the detention of about one day lawful, not by considering the Wisconsin cases allowing delay, but by citing cases where the federal courts found longer delays not to be in violation of Rule 5(a). However, in the two cases cited the court merely said that all of the delay was not relevant to the admissibility of the confession; in one most of the time lapse was after the confession was received, and in the other most of the delay preceded the confession, but in this case state officers held the suspect for some time before federal authorities were notified.

[35] 302 Mich. 484, 5 N.W.2d 435 (1942).

he applied on the contract; he had materially increased the amount of his insurance coverage shortly before the fire; he was the last person known to leave the building and the only person with a key; and evidence of arson was found in the building. The suspect was placed under arrest on Monday. On Tuesday the prosecutor refused a warrant and asked for further investigation. On Thursday the suspect was taken into court on a writ of habeas corpus, and the judge directed that he be charged or released by 3:00 P.M. The prosecuting attorney again refused to approve a warrant, stating that he wanted proof that the suspect was in the area at the time of the fire. In subsequent false imprisonment litigation the supreme court approved the lower court's referral of the reasonableness of detention question to the jury (which found the length of time reasonable). The court said: "The record leaves no doubt that the officers in good faith were energetically endeavoring to discover the true facts and circumstances throughout the short period during which appellant was in custody." [36]

The court did not expressly state that the investigation was (or should be) for purposes of obtaining evidence to charge, although the facts make it clear that the police were attempting to obtain evidence to satisfy the prosecutor. A more recent Michigan decision suggests such a limitation. In *People v. Hamilton,*[37] the police, investigating the murder of Hirmiz, questioned the decedent's wife, who had been found at the murder scene bound hand and foot. She contended that a stranger had entered the apartment and killed her husband, but upon further questioning the police detected some flaws in her story. A man named Hamilton, a friend of the family, arrived on the scene shortly after the police and was arrested with Mrs. Hirmiz. The arrests occurred Friday morning, and on Saturday morning Mrs. Hirmiz confessed that she and Hamilton had committed the murder. Using her confession, the police then questioned Hamilton, who finally gave a confession the following Monday evening.

The primary concern of the court[38] seems to be the fact that the

---

36 302 Mich. at 489, 5 N.W.2d at 437.

37 359 Mich. 410, 102 N.W.2d 738 (1960). Decided after the field observations in Michigan were concluded, the Hamilton case is the first state case adopting the Mallory sanction of excluding a confession obtained during an illegal detention. It illustrates well that the appropriateness of the Mallory norm and that of the Mallory sanction are two quite separate and distinct questions.

38 Some of the court's language suggests the adoption of the requirements of Rule 5(a) as well as the exclusionary aspects of the Mallory rule. There are statements suggesting that the Michigan rule is now the equivalent of the federal standard: "[T]he reasoning of Mallory . . . and Upshaw . . . should be inosculated with quoted sections 13 and 26 [the Michigan statutes requiring production before the magistrate 'without unnecessary delay'] quite as firmly as if written therein. . . . Said

police had sufficient evidence to charge Hamilton with murder prior to the time of his confession:

> *Hamilton's continued detention . . . was unlawful because* the delay was unnecessary, and unlawful because its manifest purpose was that of "sweating" a confession after *the officers were fully enabled to complain and arraign . . .* Here the delay *(from and after, at least, the time of Mrs. Hirmiz' confession)* was "unnecessary" as a matter of law. . . . Hamilton should have been taken before a magistrate no later than Saturday afternoon, immediately following the confession of his codefendant.[39]

The Wisconsin court has also judged the propriety of detention according to whether it was necessary to gain sufficient evidence for charging. In *Peloquin v. Hibner*[40] the plaintiff was held while her co-suspects were apprehended and brought back to the county where all could be questioned and their stories checked. The court noted that there were grounds for the arrest and added that the two-day detention was proper.

> This was the earliest opportunity the sheriff had to obtain statements from the Peloquins and to check their statements with the information he had obtained up to that time relative to the bank robbery. The reasonableness or unreasonableness of the period of detention must be determined from the facts and circumstances in each case. There is no suggestion that the sheriff and the district attorney of Columbia county did not expedite their investigation following the examinations on Monday night, with due diligence and dispatch. *The defendants [police] and the district attorney were entitled to a reasonable time* on Tuesday, June 1st, as a matter of law, *to determine whether to make a formal complaint against the plaintiff or release her from custody.*[41]

The implication in *Peloquin* is that in some cases where there are grounds to arrest it is necessary to obtain further evidence be-

---

sections 13 and 26, and Rule 5(a) of the Federal Rules of Criminal Procedure . . . are quite alike and equally mandatory." Id. at 415, 416, 102 N.W.2d at 741-742.

That the court did not really adopt the federal standard seems clear from the more recent case of People v. Harper, 365 Mich. 494, 113 N.W.2d 808 (1962).

[39] People v. Hamilton, *supra*, at 416-417, 102 N.W.2d at 742 (1960). [Emphasis supplied.] Although, as suggested earlier, one major difference in the arrest and charging standards is that rules of evidence must be applied at the time of the latter determination, Hamilton cannot be explained on this basis, as the confession of Mrs. Hirmiz would not have been admissible against Hamilton. People v. Wysocki, 267 Mich. 5, 255 N.W. 160 (1934). Perhaps the case is explainable by the fact that at the time of arrest there were grounds for charging as well but that in view of Hamilton's denials he was properly not immediately charged until Mrs. Hirmiz' confession, though not admissible, further implicated him. See discussion at p. 327. The court does not disclose the basis of Hamilton's arrest, however.

[40] 231 Wis. 77, 285 N.W. 380 (1939).

[41] 231 Wis. at 86-87, 285 N.W. at 385. [Emphasis supplied.]

fore charging and that reasonable detention for this purpose is proper. This is further supported by *State v. Francisco*,[42] in which a 17-year-old girl told of having sexual relations with her step-father. On this evidence the stepfather was arrested and was questioned in the district attorney's office for an hour prior to his initial appearance before the magistrate. In response to the defendant's reliance on the *McNabb* case,[43] the court said:

> Was the mere taking of defendant to the district attorney's office for questioning a violation of his constitutional rights? It would appear that *the district attorney had not made up his mind to prosecute at the time he sent for the defendant.* The intelligence of the girl was below normal. The district attorney had the duty of checking her story, and the method selected by him was not unreasonable.[44]

Thus both Michigan and Wisconsin recognize a right of detention following a valid arrest when it is necessary to obtain additional evidence before making the charging decision. No fixed time period can be set to apply to every case; a detention does not automatically become unreasonable because of the passage of two hours, ten hours, twenty-four hours, or any other span of time.[45] The investigation must be carried on with "due diligence and dispatch," [46] and if the police have made no progress after a time they may be obligated to release the suspect.[47] The nature of the crime is a factor, so that offenses usually requiring detailed investigation may justify a longer detention.[48]

In contrast to these cases from Michigan and Wisconsin, the Kansas decisions contain no direct holding as to the propriety of detention for purposes of obtaining evidence sufficient for charging, although dicta in a few cases suggest that such detention is

[42] 257 Wis. 247, 43 N.W.2d 38 (1950).

[43] McNabb v. United States, 318 U.S. 332, 63 Sup. Ct. 608, 87 L. Ed. 819 (1943), was the forerunner of the Mallory case and held that noncompliance with Rule 5(a) necessitates exclusion of the confession obtained thereby.

[44] State v. Francisco 257 Wis. 247, 252, 43 N.W.2d 38, 40-41 (1950). [Emphasis supplied.]

[45] Geldon v. Finnegan, 213 Wis. 539, 252 N.W. 369 (1934). Rather, the circumstances of the particular case must be considered. Peloquin v. Hibner, 231 Wis. 77, 285 N.W. 380 (1939).

It is interesting to note that a movement in Wisconsin to adopt the Uniform Arrest Act detention provision there, allowing twenty-four hours and forty-eight additional hours upon good cause shown to a judge, was defeated primarily because of the opposition of law enforcement officers, who viewed the flexible rule as more desirable.

[46] Ibid.

[47] Leisure v. Hicks, 336 Mich. 148, 57 N.W.2d 473 (1953).

[48] Thus: "The crime of arson, of which plaintiff was suspected, is generally one requiring detailed and sometimes prolonged investigation." Mooradian v. Davis, 302 Mich. 484, 488-489, 5 N.W.2d 435, 437 (1942).

considered illegal. In the early case of *State v. Beebe*,[49] the court said:

> Under our system of criminal jurisprudence we are of the opinion that no person can be deprived of his liberty on account of some criminal charge against him except by virtue of some written authority therefor, except in cases where the accused may be arrested before any warrant has ever been issued. But even in cases where the accused may be arrested without warrant, he must be immediately taken before a magistrate, and a complaint be filed against him, and a warrant issued wherewith to hold him, or the custody of him would become unlawful.[50]

In more recent cases defendants have attempted to have their statements excluded because they were made prior to the initial appearance before the magistrate. In *State v. Smith*[51] and *State v. Vargas*,[52] both of which involved admissions given the day following arrest and before complaint, warrant, or initial appearance, the court merely held that such statements were admissible if freely made without inducement or duress. In neither of these cases did the court indicate its view of the propriety of the detention.

C. Consequences Where Practice Is Recognized by Law

The fact that detention for purposes of investigation is recognized in Michigan and Wisconsin and not in Kansas provides a basis for comparing the effect of the different views on day-to-day law enforcement practice. The distinction is somewhat blurred, however, because communication of the decisions of appellate courts to the police who are expected to adhere to them is almost always inadequate. Police manuals and training materials often do not attempt a careful statement of the decisions, and those which do are not always kept current. In addition, much police material is drafted without reference to any particular jurisdiction and consequently fails to reflect important variations in state law.

However, unlike the Kansas police, the police in Michigan and

49 13 Kan. 589 (1874).

50 13 Kan. at 595. This dictum was quoted in the more recent case of Whalen v. Cristell, 161 Kan. 747, 173 P.2d 252 (1946), though the facts there concerned detention after initial appearance without preliminary hearing as required by statute.

Similarly, dictum in Crebs v. Amrine, 153 Kan. 736, 746, 113 P.2d 1084, 1090 (1941), a writ of habeas corpus case in which the petitioner alleged he had been beaten while in jail, said that there was "no authority in law . . . for holding persons in custody more than a few hours at most without a warrant for their arrest as contemplated by law."

51 158 Kan. 645, 149 P.2d 600 (1944).

52 180 Kan. 716, 308 P.2d 81 (1957).

Wisconsin are generally of the view that they do have authority to detain a suspect for investigation after arrest. They usually indicate that the authorized detention is for a "reasonable time up to seventy-two hours." Thus, where there are grounds for arrest and police believe that the necessary investigation can be completed within this time, they make the arrest and proceed with the investigation, reasonably confident that if the custody is challenged by a writ of habeas corpus they will be allowed to complete the investigation. Special steps, such as the vagrancy arrest or the probation or parolee hold, are taken by the Michigan and Wisconsin police only in the very few instances in which they believe that it is necessary to detain the suspect for longer than the seventy-two-hour maximum which they believe a court will allow.[53]

Testing the validity of a detention is possible by means of a writ of habeas corpus.[54] The writ is commonly resorted to, particularly in Detroit,[55] in cases in which the police are actively pursuing an investigation in the hope of obtaining evidence sufficient to charge. In Detroit an attorney, on learning that a client is being held by the police, fills in a printed form for the writ petition and the writ and takes them to the clerk of Recorder's Court. The clerk notes on the petition that he has seen it and then notifies the appropriate supervisory police officer in the division holding the suspect. The attorney takes the petition and writ to one of the judges, who immediately signs the writ.[56] Most writs are applied for early in the morning, and in such cases the hearing is usually set for 11:00 A.M. When writs are applied for later in the morning the hearing is usually set for 2:00 P.M., although some judges will schedule hearings any time during regular hours. Hearings are often set on short notice, leaving the investigating officer little time to get to court.[57] Often, if the officer arrives before the time set for the hearing, he will contact the judge in his chambers and explain at

---

[53] Because these practices are much more common when there are not even grounds for arrest, they are described and considered in more detail in Chapter 16. The various controls and sanctions are considered in Chapters 18 through 20.

[54] Mich. Stat. Ann. §§27.2250 to 27.2270 (1938); Wis. Stat. §§292.01 to 292.21 (1955).

[55] In 1956, for example, the Detroit Recorder's Court handled a total of 5274 habeas corpus writs (compared with 6380 felony cases and 20,452 misdemeanor cases). The vice bureau alone was required to respond to 1125 writs that year, and one of the department's fifteen precincts received about 400 writs during this period. However, many of these writs were used in Detroit to terminate the detention of persons being held purely for deterrent or punitive purposes. See Part V.

[56] One of the judges indicated that they always sign these writs. Refusal by a judge to grant a writ legally applied for subjects him to $1000 damages to the party aggrieved. Mich. Stat. Ann. §27.2260 (1938).

[57] Detectives who are conducting investigations away from their headquarters are required to phone in hourly in order to learn if any writs have been issued on cases they are investigating.

that time why continued custody is needed, perhaps giving the investigation report to the judge to read. At this time the officer will give to the judge any information he does not want to disclose in court because it would reveal the status of the case to the defendant and his attorney.[58]

At the hearing in open court, attended by the officer, the prisoner, and the prisoner's counsel, the officer will state briefly the need for additional time to conduct an investigation. The judge then determines (a) how much additional time is to be allowed the police before they must discharge the prisoner or obtain a warrant charging him with an offense and (b) whether the prisoner is to be kept in custody during this period.[59]

The judge allows additional time for investigation by granting an adjournment or continuance (the terms are used interchangeably by the judges) for a fixed period, usually twenty-four or forty-eight hours. A lesser time may be set if it is clear that the investigation is almost concluded.[60] As a general rule adjournments will not be granted for more than forty-eight hours. The hearings are usually brief and without any detailed inquiry into the circumstances of the particular case. One of the judges explained the criteria he employs in setting the time for investigation as follows:

> Fundamentally, a defendant should be charged within a reasonable time after his arrest. The reasonableness of the time depends entirely on the circumstances of the case. For example, in a murder case the police should be given the opportunity of three or four days in which to investigate. On the other hand, if the charge is relatively minor — grand larceny, for instance — then the reasonableness of time should be about two days. In other words, the length of time given the police officer to investigate varies in direct proportion to the seriousness of the offense under investigation.

Although bail is set in a majority of the habeas corpus hearings in Detroit,[61] it is not usually set in cases involving a continuing police investigation.[62] In these cases, if the judge believes that

---

[58] If the officer does not have an opportunity for such a conference, or if he feels he is not conveying his point to the judge in the course of the hearing, he may request a brief adjournment of the hearing. He will then contact an assistant prosecutor and explain the case to him. The assistant prosecutor will appear to argue for no bond or high bond.

[59] Defense counsel do not inquire into the adequacy of the grounds for arrest at this time, nor do the judges ordinarily make such inquiries.

[60] Some cases were observed in which the officer indicated that all that remained to be done was to consult with an assistant prosecutor. The judge in such cases adjourned the hearing for a half hour.

[61] If a person is found to be legally committed, the judge is to "proceed to let such party to bail, if the case be bailable." Mich. Stat. Ann. §27.2274 (1938).

[62] It is usually set in cases where the individual is being detained for deterrent or punitive purposes. See Part V. Instances were noted in which bail was granted

continued custody is necessary for an adequate investigation, he will either set no bail or set bail sufficiently high to preclude release. The necessity for continued detention may relate to in-custody interrogation, a lineup, or preventing the suspect from warning his confederates. If the investigating officer does not indicate to the judge that continued custody of the suspect is necessary for an orderly investigation, the judge will set bail.[63]

While these procedures are most frequent in Detroit, they also occur in other Michigan municipalities.[64] Milwaukee police are not frequently called upon to respond to writs of habeas corpus, but when they are, the continuance device is employed there as well.[65]

The remand of suspects to the police can be supported on the basis of Michigan and Wisconsin appellate cases discussed earlier.[66]

---

upon the provision that the person report back to the police station, but these were likewise not cases where the detention was for purposes of investigation. The persons were to return to the station so that they could be lectured by the inspector.

[63] An example of a case in which the investigation was to continue but continued custody was not necessary is that of a man arrested for writing bad checks. The police indicated that they wanted an additional forty-eight hours to see if any more checks were discovered, so the suspect was released on bail.

[64] In Pontiac local attorneys rarely use the writ in an attempt to free suspects from in-custody investigation. If an attorney does petition for a writ, the local judge will tell him to "cool his heels" while the police continue with the investigation.

[65] One high official in the Milwaukee department was interviewed on the subject. He indicated that an attorney does occasionally produce a writ of habeas corpus, but the judges refuse to grant them and usually give the police twelve additional hours in which to complete their investigation if they can prove constant and continuous investigation. His reference is apparently to an adjournment or continuance of the hearing on the writ under the circumstances recited. An appellate case from Milwaukee recites facts in accord with this view. State v. Babich, 258 Wis. 290, 45 N.W.2d 660 (1951).

[66] There are, nonetheless, expressions of disbelief that such practices exist: "If *habeas corpus* was brought, we believe that no court would permit custody without committal to be continued an instant because of the desirability of interrogation or the inadvisability of warning confederates. We know of no case which could be cited to bar the writ on such grounds." Memorandum by A.B.A. Committee on the Bill of Rights, 1944, reprinted in Confessions and Police Detention, Hearings before the Subcommittee on Constitutional Rights of the Committee on the Judiciary, United States Senate, 85th Cong., 2d Sess., pursuant to S. Res. 234, Mar. 7 and 11, 1958, 37-38.

The practice has come to the attention of the supreme courts of both Michigan and Wisconsin, and neither court has criticized it. Mooradian v. Davis, 302 Mich. 484, 5 N.W.2d 435 (1942); State v. Babich, 258 Wis. 290, 45 N.W.2d 660.

More recently, since the practices were observed by the field researchers, the Michigan Supreme Court has once again had the practice brought to its attention. A person was arrested in Detroit for investigation in connection with a murder. On the day following his arrest, an attorney caused a writ to be issued in Recorder's Court, and, at the request of the police, the judge adjourned the hearing until the following morning to give the police additional time to conduct their investigation concerning the defendant's denial that he had been in the vicinity at the time of the crime. On the next day the hearing was adjourned for an additional forty-eight hours because the police informed the judge that the defendant had named another

That is, if, as these cases state, the police can sometimes detain after arrest for the purpose of obtaining information sufficient for charging, then a judge might have occasion at a habeas corpus hearing to remand the suspect. Such a remand is consistent with these cases if the judge finds (a) that sufficient grounds for arrest exist, (b) that sufficient grounds for charging do not exist, and (c) that the permissible time for investigation has not expired.[67] Whether the judge is under a duty to set a time limit on the continuing investigation is not decided in the reported cases, but this is usually done in practice, particularly in Detroit, and this prevents the suspect from having to petition for further writs until charged or released.

In Michigan and Wisconsin, then, it seems proper to deny bail at a writ of habeas corpus hearing if the proper time for investiga-

---

person in whose company he was when he last saw the victim, but they had not had an opportunity to question the person. The case reached the Michigan Supreme Court before trial upon an appeal from a denial of defendant's motion to quash the information charging murder. As to the defendant's claim that his detention for four days between arrest and arraignment was unlawful, the court said that once the defendant was brought before a judge on the writ the legality of the detention no longer depended upon the original commitment, as from that point on the defendant's liberty was the exclusive responsibility of the judge who issued the writ. However, the court noted that their appellate jurisdiction had not been invoked to review the proceedings on the writ. Accordingly, the court affirmed the denial of defendant's motion and expressly stated that it was not considering the propriety of the two adjournments of the hearing on the writ. People v. McCager, 367 Mich. 116, 116 N.W.2d 205 (1962).

One apparent consequence of the McCager case is the issuance by the Michigan Supreme Court of an "Order of Superintending Control — Habeas Corpus Proceedings," dated March 7, 1963, 42 Mich. St. Bar J. No. 4, 56 (April, 1963), which, inter alia, directs all inferior courts that "adjournments may be granted upon respondent's request only for such brief delay as may be necessary to permit respondents [sic] to prepare written answers (unless waived by petitioner) or to present to the court or judge issuing the writ or order testimonial or documentary evidence to establish the cause of detention as of the time for answer." Also, since it was said in McCager that responsibility for the prisoner passes to the judge issuing the writ, the order directs that in the event of a brief adjournment "the prisoner shall be advised by the judge . . . that he has a right to counsel and that he need not incriminate himself."

Of course, while the judges have remanded suspects to police custody under the guise of an adjournment of the hearing, they might well accomplish substantially the same result by holding the hearing immediately and deciding that the detention is lawful under the cases authorizing the police to seek evidence for charging after a lawful arrest. Were they to do this, however, the judges would be more obliged to first determine that there were grounds for arrest (which is not now done) and to use more care in deciding whether the police are seeking grounds for charging and whether the time for such investigation has already expired.

[67] The practice in these states, then, could be criticized on the grounds that (1) defense counsel and judges have neglected to insure that at least the original arrest was legal, and (2) the need for further investigation is not as carefully considered as it should be and is often in part based upon information received ex parte in the judge's chambers.

tion has not expired. The provisions for bail in the habeas corpus statutes are not inconsistent with this conclusion,[68] nor are the general bail statutes.[69] Indeed, the release of a person on bail in such a situation would be inconsistent with these appellate decisions.[70]

There are instances in which the judge at the hearing grants the police additional time for investigation and at the same time releases the suspect on bail. This may occur when time for further investigation is needed, but the investigation does not require the continued custody of the suspect. For example, it may become apparent that a decision as to charging will be possible after the tracing of certain property found on the suspect's person at the time of arrest. Under these circumstances, it might be contended that the suspect should be released outright, that he should be released on bail, or that he should not be released until the investigation is completed. The first alternative is consistent with the assumption that a person ought not have to pay to gain his release when there is not enough evidence to charge him and his presence is not essential to the ongoing investigation. The second is consistent with the assumption that allowing arrest of one who cannot be charged is for the purpose of insuring his appearance when the investigation is completed. The third position stresses even more the importance of insuring the continued availability of the suspect. The alternative required by law has not been determined by the appellate courts in the two jurisdictions under discussion.[71]

68 The Michigan and Wisconsin habeas corpus statutes approve bail "if the case be bailable." Mich. Stat. Ann. §27.2274 (1938); Wis. Stat. §292.23 (1955). Thus, it would appear that no right to bail is given which does not otherwise exist.

69 The general statutes on bail merely refer to cases where the person has been "charged" or where a "warrant issued." See Mich. Stat. Ann. §28.888 (1954); Wis. Stat. §954.034 (1955).

70 The Michigan court has indicated that absolute release under such circumstances is not proper. Hammitt v. Straley, 338 Mich. 587, 61 N.W.2d 641 (1953).

71 In Michigan and Wisconsin there are nearly identical statutes which state that "until judgment be given upon the return" the judge "may either commit such party to the custody of the sheriff . . . or place him in such care, or under such custody, as his age and other circumstances may require." Mich. Stat. Ann. §27.2276 (1938); Wis. Stat. §292.25 (1955). In the recent McCager case in Michigan, discussed in note 66 *supra*, the court quoted with approval a statement by the United States Supreme Court that the prisoner is in the custody of the judge from the time of his production until the case is finally disposed of and that "pending the hearing he may be bailed *de die in diem*, or be remanded to the jail whence he came, or be committed to any other suitable place of confinement under the control of the court." People v. McCager, 367 Mich. 116, 123, 116 N.W.2d 205, 208 (1962).

The relevance of this language to the remand practice discussed in the text above is unclear, as the remand (though characterized as a "continuance") occurs not because of any inability to decide the legality of the present detention but rather because it is thought that time for further in-custody investigation is needed. There is no showing by the police that the validity of the present detention cannot immediately be determined; rather, there is a somewhat imperfect inquiry into the need

D. Consequences Where Practice Is Not
Recognized by Law

In contrast to police in Michigan and Wisconsin, Kansas officers were frequently heard to complain that they have no authority to detain persons after arrest for purposes of further investigation. Officers in Kansas assumed that they were required to take the arrested person before a magistrate "immediately," and they criticized the requirement as unrealistic. While use of the writ of habeas corpus was not frequently observed in Kansas, in the few cases noted the judges did not grant a continuance to allow police further time for investigation.

In-custody investigation is nonetheless a regular practice in Kansas, just as in the other two states, although there are indications that police in Kansas are somewhat more reluctant to resort to it than police in Michigan and Wisconsin. Sometimes Kansas police choose a noncustody alternative when one is available,[72] and in-custody investigation is usually resorted to only after other means fail.[73]

In cases in which police want to make an investigation of a suspect which will take more than a few hours, certain techniques are used to satisfy the requirement that he be arraigned shortly after the arrest and at the same time to permit the police to hold him thereafter on what appears to be a legitimate detention. The most

---

for a continuation of custody in order to obtain additional evidence sufficient for charging.

One apparent consequence of the McCager case has been the supreme court order discussed in note 66 *supra*. After directing that only brief continuances be granted, the court added: "Because determination of legal cause of detention in habeas corpus proceedings must be made expeditiously, with no more than such brief delay as above indicated, the question of release of a prisoner on bail pending hearing should not arise until after determination that legal cause exists for detention. Thereafter, if the offense for which the prisoner is detained is bailable, release may be ordered on bail notwithstanding the existence of legal cause for detention." 42 Mich. S. Bar J. No. 4, 56 (April, 1963).

[72] For example, in one case a large number of grease guns were stolen from a warehouse, and the circumstances suggested an inside job. Later a local lumber dealer notified the police that a person had offered to sell him a number of grease guns at an extremely low price. He was able to furnish only a general description, but the owner of the warehouse indicated that he had an employee who fitted the description. The suspect was not arrested; rather the police arranged for the warehouse owner to take a photograph of his entire crew on the pretense that it would be used for advertising purposes, and this photograph was then shown to the lumber dealer in order to determine whether the suspect was responsible.

[73] For example, four months after an unwitnessed robbery-murder, after the analysis of all evidence at the crime scene had not revealed the responsible party, the police arrested a man known to have had possession of the murder weapon some time before the murder.

common is that of detaining the suspect on a charge of violating the city vagrancy ordinance. In both Wichita and Kansas City, persons whom the police wish to investigate on suspicion of a felony are often handled in this way. After arrest the suspect is booked on "vagrancy and investigation," and a high bail is set. When the case reaches the city police court the following day,[74] a continuance is granted (often for a week) while the investigation continues. The local police judges require only that the police indicate what specific offense is being investigated.[75] At the conclusion of the investigation, the person is either released or held for a state warrant on the serious charge which was being investigated.

Holding the person on a charge of violating the city vagrancy ordinance, while circumventing the apparent requirement of immediate warrant and appearance before a magistrate where the arrest is for a state offense, would ordinarily not be a useful alternative if the suspect were treated as the usual ordinance violator. By statute, a police chief is to set bail immediately for ordinance violators arrested without warrant.[76] This is the usual practice in Wichita, and there is no difficulty in finding a bondsman. A list of suggested bail amounts for the common ordinance violations exists in the Wichita department for the guidance of the station lieutenant or desk sergeant who sets the bond. The highest suggested amount is $500, except in the case of vagrancy, for which the schedule provides for a range between $100 and $1000. While an ordinary vagrant must post a $100 bond, bond is set at $1000 when it is desired that the person be held for investigation. This amount is usually sufficient to hold the suspect, but sometimes bond is set at $2000 cash or $4000 property, an amount which the bondsmen will not consider. In any event, the bondsmen tend to cooperate with the police and often "vanish" on learning that the person is being held for investigation.

The uncertainty on the part of police about the propriety of this method of achieving in-custody investigation is reflected in their hesitation to acknowledge its use.[77] However, in Wichita even the

---

74 Apparently there is no delay in this regard. In fact, it is the duty of the station lieutenant in Wichita to see that all persons charged with vagrancy go to court the first court date after arrest. Wichita Police Dept., Duty Manual 40 (undated).

75 The police usually comply with this requirement, although they sometimes hold a man for no specific offense, but just because he "looks like he is no good."

76 Kan. Gen. Stat. §13-623 (1949).

77 Thus some Wichita police officers denied that the procedure was ever used. However, a defense attorney and a local newspaperman both asserted that it was frequently resorted to, and a considerable number of "vagrancy and investigation" bookings were noted in the narcotics case file. Similarly, a Kansas City detective said the practice was not employed, though a local parole officer indicated the con-

police duty manual provides booking for "vagrancy and investigation" where "there is some specific case under which the person should be investigated, or there is some specific reason for general investigation." [78]

Occasionally the same result is reached without charging vagrancy. For example, on one occasion a murder suspect was brought into the police court in Kansas City for an "informal arraignment," at which a high bail was set and the suspect was remanded to police custody, although there had been no warrant issued at that time. The judge explained that although he did not have jurisdiction to act as a magistrate in murder cases,[79] this method had been effective for allowing police to continue their investigation.[80] Such a practice seems clearly contrary to the Kansas statute requiring that city police turn over persons arrested for a state offense to the county sheriff "immediately" after arrest.[81]

Both of these techniques require the cooperation of local police justices and have proved fairly successful. Although bail is set in both situations, if police want to investigate, it is set so high that the suspect is unlikely to be able to put it up. In the rare case in which the suspect has funds, he is likely to use them to make bail rather than to retain counsel and attempt to gain his outright release by habeas corpus. Bail in these cases serves as a safety valve, preventing the detention practices from coming to the attention of judges in the state criminal justice system.

In Kansas, suspects are not remanded to the police at a habeas corpus proceeding. For this reason, Kansas police try to avoid such proceedings. On some occasions police deny, in response to a call from counsel, that a particular suspect is in custody. And, even though a Kansas statute requires that a person in custody be allowed to confer "immediately" with counsel "upon request," [82] the opportunity to contact counsel is sometimes denied by delaying the booking process[83] until the in-custody investigation has been

---

trary, and numerous "vagrancy and investigation" charges were to be found on the police court docket.

[78] Wichita Police Dept., Duty Manual 11 (undated).

[79] Police courts can only try city ordinance violations. Kan. Gen. Stat. §13-602 (1949). However, a police judge can issue a warrant in a felony case. Kan. Gen. Stat. §§62-201, 62-601 (1949).

[80] A similar practice was noted elsewhere in the state; thus a person is sometimes taken before a justice of the peace, who sets a high bail and returns the suspect to police custody, although no warrant has been issued and no charging decision made.

[81] Kan. Gen. Stat. §13-623 (1949).

[82] Kan. Gen. Stat. §62-1304a (1949).

[83] In Wichita the right to make a phone call is part of the booking process, and the interrogation form used indicates the name of the defendant's attorney and states whether he has been notified.

completed. This tactic is limited to those cases in which the police fear they will have to respond to a writ of habeas corpus or will have their interrogation interrupted by the attorney.[84] On other occasions this fear leads to the suspect's being placed in a jail other than that of the department holding him. However, as one officer observed, this is "touchy business" and consequently is rarely resorted to.

The fact that Kansas police, lacking express authority to detain for investigation, resort to the described tactics does not prove the necessity of in-custody investigation. It does indicate, however, that the police there believe that in-custody investigation is necessary for effective law enforcement. Moreover, it demonstrates that denying express authority to detain for investigation will not eliminate the practice when alternative methods are available to achieve the same objective.

---

[84] The undersheriff in one Kansas county said, "There just are times when this has to be done, because you'd be surprised how quickly defense attorneys will flock like flies to a corpse. I don't know how they get here so fast, but once they get hold of them we're done."

CHAPTER 16

Custody of a Person Who Cannot
Be Arrested for the Crime Suspected

In current criminal justice administration it is not uncommon for persons suspected of criminal conduct to be detained by the police for purposes of investigation although there are not adequate grounds for arrest for the crime suspected. Sometimes this is done without any effort by the police to justify the arrest on another basis. Such detentions occur most often in cases in which the police believe that an in-custody investigation will furnish the additional evidence needed to prosecute the suspect. The risk of a tort action against the officer in such cases is not ordinarily very great,[1] and, since in a large number of cases the suspect is not likely to be carrying critical evidence, the police are willing to sacrifice whatever physical evidence might be uncovered in return for the opportunity to conduct an in-custody investigation. Prior to *Wong Sun v. United States*,[2] at least, an admission obtained incident to an unlawful arrest was admissible.

In other instances police use an alternative to making an arrest, without adequate grounds, for the suspected offense. One alternative is to detain the suspect briefly, usually on the street but occasionally at the station, without telling him that he is under arrest and without recording the detention as an arrest. A second alternative is to "invite" the suspect to the station. In such cases, it is usually at least questionable whether the suspect is given any choice. A third alternative is to make a formal arrest, not for the suspected offense, but for another, minor, offense or for violation of a condition of the suspect's parole or probation.

Wong Sun v. United States makes these alternatives and the question of their propriety of vital importance in current law enforcement. In *Wong Sun*, the court held that the admissibility of a suspect's statement made incident to an arrest is dependent

[1] On the deterrent effect of possible tort liability, see Chapter 20.
[2] 371 U.S. 471, 83 Sup. Ct. 407, 9 L. Ed. 2d 441 (1963).

upon the legality of the arrest.   The case, if broadly construed,[3] means that police will no longer be able to arrest on inadequate grounds for the offense suspected and use in evidence the results of the subsequent in-custody investigation.   It is therefore likely that there will be greater reliance upon the alternatives mentioned above.[4]

[3] The court said that "verbal evidence which derives so immediately from an unlawful entry and an unauthorized arrest as the officers' action in the present case is no less the 'fruit' of official illegality" than tangible evidence uncovered by search. 371 U.S. at 485, 83 Sup. Ct. at 416, 9 L. Ed. 2d at 454.   Thus it is not entirely clear that the same result must be reached when the statement is given some time after the arrest or that it must be reached when the circumstances of the arrest are not such as to prompt a statement.   In Wong Sun the court stressed the fact that the defendant gave the statement immediately after arrest and that the arrest was carried out by six or seven officers, who entered his house by breaking the door, went into his bedroom where his wife and child were sleeping, and immediately handcuffed the defendant.

See United States v. Burke, 215 F. Supp. 508, 511 (D. Mass. 1963), where Judge Caffrey held: "I do not read the recent decision in Wong Sun . . . or any other opinion of the Supreme Court, as ruling that as a matter of law a person who is illegally arrested is thereby rendered legally incapable of making any voluntary admission or any voluntary surrender of property on his person by reason of the illegal arrest.   I believe that whether or not an admission or a surrender of property made after an illegal arrest is voluntary and therefore admissible in evidence, or involuntary and therefore inadmissible, is to be decided on a motion to suppress as a question of fact . . . in the resolution of which the trier of fact should have in mind the 'oppressive circumstances' . . . surrounding the illegal arrest and should require clear and convincing evidence that the admission or surrender is the product of an intervening independent act of the defendant's free will."

Even if Wong Sun is not broadly construed, the alternatives may also become important in view of the most recent case of Escobedo v. Illinois, 378 U.S. 478, 84 Sup. Ct. 1758, 12 L. Ed. 2d 977 (1964).   The court held that, at least when certain other circumstances are present, there is a constitutional right to counsel at the police station when "the investigation is no longer a general inquiry into an unsolved crime but has begun to focus on a particular suspect" and "the suspect has been taken into police custody."   If the court views arrest of a person on a particular charge as of necessity meaning the investigation of that charge has focused on him, then the alternatives discussed herein may be of considerable importance, particularly if the notion expressed in Massiah v. United States, 377 U.S. 201, 84 Sup. Ct. 1199, 12 L. Ed. 2d 246 (1964), is also applicable.   In Massiah, the court held that, at least as to the right of counsel after indictment in a federal prosecution, the protection afforded by the right to counsel required exclusion of all statements received without the presence or consent of counsel.

[4] Under Mapp v. Ohio, 367 U.S. 643, 81 Sup. Ct. 1684, 6 L. Ed. 2d 108 (1961), the Supreme Court of the United States may be concerned with state police practices of the type described.   The court has emphatically declared that the standard of reasonableness under the Fourth and Fourteenth Amendments is the same, Aguilar v. Texas, 378 U.S. 108, 84 Sup. Ct. 1509, 12 L. Ed. 2d 723 (1964), and it may well be that this means not only that federal standards govern the definition of probable cause but also that they govern on the issue of when an arrest has been made.   The federal courts have generally been more restrictive on the stopping and questioning and consent issues than have many state courts.   Kamisar, Illegal Searches or Seizures and Contemporaneous Incriminating Statements: A Dialogue on a Neglected Area of Criminal Procedure, 1961 U. Ill. L.F. 78, 115-120.

A. Short Detention Not Considered an Arrest

Brief on-the-street or at-the-station detention without a formal arrest occurs fairly regularly in each of the jurisdictions observed. However, there is no express legal authority for these practices in any of these states. Whether police should have such power has long been a matter of debate. Most of the argument has focused upon Section 2 of the Uniform Arrest Act, proposed in 1942 by the Interstate Crime Commission but adopted in only three states.[5] That section provides:

(1) A peace officer may stop any person abroad who he has reasonable ground to suspect is committing, has committed or is about to commit a crime, and may demand of him his name, address, business abroad and whither he is going.

(2) Any person so questioned who fails to identify himself or explain his actions to the satisfaction of the officer may be detained and further questioned and investigated.

(3) The total period of detention provided for by this section shall not exceed two hours. The detention is not an arrest and shall not be recorded as an arrest in any official record. At the end of the detention the person so detained shall be released or be arrested and charged with a crime.[6]

1. *"Field interrogation."* [7]

Illustration No. 1: Officers on patrol at 3:00 A.M. observed a man with a package walking slowly through a residential neighborhood in which a number of burglaries had been committed in recent months. They stopped the man, quickly frisked him for weapons, and then explained that because of the recent burglaries they had to check on persons out late at night. They asked him if he would cooperate by explaining his presence. The suspect said that he was on his way home from work on the night shift, and he showed his employee identification card for a nearby factory. When asked about the contents of the package, he answered that he had purchased two bottles of wine on his way to work, and he opened the

---

[5] Del Code Ann., tit. 11, §1902 (1958); N.H. Rev. Stat. Ann. §594.2 (1960); R.I. Gen. Laws, tit. 12, chap. 7 (1956).

[6] The act is reprinted in its entirety in Warner, The Uniform Arrest Act, 28 U. Va. L. Rev. 315, 343-347 (1942).

[7] A study of the practice of "field interrogation," as a significant investigative technique in current law enforcement, will be found in the volume on Detection of Crime. It is discussed here as another in-custody investigation procedure deserving consideration as an alternative to or complement of the other forms of custody treated in this chapter.

packages and displayed the bottles. One of the officers then prepared a brief field interrogation report, noting the name of the man and the time, place, and circumstances of the stopping. The man was then allowed to go his way.

The momentary stopping of a suspect on the street in order to make inquiries concerning his identity or his actions is a practice referred to by police as "field interrogation." [8] It is a fairly common practice in Kansas, Michigan, and Wisconsin, especially at night. A frisk of the suspect occurs as an incident to the questioning when the officer deems it necessary for his own protection. Reports are often made of these field interrogations and may prove useful in a later investigation. For example, if a burglary is reported in an area in which a suspicious person was questioned, the police have on record a suspect who can be investigated further.

Police sometimes check on the suspect at the time they stop him on the street, by calling headquarters to see if he is wanted or by checking out his story by whatever methods are available. While the detention usually lasts only a matter of minutes, making a check of police records or of the suspect's story may require additional time. If the suspect's story does not check out, if he cannot provide adequate identification, or if he refuses to answer the officer's questions, he is usually taken to the station for further investigation.

The mere asking of questions by an officer without any restraint of the suspect seems clearly lawful.[9] However, in many field interrogations a suspect may conclude either that he is presently under restraint or that his failure to cooperate will result in restraint.[10] The important question therefore is whether a brief restraint is proper when sufficient grounds for arrest do not exist.[11]

Because of the manner in which the cases have reached appellate courts and because of the traditional judicial approach to field

---

[8] See Bristow, Field Interrogation (1958).

[9] See Note, 37 Mich. L. Rev. 311 (1938).

[10] "Custody is 'an actual restraint of the person to be arrested,' which occurs at the moment an individual is no longer a free agent to do as he pleases. . . . Often this is not easy to determine, as where an officer says to a pedestrian, 'Just a minute, I want to ask you a few questions.' Were a civilian to ask such a question there would certainly be no restraint, but what on their face are merely words of request take on color from the officer's uniform, badge, gun and demeanor." Foote, The Fourth Amendment: Obstacle or Necessity in the Law of Arrest?, 51 J. Crim. L., C. & P.S. 402, 403 (1960).

[11] Of course, in many states it is uncertain whether a police officer can resort to field interrogation even when there are sufficient grounds for arrest. Some courts would probably refuse to recognize any privilege of detention notwithstanding the grounds for arrest for the simple reason that the officer failed to go through the mechanics of making an arrest. Discussion of this will be found in the volume on Detection of Crime.

interrogation,[12] many courts have not squarely faced the issues which are involved. Rather, courts have used an oversimplified "single problem" approach, assuming, without analysis, that such a practice is improper absent grounds for arrest because "any restraint of liberty is an arrest." [13]

Decisions made at different stages in the criminal justice process vary in their effect upon the person being dealt with. Generally, it can be said that decisions carrying more serious consequences for the individual require a greater degree of certainty that he is in fact guilty. This suggests that the propriety of field interrogation where there are insufficient grounds for arrest may depend upon whether the harmful effects are substantially less than those which result from a formal arrest.[14] It may be significant in this respect that the field interrogation usually results in a much shorter period of detention than formal arrest,[15] that the suspect does not have an

[12] It appears that few false arrest actions are brought. "I believe that the relative dearth of authority in point can be explained by the fact that few litigants have ever seriously contended that it was illegal for an officer to stop and question a person unless he had 'probable cause' for a formal arrest." United States v. Bonanno, 180 F. Supp. 71, 78 (S.D.N.Y. 1960). If an action is brought, the officer is likely to attempt to bring himself within the one generally recognized privilege category by asserting that an arrest was made. Similarly, in cases in which the suspect is trying to exclude evidence found in a frisk incident to the interrogation, the prosecution will argue that there has been a search incident to a lawful arrest. See Remington, The Law Relating to "On the Street" Detention, Questioning and Frisking of Suspected Persons and Police Arrest Privileges in General, 51 J. Crim. L., C. & P.S. 386-387 (1960).

[13] People v. Esposito, 194 N.Y.S. 326, 332 (1922). Other cases holding that there is no right to question are: Arnold v. State, 255 App. Div. 422, 8 N.Y.S.2d 28 (1938); People v. Tinston, 6 Misc. 2d 485, 164 N.Y.S.2d 544 (1951); Shirey v. State, 321 P.2d 981 (Okla. Crim. App. 1958); Commonwealth v. Balanzo, 261 Pa. 507, 104 Atl. 683 (1918); Commonwealth v. Doe, 109 Pa. Super. Ct. 187, 167 A.2d 241 (1933); Travis v. Bacherig, 7 Tenn. App. 638 (1928).

[14] It could be argued that this approach is equally apropos for determining whether the practice is contrary to the constitutional prohibition against "unreasonable" seizures. For a different view, see Foote, The Fourth Amendment: Obstacle or Necessity in the Law of Arrest?, 51 J. Crim. L., C. & P.S. 402 (1960), and Foote, Safeguards in the Law of Arrest, 52 Nw. U.L. Rev. 16, 36 (1957). The issue was presented to the Supreme Court in Henry v. United States, 361 U.S. 98, 80 Sup. Ct. 168, 4 L. Ed. 2d 134 (1959), and Rios v. United States, 364 U.S. 253, 80 Sup. Ct. 1431, 4 L. Ed. 2d 1688 (1960), but the cases were decided upon other grounds.

The same approach might also be used to determine the validity of other investigative devices such as the active detection methods that the police must use against prostitution, homosexuality, sale of narcotics, and the like. It was observed that some judges were throwing out cases for supposed "entrapment" or "enticement," not because entrapment had occurred in the strict legal sense, but because it became apparent that the police were not being sufficiently selective in deciding whom to approach. The issue of how selective the police actually should be might be viewed in terms of the possible harmful effects upon those approached.

[15] The stopping and questioning of a person on the street usually takes only a few minutes, while a person taken to the station is often detained several hours or more. The distinction does not hold true in all cases, however. Sometimes persons who have been arrested are released almost immediately, and a person stopped

arrest record, although a field interrogation report bearing his name may be filed,[16] and that the suspect will undoubtedly not consider himself under arrest,[17] and consequently can in all honesty answer in the negative if later asked whether he has ever been arrested.[18]   How much weight ought to be given to these factors has not been decided by courts which have dealt with the right of the police to stop and question suspects.[19]   As the pressure to minimize in-custody investigations increases, it becomes more important to know what rights of investigation exist prior to the taking of custody.

2. *Brief unrecorded detention at the station.*

Illustration No. 2: An officer observed on the street a man who fitted a very general description in the daily bulletin of the person responsible for a recent armed robbery. The suspect had no identification on his person but denied that he was the man named in the bulletin. The officer contacted head-

---

on the street may be detained for a substantial period of time if the investigating officer is awaiting the arrival of witnesses or a report from headquarters.

See United States v. Mitchell, 179 F. Supp. 636 (D.D.C. 1959), where the court said that no arrest had been made when an officer stopped, questioned, and obtained the identification of a person carrying a sack at 5:30 A.M., but that an arrest did occur when the officer asked the suspect to accompany him to a call box for the purpose of checking the story given.

16 Also relevant is the permanency of arrest records and field interrogation records in cases not ultimately resulting in further action. Some states have legislated on this subject, e.g., Mich. Stat. Ann. §4.463 (1961), requiring the return of arrest records where the person arrested was not brought to trial, or if brought to trial, was acquitted; N.Y. Code Crim. Proc. §944 (Supp. 1962), Ohio Rev. Code §5149.06 (1954), Ill. Rev. Stat., chap. 38, §780e (1961), all requiring return of photographs, fingerprints, and other records of identification under certain circumstances. It is not clear whether the underlying policy of such statutes requires their application to field interrogation reports.

For a more complete discussion of these statutes, including similar provisions found in England and Australia, see 22 Calif. Assy. Interim Comm. Reps. 1959-1961, No. 1, Report of Assy. Interim Comm. on Crim. Proc. 58-71 (1961).

17 "A layman, if asked if he had even [sic] been arrested, would not be likely to describe situations where he had been stopped by a police officer . . ."   United States v. Bonanno, 180 F. Supp. 71, 78 (S.D.N.Y. 1960).

18 However, employment forms may also inquire as to nonarrest police detentions. See note 29 *infra.*

19 The cases are cited in Remington, The Law Relating to "On the Street" Detention, Questioning and Frisking of Suspected Persons and Police Arrest Privileges in General, 51 J. Crim. L., C. & P.S. 386, 391 nn. 30, 31 (1960).

Of course, if a new "step" in the process were recognized, it would be necessary to articulate and define the probability of guilt required. If something less than "reasonable grounds" or "reasonable cause" to believe were needed, precisely what quantum of evidence would be enough? The Uniform Arrest Act proposes "reasonable grounds to suspect," which on one occasion has been interpreted as synonymous with the arrest norm. DeSalvatore v. State, 163 A.2d 244 (Del. Sup. Ct. 1960). It would obviously be difficult to develop a workable test, but, as has been observed, "the obvious difficulty of the task does not justify the easy alternative of ignoring the issue." Remington, *supra,* at 392.

quarters on a nearby call box and was instructed to bring in the suspect. While the suspect was being brought to the station, the desk sergeant contacted an off-duty detective of the robbery detail, who he knew could positively identify the wanted man, and asked him to come to the station. The suspect was held at the station without booking for about an hour, after which time the detective appeared and determined that he was not the wanted man. The suspect was then released without any record being made of the incident.

Although it is apparently a less common practice than field interrogation, the police in Kansas, Michigan, and Wisconsin do sometimes take suspects to the police station for a brief period of investigation without recording the incident as an arrest. Occasionally a suspect is taken to the station and immediately viewed in a lineup by a victim or a witness. These detentions are usually restricted to cases in which the suspicious circumstances can be explained by brief questioning by a supervisory officer or a detective familiar with the offense, by a quick check on the identity of the suspect, or by a prompt evaluation of certain physical evidence. In some instances this procedure is followed even though there is sufficient evidence to support an arrest of the suspect.[20] However, in many cases grounds for arrest are lacking, so that the question, as with field interrogation, is whether such detention is proper absent adequate evidence for arrest. This issue has received even less attention from the courts than the issue of on-the-street detention.[21] No appellate court has yet ruled on the Uniform Arrest Act

[20] If there are grounds for arrest, then it would seem proper for a police officer to detain a suspect in a manner which does not include all the attributes of the usual arrest, so long as he does not deny him any of the protections available to arrested persons. However, some courts might find this practice illegal even though there were grounds for arrest and for the actual detention, because there was no booking. Yet, if the police refrain from formal arrest when an arrest could legally be made, in order to give the suspect the opportunity to exculpate himself before his involvement can be publicized, then, it is argued, they have acted for the suspect's benefit and should not be charged with illegality. "This is not just an abstract proposition. Consider the case of a man suspected of a sexual assault against a minor. The child gives the name of a man living in the same building. Her story seems plausible to the police for the man had access to the child. Clearly, the police at that point would have a sufficiency of evidence to arrest the man formally and bring him before a magistrate for arraignment. Clearly also, the newspapers would have the right to state that the man had been arrested for a sexual attack. His friends, his business associates, his neighbors would be made aware of the charge by the publicity and the police activity and forever after he would have a record for having been arrested for a sexual crime." United States v. Bonanno, 180 F. Supp. 71, 82 (S.D.N.Y. 1960).

[21] As with field interrogation, there has been a tendency to say either that if the detention is not an arrest it is legal or that the detention must be considered an arrest in order to allow suit for its abuse. The former approach is found in 180 F. Supp. at 77, where it is said: "It is axiomatic that before a finding can be made

two-hour detention provision in a case where grounds for arrest were lacking.[22]

A court recognizing a right of field interrogation would not necessarily approve taking a suspect to the station, since the brief detention at the station has many of the characteristics of a formal arrest.[23]   Such detention makes possible investigative methods similar to those which may follow a formal arrest, particularly intensive in-custody interrogation.[24]   The detention may be of short duration, but the suspect is not ordinarily told that he will be released promptly.

The mere fact that the detention is not called an arrest by police is no basis for distinguishing it from practices which police do refer to as arrests.[25]   But the fact that it is not recorded as an arrest

---

that there has been an *illegal* arrest, a showing must be made that there has been an arrest." However, Judge Kaufman later observes that to rely solely upon the fact that no arrest was made, in the common meaning of the word, would be to fall into a "semantic trap." 180 F. Supp. at 78.

The other approach referred to above appears in Foote, The Fourth Amendment: Obstacle or Necessity in the Law of Arrest?, 51 J. Crim. L., C. & P.S. 402, 404 (1960), where the holding in Bonanno is criticized: "It is apparent, however, that such a construction is absurd, for inasmuch as it makes the officer's intent the controlling factor, it would substitute the policeman for court and law as a protector of liberty. Seizures or arrests without probable cause would be illegal only if the officer ultimately entered a formal charge of crime on insufficient evidence . . ."

[22] In DeSalvatore v. State, 163 A.2d 244 (Del. Sup. Ct. 1960), it seems clear that there were adequate grounds for arrest notwithstanding the reliance by the police on the language of the act. In Schaffer v. State, 184 A.2d 689 (Del. Sup. Ct. 1962), the court merely upheld a consent search after the two hours had expired, and no comment on the provision was necessary.

Indeed, it is far from clear that the Uniform Arrest Act contemplates detention at the station on grounds insufficient for arrest. It must be remembered that the act does not allow at-the-station detention on "reasonable grounds to suspect," except when these grounds (which were the basis for the field interrogation) are accompanied by the suspect's failure to identify himself or explain his actions satisfactorily. An arrest in such a case might well be legal without resort to the language of the act. While refusal to answer a question put by a police officer does not in itself furnish grounds for arrest, State v. Gibbs, 252 Wis. 227, 31 N.W.2d 143 (1948), and while some courts have asserted that "no adverse inference may be drawn" from a refusal to answer, Poulas v. United States, 95 F.2d 412, 413 (9th Cir. 1938) (and see United States v. Bonanno, 180 F. Supp. 71, 86 n.21 [S.D.N.Y. 1960], where the court uses this assertion as support for nonarrest detention at the station), the majority view seems to be that it is appropriate to consider the refusal along with other evidence. E.g., Dickerson v. United States, 120 A.2d 588 (D.C. 1956); People v. Simon, 45 Cal. 2d 645, 290 P.2d 531 (1955).

[23] Even if a court were convinced that a nonarrest detention at the station is less severe than a formal arrest, it might be hesitant to recognize authority to so detain because of concern over administrative feasibility. The question is whether the police could be expected to understand and apply three distinct probability of guilt standards, one for field interrogation, one for nonarrest detention, and one for actual arrest.

[24] This argument is well stated in Foote, Safeguards in the Law of Arrest, 52 Nw. U. L. Rev. 16, 38 (1957).

[25] This point is, of course, emphasized by those opposed to authorizing such de-

and may not be thought of by the individual as an arrest may be of importance.[26] Judge Kaufman, in *United States v. Bonanno*,[27] said that a layman, if asked if he had ever been arrested, would not be likely to describe as an arrest even situations where his questioning had been continued at a police station.[28] It is questionable whether this is so, however. Moreover, with various types of questionnaires, including those for employment, increasingly being revised to ask whether the individual has been "arrested or detained," [29] the distinction between "detention" and "arrest" appears to lose much of its significance.[30] Unrecorded detention may, in fact, carry added risks for the individual. Although immediate booking may operate to the disadvantage of the suspect by giving him an arrest record, it can also operate to his advantage by making his detention visible and thus less subject to abuse.[31] In the

---

tention, e.g., Foote, The Fourth Amendment: Obstacle or Necessity in the Law of Arrest?, 51 J. Crim. L., C. & P.S. 402, 403 (1960), but it is also granted by those who support it: "Thus, an immediate problem of definition arises. Joined to that problem, is the danger that the defining process will cast an air of deceptive simplicity over the broader task actually faced by the Court. One must never forget that this is a decision on the rights of individuals and the duties of government, and not an abstract exercise in definition." United States v. Bonanno, 180 F. Supp. 71, 77 (S.D.N.Y. 1960).

26 The extent to which the lack of record is a significant factor may depend to some extent on the permanency of arrest records. See note 16 *supra*.

27 United States v. Bonanno, 180 F. Supp. 71 (S.D.N.Y. 1960).

28 180 F. Supp. at 78.

29 The Application for Federal Employment, Standard Form 57 (Revised May, 1954) asked: "Have you ever been arrested, charged, or held by Federal, State, or other law-enforcement authorities for any violation of any Federal law, State law, county or municipal law, regulation or ordinance?" The newer Form 57 (Revised March, 1961) inquires: "Have you ever been arrested, taken into custody, held for investigation or questioning, or charged by any law enforcement authority?"

In 22 Calif. Assy. Interim Comm. Reps. 1959-1961, No. 1, Report of Assy. Interim Comm. on Crim. Proc. 57 (1961), it is noted that the employment application form used by the state personnel board asks: "Have you as a juvenile or adult ever been detained by law enforcement officers, or arrested, or convicted of any offense other than traffic violations?" The committee recommended that it be made unlawful for any employment application form used by the state to ask whether the applicant has ever been detained or arrested.

30 "The fact remains that . . . the [Uniform Arrest] act does not wholly eliminate the ignominy which results from a conventional arrest and charge of crime. Inferences are bound to be drawn against anyone who is taken to a police station against his will to be investigated, and the attempt to minimize this stigma is more apparent than real." Foote, Safeguards in the Law of Arrest, 52 Nw. U.L. Rev. 16, 37 (1957).

31 For instances of abuse when there is no booking, see page 340.

If certain rights were attached to booking, it would be questionable whether they should be withheld from the suspect who is not booked. In California a statute allowing the person to use the telephone "immediately after he is booked" has been recently amended to read "immediately after he is booked, and, except where physically impossible, no later than three hours after his arrest." Calif. Penal Code §851.5 (Supp. 1961).

observed jurisdictions, a suspect whom the police merely detain is not booked at all.[32]

B. "VOLUNTARY" CUSTODY

Illustration No. 3: A police officer was informed by a merchant that a pair of gloves was taken from his store while three customers were there. The officer approached one of the three and said, "I would like to see you down to the station for a minute." The suspect accompanied the officer to the station, where the officer explained in detail the nature of his suspicions. The suspect consented to a search of his person and left the station when the gloves were not found.

Police, suspecting a person of an offense but not having grounds for arrest, may "invite" or "request" him to come to the police station to facilitate further investigation. The practice was not observed so frequently as that of consent-search,[33] but *Wong Sun* may cause an increase in its use just as the traditional exclusionary rule has fostered the consent-search practice.[34] In consent-detention cases the police do not require the suspect to indicate his consent in writing as they sometimes do in consent-search cases.

If a suspect does in fact agree to accompany an officer to the station in order to exculpate himself, the fact that the police have chosen to proceed in this fashion is hardly subject to criticism. Indeed, police have been criticized for not employing the consent-detention technique more frequently in investigations.[35] The difficulty is in determining whether there was in fact consent in a particular case.

Prior to *Wong Sun* a statement was admissible without regard to whether the suspect did in fact consent to his detention. As a

[32] The "suspicion of" booking is usually employed in cases of arrest where further investigation is contemplated. See page 302. Some police officers justified this booking on the ground that it had less effect on the suspect than a booking "on the nose." For a similar view by a California district attorney, see Barrett, Police Practices and the Law — From Arrest to Release or Charge, 50 Calif. L. Rev. 11, 27-28 n.73 (1962).

[33] Because the police frequently attempt to justify searches on the basis of supposed consent, it appears that the courts are becoming more strict. See People v. Zeigler, 358 Mich. 355, 100 N.W.2d 456 (1960). Discussion on the consent-search practice in general will be found in the volume on Detection of Crime.

[34] California best demonstrates this cause and effect relationship. After the state supreme court adopted the exclusionary rule, a host of consent cases reached the courts there. See Collings, Toward Workable Rules of Search and Seizure — An Amicus Curiae Brief, 50 Calif. L. Rev. 421, 447 (1962); Kamisar, Illegal Searches or Seizures and Contemporaneous Incriminating Statements: A Dialogue on a Neglected Area of Criminal Procedure, 1961 U. Ill. L.F. 78, 116

[35] See Perkins, Elements of Police Science 302 (1942).

consequence appellate courts have seldom had occasion to consider the practice.[36] In the states studied the only case is the Wisconsin decision of *Gunderson v. Struebing*,[37] the facts of which are given in Illustration No. 3. The court held that it was error for the trial judge to direct a verdict against the police officer:

> . . . [T]here was no array of force exhibited by the officer such as would warrant, necessarily, the plaintiff in believing that if he did not obey the invitation to go to the police station he would be arrested or restrained of his liberty. . . .
>
> If the officer, in the discharge of his duty, in good faith invited plaintiff to the police station for the purpose of interrogating him and investigating the charge, with a view of deciding upon future action, and without any intention at that time of putting plaintiff under arrest or restraint, no case was made by plaintiff . . .[38]

Courts have had difficulty in giving meaningful content to the concepts of consent and voluntariness.[39] In this situation, determining the officer's intention or the suspect's state of mind is difficult unless, for example, the suspect's lack of consent is evidenced by physical resistance on his part. This is unlikely, however, and certainly is not the only situation which adequately demonstrates lack of consent.[40]

The issue in an individual case is likely to be further complicated by inconsistencies between the story of the suspect and of the officer as to what transpired before the suspect accompanied the officer to the station.[41] Even when there is agreement as to what the officer said, the same words may, depending upon how they are

---

[36] Of course, where federal officers are concerned, whether an arrest had in fact been made could be of some importance, as under the Mallory rule delay in bringing the arrestee before the commissioner results in the confession received during the delay being barred. Only one relevant federal case has been found: United States v. Vita, 294 F.2d 524 (2d Cir. 1961).

[37] 125 Wis. 173, 104 N.W. 149 (1905).

[38] 125 Wis. at 176-177, 104 N.W. at 150.

[39] Wigmore found "voluntariness" an inadequate test of when a confession is testimonially trustworthy and said that "it is not serviceable as a rule of thumb, for its significance is so indefinite and loose that it does not of itself supply a solution for the various situations with their graduated differences." 3 Wigmore, Evidence §826 (3d ed. 1940). The American Law Institute avoided use of the phrase "incapable of giving consent" in the draft of a model statute on rape and related offenses, stating that "any formulation in terms of capacity to give legal consent is rejected here because it provides no meaningful guide to decision." Model Penal Code §207.4, Comment (Tent. Draft No. 4, 1955).

[40] Stroud v. Commonwealth, 295 Ky. 694, 175 S.W.2d 368 (1943); Dade v. State, 188 Okla. 677, 112 P.2d 1102 (1941); State v. Warfield, 184 Wis. 56, 198 N.W. 854 (1924).

[41] See United States v. Vita, 294 F.2d 524 (2d Cir. 1961), where the detention was upheld on the basis that it was voluntary. The opinion relates that there was a substantial difference in the testimony of the defendant and the F.B.I. agents as to what was said before the defendant accompanied them to headquarters.

said, be interpreted as either a request or a command. The statement made in *Gunderson*, "I would like to see you down to the station a minute," could be either, depending on how it was said.[42]

In the consent-search cases courts have been hesitant to infer consent where the circumstances were such that the suspect must have known that the search was bound to produce incriminating evidence: "[N]o sane man who denies his guilt would actually be willing that policemen search his room for contraband which is certain to be discovered."[43] This is less likely to be crucial in the in-custody investigation cases because, while the finding of the physical evidence is an obvious consequence of a search, the suspect may not anticipate making an admission when he accompanies the officer to the station.

The character of the suspect may also be an important consideration. One trial judge, discussing consent-searches, said: "Some people who live in the slum areas of the city are deathly afraid of the police, and they may consent to almost anything out of this fear." This seems equally relevant in the detention cases.[44] When the suspect is a member of a lower social or economic class, it is important whether he is told by the officer that he cannot be arrested, that he is under no obligation to go to the station, and that the investigation at the station may either clear him or provide evidence justifying his continued detention. Whether the suspect was warned of his rights has always been important in determining the voluntariness of a confession,[45] and more recently some courts have indicated that a failure to warn may itself be a basis for excluding a statement of a suspect in custody[46] or physical evidence obtained in an alleged consent-search.[47]

[42] Gunderson v. Struebing, 125 Wis. 173, 175, 104 N.W. 149, 150 (1905). See the recent Supreme Court case of Culombe v. Connecticut, 367 U.S. 568, 81 Sup. Ct. 1860, 6 L. Ed. 2d 1037 (1961), where each of two suspects was asked to appear at headquarters because the lieutenant "wanted to talk to him." This supposedly voluntary appearance lasted eight hours, during which time the suspects were questioned and viewed by holdup victims.

[43] Higgins v. United States, 209 F.2d 819, 820 (D.C. Cir. 1954).

[44] This factor is often emphasized in the federal courts, which generally have been more strict than state courts in the consent cases. United States v. Martin, 176 F. Supp. 262 (S.D.N.Y. 1959); United States v. Haas, 106 F. Supp. 295 (W.D. Pa. 1952); In re White, 98 F. Supp. 895 (S.D. Miss. 1951).

[45] See Payne v. Arkansas, 356 U.S. 560, 78 Sup. Ct. 844, 2 L. Ed. 2d 975 (1958), where the confession was barred because of the failure to warn the suspect that he could remain silent, along with other factors, and Crooker v. California, 357 U.S. 433, 78 Sup. Ct. 1287, 2 L. Ed. 2d 1448 (1958), and Ashdown v. Utah, 357 U.S. 426, 78 Sup. Ct. 1354, 2 L. Ed. 2d 1443 (1958), where the giving of such a warning was a factor considered by the court in upholding the admissibility of the confession.

[46] E.g., "A confession is inadmissible unless accused was advised of his rights under the law and it is shown the confession was made voluntarily." State v. Seward, 163 Kan. 136, 144, 181 P.2d 478, 484 (1947) (dictum).

[47] E.g., People v. Zeigler, 358 Mich. 355, 364, 100 N.W.2d 456, 461 (1960).

C. ARREST FOR ANOTHER OFFENSE

Illustration No. 4: Officers responding to a call regarding a prowler in a residential neighborhood stopped a man running away from the scene. The suspect was unable to account for his presence in the area and admitted that he was not currently employed. He was arrested, booked on a vagrancy charge, and convicted of vagrancy the next day. The suspect was investigated in connection with a number of unsolved burglaries while serving his ten-day sentence.

When there are not sufficient grounds to arrest for the offense suspected, police sometimes obtain custody by making an arrest for a lesser offense which the suspect has committed. The more serious offense can be investigated while the suspect is in custody awaiting trial for the less serious offense or while he is serving a jail sentence following conviction for the lesser offense.

One variation, observed in Milwaukee, is the so-called ten-day vag check. If the detective in charge of a case is uncertain whether there are adequate grounds to arrest for the serious offense, he obtains a warrant for vagrancy from the district attorney's office. When the case reaches court an assistant district attorney or a police officer appears and asks for a ten-day continuance, which is granted by the judge. If the suspect objects to the continuance or is likely to be able to make bail, prosecution proceeds on the vagrancy charge and a ten-day jail sentence is imposed. If there is no objection to the continuance, the in-custody investigation takes place and the suspect is either prosecuted for the more serious charge or released.

In some other Wisconsin communities, a conviction of vagrancy is always attempted in these cases. If the investigation is completed before the suspect reaches court on the vagrancy charge, he is still convicted but his sentence is suspended. If the investigation has not been completed at the time he is convicted, a ten-day sentence is imposed. If the suspect is cleared before the ten days elapse, he is immediately released.

Somewhat similar practices, described earlier,[48] are found in Kansas. No such regular practice has developed in Michigan, although occasionally it does appear that arrests for minor offenses are used in cases where the officer suspects that a felony has been committed.

If there are insufficient grounds to justify an arrest for a minor offense, this practice is not available as a way of attempting to

[48] See page 338.

achieve a lawful in-custody investigation. But many states have statutes or local ordinances which make a person who is found under suspicious circumstances guilty of a crime if he fails to explain his presence adequately.[49] It is obvious that those statutes and ordinances were enacted, or at least remain on the books, precisely because they do make it possible for police to proceed lawfully when the circumstances are sufficiently suspicious but the evidence is inadequate to warrant an arrest for a serious offense.[50]

[49] See Foote, Vagrancy-Type Law and Its Administration, 104 U. Pa. L. Rev. 603 (1956); Lacey, Vagrancy and Other Crimes of Personal Condition, 66 Harv. L. Rev. 1203 (1960); Perkins, The Vagrancy Concept, 9 Hastings L.J. 237 (1958); Sherry, Vagrants, Rogues and Vagabonds — Old Concepts in Need of Revision, 48 Calif. L. Rev. 557 (1960); also Notes, 23 Calif. L. Rev. 506 (1935), 49 J. Crim. L., C. & P.S. 562 (1959), 6 St. Louis U.L.J. 247 (1960), 59 Yale L.J. 1351 (1950).

[50] "The underlying purpose [of the vagrancy laws] is to relieve the police of the necessity of proving that criminals have committed or are planning to commit specific crimes." N.Y. Law Revision Comm'n Report 591 (1935). The police stressed this same point in testimony to the Congress prior to congressional revision of the District of Columbia vagrancy provision. H.R. Rep. No. 1248, 77th Cong., 1st Sess. 1 (1941).

Also interesting on this point of legislative recognition of the use of these provisions to investigate and arrest suspicious persons is the California experience. A modern disorderly conduct statute was drafted eliminating anything comparable to the then existing vagrancy provisions defining as a vagrant "every person who roams about from place to place without any lawful business" and "every person who wanders about the streets at late or unusual hours of the night, without any visible or lawful business." Cal. Penal Code §647. Governor Brown vetoed the bill, giving the following explanation: "The bill proposed to repeal subdivisions 3 and 6 [those quoted above] of the present law without substituting any kind of control over those whose conduct afforded occasion for legitimate suspicion. I am aware that police action in this regard has led to criticism, and I agree that the present law should be revised. But I do not think that the possibility of abuse justifies completely denying any controls at all. Legislation in this area would be effective if it gave some definition of authority and obligation to which the private citizen and the policeman could reasonably and fairly conform."

The draftsman then suggested an amended bill which would describe as a disorderly person one who "loiters or wanders upon the streets or from place to place without apparent reason or business and who refuses to identify himself and to account for his presence when requested by any peace officer so to do." See Sherry, Vagrants, Rogues and Vagabonds — Old Concepts in Need of Revision, 48 Calif. L. Rev. 557, 562 n.38, 568-569, 569 n.67, 571 n.73 (1960). This language, with the qualifying phrase "if the surrounding circumstances are such as to indicate to a reasonable man that the public safety demands such identification," was adopted. Cal. Penal Code §647 (Supp. 1961).

How a legislature might be considering procedural problems when drafting such substantive legislation is also demonstrated by the comments to the Model Penal Code provision on "suspicious loitering": "The proposals here made to penalize what might be called 'suspicious loitering,' are all that would be left in the law of that ancient protean offense designated 'vagrancy,' if indeed even this much should be retained in a code of substantive penal law. The reasons for doubt on that score are that a statute which makes it a penal offense for a person to fail to identify himself and give an exculpatory account of his presence is in effect an extension of the law of arrest, and trenches on the privilege against self-incrimination. It authorizes arrest of persons who have not given reasonable ground for believing that they are engaged in or have committed offenses. Alternatively, it can be re-

The vagrancy statutes in the jurisdictions studied are representative of those found elsewhere. The Kansas statute covers those "found loitering without visible means of support";[51] the Wisconsin provision includes one "found in or loitering near any structure, vehicle or private grounds . . . without the consent of the owner and . . . unable to account for his presence";[52] and, although Michigan has no vagrancy statute, it does have a "disorderly person" offense,[53] which by definition includes "any vagrant," meaning those who were vagrants at common law.[54] It is not clear whether this includes those who cannot give a satisfactory account of their presence.[55]

State legislation may be complemented by local ordinances directed to the same problem. A Wichita ordinance defines a vagrant as "any person who knowingly associates with persons having the reputation of being thieves, burglars, pickpockets, prostitutes, or immoral women, or gambling houses or places for the reception of stolen property."[56] A Kansas City ordinance covers "any per-

---

garded as a legislative determination that in 'suspicious' circumstances, failure to respond to police inquiries supplies reasonable ground. In either view, extension of the law of arrest might be regarded as a matter for a code of procedure rather than an end to be achieved indirectly by creating a substantive offense of failure to respond to the police." Model Penal Code §250.12, Comment (Tent. Draft No. 13, 1961).

[51] Kan. Gen. Stat. §21-2409 (1949). This statute has been challenged in the Kansas Supreme Court on one occasion, and the court held: "While idleness or unemployment may not of themselves be punished in cases where these are united in one person, the legislature has the power to declare him a vagrant and to affix reasonable punishment." In re Clancy, 112 Kan. 247, 252, 210 Pac. 487, 489 (1922).

In addition, the state has granted to first, second, and third class cities the right to arrest as vagrants "persons found in said city without visible means of support, or some legitimate business." Kan. Gen. Stat. §§13-425, 14-430, 15-436 (1949).

[52] Wis. Stat. §947.02(2) (1955). Proposed but not enacted was another section of the vagrancy statute which would define a vagrant as "a person who loiters on the streets, whose actions give rise to suspicion of wrongdoing and who is unable to give a satisfactory account of himself." 5 Wis. Legis. Council, Judiciary Committee Report on Criminal Code 210 (1953). This section seems clearly to reflect a desire by the draftsmen to give police authority to arrest suspicious persons.

Prior to the effective date of the Wisconsin recodification, July 1, 1956, and during a part of the period of observation in that state, the vagrancy provision included "persons having no visible occupation and unable to give a satisfactory account of themselves." Wis Stat. §348.351 (1953).

[53] Mich. Stat. Ann. §28.364 (1938). This statute also covers "any person who engages in an illegal occupation or business," but the provision making recent reputation prima facie evidence of this fact has been determined to be unconstitutional. People v. Licavoli, 264 Mich. 643, 250 N.W. 520 (1933).

[54] In re Jordon, 90 Mich. 3, 50 N.W. 1087 (1892); In re Way, 41 Mich. 299, 1 N.W. 1021 (1879).

[55] Compare Lacey, Vagrancy and Other Crimes of Personal Condition, 66 Harv. L. Rev. 1203, 1207 (1953), with 3 Wharton, Criminal Law and Procedure §954 (Anderson ed. 1957) and Annot., 14 A.L.R. 1462, 1483 (1921).

[56] Wichita City Ord., vol. I, p. 350.1, §18-52. The Wichita city attorney indicated

son who intentionally trespasses on the property of another person in the night time or in the day time without giving a satisfactory account of himself." [57]   A Detroit ordinance includes "all able-bodied persons who, not having visible means of support, are found loitering or rambling about . . . and not giving a good account of themselves." [58]

A number of these provisions are of doubtful constitutionality. Defining a crime in terms of one's reputation[59] or associations[60] is questionable, and "failure to account" provisions may have to be narrowly construed to survive constitutional attack.[61]   The constitutional issue has not arisen, and, because of the value of such statutes for police investigation, they are likely to survive even the most thorough criminal code revision.[62]   Police do not attempt to enforce these provisions fully but limit arrests to persons they wish to investigate.

---

that he had some doubts as to the constitutionality of this ordinance.   His fears would appear to be well-founded.   See cases cited in note 60 *infra*.

[57] The ordinance further states that one "who goes from place to place, sleeping in sheds, out houses, rail-way cars, or in open air, or who shall be engaged in any unlawful act or calling whatsoever, or who shall be found loitering without visible means of support and who shall refuse to work when work at fair wages shall be procured in the community, or who shall threaten violence or personal injury to fellow workmen or to employees or labor or who shall be a habitual beggar shall be deemed a vagrant. . . .   On trial of any person being charged with being a vagrant, it shall be competent testimony to show the general reputation of the person, touching the matters charged against him."   Kan. City Rev. Ord., chap. 9, art. 17 (1950). Whether an ordinance of such broad scope could be successfully challenged in Kansas as unconstitutional is not clear.   In In re Kellam, 55 Kan. 700, 41 Pac. 960 (1895), an arrest was defended on the basis of a state statute allowing arrest "upon reasonable suspicion that an offense has been committed" and a city ordinance allowing arrest of "all persons found under suspicious circumstances, who cannot give a good account of themselves."   The state statute was found unconstitutional and the arrest held illegal without any further mention of the city ordinance.   No Kansas case was found considering the legality of the "general reputation" provision, but see discussion of a similar Michigan provision in note 53 *supra*.

[58] City of Detroit Comp. Ord., chap. 223, §1 (1954).

[59] People v. Licavoli, 264 Mich. 643, 250 N.W. 520 (1933), and, generally, Lacey, Vagrancy and Other Crimes of Personal Condition, 66 Harv. L. Rev. 1203 (1953).

[60] People v. Belcastro, 356 Ill. 144, 190 N.E. 301 (1934); Hechinger v. City of Maysville, 22 Ky. L. Rep. 486, 57 S.W. 619 (1930); Ex parte Smith, 135 Mo. 223, 36 S.W. 628 (1896).   See Annot., 92 A.L.R. 1228, 1230 (1934).

[61] A Denver ordinance provided that one "who is found abroad at late or unusual hours of the night without any visible or lawful business" may be required to give "a satisfactory account of himself" or be deemed a vagrant.   Interpreting the ordinance in such a way as to be consistent with constitutional rights, the supreme court of Colorado held that it did not apply to a person "conducting himself in such manner as not to give reasonable grounds for belief that his purpose . . . is an unlawful one."   The phrase "without a lawful business," according to the court, means "that his conduct or the circumstances of his presence constitute an offense or the suggestion of an intent to commit an offense."   Dominguez v. Denver, 363 P.2d 661 (Colo. Sup. Ct. 1961).

[62] For the interesting California experience, see note 50 *supra*.

Other minor offenses, not defined in terms of suspicious conduct, may also serve as a basis of arrest, even though usually not proceeded against, if they will serve to legitimize in-custody interrogation.[63]

The legitimacy of arresting for minor offenses in order to investigate major crimes has seldom been considered by appellate courts.[64] An exception is a California case in which the testimony of the arresting officers plainly revealed that the vagrant would not have been arrested except for the desire to investigate. The court said:

> Whether this is an entirely commendable attitude toward appellant's class of misdemeanants we need not stop to consider, but we think the admitted fact that the appellant would not have been arrested if he had confined himself to vagrancy did not render his arrest for that offense illegal.[65]

In sharp contrast is the following attitude of an English court:

> It seems to me to be an abuse of the process of the criminal law to use the purely formal charge of a trifling offence upon which there is no real intention to proceed, as a cover for putting the person charged under arrest, and obtaining from that person incriminat-

[63] On the host of criminal statutes which do not receive full enforcement, see Part II.

[64] There is language by the Michigan court, however, which suggests that the practice may be improper: "an arrest made for one purpose cannot be justified by another." Donovan v. Guy, 347 Mich. 457, 463, 80 N.W.2d 190, 193 (1956). See also Malcolmson v. Scott, 56 Mich. 459, 465, 23 N.W. 166, 168 (1895). It would also seem possible to draw an analogy between the present situation and that in Malcolmson, where the court held illegal an arrest on less than reasonable cause for an out-of-state offense, rejecting the officer's defense that he reasonably believed the offender had violated the law of Michigan. The court said: "It makes no difference whether defendants did or did not suppose the plaintiff had violated the laws of this State, unless they proposed to prosecute him here."

The practice in Kansas may conflict with the statutory definition of arrest there: "the taking of a person into custody, that he may be held to answer for a public offense." Kan. Gen. Stat. §62-1201 (1949). The Kansas court, in dicta, has said: "We may assume for present purposes that an arrest . . . to accomplish some ulterior purpose not connected with the arrest, would present a situation where rules pertaining to abuse of process might be applied. The present petition however does not make such a charge. There is no allegation whatever, nor any warranting an inference that when the arrest was made for drunkenness and possession of liquor, the arresting officer or any other defendant had any motive, malicious or otherwise, to use the arrest as an excuse to apprehend the plaintiff and then to hold her on any other charge or for any other purpose." Welch v. Shepherd, 169 Kan. 363, 367, 219 P.2d 444, 447 (1950). In a false arrest case, however, the court has said that "if the arrest was lawful the motive for it [is] immaterial," Atchison, T. & S.F. Ry. v. Hinsdell, 76 Kan. 74, 76, 90 Pac. 800, 801 (1907), but has also stated that "the law contemplates that an arrest . . . is a step in a public prosecution." Garnier v. Squires, 62 Kan. 321, 325, 62 Pac. 1005, 1007 (1900).

[65] People v. Craig, 152 Cal. 42, 47, 91 Pac. 997, 1000 (1907).

ing statements, not in relation to the charge laid . . . but in relation to a more serious and altogether different offence.[66]

Support of the practice is undoubtedly based on the belief that
statutes such as those concerning vagrancy were adopted and are
retained by legislatures to serve an investigative purpose.[67] However, the wisdom of adopting substantive provisions to solve procedural problems is debatable:[68]

> If it is necessary to . . . legalize arrests for mere suspicion, then
> the grave policy and constitutional problems posed by such sugges-
> tions should be faced. If present restrictions on the laws of at-
> tempts or arrest place too onerous a burden upon the police be-
> cause of the nature of modern crime, then such propositions should
> be discussed and resolved on their merits as, for example, the pro-
> posals in the Uniform Arrest Act.[69]

[66] Rex v. Dick, [1947] 2 D.L.R. 213, 225, quoted in Culombe v. Connecticut, 367
U.S. 568, 632 n. 95, 81 Sup. Ct. 1860, 1895 n. 95, 6 L. Ed. 2d 1037, 1075 n. 95 (1961).
In Dick the judge used his discretionary power to exclude from evidence the statements made by the prisoner, who had been charged with vagrancy, cautioned
concerning that offense only or not at all, and then questioned with the purpose
of eliciting information about the murder of which she was suspected.

[67] See note 50 *supra*. Probably best suited to this purpose, however, are not the
usual vagrancy statutes, but provisions such as that recommended but not adopted
in Wisconsin which declares as a vagrant "a person who loiters on the streets, whose
actions give rise to suspicion of wrongdoing and who is unable to give a satisfactory
account of himself" or that found in the Model Penal Code which states: "A person who loiters or wanders without apparent reason or business in a place or manner not usual for law-abiding individuals and under circumstances which justify
suspicion that he may be engaged or about to engage in crime commits a violation
if he refuses the request of a peace officer that he identify himself and give a reasonably credible account of the lawfulness of his conduct and purposes." See 5 Wis.
Legis. Council, Judiciary Committee Report on Criminal Code 210 (1953); Model
Penal Code §250.12 (Tent. Draft No. 13, 1961).

However, the commonest judicial explanation of the place of vagrancy in a penal
code is that it is used in cases of suspected future rather than past criminality. But
many of the appellate cases disclose that the latter purpose was the real reason for
the arrest. See Foote, Vagrancy-Type Law and Its Administration, 104 U. Pa. L.
Rev. 603, 625, 628-629 (1956).

[68] For example, compare: "Arrest of a person who is not known to have committed a crime simply to discover whether he might possibly have done so some-
place . . . is clearly unjustifiable," Comment, 23 Calif. L. Rev. 506 (1935), with: "If
a crime is specified for which the officer has power to arrest on reasonable suspicion,
the mere fact that the person arrested is subsequently charged with a different
crime does not make the arrest wrongful, for *non constat* that the officer did not
reasonably believe that the stated crime had been committed when he made the
arrest. . . . So it seems that an otherwise valid arrest on a minor charge is not
rendered illegal by the fact that the real or principal motive of the police is to
prevent the suspect's escaping from justice on some major charge which they are
preparing against him. . . . This means that there is no legal objection to the
practice of making a 'holding charge,' provided of course that the holding charge
is a genuine one and that it operates to justify the detention." Williams, Requisites of a Valid Arrest, 1954 Crim. L. Rev. (Eng.) 6, 17.

[69] Foote, Vagrancy-Type Law and Its Administration, 104 U. Pa. L. Rev. 603, 649
(1956). A similar position is taken in Note, 59 Yale L.J. 1351 (1950).

The answer may depend upon whether there are effective alternatives available.[70]

The problem is somewhat different when the lesser offense is not one adopted by the legislature to serve an investigative purpose. When objection is made, it is not to the form of the statute but to the use to which it is put in day-to-day enforcement. However, this objection does not require the repeal of the provision, since any statute is susceptible to selective enforcement.[71] If the practice is to be controlled, the arresting officer's motive has to be ascertained in each case, which is not an easy task.[72]

D. ARREST FOR PROBATION OR PAROLE VIOLATION

Illustration No. 5: The police received information which led them to suspect that a man presently on probation had

---

[70] The various alternatives are set forth in the Model Penal Code comments, and the difficulties of each of them are also discussed there. In brief, the alternatives are: (1) making the suspicious actions a criminal offense; (2) making suspicions the basis for police inquiry to which the actor must respond (the code position); (3) making suspicions the basis for a brief detention period (the Uniform Arrest Act position); (4) allowing the police to order suspicious persons to "move on"; or (5) allowing the police merely to make inquiries, with a view to having the person's identity established if it is later learned that an offense has been committed. Model Penal Code §250.12, Comments (Tent. Draft No. 13, 1961).

[71] On the fallacy of arguing for repeal of a provision (or for exclusion from a proposed code) because of the possibility of selective enforcement, see Remington and Rosenblum, The Criminal Law and the Legislative Process, 1960 U. Ill. L.F. 481, 493-494. For a criticism of this view, see Kadish, Legal Norm and Discretion in the Police and Sentencing Processes, 75 Harv. L. Rev. 904, 911-912 (1962).

[72] See United States v. Carignan, 342 U.S. 36, 72 Sup. Ct. 97, 96 L. Ed. 48 (1951), in which defendant was arrested for assault with intent to commit rape, questioned on that offense, identified by the victim of that offense, and then committed on that charge. In the course of this commitment he was questioned about an outstanding murder case, and his confession was later challenged in court. Justice Douglas, in a concurring opinion in which he is joined by Justices Black and Frankfurter, said: "Another time-honored police method for obtaining confessions is to arrest a man on one charge (often a minor one) and use his detention for investigating a wholly different crime. This is an easy short cut for the police. How convenient it is to make detention the vehicle of investigation! Then the police can have access to the prisoner day and night. Arraignment for one crime gives some protection. But when it is a pretense or used as the device for breaking the will of the prisoner on long, relentless, or repeated questionings, it is abhorrent. We should free the federal system of that disreputable practice which has honeycombed the municipal police system in this country. We should make illegal such a perversion of a 'legal' detention. . . . We are framing here a rule of evidence for criminal trials in the federal courts. That rule must be drawn in light not of the facts of the particular case but of the system which the particular case reflects. Hence, the fact that the charge on which this respondent was arraigned was not a minor one nor one easily conceived by the police is immaterial." 342 U.S. at 46-47, 72 Sup. Ct. at 102, 96 L. Ed. at 55. The justices are apparently saying that it is so difficult to establish in each case that the arrest on the first offense was motivated by a desire to investigate the latter offense that a statement obtained in such manner should be excluded even absent such proof.

committed statutory rape. The information was in the form of rumor, and no one appeared to have any more direct knowledge of the situation. The case was particularly difficult from the investigation standpoint, as the girl thought to be involved had since been committed to a mental institution. The police placed the suspect under arrest, booked him "hold for probation authorities," and interrogated him concerning the suspected statutory rape offense.

The "probation hold" or the "parole hold" [73] is sometimes used as a basis for arrest when police do not have sufficient evidence to make an arrest for the new offense of which they suspect the probationer or parolee. It is used particularly when police need an exceptionally long period of detention for investigation.

The probation hold, as employed in Detroit, is merely another kind of booking and indicates that the person in custody is being held by the police for the probation authorities. Sometimes the hold is used for investigative purposes with the consent and concurrence of the probation authorities, but on other occasions the police themselves file a hold on the suspect, placing the hold in the name of the probation department and signing the name of one of the probation officers, without his knowledge. Members of the probation department differed in their reactions regarding the propriety of the probation hold practice.[74] The period of detention is about a week or ten days.

In Milwaukee the Division of Corrections of the state department of public welfare has an officer assigned to liaison with the Milwaukee Police Department. Each morning he checks to see whether any parolees have been arrested. If so, he interviews them briefly and learns the circumstances of their arrest and the name of their parole agent. He usually places a hold on the suspect, which means that a request for detention form is given to the law enforcement agency, authorizing them to continue to hold the person until his parole agent can make a further disposition of the case. However, the procedure is sometimes used at the request of the police to facilitate investigation of a new offense. In such a case the police make their desire known to the parole agent, who places a hold on the parolee. The time limit for such a hold is a

[73] The fact that the suspect is a probationer or parolee is usually determined by a routine check of police records, by finding a card indicating same in the suspect's wallet, by questioning him, or by contacting the probation or parole authorities.

[74] The deputy chief probation officer felt that this was a serious problem and said that he is constantly telling the police that if they cannot hold the suspect the probation department does not want him either. However, another supervisor in the department said that police use of this device was sporadic and not a matter of serious concern to the department.

matter of agreement between the police and parole authorities; it has sometimes been stated to be ten days and sometimes fifteen days.

The extent to which this device is also used for probationers in Milwaukee is not clear.[75] Most probationers in Milwaukee County are under the supervision of the county probation department, while parolees are under the supervision of the state department of public welfare.

The hold appears to be effective in both Detroit and Milwaukee. The probationer or parolee suspected of a new offense usually has done something which constitutes a violation of a condition of his parole or probation.[76] But in other instances, such as when the arrest is based solely upon his past record, he may be warned that failure to cooperate will lead to revocation.[77] Because of the risk of revocation, these detentions are rarely challenged by the probationers and parolees.

The status of these "holds" is doubtful because the rights, duties, and privileges of probationers and parolees are at best uncertain. No express authority for the practice exists, although statutes providing that parolees and probationers remain in the legal custody of state authorities are arguably some support.[78] However, it is not certain to what extent such statutes contemplate

---

[75] One probation officer reported an instance in which the police requested from her a "probation hold" which she refused. The female probationer involved had been convicted of possession of marijuana, and the police now knew that she was again associating with narcotics users. While this undoubtedly constituted a probation violation, the probation officer asserted that if the police had sufficient evidence they could proceed on their own right, and if they did not she felt that lending her authority to their investigation would destroy her relationship with this probationer.

[76] For example, see preceding footnote.

[77] In a rural Wisconsin county the sheriff was investigating the break-in of a safe. He was aware of only one safecracker in the area, a man who was presently on parole for his past offense. On the basis of this fact alone the sheriff arrested the man. The suspect was questioned for several hours but continually protested his innocence. The sheriff called the state parole officer operating in that county and informed him that he did not have sufficient evidence to arrest the parolee and that he would have to release him soon. He asked the parole officer to come to the office and assist in the investigation. The parole officer did so and informed the parolee that he would have to take a lie detector test or his parole would probably be revoked for lack of cooperation. At this point the parolee admitted his guilt. Perhaps because of the questionable tactics leading to the confession, no attempt was made at a new prosecution; rather, the department of public welfare revoked his parole.

[78] In Michigan it is expressly stated that a person on parole is in the legal custody of the commission, Mich. Stat. Ann. §28.2308(38) (1959), but no similar statutory language as to probationers has been found. In Wisconsin both probationers and parolees remain in the legal custody of the department of public welfare. Wis. Stat. §§57.02, 57.06 (1955).

the arrest or continued detention of suspected violators by the police.[79]

Even if there is a legal basis for the hold when used incident to determination of the question of revocation, use of the procedure for the sole purpose of allowing the police to investigate another offense is questionable. The problem is similar to that which exists when an arrest is made for a minor offense in order to make possible an in-custody investigation of a suspected serious offense. Perhaps, however, there is more basis for supporting the probation or parolee hold. The fact that the parolee or probationer is suspected of a serious offense is of concern to the parole or probation officer, because commission of such an offense inevitably results in revocation. Thus the investigation of these suspicions is directly related to the public protection aspects of probation and parole.

[79] In Wisconsin three statutory provisions, Wis. Stat. §§57.025(6), 57.04(2), and 57.06(3) (1955), deal with taking custody of probationers in Milwaukee County, of misdemeanant probationers elsewhere in the state, and of parolees from state prison and house of correction, respectively. In none of the three statutes is it expressly stated that a police officer may arrest. In regard to Milwaukee probationers, it is provided that "an officer may arrest any probationer and hold him in the county jail for a reasonable time," but the context makes it appear that the reference is to probation officers. A misdemeanant probationer may be taken into custody by "the department or officer . . . to prevent his escape, to enforce discipline for violation of probation and [he may be taken] into court . . ." but again the context does not suggest that the reference is to action by a police officer. The section on felon parolees states that "any officer may, without order or warrant, take the prisoner into custody whenever it appears necessary in order to prevent escape or enforce discipline or for violation of parole." In this case, the meaning of the phrase "any officer" is not at all clear. After Milwaukee police recently arrested a parolee, representatives of the Milwaukee District Attorney's office and of the state attorney general's office took the view that the phrase referred not only to probation and parole officers of the state department of public welfare but to any peace officer. The matter apparently did not reach court.

In Michigan it is provided by statute that "the court may, in its probation order or by general rule, provide for the apprehension, detention and confinement of any probationer accused of violation of any of the conditions of probation or of conduct inconsistent with the public good." Mich. Stat. Ann. §28.1134 (1954). The context of the statute makes it appear that such apprehension, detention, and confinement is to be based upon conduct which warrants having the probationer brought into court for a determination of whether his probation should be revoked. There is no reference to the police as the parties to make such apprehension, although presumably a local court might so state in its general orders. The Detroit Recorder's Court has not done this.

It is said that there is considerable disagreement among parole officials over whether their making arrests impairs their rapport with the parolees and that consequently some officers "delegate the arresting of parolees to the local police, state police, or other officials who have no connection with the parole agency . . ." Giardini, The Parole Process 245 (1959).

CHAPTER 17

Continued Custody of a Person Who
Can Be Charged

If there is sufficient evidence to charge the suspect with an offense, further detention is obviously not a prerequisite to the charging decision. The prosecutor can authorize the issuance of a warrant with confidence that he can obtain a bindover at the preliminary hearing and survive defendant's motion to dismiss if one is made at the trial. However, it is not uncommon in the three states studied for persons to be kept in police custody prior to their initial appearance before the magistrate even in cases where the evidence is adequate for charging. This continuation of custody and delay in charging and initial appearance may serve one of a number of purposes: (a) in a case such as a serious assault in which the victim may die within a short period of time, the prosecutor can determine what offense should actually be charged; (b) the prosecutor is able to check further on certain policy aspects unrelated to evidence of guilt, such as whether the victim in certain types of cases still desires prosecution; (c) the case can be "nailed down" by further investigation, perhaps resulting in a confession, which greatly increases the likelihood of conviction; or (d) the police can conduct further investigation with a view to solving other offenses or discovering the identity of other offenders.

When custody is continued for any of these reasons, the suspect is usually held on an "investigation of" booking until the objectives of the continued custody are met or it is thought that no further delay can be allowed. Police in Michigan and Wisconsin assume that they have a right to delay the initial appearance before the magistrate for seventy-two hours when it is necessary to do so to obtain evidence required for charging. They make the same assumption in a case in which there is sufficient evidence to charge but further delay is desired for other reasons. If a period longer than seventy-two hours is thought necessary, special steps are often taken to justify the prolonged detention. Because these special procedures, such as the "ten-day vag check" or probationer or parolee hold, are also used for other purposes, they have been described in detail earlier.[1]

A. Delay to Decide the Specific Offense to Be Charged or to Consider Policy Factors Relevant to the Charging Decision

There are recurring situations in which detention is continued because further time is needed to decide upon the particular offense to be charged or to consider policy factors bearing upon the desirability of prosecution. This kind of detention does not pose problems as difficult as those involved when a detention results from a desire to gather additional evidence of guilt. Detention to consider further the desirability of prosecution for a particular offense is not so common as detention for investigatory purposes, and consideration of policy questions can take place even if the suspect is released on bail. But the practice is nonetheless significant and is one which has largely escaped the attention of appellate courts.[2]

1. *The specific offense is not presently known.* Extension of custody because the exact nature of the charge is undetermined may occur in cases in which the extent of a victim's injuries is not yet known or when a substantial amount of data must be evaluated, as in large-scale conspiracy cases.

> *Illustration No. 1:* An officer went to an assistant prosecutor to obtain an assault and battery warrant. They discussed the possible nature of the charge, since the youth who had been beaten by the man in custody had suffered a broken nose and an eye injury requiring surgery. They decided that

1 See pages 338, 354, and 360.

2 However, one recent case of interest is Czap v. Marshall, 315 F.2d 366 (7th Cir. 1963). The plaintiff brought a tort action in federal court for his arrest and confinement by Wisconsin police officers. The plaintiff was involved in an ongoing dispute with his parents and other members of the family concerning his right to certain property in the possession of his parents. The police, called to the parents' farm, where an auction was in progress, observed the plaintiff engaged in a heated argument with other members of the family. They were told that he had beaten his sister, and they observed that she had bruises on her face and was bleeding. The sister indicated that she would sign a complaint, and when the plaintiff refused to promise the officers that he would make no more trouble he was arrested. He arrived at the jail at 2:50 P.M. Sunday and was released by the district attorney about noon the following day. The district attorney did not make the charging decision until the victim's wishes could be determined. He decided not to charge because members of the family "refused, as often happens in family rows, to sign a complaint." The court, without discussion of the circumstances of the detention, held the delay lawful.

the conduct was more serious than assault and battery but that it would be best to determine the charge after the results of the operation became known. The assistant prosecutor told the officer to hold the man in custody until that time.

Illustration No. 2: Officers, called to the scene of a stabbing, arrested the offender and had the victim transported to the hospital. The offender was detained for two days while detectives checked to see if the victim was going to die.

Illustration No. 3: Fourteen members of a gambling conspiracy were arrested after two months of surveillance. The prosecuting attorney indicated that it would take a few days to prepare the necessary papers in the case to reflect properly all the charges against each of the suspects. Thus the police made no attempt to take them before a magistrate.

In contrast to those cases in which custody is required for purposes of investigation, all that is involved here is a delay of the charging decision in order to avoid having to amend the charges later. But, because release on bail does not ordinarily occur until the suspect is brought before the magistrate, the delay in charging results in additional detention of the suspect unless he is released on habeas corpus.[3] Detention is not necessary for investigative purposes in these cases, but there is no existing procedure for releasing a person on bail upon a showing by the prosecutor that, although the person could be charged, some delay is necessary before the actual charge can be determined.

2. Policy factors require consideration. Consideration of policy factors is just as important at the charging stage[4] as it is at the arrest stage.[5] Consideration of relevant factors by the prosecutor may take time and thus prolong the detention.

Illustration No. 4: A Negro was arrested for felonious assault upon an acquaintance. The prosecutor indicated that he would prosecute only if this was the victim's desire. A detective was sent to the hospital to determine the victim's wishes. He was told: "I want to see whether I die first." A few days later, after it appeared he would survive, the victim indicated that he did not desire prosecution. The offender was then released.

The victim's desire often determines whether the offender is proceeded against. If, at the time of the crime, the victim indi-

---

[3] Such was the case with the conspiracy defendants discussed in Illustration No. 3. They were brought into court on a writ of habeas corpus, and bail was set on each of them, but the prosecutor was given a week to draw up the warrants.

[4] Discussion of the factors considered by prosecutors will be found in the volume on Prosecution.

[5] See Part II.

cates that he does not desire prosecution, there may be no arrest.[6] If an arrest has been made and the victim's desire is thought to be an essential factor, the charging decision may be delayed until the wishes of the victim can be ascertained. When the victim has been hospitalized, this may take several days.

> *Illustration No. 5:* Two young servicemen were arrested for stealing hubcaps. The prosecutor felt that it would be unwise to charge them in view of their prior clean record and the fact that a conviction would prevent their honorable discharge from the service. He concluded, however, that prior to making this decision it was desirable to arrange for the complainant and the arresting officer to discuss the matter with him. The youths were detained until such a meeting could be arranged.

Sometimes an arrest is not made because it may in itself cause a disproportionate amount of harm to the individual.[7] However, this issue is not likely to arise until after arrest and therefore is most frequently considered in relation to the charging decision. Deciding whether an offender will be excessively harmed by prosecution often takes time, particularly if it is thought necessary to discuss the matter with the victim or others.

Continued custody of the suspect is not essential in order to consider policy questions of this kind. The suspect could be immediately charged, brought before a magistrate, and released on bail. The case could later be dropped on a nolle prosequi if this seemed appropriate as a matter of policy. However, this would require the concurrence of the trial judge, and, more important, the fact that the suspect was actually charged might cause further unnecessary damage to his reputation. Although such persons would probably appear if released without bail,[8] it is not the practice to make such releases.

B. Delay to Obtain Evidence Against the Suspect Beyond That Needed to Charge Him

> *Illustration No. 6:* A reliable police informant reported that a man had recently admitted to him that he was responsible for an unsolved burglary. The police arrested the person on learning that he had been convicted of burglary in

---

[6] See page 114.

[7] See page 137.

[8] Certainly the risk of flight is usually slight in these cases. However, in those cases in which the nature of the offense would make public prosecution unduly harmful, the police often feel continued custody is necessary because of some risk that the offender will attempt suicide. See page 185.

the past. The suspect vigorously denied being involved and gave an alibi. Police investigation proved the alibi false, and the suspect remained silent when the informant repeated the accusation in his presence. A watchman, who was on duty where the offense was committed, viewed the suspect and said that, although he could not make positive identification, the man generally resembled a person whom he had seen loitering in the vicinity on the night of the burglary. It appeared that the suspect could now be charged, but the police continued custody in the hope that they could obtain a confession and thereby make conviction more likely.

In many cases there is sufficient evidence to charge a suspect but further in-custody investigation may increase the probability of conviction. Some courts apparently view a continuation of detention in such cases as proper,[9] and some prosecutors have objected to limitations upon the length of detention on the ground that this type of investigation is essential.[10] However, there is apparently no authority in Kansas, Michigan, or Wisconsin for delaying the appearance of a suspect before a magistrate in order to increase the probability of conviction. The Kansas court has said that an arrested person "must be immediately taken before a magistrate";[11] the Wisconsin court has approved detentions only for the purpose of deciding whether to charge;[12] and the Michigan court recently has resolved a prior ambiguity[13] by stating that "continued detention . . . after the officers were fully enabled to complain and arraign . . . was 'unnecessary' as a matter of law." [14]

Judicial recognition of the propriety of delay when necessary to decide whether to charge a suspect does not necessarily imply approval of delay to obtain evidence beyond that needed for charging. The need may not be so great in the latter circumstance, and there may be greater necessity for judicial intervention when a person is accused of a crime than when he is merely a suspect.

[9] E.g., People v. Kelly, 404 Ill. 281, 89 N.E.2d 27 (1949).

[10] Coakley, Restrictions in the Law of Arrest, 52 Nw. U.L. Rev. 2 (1957); Statement of Oliver Gasch, U.S. Atty. for the District of Columbia, in Admission of Evidence (Mallory Rule), Hearings Before a Subcommittee of the Committee of the Judiciary, U.S. Senate, 85th Cong., 2d Sess., on H.R. 11477, S.2970, S.3325, and S.3355, July 17 and 30, 1958, p. 22.

[11] State v. Beebe, 13 Kan. 589, 595 (1874).

[12] State v. Francisco, 257 Wis. 247, 43 N.W.2d 38 (1950); Peloquin v. Hibner, 231 Wis. 77, 285 N.W. 380 (1939).

[13] In Mooradian v. Davis, 302 Mich. 484, 5 N.W.2d 435 (1942), the court failed to state specifically whether the delay in question was (or must be) for purposes of obtaining evidence for charging. However, it was the prosecutor who directed that further investigation be conducted in this case.

[14] People v. Hamilton, 359 Mich. 410, 416-417, 102 N.W.2d 738, 742 (1960).

However, courts have not given attention to whether such a distinction is proper.

The importance to the police of in-custody investigation is greater when the evidence they have is insufficient to charge. For example, time may be needed to learn the true identity of one who resembles a wanted person but will not identify himself; to check the serial numbers on a bankroll in the possession of a well-known hoodlum; to determine whether a break-in has occurred in the area in which a suspect was found lurking; to confront a suspect with his accuser; to check the stolen property file on an expensive ring worn by a known burglar; to compare the suspect's fingerprints or shoe prints with those found at a crime scene; to determine whether the suspect's alibi is true; to hold a lineup; to give a handwriting or a drunkometer test; to conduct a thorough search; to watch for withdrawal symptoms in a former addict found with fresh scars; to question an unemployed man carrying a toy gun and a large sum of money about recent unsolved holdups; or to analyze a powder which appears to be a narcotic.

In situations such as these a prosecutor would not and probably should not charge the suspect until the appropriate investigation has provided a connection between the suspect and a particular offense.[15] Without the investigation it may not be clear whether any crime has been committed,[16] whether the suspect has been connected with any particular outstanding offense, or whether any one suspect is more probably guilty of a particular offense than other suspects. But in most of these situations even an investigation which produces evidence sufficient to charge will not necessarily insure conviction. The traced stolen property, the accusation repeated in front of the suspect, the alibi proved false, and many other results of in-custody investigation may establish probable cause to believe the suspect guilty but may not be sufficient to persuade a trier of fact "beyond a reasonable doubt." For conviction there must be "no reasonable explanation of the facts proven except upon the hypothesis that the accused committed the crime

15 The "probable cause" test requires that "the evidence worthy of consideration, in any aspect for the judicial mind to act upon, brings the charge against the prisoner within the reasonable probabilities." State v. Hanley, 248 Wis. 108, 111, 20 N.W.2d 719, 720 (1945).

16 In some states such a showing is necessary even to get by the preliminary, as it must be established at that time that "the offense charged had been committed, and that there was probable cause to believe that the defendants were guilty." People v. Asta, 337 Mich. 590, 609, 60 N.W.2d 472, 482 (1953). While this is seldom a problem, it can be in cases involving negligent homicide, obscene literature, and the like, where usually the only question to be decided is whether any crime has been committed.

charged." [17]   The basic question, then, is whether delay for the purpose of eliminating other reasonable explanations is justified where there are sufficient grounds for arrest and for charging the suspect.

In England the fact that the status of the individual has changed from "suspect" to "accused" is viewed as being important.[18]   At that point he gains added rights.[19]   A similar view was once ex-

[17] Emery v. State, 92 Wis. 146, 151, 165 N.W. 848, 880 (1896). See 9 Wigmore, Evidence §2497 (3d ed. 1940); McBaine, Burden of Proof: Degrees of Belief, 32 Calif. L. Rev. 242 (1944).

[18] "The inquiry that is conducted by the police divides itself naturally into two parts, which are recognizably different, although it is difficult to say at just what point the first part ends and the second begins. In the earlier part the object of the inquiry is to ascertain the guilty party and in the latter part it is to prove the case against him. The distinction between the two periods is in effect the distinction between suspicion and accusation. The moment at which the suspect becomes the accused marks the change.

"The first phase of the inquiry is in England accepted as belonging solely to the administrative process. It has not been subjected to any form of judicial restraint. On the contrary the freedom of the police has been judicially declared. . . .

"The second phase of the inquiry begins when the suspect becomes the accused. If thereafter questions are asked of the accused, the main object must be to obtain proof against him by means of admissions. This makes it a proper subject for judicial restraint. . . .

"What test is employed to decide the moment when the suspect becomes the accused? If the first part of the inquiry were simply a matter of selecting the right person from a number of suspects, the dividing line would be easy to draw. But . . . that is rarely the case. When, for example, a man has been assaulted or a woman raped, the individual alleged to be the criminal is often identified, and then there is no question of charging anyone except him. But the police cannot charge him until they have reasonable grounds for thinking not only that he committed the act alleged but also that he was guilty of the crime. The first interview with him must almost inevitably be begun on the footing that he is still a suspect; admitting that he was the person involved, he may say in the case of rape that the woman consented or in the case of an assault that he was acting in self-defense. It then becomes the task of the police to check his statements, and when they are doing that they are engaged in the twofold task of ascertaining whether he is guilty and of collecting the evidence which, if he is charged, will be used to prove his guilt. In such a case it is hard to know where to draw the line, but nevertheless there will be a point when the police become sufficiently convinced of his guilt that their subsequent inquiries are directed toward acquiring legal proof of that which they already believe." Devlin, The Criminal Prosecution in England 31, 33-34 (1958).

[19] Under the Judges' Rules, the "accused" must be administered a caution that he need not say anything and that any statement made will be taken down and may be used in evidence. The rules are reproduced and discussed in detail in Devlin, ibid.

Proponents of Mallory sometimes cite the English system as proof that law enforcement is not hampered by requiring arrest only on grounds for charging and by denying a right to interrogate those in custody. However, close observers of the English system point out that such is not the practice. Williams, Questioning by the Police; Some Practical Considerations, 1960 Crim. L. Rev. (Eng.) 325; Williams, Arrest for Felony at Common Law, 1954 Crim. L. Rev. (Eng.) 408; Smith, Questioning by the Police: Some Further Points — I, 1960 Crim. L. Rev. (Eng.) 347; Memorandum by Street in Confessions and Police Detention, Hearings Before the Subcommittee on Constitutional Rights of the Committee on the Judiciary, U.S. Senate, 85th Cong., 2d Sess., pursuant to S. Res. 234, March 7 and 11, 1958, p. 13.

pressed by four justices of the United States Supreme Court when they said that they would hold that a constitutional right to counsel arises when the person in custody is an "accused" rather than merely a "suspect," [20] but the court has now apparently defined the right in even broader terms.[21] The distinction has been explained on the basis that once the individual is no longer a mere suspect there is a "declaration of war," and "the police . . . are no longer representing themselves to the man they are questioning as the neutral inquirer whom the good citizen ought to assist," but are now "the prosecution and are without right, legal or moral, to further help from the accused." [22]

One way, in practice, of assuring a period of detention sufficient to conduct an adequate in-custody investigation is by means of a vagrancy conviction or a probation or parole hold. Whether the use of these alternatives would justify an otherwise improper detention of a suspect who can be charged has not been decided,[23] although two members of the United States Supreme Court have spoken to this issue in a recent case in which a suspect was arrested for questioning in regard to an unwitnessed double murder-robbery. The arrest was made on Saturday night. On Monday morning the suspect was booked for breach of the peace and on Tuesday morning he was taken into police court on this charge. At the suggestion of the investigating officer, the prosecutor moved for a continuance, which was granted without the defendant having an opportunity to contest the motion or participate in the proceedings in any way. Of this procedure Justice Frankfurter and Justice Stewart said:

[20] Spano v. New York, 360 U.S. 315, 79 Sup. Ct. 1294, 3 L. Ed. 2d 1259 (1959). Though the Spano case was concerned with a person who was indicted prior to arrest, the justices saw a right of counsel arising because the person had been "formally charged" and because it was not a case "where the police were questioning a suspect in the course of investigating an unsolved crime."

This approach is now followed in New York. People v. DiBiasi, 7 N.Y.2d 544, 166 N.E.2d 825 (1960). For a careful study of the growth of the New York rule out of the Spano case, see Rothblatt and Rothblatt, Police Interrogation: The Right to Counsel and to Prompt Arraignment, 27 Brooklyn L. Rev. 24 (1960).

Also, there is some evidence that the Supreme Court, in determining the admissibility of a confession, may be more strict when it appears that the state officers already had evidence clearly adequate to charge. See Haynes v. Washington, 373 U.S. 503, 83 Sup. Ct. 1336, 10 L. Ed. 2d 513 (1963).

[21] The court's most recent declaration that there is a constitutional right to counsel, at least when certain other facts are present, when "the investigation is no longer a general inquiry into an unsolved crime but has begun to focus on a particular suspect [who] . . . has been taken into police custody," seems quite different from the "formally charged" test expressed in Spano. Escobedo v. Illinois, 378 U.S. 478, 84 Sup. Ct. 1758, 12 L. Ed. 2d 977 (1964).

[22] Devlin, The Criminal Prosecution in England 37 (1958).

[23] See pages 354 and 360.

Instead of bringing him before a magistrate with reasonable promptness, as Connecticut law requires, to be duly presented for the grave crimes of which he was in fact suspected (and for which he had been arrested under the felony-arrest statute), he was taken before the New Britain Police Court on the palpable ruse of a breach-of-the-peace charge concocted to give the police time to pursue their investigation. This device is admitted. . . . [I]t kept Culombe in police hands without any of the protections that a proper magistrate's hearing would have assured him. Certainly, had he been brought before it charged with murder instead of an insignificant misdemeanor, no court would have failed to warn Culombe of his rights and arrange for appointment of counsel.[24]

Their reasoning is most interesting, as it would seem to apply even though the charge on which the suspect is actually taken into court is fully substantiated, and even though the person's detention is brought about by actual conviction. It appears to be the view of Justices Frankfurter and Stewart that, whatever other legal reasons might exist for detention, if it is used for investigative purposes it must include the protections ordinarily available to one arrested and detained for the offense being investigated.

C. DELAY TO INVESTIGATE OTHER OFFENSES

Illustration No. 7: A man arrested while committing a burglary was placed in a lineup for viewing by detectives from different precincts. He was then interrogated by the detectives about outstanding burglaries in their respective areas of responsibility. Each detective carried a bound volume containing reports on unsolved burglaries in his geographical area, and asked the man about them one at a time. As a result of the questioning seven additional burglaries were cleared.

Suspects are frequently not charged and brought before the magistrate even though there is sufficient evidence for charging, because the police wish to question them about an offense other than the one for which they were apprehended. Because the initial appearance before the magistrate is likely to result in release on bail, an in-custody investigation must be conducted before this time.[25]

24 Culombe v. Connecticut, 367 U.S. 568, 631-632, 81 Sup. Ct. 1860, 1895, 6 L. Ed. 2d 1037, 1074-1075 (1961).

25 Even if the person fails to make bail, questioning after the initial appearance is often more difficult. The remand may be not to the city department but to the county jail. See page 402. Also, there is authority to the effect that further investigation of other offenses after remand is improper if methods not usable against those free on bail are employed. Recently a federal court enjoined the Philadelphia police from placing a man, held for lack of bail on a rape charge, in a lineup to be viewed by victims of other rapes. Said the court: "The constitutional authority for

Questioning about other offenses usually takes place when the offense for which the arrest was made suggests that the suspect has in the past committed other offenses of the same type or that he has committed an offense of greater magnitude.[26] When a person is arrested for an offense such as burglary or robbery, it is usually assumed that he may also be responsible for other similar offenses. Because there are usually many known, unsolved burglaries and robberies, an attempt is made to determine whether any of them were committed by the suspect.   Interrogation by precinct detectives, personnel of specialized agencies,[27] or by officers of another police department in the area[28] is the investigative technique most

---

the State to distinguish between criminal defendants by freeing those who supply bail pending trial and confining those who do not, furnishes no justification for any additional inequality of treatment beyond that which is inherent in the confinement itself." Butler v. Crumlish, 229 F. Supp. 565, 567 (E.D. Pa. 1964).

[26] It would be well to note that we are not here concerned with the arrest for one offense for the specific purpose of investigating another, as discussed on page 354.

[27] If precinct detectives are conducting the interrogation, they first go over outstanding similar offenses within the precinct.   Particular attention is usually given to offenses in which the modus operandi was similar to that used in the offense for which the person was apprehended.   If interrogation on these offenses is fruitful or if the person is known to have been operating elsewhere in the city, the precinct detectives may take the suspect to other precincts and review their outstanding cases. In one such case in Detroit the detective took the arrested man to a neighboring precinct and obtained from the detective lieutenant on duty records of all outstanding breaking and entering cases for 1956, numbering approximately 300.   Speaking to the defendant, the detective said: "Now, remember, listen to these carefully. Remember, you're going to tell me whether any of these jobs are yours or the jobs of any of the other boys in your group." The detective then proceeded to read off the names and addresses of the premises that were broken into and then read the officer's report describing the items taken.   The detective read only those reports involving premises in the general area in which the men operated.

After the precinct has sufficient information on the case for which the arrest was made, they might send the suspect to a specialized bureau for interrogation concerning similar offenses.   For example, persons arrested for auto theft are transferred to the auto recovery squad at headquarters for questioning about other auto thefts. Similarly, persons arrested for breaking and entering or robbery are transferred to the holdup bureau.

[28] A very complex case, involving larceny and burglary of scrap iron and tools from various electrical substations throughout the county, was handled by the Milwaukee County sheriff's office.   When the case was solved, it led to the clearance of about fifteen other larcenies which had occurred in the past year. Giving in to the demands of the defense counsel of the three youths involved, the sheriff's department rushed through their interrogation in one day and just prior to the closing of court took statements summarizing all the larcenies and burglaries to which the youths admitted, and the men were taken into court that day. They were released on bail. That evening an article appeared in the newspaper concerning the arrests, and the next day the department received calls from the Milwaukee Police Department, the Racine County sheriff's office, and the West Allis Police Department, each stating that they were interested in questioning the men.   In addition, the sheriff's department, in completing their investigations, discovered that there were several other cases in which they felt the men were involved. They investigated these and rearrested the men the following day. While the men were detained in the jail, the Racine County

often employed. The usual procedure is for the interrogating officer to read through a list of uncleared offenses similar to the one
for which the suspect was arrested, asking him about them one by
one. Such interrogations often prove successful. This is particularly true in Detroit, where the interrogating detectives stress the
fact that any additional offenses admitted are "free offenses" in
that there will be no prosecution for them. This is because con-
secutive sentences cannot be imposed under Michigan law and
thus there is little advantage, from a prosecution point of view, in
charging more than a single offense.[29] Often a considerable number of offenses are admitted and placed on a "clean-up sheet." For
example, one suspect admitted the commission of 127 felonies.

> *Illustration No. 8:* A man was arrested for indecent expo-
> sure, and a copy of the arrest report was sent to the homicide
> bureau of the police department. The man was booked on
> the offense for which he was arrested and on "investigation of
> murder." This procedure had been followed over a four-year
> period with all persons arrested for sex offenses, because of
> two unsolved sex slayings in the community. The next morn-
> ing the man was interrogated by homicide detectives about
> the two crimes, and after a short time he admitted to one of
> the killings.

The fact that a person is known to have committed a certain
kind of offense often makes him a suspect with regard to a more
serious unsolved offense. For example, a person arrested for carrying a concealed weapon is usually questioned concerning recent
holdups. A similar practice is employed with regard to sex offenders when there is a serious unsolved sex offense.

Whether the police are concerned merely with clearing their
books of many offenses so that they may direct their resources to
other outstanding crimes, or whether their aim is to solve and
make possible the prosecution of certain serious offenses, the prac-

---

sheriff's department sent a representative to question them, and they admitted to
several larcenies in that county.

This case is particularly interesting because of the rearrest feature, which really
makes it a different kind of case from that presently under discussion. But it raises
the same question: does the fact that the person can be charged with one offense
justify detention for interrogation for other similar offenses? If so, must there first
be "reasonable grounds to believe" that they have perpetrated the others?

The calling in of other agencies occurs more frequently in rural areas. For example, after Bloomfield Township (Michigan) police had apprehended a man while he
was burglarizing a school, they called in the state police, who then questioned the
man concerning similar offenses in that part of the state. The suspect admitted
about ten burglaries in the area.

[29] 2 Ops. Mich. Atty. Gen. 1955-56 No. 2381 (1956); In the Matter of Lamphere, 61
Mich. 105, 27 N.W. 882 (1886); In the Matter of the Petition of Bloom, 53 Mich. 597,
19 N.W. 200 (1884).

tice described is of considerable significance.   But appellate courts have not had occasion to give careful attention to whether detention for this purpose is proper.   This issue is more complicated in jurisdictions such as Michigan or Wisconsin, where some delay for purposes of in-custody investigation is proper when reasonably necessary in order to decide whether to charge the suspect.   In this connection, the following two problems merit consideration:

(1) If police arrest a person suspected of burglary and obtain sufficient evidence to charge him with the burglary, is a further delay justified if, in the process of investigation, they develop reasonable grounds to believe the suspect has also committed a murder? [30] It has been argued that, in such a case, a person should not be immune from further investigation, unless one takes the view that in-custody interrogation is inherently coercive.[31]   However, there may be some risk that if a further delay were authorized it would be used primarily to "nail down" the burglary case under the pretext of investigating the suspected murder.[32]

(2) Is the situation different if the police suspect the arrested burglar of murder but lack sufficient evidence of murder to justify even an arrest for that crime? [33]   If further detention were allowed

---

[30] A slightly different problem has arisen in England.   There, the accused is not to be interrogated after arrest concerning the offense of which he is accused.   However, it is not clear whether the police can interrogate concerning other offenses.   See Brownlie, Police Questioning, Custody and Caution, 1960 Crim. L. Rev. (Eng.) 298.

[31] Ibid.

The stricter Mallory rule appears to be based in part on this assumption, and under Mallory it appears that such a detention is not proper.   Thus, in United States v. Mitchell, 322 U.S. 65, 64 Sup. Ct. 896, 88 L. Ed. 1140 (1944), the court concluded that, when a confessed burglar was further detained while the police cleared up thirty other housebreakings and recovered the property, "undoubtedly his detention during this period was illegal."   322 U.S. at 70, 64 Sup. Ct. at 898, 88 L. Ed. at 1143.   The court admitted the earlier confession on the burglary for which the man was arrested, refusing to apply any sort of ab initio doctrine.

As a result of the ruling in Mitchell, District of Columbia police have been cautioned not to jeopardize their case by attempting to clear other offenses.   The U.S. Attorney's office instructed that in a case such as Mitchell "you'd better be sure of the bird in hand and not go after the bird in the bush."   However, it was also pointed out: "Now, of course, you recover property in many cases where you don't prosecute for that particular offense.   To the extent that you can continue to do that without jeopardizing your main criminal case, you should do it."   Admission of Evidence (Mallory Rule), Hearings Before a Subcommittee of the Committee of the Judiciary, U.S. Senate, 85th Cong., 2d Sess., on H.R. 11477, S. 2970, S. 3325, and S. 3355, July 17 and 30, 1958, p. 400.

The District of Columbia police have objected to the Mallory rule on the grounds that it prevents them from investigating other offenses.   See criticism by the chief of police there, id. at 42, and the deputy chief, Scott, The Mallory Decision and the Vanishing Rights of Crime Victims, Police 61 (May-June 1960).

[32] Also, if successive periods of detention were allowed to investigate other offenses without interruption and without the suspect being brought before a magistrate, the circumstances tending toward coercion would be likely to increase.

[33] If the dividing line between proper and improper detention to investigate other

in such a case, the justification would probably be that brief extension of custody is not the equivalent of arrest itself in terms of interference with the person and thus can be allowed on something less than grounds for arrest. However, under this view it would seem that the added detention allowed would have to be most brief and would probably have to be limited to giving the arrestee an opportunity to admit other offenses.[34]

D. Delay to Investigate Other Offenders

Illustration No. 9: A police officer observed an armed robbery in progress. The three robbers fled when they saw the approaching patrol car, but the officer managed to apprehend one of them. At police headquarters the offender's appearance before a magistrate was delayed so that he could be questioned regarding the identity of the other two robbers.

Illustration No. 10: An officer on patrol observed a man throw a small, shiny object into the bushes as the officer approached him. The officer picked up the object, which was a piece of tinfoil containing what appeared to be narcotics. The offender was arrested and taken to the station, where a chemical test quickly confirmed that the substance was a narcotic. The offender was then interrogated by officers in the narcotics bureau, who hoped to learn his source of supply.

When the suspect is arrested for a crime committed by a number of persons, the initial appearance before the magistrate may be delayed to permit an investigation designed to disclose the identity of the other persons involved. The same procedure is employed when the nature of the offense makes it apparent that the offender must have dealt with an organized criminal operation, as is true in narcotics and policy cases. Generally these detentions are not

---

offenses depends on whether an arrest could be made for them, the critical question in many cases will be when grounds to charge for one offense give reasonable grounds to believe that the person has committed one or more other offenses. For example, can a person arrested and able to be charged with a burglary-safecracking be questioned about a murder which occurred in the course of another attempted safecracking in a building next to that in which he was previously employed? Can he also be questioned as to fifteen outstanding safecrackings with a similar modus operandi which occurred in the same general area? These were the facts in Trilling v. United States, 260 F.2d 677 (D.C. Cir. 1958), and questioning there was held to be improper under Mallory. Similarly, can a sex offender be questioned about an unsolved sex slaying? See Illustration No. 8. While these questions are not easy to answer, the test is identical to the one which the police must employ every day in determining whether they have adequate grounds for arrest.

34 Thus, Judge Prettyman, concurring in Trilling, 260 F.2d at 697, 708, stressed that the confessed safecracker was not interrogated at length about other similar offenses but rather was asked "just one question about each of these crimes."

lengthy because it is usually possible to persuade the suspect to name his confederates, or it becomes apparent that he will not do so. If the suspect does identify his confederates, his appearance before the magistrate may be further delayed until the others are arrested. This may be done to prevent the confederates from being alerted, as they may be if the suspect appears before the magistrate and is released on bail. A delay may also make it possible to interrogate the confederates, after their arrest, in the presence of the suspect who has identified the others as his accomplices.

The legality of detention to identify other offenders is not clear in Michigan or Wisconsin.[35] Although the potential value of such detention to the investigation of crime is obvious, the propriety of retaining in custody a person who can be charged and who is not, himself, suspected of another offense, is subject to question. But, as in the case where the individual is merely suspected of (but could not be arrested for) a second offense, it might be argued that some slight extension of the otherwise legal detention period is not a significant interference with his liberty and is therefore justified in view of the possible benefits to be derived.

One way to approach this problem is by analogy to the other powers to detain persons who may be in a position to identify criminal offenders. Courts and prosecutors in the three states have power, under certain circumstances, to detain persons and compel them to give information concerning criminal offenses or offenders. Thus, in Michigan, the one-man grand jury provision allows a judicial officer, following the filing of a complaint or after application of the prosecutor, to require a person to appear before him and testify, where the judge has "probable cause to suspect" that a crime has been committed and that the person can give material evidence.[36] Similarly, in Wisconsin, there may be a John Doe proceeding upon complaint that there is "reason to believe" a crime has been committed, and persons who might be able to provide information can be called to testify.[37] In certain circumstances the county attorney in Kansas may himself subpoena persons whom "he shall have any reason to believe have any information concerning or knowledge of" an offense, and he may receive their testimony.[38] The provisions of the three jurisdictions are similar in that they allow compelled appearance and actual testimony under oath of persons who might be able to give information concerning

[35] It would appear to be clearly improper under the Mallory rule, however. The District of Columbia police criticized the rule on this score at the same time they objected to not being able to question on other offenses. See page 375 *supra*, note 31.

[36] Mich. Stat. Ann. §28.943 (1954).

[37] Wis. Stat. §954.025 (1955).

[38] Kan. Gen. Stat. §62-301 (1949).

offenses as to which there is not sufficient evidence for charging.[39]

These statutes evidence legislative recognition that identifying criminals sometimes warrants the use of the power of the state over those who are likely to be able to provide the necessary information. Resort to these proceedings every time an offender is arrested whose unknown accomplices have escaped, or every time an offender is arrested who clearly has had dealings with other offenders, would be cumbersome and would present problems of granting immunity in exchange for testimony. Thus the issue of whether the police, acting for the same purpose, may properly extend an otherwise lawful detention for questioning not under oath remains important. This question takes on added significance in view of the fact that the historic trend has been one of a shift in responsibility for the investigation of suspects from the magistrate to the police.[40]

[39] The investigations in Michigan and Wisconsin are to determine if there is probable cause. People v. Birch, 329 Mich. 38, 44 N.W.2d 859 (1950); Wis. Stat. §954.025 (1955). The Kansas statute is less clear, in that it speaks of the prosecutor acting when he has "knowledge" of a criminal violation, but it would appear the investigation is for the same purpose.

[40] Devlin, The Criminal Prosecution in England, chap. 1 (1958); Barrett, Police Practices and the Law — From Arrest to Release or Charge, 50 Calif. L. Rev. 11, 45 (1962).

Controls in the Arrest-Detention
Process

The great majority of arrests are made without warrant, and in most cases the decision to arrest is made by a patrolman or other officer of relatively low rank. Similarly, most decisions to detain a suspect after arrest and to conduct an in-custody investigation are made without the specific case being reviewed by a high-ranking officer.[1] It is necessary that important responsibility be delegated to "front-line" officers because the nature of the police task is such that most decisions must be made immediately and at all hours of the day and night. Devising adequate controls over decision-making at the arrest-detention stage is therefore more difficult than it is at the prosecution, adjudication, and correctional stages, where decisions are made by a relatively small number of persons under circumstances which make careful consideration of the issues and review of the decisions practical.

This chapter is concerned with those controls over the arrest and detention decisions which are currently built into the criminal justice system and those which have been proposed as desirable. The two chapters which follow deal with the remedies and sanctions which may be invoked by a person who feels aggrieved by a decision to arrest or to detain him.

A. Visibility of Detention at Its Inception:
Booking

The booking process is usually a predominantly clerical procedure, performed immediately or soon after the suspect has been

[1] After an arrest, it is customary for a supervisory officer to review the situation briefly before the arrestee is booked and detained further. Though the supervisor may ask the suspect or the arresting officer a few questions, the review is for the most part perfunctory. If more careful review is made, it is likely to be on matters other than the probability of guilt, such as what the booking should be or whether the person should be released for some reason unrelated to guilt.

delivered to the precinct or district station. An arrest card is prepared on the suspect and is later used for posting on his permanent
police record. Depending on the severity of the offense, the suspect may be fingerprinted, photographed, and requested to supply
a handwriting sample. An entry is made on the police "blotter"
or "arrest book," indicating the name of the person arrested, the
date and time of the arrest, the offense involved, and whether
the suspect is to be further investigated before a warrant is sought.[2]
Later developments, such as charge or release, are also likely to be
entered on this record.[3]

The booking process operates to the detriment of the suspect
in that it results in his having an arrest record.[4] But there are
benefits. The fact that a permanent record is made is some check
upon abuse. Booking makes it possible for friends, counsel, and
others to learn that the suspect has been arrested.[5] This visibility
can be maintained even in a large department if there is a central
information desk at which records of all bookings are kept.[6]

Although booking operates as a safeguard in this way, it is not
generally required by law. Its primary function is considered to
be record-keeping, and any statutory requirements concerning it
are likely to be aimed at improving criminal identification procedures. Thus a statute may require the taking of fingerprints and
photographs under certain circumstances,[7] but still not compel the
prompt making of a permanent and public record of arrests. Failure to book a suspect is likely to be criticized by a court only if it
is coupled with a rejection of the suspect's demand to contact coun-

[2] The fact that the case requires further investigation is indicated by not booking "on the nose" but by booking on "suspicion of" or "investigation of" a certain
offense. See page 302.

[3] It is common to record the reason for release and the time of release. In Detroit
the fact that the charging decision has been made is indicated by re-registering
the prisoner "on the nose" for the offense charged.

[4] See page 347.

[5] Also, important rights or privileges may be declared by law to arise at the time
of booking. If this is so, the booking takes on added importance. But the fact
that these rights arise at the time of booking may be added reason for the police
to delay the booking process. It is interesting that in California a statute allowing
the arrested person to use the telephone "immediately after he is booked" has been
amended recently to read "immediately after he is booked, and, except where physically impossible, no later than three hours after his arrest." Cal. Penal Code §851.5
(Supp. 1963).

[6] In Detroit at police headquarters there is such a central information desk which
keeps a current record of all persons being held by the Detroit department, including the precincts at which they are held and the charges on which they are
booked.

[7] E.g., Mich. Stat. Ann. §4.463 (1954), requiring fingerprinting of persons arrested
for offenses not cognizable by a justice of the peace and forwarding of a copy of
the fingerprints to the state bureau of criminal identification.

sel[8] or with refusal to allow counsel to contact his client by deny-ing that he is in custody.[9] Thus, although the police do book suspects promptly in the usual case, they do not feel obligated to do so. They may delay the booking process if it would require interruption of an ongoing interrogation, would result in counsel interrupting an investigation by resort to habeas corpus, or would alert the suspect's accomplices that they were wanted or being in-vestigated. In one instance, for example, a conspiracy squad officer asked the desk officer to "shut his eyes" to persons who might be brought in during the afternoon. As a consequence, twelve co-conspirators in a gambling syndicate arrested early in the after-noon were not booked until after four o'clock in order to prevent a hearing on a writ of habeas corpus before the following morning, thus making it possible for the police to interrogate the suspects and cross check their stories immediately after arrest and without interruption.[10]

Delayed booking was most frequently observed in Kansas, prob-ably because the courts in that state have not recognized any right to detain an arrested person for further investigation. The princi-pal concern of Kansas police is to keep counsel from challenging the detention until the necessary investigation has been completed. Juvenile suspects may be immediately interrogated without book-ing in order to obtain a statement before the parents are notified.[11]

If a suspect is booked, it is possible for the record to be altered later. For example, a suspect was arrested on December 12 for grand larceny. After a brief investigation it became apparent that prosecution for grand larceny was not possible. However, other information was received indicating that the suspect was wanted in Mississippi for passing bad checks. A wire was sent to the Missis-sippi authorities, but by December 17 no reply had been received. The lieutenant in charge signed a discharge card on the suspect and then told the turnkey to hold the man a while longer but to

8 This is an important factor in determining whether a confession was obtained in violation of due process. Lisenba v. California, 314 U.S. 219, 62 Sup. Ct. 280, 86 L. Ed. 166 (1941).

9 This is also a factor in determining whether a confession was obtained in vio-lation of due process. Haley v. Ohio, 332 U.S. 596, 68 Sup. Ct. 302, 92 L. Ed. 224 (1948). Although this practice was not observed, a recent Michigan case discloses an instance in which Detroit police repeatedly denied an attorney the right to see a suspect by detouring the attorney to various offices on different floors of the head-quarters building. People v. Hamilton, 359 Mich. 410, 102 N.W.2d 738 (1960).

10 In the case described the statements were obtained that evening, and at a writ hearing the next day the police agreed to the release of all the arrestees on bond, as all that remained to be done was the paperwork involved in charging.

11 The Kansas court has been critical of this practice. State v. Seward, 163 Kan. 136, 181 P.2d 478 (1947).

write him off the books in order to avoid the possibility of having to answer to a writ.

The fact that efforts are sometimes made to avoid immediate booking is an indication that booking does afford a certain amount of visibility to the detention and thus is some safeguard for the person detained.

B. JUDICIAL CONTROL OF DETENTION AT ITS INCEPTION

In recent years some attention has been given to the possibility of structuring the criminal justice system so that an arrested person would be brought immediately before a magistrate for a decision or whether there were adequate grounds for the arrest and, if so, whether there is need for in-custody investigation. If the magistrate were to find that the arrest was lawful and that there is need for in-custody investigation, he would remand the suspect to the custody of the police, setting a maximum time for the detention. The magistrate could warn the suspect of his rights and remand him to an agency which does not have responsibility for conducting the investigation. A form of remand to police custody is expressly provided for in a few states[12] and in some other countries, including England.[13] A remand plan has been suggested as a desirable alternative to the *Mallory* rule,[14] and there is evidence that some judges in the District of Columbia do follow a practice of remanding a suspect to police custody in certain cases.[15]

The immediate appearance-remand system is not provided for

12 Del. Code Ann., tit. 11, §1911 (1953); N.H. Rev. Stat. Ann., chap. 594, §§594:20, 594:22, 594:23 (1955); R.I. Gen. Laws, tit. 12, §12-7-13 (1957).

13 For example, in England, under the Magistrates' Courts Act §§6, 38, and 105, an arrestee is to be brought before a magistrate "as soon as practicable" (a normal standard of twenty-four hours is set, with special screening otherwise), but the magistrate has the power to remand the accused in custody without bail for a period not exceeding three days, if remand is to the police, or for a period not exceeding eight days, if remand is to prison. In France, under the new code, if it is necessary to hold a person for more than twenty-four hours, he is to be taken before a *procureur de la République,* who can authorize a further twenty-four hour period; see Berg, Criminal Procedure: France, England, and the United States, 8 DePaul L. Rev. 256, 286-287 (1959). In Japan, the normal rule is that detention for investigation shall not exceed ten days, but where a judge finds that "unavoidable circumstances" exist, the detention may be extended ten or, in the case of certain specified crimes, fifteen days; see Dando and Tamiya, Conditional Release of an Accused in Japan, 108 U. Pa. L. Rev. 323, 323-324 (1960).

14 Comment, 68 Yale L.J. 1003 (1959).

15 In Goldsmith v. United States, 277 F.2d 335 (D.C. Cir. 1960), the commissioner remanded the suspect for a three-hour period; in Jackson v. United States, 285 F.2d 675, 677 (D.C. Cir. 1960), the "case was put over for one day" and the defendant returned to police custody. However, in Trilling v. United States, 260 F.2d 677 (D.C. Cir. 1958), where the suspect was returned to the police without the express consent of the magistrate, Judge Bazelon, in a concurring opinion, took the posi-

by law in Kansas, Michigan, or Wisconsin. Although Kansas law apparently contemplates an "immediate" appearance,[16] there is nothing in the law of that state to indicate that the police are entitled to have the suspect returned to their custody when there is need for in-custody investigation. The appellate case law in Michigan and Wisconsin does recognize the right of police to conduct an in-custody investigation prior to the initial appearance before the magistrate.[17] The magistrate's chief function when the suspect is brought before him is to set bail, and he is not called upon to decide on the propriety of in-custody investigation in advance.

Although an immediate appearance-remand system is not utilized in practice in the three states studied, two existing practices are sufficiently related to such a system to deserve mention here. One is the writ of habeas corpus hearing, discussed in detail earlier.[18] It often results in remand, as the judge is usually willing to return the suspect to police custody for a brief period of time if the police indicate a need for further investigation. However, the basic difference between these continuances and a remand system is that the habeas corpus proceeding requires petition by the suspect or his counsel, while a remand system would require the magistrate, as a matter of routine in all cases, to decide whether further in-custody investigation is justified. Also, in habeas corpus hearings it is not the practice for the magistrate to decide whether there were adequate grounds for arrest or to carefully consider whether there is in fact any need for further in-custody investigation.

The other practice which has relevance to a remand system is that of regular initial appearance before the magistrate, which in current practice normally follows, rather than precedes, in-custody investigation. In this case too there is no review of the adequacy of the grounds for arrest. Such consideration as the magistrate gives to in-custody investigation is limited to cases where the suspect cannot make bail and consequently remains in custody. In this situation the suspect may be warned of his rights[19] and is usually re-

---

tion that "the magistrate may not lawfully return him to the custody of the police." 260 F.2d at 694.

16 State v. Beebe, 13 Kan. 589 (1874).

17 See page 327.

18 See page 333.

19 Of the three states studied only Michigan has a statute which clearly contemplates that the defendant be informed of his rights by the magistrate, but these rights are not enumerated in the statute. Mich. Stat. Ann. §28.885 (1954). Even in Michigan, however, it is not common for the magistrate to give the suspect any warning except of his right to a preliminary examination. In all three states the arrestee is informed in brief terms of the nature of the charge against him, and often some reference is made at this time to the fact that the defendant may have the assistance of appointed counsel if indigent.

manded to an agency other than the police agency which was responsible for his arrest.[20]

However, neither the habeas corpus proceeding nor the initial appearance before the magistrate operates in current practice as an effective, built-in review of the propriety of the arrest or of an in-custody investigation.

C. Prohibition of Police Interrogation

Much of the concern over in-custody investigation relates to police interrogation and its abuse by third-degree methods. There have been proposals that in-custody interrogation by police be entirely prohibited because it is inherently coercive or because actual coercion is so difficult to prove.[21] Others have suggested that responsibility for interrogation be given to the magistrate.[22] Even the emphasis in the *Mallory* case was upon the confession problem,[23] suggesting that other forms of in-custody investigation might not be viewed so strictly.[24]

[20] Usually the suspect is placed in the county jail, whereas before appearance, if his arrest was by city officers, he was probably detained in the local police station lockup. See page 401.

[21] See Hogan and Snee, The McNabb-Mallory Rule: Its Rise, Rationale and Rescue, 47 Geo. L. J. 1 (1958). The authors are of the view that arrest, even on probable cause, is not a proper vehicle for the investigation of crime.

[22] This has been proposed by such persons as Dean Pound and Professors Chafee, Waite, Kauper, and Warner, and was one of the recommendations of the Wickersham Commission. See Pound, Legal Interrogation of Persons Accused or Suspected of Crime, 24 J. Crim. L. & Crim. 1014 (1934); Chafee, Compulsory Confessions, 40 New Republic 266 (1924); Fed. R. Crim. P., Preliminary Draft 249-253 (1943), and Orfield, Proceedings Before the Commissioner in Federal Criminal Procedure, 19 U. Pitt. L. Rev. 489 (1958) (both on Waite's proposal); Kauper, Judicial Examination of the Accused — A Remedy for the Third Degree, 30 Mich. L. Rev. 1224 (1932) (also containing citations to other proposals at 1240 n.81); Warner, How Can the Third Degree Be Eliminated, 1 Bill of Rights Rev. 24 (1940); National Commission on Law Observance and Enforcement, Lawless Enforcement of the Law, No. 11, p. 5 (1931).

Magisterial interrogation has been criticized as unrealistic and unconstitutional: "Proposals to have judicially supervised interrogation seem unrealistic. They ignore the likelihood of silence in response to official warnings. There is no assurance that the judicial questioner will be skilled. The defendant's silence or bungled questioning would not help the police to solve crimes . . ." Beaney, The Effective Assistance of Counsel. in Harding et al., Fundamental Law in Criminal Prosecutions 52-53 (1959). "Such a procedure, being inquisitorial, would be in direct conflict with the American accusatory form of criminal procedure. . . . Indeed, it would be in violation of the constitutional privilege against self-incrimination." Moreland, Some Trends in the Law of Arrest, 39 Minn. L. Rev. 479, 487 (1955).

[23] The court condemned the use of "an interrogating process at police headquarters" or "a process of inquiry that lends itself . . . to eliciting damaging statements," and said they could not "sanction this extended delay, resulting in confession . . ." They added that what brief delay was to be allowed "must not be of a nature to give opportunity for the extraction of a confession." Mallory v. United States, 354 U.S. 449, 454-455, 77 Sup. Ct. 1325, 1 L. Ed. 2d 1469 (1957).

[24] See Payne v. United States, 294 F.2d 723 (D.C. Cir. 1961), where the defendant

Police in-custody interrogation is not prohibited in Kansas, Michigan, or Wisconsin. In fact, all state courts agree that in-custody interrogation does not itself render a suspect's confession inadmissible,[25] and appellate opinions frequently make reference to the importance of such interrogation to effective law enforcement.[26]

The importance of interrogation is evident in current police

---

was identified in a lineup held during an illegal detention. The court refused to decide whether evidence of the victim's identification in the lineup could have been introduced but said that in any event it was not reversible error to permit the victim to make identification at the trial.

An earlier decision, subsequent to McNabb but prior to the Mallory case, held that physical evidence obtained in the course of a search during a detention in violation of Rule 5(a) was inadmissible. The court in United States v. Klapholz, 230 F.2d 494, 498 (2d Cir. 1956) said: "Since the rule was one formulated by the Supreme Court as a deterrent to detentions in violation of Rule 5(a), we think that it extends to *all evidence* obtained by federal agents through access to persons while detained in violation of Rule 5(a)." The case is criticized in Note, 66 Yale L.J. 270 (1956).

The District of Columbia police, governed by Mallory, were cautioned merely to avoid a combination of interrogation and other than brief detention. See the lectures given to them, reprinted in Admission of Evidence (Mallory Rule), Hearings Before a Subcommittee of the Committee of the Judiciary, United States Senate, 85th Cong., 2d Sess., on H.R. 11477, S. 2970, S. 3325, and S. 3355, July 17 and 30, 1958. However, it is unclear whether Mallory has had even this effect upon the District of Columbia police, or whether they use greater pressures in hopes of obtaining an early confession, with even untimely confessions sought because the fruits thereof may further the police investigation.

25 For citations to cases in all states, see Culombe v. Connecticut, 367 U.S. 568, 590-594 n.38, 81 Sup. Ct. 1860, 6 L. Ed. 2d 1037 (1961).

26 For many citations, see Culombe v. Connecticut, 367 U.S. at 579 n.17. Justice Frankfurter observed in that case: "Despite modern advances in the technology of crime detection, offenses frequently occur about which things cannot be made to speak. And where there cannot be found innocent human witnesses to such offenses, nothing remains — if police investigation is not to be balked before it has fairly begun — but to seek out possibly guilty witnesses and ask them questions, witnesses, that is, who are suspected of knowing something about the offense precisely because they are suspected of implication in it." 367 U.S. at 571, 81 Sup. Ct. at 1861, 6 L. Ed. 2d at 1040.

Some would contend that the experience under Mallory — in fact since McNabb v. United States, 318 U.S. 332, 63 Sup. Ct. 608, 87 L. Ed. 819 (1942) — demonstrates the contrary: "The techniques of the Federal Bureau of Investigation have proved that secret prolonged interrogation is dispensible." Rothblatt and Rothblatt, Police Interrogation: The Right to Counsel and to Prompt Arraignment, 27 Brooklyn L. Rev. 24, 67 (1960). However, even disregarding the better training and equipment of the FBI, it may well be that the law enforcement task in a large city is substantially different from that faced by the FBI and that separate consideration should be given to the kinds of criminality with which this force must deal and those handled by the other federal police agencies. See the colloquies between Sen. Carroll and witnesses Oliver Gasch (U.S. Attorney for D.C.), Robert Murray (Chief, Metropolitan Police Dept., D.C.), and Irving Ferman (Director, D.C. Chapter A.C.L.U.), in Hearings Before a Subcommittee of the Committee of the Judiciary, United States Senate, 85th Cong., 2d Sess., on H.R. 11477, S. 2970, S. 3325, and S. 3355, July 17 and 30, 1958. There has been some judicial recognition that the problems of a large city might justify in-custody interrogation under circumstances which would not warrant its use elsewhere. E.g., Bailey v. Loomis, 228 Mich. 338, 200 N.W. 148 (1934).

practice. Although it is often used before all other means of investigation have been tried, in many cases every other means has been exhausted, leaving in-custody interrogation as the only remaining means of solving a serious offense.[27]   Often there are no witnesses or physical evidence available to identify clearly the offender.   Police in each of the states studied are of the view that prohibition of all in-custody interrogation would seriously impair the performance of their tasks.[28]

In the great majority of in-custody interrogations observed, the possibility of coercion appeared slight. In many instances the suspect is merely confronted with the evidence against him or with evidence inconsistent with his prior statements and is asked to give an explanation. Often he is just given an opportunity to admit to other outstanding offenses recited to him. Lengthy, continuous questioning is the exception rather than the rule. In practice the interrogating detective often terminates the questioning after a brief period to appear in court or elsewhere on other cases or to check upon statements already given by the suspect.

The issue is easily stated, but it raises questions not easily resolved. Does the possibility of coercive in-custody interrogation in a limited number of cases pose a sufficiently serious risk to warrant prohibition of all in-custody interrogation, even though it is the only means of solving many crimes? There is no doubt that total prohibition of in-custody interrogation would have a substantial impact on law enforcement.

Resolution of the issue on doctrinal grounds is not likely to occur. Although it is sometimes asserted that in-custody interrogation violates the privilege against self-incrimination,[29] history seems to support Wigmore's description of the privilege as "an *option of refusal,* not a prohibition of inquiry." [30] If this is cor-

---

[27] For example, in a case observed in Kansas the police were investigating the robbery-murder of an aged recluse. The investigation had been pursued for about two months, with careful and elaborate analysis of all physical evidence found at the murder scene. Information was then obtained that the murder weapon had been in the possession of a particular man some months before the murder. Although the man asserted that the gun had been stolen from him several months before, he was arrested and interrogated.

[28] Police elsewhere have also frequently made this assertion. See the views collected in Weisberg, Police Interrogation of Arrested Persons: A Skeptical View, 52 J. Crim. L., C. & P.S. 21, 27 (1961). The argument that interrogation is the only means of solving some crimes is also presented in Inbau, Police Interrogation — A Practical Necessity, 52 J. Crim. L., C. & P.S. 16 (1961).

[29] Morgan, The Privilege Against Self-Incrimination, 34 Minn. L. Rev. 1, 27-30 (1949).

[30] 8 Wigmore, Evidence §2268 (3d ed. 1940). On the history of this principal see Meltzer, Required Records, the McCarran Act and the Privilege Against Self-Incrimination, 18 U. Chi. L. Rev. 687, 694 (1951).

rect, then the privilege is inapplicable to in-custody interrogation not under oath.[31]

Although the Kansas position is unclear,[32] both Michigan and Wisconsin hold to the view that an inference of assent may be drawn from silence when the circumstances are such that a suspect could be expected to deny an accusatory statement if it were not true.[33] Thus it seems that neither the Michigan nor the Wisconsin

---

[31] Thus the courts in both Wisconsin and Michigan have held that the privilege applies only to prevent testimonial compulsion, People v. Placido, 310 Mich. 404, 172 N.W.2d 230 (1945); City of Barron v. Covey, 271 Wis. 10, 72 N.W.2d 387 (1955), and that the self-incrimination rule does not make statements made to the police while in custody inadmissible, People v. LaPanne, 255 Mich. 38, 237 N.W. 38 (1931); People v. Brockett, 195 Mich. 169, 161 N.W. 991 (1917); State v. Smith, 201 Wis. 8, 229 N.W. 51 (1930); McDonald v. State, 193 Wis. 204, 212 N.W. 635 (1927). But if the person in custody is asked to give a sworn statement, then he must be informed of the fact that he need not do so. Bianchi v. State, 169 Wis. 75, 171 N.W. 639 (1919).

Other investigative techniques, such as taking blood samples, State v. Kroening, 274 Wis. 266, 79 N.W.2d 810 (1956), or urine samples, City of Barron v. Covey, 271 Wis. 10, 72 N.W.2d 387 (1955); giving coordination tests or medical examinations, Green Lack County v. Domes, 247 Wis. 90, 18 N.W.2d 348 (1945); or requiring the suspect to put on certain clothing, Rogers v. State, 180 Wis. 568, 193 N.W. 612 (1923), are also not in violation of the privilege.

While the Kansas court has on one occasion suggested in dicta that police questioning constitutes a violation of the privilege, Clafin v. State, 154 Kan. 452, 115 P.2d 773 (1941), statements made while in custody are admitted in that state if voluntary. In the recent case of State v. Fields, 182 Kan. 180, 185, 318 P.2d 1018 (1957), the court held admissible testimony by an officer of what a suspect told him after arrest, saying, "The Clafin case involved an involuntary statement, which is not in this case." Similarly, it was not a violation of the privilege to admit as evidence an accident report filled out by an officer on the basis of the arrestee's statements, City of Wichita v. Hibbs, 158 Kan. 185, 146 P.2d 397 (1944), or to allow persons whom a suspect denied knowing or seeing to come in to identify him, State v. Smiley, 167 Kan. 261, 206 P.2d 115 (1949).

[32] In State v. Boswell, 119 Kan. 670, 240 Pac. 848 (1925), where it was admitted on trial that the defendant refused to answer the sheriff's questions concerning a certain robbery, the court, after observing that the situation was one in which answers were naturally to be expected, noted that there was a division of opinion around the country on whether silence in response to questioning while in custody can be received in evidence as an admission. The court then merely observed that the abstract did not show whether the defendant had been arrested before or after the conversation in question. This is the extent of the opinion, but the syllabus written by the court says: "The fact that the defendant in a criminal case had refused to answer questions relating to the offense charged, at a time when he was under suspicion but had not been arrested, is held to have been properly admitted in evidence against him."

This case therefore leaves unresolved the admissibility of silence in response to police questioning while in custody. No other cases on this point have arisen in this state.

[33] People v. DeBolt, 269 Mich. 39, 256 N.W. 615 (1934); Gullickson v. State, 256 Wis. 407, 39 N.W.2d 442 (1950). Generally this requires that an accusation be made directly to the suspect. Riger v. State, 249 Wis. 201, 23 N.W.2d 456 (1945). The Wisconsin court has even allowed into evidence the fact that the suspect's denial "was a qualified one and was not as direct and spirited as might be expected from one who was accused of so serious a crime," McDonald v. State, 193 Wis. 204, 208,

court assumes that the privilege against self-incrimination applies in the police station.[34]

However, resolution of the difficult issue of the propriety of in-custody interrogation seems clearly to call for careful assessment of the consequences of either alternative rather than debate over the historical applications of the privilege against self-incrimination. If in-custody interrogation is prohibited, the task of built-in controls would be to prevent it from occurring; if it is allowed, the task of built-in controls would be to prevent abusive interrogation.

D. Controls on Police Interrogation

1. *Warning of rights.* It has been suggested that the matter of the privilege against self-incrimination at the police station comes down to a question of whether the police have a duty to warn a suspect of his rights.[35] In the three jurisdictions studied, there is considerable uncertainty in the law as to when, if ever, the police must warn a suspect that he is not required to answer. In Kansas the court has said that a confession is not barred merely because of a lack of warning,[36] but recent dictum is to the contrary.[37] Dicta

---

212 N.W. 635 (1927), while the Michigan court would not allow consideration of defendant's response that he had nothing more to say when he had earlier denied his guilt. People v. DeBolt, *supra.*

Refusal to consent to some other investigative procedure while in custody may also be admitted into evidence This is true, for example, of a refusal to give a urine sample. City of Barron v. Covey, 271 Wis. 10, 72 N.W.2d 387 (1955). It is apparently true of all investigation not covered by the self-incrimination privilege. State v. Kroening, 274 Wis. 266, 79 N.W.2d 810 (1956), referring to the Covey case, stated, "Obviously, . . . if the privilege protected such facts, defendant's refusal to disclose them would not be admissible evidence." 274 Wis. at 271, 79 N.W.2d at 814.

The majority of the courts of other states would appear to conform to the Michigan-Wisconsin position, but some courts say that the fact of custody must be considered in deciding whether the defendant's silence shows admission of the allegation, and others refuse to apply the implied admission doctrine to persons in police custody. Note, 5 Stanford L. Rev. 459 (1953).

34 While the implied admission doctrine is understandable if the privilege does not apply to questioning at the police station, the observed practice makes apparent the need for careful consideration of all the circumstances before concluding that either silence or a qualified denial is evidence of guilt. The silence of a suspect may be explainable on numerous grounds, one of which might be that counsel has already cautioned him to remain silent. A less than vigorous denial sometimes may only evidence the confusion of a suspect being subjected to questioning by a group of officers.

35 Morgan, Maguire and Weinstein, Cases and Materials on Evidence 763 (4th ed. 1957).

36 State v. Criger, 151 Kan. 176, 98 P.2d 133 (1940).

37 "A confession is inadmissible unless accused was advised of his rights under the law and it is shown the confession was made voluntarily." State v. Seward, 163 Kan. 136, 144, 181 P.2d 478 (1947). No reference was made to Criger, and the ulti-

in both Michigan and Wisconsin have indicated warning may be necessary, particularly in the case of one who, by reason of limited intellect or education, may be unaware of his rights.[38] The

---

mate holding was only that the trial judge had admitted the confession without considering whether it was voluntary and that the judge had not instructed the jury on the manner in which the confession should be considered.

This dictum was relied upon by a defendant in a later case, but the court observed that the issue could not be raised since the defendant did not claim that his statement was involuntary, as he testified at the trial that he made th̶ ̶ ̶ ̶ ̶ ̶ ̶ ̶ ̶ ̶ ̶ protect his daughter. State v. Barnes, 164 Kan. 424, 190 P ̶ ̶ to warn was asserted as a defense in another case, but th̶ statements of defendant overheard by the police w̶ and not a confession, and that therefore they w̶ even if they were not preceded by a warning P.2d 1071 (1956). The defendant in that c̶ ment while in his car, and he then drove Officers at the scene heard the defendant m̶.   ̶ ̶ ̶ ̶ ̶ ̶ ̶ ̶ ̶ ̶ ̶.

It might be asked whether the Stewart hold̶ ̶ ̶ts one of the following three possible views as to when warning ne̶ ̶ e given: (1) where the defendant has not changed his character from susp̶ ̶ ̶ ̶ o accused (the English view, see page 370); (2) where the confession was not in̶ response to questioning by an officer and therefore was clearly a voluntary statement; or (3) where the defendant has not yet been taken into custody.

In the only other cases which have arisen since that time, the court has observed that the defendant in each instance was advised of his constitutional rights before he made any statement. State v. Robinson, 182 Kan. 505, 322 P.2d 767 (1958); State v. Vargas, 180 Kan. 716, 308 P.2d 81 (1957).

38 There is no Michigan appellate case in which a confession was held inadmissible upon the ground that a warning was not given. However, in the course of holding confessions admissible, the court has taken note of the fact that the suspect was fully warned of his rights prior to questioning. People v. Collins, 303 Mich. 34, 5 N.W.2d 556 (1942); People v. Rubel, 221 Mich. 142, 190 N.W. 635 (1922). In People v. Brockett, 195 Mich. 169, 179, 161 N.W. 991, 994 (1917), the court noted that for confessions to be admissible "they should come from the defendant under such circumstances as show them to be made of his free will, and *with full and perfect knowledge of their nature and consequences,* free from the dictation and coercion of others." [Emphasis supplied.]

The practice of warning has also been emphasized by the recent case of People v. Zeigler, 358 Mich. 355, 100 N.W.2d 456 (1960). There the court was concerned with the problem of alleged searches by consent. The court said that a search would be held voluntary where the suspect was warned of his rights, namely that he need not submit to the search, and that if he did consent the fruits thereof would be used in evidence against him. However, the court then went one step farther and held that the trial court erroneously admitted into evidence the fruits of the search in the instant case, though the suspect had actually handed the officers the evidence when they asked to search him, noting that no such warning had been given. This suggests that the court may be moving toward an absolute requirement of warning which might also apply to in-custody statements.

The Wisconsin court, in holding statements admissible, has noted that warning was given, e.g., State v. Goodchild, 272 Wis. 181, 74 N.W.2d 624 (1955); Potman v. State, 259 Wis. 234, 47 N.W.2d 884 (1951); Kiefer v. State, 258 Wis. 47, 44 N.W.2d 534 (1950); State v. Francisco, 257 Wis. 247, 43 N.W.2d 38 (1950), and failure to warn has been a factor in holding a confession inadmissible, e.g., Lang v. State, 178 Wis. 114, 189 N.W. 558 (1922).

The Wisconsin court has on one occasion observed that no warning is necessary where the defendant understands his rights, Esterra v. State, 196 Wis. 104, 219

United States Supreme Court's recent holding in the *Escobedo* case may well make warning by the police a prerequisite to the admission into evidence of a confession from a suspect in custody who has not consulted with counsel.[39]

In Wisconsin, where the dicta on warning have been followed by cases declaring that warning is not necessary, interrogations were observed in which the suspect was not warned of his right to remain silent.[40] The practice varies, however. Although Milwaukee police are instructed to warn a suspect before taking a state-

---

N.W. 349 (1928), and has since asserted that there is no duty to warn a person in custody, State v. Stortecky, 273 Wis. 362, 77 N.W.2d 721 (1956). The earlier dictum has recently (since the observed practices) been interpreted by the court as implying that "a confession would be inadmissible if obtained from a person of such limited education or mentality that he was unaware of such right against self-incrimination, and was not informed of the same by law enforcement officers before obtaining his confession." State v. Bronston, 7 Wis. 2d 627, 642, 97 N.W.2d 504, 512 (1959). See also Holt v. State, 17 Wis. 2d 468, 117 N.W.2d 626 (1963).

[39] Said the court, "We hold, therefore, that where, as here, the investigation is no longer a general inquiry into an unsolved crime but has begun to focus on a particular suspect, the suspect has been taken into police custody, the police carry out a process of interrogations that lends itself to eliciting incriminating statements, the suspect has requested and been denied an opportunity to consult with his lawyer, and the police have not effectively warned him of his absolute constitutional right to remain silent, the accused has been denied 'the Assistance of Counsel' in violation of the Sixth Amendment to the Constitution as 'made obligatory upon the States by the Fourteenth Amendment,' Gideon v. Wainwright, 372 U.S., at 342, and that no statement elicited by the police during the interrogation may be used against him at a criminal trial." Escobedo v. Illinois, 378 U.S. 478, 490-491, 84 Sup. Ct. 1758, 1765, 12 L. Ed. 2d 977, 986 (1964).

Escobedo does not make clear — and this ambiguity may have been deliberate — whether a confession will be admissible when counsel was denied but the police gave a warning. However, the court does say that their prior holding in Crooker v. California, 357 U.S. 433, 78 Sup. Ct. 1287, 2 L. Ed. 2d 1448 (1958), does not compel a contrary result in the instant case, as in Crooker the suspect "was explicitly advised by the police of his constitutional right to remain silent and not to 'say anything' in response to questions . . ." Escobedo v. Illinois, *supra* at 491-492, 84 Sup. Ct. at 1765, 12 L. Ed. at 986.

It has been argued that to impose an absolute requirement of warning is undesirable because it would interject an additional fact question into the criminal trial. Statement of Judge Holtzoff, in Confessions and Police Detention, Hearings Pursuant to S. Res. 234 Before the Subcommittee on Constitutional Rights of the Committee on the Judiciary, 85th Cong., 2d Sess. 8 (1958).

[40] Interrogation without warning was noted when observing the police and the district attorney in Milwaukee, and was also noted in Wauwatosa, Ashland County, Clark County, and Eau Claire County.

The following rather unusual situation from Milwaukee illustrates one way in which the failure to warn may bring the statement obtained into question. The defendant, who was charged with two counts of assault to commit murder, gave a free and voluntary confession which was taken down in writing. At the conclusion, the defendant was asked whether he had given the confession freely and voluntarily. He replied: "No, I haven't." The inspector then asked him what physical force had been used. The defendant replied, "None." "What other force have we used?" the inspector asked. The defendant replied, "You arrested me and proceeded to ask me questions which I had to answer."

ment,[41] they do not always do so. Some Wisconsin trial judges occasionally bar a confession from evidence because the police have failed to give a warning.[42]

By way of contrast, the usual practice in Kansas is to give a warning, and warnings are also frequently given in Michigan. Whether

---

[41] Milwaukee Police Dept., Rules & Regulations, Rule 30, §42 (1950), reads: "When a confession is freely and voluntarily made by a prisoner, after he has been informed that any statement he makes may be used against him, and is made without having been induced by any promise, threat or fear, it is of the highest order of evidence. . . ."

Milwaukee Police Training School, The Law of Evidence 4 (July, 1951) says: "Though it is customary (and required, where possible, in this Department) to warn a prisoner when he is about to make a confession, that he is not bound to do so, the omission of such warning does not thereby make his confession inadmissible."

Similarly, Pocket Manual for Wisconsin Sheriffs and Deputies 19 (1950) says: "It is the best practice to inform the prisoner of his constitutional rights to refuse to answer questions or otherwise incriminate himself, since it is presumed that many persons do not know these things."

However, inclusion of such advice in police manuals and training materials appears to be the exception rather than the rule. Examination of about fifty such documents disclosed that over seventy-five per cent of them did not include a provision on warning. Among those in which no warning provision was found were those from: Baltimore, Md.; Berkeley, Cal.; Birmingham, Ala.; Carson City, Nev.; Charleston, W.Va.; Cincinnati, Ohio; Columbia, S.C.; Columbus, Ohio; Des Moines, Iowa; Honolulu, Hawaii; Indianapolis, Ind.; Miami, Fla.; Minneapolis, Minn.; New Haven, Conn.; New York, N.Y.; Oakland, Cal.; Philadelphia, Pa.; Phoenix, Ariz.; Raleigh, N.C.; Richmond, Va.; St. Louis, Mo.; San Francisco, Cal.; Seattle, Wash.; Sioux City, Iowa; Toledo, Ohio; and Washington, D.C.

[42] The following colloquy between judge and prosecutor took place in Madison at a preliminary hearing:

The Court: Why wasn't he advised of his constitutional rights?

Asst. D.A.: Your Honor, we didn't think it necessary. . . .

The Court: Now just a minute on that score. I'm very much concerned about it. The law requires any individual brought into this court charged with a felony must be advised of his constitutional rights by the court. Now, here is one who is being asked to give his version of what happened, and frankly, I have just glanced informally at Exhibit I which has been offered. Certainly I would have thought that the defendant should have been advised of his rights. The whole purpose of this examination was to determine whether or not the defendant was guilty of the charge as later set forth in the complaint. Now, I think it is certainly the practice of the district attorney's office, at least as long as I have known, that when they bring somebody in for questioning, even though he hasn't been in an accident, to advise him first of all — I'm quite sure the police department does — on the numerous statements brought before me every day, he has been advised of his rights — and he doesn't have to answer unless he wishes to do so. . . .

Asst. D.A.: Your Honor, if I might say, that is a practice which sometimes I say we follow, and sometimes we don't.

The Court: I appreciate there are difficult situations arise before the police department and the district attorney's office in which sometimes they have difficulty in ascertaining the true facts in a case, but still the defendant is given the right, and must be given the right — he must be advised of his rights.

At that point the judge held the confession inadmissible because no warning had been given.

the dicta of the courts in these states account for this is unclear; the police frequently said that they gave the warning not because the law required it but because they hoped to increase the value of the statement received.[43] Warning in these states is more likely in the later stages of the development of a case than it is prior to questioning at the scene, on the way to the station, or immediately upon arrival at the station.[44]

In the usual warning given in Michigan the suspect is told (1) that he need not make a statement and (2) that anything he says can be used against him in court. In Kansas the suspect is usually also told that he has a right to contact counsel. The form of these warnings may vary, however. The police may advise the suspect that he need not make a statement by telling him that he need not say anything which would incriminate him, that he does not have to make a statement unless he wants to, or that he can refuse to answer.[45] Warning that his statement may be used in court may be phrased as: "might be held against you in court," "might be used against you," or occasionally "can be used for or against you at a later date." This last form is the equivalent of the English warning.[46] If it is intended to tell the suspect that his statement may result in his being cleared of the charge and released, it is accurate. However, if it is intended to suggest that self-serving statements are admissible in his behalf in court, then it appears to be misleading.[47] Notice of the right to contact counsel, if given, is usually made in

[43] The police added that it was common for defense attorneys to inquire whether the warning was given when a statement is introduced at the preliminary or at the trial.

[44] If a statement is received orally without the warning having been given, an assertion to the contrary is sometimes included in the transcript later signed by the suspect.

[45] It may be questioned whether the caution that the suspect need not make incriminating statements is adequate, as compared to a caution that he need not say anything. The suspect may not know what statements do tend to incriminate him. Observed the United States Supreme Court in the recent Escobedo case: "Petitioner, a layman, was undoubtedly unaware that under Illinois law an admission of 'mere' complicity in the murder plot was legally as damaging as an admission of firing the fatal shots." Escobedo v. Illinois, 378 U.S. 478, 486, 84 Sup. Ct. 1758, 1762, 12 L. Ed. 2d 977, 983 (1964). Also, note how the court, by use of the language quoted in note 39 supra, delineated its holding and distinguished Crooker.

[46] The English Judges' Rules, intended as judicial guidance of proper questioning techniques, would have the warning be: "You are not obliged to say anything unless you wish to do so, but whatever you say will be taken down in writing and may be given in evidence." The rules caution the police: "Care should be taken to avoid any suggestion that his answers can only be used in evidence against him, as this may prevent an innocent person making a statement which might assist to clear him of the charge." See Devlin, The Criminal Prosecution in England, chap. 2 and Appendix, 138 (1958).

[47] While such a statement would generally not be admissible, when the prosecution introduces the confession the entire confession, including self-serving statements, must be admitted. People v. Hepner, 285 Mich. 631, 281 N.W. 384 (1938).

very general terms,[48] and no indication of the exact extent of this right is given.[49]

2. *Access to counsel.*   In the usual case, the booking process itself includes an opportunity for the suspect to call an attorney. This practice was observed in several cities, including Wichita, Kansas City, Detroit,[50] and Milwaukee.[51]   Thus retained counsel often do enter a case shortly after arrest and immediately confer with their clients or are present when the case reaches the district attorney's office.[52]   In Milwaukee, they may actually sit in on the police interrogation.[53]   Indigent suspects are not afforded counsel at these early stages.

Police are periodically reminded of their duty to obtain statements from persons who are arrested.[54]   In cases in which obtaining a statement is particularly important, counsel is likely to be kept from contacting the suspect until the interrogation has been completed.[55] This is usually accomplished by proceeding with the interrogation immediately without mentioning counsel, thus implying that there will not be an opportunity to contact counsel until after the interrogation is completed.[56]   Other, less frequent

[48] Suspects are told that they "could have an attorney," that they are "entitled to an attorney," or that they have a "right to counsel" or a "right to an attorney."

[49] The suspect is not told whether this means that he can merely inform an attorney that he is in jail, that he can confer with the counsel before any questioning is undertaken, or that he can have counsel present during the course of the questioning. The one exception to this is when the suspect is a juvenile. In all such cases observed, the youths were told that they were entitled to have an attorney present.

[50] This is in accord with the department rule that: "Prisoners, unless intoxicated or otherwise incompetent, shall be permitted to use the telephone or be given other proper facilities for notifying their relatives, friends and legal counsel." Detroit Police Dept., Revised Police Manual, chap. 16, §59 (1955).

[51] The regulation there reads: "Prisoners shall upon request be given proper telephone facilities for notifying their friends, relatives, or counsel, as soon as circumstances permit." Milwaukee Police Dept., Rules & Regulations, Rule 32, §5 (1950).

[52] This is probably in order to bargain for a lesser charge. Discussion of this will be found in the volumes on Prosecution and Conviction.

[53] At that point counsel may prevent a statement from being taken or he may be satisfied to have the opportunity to sit in on the taking of a statement, viewing this as one form of discovery.

[54] E.g., Milwaukee Police Dept., Rules & Regulations, Rule 30, §42 (1950).

[55] Police may also prevent counsel from entering the case prior to the interrogation when knowledge that the suspect is in custody would hamper the investigation, because other culprits not in custody might either escape or destroy evidence. Such is often the case in conspiracy and organized gambling cases.

[56] Only one case was observed where the suspect refused to answer any more questions until he had seen an attorney. The detectives put him back in a cell and checked the information that they had already received, which proved the suspect's alibi to be true.

The police in Detroit do not attempt to obtain a formal statement if the suspect asserts a desire for counsel. However, requests for counsel are not encouraged,

police practices include delaying the booking process until after the interrogation; telling the suspect outright that he cannot contact counsel until after he has given a statement;[57] and offering to undertake the job of contacting counsel and then telling the prisoner that the attorney cannot be found. Actually turning away counsel who appears at the station to talk with his client is not a common occurrence. Only one such instance was observed, and in that case the suspect had not yet even been booked.[58]

---

though recently placards have been prominently displayed in all precincts in Detroit telling arrestees: "You are entitled to use the telephone." 28 Detroit Lawyer 21 (1960). If an attorney is already in the case, the taking of a formal statement is usually cleared with him.

[57] In one observed case a Milwaukee assistant district attorney reprimanded the police for not having followed this procedure. He said: "What in heck happened that you guys didn't get a statement from this fellow before you brought him up here? You know that we want a statement taken by you people downstairs, because the longer you wait the more chance defendants are going to have to get an attorney . . . If you fellows hadn't made such a big exposition of this thing, wasting so much time, we could have had a statement from this defendant."

One Milwaukee defense attorney confirmed that this was the practice. He said: "The police department will get defendants to make statements. By the time they get them to the district attorney's office, statements already are taken and you don't have a chance. I would say that as a matter of fact, the police department will try to encourage the defendant to make a statement prior to communicating with his or her attorney."

[58] The Kansas deputy in this case told the attorney that the police certainly had a right to "print and mug" suspects before they see counsel. It was clear, however, that the police also wished to question the suspect.

A recent appellate case discloses an instance in which Detroit police repeatedly denied an attorney the right to see a suspect by detouring the attorney to various offices on different floors of the headquarters building. People v. Hamilton, 339 Mich. 410, 102 N.W.2d 738 (1960). Such a practice is clearly contrary to Detroit police regulations: "A parent, husband or wife, or an attorney employed by or in behalf of a prisoner, shall not be denied the right to see and advise the accused. Other visitors may be allowed at the discretion of the officer in charge. Attorneys applying at Station Houses for permission to see a prisoner for whom they claim to be counsel shall be given an opportunity to do so, provided the prisoner desires such counsel. In all cases the prisoner shall be brought from the cell to some proper place in the Station where he may consult with his counsel in private." Detroit Police Dept., Revised Police Manual, chap. 16, §61 (1955). Compare the Milwaukee provision, which qualifies this right: "Counsel, relatives or friends of any prisoner shall upon request be allowed a personal interview with him as soon as circumstances permit . . ." Milwaukee Police Dept., Rules & Regulations, Rule 32, §6 (1950).

Hamilton is contrary to the observed practice. After providing proper identification, attorneys at all times observed were allowed to visit with their clients at both precinct and central detention quarters. One prominent Detroit defense attorney said that the police there are very liberal in allowing attorneys to consult with clients and that he had never been denied the opportunity to talk with a client at a reasonable time. No instance was observed in which counsel appeared shortly after arrest in an attempt to interrupt the interrogation of the suspect in order to consult with him. Rather, in cases where counsel had been notified, he would interrupt the investigation by bringing a writ of habeas corpus. In such cases, counsel and the suspect would usually consult briefly at the hearing.

It has been observed that "it is impossible to say just when the right to counsel begins." [59]   In Kansas, Michigan, and Wisconsin,[60] as in most states, a statement is not inadmissible merely because the suspect was not at the time represented by counsel.[61]   In 1958 the Supreme Court of the United States was directly faced with the allegation of denial of a constitutional right to counsel at the police station, but held that for lack of counsel to violate due process it must appear that it would so "prejudice" the defendant "as to infect his subsequent trial with an absence of 'that fundamental fairness essential to the very concept of justice.'" [62]   The court in 1964, in the *Escobedo* case, did find a violation of a constitutional right to counsel at the police station, necessitating suppression of the suspect's confession, but very cautiously limited the holding to the facts of that case: "where, as here, the investigation is no longer a general inquiry into an unsolved crime but has begun to focus on a particular suspect, the suspect has been taken into police custody, the police carry out a process of interrogations that lends itself to eliciting incriminating statements, the suspect has requested and been denied an opportunity to consult with his lawyer, and the police have not effectively warned him of his absolute constitutional right to remain silent . . ." [63]

[59] Beaney, The Right to Counsel in American Courts 127 (1955). On this problem generally, see id. at 129, 207, 210-212; Allen, The Supreme Court, Federalism, and State Systems of Criminal Justice, 8 DePaul L. Rev. 213-255 (1959); Beaney, Right to Counsel Before Arraignment, 45 Minn. L. Rev. 771-782 (1961).

[60] State v. Criger, 151 Kan. 176, 98 P.2d 133 (1940); State v. Ralston, 131 Kan. 138, 289 Pac. 409 (1930); People v. Hoaglin, 262 Mich. 162, 247 N.W. 141 (1933); People v. LaPanne, 255 Mich. 38, 237 N.W. 38 (1931); State v. Francisco, 257 Wis. 247, 43 N.W.2d 38 (1950).

[61] However, in New York a confession from an "accused" without counsel has been barred. People v. DiBiasi, 7 N.Y.2d 544, 166 N.E.2d 825 (1960). See discussion of the distinction between "suspect" and "accused" at page 370. Also, in Indiana, where the state constitution has been interpreted as giving a right to counsel at the police station, a confession would most likely be barred on this basis alone. Dearing v. State, 229 Ind. 131, 95 N.E.2d 832 (1951); Suter v. State, 227 Ind. 648, 88 N.E.2d 386 (1949); Batchelor v. State, 189 Ind. 69, 125 N.E. 773 (1920). Dicta can also be found in cases from other states suggesting that the courts there might so hold. Rothblatt and Rothblatt, Police Interrogation: The Right to Counsel and to Prompt Arraignment, 17 Brooklyn L. Rev. 24, 33 n.40 (1960).

[62] Crooker v. California, 357 U.S. 433, 439, 78 Sup. Ct. 1287, 2 L. Ed. 2d 1448 (1958); Cicenia v. Lagay, 357 U.S. 504, 509, 78 Sup. Ct. 1297, 2 L. Ed. 2d 1523 (1958). The court appears to have left the law as it was before: in determining whether a confession has been obtained in violation of due process it is relevant to inquire whether the police refused the suspect's request for counsel, Lisenba v. California, 314 U.S. 219, 62 Sup. Ct. 280, 86 L. Ed. 166 (1941), or whether they denied retained counsel an opportunity to consult with his client, Haley v. Ohio, 332 U.S. 596, 68 Sup. Ct. 302, 92 L. Ed. 224 (1948).

[63] Escobedo v. Illinois, 378 U.S. 478, 490-491, 84 Sup. Ct. 1758, 1765, 12 L. Ed. 2d 977, 986 (1964). It is difficult to say at this writing precisely what effect Escobedo will have, although it is not at all unlikely that it will ultimately lead to a very broad right-to-counsel-at-the-police-station rule. However, the present opinion suggests

State courts seldom deal with the question except in the context of testing whether a confession meets the requirements of due process. Some cases seem to recognize a right to contact counsel but do not provide a remedy for the suspect who is not allowed this right. For example, the Michigan court has declared that denying a suspect contact with an attorney and denying the attorney access to the suspect is "forbidden by the [Michigan] constitutional guaranty of due process of law," but held that this would not alone bar the confession.[64] The Kansas court has said:

> The conduct of the sheriff in refusing access to the defendant and to unmolested and private consultation with him was peculiarly reprehensible. It was tantamount to oppression in office, of a character which standing alone would have seriously imperiled the success of the state's case; and for which a civil action against the sheriff personally has sometimes been upheld.[65]

But a defendant, relying upon this language in a recent case, failed to persuade the court to hold his confession inadmissible.[66]

Of the three states studied, only Kansas has a right to counsel statute.[67] It is similar to those found in about half of the states.[68] It states that

> . . . any person held in restraint of his liberty pending trial or held for investigation in any jail or other place of confinement in this state, shall be permitted upon request to immediately confer privately with an attorney of his choice in the same room with such attorney and without any barriers between such person and his attorney, and without any listening in or recording devices.[69]

---

the court is not at all certain how far it should go. The language quoted in the text above will not make it difficult for the court itself or for lower courts to distinguish from Escobedo cases in which any of the following facts are present: (a) the investigation has not focused on a particular suspect; (b) the police have merely asked a few questions, as opposed to any sustained interrogation which "lends itself to eliciting incriminating statements"; (c) the suspect has not asked for a lawyer; (d) the suspect is indigent and cannot afford a lawyer; or (e) the police have fully warned the suspect as to his right to remain silent.

64 People v. Cavanaugh, 246 Mich. 680, 686, 225 N.W. 501, 503 (1929).

65 State v. Oberst, 127 Kan. 412, 423, 273 Pac. 490 (1929).

66 State v. Vargas, 180 Kan. 716, 308 P.2d 81 (1957).

67 Subsequent to the time of the field observations such a statute was also enacted in Wisconsin. Wis. Stat. §946.75 (1961) provides: "Whoever shall, while holding another person in custody and if that person requests a named attorney, deny that other person his right to consult and be advised by an attorney at law at his own expense, whether or not such person is charged with a crime, may be fined not less than $100 nor more than $1,000 or imprisoned for not less than 10 days nor more than 6 months, or both."

It is interesting that the statute expressly recognizes a right to counsel before charging. However, in view of the language "named attorney," it is unclear whether the police must afford the suspect means of learning the name of an attorney.

68 The statutes are collected and analyzed in Comment, 1962 U. Ill. L.F. 641.

69 Kan. Gen. Stat. §62-1304a (1949).

The penalty for violating this statute is a fine of from $50 to $500 or up to thirty days' imprisonment or both, and the officer is also subject to "immediate removal from office." [70]

Although too little is known about the effect of the Kansas statute to permit meaningful generalization about the effectiveness of this kind of legislation, it is interesting to note that Kansas police do not allow suspects to contact and consult counsel any more often than do police in Michigan or Wisconsin. Indeed, while Detroit and Milwaukee police are instructed to allow suspects to contact an attorney,[71] no such directive appears in the Wichita or Kansas City manuals. Kansas police seem generally unaware of the statute,[72] although it has been in effect since 1943.

Of crucial importance, from the point of view of the law enforcement officer, is the effect which the presence of counsel will have upon the success of an in-custody interrogation. Opinion differs on whether counsel would routinely instruct suspects to remain silent.[73] Cases were noted in Milwaukee in which the suspect gave a statement to the police with the full approval of counsel who was present during the interrogation.[74] However, observed police

[70] Id. §62-1304b. The statutes elsewhere provide for criminal penalties or a civil forfeiture to the person aggrieved. However, none of these statutes have been interpreted as requiring exclusion of a confession obtained when counsel was denied. See cases cited in Rothblatt and Rothblatt, Police Interrogation: The Right to Counsel and to Prompt Arraignment, 17 Brooklyn L. Rev. 24, 61 n.174 (1960).

[71] See notes 50, 51, and 58 *supra*.

[72] Indeed, there is some evidence that the highest court of the state is likewise unaware of this statute. In Converse v. Hand, 185 Kan. 112, 114, 340 P.2d 874, 876 (1959), the court said: "There is nothing in the law of this state guaranteeing counsel at that stage of the proceedings." It might have been more appropriate to observe only that denial of counsel at that stage did not vitiate the entire proceedings.

[73] Justice Jackson, in an often-quoted statement, declared that "any lawyer worth his salt will tell the suspect in no uncertain terms to make no statement to police under any circumstances." Watts v. Indiana, 338 U.S. 49, 59, 69 Sup. Ct. 1347, 93 L. Ed. 1801 (1949) (conc. opinion). But it has been said that this notion "incorrectly presupposes that every person investigated or arrested in regard to a crime is guilty and that the function of the lawyer is to keep the law enforcement officers from learning the truth," so that it may often occur that a lawyer "does advise his accused client to make a full disclosure of all facts and thus assist in the solution of the crime under investigation." State v. Braasch, 119 Utah 450, 463, 229 P.2d 289, 295 (1951). Similarly, Weisberg has said: "Since silence inevitably invites suspicion, it is not unreasonable to suppose that in many cases where the suspect is innocent his lawyer will advise him to answer questions in order to clear himself as quickly as possible and assist the police. Moreover, the lawyer's advice may be different if he is present at the interrogation. It is one thing to dispense general advice to a suspect from whose interrogation the lawyer will be barred and quite a different matter to counsel silence or answers to particular questions when the lawyer hears them as they are asked." Weisberg, Police Interrogation of Arrested Persons: A Skeptical View, 52 J. Crim. L., C. & P.S. 21, 44 (1961).

[74] It must be noted that this practice was not frequently observed, and is apparently likely to occur only when counsel is convinced of his client's innocence or when he feels that the guilty client's best chance for lenient treatment at the charging or sentencing stage lies in full cooperation with the police.

practice is not generally revealing in this regard, primarily because police usually prevent contact with counsel in cases where interrogation of the suspect is believed to be important.   There is no doubt, however, that some suspects with prior contacts with the law remain silent without the advice of counsel while other suspects do talk even though they have been allowed to contact counsel.

Another reason which police have for denying the suspect the opportunity to contact counsel immediately is that they want to prevent interruption of an in-custody investigation by a writ of habeas corpus.   Except in the case of the professional criminal, whose disappearance alerts retained counsel that he has been arrested,[75] habeas corpus is dependent upon an opportunity to contact counsel after arrest.

3. *Neutral observers.*   Observation makes it clear that it is often difficult to determine later, with any degree of certainty, what actually happened during interrogation of a suspect.   Some defendants, hoping to have their confession excluded from evidence, make false allegations of police misconduct.   Nor is the testimony of police officers always reliable.   An officer may misrepresent the situation in order to ensure conviction of one who he is convinced is guilty.   Concern about this[76] has led to the suggestion that provision be made for a neutral observer who can later report what transpired.[77]   Doubts about the desirability of this kind of proposal

---

[75] Thus it was observed that when a "bagman," or numbers carrier, failed to appear at his regular stops, the syndicate would take steps to obtain a writ of habeas corpus.   Writs sometimes reached the station before the arrestee and were sometimes received on persons who had not even been arrested.

[76] "Measured by legal standards, the most unique feature of police station questioning is its characteristic secrecy.   It is secrecy which creates the risk of abuses, which by keeping the record incomplete makes the rules about coercion vague and difficult to apply, which inhibits the development of clear rules to govern police interrogation and which contributes to public distrust of the police. . . .   No other case comes to mind in which an administrative official is permitted the broad discretionary power assumed by the police interrogator, together with the power to prevent objective recordation of the facts.   The absence of a record makes disputes inevitable about the conduct of the police and, sometimes, about what the prisoner has actually said." Weisberg, Police Interrogation of Arrested Persons: A Skeptical View, 52 J. Crim. L., C. & P.S. 21, 44 (1961).

[77] Weisberg, id. at 45. See also statement of J. R. Scullen in Confessions and Police Detention, Hearings Before a Subcommittee on the Constitutional Rights of the Committee of the Judiciary, U.S. Senate, 85th Cong., 2d Sess., pursuant to S. Res. 234, March 7 and 11, 1958, p. 177. Although the observer is apparently usually conceived of as an administrative officer, it has also been suggested that defense counsel might perform this task: "The real problem [of police interrogation] is the need for protection against police third degree methods, culminating in a coerced confession. The value of having counsel present during the police interrogation lies not in his being trained in the law, but in the protection against coercion afforded by his mere presence." Note, 107 U. Pa. L. Rev. 286, 288 (1958). For a similar view expressed by the Supreme Court, see Haley v. Ohio, 332 U.S. 596, 68 Sup. Ct. 302, 92 L. Ed. 224 (1948).

are expressed by those who believe that successful interrogation requires privacy.[78]

Observers are not used in Kansas, Michigan, or Wisconsin. However, in Wisconsin, interrogations are sometimes conducted in the presence of defense counsel.[79]   In Milwaukee, newspaper reporters are often present at interrogations; they enter interrogation rooms without asking permission, and there is no effort on the part of the police or the prosecutor to limit their involvement.[80]   Although reporters are not present at a large number of interrogations, the fact that they are freely admitted suggests that the police do not view their presence as an impediment to successful questioning.   There is evidence that Milwaukee newspapers, as a consequence of their reporters' firsthand knowledge of the practices of

---

Apparently this is not required by the law of any of the states. However, some foreign jurisdictions recognize a right of the suspect to call in a friend or relative. Mueller, The Law Relating to Police Interrogation Privileges and Limitations, 52 J. Crim. L., C. & P.S. 2, 13 (1961).

[78] Inbau and Reid, Lie Detection and Criminal Interrogation 142 (3d ed. 1953); Inbau, Police Interrogation — A Practical Necessity, 52 J. Crim. L., C. & P.S. 16, 18 (1961). In response to this, it is argued that "It is secrecy, not privacy, which accounts for the absence of a reliable record of interrogation proceedings in a police station." Weisberg, Police Interrogation of Arrested Persons: A Skeptical View, 52 J. Crim. L., C. & P.S. 21, 44 (1961).

[79] There is some basis for predicting that this might soon be declared a requirement under the constitutional right to counsel. In Massiah v. United States, 377 U.S. 201, 84 Sup. Ct. 1199, 12 L. Ed. 2d 246 (1964), the court held that the defendant's Fifth and Sixth Amendment rights were violated by use of evidence against him of incriminating statements which he made to a co-defendant after their indictment and their release on bail and in absence of defendant's retained counsel and which were overheard on a radio by a government agent without defendant's knowledge that the co-defendant had decided to cooperate with the government and had permitted the agent to install a radio transmitter in his car. Although the court said Massiah was more seriously imposed upon than had he been questioned by a known officer while in custody after indictment, there was a strong indication that the same result would have been reached under the latter circumstances. The more recent Escobedo case (discussed in notes 39 and 63 *supra*), when read with Massiah (which it quoted), raises the question of whether the requirement that counsel actually be present during interrogation will be applied to the states and to cases of pre-indictment investigation.

[80] For example, on one occasion two suspects thought to be responsible for a recent wave of holdups were arrested. One of the two gave a full confession, and not only was the questioning witnessed by a group of newsmen, but a part of his statement was recorded for later release over the air.

It has been questioned whether it would be wise, as a general proposition, to make police interrogations public: "A third choice would lie in making police questioning a public matter, by permitting the public (and thus the press and ultimately perhaps newsreel and TV photographers) to be present. But the price to be paid would be so high in terms of detriment to the suspect and the community (the investigating state authority) as to render such a plan worthless in practice." Mueller, The Law Relating to Police Interrogation Privileges and Limitations, 52 J. Crim. L., C. & P.S. 2, 13 (1961).

the police department, are likely to discount allegations of police misconduct in in-custody interrogations.

While both the Kansas and Michigan courts have condemned the failure to contact parents immediately after the arrest of a juvenile suspect,[81] none of the three states studied has had occasion to decide whether parents need to be present during interrogation of a juvenile.[82] Only a few cases involving juvenile suspects were

---

[81] In the Michigan case of People v. Cavanaugh, 246 Mich. 680, 225 N.W. 501 (1929), where the juvenile suspect was told by the police that he could not see his parents, and the boy's father was refused the right to see him after appearing at the jail, the court stated the rule to be: "In this State a parent may not be denied the right to see and have conversation with a child in jail and accused of crime." 246 Mich. at 688, 225 N.W. at 503. Although the denial of this right was not considered sufficient in itself to justify exclusion of the confession, it was a factor considered in determining its voluntariness. The Kansas court has taken a similar approach in State v. Seward, 163 Kan. 136, 181 P.2d 478 (1947).

[82] One position was stated in a federal Children's Bureau publication, as follows: "Because of the child's presumed immaturity, special safeguards should be thrown around a police officer's interview with a child in investigating a delinquent act. . . . Before being interviewed, the child and his parents should be informed of his right to have legal counsel present and to refuse to answer questions if he should so decide. In cases where waiver [to the criminal court] is possible, he should also be cautioned that if he answers, his answers may be used not only before the specialized court but possibly in a criminal court. Where a child has been questioned alone by a police officer, without having been given an opportunity to secure the presence of his parents, guardian, or counsel, his statement during such interview should be presumed to have been induced either by the child's immaturity or by the idea that they would be used only in the specialized court and they should, therefore, unless the presumption is overcome, be excluded from admission before a criminal court in which the child may be a defendant. Whenever possible and especially in the case of young children, no child should be interviewed except in the presence of his parents or guardian. This should always be the policy when a child is being questioned about his participation or when a formal statement concerning the child's participation in the alleged delinquent act is being taken." Standards for Specialized Courts Dealing with Children, Children's Bureau, Department of Health, Education and Welfare, 38-39 (1954), quoted in Harling v. United States, 295 F.2d 161, 163 n.12 (D.C. Cir. 1961).

A recent Federal Court of Appeals case establishes a new rule with prospective application only: statements of a juvenile in custody in response to official interrogation cannot be admitted in a subsequent criminal proceeding. Harling v. United States, *supra*. It is not stated whether the youth's parents had been contacted in this case or whether they were present at the time of the questioning, although they apparently were not. The court was concerned with the necessity of "insulating" the juvenile proceeding (all that occurred before waiver) from the subsequent criminal proceeding. The court was clearly troubled because the defendant's statement, had the defendant been an adult, would probably have been excluded under Rule 5(a) and the Mallory rule, but Rule 5(a) is not applicable to juvenile detentions. However, the court rejected their earlier position that in such a case the question was whether Rule 5(a) would have been violated at the time of the confession if applicable and held that the confession could not be admitted even if there was no "unnecessary delay." It is not clear, though, whether the court would reach the same result in a case establishing that the juvenile's parents were consulted and present at the time of questioning. The court's concern with allowing the juvenile detention to "serve as an adjunct to and part of the adult criminal process" suggests that they would.

observed in Kansas and Wisconsin, and in all of them the police proceeded directly with the questioning without first allowing the youths to contact their parents and without having the parents present.[83] Detroit police regulations require that the parents of any juvenile taken into custody be notified immediately,[84] and no instances were observed in which this regulation was not complied with. These regulations do not state that the parents must be present during the questioning, however,[85] and this is not the practice. But, if youths are being interrogated for purposes of obtaining a formal statement, a member of the juvenile bureau is usually called in to observe the questioning.[86]

4. *Division of responsibility for custody and investigation.* The suggestion has been made that where responsibility for the custody of the suspect is placed with an agency other than that charged with the task of investigation, the risk that improper methods will be used is lessened.[87] It has been recommended, therefore, that suspects not be allowed to remain in the custody of local police.[88]

No similar outright exclusion has been found in any state cases. Cf. State v. Smith, 32 N.J. 501, 161 A.2d 520 (1960).

83 The Milwaukee police regulations require notification of and interview with parents "as soon as circumstances permit." See notes 51 and 58 *supra.*

84 "When any juvenile is taken into custody, the officer in charge of the Station shall notify the parents or guardian and the Information Clerk immediately. . . . The officer in charge shall make certain that the parents or guardian of a juvenile are notified when such juvenile is sent to the Wayne County Juvenile Detention Home, after which he shall record such notification in the desk blotter." Detroit Police Dept., Revised Police Manual, chap. 18, §6 (1955). The manual also states that parents may be notified by the prisoner and that they may visit him. See notes 50 and 58 *supra.*

85 The Detroit manual does require that any interrogation of youths at their school be in the presence of the principal or his representative. Id. at chap. 18, §15.

86 This might not be done, however, if it does not appear that prosecution is contemplated or if the questioning is merely of a preliminary nature.

87 Lord Justice Devlin has stressed the importance in the English system of the fact that the C.I.D. or "detective branch" of the service is responsible for the investigation, while custody upon arrest is in the hands of the "uniformed branch," and, upon remand by the magistrate, in the hands of the prison service, "a distinct body of men from the police, men who have no more interest in the detection and punishment of crime than the ordinary citizen . . ." Devlin, The Criminal Prosecution in England 81-82 (1958).

88 "It would, however, be a step towards preventing possible abuses if the accused were removed from the custody of the police. Only long familiarity causes us to accept without surprise the arrangement under which a suspect is placed in the absolute power of those whose duty it is to obtain evidence against him. Consider: we employ police to investigate crime, and expect them to attain a measure of success in the apprehension and conviction of criminals; at the same time, we allow those who are arrested to remain for a time in the custody of the police themselves. . . . The conclusion is that where a local jail is available, it should be made a rule that persons arrested should be lodged forthwith in this jail rather than in a police cell. This would mean that the physical safety of the accused person would be the responsibility of a different set of officials from the police." Williams,

In Kansas, Michigan, and Wisconsin local police retain custody of a suspect until the initial appearance before a magistrate. Although a Kansas statute provides that persons arrested for a state offense "shall be immediately turned over to the sheriff of the county," [89] it is not uncommon for city police there to keep the suspect in the city jail when they desire to conduct an in-custody investigation.[90] There is no such statute in Michigan or Wisconsin. In Detroit, suspects are usually kept in precinct detention quarters during the investigation or are removed to central detention for investigation by a specialized bureau. In Milwaukee, suspects are occasionally detained briefly for investigation at a district station, but are usually held at police headquarters for the convenience of the detectives assigned there.

Detention subsequent to the initial appearance before the magistrate, in cases where the suspect cannot make bail, is in the county detention facilities. Thus, in those cases originated by city police, the investigative and detention responsibilities are at that point separated, as the county sheriff is by law responsible for the operation of the county jail.[91] However, in practice it does not appear that the shift in custody hampers in-custody investigation. City police detectives find it equally possible, although less convenient,[92] to interrogate a suspect in the hands of county officials as one in the city jail. There is no indication that county jailers refuse to allow the suspect to be removed from his cell for questioning, a lineup,[93] or re-enactment of the crime.[94] However, the

---

Questioning by the Police: Some Practical Considerations, 1960 Crim. L. Rev. (Eng.) 325, 345-346.

[89] Kan. Gen. Stat. §13-623 (1949).

[90] Since the police in Kansas, unlike police in the other two states, have no expressly recognized right of postarrest, pre-appearance detention for investigation, detaining a suspect in the city jail insures lower visibility of a practice of questionable legality.

[91] Kan. Gen. Stat. §§19-811, 19-1903 (1949); Mich. Stat. Ann. §5.868 (1961); Wis. Stat. §59.23 (1955).

[92] The inconvenience may arise from the purely administrative steps which might be required before the police are allowed to see the suspect, or it may be due to the distance between the county jail and the particular city police headquarters. Sometimes the latter factor is not a problem; in Milwaukee, for example, the county jail and the city police headquarters are in the same building.

[93] In Goldsmith v. United States, 277 F.2d 335 (D.C. Cir. 1960), the magistrate did not merely remand the defendants to the U.S. marshal after appearance, as was usually done, but rather remanded them in the custody of the marshal and the police so that the defendants could be confronted by the complainant.

[94] In Culombe v. Connecticut, 367 U.S. 568, 81 Sup. Ct. 1860, 6 L. Ed. 2d 1037 (1961), after the suspect's initial appearance on a murder charge, the judge obtained the defendant's consent to be returned to state police custody rather than to be detained in the county jail. The police wanted to take the defendant to various crime scenes. Also see Goldsmith v. United States, 277 F.2d 335 (D.C. Cir. 1960), where the magistrate's order placing the defendant in the custody of the marshal

county officer is more likely to keep a record of the time and length of any questioning[95] and may be present during the interrogation.[96]

E. Visibility of Detention at Its Conclusion: Police Release

It is not uncommon for the police to release a suspect when they decide after arrest that the evidence does not justify prosecution.[97] A suspect may be released by the station officer immediately upon his arrival at the station[98] or shortly thereafter following a brief investigation. He may be released by the detectives after a more extensive investigation has cleared him or failed to provide sufficient evidence to charge him. Release is a formalized function generally delegated to supervisory officers.[99] It is not common practice to obtain a waiver from the suspect of any right which he may have to sue for false imprisonment.

It is clearly proper in many cases to release a person without re-

---

and the police stated that it was "for the purpose of obtaining certain pieces of evidence, . . . confronting them with the complainant and for the further purpose of having them re-enact the offense." 277 F.2d at 339.

95 Jailers were observed to keep records on the time of visit and the identity of visitors, including officers from other departments.

In Jackson v. United States, 285 F.2d 675 (D.C. Cir. 1960), the court, in considering the admissibility of a post-hearing statement received by the District of Columbia police, noted: "Jail procedure required the officers to fill out a form to make a matter of record the name of the person to be interviewed and the purpose. The form was then to be presented to the prisoner who was free to consent or to decline to be interviewed. The form used in this case reads: 'Mr. Smithson: This is District of Columbia Jail RC No. 632 Resident Supervision, Jail Division, request. I hereby request to interview the following: Name of Inmate: Lester Lorenzo Jackson. DCDC No. 130206. Location: C.B.2. Purpose: Investigation. Agent or Representative of MPD.C. I consent to this interview.' This is checked. Signed, 'Lester Jackson. Time in — 12:55. Time out: 2:29 P.M. Officer in Charge, December 16, 1958, Weldon B. Drake, Detective Douglas Smith, Robbery Squad, Detective Donald J. Allen, Robbery Squad.'" 285 F.2d at 677-678.

96 Thus, in Jackson, the court noted that "after appellant had so consented in writing, he was brought to the jailer's office. A jail official, the two officers and Jackson thus were present." 285 F.2d at 678.

97 Release by the court occurs only when the suspect has been brought into court on a writ of habeas corpus. Release by the prosecutor occurs only when the prosecutor disagrees with the conclusion reached by the police investigators that there is sufficient evidence to charge the suspect.

98 For example, in Milwaukee the arresting officer is to take the suspect to the nearest district station, where the commanding officer is to determine whether the arrest is proper. Milwaukee Police Dept., Rules & Regulations, Rule 30, §34 (1950). If the commanding officer thinks that there is not sufficient basis for arrest, he may release the prisoner. Id. at Rule 7, §4.

99 In Detroit, the investigating officer may decide that release is proper, but the reason for release must be noted on the arrest ticket and countersigned by the officer's immediate superior and the officer in charge. Detroit Police Dept., Revised Police Manual, chap. 16, §§94, 98 (1955).

sort to prosecution. In a system in which arrests are properly made upon a lesser probability of guilt than is required for charging, it is apparent that there will be occasions calling for the release of persons without charging them because investigation has failed to disclose further evidence of guilt. Even if the same evidentiary standard is applicable at the arrest and charging stages, some persons will be released without being charged because evidence exculpating them is uncovered after their arrest.[100]   But it may be asked whether the release function is properly performed by the police.

Unlike some state courts,[101] the Kansas, Michigan, and Wisconsin courts do not impose tort liability upon an officer merely because he releases a suspect without bringing him before the magistrate.[102] This seems justified, as in the ordinary case police release is advantageous to the suspect. Were the suspect retained in custody until the prosecutor or judge made the decision to release, a

---

[100] "For instance, a person suspected of crime may be taken into custody by an officer without a warrant, the arrest being entirely justifiable because of the existence of probable cause to believe him guilty. Before he can be taken before a magistrate it may happen that circumstances develop showing his innocence. There can be no doubt that on all accounts he ought to be at once discharged." Atchison, Topeka & Santa Fe Ry. v. Hinsdell, 76 Kan. 74, 80, 90 Pac. 800, 802 (1907).

[101] Bohlen and Shulman, Effect of Subsequent Misconduct upon a Lawful Arrest, 28 Colum. L. Rev. 841, 853-855 (1928); 1 Harper and James, Torts §3.22 (1956).

[102] There is an express holding to this effect in Kansas. Atchison, Topeka & Santa Fe Ry. v. Hinsdell, 76 Kan. 74, 90 Pac. 800 (1907). The Michigan court has not ruled on the precise question, but has rejected the ab initio doctrine, usually used to impose liability, under other circumstances. Oxford v. Berry, 204 Mich. 197, 170 N.W. 83 (1918); Friesenhan v. Maines, 137 Mich. 10, 100 N.W. 172 (1904). The court said in both cases that they would not employ the doctrine to make an arrest illegal because of subsequent illegal detention, and has cited Hinsdell with approval, Oxford v. Berry, *supra*. The Wisconsin court has likewise not considered the matter, but has upheld an arrest where the facts disclosed that the police subsequently released the suspect, Peloquin v. Hibner, 231 Wis. 77, 285 N.W. 409 (1939).

The Wisconsin Attorney General has advised the police there that release is not unlawful: "After the arrests have been made and other facts and circumstances are presented which convince the officer that no prosecution can be successfully maintained or should not be maintained, there is no reason why the prisoner should not be discharged. So far as the vindication of the law is concerned and the interests of the people or state, I see no objections to this practice. The prisoner who has been arrested has been deprived of none of his constitutional rights. If he has been falsely imprisoned, he may have his remedy by an action against the officer for false imprisonment in a case where his discharge was made by the officer without adjudication of a court as well as when his case is brought before a court and a discharge effected in that way." 21 Ops. Wis. Atty. Gen. 782, 783 (1932). However, the police there have sometimes been cautioned to take the person before a magistrate unless a waiver is obtained. Platz and Bowers, Powers and Duties of Law Enforcement Officers of Wisconsin, Relating to Arrest, Search and Seizure 17 (1956). This document has frequently been used in local police schools and other training sessions. Another frequently used police text indicates that police release is proper except when the person demands to be taken before a magistrate. Dax and Tibbs, Arrest, Search and Seizure 96 (rev. ed. 1950).

substantial delay might occur, particularly if the arrest was made at night or on the weekend, when prosecutors' offices and courts are closed. Of course, as pointed out in a Kansas case, a suspect might have an action against the officer if he was denied an opportunity to clear his name by appearing before a magistrate when he asked that he be allowed to do so.[103] Such an opportunity is not likely to be requested by many suspects, however.

If release by police is improper, it must be because it has an adverse effect on the functioning of the criminal justice system, rather than on the suspect. It is arguable that since a decision to release is in effect a decision not to charge,[104] it should be made by the prosecutor and not by the police. A decision to charge ordinarily requires the concurrence of the prosecutor, and it might be said that a decision not to charge should also be the responsibility of the prosecutor, as he is better equipped to determine whether essential evidence is lacking or whether valid policy reasons exist for not proceeding to prosecution.[105] It is also arguable that all persons arrested should be brought before a judicial officer, even if release appears proper, as a control over police practice.[106] If the

[103] "Of course, if the person thus arrested will not accept his release, and demands to be taken before a magistrate, his wish should be respected, but in the absence of any such demand the simple act of a constable in thus releasing a person against whom he finds no evidence of guilt would not of itself suffice . . . as the basis of a claim for damages." Mayer v. Vaughan, Q.R. 11 K.B. 340, quoted in Atchison, Topeka & Santa Fe Ry. v. Hinsdell, 76 Kan. 74, 79-80, 90 Pac. 800, 802 (1907).

[104] Because this is so, more detailed treatment of the observed practice of release by the police, including description of the kinds of cases in which such releases are granted, will be found in the volume on Prosecution.

[105] Prosecutors generally exercise a broad range of discretion in deciding which of the guilty should actually be subjected to prosecution. See Inbau and Sowle, Cases on Criminal Justice 33-35 (1960); the series of articles by Baker and DeLong, 23-26 J. Crim. L., C. & P.S. (1933-1936); Munro, Functions of a Prosecuting Officer, 11 U. Det. L. Rev. 1 (1927); Snyder, The District Attorney's Hardest Task, 30 J. Crim. L., C. & P.S. 167 (1939). A detailed analysis of the exercise of this discretion in the observed jurisdictions will be found in the volume on Prosecution.

As has been noted in Part II, a substantial amount of discretion is also assumed by the police in deciding which of the guilty to arrest. Some view the exercise of such discretion by the police to be improper, Goldstein, Police Discretion Not to Invoke the Criminal Process, 69 Yale L.J. 543 (1960). Although it might be argued that discretion at the arrest stage must as a practical matter be exercised by the police rather than the prosecutor, see page 72, postarrest selection apparently could be made the sole responsibility of the prosecutor.

[106] "The Cleveland practice bypasses the requirement that all persons taken into custody be brought before a judicial officer; and while this may be a kindness to the released suspects in some or many cases, it has the undesirable feature of making it very difficult to determine what the police are doing and thus handicaps control of police practices." Foote, Safeguards in the Law of Arrest, 52 Nw. U. L. Rev. 16, 25 (1958).

In a recent federal case based upon what the court viewed to be Wisconsin law, the court assumed that it was not even correct procedure for an arrestee to be taken

police were aware that every person arrested must be brought before a magistrate, this added visibility given to their procedures might contribute to a more careful weighing of the evidence prior to arrest. Whether either of these considerations justifies the added inconvenience to the suspect is debatable. Because a tort action is for compensation of an injured party,[107] cases denying recovery to the suspect who is released do not necessarily sanction the police practice. Unlike some states,[108] Kansas, Michigan, and Wisconsin do not have statutes expressly authorizing release by the police.

---

by the police to the prosecutor, where a decision was made to release him. "It is true, as plaintiff points out, that he never was taken before a magistrate, as the law requires. It is not discernible, however, how plaintiff sustained any damages by being taken before the district attorney, who ordered his discharge, rather than before a magistrate, who could have rendered him no more favorable service." Czap v. Marshall, 315 F.2d 766, 770 (7th Cir. 1963).

[107] However, some courts have allowed recovery for release even where the person has suffered no damage. Such a result appears questionable, unless release is wrong even though there is no damage and there is no other effective sanction. See Bohlen and Shulman, Effect of Subsequent Misconduct upon a Lawful Arrest, 28 Colum. L. Rev. 841, 843-846 (1928).

[108] E.g., Calif. Penal Code §849(b) (1961): "Any peace officer may release from custody instead of taking such person before a magistrate, any person arrested without a warrant whenever . . . he is satisfied that there is no ground for making a criminal complaint against the person arrested. Any record of such arrest shall include a record of the release hereunder and thereafter shall not be deemed an arrest but a detention only."

CHAPTER 19

Immediate Challenge of Arrest or
Detention: Habeas Corpus

In theory, the writ of habeas corpus should serve as a method for a suspect to challenge the validity of his detention either by showing that grounds sufficient for arrest are not present or by showing that the time reasonably necessary for an in-custody investigation has expired and he ought therefore to be released.

In practice, the writ does not effectively serve either function. Instead of making careful inquiry into the validity of the detention, the judge typically fixes, by rule of thumb, a time limit within which the police must either charge or release the suspect. This results in an informal hearing-remand system which is apparently consistent with the detention law of Michigan and Wisconsin.[1]

A. AVAILABILITY OF THE WRIT

As a practical matter, a writ of habeas corpus is available to a suspect only if he has counsel. Thus, except in the case of the professional criminal, whose counsel is likely to know when his arrest takes place, access to a writ is dependent upon access to counsel, a matter discussed in Chapter 18.

The indigent suspect is not likely to resort to the writ, because he knows he cannot afford to retain counsel.[2] Therefore the police usually do not have to fear challenge of the detention of such a suspect. Moreover, the indigent suspect can often be held as a vagrant, which gives an added air of legitimacy to the detention which is in fact for purposes of investigating a serious offense.[3]

Thus the writ of habeas corpus does not pose a threat to in-custody investigation in the majority of cases. Police in both

1 See page 333.
2 In some of the observed hearings in Detroit, counsel fees were as much as $75.
3 On these practices, see pages 338, 354, and 371.

Wichita and Milwaukee commented that writs of habeas corpus are uncommon. And, while the Detroit Recorder's Court hears over 5000 writs a year,[4] the detention in a large number of these cases is not for investigation but is being used as a sanction against prostitution, gambling, and other offenses for which it is difficult to obtain a conviction.[5]

Even when the writ is used, the hearing may not be held until after the police have had an opportunity to conduct an in-custody investigation. In Detroit, however, some hearings are set very promptly, leaving the investigating officer little time in which to reach the court.[6] Habeas corpus hearings are usually scheduled for 11:00 A.M. if the writ is asked for at the opening of court that morning, and for 2:00 P.M. if the writ is requested later in the day. Knowing this, police are able to insure a substantial period of time for investigation by making an arrest during late afternoon, since no hearing will be held until the following morning. Or the arrest may be made on a weekend or holiday to afford more than one day of uninterrupted investigation.

B. Challenge of the Grounds for Arrest

Because the writ challenges the validity of the detention rather than the legality of the original arrest,[7] it is not an appropriate means for challenging an arrest on insufficient grounds if at the time of the hearing there is sufficient evidence of guilt available to the police. However, some hearings are held soon after arrest when there is no evidence other than that available to the arresting officer. In such a situation one might expect the detention to be challenged on the ground that the arrest was illegal.[8] This does

---

[4] In 1956, the court heard 5274 writs. City of Detroit, Annual Report for Recorder's Court 1 (1956).

[5] See Part V for a detailed description and analysis of these practices.

[6] The first step an attorney must take in securing a writ is to notify the clerk of court, who in turn immediately notifies the police department. Nevertheless, the officer investigating the case must often hurry to reach court in time for the hearing. Detectives on duty are required to phone in every hour to learn if any writs have been received on their cases. Sometimes off-duty detectives have to be notified to appear in court outside their regular working hours.

[7] Kan. Gen. Stat. §60-2201 (1949); Mich. Stat. Ann. §27.2250 (1938); Wis. Stat. §292.01 (1955).

[8] The Michigan court has expressly stated that such a question can be raised and passed upon in a habeas corpus proceeding. Hammitt v. Straley, 338 Mich. 587, 61 N.W.2d 641 (1953). The court there said that such a determination would be res judicata on the question of probable cause to arrest, but that in the instant case "there was no hearing intended by the statute, to ascertain whether the arrest without a warrant was justified by the information which had been received by the officer before the arrest." 338 Mich. at 599-600, 61 N.W.2d at 647.

Because a prior holding, to be res judicata, must be "upon the same matter in

not occur in practice, however. Rather, the magistrate merely sets a time by which the police must either charge or release the suspect. One judge, asked why the grounds for arrest were not inquired into, responded only by saying that there should be time for investigation. Defense attorneys, when asked why they did not challenge the arrest in some cases, said that they felt this would be inappropriate and that the judges would not listen to such an argument.

C. CHALLENGE THAT THE TIME FOR INVESTIGATION HAS EXPIRED

Defense counsel rarely contend that the suspect is entitled to immediate release without bail. In Detroit, at the occasional writ hearing held after the suspect has already been in custody for a substantial period of time, the magistrate is likely to be sympathetic to a claim that the time for investigation has expired.[9] However, at the usual writ hearing the suspect has been in custody less than a day. In these cases defense counsel are usually content to argue that the investigation can be pursued without the presence of the suspect. In this situation counsel requests that the suspect be released on bail.[10] If this fails, as is likely when the police insist on the need for additional in-custody investigation, counsel will ask the judge to set a time by which the in-custody investigation must be concluded.

Defense counsel do not attempt to discover the exact state of the police investigation. Consequently the magistrate's decision is not necessarily based upon an accurate picture of the investigative needs. The police are able to influence the decision because they are represented at the hearing by the officer investigating the case, who has full knowledge of the facts. In addition, the police officer sometimes may advise the magistrate on the need for investigation in his chambers before the hearing. In contrast, counsel for the suspect has often not even conferred with his client and knows little about the case.

It has been said that judicial officers generally do not possess sufficient expertise on the subject of investigation techniques to

---

issue," Tucker v. Rohrback, 13 Mich. 73, 75 (1864), it must be doubted whether the habeas corpus determination would control unless no additional information had come to light between arrest and the hearing.

[9] In observed cases of this kind, if the officer indicated that nothing remained except to obtain the prosecutor's approval of a warrant, the judge would adjourn the hearing for a half-hour for this purpose.

[10] On the propriety of requiring a suspect to post bail when his custody is not necessary to the continuing investigation, see page 337.

determine accurately what constitutes a reasonable time for investigation.[11] Whether or not this is true, in practice the judge usually defers to the investigating officer. Thus the hearings do not afford an opportunity for determining whether the appropriate time for investigation in the particular case has expired. Rather, they serve only to set the outer limits on police custody without careful consideration of the individual case. As a consequence, the result of any hearing is fairly predictable. In Detroit, the judge will usually continue the case for the seventy-two hour rule-of-thumb maximum.[12] In Milwaukee, the police indicated that the judge will usually give them twelve additional hours to complete their investigation.

The writ of habeas corpus, therefore, has not proved to be an especially effective means for challenging the grounds for arrest or detention in individual cases. However, the possibility of a writ being issued often makes the police hesitant to continue a detention beyond seventy-two hours without a vagrancy charge or probation or parolee hold. Generally, the police seem to feel that the continued liberality of the judges in acceding to their requests for time for investigation can be assured only by avoiding clear and gross violations of proper detention norms.

[11] See Weisberg, Police Interrogation of Arrested Persons: A Skeptical View, 52 J. Crim. L., C. & P.S. 21, 39 (1961).

[12] Actually, the usual continuance was for forty-eight hours, but the suspect had most likely been in custody a day or a major portion of a day. Of course, if the police admitted that this amount of time was not needed, a shorter time would be set.

CHAPTER 20

Sanctions Designed to Deter
Improper Arrest or Detention

The issue of what sanctions are needed to deter the police from making unlawful arrests or unlawfully detaining suspects has been much debated. Unlike many important issues in criminal law administration, the question has been dealt with frequently by appellate courts.

Certain sanctions, such as tort liability, place a penalty directly upon the police officer. But the objection has been made that there are so many barriers to ultimate recovery by the injured party that such sanctions are ineffective.[1] Others have objected to them on the grounds that, since arrest is viewed as a ministerial function, the officer who acts in good faith but deviates from the established legal norms should have the immunity possessed by many other public officers.[2]

Other sanctions have no direct effect upon the officer but do influence the outcome of the criminal prosecution. Since *Weeks v. United States*,[3] the wisdom of excluding trustworthy and probative evidence, solely because the police acted illegally in obtaining it, has been debated. Most of the concern has related to the exclusion of physical evidence obtained by an unlawful search,[4] but in recent years the *McNabb-Mallory* line of cases has given rise to vigorous controversy over the exclusion of a trustworthy confession because the police failed to bring the suspect promptly before the magistrate.[5] Recently the United States Supreme Court considered a

1 Foote, Tort Remedies for Police Violations of Individual Rights, 39 Minn. L. Rev. 493 (1955).

2 3 Davis, Administrative Law §26.03 (1958).

3 232 U.S. 383, 34 Sup. Ct. 341, 58 L. Ed. 652 (1914).

4 For a recent debate, see The Exclusionary Rule Regarding Illegally Seized Evidence: An International Symposium, 52 J. Crim. L., C. & P.S. 245 (1961).

5 See Admission of Evidence (Mallory Rule), Hearings on H.R. 11477, S. 2970, S. 3325, and S. 3355 Before a Subcommittee of the Senate Committee on the Judiciary, 85th Cong., 2d Sess. (1958); Confessions and Police Detention, Hearings Pursuant to S. Res. 234 Before the Subcommittee on Constitutional Rights of the Senate Com-

heretofore "neglected area of criminal procedure" [6] and held in *Wong Sun v. United States*[7] that an illegal arrest in at least some circumstances will require exclusion of subsequent statements by the arrestee. Most physical evidence and most confessions are obtained following, and often as an incident of, arrest. The threat to exclude physical evidence or a confession is thus directly related to the question of the propriety of the arrest.

The emphasis in this chapter is upon the effect of the various sanctions existing in Kansas, Michigan, and Wisconsin.

A. Tort Liability

An officer may be subjected to a tort action because it is alleged that he made an arrest on insufficient grounds or that he improperly detained the suspect following his arrest.[8] Police officers interviewed in Kansas, Michigan, and Wisconsin seldom expressed any concern over the threat of false imprisonment actions against them. Such actions are extremely rare. The Wichita City Attorney indicated that few have been brought there. The records of the assistant corporation counsel who represented the police department in Detroit disclosed an average of only ten false imprisonment suits against officers per year over an eight-year period. In Milwaukee only thirteen civil actions were brought over a five-year period,[9] and other Wisconsin police agencies also reported that few

---

mittee on the Judiciary, 85th Cong., 2d Sess. (1958); Mallory and Durham Rules, Investigative Arrests and Amendments to Criminal Statutes of District of Columbia, Hearings on H.R. 7525 and S. 486 Before the Senate Committee on the District of Columbia, 88th Cong., 1st Sess. (1963). Most of the testimony, both pro and con, was addressed to the desirability of an exclusionary rule, rather than to the correctness of the Mallory norm.

6 Kamisar, Illegal Searches or Seizures and Contemporaneous Incriminating Statements: A Dialogue on a Neglected Area of Criminal Procedure, 1961 U. Ill. L.F. 78.

7 371 U.S. 471, 83 Sup. Ct. 407, 9 L. Ed. 2d 441 (1963).

8 Even if the original arrest was proper it does not necessarily follow that the detention was proper. Leisure v. Hicks, 336 Mich. 148, 57 N.W.2d 473 (1953). This proposition is also supported by the manner in which the Wisconsin court approached the issues in Peloquin v. Hibner, 231 Wis. 77, 285 N.W. 380 (1939), and Schoette v. Drake, 139 Wis. 18, 120 N.W. 393 (1909).

9 There are indications that more suits have been brought, or at least threatened, in more recent years. In April, 1959, it was reported that false arrest suits were pending against Milwaukee police to the sum of $523,000. Wis. State Journal, April 8, 1959, section 1, p. 3, col. 3. While many of the suits have no foundation, their increasing number is said to be undermining the morale of the police department there. Milwaukee Journal, Feb. 10, 1959, section 2, p. 15, col. 4.

The amount claimed in damages in threatened lawsuits gives no indication of the amount actually recovered, however. Over a twelve-year period tort claims against police misconduct in Los Angeles have averaged approximately one million dollars a year. However, the plaintiffs have lost 91 percent of the cases, and reactions were ever actually commenced.[10]   In all three states, it is unusual for a suit to be brought without an allegation that the officer used extreme physical force and violence.[11]

These figures show that the tort sanction is rarely used, and the officers' lack of concern suggests that it is not an effective deterrent. The infrequency of tort actions might seem surprising, since even if a large city police department were to take all possible care to prevent illegal arrests and detentions "some police illegality is an inevitable concomitant of law enforcement." [12]   Among the apparent reasons why more false imprisonment cases do not reach the courts are the following: (1) events subsequent to an arrest affect the availability of the remedy or the likelihood of recovery; (2) there is seldom a readily available source of monetary recovery; (3) a jury may be more sympathetic to the police officer than to what appears to them to be a criminal-plaintiff; and (4) the innocent plaintiff will probably be offered a settlement to induce him not to take his claim to court.

1. *Importance of events subsequent to arrest.* Existing tort law is ambiguous concerning the basic theory under which a person has a right to recover. There are two possible alternatives. One is that liability is primarily a sanction against unlawful arrest, in which case the main issue is the sufficiency of the evidence at the time of arrest. The second alternative is that liability is limited to situations in which the plaintiff has actually suffered as a consequence of an unlawful arrest. This makes it important to determine whether the plaintiff was in fact innocent of criminal conduct. If the civil action is available only to innocent persons, its effect as a deterrent is lessened, because the vast majority of persons who are arrested, lawfully or unlawfully, are in fact guilty.

a. *Effect of conviction*

---

coveries have averaged only one-twentieth of one percent of the total amount claimed. Coakley, Restrictions in the Law of Arrest, 52 Nw. L. Rev. 2, 5 (1958).

10 Officers in the Eau Claire department could recall no civil actions against members of the department for false arrest. The director of law enforcement of the motor vehicle department, in charge of the state traffic patrol, could not recall any actions against members of the patrol during his fifteen years with the organization. The director of law enforcement in the conservation department estimated that approximately twenty actions had been brought in his twenty-five years with the department.

11 This may well be because absent physical injuries the plaintiff is unlikely to be able to show sufficient damage to make the suit worthwhile. Few prospective plaintiffs in actions for improper arrest or detention "are persons who are respectable in the sense that they have . . . acquired the kind of reputation which will be 'damaged' by illegal police activity." Foote, Tort Remedies for Police Violations of Individual Rights, 39 Minn. L. Rev. 493, 500 (1955).

12 Id. at 515.

In Wisconsin, the right to recover for an unlawful arrest "is not waived by pleading guilty to the charge upon which the arrest was made." [13] In contrast, the Kansas court, in *Hill v. Day*,[14] stated:

> Where a court possesses the power and jurisdiction to hear the evidence and determine the guilt or innocence of the defendant and to punish if found guilty, a judgment of conviction in such court obtained without perjury, fraud or corruption, is a conclusive determination that there was probable cause for the arresting and prosecuting officers to believe the defendant guilty of the alleged offense.[15]

The conviction of a person does not necessarily mean that adequate evidence was available to the arresting officer at the time of arrest. This point is implicitly recognized in early Michigan cases holding that conviction was only prima facie evidence of the existence of probable cause at the time of the arrest and allowing plaintiffs to recover even though they had been convicted.[16] More recently, however, the Michigan court has held that conviction, even if later set aside on appeal, is conclusive evidence of the existence of probable cause and is a complete defense in the civil action.[17] Courts in other states are divided.[18]

In Michigan, the statutes seem to provide that an officer is not liable to a guilty felon regardless of how little evidence was available at the time of the arrest. In addition to allowing a felony arrest upon reasonable cause, the statute authorizes an arrest "when such person has committed a felony." [19] The meaning of the provision is not clear.[20] It has never been interpreted by the Michigan

13 Hotzel v. Simmons, 258 Wis. 234, 241, 45 N.W.2d 683, 686 (1951). The arrest was by a train conductor, rather than a regular law enforcement officer, but the court did not base their conclusion on this fact.

14 168 Kan. 604, 609-610, 215 P.2d 219, 223 (1950).

15 The plaintiff was denied recovery even though on appeal of the police court conviction the city dismissed the case.

16 Larson v. Feeney, 196 Mich. 1, 162 N.W. 275 (1917); Schnider v. Montross, 158 Mich. 263, 122 N.W. 534 (1909); McCullough v. Greenfield, 133 Mich. 463, 95 N.W. 532 (1903).

17 Doak v. Springstead, 284 Mich. 459, 461, 279 N.W. 898 (1938). The court correctly asserted that "the liability of the defendants rests upon the question of whether or not defendant Springstead had probable cause to believe the plaintiff to be guilty of committing a misdemeanor at the time of the arrest," but liability was actually determined on the basis of whether there had been a conviction.

18 Note, 27 Notre Dame Law. 252 (1952); Foote, Tort Remedies for Police Violations of Individual Rights, 39 Minn. L. Rev. 493, 507-508 (1955).

19 Mich. Stat. Ann. §28.874(b) (1938).

20 Waite, Some Inadequacies in the Law of Arrest, 29 Mich. L. Rev. 448 (1930). It has been asserted that such a provision does not violate the constitutional bar against unreasonable seizures of persons. Waite, Public Policy and the Arrest of Felons, 31 Mich. L. Rev. 749 (1933).

court[21] or by any state court, although similar statutory language exists in many states.[22] Certainly the language is not a meaningful standard of conduct for a police officer, since he can act only upon the evidence available to him at the time of arrest. Thus the language apparently means that proof of guilt is a defense in a tort action.[23]

[21] The commissioner of police in Detroit sought an interpretation of this language on two occasions. In one the language was never brought to the supreme court's attention due to an error in the prosecutor's office, People v. Stein, 265 Mich. 610, 251 N.W. 788 (1933), and in the other the case was decided upon other grounds, People v. Lewis, 269 Mich. 382, 257 N.W. 843 (1934). Waite, The Law of Arrest, 24 Tex. L. Rev. 279 (1949).

[22] ALI Code of Criminal Procedure 234 (1931); Waite, The Law of Arrest, 24 Tex. L. Rev. 279, 293 (1949); Warner, The Uniform Arrest Act, 28 Va. L. Rev. 315, 333 (1942). Only two cases were found in which the court expressly referred to this section of the arrest law, and there it was merely noted that, whatever the provision means, it does not justify a search incident to an arrest made upon less than reasonable cause. People v. Brown, 45 Cal. 2d 640, 290 P.2d 528 (1955); People v. Estrialgo, 233 N.Y.S.2d 558 (Sup. Ct. 1962).

[23] It has been asserted that this statutory provision is merely a codification of the common law of arrest. Waite, The Tennessee Law of Arrest, 2 Vand. L. Rev. 509, 571 (1949). Some early judicial declarations of arrest law tend to support this view. Thus an early Michigan case, while not deciding this particular point, said: "The question whether an arrest can be made without warrant has been decided from time to time according to the various circumstances of each particular case, many of which may be found in 2 Hale, P.C. 72-105. The principles recognized in the cases are: (1) *Any person may arrest another who* is actually committing, or *has actually committed, a felony;* (2) He may arrest any person whom he suspects on reasonable grounds to have committed a felony, if one has actually been committed; (3) Any constable or sheriff may arrest any person whom he suspects, on reasonable grounds, of having committed a felony, whether in fact a felony has been actually committed or not." [Emphasis supplied.] People v. McLean, 68 Mich. 480, 485, 36 N.W. 231 (1888). See also cases cited in 1 Harper and James, Torts 280 n.24 (1956).

However, if this provision is intended as a defense, it has no place in the law of arrest itself: "To assert that a person who is actually guilty of a felony has no right of recovery against an arresting officer does not require the enactment of legislation giving an officer the power to arrest a person, actually guilty, where there are no reasonable grounds to justify the officer's belief." Remington, The Law Relating to "On the Street" Detention, Questioning and Frisking of Suspected Persons and Police Arrest Privileges in General, 51 J. Crim. L., C. & P.S. 386, 389 (1960).

The Restatement formulation is that the officer "is privileged to arrest another . . . if the other has committed the felony for which he is arrested," which does emphasize somewhat that it is a privilege rather than a rule of conduct. Restatement of Torts §119, applicable to peace officers per §121 (1934).

It is interesting to note that the Restatement recognizes no similar privilege in respect to misdemeanors in fact committed, nor do the common statutes such as that found in Michigan. Yet both the Kansas and Michigan cases declaring conviction conclusive proof of probable cause are misdemeanor cases, where probable cause was not the test for arrest in the first instance. It has been suggested that the Michigan position is consistent with the prior Michigan case, McCullough v. Greenfield, 133 Mich. 463, 95 N.W. 532 (1903) (see text at note 16), if the rule is considered to be that probable cause (established by conviction) is a defense to a misdemeanor arrest unless the misdemeanor clearly did not occur in the view of the officer. Note, 27 Notre Dame Law. 252 (1952).

Making conviction or proof of guilt a bar to tort recovery[24] can be rationalized:

> On occasion an unjustified arrest will luckily result in the apprehension of the right man. . . . What is believed to be the sounder rule, however, holds that if the person arrested is in fact guilty of the felony for which he is arrested, the privilege exists irrespective of the reasonableness of the actor's belief. . . . The arrest of the guilty man should not be the basis of an action looking toward the recovery of damages for the invasion of his interest for the obvious reason that he has sustained no wrong.[25]

This view has been criticized, particularly when put forward as a standard of conduct, on the grounds that it may suggest to the police officer that he can "go ahead and make an arrest in the hope that something will turn up which will legalize that unlawful action that has already been taken." [26]   There is some evidence that police do assume that they have acted properly if it is later established that the arrested person is guilty.[27]

Another reason has been suggested for freeing the officer of any liability when he arrests a guilty person:

> The reason back of the rule that the arrest of the guilty felon is privileged is not based upon a desire to protect one who has made a lucky guess, but goes far beyond that.   One experienced in the practical problems of law enforcement, but perhaps with inadequate training in the art of self-expression, finds it difficult to convey his ideas on this subject to judge and jury who seldom have had any actual experience in the apprehension of wrongdoers.   As stated by one author the officer "is unable to paint a word picture of the considerations which led him to guess the guilt of the man arrested, that will enable the judge to realize that he would have done the same thing had he been in the officer's place." [28]

Observation of current practice suggests that this is a factor of real significance.   Arrests are sometimes made upon a set of facts which

---

24 We are here concerned only with the question of whether conviction or guilt should bar tort recovery when the tort plaintiff is contending that the officer did not have sufficient evidence upon which to base the arrest. If the officer resorts to other misconduct, such as the use of excessive force or improperly extended detention, it seems clear that even the guilty should be entitled to recovery. The courts have so held: Larson v. Feeney, 196 Mich. 1, 162 N.W. 275 (1917); Note, 27 Notre Dame Law. 252 (1952); 22 Am. Jur., False Imprisonment §83 (1939).

25 1 Harper and James, Torts 280 (1956).

26 Ploscowe, A Modern Law of Arrest, 39 Minn. L. Rev. 473, 475 (1955). Special concern was voiced there about the Uniform Arrest Act provision that the arrest is lawful even if the officer charges the wrong offense or gives a reason that does not justify the arrest.

27 The observed practices suggest that this is particularly true with regard to arrests for purposes other than prosecution. See Part V.

28 Perkins, Criminal Law 871 (1957).

to the average person would not suggest criminal conduct, but which leads an experienced officer to the reasonable conclusion that a crime has been committed. Unless the officer can relate, in a convincing manner, how his skill and experience contributed to his conclusion,[29] the arrest will appear to be without adequate evidentiary basis.[30]

The rule that conviction frees the officer from liability does cause difficulty in administration by producing conflict between the police and agencies later in the process. When aware that conviction insures against tort liability, police are apt to be critical of a dismissal by a prosecutor or judge in cases where there is adequate evidence to convict. A decision not to charge[31] or not to convict[32] may be based upon policy considerations unrelated to evidence of guilt. However, it is traditional not to recognize the propriety of an acquittal except on the basis of the lack of admissible evidence of guilt.[33] Because of this, trial judges' decisions to acquit may be explained in terms of insufficient evidence, which creates antagonism between the police and the court.[34]

[29] In determining whether there were "reasonable grounds" for arrest, it is most appropriate to consider the skills and experience of the arresting officer. See page 255.

[30] Officers are frequently unsuccessful in this regard when the arrest is the basis for a search. See page 480 for examples of this and its consequences. The same difficulty is probably encountered in false imprisonment actions. Assuming such difficulties, can barring the guilty from bringing an action be supported on this basis? It might be argued that such a rule protects not only the officer who cannot explain his reasonable grounds but also the one who has made a lucky guess. If this is so, then perhaps other means should be sought for giving protection only to the officer who in fact had reasonable grounds for arrest at the time it was made. Glanville Williams has noted that, in a false imprisonment action, the rule that the officer has the burden of establishing the grounds for arrest "is undoubtedly correct as a matter of legal history, but it hardly represents the social policy of the matter. The arrester must, of course, give evidence of the grounds on which he claims that his suspicion was reasonable, so that the evidential burden may be said to rest on him. . . . But in the event of a conflict of evidence, the persuasive burden should as a matter of policy be regarded as resting on the plaintiff suing for false imprisonment, for the public interest in the arrest of suspected felons is greater than the temporary inconvenience to which innocent persons may be put if mistakenly accused . . ." Williams, Arrest for Felony at Common Law, 1954 Crim. L. Rev. (Eng.) 408, 416.

It is interesting that, while conviction is not a bar in Wisconsin, the burden is on the plaintiff to show that the officer acted unlawfully, Bursack v. Davis, 199 Wis. 115, 225 N.W. 738 (1929), whereas in Michigan, where guilt is a bar, it is for the defending officer to show the arrest was legally justified. Donovan v. Guy, 347 Mich. 457, 80 N.W.2d 190 (1956); Bailey v. Loomis, 228 Mich. 338, 200 N.W. 148 (1924).

[31] A detailed description and analysis of these decisions will be found in the volume on Prosecution.

[32] A detailed description and analysis of these decisions will be found in the volume on Adjudication.

[33] State v. Evjue, 254 Wis. 581, 37 N.W.2d 50 (1949).

[34] An officer on the Detroit "bum squad" arrested a man on a charge of being drunk in public, and the defendant pleaded guilty in court. However, since the

In order to protect themselves from civil liability, police may attempt to obtain a conviction even though they would otherwise favor release. In a Kansas community a patrolman found a man asleep in a car, awakened him, determined that he was intoxicated, and then told him to drive home. The officer then arrested the man for driving while intoxicated. The chief said that the patrolman had made a very serious mistake but indicated that the case would not be dropped because of the doubt which this would cast upon the arrest. In another city in Kansas, the police arrested a man for striking his wife and also arrested the wife to insure her appearance in court the next day. They said this was done to insure the conviction of the husband and thus to prevent any false imprisonment action from being brought on the grounds that the arrest was without warrant and for a misdemeanor which did not occur in their presence.

b. *Effect of finding of probable cause at the preliminary examination*

If conviction is conclusive evidence of probable cause, and if probable cause subsequently found is an absolute defense to suit, as the Michigan and Kansas cases suggest, it may be that a finding of probable cause at the preliminary examination will also serve as a bar. No cases in point were found in either Kansas or Michigan.[35]

c. *Effect of waiver of preliminary examination*

The Kansas court has held that defendant's waiver of a preliminary examination is properly considered by a jury in a false imprisonment action, but that it does not alone conclusively establish that probable cause existed at the time of the arrest.[36] No cases in point were found in Michigan or Wisconsin.

It is not possible to state with any degree of certainty how a jury reacts to the information that the person waived a preliminary examination. However, it is doubtful that jurors ordinarily understand the function of the preliminary hearing or the significance

---

man had no prior record and was a reputable person, the judge refused the plea and found him not guilty. Later, the officer who made the arrest said, "Now what happens if some attorney gets hold of this guy and sues the department for false arrest? In this kind of case, I wish the judge would make the stipulation that he is finding the defendant guilty without prejudice. . . . This looks bad when you see it in black and white."

35 However, in dealing with a malicious prosecution case, the Kansas court said that the fact that probable cause had been found by the magistrate would be prima facie evidence of probable cause even though the case was later dismissed by way of a statement of cause for nonprosecution by the district attorney. The court expressly distinguished this from proof of conviction, which it was observed would ordinarily be conclusive. Ross v. Hixon, 46 Kan. 550, 26 Pac. 955 (1891).

36 Torson v. Baehni, 134 Kan. 188, 5 P.2d 813 (1931).

of waiver in current criminal justice administration. Some unrepresented defendants assume that a plea of guilty and a waiver of the preliminary are synonymous. In Detroit, for example, it is common for the magistrate to ask a defendant how he pleads at the initial appearance and to interpret a plea of guilty as a waiver of the preliminary hearing. Waiver, under these circumstances, is certainly relevant to the guilt of the defendant, an important issue in states where a guilty person is not entitled to recover. Perhaps giving this weight to a plea of guilty at the initial appearance makes it necessary to afford counsel to an indigent defendant at that time, although this precise issue has not been litigated.[37]

If a defendant is represented by counsel he is not likely to waive the preliminary, because it serves a valuable pretrial discovery function. But most defendants are indigent and not represented at this stage in the proceedings.[38] Many unrepresented defendants have considerable difficulty in understanding exactly what the preliminary is and what advantages or disadvantages result from waiving it. The magistrate's explanation, if one is given, is usually brief, and the nature of the question, "Do you waive a preliminary hearing?" or "Do you wish a preliminary examination or would you rather go directly to trial?" may suggest that it would be wise to waive. The defendant who is in doubt may be advised by other court personnel or by police officers to waive the preliminary.[39]

[37] In White v. Maryland, 373 U.S. 59, 83 Sup. Ct. 1050, 10 L. Ed. 2d 193 (1963), the court held that counsel has to be furnished at the initial appearance before the magistrate if the defendant is asked to plead and the prosecution attempts to use the plea of guilty as an admission of guilt by the defendant during his subsequent trial.

[38] However, in Sedgwick County, Kansas, it is the practice, although not required by law, for the magistrate to set a date for the preliminary hearing when the defendant is indigent. And, although by statute counsel need be appointed only when the information or indictment has been filed, Kan. Gen. Stat. §62-1304 (1949), they are in fact appointed in this county so that they can serve their client at the preliminary. Thus, in practice, any waiver by indigent defendants occurs immediately before the scheduled hearing and after consultation with counsel.

[39] In one case observed in Milwaukee two female defendants charged with embezzlement were asked by the judge whether they wished to waive the preliminary. The two women shrugged their shoulders, looked about in an amazed fashion, and said, "Gee, we don't know what to do." The judge said he would give them a few minutes to think it over and left the bench. The detective said to the defendants, "Look, there is nothing to this procedure. Take my word for it, just waive. When the judge gets back tell him you waive. In this way he will set your bond." The defendants still appeared uncertain, so a court attendant said, "Look, we're not trying to influence you in this matter at all, but the best thing to do is to waive the preliminary hearing. When the judge comes back tell him you waive the preliminary hearing and he will set the bond for you right now." The husband of one of the defendants came forward, and the officer told him to advise his wife to waive the preliminary. A few minutes later the judge returned, and the two defendants waived the preliminary.

Waiver occurred in a high percentage of cases in Milwaukee, and it appeared that

In practice, therefore, a waiver by some defendants may mean only that they have decided to bypass a step in the process, which is of uncertain benefit to them, in the hope of obtaining a more prompt adjudication of their guilt or innocence.

d. *Effect of posting bond*

In the perplexing Kansas case of *Hill v. Day,* after deciding that probable cause was a defense and was conclusively shown by a conviction, the court went on to say:

> Appellee also cites *City of Wichita v. Hibbs* . . . as another argument that the petition does not state a cause of action. It was there held that the giving of a bond for bail and an appeal bond constitute a waiver of any right to object to the legality of an arrest without warrant. The petition before us alleges . . . the making of both such bonds, and the Hibbs case seems to be somewhat in point.[40]

It seems clear, however, that the *Hibbs* case and its predecessors are not authority for the point stated in this dictum. In *Hibbs,* although it appears that the arrest was not made for an offense in the presence of the officer, the basis of defendant's appeal was that he could not be convicted in police court without a complaint and warrant first being filed against him. The court merely noted that by statute the defendant was entitled to a complaint in writing only "on demand," and that the giving of bond waived any defect in the oral complaint and "any right to object to the process, warrant and arrest which brought him before the court for trial." [41] The decision seems to be merely that the jurisdiction of the court cannot be challenged after bond has been given, a view expressed in earlier Kansas cases.[42]

Whether the Kansas court would expressly hold that posting bond waives a right to recovery for an unlawful arrest is not clear. Such a decision would be difficult to support, because the fact that a bond is posted is not particularly relevant to the issue of whether probable cause existed at the time of the arrest. Certainly the person should not have to remain in custody throughout the course of the criminal proceedings against him in order not to lose his civil cause of action.[43]

---

some pressure to waive was frequently exerted. A few cases were observed in Detroit where the court bailiff attempted to persuade the defendants to waive, but this did not appear to be common practice.

[40] 168 Kan. 604, 611, 215 P.2d 219, 224 (1950).

[41] City of Wichita v. Hibbs, 158 Kan. 185, 187, 146 P.2d 397, 399 (1944).

[42] Topeka v. Kersch, 70 Kan. 840, 79 Pac. 681 (1905); State v. Lewis, 63 Kan. 265, 65 Pac. 258 (1901); State v. Moselli, 49 Kan. 142, 30 Pac. 189 (1892).

[43] Indeed, if there were such a rule, the prospective plaintiff who consequently chose to remain in jail could claim a much greater amount of damages against the officer because of the substantially increased detention.

2. *Source of monetary recovery.* A civil action for false impris-onment is often impractical because there is no source of monetary recovery. Commentators have stressed such things as governmen-tal immunity, lack of assets by police officers, and limited bonding requirements.[44]

The law in Kansas, Michigan, and Wisconsin, typical of that found in other states, highlights these difficulties. There is con-siderable inconsistency in the legal requirement that officers be bonded. Statutes require bond for the officers of long tradition, such as the constable,[45] marshal,[46] or sheriff.[47] However, as to the more numerous city police, the statutes may make no mention of bonding,[48] merely provide that cities may require their officers to give bond,[49] or require a bond of the chief only, which does not cover the members of the force.[50]

---

44 "This non-availability of potentially effective legal remedy is not the outcome of the law of arrest, or of the law of torts, but rather results from the dominance of other rules. Thus it is the law of municipal corporations which bars suit against the city, as does other public law bar suits against the state. Again it is the law of municipal corporations that almost everywhere prohibits garnishment of the policeman's salary. It is the law of suretyship that limits actions upon bonds. It is the law governing the issuance of injunctions that bars equitable relief for threatened false arrest. These bodies of rules have grown from diverse sources and in response to needs other than those arising from the problem of arrest or even that of police in general. Equally clear is the fact that there has been no deliberate intention to render rules impotent by restrictive technicality. With the rise of a professional police force and of an enormous body of diversified substantive law, men have probed into this *corpus juris* for instrumentalities that might be effective under the changed conditions. Integration of the various lines of attack reveals the failure to solve the existing problem." Hall, The Law of Arrest in Relation to Contemporary Social Problems, 3 U. Chi. L. Rev. 345, 353 (1936). Hall collects the law from other jurisdictions, which creates these limitations. See also Foote, Tort Remedies for Police Violations of Individual Rights, 39 Minn. L. Rev. 493 (1955).

45 Kan. Gen. Stat. §80-204 (1949); Mich. Stat. Ann. §5.72 (1961); Wis. Stat. §§60.53, 61.29 (1955).

46 Wis. Stat. §61.28 (1955).

47 Kan. Gen. Stat. §§19-802, 19-805 (1949). The bond, to cover the sheriff and his subordinates, will be from $2000 to $20,000 as set by the county board. It covers "the arrest and the care of prisoners," Pfannenstiel v. Doerfler, 152 Kan. 479, 105 P.2d 886 (1940).

Mich. Stat. Ann. §§5.861, 5.862 (1961). The bond is to be in the sum of $10,000. It covers the arrest and treatment of prisoners, Kosowsky v. Fid. & Deposit Co. of Md., 245 Mich. 266, 222 N.W. 153 (1928). The sheriff is not responsible for the acts of his subordinates, but deputies must also be bonded in an amount set by the county board of supervisors. Mich. Stat. Ann. §5.863 (1961).

Wis. Stat. §59.13(1)(c) (1955). The bond is to be not less than $5000 nor more than $10,000. The sheriff's bond must also cover the acts of his undersheriff, jailer, and deputies, except that the sheriff may require these officers to post their own bond. In counties of population over 200,000, or in other counties where these offi-cers are chosen by civil service rather than by the sheriff, the sheriff and his sureties are not responsible for the acts of these officers except when they are acting under the express direction of the sheriff.

48 This is the case in Michigan.

49 Kan. Gen. Stat. §§13-420, 14-205, 15-208 (1949).

50 Wis. Stat. §62.09(4)(b) (1955).

Recovery is not possible as a matter of right against a governmental unit. Since the police operation is a governmental function, cities are not liable[51] and the state cannot be sued for the torts of its officers.[52] However, in Michigan the political subdivision may, if the officer acted within the scope of his authority and not from willful misconduct, pay any judgment against policemen.[53] In Wisconsin a commission may allow payment of a judgment against a state officer where it is found that the officer "acted in good faith," [54] but until recently false arrest actions were expressly excluded from a statute requiring the state and political subdivisions to pay judgments against public officers with regard to their

[51] Tzatzken v. Detroit, 226 Mich. 603, 198 N.W. 214 (1924); Flamingo v. City of Waukesha, 262 Wis. 219, 55 N.W.2d 24 (1952). Kansas has a statute imposing liability on cities and towns for mob action, Kan. Gen. Stat. §12-201 (1949), and this has been held applicable to situations where a posse was assembled by an officer, Harvey v. City of Bonner Springs, 102 Kan. 9, 169 Pac. 563 (1907), and where police officers acted unlawfully as part of a mob, Moore v. City of Wichita, 106 Kan. 636, 189 Pac. 372 (1920). However, the statute does not appear to cover an arrest accomplished by a number of officers. In Lee v. City of Kansas City, 175 Kan. 729, 732, 267 P.2d 931 (1954), recovery was not allowed where a person was killed while being pursued by eight policemen, and the court said: "To so hold would subject the city to liability every time four or more officers acted in concert to prevent what in their judgment constituted a breach of the peace. The legislature never intended any such result."

However, Wisconsin has recently abolished, as to future occurrences, the immunity doctrine, so that "it is no longer necessary to divide [a municipality's] operations into those which are proprietary and those which are governmental." The court noted that the decision could not affect Wis. Const. art. VI, §4, declaring that counties shall not be liable for the acts of their sheriffs. Holytz v. City of Milwaukee, 17 Wis. 2d 26, 39, 115 N.W.2d 618 (1962).

[52] Holzworth v. State, 238 Wis. 63, 298 N.W. 163 (1941). In Michigan it is expressly declared that no political subdivision can be made a party to such a suit either, Mich. Stat. Ann. §5.3376(2) (1958), and in Kansas the courts have held that counties cannot be held responsible, because they are an arm of the state, Wommack v. Lesh, 180 Kan. 548, 305 P.2d 854 (1957).

But, for the recent change in Wisconsin, see the Holytz case, note 51 *supra*. The court noted that under Wis. Const. art. IV, §27, the state still can be sued only with its consent.

[53] The judgment is not to be paid, however, unless a copy of the summons is served upon the political subdivision by one of the parties. Mich. Stat. Ann. §5.3376 (1958).

The statute also provides that the city may furnish legal counsel in such a case. In Detroit, an officer who receives notice of a suit against him is instructed to immediately contact the office of the assistant corporation counsel for police matters. Unless the action of the officer was clearly arbitrary, this office will undertake the defense. Over an eight-year period, that office declined to represent the officer in only one case, in which the officer was intoxicated at the time the arrest was made. If the case is settled or if a judgment is obtained against the officer, the assistant corporation counsel may petition the common council of the city for payment of the damages.

Although the process is less formalized, the state sometimes volunteers to pay judgments obtained against state police officers.

[54] The statute provides that counsel fees and costs may also be paid. Wis. Stat. §285.06 (1955).

good faith actions.[55]   The police may carry false arrest insurance,[56] but it is more common to create a form of group protection by the assessment of the entire force after a judgment has been obtained against an officer[57] or by the establishment of a fund for this purpose beforehand.[58]

3. *Sympathy for the policeman.*   The jury will often be more sympathetic toward a police officer who has made a mistake in good faith than toward a plaintiff, particularly if the plaintiff has a reputation of having engaged in criminal conduct of a type thought serious by members of the community.

As the Supreme Court of the United States has observed, the prospect of recovery for police illegality often depends, as a practical matter, upon the "moral aspects of the case." [59]   It has been pointed out that the "moral aspects of the case" frequently are not very favorable for the tort plaintiff.[60]   Unless he is a respectable citizen, the jury is likely to conclude that no substantial damage was suffered.   The reputation and past record of the plaintiff is made known to the jury.   His reputation may be admitted to impeach his credibility, to mitigate compensatory damages by showing that his reputation was not damaged, to prevent punitive damages from being assessed by showing that the police did not act maliciously, or to establish that the police did in fact have grounds for arrest.[61]

Unless the jury knows the officer has insurance, they are likely

55 Wis. Stat. §270.58(1) (1955). This statute, which has been interpreted as applying to all police officers except sheriffs, Larson v. Lester, 259 Wis. 440, 49 N.W.2d 414 (1951), has been amended since the time of the observed practice to include false arrest actions and to provide for payment of reasonable attorney's fees in false arrest cases where the governmental unit does not provide legal counsel.   Wis. Laws 1959, c. 438.

Another statute permits municipalities to pay reasonable expenses where an officer has successfully defended a civil action arising out of the performance of his duties. Wis. Stat. §331.35 (1955).

56 A Kansas deputy sheriff indicated that he carried $50,000 worth of false arrest and assault insurance through the National Sheriff's Association.   A number of other officers also indicated that they carried insurance.

57 When a $500 settlement was made through the intervention of the chief of police in a false arrest suit against three Wichita officers, each member of the department was assessed $2 to pay the settlement.

58 The Policemen's Protective Association in Milwaukee provides a fund to be used for the protection of its members in any civil action that may arise out of acts committed in the discharge of police duties. Constitution and By-Laws, Policemen's Protective Association, City of Milwaukee, art. 2, p. 3.   In Detroit, the Detroit Police Benevolent Association, an organization whose specific purpose is the payment of judgments against police officers and which maintains a fund for this purpose by periodic assessment of its members, pays most judgments or settlements.

59 Ker v. Illinois, 119 U.S. 436, 444, 7 Sup. Ct. 225, 230, 30 L. Ed. 421, 425 (1886).

60 See the excellent discussion in Foote, Tort Remedies for Police Violations of Individual Rights, 39 Minn. L. Rev. 493 (1955).

61 Id. at 504-506.

to interpret a verdict to compensate the plaintiff as a decision to penalize the police officer, which a jury may be hesitant to do if the officer acted in good faith. The Michigan Supreme Court has expressed a similar concern:

> . . . a police officer who acts in good faith in the line of duty should be protected even though overzealous in its discharge. . . . If possible, any doubt should be resolved in favor of an honest discharge of duty by peace officers, and the courts should not place them in fear of responding in damages for the lawful and proper discharge of that duty.[62]

4. Inducements not to litigate. Another reason why few cases of police misconduct actually reach the courts is that the injured party may find it to his advantage not to litigate. To some extent, the fear of police harassment undoubtedly induces some prospective litigants, particularly those who engage in a continuing course of illegal conduct, to forego suit. No instance of an express threat by the police was observed, however. Most arrests made on questionable grounds or extended detentions involved professional or habitual criminals, and these persons do not respond with tort actions against the police.

Even if an aggrieved party does decide to take action, the case may still never get into court. Detroit officers threatened with suit are advised to contact the assistant corporation counsel, who will aid in bringing about a settlement of the case. The next procedure, if the city is to pay the damages, is to petition the common council for payment, but over a seven-year period only three such requests were made. In the balance of the cases, payment was made by the Detroit Police Benevolent Association, an organization whose specific purpose is the payment of such claims against the police and which maintains a fund for this purpose by periodic assessments on its membership.

This practice is interesting for a number of reasons. First, if tort liability is intended as an economic sanction, the above procedure minimizes its effectiveness. The officer does not incur an economic loss, and, as long as the total number of claims is low, no significant loss is felt by the members of the association.[63] It would be difficult to criticize the practice on this basis; just as

---

[62] Odinetz v. Budds, 315 Mich. 512, 517-518, 24 N.W.2d 193 (1946). This language was quoted with approval in Hammitt v. Straley, 338 Mich. 587, 593-594, 61 N.W.2d 641, 644-645 (1953). This position has been criticized as failing to give substance to the criminal law philosophy that it is better that a few escape punishment than to allow too permeating police surveillance. Foote, Tort Remedies for Police Violations of Individual Rights, 39 Minn. L. Rev. 493, 502 (1955).

[63] The Detroit association's assessment was an infrequent levy of one dollar per member.

in cases where the officer is covered by insurance, whatever loss there may be in deterrence seems more than offset by the desirability of allowing distribution of the financial risk.

Secondly, because the police have this fund at hand, they are in a position to reach a settlement with the injured party without the case first reaching the courts. Courts have often indicated that settlement is to be favored,[64] and the crowded calendars make settlement of a high percentage of cases necessary. However, settlement of claims concerning police misconduct may prevent one desirable effect of the tort action. Trial of a tort action against an officer is usually attended by considerable publicity, and this added visibility to instances of misconduct may itself serve to deter violation of the legal norms.[65]

Finally, if the police are able to pay off claims without having them presented to the governing body of the municipality, another form of control is lacking. Municipal liability is often supported on the ground that "[a] community which pays the bill will not long tolerate habitual lawlessness." [66] The rationale, of course, is that the economic pressure upon local government will in turn result in pressure upon the police to conform their conduct to the law. But in Detroit very few claims, and only those in which it is clear the officer was acting in good faith, reach the council. Consequently, not only does the governing body not learn of instances of serious misconduct, but the financial loss felt by the municipal government is kept at a minimum and is not representative of the actual damage resulting from police illegality. Thus, while a statute which permits municipalities to pay claims against police may provide added deterrence by increasing the probability of injured parties pursuing their claims, it does not afford the added control that might result if prospective plaintiffs were required to submit their claims directly to the municipality.

B. Criminal Prosecution and Departmental Discipline

There are other sanctions for improper arrest or detention which are internal to the criminal justice process itself. The officer may be subjected to criminal prosecution or to discipline within the police department. These sanctions can be effective only if there

64 E.g., People ex rel. Terry v. Fisher, 12 Ill. 2d 231, 145 N.E.2d 588 (1957).

65 Of course, the police might argue that the kind of publicity arising out of such cases is not a "desirable side effect," in that it may involve exaggerated and untrue claims of police misconduct.

66 Hall, The Law of Arrest in Relation to Contemporary Social Problems, 3 U. Chi. L. Rev. 345, 373 (1936).

is sufficient motivation for this kind of policing by the prosecutor or police administrator.

Statutes carrying penal sanctions are often directed toward deviant police conduct of the kind described earlier. Statutes may proscribe the doing of an act by an officer when he knows it to be in excess of his lawful authority[67] or the confining of a person by an officer when he knows he does not have authority to do so.[68] Unlike tort liability, these statutes are directed toward deliberate violation of arrest and detention laws and do not authorize punishment of officers acting in good faith. Other statutes penalize specific acts of misconduct, such as concealing a prisoner entitled to a writ of habeas corpus[69] or denying a prisoner the right to consult with counsel.[70]

No instance of a criminal prosecution against a police officer was noted, and police did not voice any concern over the threat of criminal prosecution. Indeed, there sometimes appeared to be complete ignorance of the fact that certain practices are prohibited by statutes carrying penal sanctions.[71] This situation casts doubt upon the effectiveness of the criminal sanction as a deterrent.[72]

The reasons for the infrequent use of the criminal sanction are fairly obvious.[73] First, the injured party is not likely to seek criminal prosecution, as the inducements found in the false imprisonment action are not present here. Secondly, "policemen and

[67] E.g., Wis. Stat. §946.12 (2) (1955), which provides for a fine and imprisonment of an officer who "[i]n his capacity as such officer or employe, does an act which he knows is in excess of his lawful authority or which he knows he is forbidden by law to do in his official capacity . . ."

[68] E.g., Wis. Stat. §940.30 (1955): "Whoever intentionally confines or restrains another without his consent and with knowledge that he has no lawful authority to do so may be fined not more than $1,000 or imprisoned not more than 2 years or both."

[69] E.g., Mich. Stat. Ann. §27.2292 [1948 (revised, 1963)]: "Anyone having in his custody . . . any person . . . entitled to a writ of habeas corpus . . . who shall with intent to elude the service of any such writ, or to avoid the effect thereof, transfer any such prisoner to the custody, or place him under the power or control of another, or conceal him, or change the place of his confinement, shall be deemed guilty of a misdemeanor."

[70] See the Kansas statute quoted at page 396. The statutes elsewhere are collected and analyzed in Comment, 1962 U. Ill. L.F. 641.

[71] In Kansas, although denial of counsel at the police station is prohibited by penal statute, the practice of denying counsel continues, and no officer indicated that he knew of the statute. In Michigan, while officers said that transferring the suspect to avoid a writ was "tricky business," no mention was made of the statute setting penalties for such conduct.

[72] Foote, Tort Remedies for Police Violations of Individual Rights, 39 Minn. L. Rev. 493 (1955); Hall, The Law of Arrest in Relation to Contemporary Social Problems, 3 U. Chi. L. Rev. 345 (1936); Note, 100 U. Pa. L. Rev. 1182, 1211 (1952).

[73] Apparently penal sanctions have proved ineffective throughout the world. Study on the Right of Everyone to Be Free from Arbitrary Arrest, Detention and Exile, Commission on Human Rights, U.N. Doc. E/CN.4/813, p. 209 (1961).

prosecutors do not punish themselves"[74] for conduct thought by them to be understandable even if perhaps improper.

Sanctions may also be imposed from within the police department itself. Discharge, suspension, forfeiture of pay, reprimand, or similar penalties can be employed to deal with varying kinds of misconduct. However, departmental discipline is not often used in arrest situations,[75] particularly if the person arrested is in fact guilty. Even when an innocent person is arrested, departmental discipline is unlikely if the officer's conduct does not deviate greatly from practices commonly tolerated in the department.

Discipline, when it occurs, is most likely to be used against the officer who has used extremely poor judgment and has put the entire department in a bad light. It may also be used if it is necessary to placate persons bringing external pressures to bear upon the department. Thus an indignant citizen may present his complaint not to the police department but to another agency higher in the governmental structure. Consequently a through-channels inquiry may be made, which will require a report from the police department as to what action has been taken against the officer involved.[76] Or the injured party may report the incident to an organization which has the power to bring some pressure to bear on the department, in which case disciplinary action may again be taken.[77] It is important to note that in these cases the department may take disciplinary action even though the officer was complying with the informal and unwritten rules of the department.

C. The Exclusion of Evidence

There has been long and vigorous debate over exclusion of evidence as a sanction to induce police to conform their practices

---

[74] Foote, Tort Remedies for Police Violations of Individual Rights, 39 Minn. L. Rev. 493 (1955).

[75] Id. at 494-495.

[76] For example, in one instance Michigan state troopers made an arrest without warrant for a misdemeanor which did not occur in their presence. A letter of protest was sent to the office of the governor by the father of the arrested youth, which resulted in an inquiry being passed down through channels to the supervisor of the officers involved. The supervisor reprimanded the officers and reported on his action.

[77] A Negro woman suspected of being a prostitute was arrested by a Detroit officer (probably for purposes other than prosecution, see Chapter 22). It was later decided that the officer had erred, and the woman was released shortly after her arrival at the station. However, she reported the matter to the local chapter of the N.A.A.C.P., and that organization filed a formal complaint. It was indicated that if the arresting officer could not give a satisfactory explanation of his action, the case would be referred to the police trial board. The circumstances of the arrest strongly suggest that the arresting officer took precisely the action which was expected of him by his superiors.

to the requirements of law. The argument against exclusion is summed up most succinctly in Justice Cardozo's terse comment: "The criminal is to go free because the constable has blundered." [78] The argument for exclusion is based on a belief that it serves to prevent the government from profiting by its own wrong, to preserve the integrity of the judicial process, and particularly to deter further illegal acts by police.

To a degree, assumptions as to the necessity of an exclusionary rule are influenced by the adequacy of alternative sanctions for deterring police misconduct.[79] The earlier discussion of tort liability, criminal responsibility, and departmental discipline is therefore relevant to the issue of the exclusionary rule.

It is difficult to assess the effectiveness of the exclusionary rule in practice. It is clear that the rule does have a significant impact upon police practice in some situations. It is equally clear that it does not produce police conformity with the requirements of law in all cases. The extent to which the exclusionary rule does achieve its objective[80] depends upon a number of factors, which may vary from case to case:

[78] People v. Defore, 242 N.Y. 13, 21, 150 N.E. 585, 587 (1926).

[79] Thus the Supreme Court held Weeks inapplicable to the states, saying: "The jurisdictions which have rejected the *Weeks* doctrine have not left the right to privacy without other means of protection. . . . We cannot, therefore, regard it as a departure from basic standards to remand such persons, together with those who emerge scatheless from a search, to the remedies of private action and such protection as the internal discipline of the police, under the eyes of an alert public opinion, may afford." Wolf v. Colorado, 338 U.S. 25, 30-31, 69 Sup. Ct. 1359, 1362, 93 L. Ed. 1782 (1949). Then, in one of the leading state cases adopting the exclusionary rule, the court said: "If the unconstitutional [sic] guarantees against unreasonable searches and seizures are to have significance they must be enforced, and if courts are to discharge their duty to support the state and federal Constitutions they must be willing to aid in their enforcement. If those guarantees were being effectively enforced by other means than excluding evidence obtained by their violation, a different problem would be presented. . . . Experience has demonstrated, however, that neither administrative, criminal nor civil remedies are effective in suppressing lawless searches and seizures." People v. Cahan, 44 Cal. 2d 434, 447, 282 P.2d 905, 913 (1955). The Supreme Court, in recently overturning Wolf, took note of this language in Cahan, and then said: "The experience of California that such other remedies have been worthless and futile is buttressed by the experience of other States. The obvious futility of relegating the Fourth Amendment to the protection of other remedies has, moreover, been recognized by this Court since *Wolf*. See *Irvine v. California . . .*" Mapp v. Ohio, 367 U.S. 643, 652-653, 81 Sup. Ct. 1684, 6 L. Ed. 2d 1001 (1961).

Even some opponents of exclusion have granted that other effective remedies are not readily available. See Kamisar, Public Safety v. Individual Liberties: Some "Facts" and "Theories," 53 J. Crim. L., C. & P.S. 171, 182 n.83 (1962). Proponents of exclusion admit that their case would be weakened were other effective sanctions readily available. Id. at 183; Paulsen, The Exclusionary Rule and Misconduct by the Police, 52 J. Crim. L., C. & P.S. 255, 261 (1961).

[80] "[I]t would seem that the ultimate test of the exclusionary rules is whether they deter police officials from engaging in the objectionable practices. For if, as some assert, reversals of convictions in this area have had no substantial effect on police

(1) Whether the police know the legal requirements well enough to conform to them.[81] It is clear, at least in the jurisdictions studied, that the police often are not aware of the norms laid down by the appellate courts of their states. Although, generally speaking, there is greater awareness of the attitudes of the local judiciary with respect to specific arrest and detention practices, these attitudes come to the direct attention of only those officers appearing in court. Communication to the rest of the department, if it occurs, is usually only by word of mouth.

(2) Whether police desire a conviction sufficiently to take the steps necessary to conform to the requirements of the law. It is sometimes said that police are not concerned with conviction once a case is solved.[82] However, in the jurisdictions studied officers frequently indicated a strong interest not only in solving a case but in ultimately bringing about the conviction of the offender. In situations involving serious offenses, the police are highly critical of instances of acquittal on any ground if it appears certain that the defendant is guilty. In certain other cases, such as minor gambling violations, the desire for conviction may not be strong enough to induce compliance with existing norms. This is particularly likely to be true when the consequences of conviction are slight and the means of obtaining a conviction place great demands upon available police resources.[83]

(3) Whether there are short cuts to conviction. It is possible to create the impression that legal requirements have been complied with. This can be done, for example, in situations where arrests and searches are made upon inadequate grounds but the officer testifies later that the person arrested fitted a general description given in a police bulletin of a person wanted by the police. This process of making the law fit what was done, rather than conforming the practice to the requirements of law, produces an appearance of conformity and thus may make it possible to achieve conviction without having, at the same time, to change the practice.

The vigor of the debate over the merits of the exclusionary rule, at least as applied to searches, will no doubt diminish because of

---

conduct, then the consequent gains even in terms of popular respect for law are tenuous, indeed." Allen, Due Process and State Criminal Procedures: Another Look, 48 Nw. U. L. Rev. 16, 34 (1953).

[81] See Waite, Judges and the Crime Burden, 54 Mich. L. Rev. 169, 194 (1955), for the view that police generally are not aware of the procedures necessary to prevent exclusion.

[82] Inbau, Restrictions in the Law of Interrogation and Confessions, 52 Nw. U. L. Rev. 77, 78 (1957); Inbau, The Confession Dilemma in the United States Supreme Court, 43 Ill. L. Rev. 442, 461-462 (1948).

[83] This matter is explored in greater detail in Chapter 24.

Mapp v. Ohio,[84] which held that the exclusionary rule is binding upon the states. Even so, there remains the question of the extent to which the rule will be applied in new situations. Therefore the merits and effectiveness of the rule remain matters of importance.[85]

1. *Exclusion because of illegal taking of custody.* At the time police practices were observed,[86] the exclusionary rule had been adopted in Wisconsin,[87] rejected in Kansas,[88] and modified by constitutional amendment in Michigan so as not to be applicable to nondwelling searches for weapons or narcotics.[89] The Wisconsin and Michigan exclusionary rule did appear to have an effect upon some search practices[90] and to contribute to the development of the practice of arresting for purposes other than prosecution.[91] It did not, however, affect the decision to take a suspect into custody where the primary motive of the officer was to make an arrest, conduct an in-custody investigation, and subject the suspect to prosecution. Usually, in such cases, the officer was willing to sacri-

---

84 367 U.S. 643, 81 Sup. Ct. 1684, 6 L. Ed. 2d 1001 (1961).

85 Attempts to show the effect of exclusionary rules usually involve use of crime statistics, which are of questionable reliability. Beattie, Criminal Statistics in the United States, 51 J. Crim. L., C. & P.S. 49 (1960). See Kamisar, Public Safety v. Individual Liberties: Some "Facts" and "Theories," 53 J. Crim. L., C. & P.S. 171 (1962), for a rebuttal of police assertions that the Cahan holding crippled law enforcement in California and that Mallory likewise affected enforcement in the District of Columbia.

86 The exclusionary rule has now been imposed upon the states as a matter of constitutional law. Mapp v. Ohio, 367 U.S. 643, 81 Sup. Ct. 1684, 6 L. Ed. 2d 1001 (1961).

87 The rule was adopted in Wisconsin in 1923 in Hoyer v. State, 180 Wis. 407, 193 N.W. 89 (1923).

88 State v. Johnson, 116 Kan. 58, 226 Pac. 245 (1924).

89 Michigan became the first state to adopt the Weeks doctrine in 1919. People v. Marxhausen, 204 Mich. 559, 171 N.W. 557 (1919). The Michigan court appeared to interpret the admission of such evidence as, in itself, constituting a violation of the constitution, in contrast to the contemporary federal position that exclusion of evidence was only a judicially imposed sanction for enforcement of the constitutional provision. People v. Margelis, 217 Mich. 423, 186 N.W. 488 (1922); People v. Halveksz, 215 Mich. 136, 183 N.W. 752 (1921). This interpretation is supported by the fact that exceptions to the rule were brought about by constitutional amendment, not statute.

Following the critical reaction to the decision of People v. Stein, 265 Mich. 610, 251 N.W. 788 (1933), in which a dangerous weapon obtained during an illegal arrest was excluded, the constitution was amended in 1936 to make admissible as evidence "any firearm, rifle, pistol, revolver, automatic pistol, machine gun, bomb, bomb shell, explosive, blackjack, slungshot, billy, metallic knuckles, gas-ejecting device, or any other dangerous weapon or thing, seized by any peace officer outside the curtilage of any dwelling house in this state." Mich. Const. art. II, §10 (1908), as amended (1936). Similarly, in 1952 the constitution was once again amended by the addition of "any narcotic drug or drugs" to the exceptions.

90 Detail exploration of this matter will be found in the volume on Detection of Crime.

91 See Chapter 24.

fice whatever physical evidence might be found in exchange for the opportunity to conduct an in-custody investigation and hopefully to obtain a confession.

This situation may be significantly different in the future because of the impact of the recent case of *Wong Sun v. United States*.[92] In that case the Supreme Court of the United States excluded a statement obtained incident to an unlawful arrest. However, as emphasized by a more recent federal district court case in which a statement subsequent to an illegal arrest was not excluded,[93] the court in *Wong Sun* placed considerable emphasis upon the "oppressive circumstances" present in that case.[94] It remains to be seen, therefore, whether exclusion will be required in any or all of the following situations:

(1) After an illegal arrest the police search the arrested person, uncovering evidence which clearly establishes guilt, such as narcotics or gambling paraphernalia. After the search, the suspect either makes a confession or leads the police to other evidence of his guilt.[95]

(2) After an illegal arrest the police search the arrested person, uncovering evidence which does not clearly establish guilt, such as a toy pistol or a substantial sum of money in small bills. Subsequent to the search, the suspect either makes a confession or leads the police to more conclusive evidence of his guilt.

(3) After an illegal arrest but before any search is made, the suspect admits his guilt, which is established in whole or in part by a subsequent search.[96]

---

92 371 U.S. 471, 83 Sup. Ct. 407, 9 L. Ed. 2d 441 (1963).

93 United States v. Burke, 215 F. Supp. 508, 511 (D. Mass. 1963).

94 "The Government argues that Toy's statements to the officers in his bedroom, although closely consequent upon the invasion which we hold unlawful, were nevertheless admissible because they resulted from 'an intervening independent act of a free will.' This contention, however, takes insufficient account of the circumstances. Six or seven officers had broken the door and followed on Toy's heels into the bedroom where his wife and child were sleeping. He had been almost immediately handcuffed and arrested. Under such circumstances it is unreasonable to infer that Toy's response was sufficiently an act of free will to purge the primary taint of the unlawful invasion." Wong Sun v. United States, 371 U.S. 471, 486, 83 Sup. Ct. 407, 416-417, 9 L. Ed. 2d 441, 444 (1963).

95 For example, see Gibson v. United States, 149 F.2d 381 (D.C. Cir. 1945), where the police arrested and searched without sufficient grounds and found a supply of narcotics. Later, at the station, the arrested man was asked whether he would surrender another supply of narcotics. He said he would and led the police to his hiding place. The evidence was admitted.

96 For example, see Smith v. United States, 254 F.2d 751, 759 (D.C. Cir. 1958), where the police made an arrest for the sale of narcotics, and the arrested man admitted he had made the sale before he was searched for the marked money which he still had on his person. The court said that "without the necessity of holding that the arrest and search were proper, we believe that the admission of the inculpatory statement was proper . . ."

(4) An illegal arrest is immediately followed by a spontaneous admission of guilt, although no physical evidence establishing this guilt is found.

(5) An illegal arrest is immediately followed by an attempt to bribe the arresting officer.[97]

(6) An illegal arrest is followed by questioning at the police station. The suspect gives an exculpatory statement which is later found to contradict provable facts and which thus could be used against the arrestee.[98]

(7) An illegal arrest is followed by questioning at the police station, which results in the suspect making certain admissions or giving a confession of guilt.[99]

(8) An illegal arrest is followed by taking of fingerprints at the police station. The prints are found to be identical to those discovered at the scene of the crime.[100]

(9) An illegal arrest is followed by a lineup at the police station, at which time the victim or a witness identifies the arrested person as the guilty party.

In Brinegar v. United States, 165 F.2d 512 (10th Cir. 1948), the suspect's car was stopped by police, after which he admitted that he was illegally carrying liquor. The court said that it was not necessary to decide whether the stopping constituted an illegal arrest, as the statement would be admissible in any case. It has been noted that the approach taken by the Supreme Court in dealing with this case, 338 U.S. 160, 69 Sup. Ct. 1302, 93 L. Ed. 1879 (1949), suggests that they reject the above view. Kamisar, Illegal Searches and Seizures and Contemporaneous Incriminating Statements: A Dialogue on a Neglected Area of Criminal Procedure, 1961 U. Ill. L.F. 78, 88.

Another example is provided by People v. Macias, 180 Cal. App. 2d 193, 4 Cal. Rptr. 256 (1960), where the admission of possession of narcotics was made while the suspect was being driven to the police station for a complete search. The admission was excluded.

[97] For example, see People v. Guillory, 3 Cal. Rptr. 415 (App. Ct. 1960), where subsequent to an apparently illegal arrest and search which uncovered narcotics the arrestee attempted to bribe the arresting officers. The court held the officers' testimony concerning the bribe admissible though the search and arrest may have been unlawful.

[98] For example, see United States v. Bonanno, 180 F. Supp. 71 (S.D. N.Y. 1960), where the court emphasized the fact that the statements given to the police at the station after what the court considered to be a "stopping and questioning" were exculpatory in nature.

[99] For example, see Dailey v. United States, 261 F.2d 870 (5th Cir. 1959) and United States v. Walker, 197 F.2d 287 (2d Cir. 1952), where the courts distinguished this situation from that presented in the McNabb-Mallory line of cases.

[100] For example, see Bynum v. United States, 262 F.2d 465 (D.C. Cir. 1958), where the court excluded from evidence the fingerprints taken subsequent to an illegal arrest, drawing an analogy to search cases. The court subsequently upheld the conviction of the defendant on retrial where the comparison of prints was between those found at the crime scene and those obtained by the F.B.I. on another occasion. The court rejected the "fruit of the poisonous tree" argument that the F.B.I. prints should also be excluded because they were requested only after the prints obtained after the illegal arrest established the defendant's guilt. 274 F.2d at 767 (D.C. Cir. 1960).

Which of these cases call for exclusion under the *Wong Sun* rule remains uncertain,[101] although the reasons for exclusion are clearly more compelling in some of the situations than in others. If courts do decide that statements must be excluded in some of these situations, it will probably have a significant effect upon police practice. Presently, police are aware that an arrest, legal or not, makes possible subsequent investigation techniques such as fingerprinting, lineups, and interrogation. Before *Wong Sun*, they also knew that the illegality of the arrest would not be likely to affect the admissibility of evidence obtained during the in-custody investigation.[102]

2. *Exclusion because of illegal continuation of custody.* At the time of the field study, none of the jurisdictions,[103] indeed no state in the country,[104] followed the federal rule of excluding evidence

[101] Most appellate cases prior to Wong Sun assumed that exclusion was not required in such cases. See cases cited in notes 95 through 100 *supra*, and Kamisar, Illegal Searches and Seizures and Contemporaneous Incriminating Statements: A Dialogue on a Neglected Area of Criminal Procedure, 1961 U. Ill. L.F. 78, 81 n.16. This attitude has been traced back to Balbo v. People, 80 N.Y. 484 (1880), holding a confession obtained subsequent to an illegal arrest admissible. It has been noted that Balbo was decided at a time when no type of police illegality was sufficient in and of itself to bring about exclusion of evidence. Kamisar, *supra*, at 84, 107-114.

[102] The police in the observed jurisdictions are fully aware that exclusion results only where there has been an illegal search or where a confession has been coerced. And in the District of Columbia, where the Mallory rule prevails, the police have been instructed that a confession is admissible if there is no undue delay "whether the arrest was legal or illegal." See police lectures in Admission of Evidence (Mallory Rule), Hearings on H.R. 11477, S. 2970, S. 3325, and S. 3355 Before a Subcommittee of the Senate Committee of the Judiciary, 85th Cong., 2d Sess. (1958).

[103] The Kansas court expressly decided that it would not invalidate confessions obtained during an illegal detention, State v. Vargas, 180 Kan. 716, 308 P.2d 81 (1957); State v. Smith, 158 Kan. 645, 149 P.2d 600 (1944).

Some indication that the Michigan court might adopt an exclusionary rule was to be found in earlier cases. While these cases emphasized that a confession is not rendered invalid just because a person is in custody, e.g., People v. LaPanne, 255 Mich. 38, 237 N.W. 38 (1931), they did not inquire into the legality of the detention. The Michigan court had asserted that it would not allow a confession into evidence, even if clearly voluntary, "had improper means been used to secure it." People v. Cleveland, 251 Mich. 542, 232 N.W. 384 (1930).

In Wisconsin, the court has never found a detention time unreasonable in a confession case, and thus has never held a confession inadmissible because of illegal detention. In the great majority of these cases, however, the court has failed to consider the detention and has addressed itself only to the ultimate question of trustworthiness. Thus it is impossible to say with certainty whether the court considered the detention in these cases to be reasonable and the confessions therefore admissible, or whether it considered the detentions unreasonable but the confessions nonetheless admissible. See Note, 1960 Wis. L. Rev. 164. However, the court has recently indicated that a lesser showing than testimonial trustworthiness might be sufficient to exclude a confession. State v. Bronston, 7 Wis. 2d 627, 97 N.W.2d 504 (1959).

[104] While it is often said that the states have rejected the McNabb-Mallory sanction, e.g., Columbe v. Connecticut, 367 U.S. 568, 600, 81 Sup. Ct. 1860, 6 L. Ed. 2d 1037 (1961), it would appear that the appellate courts in a number of states, as was the case in Michigan and Wisconsin, have been rather vague as to whether they would exclude a confession on grounds other than its trustworthiness. See Roth-

solely upon the basis of an illegal continuation of custody without bringing the suspect before a magistrate. More recently, in *People v. Hamilton*,[105] Michigan has become the first state to adopt the *Mallory* sanction. The extent to which the practices observed in Michigan will change because of the *Hamilton* case is not clear. Subsequent decisions by the Michigan court make it uncertain whether illegal detention will alone suffice to require exclusion or whether there must be an additional showing of circumstances tending to establish that the statement is involuntary.[106]

Under current Michigan decisions, brief custody for such purposes as fingerprinting or holding a lineup is not likely to be characterized as illegal. Therefore, the risk of exclusion in these instances is so slight that the police are unlikely to alter their present practice of detaining for such investigations. Moreover, particularly in view of the Michigan court's subsequent emphasis on voluntariness as the test of exclusion, it may be that the court would not exclude such evidence even if obtained during a period of illegal detention. *Mallory* is sometimes explained on the ground that it is intended to keep out of evidence confessions which might be coerced but which the defendant could not prove were coerced,[107] and consequently some federal courts have admitted other forms of evidence notwithstanding an illegal detention.[108]

---

blatt and Rothblatt, Police Interrogation: The Right to Counsel and to Prompt Arraignment, 27 Brooklyn L. Rev. 24, 42-44 (1960).

[105] 359 Mich. 410, 102 N.W.2d 738 (1960).

[106] In People v. Harper, 365 Mich. 494, 503, 113 N.W.2d 808, 812 (1962), the court refused to exclude a confession received during a twelve and one-half hour delay, noting that "nothing appears to indicate the defendant's admissions and his confessional statement were other than voluntary. . . . None of the circumstances which so strongly compelled our finding Hamilton's confession was involuntary is present in the case at bar." See also People v. McCager, 367 Mich. 116, 116 N.W.2d 205 (1962).

[107] There is not complete agreement as to whether this is the basis of the McNabb-Mallory rule, however. Compare Douglas, The Means and the End, 1959 Wash. U. L.Q. 107, 113-114, with Hogan and Snee, The McNabb-Mallory Rule: Its Rise, Rationale and Rescue, 47 Geo. L.J. 1, 29 (1958).

[108] In Fredricksen v. United States, 266 F.2d 463, 464 (D.C. Cir. 1959), the suspect, after complaining that others being placed in a lineup did not resemble him, acknowledged that the victim would be able to identify him. The court said: "We believe that appellant's statement was properly admitted. It was a spontaneous and voluntary exclamation. It was in no sense sought or 'elicited'; it was not in an answer to police interrogation or in any way related to the lapse of time. Statements so volunteered without questioning before arraignment are admissible in evidence. Mallory . . . does not hold otherwise."

Similarly, in Payne v. United States, 294 F.2d 723, 727 (D.C. Cir. 1961), though the court found it unnecessary to decide whether a lineup identification during illegal detention could be admitted, it was asserted that "the suppression of the testimony of the complaining witness is not the right way to control the conduct of the police,"

If *Hamilton* does have an effect it is most likely to be in cases where the detention is for purposes of interrogation, a category into which most cases fall.[109]   In Detroit, in-custody interrogation often occurs after the suspect has been remanded to police custody by a judge who has granted a continuance at a writ of habeas corpus hearing.   The Michigan court has recently said that upon remand the custody of the suspect is based upon "the superior authority of the habeas corpus" and consequently does not require exclusion of a confession subsequently obtained.[110]   The court reached this result without considering the propriety of the adjournment of the hearing in the particular case.   Subsequently the Michigan Supreme Court has directed the lower courts that "adjournments may be granted upon respondent's request only for such brief delay as may be necessary to permit respondents to prepare written answers (unless waived by petitioner) or to present to the court or judge issuing the writ or order testimonial or documentary evidence to establish the cause of detention as of the time for answer." [111]   In the event of a brief adjournment, "the prisoner shall be advised by the judge, in the presence of respondent, that he has a right to counsel and that he need not incriminate himself." [112]   This may have a significant impact upon in-custody interrogation practice.

---

and the court added that "confrontation may be beneficial to the accused rather than damaging to him: Warren might have declared that Payne was not the man who robbed him.   Confrontation is thus a precaution against the making of baseless and unfounded charges.   It holds few of the dangers which led to the promulgation of Rule 5(a)."   Compare United States v. Klapholz, 230 F.2d 494 (2d Cir. 1956), where the court excluded physical evidence obtained in a search by supposed consent during illegal detention on the grounds that rule 5(a) compels exclusion of all evidence obtained during such detention.

109 See page 304.

110 People v. McCager, 367 Mich. 116, 124, 116 N.W.2d 205, 209 (1962).

111 Michigan Supreme Court, Order of Superintending Control — Habeas Corpus Proceedings, 369 Mich. XXX, 1, March 7, 1963.

112 Id. at 3.

PART V

The Decision to Arrest for Purposes Other than Prosecution

To be lawful, not only must an arrest be made on a proper occasion but, whether by officer or citizen, it must be made for the purpose of apprehending the person arrested and taking him before a court or public official.

HARPER AND JAMES, *Torts* §3.18 (1956)

It requires a vivid imagination to conceive of an officer making an arrest for the purpose of releasing his prisoner.

BOHLEN AND SHULMAN, Effect of Subsequent Misconduct upon a Lawful Arrest, 28 *Columbia Law Review* 841, 851 (1928)

The making of an arrest intended to culminate in release of the suspected offender rather than in his prosecution is said to be both illegal and unlikely. Yet in current criminal justice administration arrests for purposes other than prosecution are common. A wide range of offenders, including drunks, prostitutes, transvestites, gamblers, and liquor law violators, are taken into custody day after day with full intention by the arresting officers that prosecution shall not follow. The extent of this practice, the reasons for its existence, its consequences for the individual and the community, and its basis or lack of basis in law are dealt with in the chapters which follow.

These arrests are made to serve what the police perceive to be deterrent, rehabilitative, or punitive functions. The helpless drunk may be taken into custody for his own safety and not prosecuted because a criminal conviction seems, to the police, to serve no purpose. The prostitute on the street may be arrested and given a medical examination, yet not prosecuted because the evidence is inadequate. Making a case against her may be difficult and thought to serve no purpose because arrest and release are nearly as effective as arrest, prosecution, conviction, and a nominal fine. The transvestite may be arrested because he is a nuisance and a possible thief but not prosecuted because criminal conduct cannot be proved. Gamblers and liquor law violators may be taken into custody merely to keep them "on the run" rather than to prosecute them because, although they may be obviously guilty, conviction may prove impossible because of the rule requiring the exclusion of evidence illegally obtained.

To some extent these practices may reflect difficulties which are a direct consequence of utilizing the criminal justice system for the administration of what is essentially a social service. The helpless drunk, the possibly infected prostitute, or the transvestite may be subjected to the criminal justice process because more adequate welfare methods of dealing with these problems are largely lacking. As a consequence arrest may seem to be preferable to doing nothing at all.

In some instances the practice of arresting for purposes other than prosecution may be symptomatic of other difficulties existing in the criminal justice system. Police often feel justified in making arrests in situations in which they believe they are faced with insurmountable barriers to conviction resulting from overly strict limitations upon methods of obtaining evidence and overly narrow interpretations of certain criminal statutes.

The continuation of certain police practices that are not authorized by law suggests clearly that existing sanctions are not successful. The rule excluding evidence illegally obtained, now binding on the states as a consequence of *Mapp v. Ohio*,[1] is based upon the assumption that a threat to exclude evidence will induce police conformity with the requirements of law. Yet it is apparent that this sanction is bound to be ineffective when the purpose of the arrest is other than prosecution. Indeed, such practices may be encouraged rather than deterred by the threat that use of the entire criminal justice process will be impossible. To suggest this neither supports nor condemns the exclusionary rule, but does show that careful analysis is required if it and the practice of arresting for purposes other than prosecution are to be fully understood.[2]

[1] 367 U.S. 643, 81 Sup. Ct. 1684, 6 L. Ed. 2d 1081 (1961).

[2] It is particularly important in regard to the material in this part to reiterate a point stressed in the Editor's Foreword. When reference is made to "current practice," it means those practices current during the mid-1950's when the field research was done. Substantial changes have since taken place in these practices. They are stressed here because understanding what they were and why they existed during the mid-1950's is important to those who desire to understand the problems facing criminal justice administration today and in the future.

CHAPTER 21

Arrest of an Intoxicated Person
for His Own Safety

Drunkenness in one form or another is a major police concern. The Uniform Crime Reports indicate that nearly 40 per cent of all reported arrests are for drunkenness.[1] A substantial number of the arrests made in Michigan, Kansas, and Wisconsin are in this category. The large number of arrests for drunkenness is particularly impressive because it is evident that many persons found in an intoxicated condition by the police are not arrested and thus are not reflected in the arrest statistics.[2] In Kansas and Michigan, notwithstanding broadly phrased statutes prohibiting public intoxication,[3] nonhabitual drunks are rarely arrested unless they cannot care for their own safety or are likely to cause harm to another. The corresponding statute in Wisconsin[4] is more narrowly defined and, as a consequence, more accurately reflects existing police practice.

Of those arrested for drunkenness, not all are subject to prosecution. The drunk who has actually caused harm to others, who has made an extreme nuisance of himself, or, perhaps, who is habitually drunk in public may be prosecuted. In other situations, however, the drunk has been arrested for his own safety because he needs protection from the cold, because he has fallen and injured himself, or because he is likely to become the victim

---

[1] Moreover, the second largest category of arrests is disorderly conduct, which undoubtedly includes many drunks. Statistics for five recent years are:

Year	Drunkenness Arrests	Disorderly Conduct Arrests
1961	36.3%	11.3%
1960	36.1%	12.2%
1959	38.7%	12.4%
1958	38.8%	12.1%
1957	40.2%	11.7%

Department of Justice, F.B.I., Uniform Crime Reports (1957-1961).

[2] See page 108.

[3] Kan. Gen. Stat. §41-802 (1949); Mich. Stat. Ann. §28.364 (1938).

[4] Wis. Stat. §947.03 (1955).

of a "jackroller." [5] This practice is reflected in different ways in major cities across the country: the Chicago officer may enter "drunk-safekeeping" or "drunk-down" on his arrest slip;[6] a Philadelphia officer may release the man to a friend and indicate on a form that his arrest was "for his own protection";[7] the Detroit policeman uses the revealing term "golden rule drunk" to describe the man arrested for his own safety.

Prosecution, conviction, and sentence may follow the arrest of some persons who are drunk and who are taken into custody for their own protection. However, prosecution seldom follows such arrests except in some cases where the person is in such bad condition that he needs time to "dry out." In the absence of alternative facilities, a period in jail may be imposed to achieve this objective. With this exception, there has long been doubt as to whether the criminal justice process is an effective way of dealing with the chronic or occasional drunk.[8] The large number of persons in these categories would impose a very large strain on courts and jail facilities if they were routinely charged, convicted, and sentenced. As a consequence, a practice has developed [9] in some jurisdictions of arresting drunks for their own safety with the intention of releasing them the following morning without taking them to court. This police practice of invoking a part, but not all, of the criminal process is of considerable significance.

A. The Practice of Arresting Drunks for Purposes Other than Prosecution

In Detroit, intoxicated persons who are arrested but released without charge after they become sober are called "golden rule drunks." Although this procedure finds explicit recognition in the Detroit Police Manual,[10] no criteria for deciding whom to treat

---

[5] Jackrollers are criminals who rob, and sometimes sadistically beat, derelicts for the small sums of money they may be carrying.

[6] Note, The Law on Skid Row, 38 Chi.-Kent L. Rev. 22, 33 n.52 (1961).

[7] Foote, Vagrancy-Type Law and Its Administration, 104 U. Pa. L. Rev. 603, 646 n.162 (1956).

[8] See generally Pittman and Gordon, Revolving Door (1958).

[9] "The widespread and frequent practice of arrest and release without appearance in court in such cases, undoubtedly has a long history. It is much older than the Boston Police Report of January, 1851, which recites that 'persons arrested for drunkenness . . . were detained until sober and then discharged.'" Hall, The Law of Arrest in Relation to Contemporary Social Problems, 3 U. Chi. L. Rev. 345, 367 (1936).

[10] Persons being detained on this basis are recorded in a Golden Rule and Lodgers Book, rather than the Arrest Book. Recorded therein are the time and place of arrest, the name of the officer making the arrest, the time of discharge, and similar items. Detroit Police Dept., Revised Police Manual, chap. 11, §100 (1955).

as a "golden rule drunk" are set forth. The number of golden rule drunks is substantial:

	1951	1952	1953	1954	1955	1956
Golden rule drunks	9,303	8,064	8,592	7,249	6,626	5,865
Drunks prosecuted	8,443	7,840	10,181	10,124	10,513	8,665 [11]

The decision to subject a drunk to the golden rule procedure may be made by the arresting officer at the time of arrest, or it may be made by the supervisory officer at the desk in precinct head-quarters when the drunk is brought before him.[12] Indeed, in the first situation the arresting officer sometimes obtains the coopera-tion of the drunk by assuring him that he will be released the next morning.[13] In either event, golden rule drunks are held in the precinct detention quarters until the supervisory officer decides they are sober, usually the following morning. No attempt is made to require them, as a condition of release, to sign a waiver relieving the police department of liability for their detention.

The golden rule procedure is normally confined to nonhabitual drunks and is regularly applied to this class unless they are bellig-erent or "down and out," or request a more extended period of incarceration.[14] Because the procedure is thus limited, it is more commonly applied to those found outside the "skid row" area. Nevertheless, skid row drunks who are known not to have substan-tial arrest records are also likely to be "golden ruled." The "down-and-out" drunk is not processed under the golden rule, because he needs a lengthy period of incarceration for medical treatment. Other skid row drunks may request jail terms in the winter simply to secure protection from the cold weather.

[11] Detroit Police Dept., 91st Stat. Ann. Rep., Table III-B (1956).

[12] Thus on one occasion a woman in a highly intoxicated condition was brought before the lieutenant. Upon inquiry, she stated that she had a family and that she was ashamed of herself for being in her present state. The lieutenant quickly de-cided to book this woman as a golden rule drunk to be released after she had sobered up.

[13] A special detail of two officers, referred to as the "bum squad," is assigned to the "skid row" area of Detroit in an effort to keep the streets clear of drunks. On one occasion, they caught up with a drunk staggering down the street and poured the contents of his bottle in the street. "Aw, hell, boys, give me a break," the drunk pleaded, but the officers responded that he was too drunk. They added, "We will G.R.D. you if you don't have a traffic warrant, how's that?" The drunk thought this was fine.

[14] Because the golden rule decision is often made after arrest, a more detailed discussion of these criteria will be found in the volume on Prosecution. Of more immediate interest in this chapter is the effect which this policy has upon the legality of these arrests.

Although the golden rule practice is not known in Milwaukee, a somewhat similar procedure for handling intoxicated persons is used there. A city ordinance authorizes a stipulation of guilt by defendants arrested for drunkenness. Under this procedure, one arrested for drunkenness may be released when sober upon payment of $4.35. He need not appear in court, although he may later request a trial.[15] Not all drunks are allowed to stipulate guilt in this fashion. A directive from the chief of police indicates that this alternative is to be used only with nonhabitual drunks who do not have any outstanding warrants or cases pending against them.[16] Nevertheless, the stipulation procedure is sometimes made available to repeaters when the police are convinced that nothing will be gained by prosecution under state law. One individual will sometimes stipulate guilt as often as three times within a 24-hour period.[17]

Because this procedure results in a record of arrest and a record of a stipulation of guilt under the city ordinance, it differs from the Detroit practice, which dispenses with both charging and conviction. It is, nevertheless, considered at this point because it serves the identical purpose of conserving resources by permitting release without the expense of conventional processing. In a sense, it is the golden rule procedure put on a paying basis.[18]

Another practice resembling that found in Detroit was observed

---

[15] City of Milwaukee, Code of Ordinances, chap. 106, §2.

[16] "The Desk Sergeants and their assistants, at all District Stations, before permitting any person arrested for Plain Drunk to Stipulate will first ascertain from the Bureau of Identification, by calling the Record Clerk, the person's record; whether or not there are any warrants or commitments for him; and if there are any cases open and pending against him.

"If the record shows numerous arrests for Drunk, Drunk and Disorderly, or other serious offenses, such person will not be permitted to stipulate but will be held on Suspicion of Common Drunk or Vagrancy and a Warrant for such offense is to be applied for from the District Attorney's Office.

"A person arrested the average of once per month or more during the previous year for Drunk, Drunk and Disorderly or other offenses involving drinking shall be considered as being a Common Drunk." Milwaukee Police Dept., Order No. 3947 (April 14, 1955).

In 1954 in Milwaukee, 6817 persons were convicted in court for drunkenness, while 7632 stipulations of guilt were entered. City and County of Milwaukee Municipal and District Courts, 1954 Ann. Rep.

[17] This occurs frequently with respect to "old-timers" receiving their welfare, social security, and old age assistance checks. On the first Monday in each month, after these checks have been received, the volume of drunks would ordinarily be 200 to 300 per cent higher than it would be any other Monday in the month.

[18] It is not clear what is done in Milwaukee as to the drunk who does not have the necessary $4.35. There may be no reason for proceeding further with him either, unless it is desired to give him a place to stay for a time.

The Milwaukee practice may also be considered the golden rule procedure put on a legal basis, if the law requires that the police not release without a stipulation of guilt. See page 405.

elsewhere in Wisconsin. Drunken transients who are willing to leave the community are informally released after arrest without being charged, often on condition that a bond be posted.[19] One purpose of the bond is to insure that the man — if he does have a small amount of money — will not resume drinking prior to reaching his destination.[20] In addition, police in one Wisconsin city use the overnight detention procedure in cases involving local Indians personally known to them when "to carry the case any further would only result in hardship." [21]

In Wichita all persons arrested for intoxication are prosecuted. No instances of a "golden rule" or similar procedure were observed anywhere in Kansas, although vagrants who voluntarily spend the night in jail are released the following morning without being prosecuted.[22]

It is not entirely clear why the practice varies as it does between Detroit, Milwaukee, and Wichita. While the differences may be fortuitous, they probably do reflect the existence of substantially different conditions and problems in the three cities. Detroit has

19 For example, in Neillsville, Clark County, a bus driver put a drunk off the bus because he was annoying other passengers. The chief took the drunk to the station and then notified the chief in the man's home town, telling him that if the man's wife did not appear to pick him up before morning the drunk would be taken to court. The man's wife appeared and he was then released.

Similarly, Eau Claire police arrested a drunk, though he objected that he had to catch a train. His only possessions were a bus ticket and eighty-two cents. The next morning the man was released and put on the bus.

20 Ashland police arrested two drunks, one of whom had $8.99 on his person when he was booked. The chief explained that this man was on his way to Superior, so he would have one of his officers put the man on the afternoon bus. The $8.99 would be retained; the chief added a penny and accepted $9 as bond, which would be forfeited when the man failed to appear in court Monday. The man had a ticket for the bus to Superior, and the chief indicated that the bus driver would be willing to take the man only if he was without funds to purchase more liquor. The second drunk had no money in his possession, and the chief indicated that he would be released later in the day without bail or stipulation. The handling of these two cases is typical of the manner in which this department handles drunks, though in most cases the drunks have $10 for bail, which is posted prior to release.

21 The Ashland city police records disclose 527 "lodgers" for the year 1955, a large number of whom were Indians arrested for drunkenness. Their release is without use of waiver, and the decision is made by the chief in each case. A similar procedure is used by the county sheriff because, in his words, "frequently, spending a night in jail is sufficient." He went on to explain, "We know practically every family on the Indian reservation and usually we can make a judgment as to whether or not it would be desirable to take a fellow into court or release him."

22 A form used by the Wichita Police Department concerns such a practice. The form states, above a place for signature, that the undersigned is without funds and is voluntarily spending the night in jail as a "sleeper," and that he will allow a taking of fingerprints before release. Pittsburg, Kansas, booking records also disclose an occasional sleeper.

The only instance observed in which a drunk was booked as a sleeper was one where the officer had hopes of the drunk providing him with information.

the largest skid row area, reflecting the fact that more homeless drunks congregate there.   At least some of this group must be taken into custody on occasion to assure their safety.   Wichita is a smaller city[23] with fewer homeless drunks and fewer transportation difficulties.   The police can easily solve some of the problems by escorting the drunk home.   Some of the concern in Milwaukee is with the free-spending pensioner, for whom the stipulation device is perhaps better suited.

Whatever the reasons for the variations in practice, the result is a differing level of toleration for the drunk who is unable to care for himself adequately.   Wichita police, perhaps because they know that charging automatically follows an arrest, are hesitant to arrest a drunk even if he appears to be unable to care for himself. Because the stipulation device is available, Milwaukee police are more likely to arrest.   Finally, the existence of the golden rule procedure in Detroit means that arrests are made there which would not be made in Milwaukee or Wichita.

B. The Legality of the Practice

If the golden rule procedure were used only when a drunk asks to sleep in jail overnight, no question about the legality of the practice would arise.   Usually, however, the drunk is taken into custody against his will.[24]   Because the arrested person is invariably drunk in the presence of the arresting officer, grounds for arrest clearly exist.   If the legality of the arrest is questionable, it is because the officer has a purpose other than prosecution in mind, or because the later decision to release without charging is thought to be improper and, therefore, to make illegal the original arrest. Arrests have sometimes been challenged on these grounds.

The legislatures in the three states have neither expressly authorized nor explicitly forbidden the arrest and detention of intoxicated persons for their own safety.   Statutory language in both Kansas and Wisconsin seems to assume that those who are arrested should be prosecuted.[25]   On the other hand, language incorpo-

---

[23] In the 1960 census, Wichita had a population of 254,698, compared with Detroit's 1,670,144 and Milwaukee's 741,324.

[24] A Detroit officer characterized the "voluntariness" of the golden rule procedure as follows: "This is a golden rule arrest, and we usually do not make out papers on the man.   It simply amounts to letting him cool off over night.   Actually, he is free to go if he wants, and we are simply furnishing him a hotel room.   As a matter of fact, we usually lock the door, and it is far enough downstairs so that we cannot hear him rattling the doors."

[25] In direct contrast to the Michigan provision, a Wisconsin statute declares that city police "shall arrest with or without process and with reasonable diligence take before the police justice or other proper court every person found in the city in a

rated in 1895 in the Michigan statute delineating the duties of chiefs of police of cities arguably provides a basis for the golden rule procedure:

> He shall arrest upon view, and with or without process, any person found in the act of committing any offense against the laws of the state or the ordinances of the city amounting to a breach of the peace, and forthwith take such person before the proper magistrate or court for examination or trial, and *may* also without process *arrest and imprison persons found drunk in the streets.*[26]

This language suggests that, although other offenses call for both arrest and production before a magistrate, it is proper to arrest and detain drunks, but to release them without court appearance. There is no available legislative history establishing that this distinction was intended. However, in other states at about this time similar statutory changes were made for the purpose of reversing judicial decisions which held that it was illegal to arrest drunks and release them without an appearance before a magistrate.[27] The language of the Michigan statute may in part explain why intoxicated persons are released without either reaching court or stipulating guilt only in Michigan. At best, the legality of the golden rule procedure remains unclear. Courts in some states have held liable in tort police officers who have arrested intoxicated persons and released them when sober.[28] Though no cases directly in point are to be found in the three jurisdictions studied, there is enough judicial language indicating that an arrest for purposes

---

state of intoxication . . ." Wis. Stat. §62.09(13)(a) (1955). Almost identical language is found in the statute concerning village marshals, Wis. Stat. §61.28 (1955), and has been incorporated by reference into the statutes concerning town police, Wis. Stat. §60.29(7) and (21) (1955), and village police, Wis. Stat. §61.31(2) (1955).

Kansas has no provision relating directly to persons intoxicated, but a statute there defines arrest as "the taking of a person into custody, that he may be held to answer for a public offense." Kan. Gen. Stat. §62-1201 (1949).

[26] Mich. Stat. Ann. §5.1674 (1949). (Emphasis supplied.)

[27] In Massachusetts, a false arrest recovery under these circumstances was upheld, Brock v. Stimson, 108 Mass. 520 (1871), after which the legislature changed the statute to read that the officer "may" make a complaint, rather than "shall." But shortly thereafter the court upheld another recovery on similar facts, asserting that "shall" and "may" were equivalent terms. Phillips v. Fadden, 125 Mass. 198 (1878). Finally, in 1891 the Massachusetts legislature passed a special statute to deal with the situation. The present statute, in subtantially the same form, is Mass. Ann. Laws, chap. 272, §§44-46. See page 448, note 42.

[28] For example, using both the trespass ab initio doctrine and a statute stating an officer "shall" make a complaint, the court in Brock v. Stimson, *supra,* held that where an officer found a person intoxicated, took him to the station, and then discharged him when sober, the arrest was only "a preliminary step towards taking the prisoner before a court. The defendant . . . having failed to do this, cannot justify the arrest, . . ." 108 Mass. at 522.

other than prosecution is improper[29] to put the "golden rule" and similar practices in an uncertain status.

C. Desirability of the Practice

Perhaps the most desirable means of protecting the helpless drunk would be through a process divorced from the criminal justice system. The American Law Institute's Model Penal Code Advisory Committee favored deleting the section on public drunkenness

> . . . so as to preclude the handling of non-disorderly drunks through the usual facilities of law enforcement, *i.e.,* police station and jail, and to require that such persons be taken to their homes or to hospitals, where drunkenness can be differentiated from epileptic attacks or other pathological conditions.[30]

Such an alternative is feasible when adequate facilities are available. In New York City it is reported that the public drunkenness statute is not used and that only the person who is both drunk and disorderly is arrested.[31] Drunkenness arrests, therefore, are less than 15,000 a year.[32] The New York City Department of Welfare operates a shelter which supplies lodgings for six hundred persons,[33] and it apparently serves as a haven for many who, in Detroit, would be "golden ruled." Even though this alternative is a noncriminal process, it does require both taking and holding the drunk in custody against his will.[34]

When adequate noncriminal facilities are lacking, the arrest-

[29] "It makes no difference whether defendants did or did not suppose the plaintiff had violated the laws of this State, unless they proposed to prosecute him here." Malcomson v. Scott, 56 Mich. 459, 465, 23 N.W. 166, 168 (1885). "The law contemplates that an arrest either by an officer or a private person, with or without warrant, is a step in a public prosecution, ..." Granier v. Squires, 62 Kan. 321, 325, 62 Pac. 1005, 1007 (1900). See Bergeron v. Peyton, 106 Wis. 377, 82 N.W. 291 (1900). None of these cases dealt directly with the drunk release situation.

[30] Model Penal Code §250.11, Comment (Tent. Draft No. 13, 1961). The Council was divided on the issue, but a majority favored retaining the section on public drunkenness.

The mistaking of an epileptic or other sick person for a drunk sometimes occurs. See Illustration No. 5 at page 240.

[31] Murtagh, The Derelicts of Skid Row, 209 Atlantic Monthly 77, 80 (March, 1962).

[32] As compared with nearly 100,000 a year in Los Angeles. Ibid.

[33] Id. at 79.

[34] "Chief Parker may well ask: 'Would you then continue to permit the derelict to lie in the gutter?' The answer is simple. I would arrest the unfortunate who is a menace to the community, such as the derelict who is loud and boisterous or assaultive. I would have the police escort others for their own safety to a public shelter, . . . there to remain, perhaps, for the cooling-off period of six hours." Id at 81.

release process is perhaps the best available means of caring for the drunk. As Jerome Hall has written,

> . . . the police conduct serves as a crude prophylaxis and as a minor benefit to the arrestees, in providing a night's lodging and time to become sober. In the absence of substantial social reform providing adequate treatment of . . . [intoxicated persons], the present police practice, crude as it is, can hardly be abandoned.[35]

This is an instance in which the criminal justice process is used, by default, to perform what is essentially a social service.[36] In doing so, must the police invoke the entire criminal process when it seems that little will be achieved by prosecution, conviction, and sentence?

If so, it is presumably because the legislature has said that prosecution and court appearance is a normal consequence of arrest even in situations where it seems that nothing will be contributed beyond what is achieved by the arrest alone. The alternative is to assume that there are situations in which the legislature has contemplated that arrest itself may achieve the objective which underlies the criminal statute. For example, the Model Penal Code declares a person guilty of an offense "if he appears in any public place manifestly under the influence of alcohol . . . , to the degree that he may endanger himself or other persons or property, or annoy persons in his vicinity." [37]   The comments to the section state:

> In most cases, the drunk will have been guilty of some other category of disorderly conduct, but *it seems necessary to provide a basis for police action* for those who, for example, are in a drunken stupor but not otherwise making a nuisance of themselves.[38]

Even if it is assumed that the legislature has contemplated that there may be situations in which arrest and release is proper, it may be that the decision is one which ought properly to be made by a judicial officer. Indeed, at least one court has characterized selection for release by the police as "the best description of des-

---

[35] Hall, Police and Law in a Democratic Society, 28 Ind. L.J. 133, 156 (1953).

[36] Such overloading of the criminal justice system by using it as a device for the administration of social services can have serious consequences, including (a) deterioration of social services, (b) impairment of law enforcement, and (c) corruption of agencies of criminal justice. See the excellent discussion of this in Allen, The Borderland of the Criminal Law: Problems of "Socializing" Criminal Justice, 32 Social Serv. Rev. 107 (1958).

On the specific question of using the criminal process to care for drunks, see Hall, The Law of Arrest in Relation to Contemporary Social Problems, 3 U. Chi. L. Rev. 345, 354-355, 367-368 (1936).

[37] Model Penal Code §250.11 (Tent. Draft No. 13, 1961).

[38] Id., Comment. (Emphasis supplied.)

potism," [39] even though the particular decision may seem clearly to benefit the individual involved.[40]   This is another situation where the question of the desirability and feasibility of genuine judicial participation in an essentially routine day-to-day decision is not easily resolved.

A few states have legislated on this problem in a way that recognizes the power of the police to grant releases.   In Delaware, New Hampshire, and Rhode Island, by virtue of a provision of the Uniform Arrest Act, and more recently in California by a similar enactment, the police may release persons arrested for drunkenness when "no further proceedings are desirable."[41]   By comparison, a Massachusetts statute allows police release if the arrestee has not been arrested four times in the past year for drunkenness, but the officer must make a complaint to court, where the judge then decides whether to do anything further under those circumstances.[42]

On the basis of available knowledge, it is doubtful whether meaningful judicial participation in the decision as to whether to release the drunk is feasible.   A recent empirical study of enforcement in Chicago's skid row pointed out that, while the police arrest drunks for their own safety, all those arrested are taken to court.[43]   It is unclear why this is so, in view of the similarity of the problem there to that in Detroit, unless it is a result of the declaration by one Illinois court that overnight detention may not

[39] State v. Parker, 75 N.C. 249, 250, 22 Am. Rep. 669, 670 (1876).

[40] Courts have held that the decision is not the officer's to make: e.g., State v. Parker, *supra;* Brock v. Stimson, 108 Mass. 520 (1871).

[41] Variations of the Uniform Arrest Act have been enacted in Delaware, New Hampshire, and Rhode Island.   Thus, in Delaware, release is possible by "[a]ny officer in charge of a police department or any officer delegated by him . . ." Del. Code Ann., tit. 11, §1910 (1953).   In New Hampshire, release may be by the arresting officer or his superior.   N.H. Rev. Laws §594:18 (1955).   In Rhode Island, "[t]he officer in charge of any police station may release any person in his station who has been arrested without a warrant."   R.I. Ann. Laws, tit. 12, §7-12 (1956).   See Warner, The Uniform Arrest Act, 28 Va. L. Rev. 315, 337, 346 (1942).   In California "any peace officer" may make the release.   Cal. Penal Code §849 (Supp. 1961).

[42] The statute provides that a person found intoxicated "may" be arrested and "kept in custody in a suitable place until he has recovered from his intoxication." When the person is sober, the police have a duty to inform him that he has a right to make a written request for release.   In towns where there is no probation officer the police officer "may" grant release, or in towns with a probation officer that officer "may" direct release, provided the officer in either instance believes that the person gave his true name and address, that he will appear on a summons, and that he has not been arrested four times in the past year for drunkenness.   The arresting officer incurs no liability where release is granted in this way.   But, notwithstanding release, whoever arrests "shall" make a complaint at the next session of court, at which time the court may issue a summons or warrant for appearance, or if the court is satisfied that the accused has not been arrested for drunkenness four times within the year, then it "may" dismiss the complaint.   Mass. Ann. Laws, chap. 272, §§44-46.

[43] Note, The Law on Skid Row, 38 Chi.-Kent L. Rev. 22 (1961).

be used as a device for sobering up an intoxicated arrestee.[44]   In any event, the Chicago judge always assumes the guilt of the derelict brought before him, and the only issue is whether further incarceration is called for.   "Many trials are shorter [than one minute], some consisting of calling the defendant's name and, in the same breath, telling him, 'Go on home.' "[45]   Another study of the Chicago procedure asserts that it

> . . . serves only two useful functions — (1) to protect the drunken man from exposure to the elements, and (2) to cull out the ones who are too weak, too sick, or too mentally deteriorated to be "turned back to pasture" for another day in the taverns.   It does nothing to help any man to stop drinking.   The Referee at Monroe Street Court screens one hundred twenty-five to two hundred men in less than one-and-a-half hours, which gives him between forty-five seconds and one minute per "client."[46]

The operations of other metropolitan criminal courts of first instance suggest that such summary procedures could be expected in most major cities if all drunks were taken into court.[47]   While it has been asserted that a judicial hearing is necessary to "protect alcoholics from abuses in the system of arrest and detention,"[48] it is extremely questionable whether any such protection is afforded under the abbreviated hearing now customarily given.

44 Markey v. Griffin, 109 Ill. App. 212 (1903).   However, the case also declares that the arrestee has an absolute right to bail regardless of his state of intoxication.   The prevailing rule elsewhere is to the contrary, Annot., 79 A.L.R. 13, 20 (1932), and the reported practice in Chicago is to deny bail to intoxicated persons except when release to a responsible relative or friend is possible, Note, The Law on Skid Row, 38 Chi.-Kent L. Rev. 22, 43 (1961).

45 Id. at 37 n.67.

46 Bogue and Schusky, The Homeless Man on Skid Row 88 (1958), quoted in Plunkert, Skid Row Can Be Eliminated, 25 Fed. Prob. 41, 42 (June, 1961).

47 Note, Metropolitan Criminal Courts of First Instance, 70 Harv. L. Rev. 320, 329-335 (1956).

48 Chicago officers are reported as having expressed a preference for the system there on this basis.   Note, The Law on Skid Row, 38 Chi.-Kent L. Rev. 22, 38 (1961).

CHAPTER 22

Arrest to Control the Prostitute

Prostitution exists in a number of different forms, from the "call girl," to the girl in a house of prostitution, to the streetwalker. Prostitution in any of these forms can be a serious problem, particularly when linked with organized crime, and is of continuing concern to agencies charged with the law enforcement task.

In many respects, however, the streetwalker, predominantly a product of lower-class neighborhoods in large cities, presents the most serious problem. The woman engaging in solicitation in public places, unlike the call girl or house prostitute, creates a nuisance plainly visible to the public. It is this nuisance aspect of prostitution that the common law proscribed,[1] and there is some current thought that only solicitation in public places should be prohibited.[2] Thus, the Wolfenden Report noted:

> We are concerned not with prostitution itself but with the manner in which the activities of prostitutes and those associated with them offend against public order and decency, expose the ordinary citizen to what is offensive or injurious, or involve the exploitation of others.
>
> . . . we are not attempting to abolish prostitution or to make prostitution in itself illegal. We do not think that the law ought to try to do so; nor do we think that if it tried it could by itself succeed. What the law can and should do is to ensure that the streets . . . should be freed from what is offensive or injurious and made tolerable for the ordinary citizen who lives in them or passes through them.[3]

[1] Public solicitation was technically unlawful only when done to the "annoyance" of the person solicited. Great Britain, Home Office, Report of the Committee on Homosexual Offenses and Prostitution 82-87 (1957). See also Bishop, Criminal Law §§1106-1112 (5th ed. 1872).

[2] Such is the position taken in the British Street Offenses Act, 1959, 7 & 8 Eliz. 2, c. 57. The Model Penal Code section on prostitution was recommitted for consideration of this view. Model Penal Code §251.2, Status of Section (Proposed Official Draft, 1962).

[3] Great Britain, Home Office, Report of the Committee on Homosexual Offenses and Prostitution 80, 95 (1957).

Even if the legislature makes other forms of prostitution criminal,[4] the streetwalker remains the major problem for the policeman. Public knowledge of the existence of streetwalkers results in pressures on the department for action. These are in turn translated into pressures on precinct supervisors and on individual patrolmen to keep their areas "clean." The concern in this chapter is with police attempts to control the streetwalker by resorting to arrest without thought of prosecution.

A. THE PRACTICE OF ARRESTING PROSTITUTES FOR PURPOSES OTHER THAN PROSECUTION

Suspected prostitutes are clearly the largest category of offenders arrested in Detroit for purposes other than prosecution. Practically all of these arrests are made in one city precinct, in a relatively small area where streetwalking by individual prostitutes flourishes. There are no houses of prostitution; rather, patrons are solicited on the streets and in taverns and other public places, and then escorted to nearby rooms.

The arrest of suspected prostitutes without intent of prosecution is almost exclusively a practice of the precinct officer.[5] While some of these arrests are made by regular patrol car officers, a great majority of them are brought about by officers assigned to the precinct "whore squads." These officers operate with unmarked cars, and although they are uniformed, they remove their caps to prevent easy identification. Members of these squads do not conceal their identity to the extent of plainclothes officers attempting to make accosting and soliciting cases.[6] They are interested only in preventing the girls from seeing them approach in time to take shelter in some nearby residence.[7] Each night these squads arrest from forty to fifty women believed or known to be prostitutes. Most of these women are arrested as they are standing in doorways or on street corners, or while they are slowly walking down the street. On occasion, they are pursued into residences in the area or are arrested while sitting in a restaurant or other public place.

4 See American Social Hygiene Assn., Digest of State and Federal Laws Dealing with Prostitution (1942, with 1950 Supp.).

5 Officers in the vice bureau, central services division, concentrate on making accosting and soliciting cases for court. The precinct cleanup squads also work on making such cases.

6 A discussion of this will be found in the volume on Detection of Crime.

7 On one occasion the officers were having difficulty in apprehending many of the prostitutes because they would run into doorways and pull shut heavy doors of metal sheeting. The officers solved this problem by obtaining "the master key," a sledge hammer, and putting it to use.

Occasionally the officers see and arrest a girl as she is in the process of making a contact with a man.[8]

A booking of D.P.I. (Disorderly Persons Investigation[9]) is always used in this precinct for prostitutes who are not to be prosecuted. In other precincts, where prostitution is far less of a problem, the bookings are either D.P.I. or "investigation of larceny from the person." The latter booking is based upon the fact that many of these girls participate in the "Murphy game."[10] The procedure is the same whichever entry is made. The women are not searched at the time of booking at the precinct, but are immediately placed in a large detention area reserved for women prisoners. When the number of D.P.I.'s reaches ten, the patrol wagon transports them to the women's detention quarters located at police headquarters. There the women are searched and fingerprinted.

On the morning after arrest (except Sundays), a registered nurse reports to the women's detention quarters at 6:30. She immediately takes a smear and culture on each girl with a D.P.I. booking, and if the girl is not a "regular customer" a treatment record is prepared. By 8:00 A.M. the girls are ready for a brief examination by a doctor, also an employee of the city health department. The results are obtained from the laboratory before 11:00 A.M. At this time the girls are called out one at a time for a brief interview with a patrolman from the vice bureau. This officer observed that most of them "would not tell me the right time of day." However, he does manage to build some pandering cases on information obtained from those few, usually inexperienced, prostitutes who will identify their pimps. The infected prisoners are given medication and are asked to report back the next day, which most of them do. In fact, they are not released if they refuse to take medication or refuse to promise to return the following day.[11]

---

[8] While cruising in the precinct, the squad on one occasion observed a known prostitute on a street corner speaking to two men in a parked car. The driver of the squad car called to the girl by her first name, and she came to the car. While leaning on the car window, she complained that the officers were taking her in awfully early and that she had not been able to make any money. She asked if she could be allowed to work for a while longer because she had been locked up over the weekend and had only thirty cents in her possession. The officers placed her in the car and transported her to precinct headquarters, where she was booked under D.P.I.

[9] The name is derived from the Michigan statute on disorderly persons, discussed at page 460.

[10] The "Murphy game" is a racket in which the prostitutes and their male employers or friends endeavor through trickery to relieve the men who frequent this area of whatever funds they may have.

[11] In Kansas, where the right to detain for medical examination is clear, the court has held that continued detention until the person voluntarily agrees to undergo

Ordinarily, most of these women are back on the street by 11:00 A.M.

The magnitude of this program is indicated by the fact that arrests of the above type often comprise nearly half of this precinct's total arrests. For example, an analysis of all of the bookings in this precinct for a typical two-day period disclosed a total of 75 arrests, 34 of which were D.P.I.'s. The "cleanup squad," charged with vice enforcement at the precinct level, reported 2942 D.P.I. arrests in a six-month period, in which time arrests for accosting and soliciting totaled only 53.[12] There are no departmental statistics which accurately portray how many D.P.I. arrests are made in comparison with the number of prostitutes arrested for purposes of prosecution.[13]

B. Criteria for Selection of Those Who Are Arrested

The objective of the police is to arrest women presently working as prostitutes, who have been or will be guilty of accosting and soliciting, regardless of whether the offense takes place in view of the officer or whether the girl is actually on the street for this purpose at the time of arrest. However, the officers do require some indication that the woman is in fact a prostitute before making an arrest.

For purposes of comparison, it is helpful to identify the amount of evidence of guilt that the police generally feel is necessary in order to make an arrest for accosting and soliciting which will result in prosecution and conviction. First, it is necessary to establish the word, act, or deed by the woman which constitutes the actual accosting, and which shows that the woman accosted the officer and not vice versa. Second, the officer attempts to determine the nature of the immoral act suggested by the woman. Third, the officer is expected to establish the fee requested by the

---

treatment is improper, the proper procedure being to use force when necessary. Welch v. Shepherd, 165 Kan. 394, 196 P.2d 235 (1948).

12 Not all of the accosting cases involve prostitutes, as the same offense category is used for accosting by homosexuals. It has been estimated that 60 per cent of the accosting cases involve prostitutes.

13 For example, while in 1956 a total of 1512 accosting cases were recorded, it is estimated that 40 per cent were homosexuals. All investigation arrests are reported together without regard to offense, so it cannot be determined how many of the 26,696 investigation arrests are D.P.I. cases. Detroit Police Dept., 91st Stat. Ann. Rep. (1956). It was indicated that after the local bar complained about the large number of arrests for investigation, these arrests were subdivided, and a "major portion" of them were found to be D.P.I. cases.

prostitute. If any one of these is lacking, it is not likely that an accosting arrest will be made.[14]

In contrast, a considerable number of the D.P.I. arrests are made upon the basis of the woman's reputation and past record. Thus, if a woman is found in an area in which prostitution is practiced and it is known or thought that she has a past record of arrests for accosting and soliciting or D.P.I., she will be taken into custody.

Often the fact that the girl is a prostitute will be substantiated by the girl herself. She may object to being taken in before she has been able to make any money, or else may object upon the ground that she "was not hustling today." But when a woman is arrested upon the basis of her past record, the officers are not concerned with whether or not she is presently soliciting. Prostitutes may be arrested even if they are in a restaurant or on the street for some other purpose at the time of their arrest.[15] While the prostitutes seem resigned to the fact that they are going to be "D.P.I.'d" if found on the street for purposes of prostitution, they object to this when they consider themselves "off duty." One prostitute brought before the station lieutenant asked, "Is it fair to take us out of the restaurant while we are eating?"

Other women, even in the absence of any knowledge on the officer's part as to a past record, will be arrested when found late at night in areas with a high incidence of prostitution. In such an area, the mere fact that a woman is slowly walking down the street, standing on a corner, or standing in a doorway may be the basis for arrest. In the colder months the prostitutes in these areas are often recognizable by their typical dress for protection against the weather — white leather coats and high boots.[16]

---

14 For example, an officer picked up a girl who asked for a ride, and she indicated that she was willing to "turn a trick." The girl told the officer, "My family has been down on the luck lately and we need some money for food. Can I borrow about $25 from you for groceries?" When the officer said he could go as high as $10, the girl realized that he was trying to get her to state a flat price, so she feigned anger and left the car.

15 Thus the following transpired in Recorder's Court:
JUDGE: The defendant's record shows about 30 arrests.
DEFENDANT: Yes, if you're counting D.P.I.'s and all that.
JUDGE: Don't they count?
DEFENDANT: Sometimes I was only going to the grocery store.

16 As to arrest of these persons, one high official in the Detroit department said: "Now if our police patrol certain areas in this city and they find two women standing on a corner, they go back an hour later and those two women are still standing there, they go back in another hour and those women are still there, and they have been persons theretofore arrested as prostitutes, what conclusion do the police come to? They are prostitutes. Yet, they have seen no active prostitution, there has been no accosting and soliciting, there has been no offense committed by the prostitutes in the presence of the officer." Actually, D.P.I. arrests are not based upon such detailed observations by the police. In the case described, the usual practice would

The arrest of women just because they are on these streets at night undoubtedly results in some women being unintentionally subjected to the D.P.I. process, although this does not seem to occur frequently. Often the officers will question the suspect in an attempt to determine if she is in fact a prostitute. It is not uncommon for them to detect some flaw in an elaborate story given by the woman. When confronted with the inconsistency, the woman frequently admits that she is a prostitute. Sometimes the police check the woman's story and learn that she is going to or from a legitimate job, in which case no arrest is made. The mere fact that the woman has no regular employment may result in her being D.P.I.'d even without further evidence that she is a prostitute.[17]

If the woman is accompanied by or is talking to men, she is likely to be arrested unless the men are relatives. Usually she is questioned to determine if she knows all her male associates. Often she can name one but not the other, which leads the officers to believe that she is a prostitute and that one of the men is her pimp. A woman who stops to talk to men in a car will usually be suspect. Association of a woman with men of another race usually results in an immediate conclusion that she is a prostitute. If a Negro woman is found in the company of a white man, she is usually confronted by the police and taken to the station unless it is clear that the association is legitimate.[18]

While officers assigned to the "whore squads" are skilled in determining who is in fact a prostitute, some arrests are made of women who are not prostitutes. Review of these arrests at the precinct station by the lieutenant in charge does not always follow as a matter of course. If the lieutenant is involved in some other task, the woman will be sent directly to the lock-up. When there is review, the lieutenant usually waves on the known prostitutes, but may question the others. Even this varies according to which lieutenant is on duty. Some lieutenants lock up all the women brought in, and if they complain, they are told that this is a mere check and that they will be released in the morning. Often questioning by the lieutenant will establish that the girl is a prostitute.

---

have been to pick up the women when they were first observed in this area of high prostitution, even if the officers were not aware of any past record.

[17] One nineteen-year-old girl walking down the street at a slow pace was brought in after she indicated that she did not work and lived with her parents. No attempt was made to check her record, and the station lieutenant said, "Well, my girl, we have found a home for you. Lock her up and we'll check on her. If we are wrong, we'll apologize."

[18] One such case, even though it resulted in release at the station by the lieutenant, had some important repercussions. See page 489.

Occasionally either questioning or a check of the girl's record will convince the lieutenant that the girl should be released immediately. Even with the most cautious lieutenant on duty, it is presumed that the girl brought in is a prostitute, and she is released only if it is quite definitely shown that she is not.

C. Reasons for the Practice

While part of the process involves a health examination, it is clear that the police view this as merely a side benefit, and that the practice of arresting suspected prostitutes without intent of prosecution is thought necessary by the police as the only effective means available to deal with prostitution. Said one key official in the department, "Disorderly persons investigation arrests, as practiced primarily in one of the precincts, is a harassment program. The police department has no other means of dealing with prostitution." Similarly, another department official emphasized that an officer makes a D.P.I. arrest to accomplish several purposes:

> First, to get them off the street; second, as a means of harassment. It's a deterrent. They know when certain officers are on the job they are very likely to be picked up and they won't go over on that corner. These particular women I referred to are not only prostitutes but they are decoys for the so-called Murphy game. There have been persons murdered who came into contact with them. As a general rule, in fact almost invariably, these women are out there at two o'clock when the saloons close, when the prospective customers have a lot of liquor in them. They don't want to go home; they are looking for strange experiences. And we've had murders. We had one fellow that was found in an ashcan. Now what should we do under those circumstances? There's our problem — we have no crimes committed in the presence of the police officer, nothing that legally warrants the arrest. Shall we say, "Well, now because our hands are tied, we are going to let these women alone"?

Thus, the police view the program as a way of removing prostitutes from the street, and thereby also decreasing the amount of other potential criminal activity.

The prostitution problem is more serious in Detroit than in any of the other cities studied, because of the hundreds of single-girl prostitution operations. These girls are viewed as a considerable nuisance by the precinct officers. Consequently they react with a program intended to bring about a satisfactory short-term result.

By comparison, Wichita vice officers indicated that they were troubled with prostitution only a few times a year. The girls there are transients, few in number, and certain to move on once discovered.[19] Prosecution has always proved effective and puts little burden on the system, since the girl pleads guilty and leaves town, which is the desired result.[20] Detection is difficult, but Wichita officers have been successful in building cases against the few prostitutes by using paid informants and undercover officers, and by watching through transoms and windows of suspect hotel rooms.

Milwaukee does not appear to have a serious prostitution problem. The prostitutes are not streetwalkers, but operate out of hotels or similar quarters, and consequently the community pressures for police action are not great.

To better understand current practice,[21] three different methods provided by law for dealing with prostitutes will now be briefly discussed: (1) arrest and prosecution for accosting and soliciting; (2) arrest and prosecution on a charge of "common prostitute"; and (3) arrest and detention under health regulations.

1. *Arrest and prosecution for accosting and soliciting.* A detailed discussion of the problems of the Detroit police in making an accosting and soliciting case which will lead to conviction will be found in another volume.[22] That discussion indicates why the police do not view this as an effective means of dealing with the great number of prostitutes. In the first place, limitations upon resources make it difficult to build cases against a significant number of the prostitutes. Secondly, the actual making of a case by a police officer presents many difficulties. The statutory definition of the offense requires that the woman "accost, solicit or invite another . . . by word, gesture or any other means, to commit prostitution . . ."[23] On the basis of their experience in the local trial courts, the police have concluded that they must prove the

[19] The city attorney and police court judge in Wichita said that any prostitutes found in the area (and it was noted they could be found in five or six second-rate hotels) were only transients, never remaining in the city for more than a week or two. It was stated that a survey by a national organization had concluded that prostitution was at an irreducible minimum in Wichita.

[20] The usual procedure in Wichita is for prostitutes to make immediate bail and later be pleaded guilty by an attorney, by which time the girl has left the state. The girls regard this as a mere operational hazard, and their pimp usually has a special fund for such contingencies and has told the girls which attorney and bondsman to call. These girls follow a regular circuit in Texas, Oklahoma, and Kansas.

[21] Probably not all observers of the Detroit procedures would agree on the direction of the cause and effect relationship. Some would contend that the great prostitution problem accounts for the D.P.I. program; others would take the position that prostitution continues to be a problem because the D.P.I. program, rather than prosecution and conviction, continues to be employed.

[22] The volume on Detection of Crime.

[23] Mich. Stat. Ann. §28.703 (1949).

woman was the initiator, that the specific nature of the immoral act was suggested, and that the specific price was agreed upon. Not only is the experienced prostitute often able to identify plain-clothes officers,[24] but she may routinely avoid making any statements encompassing all three elements.[25]

As a consequence, the police have considerable difficulty obtaining convictions in accosting cases.   Judges frequently dismiss such prosecutions, giving as a reason the defense of entrapment, or "enticement" in situations where it is doubtful whether the doctrine of entrapment, as defined in appellate opinions, is applicable.   According to the police, dismissals have been granted in accosting cases where the officer used a Cadillac, because "everyone knows that the police officers use cheap cars"; where the officer disguised himself as a taxi driver or uniformed laborer; where the officer made a telephone call to a number which he had obtained and which he was told belonged to a prostitute; where the officer stopped his car beside a prostitute on a street corner when she had not beckoned to him; and where the officer bought the girl a few drinks or otherwise spent some time with her before the accosting.

Some police attribute the difficulty to the fact that some judges do not properly understand the doctrine of entrapment.   However, it seems apparent that the frequent dismissals on grounds of entrapment are merely symptoms reflecting a much deeper difference of opinion between the police and the judges.   Such dismissals are often attributable to a variety of assumptions or opinions about the prostitution problem.   Some judges believe that unorganized prostitution is not a serious offense, that vice in Detroit is at an irreducible minimum, and that consequently there is too great an allocation of police time and resources to vice enforcement and too little to crimes involving serious harm to persons and property.   Another view is that the individual prostitute is to be "pitied" rather than "persecuted" by prosecution and conviction.   Some judges feel that the methods used by police to induce women to solicit prostitution are overly aggressive, even if not technically sufficient to constitute entrapment.   One judge labels this "enticement" rather than "entrapment."

The police appear to be partly responsible for the difficulty. They have not always been properly instructed in making accost-

24 In one accosting case the defendant asserted that she was careful not to accost the plainclothes officers because "they look just like police."   The judge noted her extensive record, and defense counsel said this was why she could detect them.   In another case the girl spotted the officer's call box key on his ignition key ring and got out of the car immediately.

25 Sometimes the officers will pick up a girl who speaks of money as a "loan" and will not state a flat price.

ing cases,[26] and some cases have been presented in which these re-actions against police methods might be expected.[27] The difficulty is compounded because the police, knowing of the judicial hos-tility, sometimes feel compelled to embellish their testimony to make a better case. The judge is often able to detect this, and may conclude that the officers probably are also distorting other aspects of the case. These factors often contribute to minimum fines being imposed in cases where a conviction is obtained.

The judicial concern with the accosting and soliciting cases is not reflected in a similar attitude toward the D.P.I. program. Judges who are aware of the D.P.I. program informally approve of it. They feel that the police department is simply making an at-tempt to cut down the nuisance aspect of prostitution, particularly in areas of the city where law-abiding citizens are likely to be ac-costed. Thus, while the D.P.I. program may have been originally attributable to the refusal to convict in accosting cases, it now ap-pears that the reluctance to convict is in part due to an attitude by the courts that the D.P.I. program is an adequate alternative. As a consequence, police rely heavily on the D.P.I. program as a method of control. One high-ranking police official said that he felt the situation could be changed only through an interchange of infor-mation at the highest level and a forthright disclosure of the views of the police, the prosecutor, and the courts.

2. *Arrest and prosecution on charge of "common prostitute."* It is apparent that the Detroit police believe it desirable to take official action against women whose provable conduct does not con-stitute "accosting and soliciting," as that phrase has been inter-preted judicially. Police action is in fact taken against women whose past record and present conduct indicate that they are en-gaged in prostitution, even though there is no evidence of actual accosting and soliciting. It is doubtful whether Michigan law provides a basis for such arrests.

Vagrancy and disorderly persons statutes are sometimes drafted to include classes of undesirable persons against whom it is difficult to obtain direct evidence of the commission of a crime. Although

[26] The inspector in the vice bureau said he felt that precinct officers often did not know how to make accosting cases, and he indicated that he was trying to ac-quaint superior officers in the precincts with the proper techniques.

[27] This does not necessarily mean that entrapment was involved, however. A case frequently cited when the judges discussed police actions in making accosting cases was one in which the officer, after a couple of dates with a grandmother, received her consent to go to a hotel room with him for $10, the consent taking place after a night of drinking. While the judges are relating these extreme cases among them-selves, the police tell each other of some of the extreme actions by the court. The dismissal because of the use of the Cadillac is an example. In this way the ani-mosity between the police and the judges continues to grow.

there is doubt that status can constitutionally be made a crime,[28] such statutes remain in the books and may thus constitute an alternative ground for police action.

Michigan does not have a vagrancy statute, but does have a statute defining disorderly persons, and included in the definition is "any common prostitute." [29]   Similarly, cities and villages have been given power to pass ordinances for the arrest and punishment of "common prostitutes." [30]   While the D.P.I. program takes its name from the disorderly persons statute, no one asserted that D.P.I. arrests were legal because the women arrested were common prostitutes, nor were any arrests on this charge observed.[31]

It is doubtful whether the "common prostitute" provision can be used to deal effectively with the streetwalking problem.   The phrase has not been defined by the Supreme Court of Michigan,[32] and it is improbable that the court would construe the phrase to make it possible to invoke the criminal process against persons believed to be prostitutes because of their reputation or past record or because of generally suspicious conduct in an area with a high incidence of prostitution.   A provision that "proof of recent reputation for engaging in an illegal occupation or business shall be prima-facie evidence of being engaged in an illegal occupation or business" has been declared unconstitutional by the Michigan court.[33]

A few early Michigan cases, in which persons arrested as prostitutes were successful in tort actions against the arresting officers, suggest that the "common prostitute" provision could not be applied to most of the girls booked under D.P.I.[34]   One case makes it quite clear that the mere presence of a woman alone late at night

28 See Annot., 92 A.L.R. 1228 (1934).

29 Mich. Stat. Ann. §28.364 (1949).

30 Mich. Stat. Ann. §§5.1285, 5.1740 (1949).

31 The police charged eighteen persons in court as common prostitutes in 1956, and fifteen were convicted.   Detroit Police Dept., 91st Stat. Ann. Rep., Table V (1956). Fourteen of the common prostitute arrests were recorded by the vice bureau.   Id. at 65.   It is not known what factors were considered in either the arrest or the conviction.

32 One definition by a court elsewhere is that a common prostitute is one "who holds herself out as a person who is anxious and willing to engage in acts of prostitution either by her habitude in a known place of prostitution, or by acts, conduct or signs, whose meaning men of like disposition instinctively know or understand, . . ." Burns v. City of Columbus, 30 Ohio Dec. 618, 623 (C.P. 1912).

33 People v. Licavoli, 264 Mich. 643, 250 N.W. 520 (1933).

34 These cases, however, fail to approach directly the problem, as in none of them is the "common prostitute" language referred to.   In addition, the officer's position in terms of a right to arrest was weakened in all three cases.   In two of the cases the court noted that the officer walked away from the alleged prostitute without effecting an arrest and then came back and placed the girl under arrest, and in the third case the girl was released by the lieutenant at the station after only a few questions which convinced him that the girl was not a prostitute.

in an area of Detroit which has a high incidence of prostitution does not justify arrest.[35] However, the arrest in that case was based upon less evidence than often is present in the D.P.I. cases. The woman arrested had no reputation or record as a prostitute, but merely left her husband's tavern at 12 o'clock midnight and walked down the street without indicating in any way that she was plying a prostitute's vocation. Two other cases are even more restricting, as they appear to hold that the girl's reputation or prior record is not a factor which may be considered. In one, the officer testified that the woman had a reputation as a prostitute and that at the time of arrest and other times she was found in a suspicious quarter of the city at a late hour of the night. The court said:

> It is true that an officer, as a conservator of the peace, may arrest street-walkers or common prostitutes who are on the street plying their vocation; but a mere suspicion that they are doing so, where there is no act indicating that the party is there for that purpose, will not justify the arrest . . .[36]

The court did not indicate what kind of an act short of an actual accosting would be sufficient. In the other case it was said that the fact the plaintiff had four prior convictions for streetwalking did not enlarge the officer's arrest powers.[37] While both of these cases are questionable authority because of other facts noted by the court,[38] they do make it doubtful that the Detroit prostitutes can be proceeded against as "common prostitutes" on the basis of the information at hand when D.P.I. arrests are made.[39]

[35] Klein v. Pollard, 149 Mich. 200, 112 N.W. 717 (1907). This case arose in that part of Detroit in which the current prostitution problem is most serious, and the defendant's brief recites that because of the problem 400 women of "known bad repute" had been arrested in the area.

[36] Pinkerton v. Verberg, 78 Mich. 573, 586, 44 N.W. 579, 583 (1889).

[37] Larson v. Feeney, 196 Mich. 1, 162 N.W. 275 (1917). The plaintiff had coughed and said, "Hello there, kid," to the officer.

[38] In Pinkerton, *supra* note 36, the court noted that the girl was released without prosecution and that the officer made the arrest when the girl had given him "some sauce" and after he had once walked away from her. In Larson, *supra* note 37, the court also emphasized the fact that the officer must have thought the grounds insufficient since he walked away without making an immediate arrest.

[39] Perhaps consideration might be given to the more general "disorderly person" definition. No other defining term in the state statute seems appropriate except "any vagrant." Mich. Stat. Ann. §28.364 (1949). This has been determined to include persons who are vagrants at common law, In re Way, 41 Mich. 299, 1 N.W. 1021 (1879), which includes persons without lawful visible support who do not work for a living though able to do so. Also, the Detroit disorderly persons ordinance includes "all able-bodied persons who, not having visible means of support, are found loitering or rambling about . . . in the open air, and not giving a good account of themselves." Detroit Compiled Ordinances of 1954, chap. 223, §1. The fact that the woman does not have a lawful job is often known, and she is sometimes told that she will be picked up until she obtains a legitimate job. However, these provisions can hardly mean that all women must have employment, and claims that

3. Arrest and detention under health regulations. A Michigan statute provides:

> Every person arrested and charged with committing an act of prostitution in violation of sections [28.703, 28.704, 28.705, 28.707, 28.710, which are the accosting and soliciting and similar provisions] or any city or village ordinance prohibiting prostitution, shall be examined by the local health officer . . . Any such person so taken into custody may be detained . . . until such examination shall be made by the local health officer, and diagnosis established, but not for a period of more than five [5] days.[40]

This statute does not itself afford a ground for arrest, but merely allows detention of persons otherwise arrested *and* charged. Police officers in some cities without a D.P.I. program have made particular note of the fact that the quarantine law gives them no arrest authority. In Detroit it is also realized that these statutes give no arrest authority, but they are cited as some justification for the D.P.I. program, together with the local ordinance, which provides:

> All persons known to be common prostitutes or reasonably suspected and believed to be such . . . shall be deemed to be suspected cases [of venereal disease] and shall be subject to arrest and to examination at such places and times as the Commissioner of Health may direct.[41]

The constitutionality of such a provision has not been determined by the Michigan Supreme Court. Here again the phrase "common prostitute" is used, and it is not clear that an arrest for health purposes can be made on less evidence than that required for an arrest for a crime.[42]

---

the women are married or living with their parents are sometimes received when their employment is inquired into.

[40] Mich. Stat. Ann. §14.345(3) (1949).

[41] Detroit Compiled Ordinances of 1954, chap. 173, VIII, §1.

[42] Health provisions of a more limited scope have been judicially approved in Kansas in Welch v. Shepherd, 165 Kan. 394, 196 P.2d 235 (1948). The full procedure is set forth therein. Section 65-128 of Kan. Gen. Stat. (1949) allows the state board of health to designate infectious diseases and prescribe rules for their isolation and quarantine; and Rule 11,337 of the board designates the common venereal diseases as communicable and orders local health officers to investigate suspected cases. This rule gives local authorities the power to isolate and examine persons "reasonably suspected," and adds, 'Owing to the prevalence of such disease among pimps and prostitutes, all such persons may be considered in the above class."

Wichita City Ordinance 6009, §8 reads: "It is hereby made the duty of the City Physician and he is hereby directed and empowered: (a) To make examinations of persons reasonably suspected of having syphilis in the infectious stages or gonococcus infection (owing to the prevalence of such disease among prostitutes, all prostitutes may be considered within the above class)."

The court in the Welch case noted: "If the question before us were the validity of these ordinances and the right and duty of the city health officer to examine

Such provisions do, however, provide one of the major rationalizations for the D.P.I. program. Said one high official in the police department:

> We use this as an excuse. The Commissioner of Health has the authority to detain prostitutes for physical examination. Of course, our practice goes far and beyond this provision, but we lock the prostitutes up under this provision.

When it was suggested that the average officer does not justify the practice on this basis, he added:

> Let me put it this way. Under the present setup, I seek refuge in the feeling that until such time as a court of competent jurisdiction proves us wrong, we can continue engaging in this practice. If, however, we are ever subject to attack, I would use the two provisions which I have cited in defense of the practice.

D. The Legality of the Practice

Whatever the justification for the practice of arresting and releasing prostitutes, it is evident that the practice has at best an uncertain status under the law of Michigan. Most of the arrests fail to meet the probability of guilt requirements as those are customarily defined. Certainly in most arrests there is insufficient evidence to believe a violation of the accosting and soliciting statute, as interpreted by the trial courts, has been committed. Neither the common prostitute definition nor the health provisions furnish a clear basis for the practice.

Most arrests are, however, based upon evidence which makes it quite probable the woman is a prostitute. This is true, for example, even in the situation where a Negro woman is arrested solely because she is in the company of a white man in a certain section of the city and cannot satisfactorily explain their association. Because of the conditions which prevail in this particular locale, such an association does give rise to an extremely strong inference that the woman is engaged in prostitution. But, as with the other sus-

---

persons suspected of having a venereal disease our decision would be easy. We have heretofore upheld the action of the health officer taken pursuant to such ordinances." Welch v. Shepherd, 165 Kan. at 403, 196 P.2d at 242 (1948).

The extent to which this procedure is utilized in Kansas is not clear. In Wichita the usual process is for prostitutes to make immediate bail and leave the city. However, one instance was observed in which a pick-up order from the health clinic was issued after a girl did not appear for trial. Apparently there were doubts whether this girl had in fact left the city. In contrast, the Kansas City procedure is to book prostitutes "hold for welfare and health department," and in such a case bail is not allowed. There is no evidence that the health provisions are used to arrest and detain prostitutes who could not otherwise be arrested.

picious conduct discussed, this is not sufficient evidence for arrest under either the accosting or the common prostitute provisions. Even if the statutes did allow arrest upon reasonable belief that the woman is a prostitute, the police might be subjected to severe criticism for drawing the above inference.[43]

Assuming evidence sufficient to justify the arrest, the question discussed in relation to the arrest of drunks, namely, whether a practice of arrest and release is proper, would then arise. Some courts have said that a release by police following an arrest otherwise proper makes the arrest and detention illegal.[44]   This position has been rejected in Michigan, but the court has indicated that the doctrine has application when the arresting officer had an unlawful objective in mind at the time of the original arrest.[45]   In D.P.I. cases the arresting officer typically is aware that release will follow the arrest.

In some states the legislature has specifically provided that an arrest is privileged only if made for the purpose of prosecution.[46] No such statute exists in Michigan, although this result, it may be argued, is implied from a statute indicating that the officer must take the arrested person before a magistrate and make a complaint.[47]

[43] In Philadelphia, the Police Review Board, a group of five citizens appointed to hear allegations against the police, received a complaint of an arrest allegedly based solely upon the interracial nature of a couple. As a consequence, the Board requested the police commissioner to issue a directive "pointing out that no arrest or police action should be taken or commenced solely because of the fact that there is an interracial group or couple." Philadelphia Police Review Board, First Ann. Rep. 3 (1959).

Thus, even though an arrest made upon this basis may conform to the informal policy on D.P.I. arrests, outside pressures upon the police department may necessitate the imposition of sanctions upon the individual officer who made such an arrest. See page 489.

[44] The doctrine developed because it was felt necessary to use such a fiction to determine a man's intention. Bohlen and Shulman, Effect of Subsequent Misconduct upon a Lawful Arrest, 28 Colum. L. Rev. 841, 847 (1928). The need for the doctrine today on this basis seems questionable. Release of an arrestee ought not be considered conclusive evidence of an illegal purpose at the time of arrest.

[45] Oxford v. Berry, 204 Mich. 197, 170 N.W. 83 (1918); Friesenhan v. Maines, 137 Mich. 10, 100 N.W. 172 (1904).

[46] See A.L.I. Code of Criminal Procedure §18, Comment (1930).

[47] Mich. Stat. Ann. §28.872 (1949). See Malcolmson v. Scott, 56 Mich. 459, 465, 23 N.W. 166, 168 (1885). The court has decided one case in which the facts indicated repeated arrests without prosecution for alleged liquor violations. No comment was made of this fact, but the court did indicate that the jury could have found that the police did not possess the probability of guilt required for arrest. Odinetz v. Budds, 315 Mich. 512, 24 N.W.2d 193 (1946). The requirement of a purpose to prosecute is often stated in texts on torts. See 1 Harper and James, Torts §3.18 (1956). The rule, as stated by the Restatement, is: "The arrest of another is not privileged unless the actor makes the arrest for the purpose of bringing the other before a court, body or official or otherwise securing the administration of the law." 1 Restatement of Torts §127 (1934).

CHAPTER 23

Arrest to Control the Transvestite

Private homosexual conduct between consenting adults is not in practice a matter of major concern to law enforcement agencies. Detection of such conduct is extremely difficult, and it is generally assumed that enforcement resources are better applied to other forms of criminal conduct.[1] Indeed, there is considerable current thought that such conduct is a matter of morals rather than of law, and that consequently it should not be proscribed by penal legislation.[2]

As with prostitution, however, there are aspects of homosexual conduct which are of concern to the police because of the nuisance to the public which is created. Solicitation by homosexuals in public places often causes complaints from persons who have been accosted and from the proprietors of reputable places in which such conduct occurs. The police respond to these complaints by dispatching plainclothes officers to these locations to see if they are solicited. These tactics are frequently successful in identifying those persons who are engaging in public solicitation,[3] although the police have encountered some judicial hostility to such enforcement practices.[4]

[1] "Funds and personnel for police work are limited, and it would appear to be poor policy to use them to any extent in this area when large numbers of atrocious crimes remain unsolved." Model Penal Code §207.5, Comments (Tent. Draft No. 4, 1955).

[2] See Great Britain, Home Office, Report of the Committee on Homosexual Offenses and Prostitution (1957); Model Penal Code §207.5, Comments (Tent. Draft No. 4, 1956); Model Penal Code §251.3, Status of Section (Proposed Final Draft, 1962). See also Rittenour v. District of Columbia, 163 A.2d 558 (D.C. Munic. Ct. App. 1960), holding that the D.C. Code provision proscribing any "lewd, obscene, or indecent act" did not include acts in private to one who had manifested consent.

[3] While it is said that it is impossible to identify a homosexual if he does not want to be identified, the sometimes indiscriminate public solicitation has been explained on the ground that many homosexuals are masochists and consequently want to be apprehended by the authorities. Illustrative is the case of the homosexual who accosted a detective in the men's room of City Hall, where the police department was located. Bergler, 1000 Homosexuals 156, 161 (1959).

[4] The conflict between the judges and the police is not unlike that described in the preceding chapter regarding enforcement against prostitution. Details on the

Police are also concerned with the transvestite, the person appearing in public dressed in the clothing of the opposite sex. This conduct is obviously offensive to a large segment of the community. Moreover, some transvestites and persons appearing to be transvestites use this as a method of committing other crimes, such as robbery. Detection and identification of the perpetrator after the robbery takes place is difficult.

In practice, police sometimes attempt to control the problem created by the transvestite by a program of arrest and release without prosecution. This program is the subject of this chapter.

A. THE PRACTICE OF ARRESTING TRANSVESTITES FOR PURPOSES OTHER THAN PROSECUTION

In Detroit, the police frequently arrest male homosexuals who are found on the street dressed in female attire. These persons, referred to by the police as "fags," are brought in whenever they are spotted on the street by an officer.[5] When the homosexual is brought to the station, he is booked for investigation of larceny from a person. This booking is explained on the basis that a large number of these transvestites "roll" their customers when engaged in their perverted sexual activities, and many participate in the "Murphy game," in which "johns" (men looking for girls) are tricked out of their money.[6] The homosexual is held in jail overnight, and the next morning he is questioned by a detective before release.[7] This procedure is used principally with male homo-

---

police problems in this regard will be found in the volume on Detection of Crime.

Judicial concern with enforcement tactics in this area is evidenced elsewhere as well. See Kelly v. United States, 194 F.2d 150 (D.C. Cir. 1952), holding a policeman's unsupported testimony of solicitation insufficient to convict.

[5] An officer on patrol observed a known "fag" walking down the street. The officer stopped the patrol wagon, and one of the other officers confronted the "fag." He was asked his name, and then he was asked his "bitch name," which he said was Vicki. He was placed in the patrol wagon and taken to headquarters. The officers explained that there are a large number of "queers" in this area and that they pick them up frequently when they see them on the street.

[6] Actually, some of those arrested are not true transvestites. Some persons parade in female attire solely for purposes of disguise in order to assault or rob individuals whom they have enticed into an isolated location. It is seldom possible for the police to distinguish these persons from others who actually derive sexual pleasure from dressing in the clothing of the opposite sex, and who may or may not engage in the "Murphy game."

[7] Thus, in the case reported in note 5, supra, the detective questioned the homosexual regarding his homosexual activities, and then reviewed all outstanding larceny from person cases in an effort to determine if the descriptions matched that of the defendant. When he was satisfied that none matched, the detective released the man with the approval of the sergeant. The results of the questioning were placed in the man's file, and the arrest was not removed from his record.

sexuals found on the streets dressed as females. Occasionally a female dressed as a male is accorded similar treatment. Associates of these transvestites may also be arrested on the assumption that they are homosexuals.[8]

This arrest practice is limited to transvestites and their associates and is not used with respect to other persons known to have homosexual tendencies. Members of the latter group, when they are the object of enforcement concern, are subjected to intense investigation for the purpose of making accosting and soliciting cases against them.[9] These investigations take place primarily in taverns, hotels, and public rest rooms at which homosexuals are known to congregate. Unlike the transvestites, these homosexuals have no obvious characteristics which identify them, although some do have feminine mannerisms. If an investigation of the ordinary homosexual fails to produce evidence of an actual solicitation, no arrest is made, even though the police may be convinced that the person is in fact a homosexual.[10]

B. Bases of Selection of Those Arrested

To the extent that the objective of the program is to remove transvestites from the street, there is little doubt that the police arrest the right persons.[11] Their dress makes this perfectly apparent. The few cases observed in which persons associating with transvestites were also arrested were ones in which it was clear that the association was based upon a homosexual involvement.[12]

To the extent that a purpose of the program is to arrest persons who have committed, or are intent upon committing, robbery, the methods used are much less selective. The fact that a person is dressed in the clothing of the opposite sex does not conclusively establish that he is also a robber. However, most of these arrests

8 For example, a man following a transvestite down an alley was taken into custody when he told the police that the homosexual had offered to commit an act of sodomy. On another occasion, officers entered an apartment and found a male dressed as a female, along with a number of other persons. When the others indicated that they were present for the purpose of having their hair fixed, all of them were taken into custody.

9 Further discussion of this will be found in the volume on Detection of Crime.

10 Officers assigned to the general vice section of the vice bureau in Detroit traveled to a theater for a check on homosexuals who often linger there. One of the officers entered the men's rest room and lounged about the area for approximately thirty minutes. Other officers periodically checked on him. During the course of this period the officer was not accosted. Though there were a large number of known homosexuals present, none were arrested.

11 That is, with one exception. See note 6 *supra*. But since these persons are clearly on the street for purposes of committing a violent crime, the police are not at all concerned about the fact that they are being included.

12 See, for example, note 8 *supra*.

are made in that part of the city where the "Murphy game" is most common.

C. Reasons for the Practice

Although the transvestite is booked for "investigation of larceny from the person," and although he is questioned briefly by a detective prior to release, this investigation does not appear to be the primary reason for the practice. The detectives merely take advantage of the fact that the person is in custody and conduct a brief investigation. It is usually limited to asking the homosexual a few questions and checking the descriptions of wanted criminals. Few cases are actually made in this way, but the investigation at least makes known to the transvestite the fact that his activities are not going entirely unnoticed. It also supplies an apparent justification for the arrest and detention practice.

Police experience difficulty in getting convictions in accosting and soliciting cases involving homosexuals, just as they do in the case of prostitutes. On occasion, an assistant prosecutor may refuse a warrant in such a case or the court may dismiss the case, sometimes without explanation to the officer. This action may reflect displeasure with the methods used by the police, pity for the offender, or an opinion that psychiatric treatment is a better alternative than resort to the criminal process. However, unlike the D.P.I. process for prostitutes, the arrest and release of transvestites does not result from judicial attitudes expressed in accosting and soliciting cases. The transvestite subjected to the arrest and release practice and the homosexual who is prosecuted for accosting and soliciting pose quite different problems for society.

Arrest of the transvestite appears to be explainable in part by a police desire to remove these individuals from the streets. Like the streetwalking prostitute, they can be observed by the general public. Their presence is likely to be an affront to the ordinary citizen, and the failure of the police to do something may be interpreted as an indication of lax law enforcement.

In addition, although investigation of larceny is not the predominant reason for the practice, it is true that the transvestite does frequently engage in this kind of criminal conduct and he will, on occasion, admit at the time of arrest that he was hustling "johns." Because of the embarrassing circumstances involved, the victim of such a theft rarely contacts the police. The police realize this, and as a consequence the arrest and detention of the transvestite is thought to punish him for past offenses and also to prevent, for at least a brief time, the commission of further offenses.

Police hold the transvestite in contempt. He is often subjected to ridicule at the time of arrest and usually is made to dispose of at least some of his female garb when he is booked. In contrast, other homosexuals are usually treated with courtesy. They are frequently told that no notoriety follows from arrest, and often inquiry is made as to whether the person has sought psychiatric help.

There does not appear to be any effective way specifically authorized by statute for dealing with the transvestite. Prosecution for larceny is not usually possible because of the absence of a victim willing to testify. Nor does prosecution for being a transvestite appear possible unless there is evidence of an act of accosting, which is required to make homosexual conduct criminal. Dressing in the clothing of the opposite sex is not among the kinds of conduct defined in the disorderly persons statute, nor is prosecution possible under the city ordinances.[13] Were prosecution possible, there still might be judicial reluctance to convict the transvestite unless he is viewed as more offensive and thus warranting more serious treatment than the ordinary homosexual.[14]

So far as was determined, the transvestite was not a significant problem in Milwaukee or Wichita, and therefore police procedures for handling this problem were not observed.

D. Legality of the Practice

The arrest and release of transvestites is not expressly authorized by law. The practice differs from that used for drunks in that the arrest of the transvestite clearly is not motivated by a

13 This, however, has been changed in Detroit since the time of the observations. In 1958, the disorderly persons ordinance was amended to make it unlawful for "any member of the male sex to appear in or upon any street, alley, highway, sidewalk, bridge, viaduct, tunnel, path, parkway, or other public way or place, or in, upon or about any private premises frequented by or open to the public, in the dress of the opposite sex: Provided, however, that this section shall not apply to any person while legally giving, conducting, producing, presenting, offering or participating in any entertainment, exhibition or performance." Detroit City Ordinances, chap. 223, §8-D, as amended July 29, 1958. The fact that it was so amended suggests that the general definition of a disorderly person, as given in that ordinance and the state statute, was believed insufficient. It is not known whether police tactics have changed since the amendment of this ordinance.

14 Of course, part of the judicial hostility in cases involving ordinary homosexuals is because of police methods, which would not here come into question. But another significant reason for the lack of convictions is the judicial attitude that the homosexual is to be pitied. Such an attitude would appear more proper as to those persons who occasionally accost than to the transvestite who engages in the "Murphy game." However, the judges might not note the distinction and might not be aware of the police difficulties in making a case on the larceny offense. Also, the judges might not share the police attitude that these persons must be acted against because of their participation in the "Murphy game," as the judges sometimes dismissed such cases on the basis that the victim brought about the offense by his own doing.

desire to insure his safety, and differs from that used for prostitutes in that there is no physical examination or other health factor which might be used as justification. The transvestite and the drunk situations are similar in that there is almost always conclusive evidence that the person arrested is in fact drunk or in fact a transvestite. But the central difference is that being sufficiently drunk is a crime while being a transvestite is not. Although it is known that transvestites frequently commit other crimes, such as accosting and soliciting or theft, there is ordinarily insufficient evidence that the transvestite who is arrested has in fact committed one of these crimes. The question of whether the release of the transvestite would make improper an arrest, otherwise proper, is not likely to arise therefore unless the disorderly persons or other statute is amended to make it an offense to appear on the street in the clothes of the opposite sex.[15]

[15] For the effect of release upon the legality of an arrest of a drunk, see page 444.

CHAPTER 24

Arrest as a Punitive Sanction:
Gambling and Liquor Law Violations

Social gambling is ordinarily not of concern to law enforcement officers, even though state statutes customarily are drafted in language broad enough to make it a crime. Police routinely refuse to make an arrest for such conduct.[1] However, professional gambling, which is a major activity of organized crime, is of concern to law enforcement, and consequently a large share of available law enforcement resources is devoted to the difficult task of building a case against the criminal organization which is involved.

In most large urban centers, one of the major forms of gambling, especially among minority and low-income groups, is the policy game,[2] sometimes referred to as "numbers." Bets are received daily, usually in small cash amounts, on any combination of three numbers from 000 to 999. The winning number is determined on the basis of some statistic reported daily, such as certain digits of the total amount of money bet at a particular race track. While the actual odds are 1000 to 1, most syndicates pay at 600 or 500 to 1. An elaborate organization of bet takers ("writers"), runners ("bagmen"), and clerks ("office workers") is needed in the day-to-day operation of a numbers syndicate.[3] The

1 See page 89.

2 This game received its name from "polizza," the Italian word for lottery tickets. See generally Peterson, Obstacles to Enforcement of Gambling Laws, 269 Annals 9 (May, 1950); A.B.A., Commission on Organized Crime, Organized Crime and Law Enforcement 11 (1952). See also Hearings on H.R. 3024, H.R. 8410, and S. 1658 Before the House Committee on Interstate and Foreign Commerce, 87th Cong., 2d Sess. (1962); Hearings Pursuant to S. Res. 69 Before Permanent Subcommittee on Investigations of the Senate Committee on Government Operations, 87th Cong., 1st Sess. (1961); Hearings on H.R. 468 Before Subcommittee No. 5 of the House Committee on the Judiciary, 87th Cong., 1st Sess. (1961).

3 For a more detailed description, see A.B.A., Commission on Organized Crime, Organized Crime and Law Enforcement 91-94 (1952); Jacoby, The Forms of Gambling, 269 Annals 39, 43-45 (May, 1950).

Although the terms "policy" and "numbers" are often used interchangeably, the form of lottery described above, common in Detroit, is usually called "numbers." In contrast, "policy," common in Chicago and some other large cities, involves

gross annual play on the "numbers" or "policy" has been conservatively estimated at one billion dollars.[4]

Some other forms of gambling, such as bookmaking or the operation of a gambling room, may be small operations or may be associated with an organized criminal syndicate. Making book on horse races grosses from three to five billion dollars a year.[5] Many millions of dollars are also bet annually in other kinds of gambling establishments.

Gambling and liquor law violations, which also range from small-scale to syndicate operations, present difficult enforcement problems for the police. There is customarily no victim willing to complain, furnish evidence, and testify in court. Unlike the narcotics offender, violators of the gambling and liquor laws are seldom willing to become informants. Because much of the activity takes place behind locked doors, direct observation by the police is seldom possible. Effective police detection methods often raise difficult questions of search and seizure and entrapment. Perhaps in part as a consequence of this, the arrest and release practice, described in detail in this chapter, has developed.

A. The Practice of Arresting Violators of the Gambling and Liquor Laws

In Detroit, as well as elsewhere in Michigan, the police frequently arrest persons involved in professional gambling or illegal liquor sales without any intention of subjecting them to prosecution or of bringing the case to the attention of the prosecutor. This procedure is used not only against owners, operators, and frequenters of places where gambling or illegal liquor sales are conducted, but also against bookies, numbers writers and carriers, liquor carriers, and persons similarly involved. In Detroit, these arrests are made predominantly by the "cleanup squads" in the precincts[6] and by the general vice section of the vice bureau operating out of police headquarters.[7]

---

basically the same kind of organizational structure, but the bettor selects a series of three two-digit numbers and the winners are determined by an actual drawing of numbered chits from a drum by that particular policy wheel. Winning numbers are announced by the distribution of "hit slips" by the "bagmen."

4 A.B.A., Commission on Organized Crime, Organized Crime and Law Enforcement 94 (1952).

5 Id. at 79. For a more detailed description of bookmaking operations, see Lawrence, Bookmaking, 269 Annals 46 (May, 1950).

6 Six to eight officers in a precinct are assigned to the cleanup squad. Officers so assigned work in plainclothes under the direction of the inspector in charge of the precinct. They are considered a precinct vice squad, and have as their primary function the enforcement of liquor licensing regulations.

7 At the same time, the racket squad of the vice bureau works on building

Some indication of the extent of these arrests for purposes other than prosecution is evident from the following statistics concerning the Detroit Police Department. In one precinct in which gambling and liquor violations are a serious problem, the cleanup squads made a total of 592 such arrests for gambling in a six-month period. During the same time only 24 gambling warrants were sought for the purpose of prosecuting the persons arrested. In the same six-month period 420 arrests were made for violation of the liquor laws, but only 36 of them resulted in warrants being sought.[8] The practice of subjecting these persons to arrest without prosecution occurs with the knowledge and consent of the supervisory officers of the department, who feel that this is the only means they have for coping with a difficult problem.

Police action of this type against liquor or gambling places sometimes results from a specific complaint.[9] On other occasions these places are discovered by surveillance of suspected establishments. The following is a report of a typical raid:

Passing by the establishment at approximately 1:00 A.M., the cleanup squad officers observed two men who were probably serving as lookouts in the shoeshine parlor in the front of this building. The officers traveled around the block and then pulled into an alley. Two of them walked in the front of the establishment, the shoeshine parlor, while the other two men stationed themselves at the rear door. Through the door, they could hear a large number of voices. This reporter waited at the rear of the establishment together with the sergeant and one of the other members of the cleanup crew.

In very short order, the door was opened by one of the other officers. There was a large round table in the center of this back room with 32 people gathered around it. There were cards on the table, but there was no money present. The sergeant theorized that the money was removed as soon as one of the lookout men had seen the officers. Although the officers operate in plain clothes, they are usually well known to professional gamblers in the neigh-

---

conspiracy cases for prosecution. Building such cases is also an important activity of the racket squad of the state police.

8 In 1956 a total of 1125 habeas corpus writs were received by the vice bureau, a majority of which were for persons arrested without intent of prosecution.

9 A man called the precinct, identified himself, and stated that a noisy party was being held in the apartment below, and that he could hear gambling. Armed with this information, the cleanup squad went to the address, listened at the door, and then without notice broke in and seized the cards, dice, and money. All twelve persons were arrested. The woman in possession of the apartment was booked for investigation of violation of the gambling laws, and instructions were left to release her in the morning. The others were lectured and sent on their way after a time, except that those with outstanding traffic warrants had to post the amount due prior to release.

borhood. Those present in the room continued to engage in their card game, though with the absence of cash at the table.

The sergeant then ordered that everybody in the room turn toward the wall. With two officers starting at each end of the line-up, they began to search for concealed weapons. On finding a jackknife they removed it and threw it onto the center of the table. Approximately 50 jackknives were found, but no other type of weapon. With the search of all 32 individuals completed, the officers then went through the line again taking down the name, address, birth date, and sex of each of the individuals in the room. In the meantime, one of the officers had radioed for a patrol wagon.

The patrol wagon arrived and was backed up to the rear door of the establishment. A large number of people had gathered outside to inquire about their relatives. The sergeant instructed all of them to leave or they too would be placed in the wagon. Fifteen of the 32 people were then placed in the wagon and driven to precinct headquarters. At the precinct these individuals were placed in the bull pen. The wagon then returned to pick up the others.

At precinct headquarters no effort was made to book these individuals. The cleanup squad instead listed them in their report and phoned the names in to the administrative unit of the traffic division in order to determine whether or not there were any traffic warrants outstanding on them. As a result of this check, four individuals were detained on outstanding traffic warrants. The cleanup squad also detained the owner of the premises and the individual who was operating the game. The 26 other persons were taken out of the bull pen at 2:15 A.M. and released.

A number of similar incidents were observed, both in gambling places and in "blind pigs," where liquor is sold illegally. Sometimes, especially when the gambling was a small operation taking place in a house or apartment, the police would break in without notice and actually see the money and gambling paraphernalia. On other occasions, usually when the gambling place was a larger operation employing lookouts, a considerable number of persons would be sitting around doing nothing by the time the police gained entrance. The officers in these cases entered without any pretext of complying with the legal requirements for search or entry.

Arrests are also frequently made of persons in the lower echelons of the numbers syndicate, that is, persons who write and carry numbers slips.[10] The police suspect certain persons as "writers"

10 This is the most prevalent form of gambling in Detroit, is the most highly organized, and involves the largest number of people. A numbers player may bet on one three-digit number, or as many as he chooses. The average bet is about twenty-five cents per number, and a typical player will bet on four or more numbers for a total outlay of at least one dollar. The standard odds for any one number are 500 to 1. The "writer" usually visits his customers during the morning.

or "bagmen" either because of their past record or because of their suspicious actions. They are stopped and searched, and if evidence of gambling is found they are arrested. When the "bagman" fails to make his rounds it is presumed by the syndicate that he has been picked up, so a writ of habeas corpus is promptly obtained, and at the hearing the arrestee is released on bond.[11] Similarly, persons suspected of carrying illegal liquor are stopped, searched, and then detained if the search discloses the presence of illegal liquor.

Finally, this same procedure may also be used on persons suspected of being bookies. When the police become suspicious of a particular establishment, a raid may be carried out which produces evidence of bookmaking. Here again the person is arrested and booked on "investigation of violating the gambling laws." He is released the following day if not freed earlier on a writ of habeas corpus.

Despite the fact that no prosecution is intended in these cases, automobiles, liquor, gambling money, and telephones are confiscated by the police when they are connected with the offense for which the arrest is made. If a search of a suspect and his car discloses illegal liquor or policy slips, the car is brought to headquarters at the time of arrest and later taken to the police automobile pound. The prosecuting attorney's office bases its action in automobile confiscation cases on the statute dealing with abatement of nuisances, which provides that any building, vehicle, or place used for the purpose of prostitution, gambling, or illegal manufacture or sale of liquor is declared a nuisance and shall be "enjoined and abated." [12] The prosecuting attorney's office is not

---

All bets are recorded on small tablets, with a copy of the bet being given to the bettor. The parimutuel totals of the first, second, third, and fourth races at a designated track are used in determining the first digit of the winning number. For this reason, all betting must cease before the end of the fourth race. The "writer" delivers his tickets to a substation operated by the syndicate. A "bagman" picks up the tickets from the substations and delivers them to the "office," where people known as "office workers" sort the slips to determine the winners. Only trusted employees of the syndicate know the location of the office. The winners are usually paid at the same time bet slips are accepted the following day.

[11] For example, in one case a carrier was arrested at 1:50 P.M. and the officers arrived at the vice bureau with him at 2:19. At 2:38 an attorney called to inquire about the carrier, and at 2:47 the lieutenant was notified of the writ, with a hearing set at 3:15. At the hearing the officer requested adjournment until the next day, and the carrier was released on $300 bond, subject to appearing at the vice bureau the next morning. The lieutenant indicated that the inspector would reprimand this man in the morning, and then he would be returned to court, where the writ would be dismissed.

[12] Mich. Stat. Ann. §18.901 (1949). This act has been held constitutional in People ex rel. Wayne County Prosecuting Attorney v. Sill, 310 Mich. 570, 17 N.W.2d 733 (1945). It was affirmed by an evenly divided court that a single instance of an

influenced in its decision by the fact of an illegal arrest or search and seizure. Civil actions to sell the cars are routinely brought, although it has been estimated that there is an illegal arrest or search in nine out of ten such cases.[13]

When the police raid a gambling game or arrest a numbers runner, they always confiscate any money which is found. Often runners will admit to the police what money is theirs and what money has been collected, enabling police to seize only that connected directly with gambling.[14] Some individuals sue for return of the money when they feel the amount is large enough to justify litigation. If the plaintiff can prove that the money was obtained by an illegal search, the court will order the money returned to him. In Detroit, the department secretary, who is the second deputy commissioner, decides when money is to be returned even though no lawsuit has been instituted. When the arrested person is not prosecuted, the decision as to whether to return the money is based upon his record, the nature of the crime, and the evidence of guilt (without applying the exclusionary rule to evidence illegally obtained).

---

automobile being used to transport numbers slips was sufficient for the automobile to be declared a nuisance. People ex rel. Wayne County Prosecuting Attorney v. Bitonti, 306 Mich. 115, 10 N.W.2d 329 (1943).

[13] One assistant prosecutor is responsible for bringing these actions, and in a given case he may select one of five possible alternatives:

(1) If he feels it is a very poor case, he may have the car returned to the defendant. Such is likely to be the case if only a few bet slips are found in the car of a person without a record.

(2) He may arrange with the defendant to enter into a consent decree whereby the defendant gets his car back upon payment of court costs. The consent decree orders that the defendant be permanently enjoined from using the vehicle for illegal activity and asserts that the officers are freed from any liability arising out of the seizure. The court costs range from $119 for a 1957 car to $69 for cars manufactured in 1953 or earlier. There is some doubt about the legality of these costs, as State ex rel. Wayne County Prosecuting Attorney v. Martin, 314 Mich. 317, 22 N.W.2d 381 (1946), held that attorneys' fees and statutory costs were the only authorized costs in such a proceeding.

(3) The case may actually go to court at the insistance of the defendant. This does not frequently occur, even if the search was illegal, as the defendant pays less for the consent decree costs than would be required for an attorney. Also, the crowded docket results in a delay of two or three months before the defendant can get his car back.

(4) The case may actually go to court because the state refuses to accept a consent decree. This happens only when the arrest and search was legal and the defendant has a bad record.

(5) The defendant may not appear, in which case a default decree is entered. In such an event the case is left open for six months, after which the car is declared abandoned and turned over to the police department for sale. A considerable number of the "bagmen" in Detroit use old cars for this reason.

[14] In six months, one precinct confiscated $8810.31 from 582 individuals, only 24 of whom were prosecuted. The vice bureau confiscated $33,556.16 in one year. Detroit Police Dept., 90th Stat. Ann. Rep. 65 (1955).

When an investigation reveals that a telephone on the premises has been used to convey gambling information, the officer making the arrest removes the telephone regardless of whether the arrest and search were legal. A memorandum reciting the facts is then sent to the prosecutor's office and to the telephone company, which has agreed not to reinstall a phone in such a situation until clearance is obtained from the prosecutor. The prosecutor has delegated this decision to the inspector in charge of the vice bureau.[15] When it is unclear whether the telephone was used for gambling purposes, it is not removed.

B. Bases of Selection of Those Arrested

In considering the nature and amount of evidence required by the police before an arrest is made, it is important to distinguish between persons arrested when gambling paraphernalia or illegal liquor is found and persons arrested when no such evidence is found.

When a person is searched and found to be in possession of gambling paraphernalia or illegal liquor, he is obviously guilty of an offense. If he is a low echelon member of a numbers syndicate arrested because he is found carrying numbers slips, there is clear evidence of guilt, notwithstanding the fact that it may not be admissible in court. Likewise, if during a gambling raid the police make an arrest after finding cards and money or similar evidence of gambling, there is typically clear evidence of guilt, although again such evidence may not be admissible in court. Similarly, in a raid of a "blind pig," the discovery of illegal liquor is persuasive evidence that the person arrested is an owner, operator, or frequenter.

There are situations in which arrests are made even though no physical evidence is found. One such situation is where gambling has been overheard, although the money is no longer present at the time of entry. In other situations there may be a large group of persons sitting around doing nothing at the time of entry, and it may appear reasonably certain that gambling was interrupted by knowledge that the police were approaching.

If a suspected numbers runner or writer is stopped and only a few slips are found on his person or in his home and he claims these represent his own bets, he is typically not taken into custody.

[15] In 1956 approximately two hundred telephones were confiscated by the vice bureau in Detroit.

C. REASONS FOR THE PRACTICE

One assistant prosecutor, when asked about this program, gave the following explanation:

The laws in Michigan with respect to gambling are most inadequate. This is equally true of the punishment feature of the law. A well-organized and productive gambling house or numbers racket could take in one quarter of a million dollars each week. If, after a long and vigorous period of investigation and observation, the defendant was charged with violating the gambling laws and convicted, the resulting punishment is so obviously weak and unprohibitive that the defendants are willing to shell out a relatively small fine or serve a relatively short time in prison. The Detroit gamblers and numbers men confidently feel that the odds are in their favor. If they operate for six months or a year, and accumulate untold thousands of dollars from the illegal activity, then the meager punishment imposed upon them if they are caught is well worth it. Then, too, because of the search and seizure laws in Michigan, especially in regard to gambling and the numbers rackets, the hands of the police are tied. Unless a search can be made prior to an arrest, so that the defendant can be caught in the act of violating the gambling laws, there is no other earthly way of apprehending such people along with evidence sufficient to convict them that is admissible in court. Because of these two inadequacies of the law the prosecutor's office and the police department are forced to find other means of punishing, harassing, and generally making life uneasy for the gamblers.

These appear to be the reasons for the practice. Even where a legal arrest and search are possible the police feel that little is accomplished by taking the individuals into court. As one officer observed, "The case will either get thrown out of court or else everybody will get off with a very light fine, scarcely enough to make continued operation costly to the offender." [16] In brief, the fact that the legality of arrest and search is often doubtful and the fact that a considerable financial penalty results from the requirement of bail and the confiscation of money, a car, or a telephone constitute the main reasons for the arrest and release practice.

[16] While penalties up to one year in jail or a fine of $500 are possible, Mich. Stat. Ann. §§28.533 to 28.547 (1949), the courts are not disposed to levying such penalties. In fact, because of the low sentences received, the present practice is to charge gamblers under the disorderly persons statute, Mich. Stat. Ann. §28.364 (1949), the maximum for which is 90 days or $100 fine or both, as it is known that no greater sentence would result. If the offender is engaged in gambling for a profit, he customarily receives only a money fine, and if he is a frequenter of a gambling place, he will most likely receive a suspended sentence. Detroit Police Dept., 90th Stat. Ann. Rep. 46 (1955).

Gambling and liquor offenses present greater detection difficulties than do the drunk and the transvestite. They probably are also more difficult to detect than prostitution and ordinary homosexuality, although in these cases judicial concern about undercover methods of detection has complicated the task. Gambling and liquor offenses are more likely to be the result of a syndicate operation than is prostitution of the kind observed in Detroit. Obviously the drunk and the homosexual are not involved in organized criminal activity. Although the problems of search and seizure are dealt with in detail elsewhere[17] some attention to these issues is necessary here for a proper understanding of the reasons behind the arrest and release practice used in dealing with gambling and liquor offenses.

Even a small gambling house operation, while not as well guarded as some of the larger establishments, presents investigation problems. Sometimes it is possible to approach an apartment or a house in which gambling is being conducted and to hear such activity through the door. Yet, even if hearing such an offense causes it to qualify as a misdemeanor committed in the presence of the police officer, for which a legal arrest can be made,[18] there is no attempt to prosecute upon such evidence. If the gambling was heard or even seen while the police were on private property, some judges feel that such evidence is not admissible because it was obtained while trespassing.[19] Gaining entry by means clearly lawful in order to observe and obtain evidence of the gambling is practically impossible. By statute, even entry to make a lawful arrest for a felony requires prior notice by the officer of his purpose followed by refused admittance by the occupants.[20] The Michigan law is silent on the question of the right to enter to arrest for a misdemeanor, except when necessary to prevent a breach of the peace.[21] Thus, even if there are reasonable grounds to believe that the occupants are guilty of conspiring to gamble, which is a felony, entry requires notice and refusal, by which time the money will be removed from the game. If force is used to gain entrance the evidence thus obtained is not admitted.[22]

[17] The volume on Detection of Crime.

[18] See page 236.

[19] In the volume on Detection of Crime will be found a detailed discussion of the effect of trespassing on the legality of a subsequent search.

[20] Mich. Stat. Ann. §28.880 (1949).

[21] People v. Woodward, 220 Mich. 511, 190 N.W. 721 (1922).

[22] One assistant prosecutor said it was their practice to refuse warrants "if it affirmatively appears that the officer displayed his authority as a policeman in any manner whatsoever while gaining entrance into the house." The judges hold searches illegal on the same basis.

A study of another jurisdiction concluded that 85 per cent of the arrests for

The larger gambling houses present even greater problems. In the case previously mentioned, thirty-two persons were found in the back of a shoeshine parlor. The police were fully aware of the fact that these persons had been gambling, but by the time they gained admittance the lookouts had provided adequate warning to allow all money to be removed from play. On other occasions the police have entered suspected gambling places only to find groups of twenty-five or more persons just sitting around card tables doing nothing. Police typically find it impossible to persuade anyone to sign a complaint and testify as to these gambling places. The owners make it well known to their clientele that toughs have been employed to take care of any disgruntled losers who might complain to the police.

Similar difficulties are encountered as to "blind pigs," where the doors are locked and considerable precautions are taken to insure against detection. About the only way a case can be made is for an undercover officer to gain admittance and observe the illegal sale.

Making what subsequent agencies in the process will view as a legal arrest and search is equally difficult with respect to the numbers runner. Possession of policy slips is a misdemeanor,[23] and the prosecutors and courts require that the slips actually be seen by the officer prior to arrest or search. This will rarely occur, however, since the numbers carrier, called a "bagman," carries the numbers from place to place in a brown paper bag or takes even greater precautions to conceal the slips. Even when officers do directly observe something which is the size and color of a policy slip, a warrant is often refused by a prosecutor unless the officer can state that he was close enough to have been able to actually read what was written on the slip.[24] Typically little weight is given to the fact that the experienced police officer may have developed considerable expertise in spotting policy slips.

The difficulty of investigation is compounded by the fact that police, prosecutors, and judges usually treat possession of policy

keeping gambling houses were preceded by illegal entry. Note, Philadelphia Police Practice and the Law of Arrest, 100 U. Pa. L. Rev. 1182-1216 (1952). This was in a state that did not have the exclusionary rule.

23 Mich. Stat. Ann. §28.538 (1949).

24 Officers watched a woman stop at a number of houses, each time coming out with a handful of yellow slips. When she finally saw the officers watching her, she put the slips under her blouse. She was arrested and taken to the woman's division, where a search disclosed policy slips and $14.59 in gambling money. The prosecutor refused a warrant, stating, "Those slips of paper could have been just any yellow slips of paper. I have some yellow slips of paper on my desk, but just because they are yellow and a certain size does not mean that they are bet slips. That is why I turned the recommendation down."

slips as a misdemeanor even though the mere fact of possession is substantial evidence of conspiracy, a felony,[25] since the numbers operation of necessity involves several persons acting in concert. The legal advisor to the police has emphasized this point:

> Take for instance an arrest for possession of policy slips. An officer can watch that man dealing with someone else and, instead of arresting him for possession, he can arrest him for conspiracy. Even if he doesn't know the other man, he can refer to him as John Doe, and then you've got a valid arrest . . . And if he finds in this man's possession gambling paraphernalia and he charges him with possession, academically that's a good search. But whether it will be in court is another question.

Police do not make a concentrated effort to base arrests and searches on this ground. And the prosecutors seem hesitant to conclude that the arrest can be interpreted as a felony arrest.[26]

Illegal liquor sales involve difficulties even where the contacts and sales are made outside of a building. Where the likely location for such sales is known, continued surveillance is necessary.[27] Often a search of the contact men does not produce the liquor; they usually size up the situation very carefully before reappearing with the liquor in their possession.

D. Legality of the Practice

In the situations described, there is no effort by the police to prosecute and convict the person arrested. In part the arrest and

25 The crime of conspiracy is not included in the Michigan Code, but it is a common law offense. At common law it was only a misdemeanor, but by Mich. Stat. Ann. §28.773 (1949) indictable common law offenses are made felonies, and it has been held that this includes conspiracy. People v. Smith, 296 Mich. 176, 295 N.W. 605 (1941).

26 Even if the conspiracy basis were used, not all present arrests would be legal from a probability of guilt standpoint. This is because the police, in determining who is a probable numbers carrier, use cues which have not been approved by the courts as constituting reasonable cause. For example, the police indicate that "bagmen" are spotted because they turn around and look at the police when they see them pass in their unmarked car. Yet the Michigan court has held that such a "double look" does not provide adequate grounds for search of the car. People v. Roache, 237 Mich. 215, 211 N.W. 742 (1927).

27 Said one officer: "We can't pick them up for just standing there. Therefore, we have to catch them in the act of doing something. To do this you would have to stake a man out there 24 hours a day undercover. If we do that then these people get aware of what you are doing and they suspend their operations and go to some other part of town and pick up the same thing. That way we just drive them underground." The officer making this observation was from Pontiac, where arrest for purposes other than prosecution was observed as to gamblers but not as to the liquor sellers. It appears that the liquor problem is not as great there, proportionally, as it is in Detroit; and, as the above quotation indicates, there is some desire to prevent driving this operation underground.

release practice undoubtedly reflects the fact that the methods used in detecting the offense make successful prosecution impossible. In some situations, involving minor participants in the criminal enterprise, the arrest and release practice may also reflect the view that conviction and a small money fine do not serve any very important objective.

Some of the cases could conceivably be considered as felony arrests since it is apparent that a person in possession of a sufficient quantity of numbers to indicate that he is a "bagman" is undoubtedly a member of a criminal conspiracy. Certainly there would seem to be reasonable grounds for the police to conclude that he is if consideration is given to the fact that the experienced police officer gains considerable expertise in spotting this kind of offense.[28] Typically, however, no effort is made to argue that the arrest was valid. In some other situations there clearly seems to be a lack of adequate evidence, lawfully obtained,[29] upon which to make a proper arrest.

In the cases where there are sufficient grounds to arrest and to search as an incident to the arrest, the practice then raises the issue, already discussed,[30] of whether an arrest is rendered invalid because the officer intends not to prosecute at the time the suspect is taken into custody.

[28] On experience as a factor in making felony arrests, see page 255.
[29] See discussion of this point at page 252.
[30] The law in Michigan on this point has been considered earlier. See page 404.

CHAPTER 25

Challenge of Arrest for Purposes
Other than Prosecution

The arrest and release practice involving prostitutes, transvestites, gamblers, and liquor law violators is an administrative accommodation resulting in large part from a combination of two factors: (a) the difficulty of detecting the offenses by methods which will produce evidence which will be both admissible in court and not offensive to the trial judge; and (b) the fact that conviction in the case of the offenders of these types typically results in the imposition of a small fine or other sentence which seems not particularly effective in rehabilitating the offender, deterring others, or achieving any objective beyond those served by the arrest and release practice. The cases involving intoxicated persons do not present any difficult problem of detection, but they are like the others in that conviction seems to accomplish nothing beyond what is accomplished by arrest and release.

One obvious alternative for the police in these situations would be to do nothing. In the drunk cases this would require leaving a helpless man on the street, which is an obviously undesirable course to follow. It is less clear why the police have concluded that it is impractical to adopt a policy of nonenforcement in regard to the other offenses. The frequently stated reason in prostitution cases is that the arrest and release practice does serve to prevent the syndication of prostitution and does, to a degree, control the amount of theft. There is also the advantage of medical examination and treatment of prostitutes for venereal disease. The transvestite is a nonprofessional usually left alone when in places where one expects to find transvestites, but arrested when on the street, perhaps because of the fact that such conduct is offensive to ordinary members of the community. The arrest and release practice concerning gamblers and liquor law violators seems most closely related to a desire to subject such conduct to some enforcement but an inability to do so with existing procedures because the evidence available is typically inadmissible.

Generally, existing legal sanctions do not have a substantial impact upon the arrest and release practice. Attention is given in this chapter to the extent to which the arrest and release practice is known, particularly to other agencies in the criminal justice process; to the effectiveness of certain legal remedies available to the person improperly arrested, particularly the writ of habeas corpus, the rule excluding evidence illegally obtained, and the civil action for damages; and, finally, to the impact which departmental discipline has upon the arrest and release practice.

A. Visibility of the Arrest and Release Practice

The decision to arrest for purposes other than prosecution is more conspicuous than the decision not to invoke the criminal process at all, but is less often a matter of written record than is the decision to arrest for purposes of prosecution. Those persons who are arrested and detained for a very short period and then released may not be booked, and therefore there may be no record of their having been taken into custody. This is true, for example, of frequenters of gambling places and "blind pigs." A written record is kept of those drunks who are "golden ruled," but this record is kept separate from other bookings.[1] In the case of other persons who are arrested, booked, and later released, the record is the same as that for persons who are arrested for prosecution. Therefore, one looking at the written record could not tell whether the person was taken into custody for prosecution or as part of the arrest and release practice.[2]

Although the Detroit Police Department does not officially recognize the program of arresting certain persons for purposes other than prosecution, supervisory police, the prosecutors, and the judges are aware of its existence. However, individual arrest decisions do not come to their attention, and consequently their knowledge does not necessarily extend to the specific nature or number of such arrests.

There does not appear to be any effort to define the policy systematically, even for intradepartmental purposes, nor is there any process of review and evaluation of the practices to see if they do

[1] See page 440, note 10.

[2] The bookings are all for "investigation of" some appropriate offense, just as with all arrests in which prosecution is intended but the charge has not yet been established. See page 302.

in fact achieve the desired objectives. Review of individual decisions to arrest and release is not undertaken as a matter of routine by supervisory officers. Such review as does take place at the station is often perfunctory and limited largely to ascertaining whether the persons arrested are actually prostitutes, transvestites, or within other categories of persons subject to the arrest and release procedure. In the case of gamblers or liquor law violators, the illegally obtained evidence of their guilt is deemed sufficient to bring about their detention. In the case of the transvestite, the fact that he is dressed in the attire of the opposite sex is thought to be adequate. If the supervisor makes any detailed inquiry at all, it is in prostitution cases where the true facts are more likely unclear. The "regulars" are waved on into a cell without any review, but the presence of a new face may cause the lieutenant to ask a few questions.

B. Immediate Challenge by Writ of Habeas Corpus

As is explained in earlier chapters,[3] the writ of habeas corpus is frequently used in Michigan. Its most important function is as a sort of defense-instituted initial appearance before a judicial officer, at which time bail is often set and it is determined how long the police have to either charge or release outright. But so far as arrests made for purposes other than prosecution are concerned, the writ of habeas corpus has not been an effective means of challenging such arrests. Rather, if anything, it tends to aid in making this practice a more effective sanction against those persons subjected to it.

Actually, many of the persons arrested for purposes other than prosecution do not attempt to secure their release on habeas corpus. Knowing that they will shortly be released anyway, they prefer not to go to this expense. Prostitutes in particular do not resort to the writ because they know that, even if they do, the judge will not grant their release until they have received a medical examination.

Habeas corpus is most frequently resorted to by participants in the policy racket. In fact, an application for a writ is prepared as soon as a "bagman" fails to make a stop at the appointed time. This action is prompted in part by the fact that the syndicate is not always certain whether the arrest has been made for purposes of prosecution, and also by the desire that the "bagman" be freed so that he can continue his part of the operation. But, to the ex-

3 See page 333, and Chapter 19 generally.

tent that writs are applied for, they aid the punitive aspects of arrest without prosecution. To obtain release on a habeas corpus one must not only hire an attorney but also pay the fee for a bond.[4]

During the hearing on the writ of habeas corpus, defense counsel do not attempt to challenge the lawfulness of the initial arrest. Rather their effort is directed toward obtaining the release of their client from police detention.[5] Challenge of the detention on the basis that the initial arrest was unlawful seems clearly to be appropriate under a writ of habeas corpus. It would have the advantage, from the point of view of the defendant, of entitling him to release without his having to post bail, since bail is certainly not appropriate if there are no grounds to justify taking the person into custody at all.[6] On the other hand, where the writ of habeas corpus is used to obtain the release of a person who was properly arrested, it is appropriate to condition the release upon the posting of bail. It is evident that defense counsel do not think it desirable to challenge directly the initial arrest and thus to challenge the entire arrest and release practice, perhaps because they consider the arrest and release practice preferable to the alternatives which would be used by police if the practice were successfully challenged.

C. SANCTIONS

1. *Tort action.* One possible remedy for the prostitute, transvestite, gambler, or liquor law violator who is subjected to the arrest and release process is to bring a tort action for false imprisonment against the police officer involved.[7] In some respects, the arrestee who is only detained briefly without any attempt at prosecution theoretically has a better chance of recovery than others who are arrested. There is no subsequent conviction, finding of probable cause at the preliminary examination, or waiver of pre-

---

[4] Attorneys' fees for obtaining release on a writ are often about $75. The minimum bond observed for such persons was $300, which at the 10 per cent bond fee would require $30.

[5] Mich. Stat. Ann. §27.2250 (1949).

[6] Also, challenging the arrest might provide a basis for a subsequent action for damages. A determination of lack of probable cause in a habeas corpus proceeding is res judicata in a subsequent tort action. Hammit v. Straley, 338 Mich. 587, 61 N.W.2d 641 (1953).

[7] Recovery would be possible on one or more of the following theories: (a) that the amount of evidence required by law was not present; (b) that the arrest was made by the officer for a purpose not recognized by law; (c) that the fact of release in itself is wrong, making the arrest illegal ab initio; or (d) that failure to comply with the statutory command that the arrestee be taken before a magistrate makes the arrest unlawful ab initio.

liminary examination which might impair such an action.[8] In addition, it can be argued that the fact of release itself is some evidence that there were no grounds for the arrest when it was made.

Few false arrest actions are, in fact, brought by persons arrested for purposes other than prosecution. The poor financial condition of most police officers is not the explanation, since in Detroit damages are paid by the common council or the local police organization.[9] And, at least in the case of members of a gambling syndicate, the person arrested has sufficient funds to finance such a lawsuit. Nonetheless, most of the persons who are arrested are willing to consider their arrest and the incidental costs as one of the expenses of carrying on their activity. Again this probably also reflects the attitude that the arrest and release practice, if successfully challenged, might be replaced by an enforcement practice which is more stringent. The civil actions for damages that are brought are usually by persons who are mistakenly assumed by the police to be within one of the categories subject to the arrest and release practice, but who are, in fact, respectable members of the community. Although it apparently happens infrequently, this could occur where police mistakenly conclude that a woman is a prostitute.

It is doubtful whether the golden rule drunk would have any basis for recovery even if he did bring a civil action for damages, which he does not do. In most situations, the release is to his advantage rather than detriment.[10] Money damages would be appropriate, of course, if the man arrested as a drunk was in fact not drunk and by his release was deprived of an opportunity to clear himself by appearing before a judicial officer and establishing his innocence.[11] Beyond this kind of case, if the practice is wrong it is only because the decision to release is made by the police rather than by a prosecutor or judge. Assuming this to be so, money damages might be given to those released in order to advance the proper administration of criminal justice, but it has been forcefully argued that this would be inappropriate.[12]

[8] See page 413 on the effect of these upon a false arrest action.

[9] The latter group pays most claims, particularly those in which the illegality of the police action is most evident, and thereby prevents them from reaching the council, where the police might be criticized. For more on this see page 424.

[10] The point is well made in Bohlen and Shulman, Effect of Subsequent Misconduct upon a Lawful Arrest, 28 Colum. L. Rev. 841, 854 (1928). It is there noted that no cases on the subject were found in which any such distinction between an innocent man and a guilty man was drawn.

[11] This matter is discussed in detail at page 405.

[12] "If our society and the criminal law have developed sufficiently to be willing and able to punish official misconduct, then there is no room in our tort law for

2. *Exclusion of evidence obtained by illegal arrest.* The extent to which the exclusionary rule itself causes the arrest and release practice is not entirely clear. It is apparent that the exclusionary rule is not a deterrent to improper police practices in situations where the police have no desire to prosecute and convict the person who is arrested. In some of the situations in which police use the arrest and release procedure, it is obvious that they assume that prosecution and conviction would serve no very worthwhile purpose, however easy they may be to accomplish. This is true in regard to drunks and probably also in regard to prostitutes, who customarily are only given a small money fine. In these instances, the threat to exclude evidence illegally obtained has no effect upon the practice.

In other situations, such as organized gambling, police may desire to obtain a conviction, yet that objective is difficult to achieve considering the methods which must be used to insure that the necessary physical evidence will be admissible. Some trial judges refuse to sustain an arrest unless the officer has actually seen what is written on the betting slip, a requirement which police say is impossible to comply with. In this situation police have three alternatives: (a) to expend the addition time, effort, and resources necessary to produce admissible evidence; (b) to do nothing; or (c) to subject the conduct to some enforcement but not prosecution and conviction. It seems evident that the exclusionary rule can operate to induce conformity with rules controlling police conduct only where the objective of prosecution and conviction is sufficiently important to justify the expenditure of the resources necessary to make it possible to develop and use methods which will produce admissible evidence. It is also apparent that when the trial judge by his sentencing seems to dilute the effect of conviction, or by his interpretations seems to make it excessively difficult to conform to the proper rules of police conduct, the police will tend to use alternatives to prosecution and conviction such as the arrest and release procedure.[13]

---

anomalous civil liability to a plaintiff who has suffered no harm from the misconduct." Bohlen and Shulman, Effect of Subsequent Misconduct upon a Lawful Arrest, 28 Colum. L. Rev. 841, 854 (1928). This article contains an excellent discussion of this point at 843-846.

[13] Some have questioned the desirability of the exclusionary rule on this basis: "Not one shred of evidence has been discovered to indicate that the police of Ohio and New York, where use of evidence is permitted, are worse behaved than the police of Michigan and Illinois, where it is excluded. But to the contrary, there is ample and persuasive evidence that the rule of exclusion, academically designed for improvement of police methods, has in practical application conduced to serious police misbehavior. If it did not actually beget the 'tip-over raid,' it nurtured that vicious practice to its evil florescence." Waite, Evidence — Police Regulation by Rules of Evidence, 42 Mich. L. Rev. 679, 685 (1944).

3. *Departmental discipline.* Departmental discipline is not an effective sanction against arrests for purposes other than prosecution of the kind described, since these practices are carried out with the acquiescence of supervisory officers of the department. Disciplinary action, when taken, is limited to instances in which the arresting officer has used poor judgment in deciding whom to subject to this process. This is not likely to occur with respect to homosexuals, gamblers, and liquor law violators because their identity is usually obvious. With prostitutes the process of selection is more difficult, and an officer may be reprimanded if he fails to use the minimum standards which the police generally use in determining who is a prostitute. Even if the officer does conform to customary practice, he may still be disciplined on occasion. For example, when a Negro woman is arrested as a suspected prostitute because she is found on the street at night in a particular area in the company of a white man, there is a high probability that the woman is a prostitute. This kind of arrest was made on one occasion, but the woman was released at the station after the lieutenant became convinced that her protestations of innocence were genuine. The woman subsequently complained to the NAACP and her congressman, with the result that inquiries were directed to the police commissioner. Because of the external pressure, it was indicated that the matter might be referred to the police trial board unless the arresting officer could give an acceptable explanation.

Arrest in Criminal Justice Administration:
Important Unresolved Issues

. . . I cannot concur without pointing out that the courts have been left to make rules and apply constitutional standards with little, if any, real knowledge or guidance regarding the difficulties which face the police in solving such crimes in our crowded metropolitan centers. Moreover, Congress and the legislatures have failed to make appropriate inquiry and statutory provision to meet the situation.

> Judge Lumbard, concurring
> in *Williams v. Fay*,
> 323 F.2d 65, 70 (2d Cir. 1963)

It is fair to say that courts have in fact been left without adequate knowledge or guidance concerning the problems which face police, particularly in the large cities, in the enforcement of the criminal law. It is equally appropriate to conclude that police lack an adequate understanding of the obligation which the courts have to insure that law enforcement methods conform to standards essential for the maintenance of a democratic society. And, as Judge Lumbard points out, Congress and the state legislatures have made very little effort to deal adequately with the range of issues which the arrest decision involves.

Much of the current difficulty results from the lack of adequate meaningful communication between the agencies which share the responsibility for effective and fair administration. The police feel, and not without some basis in fact, that courts do not really understand many of their problems. This results in part from the kind of sifting of information which occurs before cases reach the appellate court. The usual criminal appeal is characterized by a total reliance by counsel upon cases decided in the past, without any effort to present to the appellate court an adequate factual picture of the law enforcement context out of which the issue has arisen. Too often prosecuting attorneys proceed in litigation without even consulting the police agency to learn how the issue appears from an enforcement point of view.

On the other hand, the responsibility of the judiciary for the fair administration of the criminal law is seldom adequately understood by the police agency. The court is often thought of as a roadblock in the way of enforcement rather than as an agency sharing responsibility for the development and maintenance of a fair and effective enforcement system. Police agencies frequently seem to expend more effort in attacking judicial decisions than in trying to develop policies and practices which will achieve both effective enforcement and conformity with constitutional safeguards. In part this may result from the fact that courts seldom take the time or have the means to communicate effectively to the police what a particular decision is, the reason for it, or the implications of the decision upon police practice. As a consequence, police seldom understand the decision or the objective of the court in the particular case, and the decision does not have the desired effect upon arrest practice.

Some of the difficulty in current administration results from the long-time adherence to certain "ideals" of enforcement without serious attention to whether they are at all achievable under present circumstances. Thus some appellate courts continue to stress that use of the arrest warrant is the preferred method for making an arrest, apparently oblivious to the fact that meaningful judicial review of the evidence prior to the issuance of the warrant is unknown in many localities. Continued adherence to the myth of full enforcement of the law results in the police exercising wide discretion without acknowledging that it occurs and without attempting to explain and re-evaluate systematically the criteria by which the discretion is exercised.

Too little attention has been given to discovering how procedures work in practice and, particularly, whether they satisfactorily achieve all the objectives which they are designed to achieve. The rule excluding evidence illegally obtained may in some situations have the effect of encouraging illegal action by the police rather than deterring it. This does not mean that the exclusionary rule ought to be discarded or that courts ought not to assume responsibility for controlling police practices, but only that the unanticipated and undesired consequences which occur in practice ought to be discovered and that attention should be given to devising new and more adequate ways of preventing these consequences.

The lack of communication, the perpetuation of "ideals" without sufficient regard to their feasibility, and the continuation of rules, particularly sanctions, without adequate evaluation of their consequences in practice, combine to cause difficulty for criminal justice administration.

A. Important Problem Areas

The effort in this volume has been to give systematic attention to some important aspects of the arrest decision which are inadequately understood, or at least inadequately dealt with, in current criminal justice administration. The objective is not the indictment of police, prosecutors, or courts for their inadequacies, but a sympathetic understanding of the tasks which they face and particularly the problems which develop as they attempt together to maintain an ongoing system of criminal justice administration.

The arrest decision gives rise to a number of issues, of which the following appear to be the most important and the most in need of attention:

1. *Police discretion.* It is commonly assumed that the police can, or at least should, fully enforce the criminal law by arresting all violators. However, this is clearly not possible in current practice. One of the major objectives of the criminal justice process must be that of determining what criminal conduct is sufficiently serious to justify the use of limited enforcement resources against it. But the responsibility of the various agencies in the process for the exercise of this discretion and for the control of its exercise is, at best, ambiguous.

The intake of the criminal process is in large measure determined by the manner in which arrest decisions are made. Instances of discretionary enforcement at the arrest stage are of obvious importance to the criminal justice system, to the individuals affected, and to society as a whole. Many of the policy questions involved are a great deal more basic than many others which have received sustained attention by legislatures, courts, and administrative agencies. For example, members of certain racial groups, such as Negroes, are in many instances held to a lesser standard of accountability than are majority groups in the same community. Assaults between Negroes often do not lead to arrest because they are assumed to be a common method of settling disputes in the Negro community, while comparable assaults between whites are viewed as serious criminal behavior. Concern over civil rights in law enforcement commonly centers on police brutality against minority groups, a practice which no one would condone. But attention is seldom given to the more difficult and more basic question of whether it is desirable social policy to hold the minority group to a lesser standard of accountability than the majority group. Perhaps no more difficult question can be asked of a law enforcement agency. Yet it is an issue seldom discussed, and it is in fact uncommon for any agency even to acknowledge responsibility for any concern with it.

Another question which has not been given any sustained attention is whether police ought to take into account individual characteristics of a suspect when deciding whether to invoke the criminal process. In contrast, it is common to acknowledge the importance of individual characteristics in deciding upon an appropriate sentence, and efforts have been made to identify those characteristics which should be considered at the sentencing stage. Although this kind of information is less often available at the arrest stage, there are cases in which it is known that the suspect is a highly respected member of the community who will be greatly damaged by prosecution or even by arrest should prosecution not follow. Whether police are properly charged with balancing the gain to law enforcement which will result from invocation of the process against the harm to the particular person involved is a matter seldom dealt with, despite its quite obvious importance.

Issues involving competing law enforcement objectives are also largely ignored. The granting of immunity from arrest to some offenders in return for information about other offenses and offenders is a common police practice. However, this issue is seldom dealt with by legislatures or courts, and police rarely re-examine the practice thoroughly to insure that it is achieving sufficiently worthwhile law enforcement objectives.

Notwithstanding the great importance and significance of these and other instances of discretionary enforcement, the police have failed to evaluate carefully such enforcement policies or even to acknowledge that such practices exist.[1] Rather, most departments attempt to maintain the existing stereotype of the police as ministerial officers who enforce all of the laws, while they actually engage in a broad range of discretionary enforcement.[2]

1 Unique in this respect is the following recent declaration of policy by the Chicago department, published in a document intended for the information of members of the department and the general public: "The police must necessarily exercise discretion in the enforcement of the laws bcause of the limited resources available to them, because of the inherent ambiguity of some laws, and because there are often a number of acceptable and more effective ways of accomplishing the purpose of the law.

"Enforcement must be selective to be most effective in decreasing the number of crimes. It must be selective as to time and place; it must be directed at the locations of greatest frequency during the hours of the day, day of the week, and season of the year of greatest frequency. It must also be selective as to the relative importance of crimes." Chicago Police Department, On This We Stand 2 (1963).

2 Most police officials have long taken a defensive position with regard to the crime problem generally. An increase in crime is viewed as a mark of police failure,

It is understandable that a police administrator may be willing to have the myth of full enforcement continue. Full enforcement is consistent with impartiality, while acknowledged discretionary enforcement may be challenged [3] as unfair, inconsistent, or arbitrary. The image of full enforcement raises less of a public relations problem than does the image of the police agency as a formulator of enforcement policy. Finally, police training is an easier task in a department committed to the facade of full enforcement than in one in which it is assumed that police officers must share some responsibility for making decisions with important social implications.

Appellate cases concerned with good faith instances of discretionary enforcement are almost nonexistent; nor has the problem received careful attention from the legislatures. Existing legislation has, if anything, contributed to the uncertainty. Neither in the definition of what conduct is criminal nor in the allocation of enforcement resources to police agencies have legislatures given explicit attention to the need for discretionary enforcement. Thus the practice of unlimited discretion continues without any accountability and without any effort from the law itself to define the nature of the discretion which exists, to indicate the agency which should bear the responsibility for its exercise, or to furnish norms to guide and control the discretion thus exercised.

There are ways of recognizing police discretion and of controlling its exercise. Legislatures can give explicit attention to police discretion and prescribe criteria to guide the exercise of that discretion.[4] This is the trend at the sentencing and correctional stages of the criminal process, and there is no reason to believe that this sort

---

despite the fact that there is little evidence that police efficiency and the commission of many crimes, such as murder, are necessarily related. Therefore, it is not surprising that the police feel they are being made to carry responsibility for a level of enforcement above that which is physically possible. See Goldstein, Police Discretion: The Ideal Versus the Real, 23 Pub. Admin. Rev. 140, 143-144 (1963).

[3] E.g., Bargain City U.S.A., Inc. v. Dilworth, 29 U.S.L. Week 2002 (Pa. C.P., June 10, 1960).

[4] Apparently no such statutes are to be found presently. There are analogous provisions, however, such as those delegating powers of suspension and dispensation to administrative agencies charged with economic regulation. Also, the Model Penal Code would grant discretion to a judge not to proceed against what are characterized "De Minimis Infractions." Model Penal Code §2.12 (Proposed Official Draft, 1962).

The legislature might clarify the police task by identifying certain desired objectives of the discretionary enforcement program or by indicating what special procedures are appropriate as to certain forms of criminal conduct. For example, a recent enactment in California allows a peace officer to release where "the person was arrested for intoxication only, and no further proceedings are desirable." Cal. Penal Code §849 (1961).

of legislation would be less appropriate at the arrest stage. Courts can subject police discretion to the kind of review which sometimes occurs in regard to economic regulatory agencies. The development of an "administrative law" in the enforcement field is as important as it is in the field of economic regulation, but while the one has been given sustained attention, the other has been completely neglected. Greater legislative and judicial recognition of the importance of police discretion might in turn encourage police administrators to acknowledge its importance and attempt to devise methods of meaningful evaluation of existing policies.

The obvious complexity of the task of dealing adequately with police discretion at the arrest stage makes it all the more important that a start be made immediately.

2. *Evidentiary requirements for arrest.* Another primary task of the criminal justice process is that of identifying those persons who have in fact engaged in criminal conduct and to do this by methods which minimize interference with those who are innocent. Although the importance of this function is universally recognized, attention to it by legislatures and appellate courts has been sporadic.

Existing arrest law focuses primarily upon the amount of evidence needed to justify taking custody of a suspect. Many state statutes contain "in presence," "reasonable grounds," or similar tests, and the great majority of appellate litigation concerns the application of these standards to a variety of fact situations. There are, however, important unresolved problems because some significant, recurring situations are seldom dealt with in appellate litigation.

Prior to *Mapp v. Ohio*,[5] there was no effective way, in many states, of challenging the validity of an arrest in the criminal case. Even in states which had long recognized the exclusionary rule, courts were required to face only a limited number of the situations which confront police in day-to-day practice. Until the recent case of *Wong Sun v. United States*,[6] only physical evidence found incident to an arrest could be challenged. Therefore, only crimes involving physical evidence, such as narcotics, were likely to raise the issue of the lawfulness of the arrest. As a consequence there is a profusion of cases on the question of when information from a narcotics informant is sufficient to justify an arrest. But there is little guidance on such questions as when, if ever, an officer can arrest one or more than one member of a group of suspects each with physical characteristics fitting the description given by an eyewitness, or when an officer can make a felony arrest on the

5 367 U.S. 643, 81 Sup. Ct. 1684, 6 L. Ed. 2d 1081 (1961).
6 371 U.S. 471, 83 Sup. Ct. 407, 9 L. Ed. 2d 441 (1963).

basis of suspicious conduct which he observes. These questions, seldom considered, confront law enforcement officers daily.[7]

There is doubt as to whether the appellate judicial system is really capable of systematic development and re-evaluation of detailed rules to govern the conduct of law enforcement officers. If *Wong Sun* is ultimately broadly interpreted and generally followed, it will have the incidental benefit of creating the opportunity for appellate courts to review arrest procedures in a broader range of cases; arrests which do not lead to the discovery of physical evidence but do result in the suspect making an admission can also be challenged.[8] Even so, it is questionable whether appellate courts can fully develop detailed rules in a system where only the defendant is given the right to appeal. Indeed, even in those jurisdictions where the state can seek appellate review of a trial court order suppressing evidence, the opportunities presented to the higher courts are likely to be few. Because of the limited resources of his office, the prosecutor obviously cannot appeal in every case in which there is some basis for questioning the trial judge's decision that the police conduct was improper. The prosecutor, in selecting cases for appeal, is likely to choose the "big" cases, those involving serious crimes and the subject of greatest publicity. From the police standpoint, however, the need for clarification may be much greater as to enforcement practices used against relatively minor offenses, such as misdemeanor gambling.

Closer attention to the evidentiary requirements for arrest seems more likely if legislatures adequately articulate the broad policy objectives[9] and encourage, or perhaps require, enforcement agen-

[7] Compounding the difficulty is the fact that the status of many existing state cases remains uncertain. This is because it is not clear to what extent federal precedents on the issue of what constitutes grounds for arrest are now binding on state courts. See the language from the Ker case, note 9 *infra*. Compare: "We find nothing in *Mapp v. Ohio* to indicate that as a result of that decision the states are bound to follow the federal requirements of reasonable and probable cause instead of their own." People v. Tyler, 193 Cal. App. 2d 728, 734, 14 Cal. Rptr. 610, 613 (1961). See also People v. Mickelson, 30 Cal. Rptr. 18, 380 P.2d 658 (Sup. Ct. 1963).

[8] However, if courts read Wong Sun as not barring statements received after arrest, but only those obtained as a result of "oppressive circumstances," then the circumstances for inquiring into the lawfulness of arrest will again be limited. Wong Sun does lend itself to this narrower interpretation, and some courts have so viewed the case. E.g., United States v. Burke, 215 F. Supp. 508 (D. Mass. 1963).

[9] If, for example, it is thought desirable to authorize some form of brief detention on grounds less than those needed for arrest, this may be best accomplished by legislation, as an officer attempting to justify such a stopping in court will usually characterize it as an actual arrest, the only generally recognized detention privilege.

Another possibility, which was suggested several years ago, is that legislatures should try to identify certain specific fact situations which recur with some frequency and which are viewed as adequate grounds for arrest. Ploscowe, A Modern Law of Arrest, 39 Minn. L. Rev. 473, 475-476 (1955). Although most of the refinements of arrest law will probably always have to come from the courts which deal with the

cies to consider, develop, and publish specific rules which they will follow in practice and which they can be called upon to defend successfully or to change if an individual suspect challenges the propriety of the rule as applied in his case.

3. *In-custody investigation.* Most of the attention which has been given to in-custody investigation has centered on the issue of whether it is desirable to allow enforcement officers to convict a suspect "out of his own mouth," and upon the closely related question of whether the danger of "third-degree" methods is so great that in-custody interrogation should be prohibited. However, much of the current uncertainty about the propriety of in-custody investigation is attributable to the fact that too little attention has been given to one very basic question: Is it ever proper to arrest a suspect on the basis of evidence which is insufficient, without further investigation, for prosecution? If arrest is proper only when there is sufficient evidence to charge, then in-custody investigation is not a prerequisite to the charging decision. If, on the other hand, there are recurring situations in which it is proper to make an arrest but improper to charge without additional evidence, there is inevitably going to be pressure to conduct an in-custody investigation.[10]

In current practice in-custody investigation is common despite

---

details of specific instances of arrest, such legislation might afford added guidance to the police on those kinds of cases which have not reached the appellate courts.

In addition, data could be collected to identify situations in which arrest and search should be allowed. Legislative action could be taken on the basis of this, authorizing arrest and search in cases in which they are presently in jeopardy of being declared contrary to the guarantees of the federal Constitution. The most interesting question raised by Mapp v. Ohio, 367 U.S. 643, 81 Sup. Ct. 1684, 6 L. Ed. 2d 1081 (1961), holding the constitutional prohibition of unreasonable searches and seizures enforceable against the states through the Fourteenth Amendment, is whether the states still have some leeway in defining their own laws of arrest, search, and seizure. See Traynor, Mapp v, Ohio at Large in the Fifty States, 1962 Duke L.J. 319, 320. Although the matter is still in doubt, the Supreme Court's most recent pronouncement on the question is that "the States are not thereby precluded from developing workable rules governing arrests, searches and seizures to meet 'the practical demands of effective criminal investigation and law enforcement' in the States," and that the governing standard "implies no derogation of uniformity in applying federal constitutional guarantees but is only a recognition that conditions and circumstances vary just as do investigative and enforcement techniques." Ker v. California, 374 U.S. 23, 34, 83 Sup. Ct. 1623, 1630, 10 L. Ed. 2d 726, 738 (1963). A state legislature, with its ability to investigate, hold hearings, and otherwise bring about the collection of a vast amount of relevant data, may be in a much better position to establish the existence of "conditions and circumstances" justifying arrest in certain specific situations than is a court, which is limited to information which is brought before it by the litigants or is properly a subject of judicial notice.

[10] Obvious though this is, analysis of this kind is seldom to be found. Exceptional in this regard is the case of Goldsmith v. United States, 277 F.2d 335 (D.C. Cir. 1960). However, one commentator has denominated Goldsmith as "utterly indefensible." Broeder, Wong Sun v. United States: A Study in Faith and Hope, 42 Neb. L. Rev. 483, 493 n.40 (1963).

ambiguity about its propriety under varying circumstances. State appellate courts seldom face the issue directly,[11] and state legislatures have typically employed an ambiguous requirement that the police bring a suspect before a magistrate "forthwith," "within a reasonable time," or "without unnecessary delay." These phrases do not clearly reflect a legislative judgment on the underlying policy questions involved.

The dilemma is easy to state. There is a widely held view that conviction based on the results of in-custody interrogation is an undesirable law enforcement method because of the risks involved.[12] There is at the same time a prevalent view that a fairly conducted in-custody interrogation is both proper and indeed essential under the conditions existing in current criminal justice administration.[13] The ambiguity of current legislative and judicial formulas reflects an unwillingness to confront the issue directly.

Despite the fact that police detention has received considerable attention in recent years, little is known about some essential aspects of the problem. For example, it is sometimes erroneously assumed that, in current practice, the initial appearance of the arrested person before the magistrate enables the magistrate to review the propriety both of the arrest and of any prior or subsequent detention. This is not the case. There is seldom, if ever, any inquiry into the propriety of the arrest, and some period of police detention has already taken place. Only a few states have expressly provided for a remand system by which an arrested person is promptly brought before a magistrate, who decides whether and for how

[11] This is partly because tort actions challenging instances of such detention by the police are rare. And, because the states have not adopted the Mallory sanction of excluding statements obtained during illegal detention, the defendant's conviction is not likely to be affected by his detention after arrest. (Since the observations in Michigan the court there did adopt a Mallory-type sanction in the Hamilton case [People v. Hamilton, 359 Mich. 410, 102 N.W.2d 738 (1960)], but since then appears to have abandoned it. See page 330.) Of course, the voluntariness of a confession may depend in part upon the length of time the individual was held prior to the confession, but it is not necessary for the court to decide that the detention was proper before finding the statement voluntary or to decide that the detention was improper before concluding that the confession is inadmissible.

[12] There is, of course, the risk of a coerced confession which the defendant may not be able to challenge successfully later. See Douglas, The Means and the End, 1959 Wash. U. L.Q. 103, 114. But there are other risks as well, such as the possibility that even an innocent man may give a false alibi. Borchard, Convicting the Innocent 373-374 (1932).

[13] "Despite modern advances in the technology of crime detection, offenses frequently occur about which things cannot be made to speak. And where there cannot be found innocent human witnesses to such offenses nothing remains — if police investigation is not to be balked before it has fairly begun — but to seek out possibly guilty witnesses and ask them questions . . ." Culombe v. Connecticut, 367 U.S. 568, 571, 81 Sup. Ct. 1860, 1861, 6 L. Ed. 2d 1037, 1040 (1961).

long he may be kept in police custody before being given an opportunity to obtain his release on bail.[14] Informal remand procedures
do develop, as in Detroit, where it is common for the suspect to be
brought before a judge on a writ of habeas corpus for a determination of whether the police can continue to keep him in custody. In
such situations it might seem logical for the magistrate to decide
(a) whether the arrest was lawful, (b) whether further in-custody
investigation is needed to decide whether to charge or release the
suspect, and (c) if further in-custody investigation is needed, how
much additional time is reasonably required. In practice, however, there is no judicial inquiry into whether the arrest was lawful,
there is almost complete reliance upon the police as to the need for
further investigation, and the total time allowed is usually set by
rule of thumb as seventy-two hours without regard to the circumstances of the individual case. If the Detroit experience is typical,
then it appears that judges are no more likely to exercise supervisory control over police at the initial appearance than they are in
connection with the issuance of arrest warrants.

To the extent that observation of current practice affords an adequate basis for generalization, it seems to lead to the conclusion
that some form of interrogation of suspects is necessary in at least
certain types of cases. The questions which need to be decided
then become: What agency or agencies ought to be given responsibility for such interrogation, at what stage of the process, and
under what kinds of controls?

4. *Access to counsel and other controls on in-custody investigation.* The dilemma involved in deciding upon the propriety of
in-custody investigation is manifest in the equally difficult issue of
early access to counsel in the police station. It is said, on the one
hand, that allowing counsel during this time will impede the investigation[15] and, on the other hand, that a defendant needs a lawyer most immediately after arrest.[16] Although it has been suggested that there must be some "middle ground" which "will give
reasonable protection against improper procedures and still permit
fruitful police inquiry," [17] it is not clear how this balancing of
interests can best be accomplished.

If, as often assumed, a lawyer will always advise his client not to

14 Del. Code Ann. tit. 11, §1911 (1953); N.H. Rev. Stat. Ann. §§594:20, 594:22,
594:23 (1955); R.I. Gen. Laws §12-7-13 (1957). The remand provision is a part of
the Uniform Arrest Act, adopted in these three states with some minor variations.

15 "[A]ny lawyer worth his salt will tell the suspect in no uncertain terms to make
no statement to police under any circumstances." Watts v. Indiana, 338 U.S. 49,
59, 69 Sup. Ct. 1357, 1358, 93 L. Ed. 1801, 1809 (1949) (Jackson, J., concurring).

16 Allison, He Needs a Lawyer Now, 42 J. Am. Jud. Soc. 113 (1958).

17 Lumbard, The Administration of Criminal Justice: Some Problems and Their
Resolution, 49 A.B.A.J. 840, 843 (1963).

talk to the police, then the right to counsel at the station and any police right to conduct an in-custody interrogation are incompatible. This compounds the difficulty and is, no doubt, why courts, including the Supreme Court of the United States, have refrained from confronting the question squarely.[18]

If in-custody interrogation is proper under some circumstances, then it would appear that either access to counsel must be denied for some period of time or else counsel will have to view his function as not necessarily involving routine advice to all suspects to refuse to answer any questions. There is some evidence that the latter alternative is not completely unrealistic. Cases were noted in Milwaukee in which a suspect gave a statement to the police with the full approval of counsel, who was present during the questioning. Since the police in current practice do have an important role in the determination of whether to prosecute, how serious an offense to charge, and how serious a penalty may be imposed, such cooperation may often be beneficial to the suspect. However, it is questionable whether lawyers, who regularly advise their clients to plead guilty because it is in their interest to do so, will generally advise cooperation with the police for the same reason. For one thing, defense counsel is unlikely to have sufficient information at this earlier stage of the process to know whether cooperation or silence is the best course.

A large part of the problem of access to counsel at the police station concerns what provision, if any, should be made for providing the indigent suspect with counsel at this early stage in the process. Certainly most suspects lack sufficient funds to hire an attorney. "[I]t can be forcefully argued that if [the] law permits a financially able person promptly to secure a lawyer, but does not permit an indigent person to do so, 'there is lacking that equality demanded by the Fourteenth Amendment.'"[19] But, because of the incom-

---

[18] Previous to the recent case of Escobedo v. Illinois, 378 U.S. 478, 84 Sup. Ct. 1758, 12 L. Ed. 2d 977 (1964), but subsequent to a number of earlier cases in which the issue of counsel at the police station had been raised before the Supreme Court, it was noted that the question of when the right to counsel begins remains "as unilluminated after the Supreme Court's recent decisions as before." Kamisar and Choper, The Right to Counsel in Minnesota: Some Field Findings and Legal-Policy Observations, 48 Minn. L. Rev. 1, 33 (1963). The court's treatment of the problem in Escobedo still leaves the question in considerable doubt. See page 390 *supra*, note 39, and page 395 *supra*, note 63.

[19] Id. at 59. The reference is to Douglas v. California, 372 U.S. 353, 357-358, 83 Sup. Ct. 814, 816-817, 9 L. Ed. 2d 811, 814-815 (1963).

The pattern of the state legislation is discussed in some detail in Comment, 1962 U. Ill. L.F. 641. Although some of the statutes are not entirely clear, most of them seem to contemplate that the right arises immediately, and the only basis for denial of an opportunity to consult with counsel ever expressed by statute is where escape of the prisoner is "imminent." Id. at 649-650. Although these statutes are seldom the subject of judicial interpretation, some courts have made substantial inroads

patibility of the two positions set forth above, there is no great demand to furnish counsel for indigents immediately after arrest. The unfortunate consequence is that advice of counsel to indigent suspects is completely lacking, when it is apparent that a great deal of assistance could be furnished a suspect if counsel were available to do no more than explain to him what his rights are and what alternatives he has, and to leave to the suspect the decision, based on the facts of the particular case, of whether to cooperate with the enforcement authorities. Providing counsel at an early stage for the indigent offender may result in substantial financial cost, but this seems a less difficult problem than that relating to the compatibility between access to counsel and reasonable in-custody interrogation. Some efforts are being made to provide for early access to counsel,[20] and the problem is receiving increased attention.[21]

Little attention has been given to other possible controls and safeguards on in-custody interrogation, such as requiring that a full record be kept of the circumstances of the arrest and the detention. Booking, a step provided for in police manuals but ordinarily not expressly required by statute, has the advantage for the suspect of giving visibility to the fact that he has been arrested and is being detained. Failure to follow the usual booking process usually occurs when police believe that this will operate to their advantage. Of course, in one sense booking may also operate to the disadvantage of the suspect, since it will constitute a record of his involvement with the police. To deal with this problem, a few states have provided for the destruction or return of certain records under some circumstances, and some have also placed limitations upon access to these records.[22] Beyond these partial attempts, however,

---

upon what is apparently stated by statute to be an unqualified right. E.g., People v. Escobedo, 28 Ill. 2d 52, 190 N.E.2d 825 (1963), reversed on constitutional grounds, Escobedo v. Illinois, 378 U.S. 478, 84 Sup. Ct. 1758, 12 L. Ed. 2d 977 (1964). Even where this has not occurred, the sanctions provided do not induce strict compliance. A few of the statutes provide a civil remedy in lieu of or in addition to criminal prosecution, which is the usual sanction prescribed. Comment, *supra*, at 650-651.

20 "We are informed that . . . [the California] public defender often enters a case while the accused is in police custody and before preliminary hearing and that these practices have in no way disrupted or adversely affected the orderly prosecution of criminal cases in that state." Attorney General's Committee, Report on Poverty and the Administration of Federal Criminal Justice 38 (1963).

21 The American Bar Foundation has recently undertaken a nationwide study of representation of indigent defendants, in cooperation with the American Bar Association and other groups. See 1962 A.B.A. Rep. 468. The project includes field research in several states. For an article using some of the data from the project, see Kamisar and Choper, The Right to Counsel in Minnesota: Some Field Findings and Legal-Policy Observations, 48 Minn. L. Rev. 1 (1963).

22 On these statutes and other record-keeping problems, see Comment, 1963 U. Ill. L.F. 685.

little has been done. Largely unexplored is the basic question of precisely what kind of records, with what distribution, and of what permanency are appropriate.

There are other possible methods of control. Requiring police to notify a suspect of his right to remain silent is frequently suggested. This is common practice in some police departments but is not done in others, and opinion differs on whether such a warning seriously interferes with interrogation. It has also been suggested that, either through the use of a neutral observer or by dividing responsibility for custody and investigation, it would be possible to prevent coercive questioning or to increase the opportunity to prove such practices in court. Use of observers is commonly resisted by those who give advice on proper and effective methods of interrogation. But in Milwaukee many interrogations are open to members of the press, and this fact seems to contribute to a general confidence in the propriety of police methods. Separate responsibility for custody and for investigation is common in current practice only as to those who are further detained after initial appearance because of their inability to make bail.

5. *Judicial participation in the arrest decision.* While police need not obtain a warrant before making an arrest in felony cases or for misdemeanors committed in their presence, procuring a warrant of arrest from a judicial officer has long been considered the ideal way of invoking the criminal justice process. One court has gone so far as to say that "while the ease and practicability of obtaining the warrant of arrest" does not alone render an arrest without warrant invalid, the "availability of the safeguards afforded by an impartial, judicial magistrate is a factor bearing on reasonable, probable cause." [23] And the view has recently been expressed by one commentator that it is "imperative" that the fourth amendment be read as requiring a warrant for arrest except in limited situations in which the exigencies of the situation do not allow taking this step in advance of arrest.[24]

The assumption apparently is that greater protection for the individual is afforded by the warrant procedure, since an arrest will be made only if an impartial judicial officer, upon careful evaluation of the evidence presented to him, determines that adequate grounds for an arrest exist. But, at least in Kansas, Michigan, and Wisconsin, it is clear that the warrant process does not serve this function. Rather, the decision is made in the office of the prosecu-

[23] Clay v. United States, 239 F.2d 196, 204 (5th Cir. 1956). See also Carter v. United States, 314 F.2d 386 (5th Cir. 1963); Hopper v. United States, 267 F.2d 904 (9th Cir. 1959).

[24] Broeder, Wong Sun v. United States, A Study in Faith and Hope, 42 Neb. L. Rev. 483, 501 (1963).

tor and the judge routinely signs the arrest warrant without any independent inquiry into the facts and circumstances of the individual case.

Another common assumption is that, even in cases where the arrest is made without warrant, the initial appearance before the magistrate achieves a judicial review of the grounds for arrest. In fact, while the initial appearance does serve as an occasion for setting bail and perhaps for notice to the accused of the charge against him, it does not, in current practice, involve a judicial review of the legality of the arrest.

The difference between the stated ideal and the practice raises the question of the extent to which it is practical to structure the system so as to involve the judge at the arrest stage of the process. The reasons why judicial officers have abdicated to the police and the prosecutor their authority to determine on a case-by-case basis whether an arrest warrant shall issue and whether an arrest without a warrant was lawful are not entirely clear. In urban areas it may be explainable in part by the pressure of other demands on the available time of the judges. Also, many judges feel that other agencies can adequately perform the task. They may also rationalize this abdication on the ground that the trial of contested cases, which they view as their primary responsibility, does afford some opportunity to review arrest procedures.[25]

It is apparent that a choice must be made. If it is desirable for the trial judge to be involved in the arrest decision, new ways must be developed to make effective judicial participation feasible at this stage. The obvious alternative is to abandon the "ideal" of judicial participation in the arrest decision and structure the system in a way which will clearly give primary responsibility for these decisions to the police or prosecutor. To say this is not inconsistent with the view that the trial judge is the one with responsibility for insuring that the total criminal justice process, from detection to final release from parole, is fair, effective, and consistent. This can be achieved without the actual involvement of the judge in the arrest decision; the responsibility for fashioning arrest policies

[25] For all practical purposes, however, this review is limited to situations in which there has been a search incident to the arrest.

One consequence of the fact that judges are not interested in making arrest decisions in the first instance is that a judge may suppress evidence by declaring illegal an arrest based upon a warrant previously signed *pro forma*. Such an occurrence has been observed in one jurisdiction (not one of those studied here) on more than one occasion. Although it is common for warrants there to be prepared by the police without the concurrence of the prosecutor, many judges still tend to issue warrants as a matter of course. A subsequent hearing on a motion to suppress before the same judge may result in his deciding, in effect, that he should not have issued the warrant.

could be expressly given to police and prosecutors, and an opportunity for judicial review of those policies and their application in specific cases could be afforded, as is done in regard to other administrative agencies. This might provide a more effective and meaningful judicial control over the arrest decision and, at the same time, encourage participation by enforcement agencies in the development and articulation of enforcement policies.

6. *The exclusion of evidence as a sanction against improper police practice.* Although the trial judiciary has not been involved in a meaningful way in the arrest decision at either the warrant issuance or the initial appearance stage, it has had to decide the validity of arrests in cases in which the admissibility of evidence has been challenged, under the exclusionary rule, on the ground that it was seized as an incident to an illegal arrest. The judiciary has assumed this responsibility because other remedies were thought to be inadequate.[26]

The exclusionary rule has contributed to an increased awareness by police of constitutional requirements.[27] It has also induced

---

[26] When California adopted the exclusionary rule in 1955, the court emphasized that it was "compelled to reach that conclusion because other remedies have completely failed to secure compliance with the constitutional provisions . . ." People v. Cahan, 44 Cal. 2d 434, 445, 282 P.2d 905, 911 (1955). Six years later, the United States Supreme Court placed heavy reliance upon this language from Cahan in holding that the Constitution required the states to exclude evidence uncovered incident to unconstitutional searches. Mapp v. Ohio, 367 U.S. 643, 81 Sup. Ct. 1684, 6 L. Ed. 2d 1081 (1961).

[27] State courts which prior to Mapp admitted into evidence the fruits of illegal searches and seizures were viewed by police as approving, if not encouraging, police misconduct. At a panel discussion on the impact of Mapp in Minnesota, the point was made that arrests and searches on less than adequate grounds had always been in violation of the federal and state constitutions. The following responses are illuminating:

"CITY ATTORNEY STIDD: [Other speakers] have used the expression that prior to the *Mapp* decision the police were violating the law all along. I don't think it is really proper for us to put it that way when the courts of our state were telling the police all along that the federal rules [barring the use of illegally seiged evidence] didn't apply in Minnesota . . . The [illegally seized] evidence was being brought into [Minnesota] courts and the courts were receiving it. . . . Technically, there might have been a violation, but the [Minnesota] courts were accepting this evidence; they were getting convictions on it. I don't believe we should be critical of the police and say, see how illegal and unlawful they were all this time. . . .

"DETECTIVE ANDERSON: The thing is that the county attorneys and defense attorneys who tried these cases in Minnesota were well aware of what the procedure was, that this was in violation of the federal rule, and . . . no police officer lied upon the witness stand. If you were asked how you got your evidence you told the truth. You had broken down a door or pried a window open . . . oftentimes we picked locks. Now, we didn't like this, but this is what the mores of society dictated. . . . That this is okay, it's been going on in Minnesota since it became a state, practically, and if you didn't want to perform that way, we just couldn't use you as a police officer.

"The Supreme Court of Minnesota sustained this time after time after time. Now,

some legislative revision of antiquated arrest laws[28] and has made possible appellate court consideration of many arrest issues.[29] But, notwithstanding the existence of the exclusionary rule on the federal level for nearly half a century and in many states for almost as long, there has been no systematic attempt to measure the precise impact of that rule or to determine the limitations, if any, upon its effectiveness. Most of the attention given the exclusionary rule is devoted to arguing its merits without the benefit of any inquiry into its actual effect upon police practice.

For the exclusionary rule to be effective as a sanction, it is necessary that police know the requirements of law and have a sufficient desire for conviction to cause them to conform to these requirements. Often neither is present in practice.

In some localities police are thoroughly aware of the content of important appellate cases in their jurisdiction and in others they are completely lacking in such knowledge. Training materials often become outdated. Officers who have completed their training are not kept up to date on legal developments relevant to their work because some departments make no effort to disseminate such information to personnel at the operational level. The police also are unlikely to have an adequate understanding of the attitude of the trial courts, particularly in the larger communities. Because of the vastness and the impersonal nature of the law enforcement machinery, there is usually no direct interchange between police and courts. With many judges handling criminal cases, consistency in policy or uniformity in decision-making regarding the propriety of police practices is often lacking. The knowledge of an individual officer is, for the most part, limited to his own in-court experience. Some rulings, usually those which the officer views as being completely at variance with the practical needs of enforcement, may be passed by word of mouth through the department, but the

---

your judiciary o.k.'d it; they knew what the facts were. Your trial judges, your defense attorneys, knew, too."

Minnesota A.C.L.U. Panel on "Police Searches and Arrests in Relation to Civil Liberties," May 18, 1963; rebroadcast on KUOM, July 25, 26, 1963; recording on file at University of Minnesota.

28 The California legislature was stirred into action as a result of the Cahan case there. See Cal. Penal Code (Supp. 1963). Mapp will undoubtedly prompt action in other states, as was recently the case in Minnesota. Minn. Session Laws 1963, chaps. 849, 850. One close observer of the Minnesota situation remarked: "Prior to Mapp, few people knew what the Minnesota statutes on arrest and search and seizure provided — and still fewer cared. Hence, no suggestion of revision — although one was badly needed — for the twenty or thirty years preceding Mapp." Letter from Professor Yale Kamisar, University of Minnesota Law School, December 19, 1963.

29 Cahan prompted a flood of appellate cases on arrest, search, and seizure in California. States without an exclusionary rule prior to Mapp are just beginning to receive some judicial clarification of arrest requirements.

basis of the judge's decision often becomes distorted in the retelling. There is an obvious need for improvement of police training and for greater effort by trial judges to articulate understandable and consistent standards.

Even when police do understand what the requirements of law are, the exclusionary rule does not always induce conformity with those requirements. As Professor Barrett has pointed out, the exclusionary rule

> . . . comes into play only when a successful police search has turned up evidence which is to be offered at the trial. . . . In short, the rule has a deterrent impact only on illegal searches and those illegal arrests to which searches are incident. And it has impact on those procedures only in those situations in which the police are proceeding with the conscious purpose of securing evidence to use in prosecuting the defendant.[30]

This is clearly demonstrated by the practices described in detail in Chapter 24, whereby the police sometimes arrest and search without concern as to whether the evidence uncovered can be used to obtain a conviction.

There are a number of reasons why police may not be primarily interested in obtaining the conviction of an arrested person. In some situations they may feel that a conviction is rarely attainable because of judicial attitudes regarding the legality of the arrest and search. For example, some trial courts have consistently declared arrests of "bagmen" (persons employed by the syndicate to collect numbers slips from individual writers) to be illegal unless prior to arrest the officer has actually observed the slips. This is seldom possible. Arrests are usually based upon the fact that the individual is traveling around in an area of the city where the numbers game is a popular pastime, is making a series of stops day after day at locations where numbers writing has occurred in the past, is making these stops during the time of the day when numbers are picked up, and perhaps is carrying a package with "something" in it. Because a right to arrest and search is not recognized as proper by the trial court under these circumstances, police have developed the procedure of making arrests and searches without thought of prosecution and instead merely subject the suspects to a brief period of detention. This policy in turn results in the police being even less selective as to who is arrested and searched as a suspected numbers carrier.

Another situation in which police do not make an effort to obtain a conviction is when they believe the penalty will not be worth the

[30] Barrett, Personal Rights, Property Rights, and the Fourth Amendment, 1960 Sup. Ct. Rev. 54-55.

expenditure of the police resources necessary to obtain the conviction. If, for example, it takes days to gather evidence necessary for a gambling conviction, they do not consider it worth while if the result of conviction is only a small fine, which the gambling organization can easily write off as one of the costs of doing business. This is particularly true when these same police resources can be utilized to discover and arrest a larger number of offenders, who can be subjected to substantial sanctions without resort to prosecution. These sanctions may include brief detention in jail, seizure of the gambling paraphernalia and funds, the cost of obtaining release (attorney fees and bondsman fees), and perhaps the cost of obtaining the return of an automobile seized at the time of arrest.[31]

Finally, police often believe that law enforcement objectives can be adequately achieved by arrest without prosecution. Thus, in states where the appellate court has expressly held that commission of a minor traffic violation is not a basis for a lawful search of the driver or his vehicle, the police may choose to continue to make such arrests and searches. Indeed, in some departments a specialized unit may be assigned the task of making such stops and searches as its primary responsibility despite the court's ruling that evidence thus discovered is inadmissible. Although conviction for any serious offense which is detected will seldom be possible, a continuation of the practice is believed justified as a general crime preventive and as a means of removing dangerous weapons from circulation and recovering stolen property.

Because the exclusionary rule sometimes brings about these unanticipated and undesired consequences, it is clear that there is a need for additional methods of inducing police to conform to the requirements of law. Certainly situations in which conviction is largely unattainable or largely meaningless ought to be eliminated as far as possible. This may require a basic reconsideration of the tasks which are imposed upon police agencies under current substantive law. Equally important is an effort to define and make available lawful methods of proceeding against criminal conduct. In the preoccupation over sanctions such as the exclusionary rule, the fact is too often overlooked that a negative sanction can induce proper law enforcement behavior only if proper methods are made known and are meaningful in relation to the task which police are expected to perform.

7. *The need to take immediate custody of a suspect.* Another major objective of the criminal justice process is the treatment of the guilty by methods which are fair and just. One important and neglected way of achieving this is the limitation of the use of physi-

31 Precisely how this occurs is described in some detail in Chapter 24.

cal arrest to those situations in which it appears that there is a need to take the suspect into immediate custody. Except in the field of minor traffic offenses, legislatures have generally failed to provide expressly for the use of a notice to appear or other means of accomplishing voluntary appearance. The assumption, in both law and practice, is that need for custody is a matter which need be considered only when the arrested person is brought before a judicial officer at the initial appearance for the setting of bail. It has been said that "indiscriminate exercise of the power of arrest is one of the most reprehensible features of American criminal justice," [32] and the recommendation has often been made that the summons or other arrest alternative be more widely used.[33]

At the bail-setting stage, the sole criterion generally recognized in law as proper is the likelihood of the defendant's appearing at the subsequent proceedings. It is sometimes assumed that this ought also to be the only factor influencing the decision as to whether to make an immediate arrest. It is clear, however, that police believe it desirable to arrest and retain custody of suspects for other reasons. It is not apparent that the need-for-custody question at the time of arrest and at the time of bail-setting must be answered in identical terms. Moreover, in current practice the bail decision is not limited to consideration of the likelihood of the defendant's appearance. Because of the broad and largely uncontrolled discretion which the judge has, custody can effectively be continued for other reasons by setting a prohibitively high bail. Judges are often in fact influenced by such matters as the risk of further criminal conduct, the risk of harm to witnesses, or the destruction of evidence. Thus, while state constitutional provisions apparently preclude the express recognition in law of these factors as a basis for refusing bail, as is the situation in some other countries, the amount of bail required is and probably will continue to be heavily influenced by these factors.

Police also arrest for reasons other than insuring that the suspect will appear in court. Most important is the fact that an arrest usually makes possible a lawful search as an incident to the arrest and also makes possible an in-custody investigation. It is apparent that a continuation of the traditional approach of making the validity of a search without a warrant depend upon making a lawful arrest will have the consequence of distorting the law of arrest or the law of search or both. There are recurring situations in which it is

[32] National Commission on Law Observance and Enforcement, Report No. 8, Criminal Procedure 14 (1931).

[33] E.g., ibid.; Report of the Attorney General's Committee on Poverty and the Administration of Criminal Justice vii (1963).

desirable, from a law enforcement point of view, to search a person who has committed an offense in the officer's presence even though, absent the desire to search, there would be no necessity to take immediate custody of the suspect. In current practice an arrest is often made in order to provide a lawful basis for a search, and if evidence is found in such a case, the suspect is retained in custody because police feel that under existing legal doctrine release would cast doubt upon the validity of the arrest and the incidental search. There may be understandable reluctance on the part of legislatures and courts to limit the power of arrest to situations where there is a need to take the suspect into immediate custody in order to insure his appearance in court. The recognition of a power of search which exists apart from the making of an arrest or the possession of a search warrant would make possible the orderly development of both the law of arrest and the law of search.

The situation is different where the arrest is prompted by a desire to conduct an in-custody investigation. Here there is a direct connection between the need for custody and the making of an arrest. The basic and difficult issue, already discussed, is whether in-custody investigation, particularly in-custody interrogation, is to be recognized as a proper law enforcement method. If it is, then it would seem to follow that taking immediate custody, where sufficient grounds for arrest exist, is proper in order to afford an opportunity to conduct a proper in-custody investigation.

B. The Role of the Various Criminal Justice Agencies in Relation to the Arrest Decision

It is helpful to look at an important decision, such as the arrest decision, in terms of the functions which are, or should be, performed by the various agencies in the system. This is particularly true in criminal justice administration, as the criminal justice process is a complex one in which the important decisions of one agency affect, and in turn are affected by, the important decisions of other agencies.

Observation of current practice makes it apparent that the police play a primary role in the making of the arrest decision. However, this is a responsibility shared by the prosecutor and the trial judge, and one of the major dilemmas of current criminal justice administration is in knowing how responsibility for important decisions ought to be shared among the various agencies. It is not easy to determine whether a given system contains a healthy set of checks and balances or whether instead the actions of different agencies within the system, such as the police and the trial court, constitute a nullification of each other's efforts.

1. *The role of the police.*　In current criminal justice administration many decisions are commonly made by the police: whether to seek a warrant; whether to invoke the process in individual cases; whether to make an immediate arrest or to refrain from doing so because of the amount of force that would be required or because an alternative is available; and whether to arrest and detain for purposes related to prosecution, or for other purposes. Thus the role of the police is obviously one of primary importance.

The task of the police is complicated by the fact that they must make difficult judgments as to whether there is sufficient evidence of guilt in a particular case to make an arrest and must also decide the even more difficult question of whether it is desirable law enforcement policy, assuming adequate evidence of guilt, to make an arrest under the circumstances known to them at the time.　The latter decision requires perhaps the most difficult kind of social judgment involving community attitudes about certain kinds of conduct, certain racial and economic groups, and other factors which defy precise measurement or evaluation.　The police officer serves, for many members of the community, as the only point of contact with government, and the impressions he creates must, in the aggregate, have profound effects.

This being so, it is surprising that the public and the police themselves view the task and the responsibility of the police as a ministerial one.[34]　They are commonly compared with firemen, who share the uniform, the semimilitary organization, and the mission of safeguarding persons and property.　Even casual analysis makes apparent the fact that the analogy is entirely superficial. The objectives of controlling deviant social behavior and of saving persons and property threatened by fire are as different as any two objectives can be.　There are some possible explanations for this prevailing misconception of the police role, and it is also possible to identify some consequences of the misconception which ought to be matters of serious concern.　Some of these have already been discussed but are significant enough to warrant brief repetition.

The traditional attitudes of legislatures, appellate courts, and perhaps the public, toward police are no doubt influenced by an assumption that important policy decisions ought to be made by the prosecutor or the court.　In current administration, however, police are required to make social decisions in the formulation

[34] "One of the standards of the police in a democratic society is the . . . restriction of police to the so-called ministerial work."　Hall, Police and Law in a Democratic Society, 28 Ind. L.J. 133, 155 (1953).

and implementation of an arrest policy that are perhaps more important than those left to the prosecutor or the judge. This is particularly true in large metropolitan areas. If the objective is to have the prosecutor and the court assume full responsibility for making important policy decisions, then the structure of those agencies must be substantially changed.

As has been pointed out, police themselves contribute to the belief that theirs is a ministerial task because important decisions are more easily defended when the responsibility can be described as a ministerial one. The defensive attitude of police is no doubt further encouraged by the generally adverse publicity which police agencies receive. Press coverage is often directed at incidents that tend to discredit the police. Appellate cases involving an evaluation of police conduct typically arise only when someone objects to his treatment at the hands of the police and thus are hardly a representative sample of police behavior. Much of the scholarly writing about police has been hostile. Jerome Hall has pointed this out:

> The literature on police, including surveys and studies by various commissions, abounds in adverse criticism. It is based on an implied "bad man" theory, and assumes that by exhortation and scolding, police services can be improved. The difficulty with that approach is not so much that it is unfair to the police, but that it does not investigate the basic causes of police abuse and ineffectiveness.[35]

Police themselves contribute to this situation. Their attempt to maintain the public support necessary to their operation[36] seems to lead them to act beyond the restrictions placed upon them rather than to act within these limitations. They feel that "there is a wide discrepancy between what the people expect the police to do and what the police are permitted to do under the law," [37] and the pressure to conform to public expectations is greater than that to conform to the requirements of law. The head of one of the largest departments in the country recently said: "Let the police have the authority to do what the public expects them to

[35] Id. at 146. This is not to say, of course, that the courts have not also had their share of criticism. See, for example, Collings, Criminal Law and Administration, 1957 Annual Survey of American Law 93. The effect, however, is not the same, as the courts are generally more insulated from public pressure than are the police.

[36] "In a democratic society, the corollary is the dependence of professional police upon the public with regard to detection, evidence, financial support, and in last analysis, the police job itself." Hall, Police and Law in a Democratic Society, 28 Ind. L.J. 133, 143 (1953).

[37] Wilson, Police Authority in a Free Society, 54 J. Crim. L., C. & P.S. 175, 176 (1963).

do in suppressing crime. If we followed some of our court decisions literally, the public would be demanding my removal . . .
and — I might add — with justification." [38]

This attitude often prompts the imposition of even greater restrictions on police authority. Courts are undoubtedly influenced
by their assumption as to how police will react to legal requirements. If there is confidence that they will stay well within defined limits, their powers may be stated broadly;[39] but, if it is
thought that they will regularly exceed the limits, the tendency
is to impose severe and perhaps unrealistic limitations upon their
authority.[40]

This unhappy situation contributes to a nullification of the
efforts of the police on the one hand and the courts on the other
hand. It is a problem to which there is no simple answer, but
analysis of current administration does furnish some guidelines
for constructive action.

It seems likely that police always will have a very important
social responsibility, and it is therefore imperative that this fact
be recognized by legislatures, by appellate courts, and certainly by
the police themselves. Careful attention ought to be given to insuring that there are proper and effective ways for the police to
discharge their responsibility and that there are effective sanctions
to deter irresponsibility.

The development of police expertness should be encouraged,
and its existence should be recognized when appropriate. There
is merit in acknowledging that police may develop in the identification of certain kinds of criminal behavior a competence which
will result in their having grounds for arrest in some situations
in which the layman would lack adequate grounds.[41] There is
need, and ample precedent in other fields, for the development
of methods of communicating the existence of police expertness

[38] Id. at 177.

[39] "We like to grant large powers so as to prevent any legal quibble about their
extent, but we expect the holders of them to act fairly and reasonably and well
within them." Devlin, The Criminal Prosecution in England 16 (1958).

[40] "Among the opponents of the amendment [broadening the powers of the
police in Japan] there seems to have been this feeling: Allow the police seven miles
and they will go nine miles; therefore, if we want to keep them at seven miles, better
give them six miles." Abe, Police Detention and Arrest Privileges Under Foreign
Law — Japan, 51 J. Crim. L., C. & P.S. 429, 433 (1960).

[41] Illustrative is the kind of case discussed earlier in which some trial judges
regularly hold that an experienced officer of the gambling unit does not have reasonable grounds to arrest a man for possession of gambling paraphernalia, if the arrest
is based only on the facts that he travels about day after day in an area of the city
where policy is a popular pastime and during the time of day when policy slips are
picked up, and makes a series of regular stops, some of which are at locations where
it is known that policy writing has occurred in the past.

to trial or appellate courts which are called upon to decide arrest issues. The relationship between the court and the economic regulatory agency might serve as a model in the absence of a more highly developed proposal.[42]

Of course, even with the traditional administrative agency the court's willingness to acknowledge the expertness of the administrators depends in large measure upon the confidence which the court has in the agency involved.[43] Because this is so, it is apparent that the police need to do more in confronting directly the major social responsibilities which, perhaps by default, have become their burden. In training, in research, and in day-to-day administration, greater attention by the police to the complexities of the arrest decision is necessary. In the last analysis, it is the police who will have to establish the aura of expertise which must precede greater judicial deference to decision-making at the police level. For example, police ought to acknowledge their exercise of discretion and reduce their enforcement policies to writing and subject them to a continuing process of critical re-evaluation. Each large department has a police planning unit responsible for the formulation of basic policy, but heretofore these units have confined their attention to the evaluation of issues long a part of police thinking, such as the long-standing debate over use of one-man versus two-man squad cars. Without depreciating the importance of such operational problems, preoccupation with them at the expense of basic policy issues seems clearly unwise and certainly inconsistent with the development of a professional status for police.

It is common for police to blame the courts for not recognizing the practical problems of law enforcement. Yet the police themselves have not done all they might do to afford a basis for a more adequate understanding of important law enforcement problems[44]

---

42 That this is presently not the case is best illustrated by comparison of Bargain City U.S.A., Inc. v. Dilworth, 29 U.S.L.W. 2002 (Pa. C.P., June 10, 1960), with Moog Industries, Inc. v. FTC, 355 U.S. 411, 78 Sup. Ct. 377, 2 L. Ed. 2d 370 (1958).

43 "In one case a judge looks at a record and quickly gets the impression that the agency is in all respects the master of the situation. All the earmarks of thoroughness and fairness can be readily detected. Moreover, the judge over the years has built up confidence in the personnel of the particular agency and in its prevailing policies. In this state of mind, he spends little time studying the record. . . . The limited time of the judge, he thinks, can be better spent on another case before him, one in which he gradually develops the feeling that the complaining party may have been unjustly treated or the feeling that the direction of the policy development is much in need of judicial attention." 4 Davis, Administrative Law Treatise 234, §30.08 (1958).

44 For example, in some locales the courts view entry into handbooks by plainclothes officers posing as customers as a form of trespass, requiring exclusion of all observations and the fruits thereof. In such cases, it should be possible to evaluate

by themselves, by prosecutors, and by both trial and appellate courts. Although it is said that "the police are not a scholarly group, skilled in presenting the police point of view," [45] there are a number of capable police administrators who can make a major contribution to public understanding of the police function. To date, however, most of their efforts have been misdirected. For example, police administrators feel compelled to continue their attack upon the exclusionary rule as a sanction which results in "setting the guilty free." [46] But it is clear since *Mapp v. Ohio*[47] that illegally obtained evidence will continue to be excluded and that the need is for the development of methods for effective and lawful police action.

Finally, universities have failed to recognize the problems of the police and their role in the administration of criminal justice and as a consequence have not engaged in the kind of research and teaching required for the development of effective law enforcement in a democratic society. What little scholastic attention there has been to the field of police work has for the most part been limited to scientific methods of detection or administrative problems of police departments, both of which are important but should not preclude attention to the difficult social problems which policemen must confront in practice.

2. *The role of the prosecutor.* Although the prosecuting attorney is an important participant in the criminal justice system, he does not ordinarily play a major role in the arrest decision. However, by the manner in which he makes decisions on whether to charge arrested suspects, he may have an important indirect effect upon police practice. This is particularly so in cases in which the police view conviction as the primary objective of the arrest.

---

the practice by determining how often this technique is employed and, where it is used, how many cases have been lost as a result. Moreover, some basis could be provided for evaluating the significance of these rulings, such as by considering what available alternative methods of enforcement against this conduct exist, whether these alternatives are less or more feasible than the methods used, and whether these alternatives would constitute a greater or lesser imposition upon those being investigated.

[45] Wilson, Police Authority in a Free Society, 54 J. Crim. L., C. & P.S. 175, 176 (1963).

[46] E.g., Comments of O. W. Wilson, Chicago Superintendent of Police, at panel discussion on "How Do We Live with Mallory, Mapp, and Sun?" 1963 Proceedings, Section of Criminal Law, American Bar Association 32, 35 (1964).

The position is not a comfortable one, particularly when the police acknowledge nonconformance to the governing norms prior to application of the exclusionary rule in their particular jurisdictions. Such an admission is at least implied when the police assert that the addition of the exclusionary rule sanction, as opposed to any tightening of the legal norms, has brought an increase in crime. E.g., Parker, Police 120 (Wilson ed. 1957).

[47] 367 U.S. 643, 81 Sup. Ct. 1684, 6 L. Ed. 2d 1081 (1961).

The rural prosecutor is more likely to play a significant role in the development and carrying out of a law enforcement policy than is the urban prosecutor. He is accessible to the police and in some situations may be regularly consulted prior to arrest. The contribution of the rural prosecutor is limited primarily by the fact that he is commonly inexperienced. In contrast, the urban prosecutor seldom becomes involved in a case prior to arrest. Nor does he ordinarily have occasion to review or evaluate existing law enforcement policies and practices. His attention is usually focused upon individual cases of assumed major importance, while his often overworked and inexperienced [48] assistants find that all of their time is needed in determining charges, preparing for and appearing at trials, and conducting the routine business of the office.

Appraisal of the role of the prosecutor is made difficult because that role is inevitably more ambiguous than that of the police or the trial court. It is clear that the police are concerned with the detection of crime and the identification and apprehension of offenders; it is likewise apparent that courts must decide the issue of guilt or innocence. A prosecutor, however, may conceive of his principal responsibility in a number of different ways. He may serve primarily as trial counsel for the police department, reflecting the views of the department in his court representation. Or he may serve as a sort of "house counsel" for the police, giving legal advice to the department on how to develop enforcement practices which will withstand challenge in court. On the other hand, the prosecutor may consider himself primarily a representative of the court, with the responsibility of enforcing rules designed to control police practices and perhaps otherwise acting for the benefit of persons who are being proceeded against. Another possibility is that the prosecutor, as an elected official (while the police are increasingly appointive and the judiciary is increasingly insulated from political pressures), will try primarily to reflect community opinion in the making of decisions as to whether to prosecute. The uncertainty as to whether the prosecutor is responsible for all these tasks and as to which is his primary responsibility creates difficult problems in current administration.

Prosecutors do serve as trial counsel, at least in cases involving relatively serious crimes. The difficulty is that when certain police practices are brought into question in court the prosecutor is not likely to be in a position to articulate the relevant problems as

---

[48] See Kuh, Careers in Prosecution Offices, 14 J. Legal Ed. 175, 176-178 (1961), on the turnover in the New York County District Attorney's office and the problems caused thereby.

they appear to the police. This is because he is relatively detached from the day-to-day problems of the police and from the enforcement practice which gives rise to the legal issue. While private counsel representing a business client would believe it to be of utmost importance to consult fully with his client, prosecutors commonly proceed on the assumption that the police need not be consulted. A prosecutor who understood the problems of the police would not only be in a better position to focus the attention of the trial courts on the true nature of the issues before them, but also could better decide what issues are in greatest need of clarification from the appellate courts.[49]

There is uncertainty as to which agency has responsibility for serving as "house counsel" for the police. The prosecutor has seldom assumed this function; indeed, in many locales communication between the prosecutor and the police chief is almost nonexistent. The police, if in need of a "legal advisor," are expected to deal with the city attorney or the municipal corporation counsel, although these officers do not have responsibility for the trial of criminal cases or for arguing the propriety of police practices on appeal. However, the city attorney and the corporation counsel seldom view consultation with police as a major responsibility, and typically the relationship is limited to occasional consultation on the propriety of certain practices which might cause an action against the officer or the city. Efforts of police departments to add competent counsel to their staffs have been resisted on the ground that legal advice is adequately provided by the city attorney, corporation counsel, or prosecuting attorney.

There are occasions when the prosecutor does act, in effect, as a representative of the court in controlling police practices and in insuring maximum protection of those subjected to arrest, search, and detention. Involvement of the prosecutor in certain minor cases seems explainable only on the ground that there is a need to minimize the effect of unfair police action.[50] Yet prosecutors are sometimes criticized for not utilizing their most direct means of control: refusal to charge when the fact of prosecution would constitute tacit approval of clearly improper police conduct.[51] It is

[49] As noted earlier, even if the prosecutor can appeal from an order suppressing evidence, he may fail to select those cases which from the police point of view pose the greatest problems. Thus the prosecutor is likely to ignore misdemeanor gambling cases and appeal only in the "big" cases, those which involve serious crimes and are the subject of greatest publicity.

[50] See Chapter 2.

[51] "It is the duty of the prosecutor to know not only whom to prosecute, but *when* . . . Unhesitatingly he should refuse to go forward with the presentation of evidence which has been obtained by illegal police invasion of a private home. If

unclear, however, whether the prosecution agency should assume other tasks directly related to the protection of persons being subjected to the process. This is sometimes done, as illustrated by the existence of the Detroit Release Bureau, operated by the prosecutor's office to afford a means of prompt release without bail in minor cases.[52] If additional safeguards are added, they may conceivably be made the responsibility of the prosecutor.[53]

Response to public opinion by the prosecutor may take many forms but is most likely to involve an exercise of what traditionally has been referred to as "the prosecutor's discretion." However, this fashioning of enforcement policy by the prosecutor is essentially negative in character; the prosecutor does not directly determine arrest policies but can only eliminate certain of the cases which reach him. There would be greater impact if the prosecutor were to articulate his policies and communicate them to the police. With some exceptions,[54] the police would arrest in conformance with these policies if they knew what they were. While this feedback of the prosecutor's discretion would not eliminate the need for police discretion,[55] it would aid in accomplishing discretionary enforcement at the police level on a much more consistent basis than is presently the case.

3. *The role of the trial judge.* It is commonly assumed that judicial participation in the arrest decision requires the actual involvement of a judicial officer in each decision rather than a delegation of this responsibility to the law enforcement agencies and appropriate judicial review when law enforcement action is challenged. Thus it is often suggested that trial judges should be more directly involved in the arrest-detention process and that they should be given responsibility for many of the decisions now made by the police. It is said that arrest warrants should be re-

---

his case *depends* upon such evidence, he should dismiss the prosecution." Williams v. United States, 263 F.2d 487, 491 (D.C. Cir. 1959) (Danaher, J., conc.)

[52] See page 174.

[53] For a proposal that we "introduce into the routine of police operations . . . a responsible independent officer — judicial, quasi-judicial, or administrative — with the duty of supervising police control over persons held in custody," see Barrett, Police Practices and the Law — From Arrest to Release or Charge, 50 Calif. L. Rev. 11, 54 (1962).

[54] A nonenforcement policy announced by the prosecutor probably would not be followed by the police in those cases in which other pressures seem to demand affirmative action. For example, the police view the homosexual as a serious problem because they receive repeated complaints from offended citizens, and consequently they makes arrests even when it is known that the prosecutor does not favor prosecution of homosexuals.

[55] For one thing, unique cases not covered by the prosecutor's guidelines are bound to arise.

quired in all but emergency situations,[56] that judges should be given responsibility for conducting in-custody interrogations,[57] that in-custody investigation by the police should occur only after a judge has decided that further detention is proper and has remanded the suspect to the police,[58] and that judicial approval should be required for the release of a suspect where evidence is insufficient to charge[59] or there are policy reasons for not prosecuting.[60]

In current practice the trial judge seldom operates effectively in making the run-of-the-mill arrest and detention decisions. Where arrest warrants are used the judge does not usually even consider the evidentiary basis for the warrant. When suspects are produced by habeas corpus or at the initial appearance, there is rarely any inquiry into the basis for the arrest or for the detention. As a consequence, there is reason to doubt that meaningful judicial participation is possible as a matter of routine in arrest or detention decisions.[61]

On the other hand, judicial review of enforcement decisions does seem feasible, although currently the trial judge typically does not conceive his relationship to enforcement agencies to be analogous to his relationship to other governmental administrative agencies. Contested cases which involve rulings on evidence claimed to have been illegally obtained do call for the trial judge to decide whether the police action was proper and to do so for the express purpose of affecting police practice if found to be improper. Few trial judges, however, act as if this is their objective. Seldom is a careful inquiry made into the beneficial or detrimental aspects of a given law enforcement practice. Even if a question is asked, trial counsel are seldom able to present accurately what the current practice is and why it is followed, and the police themselves disclaim responsibility for this kind of evaluation. When

---

56 See discussion page 502.

57 E.g., Pound, Legal Interrogation of Persons Accused or Suspected of Crime, 24 J. Crim. L. & C. 1017 (1934).

58 Comment, 68 Yale L.J. 1003 (1959).

59 Foote, Safeguards in the Law of Arrest, 52 Nw. U. L. Rev. 16, 25 (1957).

60 Thus, instead of the "golden rule" drunk procedure observed in Detroit, it might be thought desirable to have these kinds of release decisions also made by a judicial officer. A few states have so provided. See Chapter 21.

61 Thus one commentator responded to the remand proposal in these words: "Judges have no special expertise in the art of criminal investigation. They are not equipped to judge the necessities of investigation in specific cases. If governed by a flexible rule clearly intended to allow some police questioning, the courts would be reluctant to second-guess police strategy in any particular case. A flexible standard would thus lead the courts to defer to police discretion." Weisberg, Police Interrogation of Arrested Persons: A Skeptical View, 52 J. Crim. L., C. & P.S. 21, 39 (1961).

a decision is made there is seldom an effort to communicate the reason to the police department, the assumption apparently being that police practice is positively influenced by the exclusion of evidence even without knowledge as to why the decision was made. With the judge not completely familiar with the law enforcement problem and the police unaware of the basis for the trial judge's decision, it would indeed be surprising if this were to constitute an effective method of supervising police behavior.

In multijudge courts there is often disparity in the views of the judges as to what constitutes proper or improper police practice. There has been considerable attention to the fact that disparity in sentencing has an adverse effect upon offenders. Disparity in decisions as to what police behavior is proper has an equally detrimental effect upon police morale. Although it seems obviously desirable to try to minimize this kind of inconsistency, there has been little effort to devise methods of achieving this objective.

The basic question is not difficult to state. Can adequate judicial control over law enforcement practices be best achieved by requiring that important decisions be made by a judicial officer or by delegating that responsibility to law enforcement agencies and devising methods for adequate judicial review of the administrative action? Currently there is a commitment to the ideal of judicial participation which is not meaningful in day-to-day administration.

4. *The role of the appellate court.* In considering the ability and opportunity of appellate courts to deal with the range of significant policy issues raised by current arrest practices, it is important to keep two points in mind. One is that whether an appellate court is confronted with an issue depends upon the relatively fortuitous circumstance of the opportunity for a defendant to raise the issue in contesting his guilt. Thus certain issues are frequently litigated and appealed while others of equal importance to law enforcement, the individual concerned, and the community are seldom raised.

Secondly, the appellate court typically hears only those cases where police practice is challenged on a somewhat narrow set of facts, and thus the picture is somewhat distorted. Appellate counsel fail to compensate for this by attempting to put the individual case in the context of the over-all enforcement policy which is involved.[62] Instead, argument is commonly confined to prior ap-

62 Sound judgments on many of the critical issues require an accumulation of knowledge which goes beyond the facts of the particular case. The propriety of particular practices is best determined by study and evaluation of the demands being made upon the law enforcement process, the methods currently being used to re-

pellate opinions. Because the court cannot itself gather the information needed,[63] it must make judgments, particularly about what is happening in current practice, upon less than adequate data. Indicative of this is the fact that it is common for appellate courts even today to cite the Wickersham Report on Lawlessness in Law Enforcement[64] in regard to the treatment of persons in custody and for the proposition that abuses can be prevented only if persons arrested are taken immediately before a magistrate. This report is over thirty years old and was itself primarily based upon appellate decisions and newspaper accounts. Thus reliance for information as to current practice is placed upon this report on the doubtful assumption that the appellate opinions were reliable evidence of current practice. Perhaps appellate opinions do give indication of the kinds of police abuses which do occur, but this does not mean that they constitute an adequate basis for assessing the legitimate needs of law enforcement.[65]

In cases which clearly involve police misconduct, the court's indignation is often expressed in sweeping language which condemns other police practices which may be quite proper. For example, in State v. Lombardi,[66] discussed earlier,[67] the court, after concluding that there was sufficient proof of serious misconduct, went on to say, without careful analysis, that the failure to arrest for an intrafamily assault where the victim did not desire prosecution constituted a failure to perform "a known, mandatory, non-discretionary, ministerial duty." [68] This serves to perpetuate the myth that police can fully enforce the law and serves also as a deterrent to an analysis of police discretion, how it is exercised, and how it should be controlled.

---

spond to these demands, and the impact which these methods have upon the individuals involved. Moreover, declaration of rules to govern at certain decision points in the process should be preceded by careful attention to the possible effect elsewhere in the process, as one significant change "may require substantial reorientation of the entire system." Ohlin and Remington, Sentencing Structure: Its Effect upon Systems for the Administration of Criminal Justice, 23 Law and Contemp. Prob. 495, 496 (1958).

[63] Professor Hurst, in his excellent study of the development of legal institutions in this country, points out: "As fact finders courts were inherently hampered by the limiting tradition of their office. It was not the proper work of judges to initiate broad solutions of public problems. The courts inherited no staff which they could use for independent fact finding. They had no independent funds with which to finance inquiries." Hurst, The Growth of American Law 412 (1950).

[64] National Commission on Law Observance and Enforcement, Report No. 11 (1931).

[65] Remington, Criminal Justice Research, 51 J. Crim. L., C. & P.S. 7, 14 (1960).

[66] 8 Wis. 2d 421, 99 N.W.2d 829 (1959).

[67] See page 80.

[68] State v. Lombardi, 8 Wis. 2d 421, 422, 99 N.W.2d 829 (1959).

In an increasing number of jurisdictions the judiciary is given the responsibility for developing the law of criminal procedure through rules of court. Most states have been influenced by the Federal Rules of Criminal Procedure. In assuming this responsibility, the judiciary is able to deal with important issues which may not necessarily arise in litigation. The difficulty is that the rule-making power is commonly limited to procedures before courts. Thus, while the issuance of an arrest warrant is included, other equally important issues, such as the requirements for an arrest without a warrant, are not dealt with.

5. *The role of the legislature.* Legislative attention to the arrest stage of the criminal justice process has been sporadic. While statutes prescribing who can issue an arrest warrant and when an arrest can be made without a warrant are common, these statutes tend to be highly imitative, suggesting that their enactment did not occur as a consequence of careful deliberation on the existing problems. It is fair to say that, with rare exception, the states have not engaged in a thorough legislative consideration of arrest issues as they exist in the particular jurisdiction. There are some reasons for this which can be identified.

Currently there is uncertainty in many states as to whether the responsibility for the development of arrest policy lies with the legislature or the judiciary. Where rules of procedure are the responsibility of the judiciary it often seems to be assumed that this relieves the legislature from the obligation of considering issues of criminal procedure except sporadically as individual issues become of current concern. The difficulty is that the judicial rule-making power typically is not extended to matters such as arrest without a warrant, so inevitably many of the arrest issues remain unresolved.

Traditionally, procedural codes have dealt primarily with details relating to the trial of contested cases and have given much less attention to issues such as those confronting the police at the arrest stage. In part this no doubt reflects the fact that lawyers have had responsibility for the development of such codes, and the professional interest of the lawyer has been concentrated on the prosecution and adjudication stages of the criminal justice process. When the drafting of procedural law is undertaken, it is often assumed that the task can be accomplished satisfactorily without involving the police.[69]

---

[69] This was the case, for example, with the recent Illinois enactment, where the first opportunity for police participation came only after the printing and distribution of the tentative final draft, just a few weeks before its introduction in the legislature. Thus the Chicago Superintendent of Police remarked, in presenting his

The neglect of the difficult policy issues at the arrest stage also reflects the fact that procedural codes have concentrated more on details than on the basic policy questions involved. For example, a great deal of attention is given to the mechanics of selecting a jury, but the statutes are usually silent or extremely ambiguous on the question of whether in-custody investigation is a proper law enforcement method.[70] This results, in part at least, from a healthy respect for the difficulty of such questions.[71] It results also

---

views on the proposed legislation: "It is important that the committee recognize that my comments here today are in the nature of first impressions. The views of the Chicago Police Department were not solicited in the drafting of the code. Until a week ago, our only knowledge of it was gleaned from newspaper accounts. We have not had time, during the past week, to study it as thoroughly as we would like, nor have we had time to devise specific alternative wording for some of the sections which are of greatest concern to us. . . .

". . . One of the real shortcomings in the past has been the failure to articulate and analyze the problems of the conscientious and able police officer who characteristically has not been consulted in the drafting process." Wilson, Comments presented at the Conference on the Proposed Illinois Code of Criminal Procedure, University of Illinois College of Law, January 12, 1963.

70 The experience in the enactment of what at this writing is the newest code of criminal procedure in the United States illustrates the difficulty. The proposed code submitted to the Illinois legislature included a section directing that "any person making an arrest without a warrant shall take the arrested person without unnecessary delay before the nearest or most accessible judge . . ." Illinois State and Chicago Bar Associations' Joint Committee to Revise the Illinois Criminal Code, Tentative Final Draft of the Proposed Illinois Code of Criminal Procedure 1963, §45-1(b). Although the "without unnecessary delay" language was to be found in the existing law, Ill. Rev. Stat. chap. 38, §660 (1961), judicial interpretation was not consistent on the question of whether this language contemplated delay for investigation in some cases. Compare the statement in People v. Jackson, 23 Ill. 2d 274, 280, 178 N.E.2d 299, 302 (1961), that the statute "cannot mean . . . the police do not have reasonable latitude to fully investigate a crime," with that in Fulford v. O'Connor, 3 Ill. 2d 490, 500-501, 121 N.E.2d 767, 773 (1954), that "the fact that there is as yet insufficient evidence to justify preferring charges against a criminal suspect is not an excuse for detention, but is precisely the evil which the statute is aimed at correcting." In the legislature, one of the principal disputes concerning the code was whether the "without unnecessary delay" phraseology should be retained or replaced by the word "forthwith." Yet selection of either of these alternative uses of language, often viewed as synonymous by the courts in Illinois and elsewhere, e.g., People v. Jackson supra, would hardly be a clear expression of legislative judgment concerning the basic issue involved. The "without unnecessary delay" language was ultimately adopted, Ill. Rev. Stat. chap. 38, §109-1 (1963), but the courts and police of the state have no greater insight into the policy underlying the choice of this phrase than they had prior to recodification.

71 Moreover, proposals in the delicate area of police-citizen relations often engender strong (and sometimes highly emotional) reactions. Legislators are understandably reluctant to act in this area, and sponsors of legislation are sometimes moved to delete controversial matters in order to insure passage.

Here again the recent Illinois experience is illustrative. When some of the proposed sections on police practices were publicly criticized by the Chicago Superintendent of Police and by the A.C.L.U. (for quite different reasons, as might be expected), the sponsoring committee made the tactical decision to eliminate these sections from the proposal forwarded to the legislature, rather than to include them

from an assumption that these issues will be taken care of by courts, particularly since most of them involve questions of constitutional law. For reasons already discussed, this assumption seems unrealistic.

To some extent the failure of legislatures to deal with important arrest issues reflects the lack of an appropriate model indicating the issues and alternative ways of dealing with them. The Uniform Arrest Act does cover many issues, but even it fails to treat police discretion and many aspects of in-custody investigation. There is no doubt that the Uniform Arrest Act has had an important effect upon the development of legislation, even in states which have not adopted the specific provisions of the act. But the issues are complicated, and the factual basis upon which the Uniform Arrest Act was drafted gives no clear indication of the needs of law enforcement and thus how they can be met without undue imposition upon the rights of individuals who may be affected.

Legislatures, particularly in the last few years, have made substantial efforts toward substantive criminal code revision. The objective has been to deal with most issues which bear importantly upon the question of what conduct should be considered a violation of the criminal law. However, very little attention has been given to the kind of enforcement problems that are created by the enactment of some criminal statutes.

> The problems of administration are inseparable from the problem of what is or ought to be the substance of what is being administered. Indeed, the character of the processes of criminal justice is formed by the substantive tasks allotted to them. A criminal law that deals centrally with gross injuries to persons and property — as Anglo-American law traditionally did — requires very different institutional processes for its administration than does a criminal law that plays a role in every sphere of social policy in which government takes a hand, as Anglo-American criminal law has increasingly come to do in the last century or so. It is in the context of a given set of tasks allotted to the criminal law that we are forced to ask, for example, what powers of arrest and interrogation the police should possess.[72]

Many illustrations are to be found in the observed practice. It is primarily in enforcing the gambling and narcotics laws that the police feel it is necessary to break into premises unannounced before critical evidence can be destroyed. It is primarily as to these offenses that informants are used, informants whose identity

---

in either their present or some revised form and jeopardize passage of the entire code.

[72] Packer, The Model Penal Code and Beyond, 63 Colum. L. Rev. 594, 604 (1963).

is concealed and whose cooperation is insured by techniques which affect the process in a variety of ways. What the legislature has not defined as criminal may likewise have considerable effect. Thus the police arrest and briefly detain the transvestite, whose appearance on the street has not been made criminal, and the prostitute, who can be prosecuted only when she "accosts and solicits." Revision of the substantive criminal code typically proceeds without concern over such enforcement problems.

C. The Need for Further Research

Without adequate knowledge of the problems facing law enforcement agencies in day-to-day administration, it is not possible to make an informed judgment of how the process ought to operate. To say this is not to contend that "simply by accumulating a big enough pile [of facts] you will learn something you did not know before." [73] The value of empirical research in this area obviously depends upon whether the factual data have relevance to the understanding and solution of important social issues. If they do, a contribution is made, even though ultimate resolution of basic social issues involves value judgments which cannot be made on the basis of facts alone.

The objective of this volume has been to put the arrest decision in the perspective of the total system of criminal justice administration. This is done on the assumption that the goal is a total system of criminal justice which is effective, fair, and consistent. It is not enough to achieve arrest practices and policies which, however adequate, do not fit in a sensible way in the over-all system.

Although it is important to understand the arrest decision as an important stage in the criminal justice process, this approach is obviously not adequate in itself. An arrest is not only an important decision in the criminal justice process; it is also likely to be a critical episode in the life of the individual who is arrested. Moreover, in the aggregate, arrest practices have an impact upon the total community and particularly upon minority groups whose primary contact with government is through the police officer. It is perhaps not an overstatement to say that arrest policies and practices have a significance for a democratic society which goes beyond the question of the effectiveness of law enforcement and beyond the interest of individual citizens in individual communities.

Research with a broad focus, such as that conducted to support

[73] This, apparently, was the belief of the early empiricists. See Hurst, Perspectives upon Research into Legal Order, 1961 Wis. L. Rev. 356, 365.

this series of volumes, is a necessary first step if important issues are to be sufficiently identified as they relate to the total system of criminal justice administration. However, once the issues are defined, further empirical research of a narrower focus and longer duration will often be a prerequisite to the proposal of specific solutions to existing problems. Until the precise causes of certain current practices can be more sufficiently pinpointed, finding adequate solutions will remain a difficult task.[74]

Empirical research often raises more issues than it resolves. The test of its value is the significance of the issues which are disclosed. The importance of this volume depends upon the significance of the issues which have been emphasized and upon the extent to which it stimulates further effort toward understanding the issues and assessing alternative means of dealing with them.

[74] Thus, as to the problem areas identified and summarized at the outset of this chapter, the following inquiries might be made:

(1) Precisely what effect does the formal law itself have upon the nature of day-to-day enforcement by the police? It is important to determine precisely to what degree the law is communicated to the police and, to the extent that it is, the degree to which the legal norms are accepted by the police.

(2) How is decision-making at the police level further affected by the anticipated reactions of administrators located farther along in the process? There is a need for greater understanding of the patterns of communication between the various agencies involved and of the extent to which current police practices are prompted by the assumed attitudes in the other agencies.

(3) How is decision-making at the police level further affected by assumptions by the police concerning the attitudes of the public? Insufficient attention has been given to the extent to which legal controls on the police can be operative when contrary to public expectations regarding law enforcement.

(4) To what extent are legal norms lacking to control important day-to-day police decisions, and, in the absence of these norms, have the police developed professional norms to insure responsible decision-making within the area of ambiguity? It is clearly important to determine the degree to which the police, in exercising the broad range of discretion delegated to them, often by default, have developed an expertise similar to that acknowledged as to administrative agencies.

(5) What kind of situations recur with some frequency in which the police obtain some evidence of criminal conduct, and what is the context of these situations in terms of the availability of further evidence to confirm or dispel the suspicion? Quantitative research, to the end of discovering how often certain recurring difficult situations come to police attention, is needed, as is analysis which puts these situations in proper context by determining whether the acquisition of further evidence is possible without interfering with the suspect.

(6) Precisely what is the degree of imposition upon those suspected of criminal conduct by certain recurring police practices? This is the other side of the coin; before the needs of law enforcement can be balanced against the rights of the individual, more knowledge about the impact upon the suspect of certain police practices is required.

(7) How effective are existing controls over police practices? Further attention is needed to the means for challenging the various kinds of police decisions, the degree to which and the reasons why certain sanctions (such as the exclusionary rule) are ineffective, and affirmative ways of inducing police conformance to legal norms.

Index